THE ROUTLEDGE HANDBOOK OF THE ETHICS OF IMMIGRATION

Immigration poses some of the major moral, economic, and political challenges of the twenty-first century. Questions of the state's responsibilities toward immigrants, open borders, security, coping with the displacement of people caused by climate change and natural disasters, and deciding who has a 'right to remain' are but some of the significant issues currently faced by governments, policymakers, and humanitarian organizations.

The Routledge Handbook of the Ethics of Immigration is an outstanding reference source to this vitally important topic. Comprising twenty-five chapters by an international team of philosophers, economists, political scientists, and legal theorists, the handbook is organized into seven clear parts:

- Open Borders or Right to Control: Theoretical Arguments
- Open Borders or Right to Control: Practical Approaches
- Culture, Language, and Institutions
- Immigration and Discrimination
- Entry, Exit, and Exploitation
- Climate, Refugees, and Protection
- Immigration Enforcement

In these sections a range of important issues are explored, such as immigration and cultural diversity, the economic aspects of immigration, discrimination, exploitation, definitions of refugee status, territory, citizenship, trafficking and gender. As such, *The Routledge Handbook of the Ethics of Immigration* will be of great interest to those studying philosophy, politics, economics, and related subjects such as law, sociology, and social policy.

Sahar Akhtar is faculty at Georgetown University, USA, and writes and teaches at the intersection of philosophy and economics. Among other works on immigration, she is the author of *Immigration and Discrimination: (Un)Welcoming Others* (2024).

ROUTLEDGE HANDBOOKS IN APPLIED ETHICS

Applied ethics is one of the largest and most diverse fields in philosophy and is closely related to many other disciplines across the humanities, sciences, and social sciences. *Routledge Handbooks in Applied Ethics* are state-of-the-art surveys of important and emerging topics in applied ethics, providing accessible yet thorough assessments of key fields, themes, thinkers, and recent developments in research.

All chapters for each volume are specially commissioned, and written by leading scholars in the field. Carefully edited and organized, *Routledge Handbooks in Applied Ethics* provide indispensable reference tools for students and researchers seeking a comprehensive overview of new and exciting topics in applied ethics and related disciplines. They are also valuable teaching resources as accompaniments to textbooks, anthologies, and research-orientated publications.

THE ROUTLEDGE HANDBOOK OF THE ETHICS OF HUMAN ENHANCEMENT
Edited by Fabrice Jotterand and Marcello Ienca

THE ROUTLEDGE HANDBOOK OF APPLIED CLIMATE CHANGE ETHICS
Edited by Donald A. Brown, Kathryn Gwiazdon, and Laura Westra

THE ROUTLEDGE HANDBOOK OF PHILOSOPHY AND POVERTY
Edited by Gottfried Schweiger and Clemens Sedmak

THE ROUTLEDGE HANDBOOK OF PHILOSOPHY AND MEDIA ETHICS
Edited by Carl Fox and Joe Saunders

THE ROUTLEDGE HANDBOOK OF THE ETHICS OF IMMIGRATION
Edited by Sahar Akhtar

For more information about this series, please visit: https://www.routledge.com/Routledge-Handbooks-in-Applied-Ethics/book-series/RHAE

THE ROUTLEDGE HANDBOOK OF THE ETHICS OF IMMIGRATION

Edited by Sahar Akhtar

LONDON AND NEW YORK

Cover image: *Close-Up Of Footprints On Rippled Sand*, by EyeEm Mobile GmbH. Courtesy of Getty Images.

First published 2025
by Routledge
4 Park Square, Milton Park, Abingdon, Oxon OX14 4RN

and by Routledge
605 Third Avenue, New York, NY 10158

Routledge is an imprint of the Taylor & Francis Group, an informa business

© 2025 selection and editorial matter Sahar Akhtar; individual chapters, the contributors

The right of Sahar Akhtar to be identified as the author of the editorial material, and of the authors for their individual chapters, has been asserted in accordance with sections 77 and 78 of the Copyright, Designs and Patents Act 1988.

All rights reserved. No part of this book may be reprinted or reproduced or utilized in any form or by any electronic, mechanical, or other means, now known or hereafter invented, including photocopying and recording, or in any information storage or retrieval system, without permission in writing from the publishers.

Trademark notice: Product or corporate names may be trademarks or registered trademarks, and are used only for identification and explanation without intent to infringe.

British Library Cataloguing-in-Publication Data
A catalogue record for this book is available from the British Library

Library of Congress Cataloging-in-Publication Data
Names: Akhtar, Sahar, editor.
Title: The Routledge handbook of the ethics of immigration / edited by Sahar Akhtar.
Other titles: Handbook of the ethics of immigration
Description: Abingdon, Oxon ; New York, NY : Routledge, 2025. | Series: Routledge handbooks in applied ethics | Includes bibliographical references and index.
Identifiers: LCCN 2024042189 (print) | LCCN 2024042190 (ebook) | ISBN 9780367479282 (hardback) | ISBN 9781032968681 (paperback) | ISBN 9781003037309 (ebook)
Subjects: LCSH: Emigration and immigration--Government policy--Moral and ethical aspects. | Immigrants--Government policy--Moral and ethical aspects. | Immigration enforcement--Moral and ethical aspects.
Classification: LCC JV6038 .R68 2025 (print) | LCC JV6038 (ebook) | DDC 325--dc23/eng/20250107
LC record available at https://lccn.loc.gov/2024042189
LC ebook record available at https://lccn.loc.gov/2024042190

ISBN: 978-0-367-47928-2 (hbk)
ISBN: 978-1-032-96868-1 (pbk)
ISBN: 978-1-003-03730-9 (ebk)

DOI: 10.4324/9781003037309

Typeset in Sabon
by KnowledgeWorks Global Ltd.

CONTENTS

Notes on Contributors   *viii*

   Introduction   1

PART I
Open Borders or Right to Control: Theoretical Arguments   9

  1 The Ethics of Immigration   11
     Michael Huemer

  2 Social Democracy's Tensions with Immigration   24
     Jason Brennan

  3 A Case for Controlled Borders and Open Doors   35
     Sarah Song

  4 Free Movement: A Human Right or a Citizenship Right?   47
     Rainer Bauböck

PART II
Open Borders or Right to Control: Practical Approaches   63

  5 Immigration and Economic Freedom   65
     Ilya Somin

  6 The Economic Case for Liberalized Immigration Policies   76
     Howard F. Chang

7 Immigration: Some Arguments for Limits 87
   Hrishikesh Joshi

PART III
Culture, Language, and Institutions 97

8 Migration as a Culture Transplant: Neoclassical
   and Institutional Channels 99
   Garett Jones

9 Language as a Criterion of Immigrant Selection 118
   Daniel M. Weinstock

10 On Migration and Backlash 128
   Michael Blake

11 The Nation, The State, and The Foreigner: Rethinking the Place
   of Nationalism in the Ethics of Immigration 140
   Lior Erez

PART IV
Immigration and Discrimination 155

12 Excluding by Race, Ethnicity, and Religion 157
   Sahar Akhtar

13 Nationality and Immigration Restrictions 167
   Rufaida Al Hashmi

14 Immigration and Social Identity Formation 177
   Amy Reed-Sandoval

15 The Ethics of Skill-Selective Immigration Policies 187
   Désirée Lim

PART V
Entry, Exit, and Exploitation 199

16 Citizenship Tests 201
   Thom Brooks

17 Temporary Migration and Worker Exploitation 211
   Michael Kates

18 Treating People as Resources: Emigration
and the Brain Drain   224
Bas van der Vossen

PART VI
Climate, Refugees, and Protection   233

19 Climate Migrants Are Not Refugees   235
Max Gabriel Cherem

20 Immigration and Climate Change   253
Dan C. Shahar

21 Refugees and the Politics of (In)Humanitarianism   266
David Owen

PART VII
Immigration Enforcement   275

22 Shining a Light in the Dark: The Urgency of Addressing
Immigration Detention in Normative Political Theory   277
Felix Bender and Stephanie J. Silverman

23 Immigration Enforcement   292
Alex Sager

24 The Economics and Ethics of U.S. Internal
Immigration Enforcement   305
Madeline Zavodny and George W. Rainbolt

25 Children, Families, and Immigration Enforcement   322
Matthew Lister

Index   *334*

CONTRIBUTORS

Sahar Akhtar is a Faculty at Georgetown University, USA, and writes and teaches at the intersection of philosophy and economics. Among other works on immigration, she is the author of *Immigration and Discrimination: (Un)Welcoming Others* (Oxford, 2024).

Rufaida Al Hashmi is a Lecturer in Political Theory at the University of Reading. She works on the ethics of migration and topics in global justice. She is writing a book, under contract with Oxford University Press, on the ways in which states select which immigrants to admit and which to exclude.

Rainer Bauböck held the Chair in social and political theory at European University Institute from 2007 to 2018 and is co-director of the GLOBALCIT and DILEMMAS projects at the EUI. He is also a corresponding member of the Austrian Academy of Sciences, where he chaired a Commission on Migration and Integration Research until 2024. He teaches as a guest professor at the Nationalism Studies Program of Central European University Vienna. His research interests are in normative political theory and comparative research on democratic citizenship, European integration, migration, nationalism, and minority rights.

Felix Bender is a Lecturer in Politics at Northumbria University. He works and has published extensively on normative questions surrounding refugeehood and asylum.

Michael Blake is Professor of Philosophy, Public Policy, and Governance at the University of Washington. He is jointly appointed to the Department of Philosophy and the Daniel J. Evans School of Public Policy and Governance. He is currently writing a short volume on the ethics of migration, and a longer monograph on the relevance of political justice to questions of meaning in life.

Jason Brennan is the Robert J and Elizabeth Flanagan Family Professor of Strategy, Economics, Ethics, and Public Policy at the McDonough School of Business, Georgetown University. He is the author of eighteen books, including, most relevantly, *In Defense of Openness*, with Bas van der Vossen.

Contributors

Thom Brooks is Professor of Law and Government at Durham University's Law School, where he was Dean (2016–2021) and visiting fellow at Yale Law School. His books include *Becoming British* (2016), *Reforming the UK's Citizenship Test* (2022), and the Jenny Jeger Prize- winning Fabian Society pamphlet *New Arrivals: A Fair Immigration Plan for Labour* (2022).

Howard F. Chang is the Earle Hepburn Professor of Law Emeritus at the University of Pennsylvania Carey Law School. He received his J.D. from Harvard Law School, his Ph.D. in economics from the Massachusetts Institute of Technology, his Master in Public Affairs from Princeton University, and his A.B. in government from Harvard College.

Max Gabriel Cherem is Professor of Philosophy at Kalamazoo College. He writes on moral and political philosophy, focusing on refugees and migration. He spent a year as a Grotius Fellow at the University of Michigan Law School where he studied refugee law, and a year as a Faculty Fellow in the Kenan Institute for Ethics at Duke University. When he reads or writes academic bios he thinks of Charlie King's 1978 song Our Life is More than Our Work.

Lior Erez is the Alfred Landecker Postdoctoral Fellow at the Blavatnik School of Government, University of Oxford. He has written on normative questions surrounding immigration and international development aid, and his current book project focuses on the political ethics of naturalization policies.

Michael Huemer is a professor of philosophy at the University of Colorado. He is the author of more than eighty academic articles in epistemology, ethics, metaethics, metaphysics, and political philosophy, as well as ten amazing books that you should immediately buy, including *The Problem of Political Authority* and *Knowledge, Reality, and Value*.

Garett Jones is Professor of Economics at George Mason University and the author of *The Culture Transplant: How Migrants Make the Economies They Move to a Lot Like the Ones They Left*, published by Stanford University Press and reviewed in *The Wall Street Journal*. His research focuses on the intersection of macroeconomics, IQ, culture, and economic institutions. Jones holds a Master of Public Administration degree from Cornell University, an MA in Political Science from UC Berkeley, and a Ph.D. in Economics from UC San Diego. He is the son of a union pipefitter.

Hrishikesh Joshi is Assistant Professor of Philosophy at the University of Arizona. He works on social and political philosophy, epistemology, and topics at the intersection of politics, philosophy, and economics (PPE). His current book project is *Should We Have Open Borders?: A Debate* with Christopher Freiman.

Michael Kates is Associate Professor of Philosophy and Director of the Pedro Arrupe, S.J. Center for Business Ethics at Saint Joseph's University. He writes on issues of labor justice and exploitation.

Désirée Lim is the Catherine Shultz Rein Early Career Professor and Associate Professor of Philosophy at Penn State, USA. She is also Associate Director of the Rock Ethics Institute. She received her doctorate in Philosophy from King's College London in 2016.

Contributors

Matthew Lister is an associate professor of law at Bond University on the Gold Coast, Queensland Australia. He previously taught at Deakin University, the University of Pennsylvania, Villanova University, and the University of Denver, and was a law clerk on the US Court of International Trade and the 3rd Circuit Court of Appeals. He holds a J.D. and Ph.D. in Philosophy from Penn, and teaches and writes on immigration and refugee law, administrative law, and other topics in legal and political philosophy.

David Owen is Professor of Social and Political Philosophy at the University of Southampton. He works widely on issues of post-Kantian philosophy as well as the ethics and politics of migration and citizenship. Recent books include the co-edited volumes 'The Political Philosophy of Internal Displacement' (Oxford UP 2024) and 'Democratic Multiplicity' (Cambridge UP 2022) as well as his authored work 'What do we owe to refugees?' (Polity, 2020).

George W. Rainbolt is Professor of Philosophy at the University of North Florida. He is the author of *The Concept of Rights* (Springer 2006) and *Freedom as Non-Constraint* (Palgrave-Macmillan 2024).

Amy Reed-Sandoval is Associate Professor of Philosophy and Participating Faculty in the Latinx and Latin American Studies Program at the University of Nevada, Las Vegas. She is the author of *Socially Undocumented: Identity and Immigration Justice* (Oxford University Press, 2020), and co-editor of *Latin American Immigration Ethics* (University of Arizona Press, 2021).

Alex Sager is Professor of Philosophy and Executive Director of University Studies at Portland State University. He is the author of *Toward a Cosmopolitan Ethics of Mobility: The Migrant's-Eye View of the World* (Springer. 2017) and *Against Borders: Why the World Needs Free Movement of People* (Rowman & Littlefield, 2020).

Dan Shahar is MBA Program Director and a Teaching Assistant Professor at West Virginia University. He is the author of *Why It's OK to Eat Meat*; co-editor (with David Schmidtz) of *Environmental Ethics: What Really Matters, What Really Works*; and author of over a dozen journal articles and book chapters.

Stephanie J. Silverman holds a DPhil in Politics and International Relations from the University of Oxford where she was a Commonwealth Scholar associated with the Centre on Migration, Policy and Society. She has published widely on immigration and imprisonment.

Ilya Somin is Professor of Law at George Mason University and B. Kenneth Simon Chair in Constitutional Studies at the Cato Institute. He is the author of *Free to Move: Foot Voting, Migration, and Political Freedom* (Oxford University Press, rev. ed., 2022), *Democracy and Political Ignorance: Why Smaller Government is Smarter* (Stanford University Press, rev. ed. 2016), and *The Grasping Hand: Kelo v. City of New London and the Limits of Eminent Domain* (University of Chicago Press, 2015). Somin has also published articles in a variety of popular press outlets, including the New York Times, Washington Post, Wall Street Journal,

Los Angeles Times, CNN, The Atlantic, and USA Today. He is a regular contributor to the popular Volokh Conspiracy law and politics blog, affiliated with Reason magazine.

Sarah Song is the Milo Rees Robbins Chair in Legal Ethics Professor of Law and Professor of Philosophy and Political Science at the University of California, Berkeley. She is the author of *Justice, Gender, and the Politics of Multiculturalism* (Cambridge, 2007) and *Immigration and Democracy* (Oxford, 2018).

Bas van der Vossen is a Professor of Philosophy and Associate Director of the Smith Institute of Political Economy and Philosophy at Chapman University. He's the co-author of *In Defense of Openness*, with Jason Brennan (Oxford University Press, 2018) and *Debating Humanitarian Intervention*, with Fernando Tesón (Oxford University Press, 2017), and *Political Philosophy: The Basics* (Routledge Press, 2024). He is also the co-editor of *Economic Liberties as Human Rights* (Routledge, 2019) and the *Routledge Handbook of Libertarianism* (Routledge, 2017). He is Associate Editor of *Social Philosophy and Policy*. Bas earned his DPhil from the University of Oxford.

Daniel Weinstock holds the Katharine A. Pearson Chair in Civil Society and Public Policy at McGill University, where he teaches in the Faculty of Law, The Department of Philosophy, the Max Bell School of Public Policy, and the School of Population and Global Health. He has published over 150 academic articles on a wide range of topics in moral, political, and legal philosophy.

Madeline Zavodny is Professor of Economics at the University of North Florida. She co-authored *The Economics of Immigration* (Routledge 2015, 2nd edition 2021) and *Beside the Golden Door* (AEI Press 2010).

INTRODUCTION

Immigration remains one of the most pressing and complex issues of our time, shaping the lives of millions of people around the globe. It provokes important questions about human rights, state sovereignty, cultural identity, and economic opportunities and growth. And it can promote or challenge our understanding of justice, equality, and freedom. This book brings together immigration scholars from a range of disciplines, including philosophy, economics, politics, and law, and presents a range of methods, theoretical approaches, and fresh views on both established and new questions.

The book comes at a time when anti-immigration sentiments have been intensifying across the globe. In countries as diverse as, Colombia, India, Hungary, South Africa, Israel, and Thailand,[1] there has been a noticeable decline in receptiveness toward immigrants, accompanied by a rise in hostility. While the proportion of people opposing immigration in Europe and the United States has remained relatively constant over the past decade, the importance placed on immigration as a political issue has significantly increased among these opponents.[2] In light of this, a central theme of the book concerns backlash against immigrants. Are anti-immigrant attitudes and nationalist sentiments morally important? If so, how? What are the economic implications if new immigrants do not share the existing culture and norms of the state? How should states morally or practically address this? These questions are the focus of several chapters in the book and implicitly run through various other chapters.

Another central theme that runs through the book is the tension between the right of states to control their borders and the rights of individuals to seek better lives beyond those borders. This tension raises classic questions—such as, do individuals have a right to move freely across borders, or does the state's right to self-determination take precedence—but the authors in this book provide new perspectives on these issues. The tension also raises questions related to the modern political landscape: How should we morally address unauthorized migrants? Should migrants who wish or need to move due to climate change be considered refugees? And, how should states handle detention while enforcing their immigration policies, especially when concerning vulnerable populations? The chapters collectively explore these questions, offering insights that challenge conventional thinking and open new avenues for understanding immigration.

DOI: 10.4324/9781003037309-1

The opening discussions in the book focus on the theoretical foundations of the immigration debate, examining the conflicting principles of open borders versus state sovereignty. The perspectives offered range from libertarian views that argue for minimal restrictions on movement to more moderate approaches that advocate for controlled borders or new framings of rights to international movement, balancing the rights of individuals with the interests of states. This exploration sets the stage for a deeper understanding of how these theoretical debates translate into real-world policies and practices.

As the discourse moves from theory to practice, the economic aspects of immigration often at the forefront of public and political debates become the focus. The chapters here center on issues such as labor markets, economic freedom, and the redistribution of wealth. They also highlight the role that empirical research plays in shaping immigration policies that are not only just but also economically viable and sustainable in the long term.

Issues of cultural integration and the impact of immigration on national identity are the next themes examined. As migration reshapes societies, it can cause significant backlash, and it inevitably brings questions about cultural integration, the preservation of national identities, and the impact on social cohesion. The chapters in this section examine how immigrants and their cultural backgrounds interact with the host society's institutions and norms and the proper role of nationalism in a morally sound immigration policy.

This discussion naturally leads to the questions taken up in the next section, concerning discrimination—one of the most morally and politically charged issues in the immigration debate. Discrimination in immigration policies can take many forms, from overtly racist or xenophobic practices to more subtle forms of exclusion based on nationality, language, or skill level, and even the creation of new identities that are in turn the subject of discrimination. These discussions are particularly relevant in a world where rising nationalism and populism often drive immigration policy.

The management of individuals into and out of borders is the next subject of the book, with the chapters on entry, exit, and exploitation exploring the ethical considerations that should guide how states manage immigration. These discussions cover a range of issues, from the criteria for granting citizenship to the rights of temporary workers and the ethical implications of the brain drain phenomenon.

Climate change is increasingly recognized as a major driver of migration, and the book addresses this issue with a focus on the unique challenges posed by climate-induced displacement. The concept of "climate refugees" challenges existing legal frameworks and raises questions for the authors about how best to protect those who are either forced to or wish to migrate due to environmental factors. The authors also explore whether the humanitarian framing of assisting refugees more broadly is adequate to address their needs.

Finally, the book turns to the issue of immigration enforcement, a topic that is both contentious and critical to the broader debate on immigration. The enforcement of immigration laws often involves practices that raise serious ethical questions, such as detention, deportation, and the separation of families. The authors in this section examine these practices from different angles, questioning the legitimacy of current enforcement methods and exploring alternatives based on various ethical principles.

By bringing together diverse perspectives and examining the issue from multiple angles—ethical, economic, legal, and cultural—the book provides a nuanced understanding of many of the challenges and opportunities that immigration presents. It provokes readers to think critically about the balance between state sovereignty and individual rights, the role of discrimination in immigration policies, and the ethical responsibilities that states have toward migrants. Ultimately, the book serves as a valuable resource for anyone seeking to understand the complex nature of immigration and the impact it has on our world.

Open Borders or Right to Control: Theoretical Arguments

The book opens with different theoretical perspectives on the debate between open borders and state sovereignty. The chapters collectively explore the tensions between individual rights and state self-determination, as they variously address the coercive implications of restricting immigration, the philosophical underpinnings of social democracy in relation to open borders, or a moderate approach aimed at respecting both the rights of some potential migrants and the interests of sovereign states.

Michael Huemer ("The Ethics of Immigration") initiates this discussion by arguing that the rights of potential immigrants are infringed because immigration restrictions subject them to harmful coercion and he challenges the conventional justifications for such restrictions. He moreover argues that unauthorized immigration is morally defensible since

The typical reasons for obeying a state's laws assume that the individual is part of the society, benefits fairly from social cooperation, or has an equal voice in governance, none of which, he argues, applies to potential migrants.

Jason Brennan ("Social Democracy's Tensions with Immigration") builds on the libertarian critique offered by Huemer. Brennan argues that the philosophical commitments and defenses of social democracy are not compatible with open borders. Because of its tension with open borders, he argues, social democracy is not as committed to an egalitarian worldview as its defenders might think it is. In contrast to a world of separate social democracies with significant immigration restrictions, he argues that a libertarian world of open borders is likely far more egalitarian.

Moving toward a more moderate perspective, **Sarah Song** ("A Case for Controlled Borders and Open Doors") advocates for a middle-ground approach between the open borders stance and the view that states have the right to control their borders. She argues for the perspective of "controlled borders and open doors." After outlining the concept of qualified state sovereignty over immigration and critically evaluating three common arguments supporting the state's right to control immigration, she presents an alternative argument centered on the value of collective self-determination.

Finally, **Rainer Bauböck** ("Free movement: A human right or a citizenship right?") offers a partial reconciliation between the competing views of free movement as a human right and the state's right to control immigration grounded in collective self-determination. He proposes that free movement should be framed as a citizenship right within the context of the international state system by building on citizens' right to leave and return. This view suggests a cooperative international framework, supported by reciprocal agreements between states that promote individual mobility, as the most realistic prospect for free movement.

Open Borders or Right to Control: Practical Approaches

While theoretical arguments figured prominently in the previous section's discussion of immigration restrictions, this section focuses more centrally on economic considerations and empirical research. The chapters engage with the debates surrounding the economic and institutional implications of immigration, presenting a range of perspectives on the benefits and challenges of liberalized immigration policies.

The discussion begins with **Ilya Somin** ("Immigration and Economic Freedom"), **who attempts to bolster the case for open borders by arguing that immigration restrictions impede** economic freedom. He considers both "negative" economic freedom, typically valued by libertarians and classical liberals, and "positive" freedom, emphasized by left-liberal thinkers, arguing that immigration restrictions undermine both types of freedoms for both immigrants and current members. Somin's analysis aims to show that a commitment to economic liberty strongly opposes the imposition of migration barriers.

Howard Chang ("The Economic Case for Liberalized Immigration Policies") furthers the broad economic case for more liberalized immigration policies. An important theme of his chapter is that even when prioritizing the interests of current citizens, the gains from trade in the labor market provided by immigrant workers justify more open admission policies. Chang emphasizes that alternative solutions to concerns like environmental protection, stable cultural communities, or the distribution of income among a society's existing members, are more effective and less restrictive than limiting immigration and do not sacrifice the gains from trade in the labor market.

In contrast to Somin and Chang, **Hrishikesh Joshi** ("Immigration: Some Arguments for Limits") presents a rationale for immigration limits. First, he draws on recent empirical research to show that the institutions we live under may be influenced by immigration policy. Second, Joshi argues that, since we commonly accept limits on freedom of movement as necessary in various significant areas of our lives, there is no compelling reason to consider such limits illegitimate when it comes to international borders.

Culture, Language, and Institutions

This section delves into the relationships between culture, nationalism, and immigration, offering an exploration of how these factors should influence and are influenced by migration policies and practices. Through examining the cultural and linguistic background of selected immigrants and the rising tide of populist and nationalist backlash against immigration, the authors collectively highlight the challenges of crafting immigration policies that are both just and politically sustainable.

Expanding the focus on the host society's institutions that was part of the subject of Joshi's chapter, **Garett Jones** ("Migration as a Culture Transplant: Neoclassical and Institutional Channels") challenges economic and related consequentialist arguments supporting open borders by exploring the extensive literature on what he refers to as "cultural transplant theory." This literature, he argues, shows how immigrants and their descendants bring specific attitudes, values, and norms that can significantly impact the institutions and productivity levels of the receiving state. Jones maintains that this phenomenon creates challenges for assimilation, potentially reducing economic growth and innovation in the most productive economies. Therefore, poorly-chosen immigration policies in those economies could, he maintains, hurt not only citizens in the receiving state but also the world as a whole, including the global poor.

Daniel Weinstock ("Language as a Criterion of Immigrant Selection") builds on the theme of cultural integration by exploring whether states can justifiably select discretionary immigrants based on whether they speak the state's dominant language. After arguing that any criteria used by states must be morally understandable even to those who are rejected based on those criteria, he maintains that, on this standard, language criteria seem permissible. While recognizing that immigrants can certainly learn the language over time, he argues that in states where the native language is vulnerable to being assimilated, selecting immigrants who already speak the language may be justifiable.

Michael Blake ("On Migration and Backlash") frames his inquiry around the growing negative sentiment about immigration based on nationalist concerns. As Blake notes, all around the world, we have seen a recent rise in populist pressure on governments to reduce migration and to remove the few migratory rights currently protected by law and political practice. Should this backlash be discounted as fleeting and irrational, or should it be accounted for as a part of an ethical immigration policy? Blake argues that states that defend the rights of migrants amidst such backlash may undermine popular support for democratic institutions and liberal governance, and may therefore be forced to choose between protecting the rights of migrants and protecting the rights of citizens. After surveying two primary approaches for how this tension might be avoided, he concludes that neither is fully satisfactory and that the problem may be more entrenched than defenders of liberal democracy would hope.

As with Blake, **Lior Erez** ("The Nation, The State, and the Foreigner: Rethinking the Place of Nationalism in the Ethics of Immigration") begins his discussion by observing the critical role that nationalism plays in contemporary migration politics. He presents a framework for examining the proper role of nationalism in the ethics of immigration, particularly in terms of inclusion and integration. By distinguishing between three key narratives regarding the relationship between nationalism and the nation-state, Erez aims to provide an argumentative roadmap that highlights nationalism's potential contribution to the ethics of immigration.

Immigration and Discrimination

Picking up on some of the cultural issues and concerns about nationalism of the last section, as well as current trends around the world, this section explores the ideas of discrimination in the context of states' immigration policies. In countries around the world, there has been a noticeable decline in receptiveness toward immigrants, accompanied by a rise in hostility. Although numerous factors, including economic considerations, could explain these attitudes, there also appears to be a growing anxiety in many places about the erosion of a shared identity.

Sahar Akhtar ("Excluding by Race, Ethnicity, and Religion") begins the section by challenging the commonplace idea that it is always wrongfully discriminatory for a state to restrict immigration on the basis of race, ethnicity, or religion. By focusing on the growing class of views that argue that discrimination is wrong when it degrades a group, and working through different examples, she aims to show that, in fact, not all cases of excluding by race, ethnicity, or religion are morally wrong.

Rufaida Al Hashmi ("Nationality and Immigration Restrictions") relates criteria such as race, ethnicity, or religion to the common practice of excluding potential immigrants on the basis of nationality. She argues that nationality-based restrictions often track restrictions based on these other criteria, which, in contrast to Akhtar, she argues are always morally wrong. Moreover, drawing from the philosophical literature on profiling, she argues that even when nationality-based restrictions do not track these other criteria, they might still be wrong.

Amy Reed-Sandoval ("Immigration and Social Identity Formation") takes the themes of identity and immigration in a novel direction, by arguing that immigration systems create social identities that are then vulnerable to oppression. Drawing from her recently developed approach to understanding immigration injustice, she argues that there is a distinction between being "legally undocumented" and being "socially undocumented," with the latter being an important source of immigration injustice. She then argues that this approach can be used to reveal and combat other forms of what she calls identity-based oppression.

Finally, **Désirée Lim** ("The Ethics of Skill-Selective Immigration Policies") connects race-based immigration restrictions to the issue of giving preferential treatment to highly-skilled migrants. Focusing on countries in the Global North, such as the United States, Canada, and Australia, she begins by describing how skill-selective immigration policies function in practice before arguing that the ethical debate over these policies largely hinges on whether they constitute wrongful discrimination. By making the comparison to restrictions based on race, she explores three approaches to understanding wrongful discrimination in the context of immigration. Ultimately, she concludes that the "Status-Harming" perspective on wrongful immigration discrimination provides the most compelling argument against skill-selective immigration policies.

Entry, Exit, and Exploitation

The chapters in this section explore distinct issues related to how states ought to manage the entry and exit of people. The discussions cover a range of topics, from the criteria and expectations placed on those seeking citizenship to the rights and treatment of temporary migrant workers, and the moral considerations surrounding the emigration of skilled individuals.

Thom Brooks ("Citizenship Tests") starts us off by providing a survey of how tests for citizenship operate in states such as the United States, Australia, and the United Kingdom. He highlights how each country has differing expectations for new citizens, reflecting their unique historical, cultural, and political contexts. Brooks concludes by offering general suggestions for a model of citizenship tests, aiming to balance the interests of the state with fairness to prospective citizens.

Turning from the formal procedures of entry to the treatment of newly admitted migrants, **Michael Kates** ("Temporary Migration and Worker Exploitation") begins with the observation that the more open a country is to migrant workers, the less extensive are their rights in comparison to citizens and permanent residents. In light of this fact, Kates asks whether it is morally permissible for states to grant temporary workers a less extensive set of rights than citizens and permanent residents. He surveys the strongest philosophical cases for limiting temporary workers' rights, ultimately rejecting them and outlining a new argument for why limiting the rights of temporary workers would be wrongfully exploitative.

Finally, **Bas van der Vossen** ("Treating People as Resources: Emigration and the Brain Drain") shifts the focus to the issue of emigration, particularly the phenomenon known as "brain drain," where highly skilled or educated individuals leave their home country for opportunities abroad. Van der Vossen challenges the idea that emigration should be restricted to prevent or reduce this loss of talent. He argues that such restrictions are among the gravest injustices in the world, emphasizing that such restrictions treat people as mere resources or property.

Climate, Refugees, and Protection

This section delves into the often-contested relationship between climate change, migration, and the protection of vulnerable populations. The authors examine the emerging discourse surrounding both "climate refugees" and refugees more generally, exploring whether current legal frameworks and humanitarian practices adequately address the unique challenges posed by each type of migration. They collectively highlight the need for a careful and differentiated approach, questioning the efficacy of existing categorizations and proposing new models for addressing the mobility needs and wants of vulnerable populations.

The section begins with **Max Cherem** ("Climate Migrants Are Not Refugees") examining whether the legal definition of a refugee or its application, should be expanded to include "climate refugees." He argues that, from a practical standpoint, using the term "climate refugee" is not an effective strategy for protecting people who want or need to move for climate-related reasons. This is because, he argues, the way individuals are harmed or wronged affects the type of corrective justice they are entitled to, which varies between refugees, climate migrants, and natural disaster victims. Thus, he maintains, climate migrants and refugees should be assisted separately, rather than being grouped together.

In a similar vein, **Dan Shahar** ("Immigration and Climate Change") challenges popular treatments of the climate crisis that envision torrents of "climate refugees" fleeing urgently across international borders. He argues these visions mischaracterize the nature of climate-induced migration and hence also immigration's role in lessening climate change harms. Rather than urgently fleeing across borders to escape climate emergencies, he argues that most people facing climate-related burdens will seek options to move in non-emergency conditions. In light of this, he claims, immigration's most important functions in a warming world will not have to do with rescuing people but with expanding options for them.

David Owen ("Refugees and the Politics of (In)Humanitarianism") turns to the subject of contemporary attempts to protect refugees, taking a more theoretical approach. He focuses on the humanitarian framing of refugees as subjects of need and argues that tensions within the discourse of humanitarianism can be exploited for inhumane ends. He ultimately offers a critique not only of the exploitation of humanitarianism but of humanitarianism itself. And he concludes by making the case for what he calls "a politics of dignity in refugee protection."

Immigration Enforcement

The enforcement of immigration laws has become a central and contentious issue in political theory and ethics. As states grapple with the complexities of migration, the measures they employ to regulate and control immigration have far-reaching consequences, not only for those seeking to enter and remain in a country but also for the ethical principles that underpin a just society. The final collection of chapters delves into various aspects of enforcement, exploring the ethical concerns and practical challenges that arise when states implement and maintain their immigration policies.

Felix Bender and Stephanie Silverman ("Shining a Light in the Dark: The Urgency of Addressing Immigration Detention in Normative Political Theory") open this section by observing that the conditions and potential harms of immigration detention are often overlooked by philosophers and political theorists. By presenting a case study of Canada's minimalist immigration enforcement system, they argue that detention is not only a fundamental part of immigration policy enforcement but also morally wrong on several grounds. Their chapter calls for a deeper normative understanding of the role detention plays in immigration ethics.

In a related vein, **Alex Sager** ("Immigration Enforcement") examines the broader legal framework surrounding immigration enforcement and highlights the ethical dilemmas arising from these practices. He argues that even if states have the right to restrict immigration, practices like detention and deportation require careful ethical scrutiny. For instance, he raises questions about the legitimacy and authority of private corporations and foreign states involved in enforcement activities. Additionally, he argues that since immigration enforcement often involves the surveillance of both citizens and immigrants, it should be assessed within the broader context of justice. Finally, he concludes by considering whether it is morally permissible or even obligatory for immigrants and their allies to resist enforcement efforts.

Madeline Zavodny and George W. Rainbolt ("The Economics and Ethics of U.S. Internal Immigration Enforcement") shift the attention to the internal mechanisms of immigration control, focusing on the case of the United States. They detail the two primary methods of enforcement currently used: employment-based and police-based enforcement. After analyzing the economic and social impacts of these strategies, Zavodny and Rainbolt propose a framework of ethical principles that should guide internal immigration enforcement in any context.

Concluding this examination of enforcement practices, **Matthew Lister** ("Children, Families, and Immigration Enforcement") explores how enforcement is applied to children and to their families. He examines a range of ethical issues posed by detention and family separation, especially in situations where some family members are citizens or authorized migrants while others are unauthorized migrants. His analysis aims to shed light on complex ethical questions that arise in the enforcement of immigration laws, particularly concerning the most vulnerable populations, and underscores the need for careful normative evaluation in these cases.

Notes

1 Crush, J., and W. Pendleton. "Regionalizing Xenophobia? Citizen Attitudes to Immigration and Refugee Policy in Southern Africa." SAMP Migration Policy Series no. 30, Southern African Migration Programme, Waterloo, ON, 2004; Gonzalez-Barrera, Ana, and Phillip Connor. "Around the World, More Say Immigrants Are a Strength than a Burden." Pew Research Center, March 14, 2019; Alesina, Alberto, and Marco Tabellini. "The Political Effects of Immigration: Culture or Economics?" Harvard Business School Working Paper 21-–069, 2020; Hainmueller, Jens, and Daniel J. Hopkins. "Public Attitudes toward Immigration." *Annual Review of Political Science* 17, no. 1 (2014): 225–49. doi:10.1146/annurev-polisci-102512-194818; https://www.pewresearch.org/global/2019/03/14/around-the-world-more-say-immigrants-are-a-strength-than-a-burden/; Singh, Priyansha, and Rohini Mitra. "Millions of Indians Seek Better Lives Abroad, but India Treats Immigrants Poorly, New Study Shows." *IndiaSpend*, January 7, 2021. https://www.indiaspend.com/governance/millions-of-indians-seek-better-lives-abroad-but-india-treats-immigrants-poorly-study-711347; Esipova, Neli, Julie Ray, and Anita Pugliese. "Syrian Refugees Not Welcome in Eastern Europe." Gallup, May 5, 2017. https://news.gallup.com/poll/209828/syrian-refugees-not-welcome-eastern-europe.aspx; Esipova, Neli, Julie Ray, and Anita Pugliese. "World Grows Less Accepting of Migrants." Gallup, September 23, 2020. https://news.gallup.com/poll/320678/world-grows-less-accepting-migrants.aspx; Gaikwad, Nikhar, and Gareth Nellis. "The Majority-Minority Divide in Attitudes toward Internal Migration: Evidence from Mumbai." *American Journal of Political Science* 61, no. 2 (2017): 456–72. doi:10.1111/ajps.12276

2 Dempster, Helen, Amy Leach, and Karen Hargrave. "Public Attitudes towards Immigration and Immigrants." ODI Working Paper 588, ODI, September 2020. https://cdn.odi.org/media/documents/Public_attitudes_towards_immigration_and_immigrants_what_people_think_why_and_how.pdf.

PART I

Open Borders or Right to Control
Theoretical Arguments

1
THE ETHICS OF IMMIGRATION

Michael Huemer

1.1 Introduction

Worldwide, there are millions of people who would like to leave the country they live in and move to a wealthier, freer, or otherwise more desirable (to them) society. Most would be vastly better off if they were able to do so. Yet governments around the world impose severe immigration restrictions, effectively trapping the overwhelming majority of people in whatever country they happened to be born in. Most citizens of first world nations, wary of the influence of foreigners, support these restrictions.[1]

On the face of it, this situation poses ethical issues. How should we weigh the interests of the individuals who wish to move to a given country against the desires of the current citizens who wish to exclude them?

In what follows, I summarize my views on two related questions: first, is it ethically permissible for the state to forcibly exclude the overwhelming majority of ordinary individuals from foreign nations who wish to enter the country? Second, if individuals find themselves legally prohibited from migrating to their desired destination country, is it permissible for them to migrate illegally? The answer to the first question is *no*, and to the second, *yes*.[2]

1.2 Why Immigration Restrictions Are Immoral

1.2.1 Starving Marvin

I begin with a hypothetical scenario:

> *Starving Marvin:* Marvin is hungry and wishes to buy some food at a local marketplace. Fortunately, there are people in the marketplace who would be happy to trade food to Marvin in exchange for something that he would be happy to give them. Unfortunately, however, Sam (who has some nephews and nieces who also do business in the marketplace and who don't like Marvin) decides to take up his rifle and forcibly block the road, ordering Marvin to return home. As a result, Marvin returns home empty-handed, where he starves.

In this story, Sam obviously acted badly. Notice that Sam did not merely *refuse to feed* Marvin; Sam actively, coercively intervened to prevent Marvin from obtaining food. Since Marvin was going to obtain food without Sam's intervention, Sam *starved* Marvin. Indeed, if the outcome was foreseeable, we might consider Sam guilty of murder. But let us just rest with the conclusion that Sam's action was very wrong. Nearly anyone, whether liberal, conservative, libertarian, socialist, etc., would agree that Sam acted wrongly; hence, this seems to be a fair starting point for ethical reasoning.

But Sam's behavior is analogous to that of, for example, the U.S. government when it forcibly prevents migrants from entering the country to work and trade. Many would-be migrants would be able to satisfy their material needs and escape oppression if they were allowed to come to the United States, where there are individuals who would be happy to trade with them. But because the U.S. government forcibly bars their entry, they must remain in a state of deprivation and danger. Notice that the government does not merely *refuse to aid* those foreigners; it actively and coercively intervenes to prevent them from trading with Americans who would like to trade with them. Since they would have been able to satisfy their needs if the government had not intervened, the government is harming them.

Admittedly, death is an extreme outcome; most will not literally die but will merely have much worse lives than they would have if the government left them alone. If you like, modify the Starving Marvin example so that Marvin merely suffers from malnutrition or some other, lesser deprivation. It remains clear that Sam acts wrongly.

1.2.2 Jobs

Against that backdrop, most of the justifications commonly given for restricting immigration are absurdly inadequate. For instance, until recently, the most popular argument for restriction cited the concern that immigrants would "steal American jobs". The vast majority of economists consider immigration overall beneficial to the domestic economy;[3] however, there is some evidence of a slight decrease in wages (of a few percent) for the least skilled American workers.[4] The government, one might argue, has an obligation to prioritize its own poor citizens over foreign nationals; hence, it should restrict immigration to prevent foreigners from competing in the labor market.[5]

This argument is analogous to the following defense that Sam might give for his actions against Marvin:

> Of course, it's very sad that Marvin is hungry. But I have to think of my own nephews and nieces first. They, too, need to trade in the marketplace. And while most of them would benefit from trading with Marvin, a few of them who are poor could be slightly disadvantaged by Marvin's bidding up the price of food. So you can see why I had to forcibly bar Marvin from reaching the marketplace.

This defense utterly fails. You may not coercively harm one person solely to prevent that individual from freely competing in the marketplace with someone else, even if the latter person is someone whom you have a special responsibility to care for. Thus, notwithstanding the government's special duties to its citizens, it may not impose severe harm on foreigners solely to prevent some of its citizens from suffering a slight disadvantage through marketplace competition.

1.2.3 Crime

The popularity of the "stealing jobs" argument seems to have waned in recent years. Today, the more common argument in public political discourse is that immigrants are likely to commit crimes; hence, the government must exclude them to protect the native-born citizens. The most common version of the argument merely cites *some crimes* committed by immigrants (sometimes just a single crime), without mentioning the overall crime *rate* among immigrants or how it compares to the native-born crime rate.[6] As it turns out, most studies find that both legal and illegal immigrants are *less* prone to commit crimes than the native-born population.[7] Illegal immigrants are especially law-abiding, committing half as many violent crimes and a quarter as many property crimes as native-born Americans.[8]

With that background, this argument for restriction is analogous to the following. Sam points out that if Marvin entered the marketplace, there was some nonzero probability that he would commit a crime there. Sam doesn't have any evidence of Marvin in particular being a criminal, but in the past, when people from Marvin's village entered this marketplace, at least some of them committed crimes, though they did so *less* often than the people who were *already* in the marketplace. On this basis, Sam claims that he had to forcibly stop Marvin from getting to the marketplace, in order to protect the people already there.

1.2.4 Culture

A third argument for restriction is that immigration from foreign nations may alter the general culture of a country in ways that the current citizens prefer to avoid. This argument is analogous to the following. Sam notes that Marvin speaks a different language, wears different styles of clothing, eats different kinds of food, and practices a different religion from most of the people currently in the marketplace. Some of Sam's nephews and nieces who trade in that marketplace dislike these things about Marvin, and they fear that Marvin might influence others to take up his own practices. Thus, Sam explains, he had to forcibly bar Marvin from reaching the marketplace.

Again, this defense of Sam's behavior is a nonstarter. A plausible diagnosis is that one may not coercively harm other people, solely to secure something that one does not have a right to – and no one has a *right* to have the culture of one's society be the way one wants it to be.

1.2.5 Property Rights

Another popular argument draws an analogy with private property. The owner of a house, for example, may choose to exclude whomever he wishes from his house. The owner need not have any special reasons for doing so; it is enough that the owner does not feel like having a particular guest at a particular time. Similarly, it is said, we have the right to exclude whomever we wish from our country and we don't need any special reasons for doing so; it is enough that we prefer not to have certain people in the country.

The agent who excludes migrants from a given country is the government of that country. Thus, the preceding argument presupposes that the government *owns the country*, in the same sense that ordinary individuals own their own houses. But the government does not own the country. Specific individuals and organizations own each particular plot of land within the country; no one owns the entire country. So the correct conclusion to draw from the homeowner example is that each individual property owner has the right to exclude migrants from *his own* land. By the same token, individual property owners also have the right to invite migrants onto their own land. Thus, if there are landlords who wish to rent apartments to immigrants, respect for property rights dictates that those migrants may occupy those apartments.

Notice the radical implications of assuming that the government has literal property rights over the entire country equivalent to those that a homeowner has over his own house. The assumption would justify migration restrictions with the same ease as it would justify *nearly any policy whatsoever*. For example, a homeowner has the right to declare that no one in his house may criticize him; therefore, we could infer that the government also has the right to prohibit anyone in the country from criticizing the government. Similarly, the government would have the right to disarm the population (a prospect particularly troubling to those on the right of the American political spectrum), prohibit poor people from voting, require everyone to worship Kamala Harris, or require everyone to smoke crack cocaine – all on penalty of being expelled from the country. These measures would all be justified in the same way, as analogous to conditions that a homeowner may impose on anyone wishing to use his house.

Perhaps it is not *the state* that owns the country but rather *the people collectively*, with the state merely acting as their agent to implement their will. Or perhaps the people merely own certain public resources, such as the roads, rather than the entire country. This might give them the right to control immigration in order to control the use of those public resources.[9] But this view runs into the same problem as the seemingly more extreme view that the state owns the country: *if* it succeeds in legitimizing immigration restrictions on the ground that the people's representatives enacted those restrictions, then it must also legitimize a host of tyrannical policies (prohibitions on criticizing the government, etc.). If the people collectively have the right to decide not to share public resources with people born in foreign countries, then they should also have the right to decide not to share public resources with people who criticize the government, people who fail to smoke crack, etc. – again, just as a homeowner may choose not to allow people who criticize the government or who fail to smoke crack into his house.

1.2.6 *Political Self-Defense*

It has recently become popular to argue that immigrants pose a *political* threat to the citizens of first world nations. Sometimes, the threat is understood to be that immigrants will vote for the wrong political party, the party opposite of the speaker's own party.[10] A more sophisticated understanding is that immigrants may import the values of their home countries, the very values that have made those countries poor, tyrannical, or otherwise undesirable places to live in the first place. If too many immigrants arrive in first world nations, they might convert the first-world nations to a worse value system, with the result that the first world nations become more like the third world nations.[11] Thus, we must exclude immigrants in order to protect ourselves.

1.2.6.1 The Threat of Incorrect Voting

Begin with the first concern, that of immigrant voting patterns. Here is an analogy:

> *Electoral Defense:* You have a neighbor who you know intends to vote for the Demoblicans in the next election. He has signs for the Demoblican party on his lawn, has a long record of voting for the Demoblicans, and has explicitly proclaimed his intention to vote for every Demoblican on the ballot in the upcoming election. You, a supporter of the Republicrats, know that the Demoblicans are the wrong party to vote for. Knowing that only a trip to the hospital will stop him from voting, you beat him up, thus sending him to the hospital for the day. This is regrettable, but, you claim, it was a necessary act of political self-defense.

This behavior seems wrong. Is it a fair analogy for immigration restriction motivated by political self-defense? Note that the action that immigrants are suspected of being about to perform is precisely the same as the action your neighbor was going to perform in the above example: voting for the wrong party. It is in fact much less certain whether and how any given immigrant will vote than it was how your neighbor would vote in the above example. The harm that you coercively impose on your neighbor in that example – a serious beating – is probably also much *smaller* than the harm that immigrants suffer by being excluded from the country. (This remains true even if we suppose that you beat your neighbor up every four years in advance of the presidential elections.) Therefore, if anything, the case for beating your neighbor is *much stronger* than the case for excluding migrants from the country. Yet the action in Electoral Defense still seems wrong.

Perhaps the action in Electoral Defense is wrong because the probability of your neighbor altering the outcome of the election was minuscule; hence, your use of force was disproportionate to the threat. By contrast, one might argue, the probability of immigrants as a class altering some election outcomes is much larger. So in that respect, the case for restricting migration is stronger. If you are moved by this concern, imagine modifying the above scenario as follows:

> *Group Electoral Defense:* As in Electoral Defense, except that you organize a large group of Republicrats to beat up *millions* of Demoblican voters on election day, thus preventing them from voting. As a result, the Republicrats are much more likely to win.

This action still seems wrong. Note that while your probability of securing your desired election outcome has gone up, the amount of harm you have coercively imposed has also increased by millions of times.

It thus seems that immigration restrictions are unjustified even if they are needed to prevent the wrong party from winning too many elections. But in fact, immigration restrictions are not even necessary for that purpose. Rather than completely excluding potential migrants from the country, the state could merely grant them legal residency without voting rights. This is the status currently possessed by millions of immigrants in the United States. Those who are concerned about immigrant voting patterns could push for tighter restrictions on who is granted *citizenship*, rather than restricting *residency*.

1.2.6.2 The Threat of Undemocratic Values

Let us now turn to the other major concern, that migrants may corrupt the values of the country to which they migrate. This is a highly speculative hypothesis, and history records no cases in which, for example, democracy has been overturned or free speech repealed due to political pressure from immigrants. The United States has had higher immigration rates at some points in its history, apparently without its values being corrupted; indeed, earlier waves of immigrants helped form the very values that we are now concerned to preserve.[12]

An opposite speculation seems about equally plausible: that immigration may *strengthen* the values of liberal democracy because immigrants are *more* likely than native-born citizens to have a strong commitment to the values for which liberal democratic societies are known. One reason this might be true is that immigrants to a liberal democratic state are people who have expressly undertaken large costs to move to that country, whereas native-born citizens merely belong to the country by default, through happening to have been born there. Immigrants are not a random sample of the societies from which they came; they are a self-selected group with a willingness to leave behind the society they grew up in, along with everyone they know, to join a new society with different customs, a different language, etc. Very few human beings are willing to do this, even when another society looks much better on purely objective metrics. On the whole, then, immigrants are probably less committed to the traditions of their birth nation and more admiring of their desired destination country than the average member of their society. They are probably more open-minded and enterprising as well.

The above is a speculative argument, but no more speculative than the opposite claim that immigrants are likely to harm democratic values. So the argument for immigration restriction is analogous to the following.

> *Values Defense:* Sam suspects that Marvin might have worse values than most of the people currently in the marketplace, and that Marvin might therefore influence people there in a negative way. Marvin has not so far done anything in particular to influence people in a negative way, nor does Sam have any concrete evidence that Marvin would do this, but it remains a plausible speculation. It is also plausible that Marvin may have better values than most of the people in the marketplace and may influence them in a *positive* way. Sam decides to forcibly bar the way to the marketplace.

Again, Sam's behavior seems wrong. Notice that if harmful coercion were so easily justified, then we would be justified in exerting harmful force against a great many people in an enormous range of circumstances. I in fact know of many people who might have bad values (with equal or greater probability to the probability of a randomly chosen immigrant having bad values), and many of them have a greater chance of influencing others than the average immigrant (for instance, many post comments on the internet, teach classes, or write editorials). Am I justified in coercively imposing on all those people harms at least as great as the harm of being forced to live in a third world dictatorship, if doing so would stop them from influencing our society's values?

Here, as in Section 1.2.6.1, you might think that the scale of the intervention matters. Perhaps you think there is a higher probability that immigrants as a class will change the values of society than that Marvin would change the values of the marketplace since Marvin is only one person. But note that a local marketplace is also much smaller than a society of millions of people, so it is far from obvious that Marvin is less likely to change the marketplace's values. Regardless, if you are moved by this concern, modify the above case as follows:

> *Group Values Defense*: As in Values Defense, except that Sam also subjects many other people to the same treatment as he gives Marvin.

This does not seem to render Sam's behavior justified.

1.3 Why Illegal Immigration Is Permissible

In my view, it is generally fine to disobey unjust laws, as long as one can do so without harming others or violating others' rights.[13] So given the injustice of immigration restrictions, it is of course acceptable to migrate illegally.

Many people, however, believe in *political obligation*, namely, a general ethical obligation to obey the law, even in cases where a given law is bad and should not have been made. For example, many think that *even if* one is unjustly overtaxed, one is nonetheless ethically obliged to pay the legally prescribed amount of tax, rather than evading one's taxes. Similarly, even if you agree with my arguments in Section 1.2, you might still think that individuals should not migrate illegally. In this section, I reject that view: *even if there is political obligation in general*, I claim, it would not apply in this specific case, that is, potential immigrants would still have no moral obligation to respect immigration restrictions.

1.3.1 *The Social Contract*

Why might we have a duty to obey the law? The best known account of this is the social contract theory, according to which political obligation arises out of a kind of contract whereby, in return for the benefits of government, citizens have implicitly agreed to pay taxes and obey the laws. Since we have a general duty to keep our promises, we are obligated in general to obey the law, even when particular laws are ill-chosen and perhaps even immoral.[14]

This would not account for (nor do most proponents of the theory advocate) an *absolute* duty to obey the law, regardless of circumstances. After all, there can be cases in which breaking a contract is justified. Thus, if the law requires you to commit murder, you should probably disobey, notwithstanding the social contract. What the social contract theory claims is that we have at least a *prima facie moral reason* (a moral reason that can in principle be outweighed in some circumstances) to obey the law, even when the law is itself unjustified.

But even if you accept the social contract theory in general, it would not apply to illegal immigrants. At the time they violate the law, they are not yet part of our society and thus are not parties to our social contract. They therefore have no moral reason, even prima facie, to respect our laws, including the immigration laws, merely as such.

But, you might object, once individuals have migrated illegally and joined our society, they *then* become subject to the social contract. So, even if the initial law violation was permissible, it is impermissible for them to continue violating the law by *remaining* in the country illegally. Once they have been present long enough to count as having accepted the social contract, they are immediately obligated to leave.

To see what is wrong with this thought, we need to review part of standard contract theory. In any contract, each party agrees to do something in exchange for some benefit provided by the other party or parties. Without some potential benefit, a contract is not binding; for example, if I promise to give you $100, but you do not agree to provide any benefit of any kind to me in exchange, then we do not have a valid contract, and no court will enforce my promise.

In the case of the social contract, citizens are said to agree to obey the laws in exchange for certain benefits that the state is to confer on them, such as protection of their rights, peaceful dispute resolution, and certain public goods. Therefore, if some alleged parties to the contract were to be excluded from all of those benefits, those parties would not be bound by the contract. And therefore, the social contract cannot obligate anyone to do things that would inherently deny them any possible benefits from the contract. Excluding oneself entirely from a given society inherently denies one any possible benefit from that society's social contract; therefore, no social contract can require anyone to completely exclude themselves from the society.

1.3.2 Gratitude

A related theory holds that political obligation arises out of the duty to show gratitude for the benefits one has received from the state. Even if one has not *agreed* to do so, it is plausible that one generally ought to show gratitude for the benefits one receives from others. In this case, some suggest, the proper way to show gratitude is to obey all the laws.[15]

Again, whatever one thinks of this as an account of political obligation, it does not apply to illegal immigrants. If they were to obey the immigration laws, they would then receive no benefits at all (indeed, as noted above, they would receive large *harms*) from the government. It cannot be that the proper way of showing gratitude for certain benefits is to completely exclude oneself from those benefits.

1.3.3 Hypothetical Consent

Some say that even if we have not actually signed any social contract, we should behave as if we had because we *would have* agreed to a social contract if we were deliberating about the structure of society in ideal conditions. This hypothetical contract would include, again, stipulations that citizens would obey the laws and pay taxes in exchange for the state's protection. The alleged facts about the hypothetical contract are meant to show something about what constitute *fair* or *reasonable* terms of social cooperation.[16]

This theory of political obligation, again, could not apply to the case of immigration law. It cannot be that the fair and reasonable terms of social cooperation include your not participating at all in the social cooperation. Accordingly, no rational person would sign on to a social contract that required him to exclude himself entirely from the society.

1.3.4 Fair Play

Another theory of political obligation holds that disobeying the law treats one's fellow citizens unfairly.[17] In order for a society to have the benefits of law and order, it is necessary that *most* people voluntarily obey the law, even when they disagree with it. Most of your fellow citizens are doing this and thereby are helping to create an orderly society, which you benefit from. If you decide to disobey the laws that you disagree with, you are refusing to take on the same cost (a restriction of your liberty) that others have undertaken. You are thus acting as a free rider on other citizens' efforts.

Once again, this theory could not apply to potential migrants deciding whether to respect the immigration laws. A key requirement for the obligation of fair play is that one receive a fair share of the benefits of social cooperation. If there is a beneficial cooperative scheme, an individual cannot be required, as a matter of fairness, to completely exclude himself from any of the benefits of that cooperative scheme.

1.3.5 Democracy

Some say that the democratic process confers authority on its outcomes.[18] That is, the reason why one should obey the law (if one lives in a society with an at least somewhat decent democratic government) is that that law was created through a democratic process that takes into account the will of the people. It is said that the democratic process is uniquely worthy of respect because only it, among all forms of government, treats all individuals as equals by giving every individual one vote. (By contrast, on this view, those living under dictatorships have no duty to respect the law.)

Once again, this theory would provide no basis for an obligation on the part of potential immigrants to respect immigration restrictions. The reason is that these potential immigrants were excluded from the democratic process. *They* were not treated as equals by the political process. To the extent that one thinks democracy treats citizens as equals by giving them equal voting power, democratic societies treat potential immigrants as *inferiors* by giving them no say on immigration policy or anything else. These potential migrants thus have no more reason to obey the law than subjects of dictatorial governments do.

1.3.6 Freedom of Association

Many believe that people possess a general right to *freedom of association*, a right to decide whom we enter into meaningful relationships with. For instance, we may decide whom to marry, whom to befriend, whom to work for, and whom to trade with. Freedom of association includes freedom *from* association, that is, the right to choose *not* to associate with those with whom we do not wish to associate. One might argue that by immigrating illegally, migrants are violating the freedom of association rights of the native-born population, who presumably wish *not* to associate with those migrants. Perhaps, therefore, it is wrong to migrate illegally. The appeal to freedom of association might also be used to defend the permissibility of laws restricting immigration.

To address this concern, we should first note that there are stronger and weaker relationships in which people can stand, and one cannot claim veto rights over all possible relationships. Consider this case:

> *Unwanted Neighbor:* I have built a cabin in an unsettled area of wilderness, where I live. You come along and build a cabin ten miles away, thereby forcing me into the relationship of "ten-mile-away neighbors" with you. You are not making me do anything in particular, nor are you interfering with anything that I am doing. Yet I simply didn't want to be ten-mile-away neighbors with anyone.

Have you violated my freedom of association rights? Presumably not. This seems comparable to the case of illegal immigrants entering the country and thereby forcing the anti-immigration members of the population into the relationship of "fellow residents of the country" with them against their will. This is an extremely tenuous relationship, which one can hardly claim rights of control over. Notice that if one had such rights, one would also have rights to enjoin native-born citizens from having children. Anti-immigrant natives can still freely choose whether or not to personally hire, befriend, marry, or trade with the immigrants, so they retain their freedom of association with respect to these personally significant relationships.

If anything, the right to freedom of association supports open borders. This is because there are members of the current population who would like to enter into relationships with immigrants – and not just tenuous relationships like "being coresidents of a nation" but personally significant relationships. There are employers who want to hire immigrants, landlords who want to rent apartments to them, and ordinary individuals who would be happy to have immigrant friends or partners. By restricting migration, the state violates those citizens' free association rights.

You might argue that immigrants force us into more significant relationships than merely that of coresidents in some large geographical area. Because the area in question is under the jurisdiction of a single government, we are also forced, through our taxes, to support the provision of public services to the immigrants, whether we want to or not. This occurs whether or not the immigrants gain citizenship and, to some extent, whether or not the immigrants even have legal residency.

I am sympathetic to the argument that this represents a rights violation.[19] But note, first, that it is a rights violation primarily attributable to *the state*, rather than to the immigrants. It is the state that forces us to pay for public services for others. Second, the rights violation, if that is what it is, occurs equally when the state provides public services to other *native-born* residents whom some taxpayers do not want to support. Yet no one argues that it is immoral for native-born citizens to remain in the country or to use public services on the grounds that doing so forces others to pay to support those services. In this respect, illegal immigrants are doing nothing different from what native-born individuals and legal immigrants are doing.

Perhaps critics will say that my mistake lies in treating freedom of association as an *individual* right. They might grant that illegal immigrants as such do not violate the rights of any particular individuals, yet they might think that illegal immigrants violate a collective right, the right of *the society* to control its membership. Perhaps the government counts as society's decision-maker; thus, the way society exercises its rights is through the government's passing laws restricting entry into the society.

In response, the rights of a group must derive from the rights of the individuals who constitute it. Individuals may grant an organization rights over themselves, but they may not, by joining a group, suspend the rights of others who do not belong to the group. Thus, for example, if it would be a rights violation for Sam to coercively restrict Marvin, then Sam also lacks the ability to morally authorize others to coercively restrict Marvin on his behalf. If Sam, Ted, and Mary all lack the right to coercively restrict Marvin, then they cannot gain that right merely by acting in concert.

For the reasons discussed above, anti-immigration individuals lack the right to coercively prevent immigrants from freely interacting with *other* individuals in the country who want to interact with the immigrants. Therefore, these anti-immigration individuals cannot acquire the right to coercively restrict immigrants merely by acting in concert.

Notice that if they could, then anti-natalists could equally well (if there were enough of them) acquire a right to reject any potential offspring of existing citizens from joining the society – and hence to either prohibit current citizens from having children or demand that the children be expelled from the society. By the same logic, one could argue that the government may eject anyone it chooses – say, members of a racial minority or partisans of a particular political view – from the society. Indeed, as in the case of the property rights argument of Section 1.2.5, the freedom of association defense of immigration restrictions would generalize to licensing virtually any policy. Whatever law one wishes to justify, one need only repackage it as a condition that "society", acting via the state, places on its membership – one must obey the law or be jailed if one wishes to be a member of that society.

1.4 Conclusion

Why do all or nearly all societies have immigration restrictions? Because most people around the world, regardless of where they live, *want* such restrictions to protect themselves from foreigners. Throughout human history, suspicion and outright hostility toward outsiders have been extremely common – hence the negative connotation of the term "outsider". It is worth reflecting on this phenomenon because we may harbor biases that influence our thinking about immigration, and we may not be able to overcome our biases unless we identify them.[20]

It is very plausible that human beings in general, across societies, are prone to emotional biases against outsiders, which leads them to look for reasons for attributing various harms and dangers to outsiders. Thus, if you sought to move to a society very different from your own, the natives of that society would likely be suspicious toward you, however innocent you might be. Their natural feelings of suspicion would lead them to imagine spurious dangers that you might pose.

Of course, if that is true of people in other human societies, it is probably true of *us*. When we feel wary of admitting foreigners to our society, it is unlikely that this is due to some entirely different cause that coincidentally happens to produce attitudes that look very similar. What is more likely is that we have the same innate suspicion of foreigners that humans throughout history have harbored, that these feelings lead us to experience a gut sense that immigration must be bad, and that we then try to devise theories and arguments to rationalize that intuition.

I have tried to explain why the most popular arguments for restricting immigration are no good. But that by itself is unlikely to change many minds; most people will just keep looking for more arguments against immigration (or perhaps abandon argument and rest with intuition) because they are antecedently convinced that *something* must justify restrictions. This is why it is important to recognize the plausibility of the theory of a general, anti-foreign bias in the human mind.

Needless to say, one would not expect to directly detect this bias by introspection; biases almost never *seem* to the subject like biases. When we devise arguments for restricting immigration, it seems to us as though we are simply reasoning to the obviously correct conclusions about migrants. But when we realize that people across societies and across times would have taken parallel views toward nearly *any* group of foreigners, including groups we regard as benign – including, say, *us* – then it becomes increasingly plausible that those of us with anti-immigration views would hold those views regardless of the particular facts or arguments that we cite. Perhaps we as a society might then recognize our stance toward immigration as a product of unfair prejudice. And perhaps we might then start to take seriously the possibility of relaxing our restrictions.

Notes

1 Gallup 2022.
2 I have earlier defended these views in Huemer 2010 and 2019, on which the present essay is based.
3 Simon 1989, 357–61; Caplan 2007, 58–9.
4 National Research Council 1997, 6–7.
5 Macedo 2008.
6 See, for example, Miller 2022.
7 For a summary, see Nowrasteh 2015.
8 Light et al. 2020, 32342.
9 See Kershnar (2000) for this view.
10 Carlson 2022.
11 Demetriou 2021, 129–34.
12 Daniels 1990.
13 For extended discussion, see Huemer 2013.
14 Locke 1980.
15 Plato 2000.
16 Rawls 1999.
17 Klosko 2005.
18 Christiano 2008.
19 See Huemer 2017a; 2017b.
20 See Caplan's (2007, 36–9) discussion of "anti-foreign bias".

References

Caplan, Bryan. 2007. *The Myth of the Rational Voter*. Princeton, NJ: Princeton University Press.
Carlson, Tucker. 2022, July 19. "The Great Replacement Is an Electoral Strategy," Fox News, https://www.foxnews.com/opinion/tucker-carlson-great-replacement-electoral-strategy, accessed November 29, 2022.
Christiano, Thomas. 2008. *The Constitution of Equality: Democratic Authority and Its Limits*. Oxford: Oxford University Press.
Daniels, Roger. 1990. *Coming to America: A History of Immigration and Ethnicity in American Life*. New York: HarperCollins.
Demetriou, Dan. 2021. "Learning All the Wrong Lessons," pp. 123–40 in *Dissident Philosophers*, eds. Allan Hillman and Tully Borland. Lanham, MD: Rowman and Littlefield.
Gallup. 2022. "Immigration," https://news.gallup.com/poll/1660/immigration.aspx, accessed November 29, 2022.
Huemer, Michael. 2010. "Is There a Right to Immigrate?", *Social Theory and Practice* 36: 429–61.
Huemer, Michael. 2013. *The Problem of Political Authority*. New York: Palgrave Macmillan.
Huemer, Michael. 2017a. "Is Taxation Theft?", Libertarianism.org, https://www.libertarianism.org/columns/is-taxation-theft, accessed November 30, 2022.
Huemer, Michael. 2017b. "Is Wealth Redistribution a Rights Violation?", pp. 259–71 in *The Routledge Handbook of Libertarianism*, eds. Jason Brennan, David Schmidtz, and Bas van der Vossen. New York: Routledge.
Huemer, MichKael. 2019. "In Defense of Illegal Immigration," pp. 34–50 in *Open Borders: In Defense of Free Movement*, ed. Reece Jones. Athens, GA: University of Georgia Press.
Kershnar, Stephen. 2000. "There Is No Moral Right to Immigrate to the United States," *Public Affairs Quarterly* 14: 141–58.
Klosko, George. 2005. *Political Obligations*. Oxford: Oxford University Press.
Light, Michael T., Jingying Hea, and Jason P. Robeya. 2020. "Comparing Crime Rates Between Undocumented Immigrants, Legal Immigrants, and Native-Born US Citizens in Texas," *Proceedings of the National Academy of Sciences* 117: 32340–47.

Locke, John. [1690] 1980. *Second Treatise of Government*, ed. C.B. Macpherson. Indianapolis, IN: Hackett.

Macedo, Stephen. 2008. "The Moral Dilemma of U.S. Immigration Policy: Open Borders Versus Social Justice?", pp. 63–81 in *Debating Immigration*, ed. Carol M. Swain. Cambridge: Cambridge University Press.

Miller, Andrew Mark. 2022, July 7. "Crimes Committed by Illegal Immigrants Surged in 2021 After Declining in Previous Years," Fox News, https://www.foxnews.com/us/crimes-committed-illegal-immigrants-surged-2021-declining-previous-years, accessed November 29, 2022.

National Research Council, Panel on the Demographic and Economic Impacts of Immigration. 1997. *The New Americans: Economic, Demographic, and Fiscal Effects of Immigration*, eds. James P. Smith and Barry Edmonston. Washington, D.C.: National Academies Press.

Nowrasteh, Alex. 2015, July 13. "By the Numbers: Do Immigrants Cause Crime?", Foundation for Economic Education, https://fee.org/articles/by-the-numbers-do-immigrants-cause-crime/, accessed November 29, 2022.

Plato. [360 B.C.] 2000. *Crito in The Trial and Death of Socrates*, third ed., tr. G.M.A. Grube, revised by John M. Cooper. Indianapolis: Hackett.

Rawls, John. 1999. *A Theory of Justice*, revised edition. Cambridge, MA: Harvard University Press.

Simon, Julian. 1989. *The Economic Consequences of Immigration*. Oxford: Blackwell.

2
SOCIAL DEMOCRACY'S TENSIONS WITH IMMIGRATION

Jason Brennan

2.1 Introduction

Many philosophers and laypeople regard libertarianism as right-wing and regard left-liberalism and social democracy as left-wing. They reason that libertarianism puts no special weight on economic egalitarianism, which they regard as essential to left-wing politics.

This chapter contends this is not quite right. Standard "right-libertarianism" rejects nationalism, including nationalism about immigration and the locus of social justice. It standardly accepts open borders as a default condition from which all deviations must be justified and puts heavy burdens on what it takes to justify such deviations. Further, as a matter of fact, a libertarian world of open borders is probably far more egalitarian than dividing the world up into low-immigration social democracies. In contrast, many left-liberals and social democrats are skeptical of open borders and free immigration. They are skeptical because they have to be; as I will discuss below, it is far from clear how their preferred institutions can allow much genuine freedom of immigration. Their explicit philosophies tend to be in tension with open borders as well.

2.2 Social Justice Nationalism

John Rawls, Ronald Dworkin, Brian Barry, and many other soi-dissant egalitarian social democrats defend a view we can call "social justice nationalism," defined here as the view that social justice concerns distributions inside countries but not between them. For instance, Rawls thinks everyone in the same "society" ought to have the same liberties, that opportunities in that society should be distributed by merit rather than luck, and that differences in income and wealth should be arranged to the maximal benefit of the representative full-time worker in that society. The "society" in question is stipulated to be the nation-state, not something more local (like the city, neighborhood, or community), and not the world as a whole. Rawlsians mostly treat national borders as a given. Rawls's theory gives only a small space for helping the poor outside one's borders.[1]

For Rawlsians, the gap between rich and poor Americans is automatically a matter of justice. The gap between Americans and Haitians is not so much. To Rawls, it does not much matter if a highly talented Haitian has far less opportunity and worse life prospects than an untalented and unmotivated American, because the two live in different countries.

We can borrow an argument from Robert Nozick to note that social justice nationalism leads to some weird or perverse implications.[2] The view suggests that we can render what the theory regards as just distribution unjust, or unjust distributions just, merely by redrawing borders. For instance, suppose a country does not realize the Difference Principle right now. Suppose the poor mostly live in the South while the Rich mostly live in the North. One way the country could suddenly realize the Difference Principle would be to divide itself into two countries. Imagine, when this happens, no one is made better or worse off. Still, since a legal boundary separates the two, the gap between rich Northerners and poor Southerners no longer qualifies as a matter of justice on Rawls's theory.

Conversely, suppose two countries both independently realize the Difference Principle, but one is much richer than the other. Suppose, for instance, that Iceland and Norway both realize Rawls's theory, but remember that Norwegians tend to be much richer than Icelanders.[3] Imagine if Norway annexed Iceland (let's say at the unanimous request of Icelandic and Norwegian voters), that this would result in all current Norwegians becoming six times richer, while Icelandic voters each become, say, sixty percent richer. Everyone in this expanded Norway is happier and richer, but the country might now qualify as unjust, per Rawls's theory. That would depend on whether the new expanded Norway could raise former Icelandic citizens' incomes even more. Suppose it could but does not. Rawls's theory would say this is unjust, while leaving the two countries separate (and worse off) was not unjust. That seems perverse. The annexation is preferable, and everyone is better off.

What could possibly justify social justice nationalism? If you are a communitarian who thinks group identities are normatively basic, then this is an easier task. But Rawls, Barry, and other left-liberals are not communitarians (supposedly). Rawls's central idea is that coercive institutions must be justifiable to all people subject to them. What it takes to justify such coercive institutions is that everyone subject to them must be treated fairly by them, have their liberties respected, and should have a sufficient stake in those institutions. For Rawls, a "sufficient stake" here means that the representative worse off person is better off than they would be in any other arrangement.

That kind of reasoning makes it hard to simply assume national borders are a given and that justice is to be assessed on the patterns of income inside national borders; instead, it seems like national borders themselves should be evaluated as just or unjust based on their distributional effects. If, as Rawls thinks, a system of property has to be justified to all subject to it, then in parallel so should the system of dividing the world up into mostly closed-border Westphalian states. The world order is, perhaps, great for Norwegians but hardly great for Haitians or Somalians. When the government of Norway puts up various restrictions to keep Haitians and Somalians from living or working in Norway, it is indeed using violent coercion and is indeed exercising power over them. On Rawls's premises, this should make this subject to concerns of social justice.

Rawls also sometimes says that social justice concerns systems of cooperation. But even in our Westphalian world, each of us is connected to billions of others in complex webs of cooperation, with some people close and others distant, with some strands thick and others thin, all organized by various overlapping formal and informal institutions, most of which regulate parts of the web but not the whole thing. Each of our webs is different, and different parts of our individual webs are governed by different institutions. Your web does not match the borders of your nation-state, and indeed, your connection to and dependence upon many people outside your borders is much greater than with many people inside.

2.3 Defining "Open Borders"

In a world of "open borders," as I use the term, everyone would have the legal right to move between countries, live in any country of their choosing, work in any country of their choosing, and to at least enjoy the same basic negative civil and economic rights as other citizens, such as a right to free speech or due process, all largely free of *exclusionary* subsidies, tariffs, and regulations.

The point of this last clause is that governments can impede immigration without directly prohibiting it. By analogy, consider the issue of free trade. Countries sometimes restrict the movement of goods across national borders by banning exports or imports or by imposing quotas. They also use tariffs and subsidies to modify prices and quantities, for the benefit of local producers at the expense of everyone else. Tariffs and subsidies allow goods to cross borders but disincentivize buyers from buying them by manipulating prices. Countries also impose predatory regulations in order to restrict imports or render imports artificially expensive and uncompetitive. Protectionism-through-regulation interferes with free trade.

Similarly, countries could have officially open borders but impose regulations on housing, schooling, medicine, and work in such a way as to make movement impossible or artificially expensive. For instance, a town might pass zoning laws that ensure only very expensive homes are built, or which ensure that no one converts their basements into apartments for rent. Or, a town might have open borders, but then pass a very high minimum wage meant to ensure lower productivity workers are never hired. These regulations are often created with the intent of keeping the poor out without literally forbidding them from moving in. A system of open borders does not merely let people cross borders but also avoids exclusionary labor or housing regulations.

2.4 Rawls on Open Borders

Rawls, the most prominent philosophical defender of left-liberal social democracy, was explicitly hostile to open and free immigration, even inside the European Union. He regarded it as policy driven by the interests of the capitalist class.[4] In a letter to Philippe Van Parijs, he wrote:

> It seems to me that much would be lost if the European Union became a federal union like the United States. Here there is a common language of political discourse and a ready willingness to move from one state to another. Isn't there a conflict between a large free and open market comprising all of Europe and the individual nation-states, each with its separate political and social institutions, historical memories, and forms and traditions of social policy. Surely these are great value to the citizens of these countries and give meaning to their life. The large open market including all of Europe is aim of the large banks and the capitalist business class whose main goal is simply larger profit.[5]

Rawls valued the sanctity of the nationalist social democratic state over open and free immigration, even when immigration was limited to Europeans with significant shared background cultures and history.

One of Rawls's main complaints is that an open European Union could destroy distinctive national identities in favor of a general European identity. That's an odd reason for Rawls to oppose open immigration inside the EU; one might expect that his liberal theory would prioritize freedom, opportunity, and economic growth for the poor over communitarian concerns about national identity. Further, he goes on to say that he favors a stationary economy. Once we get *enough* growth, no more growth is needed.

If open borders were only good for banks and cigar-smoking, top hat-wearing capitalists, then Rawls's criticisms might have more force. But, as we will discuss below, open immigration is almost certainly better for the poor than internal redistribution inside social democracies.

It's surprising Rawls was hostile to free and open movement between countries. In his own theory, freedom of movement inside a single country is a basic liberty. Rawls did not want people to remain prisoners to the unfortunate circumstances of their birth. He recognized that a rule which, say, required people to live forever in their hometowns—especially poor people born in poor places—would severely stunt their potential opportunities and inhibit their ability to lead a life authentically theirs. But that's also true of being stuck in one's home country. A random person born in, say, Nashua, New Hampshire, who was forced to live there his entire life, has much better life prospects than someone born in and forced to remain in Haiti. The Nashuan could expect to be rich by world standards even if he lived imprudently and made bad choices; the Haitian can expect to remain poor forever even if she exercised extraordinary prudence.

2.5 World Poverty Is Not a Distribution of Income Problem

Democratic Socialist Bernie Sanders once campaigned for a minimum wage of $15/hr, which implies an annual income of $30,000 for any full-time worker fortunate enough to have a job at that rate. $30,000 is low by US standards, but the now defunct website Global Rich List calculated that (even adjusting for the cost of living), an American making $30,000 is in the top 1.23% of income-earners in the world, using income tables from around 2007.[6] Similarly, GivingWhatWeCan, which uses more recent data, estimates that such an American is in the top 5% of income-earners, making 11 times the global average.[7] While the precise distribution of PPP-adjusted income in the world is slightly disputed, what's not disputed is that almost every person in the *developed* world, including those at their country's official poverty line, is much richer than most people in the world. An American at the US poverty line is still among the top 20% of income-earners world-wide.

PPP-adjusted world product (i.e., the total amount of economic production per year, adjusted to the cost of living) is about $130 trillion as of 2019.[8] That's the total value of all goods, services, government activity, and so on. Imagine, unrealistically, that I could wave a magic wand, which will convert all of this production into income, and also split all the production equally among all people, without causing *any* loss of production.

The World Bank estimates that PPP-adjusted per-capita world product, as of 2021, is $18,609.[9] That means, on this thought experiment, that if we could convert all current production into income and equally distribute it, without causing any loss of income at all, then everyone world-wide would receive $18,609.

For most people world-wide, this would be a boon. Even if mean world product per capita is $18,609, the median individual income is far lower. Most people world-wide live on far less than that.

Still, note that in 2007, Rawlsian theorist Samuel Freeman suggested that the suitable social minimum is $36,500 per American adult, which works out to just under $51,000 in 2022 USD.[10] So, Freeman effectively thinks the PPP-adjusted social minimum is about $102,000 (in constant 2022 USD) a year for a married couple. (I'm not sure how much he would add for children.) That means that, even on the parameters of this magical thought experiment, in which we imagine we somehow convert all production into income and then, without any loss, equalize world incomes, no one would have what Freeman considers enough. Keep in mind that these are PPP-adjusted dollars, so Freeman cannot say that $18,609 in Haiti counts as enough by his standards. The cost-of-living differences are already baked in.

My magic wand thought experiment gives us an extremely high *upper bound* or *overestimate* of how much workers right now could be paid under a perfectly equitable world distribution of income. In fact, not all production occurs in a form that could, in principle, be converted to income and transferred/redistributed to workers. (For instance, in the US, despite its relatively small government sector for a developed country, workers' total share of GDP is only about 42%.[11]) It's also unrealistic because, by hypothesis, once the magic wand is waved, all world production goes to workers in the form of income. Thus, in the magic wand thought experiment, by hypothesis governments, universities, and capital-building enterprises nothing and cannot even exist. The magic wand thought experiment thus asks you to imagine unrealistically that world-wide anarchism works just fine, and that current levels of production could be maintained without any capital investment or reinvestment. It's also unrealistic because equalizing all income would have at least some distortionary effects and would reduce output at least somewhat.

2.6 The Growth and Distributional Effects of Immigration

Social democracies prioritize internal redistribution over labor mobility and open immigration. They recognize they cannot afford to provide high welfare payments to just anyone who might move in. They restrict immigration in order to maintain strong welfare states.

But the economic losses from immigration restrictions are staggering. Immigration restrictions are the single most inefficient and damaging thing governments do.[12]

Many economists have published peer-reviewed estimates of the deadweight losses from immigration restrictions. They generally estimate the deadweight loss of immigration restriction to be between 50% and 150% of current world product. The mean estimate in the literature is 100% of world product.[13] Even more conservative estimates with perhaps more realistic assumptions place the losses around $50–60 trillion.[14]

The standard theory in development economics is that rich countries are rich because they have inclusive institutions which produce prosperity, and poor countries are poor because they have extractive institutions which inhibit it.[15] No one knows how to create social change to induce countries with bad institutions to switch to good. In countries with dysfunctional institutions, extractive elites benefit from their predatory institutions and thus lack the incentive to change. But an easier solution is to allow the world's poor to move where labor is scarce and where institutions are better.

The US keeps detailed records on its legal migrants. This data allows economists to compare workers who have moved to the US to their demographically identical, equally skilled counterparts who stayed home. One major economic study examined the effects of immigration to the US on workers from 42 poor countries. Workers' wages increased by factors of as low as 2.8 and as high as 15, with a median around 5. (The mean was higher than the median). That is, the median low-skilled worker from a poor country who moves to the US sees her real, cost-of-living adjusted income increase five-fold.[16]

In a world of open borders, increased immigration would probably result in lower numbers than these. Wages would increase, but diminishing marginal returns would mean the average return decreases. (When we fix any inefficiency, the first bit of fixing generally does more good than the next.) Still, by examining actual patterns of movement within free immigration zones, economists can nevertheless estimate the gains under open borders. Even then, the best estimate is that, under open borders, unskilled immigrants who move to developed countries would on average see their real (cost-of-living adjusted) income increase by least $10,000 USD/year.[17]

The welfare gains from immigration are larger than either internal redistribution (welfare states) or redistribution from rich countries to poor counties. Glen Weyl examines how differing immigration policies affect both total welfare and global income inequality. The Gulf Cooperation Countries admit a far higher number of immigrants on a per capita (and often absolute) basis than the "fortress welfare states" of the Organization for Economic Cooperation and Development Countries (OECD). This creates a natural experiment, which allows him to compare the welfare gains from immigration to internal or external redistribution.

Weyl shows that even at *current* levels of immigration, despite existing heavy restrictions on immigration world-wide, immigration already more strongly reduces global income inequality and produces higher welfare gains for the world's poor than all the redistribution *inside* or *between* countries. That is, right now, even with mostly closed borders, immigration is already doing more to reduce poverty and promote economic equality than internal welfare states or foreign aid. When Weyl estimates (using standard methods) what would happen if there were either much more redistribution or much more immigration, he again shows that immigration would do far more (in some countries, ten times more) to increase the welfare of the poor and reduce income inequality than either form of redistribution.[18]

These figures *understate* the total welfare gains, because they examine only the direct and immediate effect on workers. Immigrants also remit money to family members in their home countries. Roughly, 29% of Haiti's current GDP comes from such remittances.[19] Economists Richard Adams and John Page discovered that every 10% increase in immigrants from a poor country to a rich country leads to roughly a 2% decrease in people living in extreme poverty back in the poor country of origin, for a resulting reduction in the poverty rate by about 3.5%.[20]

2.7 Social Democracy or Open Borders?

Opening borders is a highly efficient policy, which benefits most people a great deal in the short term and benefits pretty much everyone a great deal in the long run. Nevertheless, social democrats tend to favor low levels of immigration. In the US, the Democrats, the more social democratic party, portray themselves as pro-immigration compared to the Republicans, but the debate between them concerns, in effect, whether to have 99.3% or 99.4% closed borders. Both parties are restrictionist about immigration.

One major argument against open borders is that it would bankrupt modern welfare states. Modern rich democracies, such as Norway, the United States, or the Netherlands, have expansive welfare states. Even though the "poor" in these countries enjoy pre-tax-and-transfer incomes that are much higher than the world average, the governments of these countries still regard these incomes as too low, and issue generous packages of welfare benefits, including subsidized medical care, education benefits, training, unemployment insurance, pensions, food stamps, housing subsidies, and more. A vast influx of immigrants, the argument goes, would bankrupt countries with such policies.

These worries might be mistaken. But for the sake of argument, on behalf of the other side, let's assume that the modern social democratic welfare state cannot afford to provide new immigrants from poor countries much in the way of welfare or social services.

If modern welfare states cannot afford to provide immigrants welfare benefits or government services, that need not imply that they should favor restricting immigration. After all, immigration (without welfare benefits or services) would still benefit immigrants and most current citizens, tremendously. A better solution would be to build walls *around the welfare state* rather than walls around the country.[21] This may sound callous. But it's far less callous than forbidding immigration altogether. Instead of denying immigrants safety, better employment opportunities, higher income, *and* welfare state benefits, this option only denies them the latter.

Many social democrats would balk at this. This policy proposal would create a two-tiered society, where some people work and pay taxes but are ineligible for many government-financed welfare benefits or social services, while others are eligible for such benefits because they were fortunate enough to spawn inside the right wombs. I agree this sounds and indeed is awful. (I think we should instead reduce and equalize services.) But it's awfulness not a persuasive reason to restrict immigration, when that leaves us with something even more awful. If, say, Sweden forbids Haitians from moving to Sweden, it still treats Haitians as outsiders, it still forbids them from consuming Swedish government services, and it still denies them welfare benefits. Imagine Sweden saying to Haitians, "We don't want to treat you as second-class residents, so we'll instead treat you as non-residents, which is far worse for you...and us."

2.8 Egalitarianism or Open Borders?

There is tension between social democracy and open borders, because it is unclear whether expansive welfare states can be maintained with open borders and extensive immigration from poorer countries. Indeed, this is one reason why many social democracies use indirect methods of exclusion, such as having minimum wages, high housing regulation to drive up costs, or high labor regulations. There are many ways of keeping out the people they regard as unwanted riffraff without explicitly forbidding them from coming.

There is another source of tension. The problem is that a commitment to redistribution for egalitarian outcomes tends to make richer people resent the poor.

Imagine two countries, Libertarianland and Poorland. Imagine Libertarianland is rich, with everyone making $100,000/year. Everyone in Poorland is poor, making only $2000 a year. Suppose, however, that if we allow Poorlanders to move to Libertarianland, then their real income will go up by a factor of 15. Imagine domestic Libertarianlanders' income will go up by 10%. After mass immigration, former Poorlanders now make $30,000/year, while native Libertarianlanders make $110,000 a year. (These changes are realistic, as discussed above.) Inequality inside Libertarianland has increased, but everyone is better off. Since Libertarianlanders are libertarians, not egalitarians, they think this is great. They are delighted the Poorlanders moved in, and the Poorlanders are delighted to be there.

But things are different in Egalitaria. Egalitaria is a richer social democracy, like Norway. There, everyone also makes $100,000 a year. Suppose if Egalitaria allows Poorlanders to move there, the same gross income effects would obtain as in the previous example. Poorlanders' gross, pre-tax salaries would increase to $30,000 a year, while egalitarians' gross, pre-tax salaries would increase to $110,000 a year. However, Egalitaria is committed to equal incomes. Thus, it taxes the richer residents to redistribute to the poorer. If after immigration, Egalitaria has a ratio of one former Poorlander for each long-time egalitarian, then after redistribution, income will be $70,000. For former Poorlanders, moving to Egalitaria was indeed a boon! But for domestic egalitarians, allowing mass immigration was a horrible loss to their welfare, even though mass immigration increased their gross, pre-tax-and-transfer incomes. Mass immigration *could* have led to a Pareto-superior outcome where everyone is better off and no one is worse off, but a commitment to equal outcomes turns it into a source of conflict and resentment.

This is a general problem with egalitarianism. Consider at the extreme: Imagine everyone literally had equal skill and ability. Imagine all labor has been homogenized, so that every laborer is interchangeable with every other. (Marx and others famously thought in utopia, people would indeed jump from job to job at will rather than specialize.) If so, then this leads to a perverse outcome.

In general, all identical productive inputs have diminishing marginal returns. The first $10,000 of capital produces greater returns than the next $10,000. The first laborer on the assembly line produces greater returns than the second. The first course in French language produces greater returns than the second. The first hamburger tastes better than the second.

Consider what that means for *adding new citizens*. On the stipulation of extreme equality of ability, each new member of our society in this extreme egalitarian example should produce less overall output than the last. So, if we are committed to equalizing incomes, this means each additional birth not matched with a simultaneous death should reduce each of our incomes. Rather than a birth being a cause to celebrate, a birth is a burden to bear.

2.9   The Politicized Economy and Openness

David Schmidtz and Christopher Freiman say:

> The fewer issues subject to political oversight, the less urgent the need for consensus on contentious questions. For example, selecting a "one-size-fits-all" car model is not currently a source of political conflict. Individuals browse a wide variety of cars and buy whatever best suits their needs and budget. No particular car needs to suit every member of the community. Polities do not put the question of the right car or the right shoe size to a popular vote and enforce the majority decision. In conditions of pluralism, we similarly eschew one-size-fits-all solutions to divisive political problems concerning religion, education, medicine, and so on...By contrast, when issues fall within the purview of politics—even democratic politics—minorities risk finding themselves marginalized.[22]

They think, all things equal, that the more something is subject to democratic or political control, the more it is a source of conflict and an opportunity to stifle individuality.

Consider, then, the problem of immigration, especially in a world full of racist, ethnocentric, or xenophobic people. Under an open borders policy in a capitalist society with several properties, all a would-be immigrant needs to do to acquire a place to live is to find one person willing to sell or rent her a place. All she needs to do to get a job is to find one person willing to hire her, or, alternatively, she can start her own business, which requires that she finds enough people willing to be her clients.

In contrast, the more the economy is shaped or controlled by democratic or political means, or generally, the more the economy is socialist, the more getting a place to live and getting a job becomes a political matter. In a capitalist society, an immigrant only needs to find a niche. In a socialist society, she must appeal to the majority or whoever actually holds the reins of the economy.

On this point, note the differences in incentives. Economists have long noted that markets incentivize agents to overcome prejudice. Democratic politics does not.

Competitive pressures in the market economy punish discriminatory employers and landowners by making them pay to indulge their own prejudices.[23] Employers who are unwilling to hire foreign workers would find themselves at a disadvantage relative to those who *are* willing—the latter will employ equally productive workers at a lower wage. In competitive markets, discriminatory employers, then, must follow suit or find themselves displaced by nondiscriminatory employers.[24] In fact, this is partly why anti-immigration laws exist—anti-immigration laws *mandate* that would-be employers and landowners discriminate against immigrants. If the employers voluntarily refused to hire immigrants, the laws would serve nothing but an expressive purpose.

Democratic systems contain the opposite pressure. Citizens' individual votes have no effect on the outcome of elections, and so each of them can, and nearly all of them do, use their votes *expressively*.[25] As Dan Kahan summarizes the empirical literature on voter psychology:

> The only material stake most ordinary people have in the content of their beliefs about policy-relevant facts is the contribution they make to the experience of *being* a particular sort of person. The *beliefs* a person forms about the deterrent effect of concealed-carry laws on violent crime, the contribution of human activity to global warming, and like 'facts' reliably dispose her to *act* in ways that signify her identity-defining group commitments to those who will judge her character accordingly. Failing to attend to information in a manner that generates such beliefs can severely compromise someone's well-being—not because the beliefs she will form in that case will be factually *wrong*, but because they will convey the wrong *message* about who she is and whose side she is on.[26]

People thus have perverse incentives to express loyalty to the group, antipathy toward outsiders, and other prejudiced attitudes. As voters, they can afford to indulge irrational or mistaken beliefs about immigrants and the effects of immigration. Indeed, they are often incentivized to do so. Just as a sports team fan gains status among other fans by having exaggerated and biased views of the team—say by claiming the umpire was blind when he makes an easy call against our team—political participants gain status by taking stronger and more extreme stands with less and less evidence. Politics does not provide citizens with much incentive to behave better.

2.10 Conclusion

Some left-liberal or egalitarian social democrats in fact endorse something like open borders. I am not claiming they are all economic nationalists. Nevertheless, their favored institutions—such as labor regulations, minimum wage laws, licensing laws, and the welfare state—are in tension with open borders. For many, their explicit ideologies are in tension as well. In both cases, that's an objection to their favored institutions, not to open borders. Oddly, the resulting implication is that standard right-libertarianism turns out to be left-wing compared to standard Rawlsian left-liberalism.

Notes

1. Rawls 2001.
2. Nozick 1974, 209.
3. PPP-adjusted GDP/capita in Norway is $89K; in Iceland, $69K, according to the World Bank in 2023.
4. On Rawls as a reticent socialist, see Edmundson 2017.
5. Rawls and an Parijs 2003.
6. GlobalRichList is an organization trying to induce people in the developed world to donate more to charity after realizing how rich they are. However, while GlobalRichList has an agenda, the rely on publicly available and well-used statistics, such as the World Bank's 2008 income data. (http://www.globalrichlist.com/#na)
7. https://howrichami.givingwhatwecan.org/how-rich-am-i?income=30000&countryCode=USA&household%5Badults%5D=1&household%5Bchildren%5D=0
8. https://www.cia.gov/library/publications/the-world-factbook/geos/xx.html
9. https://data.worldbank.org/indicator/NY.GDP.PCAP.PP.CD
10. Freeman 2007, 230.
11. https://fred.stlouisfed.org/series/W270RE1A156NBEA
12. See van der Vossen and Brennan 2018, chapter 11.
13. Clemens 2011, 85.
14. Stern 2006
15. Acemoglu and Robinson 2013.
16. Clemens, Montenegro, and Pritchett 2009.
17. Clemens, Montenegro, and Pritchett 2009.
18. Weyl 2018,
19. Desilver 2018.
20. Adams and Page 2005.
21. I take this phrasing from Nowrasteh and Cole, 2013.
22. Schmidtz and Freiman 2012, 425.
23. Becker 2010.
24. For research indicating discriminatory employers are more likely to go out of business, see Pager 2016.
25. Achen and Bartels 2016.
26. Kahan 2016, p. 7, italics in the original.

Works Cited

Acemoglu, Daron, and James Robinson. 2013. *Why Nations Fail*. New York: Penguin, 2013.
Achen, Christopher, and Larry Bartels. 2016. *Democracy for Realists*. Princeton University Press.
Adams, Richard H, and John Page. 2005. "Do International Migration and Remittances Reduce Poverty in Developing Nations," *World Development* 33: 1645–69.
Becker, Gary S. 2010. *The Economics of Discrimination*. University of Chicago Press.
Clemens, Michael. 2011. "Economics and Emigration: Trillion-Dollar Bills on the Sidewalk?," *Journal of Economic Perspectives* 23: 83–106.

Clemens, M.A., C.E. Montenegro, and L. Pritchett. 2009. *The Place Premium: Wage Differences for Identical Workers Across the US Border*. The World Bank.

Desilver, Drew. 2018. "Remittances from Abroad Are Major Economic Assets for Some Developing Countries," Pew Research Center, Jan. 29. Available at http://www.pewresearch.org/fact-tank/2018/01/29/remittances-from-abroad-are-major-economic-assets-for-some-developing-countries/.

Edmundson, William. 2017. *John Rawls: Reticent Socialist*. Cambridge University Press, 2017.

Freeman, Samuel. 2007. *Rawls*. Routledge Press.

John, Rawls, and Philippe Van Parijs. 2003. "Three Letters on The Law of Peoples and the European Union," *Revue De Philosophie économique* 7: 7–20.

Kahan, Dan. 2016. "The Politically Motivated Reasoning Paradigm, Part 2: Unanswered Questions," in. *Emerging Trends in the Social and Behavioral Sciences*, ed. R.A. Scott and S.M. Kosslyn

Nowrasteh, Alex, and Sofie Cole. 2013. "Building a Wall Around the Welfare State, Instead of the Country." *Cato Institute Policy Analysis* 732.

Nozick, Robert. 1974. *Anarchy, State, and Utopia*. Basic Books.

Pager, Devah. 2016. "Are Firms That Discriminate More Likely to Go Out of Business?," *Sociological Science* 3: 849–859.

Rawls, John. 2001. *The Law of Peoples*. Harvard University Press.

Schmidtz, David, and Christopher Freiman. 2012. "Nozick," in *The Oxford Handbook of Political Philosophy*, ed. David Estlund, pp. 411–428.

Stern, Nicholas. 2007. *The Economics of Climate Change: The Stern Review*. New York: Cambridge University Press.

Van der Vossen, Bas, and Jason Brennan. 2018. *In Defense of Openness*. Oxford University Press.

Weyl, Glen. 2018. "The Openness-equality Trade-off in Global Redistribution," *The Economic Journal* 128: F1–F36.

3
A CASE FOR CONTROLLED BORDERS AND OPEN DOORS

Sarah Song

3.1 Introduction

Immigration is one of the most contentious issues in contemporary politics. It implicates fundamental normative questions about the legitimacy of state power, the scope of justice, the rights of individuals and collectives, and the forms of identity and belonging. If people wish to move across international borders and settle in another country, why shouldn't they be able to? States exercise power over borders, but what, if anything, justifies this power? Do states have a right to control the movement of people into their territories? If so, how should the state's claim to control immigration be weighed against the prospective migrant's claim to enter?

This chapter takes up these questions with the aim of defending an intermediate ethical position between open borders and closed borders, what I call "controlled borders and open doors." In contrast to some nationalists who favor absolute state sovereignty over immigration, I believe the state's right to control immigration is a qualified, not absolute, right. Although members of a political community have special obligations to one another, they also have an obligation to take the interests of prospective migrants into account. Prospective migrants may have urgent reasons to move, and their interests may trump the less weighty interests of members. For example, states must open their doors to refugees and other migrants fleeing persecution and violence. At the same time, in contrast to proponents of open borders, I believe political membership is a morally significant relationship, which grounds special rights and obligations. A government may show some partiality toward the interests of its members. For instance, a government may deny admission to prospective migrants if their basic interests are protected in their home countries and doing so would protect important interests of members of the political community.

The chapter proceeds as follows. The first section discusses the intermediate ethical position of qualified state sovereignty and critically examines three arguments for the state's right to control immigration. The second section advances an alternative argument for the state's right to control immigration based on the value of collective self-determination. The third section discusses two qualifications on state sovereignty over immigration. The fourth section concludes.

3.2 State Sovereignty Over Migration

Many people take state sovereignty over migration for granted, but what, if anything, justifies the state's power over migration? In one of the earliest discussions of migration in contemporary political theory, Michael Walzer argues political membership is itself an object of distributive justice, "conceivably the most important" good because it has historically determined access to other fundamental goods (1983, 29). It is distributed by taking people in. For Walzer, it is obvious who should decide how to distribute membership: "we who are already members do the choosing" (32). But what gives citizens of a political community the right to regulate migration and membership? Walzer offers a cultural reason:

> The distinctiveness of cultures and groups depends upon closure and, without it, cannot be conceived as a stable feature of human life. If this distinctiveness is a value, as most people… seem to believe, then closure must be permitted somewhere. At some level of political organization, something like the sovereign state must take shape and claim the authority to make its own admissions policy, to control and sometimes restrain the flow of immigrants.
>
> *(39)*

Walzer suggests the state's right to control immigration rests on the value of distinctive cultures whose preservation is a central purpose of states. To use one of his examples, "Greeks driven from Turkey and Turks from Greece, after the wars and revolutions of the early twentieth century, had to be taken in by the states that bore their collective names. What else are such states for?" (42).

The state's right to control migration is strong but not absolute. Walzer outlines three qualifications. First, the right to control entry does not entail the right to control exit. Restricting the entry of people is necessary to defend "the liberty and welfare, the politics and culture of a group of people committed to one another and to their common life," but restricting exit involves coercing people who no longer wish to be members (39). Except in times of national emergency, when everyone has a duty to work for the country's survival, citizens must be free to exit their country. This "asymmetry" between exit and entry is accepted by many theorists of migration: states have a strong right to restrict entry but not to restrict exit. In the remainder of this chapter, I will focus on immigration (not emigration). The second qualification is the duty of mutual aid: a state must provide positive assistance to foreigners outside its territory if it is urgently needed, and the risks or costs of giving it are relatively low. A wealthy state might fulfill this duty by sending foreign aid and development assistance to poorer states, but in the case of "persecuted and stateless" people, the duty of mutual aid can only be met by taking them in (33, 45). Third, if democratic states choose to admit migrants to meet labor needs, "they must be prepared to enlarge their own membership" (61). Given these qualifications, we can say Walzer is not a proponent of entirely "closed borders" but rather strong state sovereignty: the state has a strong right to control immigration in accordance with its national priorities, subject only to these qualifications.

Political theorists have since developed novel arguments for the qualified state sovereignty position. I examine three accounts, all of which appeal to the value of collective self-determination but ultimately rest on other values: national identity, the right to private property, and freedom of association.

The first is David Miller's liberal nationalist theory, which develops Walzer's cultural argument in explicitly nationalist terms. The right of states to control immigration is grounded in the right of *nations* to be self-determining. Citizens are not merely co-participants in a scheme of social cooperation or subject to the same coercive legal regime; "they also relate to one another as fellow nationals, people who share a broadly similar set of cultural values and a sense of belonging to a particular place" (2016, 26). Members of the nation have an interest in the character and preservation of their national culture. Immigration generates racial and ethnic diversity, which affects the pace of change of the national culture. In earlier work, Miller says, "immigration need not pose problems, provided only that the immigrants come to share in a common national identity, to which they may contribute their own distinctive ingredients" (1995, 26). However, "immigration might pose a problem" in circumstances "where the rate of immigration is so high that there is no time for a process of mutual adjustment to occur... In such cases the education system and other such mechanisms of integration may be stretched beyond their capacity" (128). In later work, Miller points to studies suggesting that the racial and ethnic diversity generated by immigration may reduce social and political trust, which in turn may erode public support for social welfare programs and the deliberative institutions of democracy (2016, 64). The implication is that if immigration has this kind of impact, states are justified in restricting immigration for the sake of protecting their national culture.

Miller's nationalist argument rests on contestable empirical claims. If high levels of immigration do not have negative impacts on social trust, social welfare provision, or democratic participation, it seems the only reasons left for excluding migrants appeal to the goal of preserving a distinctive national identity. But a major troubling upshot is that grounding immigration control in the value of national identity may allow for racial and ethnic exclusions. Miller explicitly rejects racial exclusions: "To be told that they [immigrants] belong to the wrong race or sex (or have the wrong color) is insulting, given that these features do not connect to anything of real significance to the society they want to join" (2014, 204). Yet, race and ethnicity have historically played a central role in shaping what it means to be American, British, French, and so on. Consider the Chinese Exclusion Act, the National Origins Quota Act, and many other immigration policies animated by racial and ethnic ideologies in the U.S. (Ngai 2004; Smith 1997). Racist and xenophobic sentiments are not relics of the past; they are evident today in the rise of far-right parties in Europe and the "white nationalists" who fueled Donald Trump's rise to power. Liberal nationalists have sought to eliminate racist and xenophobic elements from their visions of national culture, emphasizing linguistic and cultural elements consistent with liberalism. Yet, the challenge for cultural nationalists remains what to do when a nation's commitment to racially exclusionary visions of national identity overtakes its commitment to liberal principles.

A second novel account of the state's right to control immigration draws on Lockean property theory. Locke began with the theological premise that God gave the earth to humankind in common and argued that individuals come to hold private property rights in land in virtue of mixing their labor with and adding value to the land (1980). Contemporary Lockeans set aside the theological premise and develop the labor theory of value. As A. John Simmons puts it, "those who innocently work to discover, make, or usefully employ some unowned good ought to be allowed to keep it (if in so doing they harm no others)...it would be wrong for others to take it away" (1992, 223). Ryan Pevnick adopts this Lockean idea to justify the state's right to control immigration. In virtue of their labor, citizens acquire property rights in their "collective accomplishments" (2011, 33):

> Like the family farm, the construction of state institutions is a historical project that extends across generations and into which individuals are born. Just as the value of a farm very largely comes from the improvements made on it, so too the value of membership in a state is very largely a result of the labor and investment of the community.
>
> *(38)*

Citizens' right of joint ownership includes the right to determine the future course of their institutions and the right to decide who can join the group (44). Pevnick suggests some qualifications on the rights of joint-owners: they cannot exclude outsiders in desperate need and children of "disliked minorities" who are born in the territory but have not yet contributed to public institutions (12, 66).

A major concern about Pevnick's account is that it conflates property rights and territorial rights of which the right to control immigration is a part (Song 2017). As the owner of my home, I can use, benefit from, and exclude people from entering it, but my ownership claim does not entail the right to determine who makes the rules governing my home and the homes of my fellow citizens. The latter is a fundamentally jurisdictional right that belongs to states. In addition, although Pevnick acknowledges states are not voluntary associations and emphasizes instead the role of labor in conferring ownership rights, consent plays an unacknowledged role. As he puts it, "In the case of illegal immigrants, by entering the country illicitly such individuals took their place in their community without the consent of the citizenry." He acknowledges unauthorized migrants make contributions through working and paying taxes, but he contends that citizens have no obligation "to pass ownership of their institutions to illegal immigrants" because the migrants have "put themselves in this situation without the consent of the citizenry" (164–5). Thus, migrants' labor is insufficient to ground a claim to joint ownership; the consent of citizens is necessary. But if we apply the same consent standard to the citizens whom Pevnick regards as joint-owners of public institutions, very few citizens would be joint-owners since their membership was not based on consent. In other words, the account presumes that the original contract of joint ownership was founded on mutual consent, and that the original members expressly or tacitly consented to pass on their institutions to future members.

A third novel argument is based on freedom of association. Christopher Heath Wellman starts with the premise that freedom of association is "an integral component of self-determination" (2011, 39–40). Freedom of association includes the right to include and exclude potential associates. Wellman quotes Stuart White on this point: "When a group of people gets together to form an association of some kind (e.g., a religious association, a trade union, a sports club), they will frequently wish to exclude some people from joining their association. What makes it *their* association, serving their purposes, is that they can exercise this 'right to exclude'" (1997, 360–1). Wellman extends the value of freedom of association beyond small-scale associations to the state itself, arguing by way of analogy:

> Just as an individual may permissibly choose whom (if anyone) to marry, and a golf club may choose whom (if anyone) to admit as new members, a group of fellow citizens is entitled to determine whom (if anyone) to admit into their country.
>
> *(2011, 37)*

Wellman acknowledges this presumptive right can be overridden by competing considerations, but he concludes,

> even if egalitarians are right that those of us in wealthy societies have stringent duties of global distributive justice, and even if libertarians are correct that individuals have rights both to freedom of movement and to control their private property, legitimate states are entitled to reject all potential immigrants, even those desperately seeking asylum from incompetent or corrupt political regimes that are either unable or unwilling to protect their citizens' basic moral rights.
>
> *(2008, 109)*

Among existing accounts of state sovereignty, Wellman's is the most absolutist, coming closest to a position of "closed borders."

The club analogy upon which Wellman's argument rests does not hold up. States are not voluntary associations; we do not freely enter them. The non-voluntariness of political membership raises the stakes of membership. Exclusion from a particular state is hugely consequential, whereas exclusion from golf clubs typically is not. If one golf club refuses to admit me, I can join another or form my own. If a state refuses to admit me, I cannot form my own nor easily join another. If no golf club will admit me, the consequences are nowhere near as dire as the consequences of being stateless. Given these differences, the burden falls on proponents to elaborate on why freedom of association is fundamental for states. Wellman says control over migration is significant because new members will have a say in determining the future course of the association. In other words, freedom of association flows from the right of collective self-determination, but Wellman does not develop the connection. Rather than relying on flawed analogies, we need to examine the idea of collective self-determination itself.

3.3 A Case for "Controlled Borders and Open Doors"

If there is a compelling argument for the right of states to control immigration, I believe it rests on the idea of collective self-determination (Song 2018). The three accounts discussed above appeal to collective self-determination, but they go awry in ignoring what is distinctive about the political community as a form of association. Collective self-determination is the moral claim of a collective to rule itself. It is recognized as a fundamental right in UN charters and covenants. Article 1 of the International Covenant on Civil and Political Rights states, "All peoples have the right of self-determination. By virtue of that right they freely determine their political status and freely pursue their economic, social and cultural development." The claim of self-determination says the legitimacy of political rule depends on authorization by the people governed by those institutions. To be legitimate, political institutions must reflect the will of the people. The people must be authors of those institutions in some meaningful way.

Any attempt to justify the state's right to control immigration based on collective self-determination must meet several challenges (Fine 2013). First, it must provide a coherent account of the collective who is to be self-determining. Second, it must connect the self-determining collective to a particular territory. Third, it must explain why the state's interest in controlling immigration outweighs the claims of prospective migrants to be admitted to the territory such that it can be said to have a general right to control immigration. I believe these challenges can be met.

First, rather than conceiving of the collective as a nation, joint-owners of state institutions, or members of a voluntary association as in the accounts discussed above, we should view the collective as "a people" engaged in the shared political project of collective self-governance. What are peoples and how are they constituted? We can identify prominent invocations of peoplehood in political documents around the world. The U.S. Constitution opens with the words, "We the People of the United States." The French Declaration of the Rights of Man and Citizen begins, "The representatives of the French people." Peoplehood is often considered synonymous with the more familiar idea of the nation, but we should distinguish them. The idea of peoplehood is more capacious. To be a member of a nation, one must share the national identity. Conceptions of nationhood tend to include a component of willingness on the part of members, a "daily plebiscite" (Renan 2018), but for nationalists, sharing the cultural attributes considered central to the national identity is essential for membership in the nation. By contrast, what is essential about peoplehood is participation in shared institutions and activities that aim at collective self-governance. Political cooperation, not cultural identity, is what defines peoplehood. By using the idea of peoplehood over nationhood, I mean to foreground political agency over cultural identity. Many nations count as peoples, but the category of peoples is broader and includes groups whose members do not necessarily share a cultural identity.

The second challenge is to explain the connection between the self-determining collective and its right to control a particular territory. The state is unique from other types of associations in being a fundamentally territorial entity. The state requires control over a particular territory to function as a state. But why is the state entitled to control access to the *particular* territory it claims for itself? To answer, we need to show that the people who are represented by the state have the right to occupy the territory in question. A state's claim of territorial rights over a particular territory depends on a prior entitlement to the area it governs. It is not the state, but the occupants of the territory who hold these prior entitlements. Only if the individuals residing in a particular place have a rightful claim of occupancy does the state, which represents those individuals, have legitimate jurisdiction over it. This right of occupancy is a pre-institutional claim of those who do not unjustly inhabit a place to reside there permanently, to make use of the area for valued practices, and to be immune from expropriation or removal (Stilz 2013). What grounds the right of occupancy is the importance of stable residence for the pursuit of life projects. The key point here is that the state's territorial rights derive ultimately from an individual's right to place. People have a right to occupy a particular place because stable residency in a particular place is necessary for personal well-being.

The most straightforward case of legitimate occupancy involves a group of people who settle on uninhabited land and reside on it continuously. This scenario is reflected in the familiar narrative of the U.S. being a "nation of immigrants." But if we look at the U.S. history, we find not only voluntary migration but also colonialism, conquest, slavery, theft of land, and the mingling of peoples over time. This complicated history generates more questions than answers about who is entitled to establish jurisdiction in any particular geographic area. For example, much territory that is today regarded as U.S. territory was annexed against the will of its original inhabitants, who were either forcibly expelled or forcibly incorporated into the territory. What are the implications for the occupancy claims of those residing on U.S. territory today and for the territorial rights claims of the U.S. government?

These are hard and important questions that can only be discussed briefly here. I do not think the legitimate occupancy condition necessarily unravels the case for the territorial rights of states. Where the agents and victims of the unjust appropriation are still alive, the agent that was causally responsible for the injustice bears the responsibility to remedy the injustice. What about cases where the perpetrators and victims of the injustice are long gone? The European settlers and government officials who expropriated Native American land are causally and morally responsible for the harms caused to Native Americans, but given that none of the original parties who perpetrated the injustices are still alive, who bears responsibility for remedying the effects of the injustice suffered by Native American descendants?

Some have argued that historical injustices should be regarded as having been "superseded," and the focus instead should be on securing the rights and well-being of current citizens (Waldron 1992). By contrast, others argue that political communities must acknowledge and respond to historical injustices by fostering the inclusion of those disadvantaged by the persisting effects of past injustices. On the latter argument, the responsibility to remedy the enduring effects of past injustices is a political responsibility that falls on all current members of the political community (Young 2011). Remedies might take symbolic and material forms, including apologies, return of stolen property, monetary compensation, and legal and constitutional provisions recognizing the self-government and land use rights of indigenous communities. The exact form that remedy should take will depend on a number of factors, including what those harmed by the past injustice want and the impact of granting the remedy on the state's obligations toward all members of the political community. There are no easy answers, but I believe the difficult questions raised by the legitimate occupancy condition can be addressed by taking historical injustice seriously.

The third challenge is to explain why the state's interest in controlling immigration outweighs the claims of prospective migrants to be admitted such that there is a general right to control immigration. There are certainly circumstances in which states are morally required to admit prospective migrants, such as in the case of refugees fleeing persecution. Refugees are a clear case of *obligatory admissions*, where the decision to admit prospective migrants is required by justice (Carens 2013). In cases where states have played a causal role in turning people into refugees, they bear a remedial responsibility to take in refugees to repair the harm they have caused (Souter 2014). Another source of the duty to assist refugees is arguably more universal in scope and distinct from the obligations of justice: this is the humanitarian concern that underpins the principle of mutual aid (Song 2018, 115). The duty of mutual aid is akin to the duty of rescue in emergencies: when someone faces the threat of serious harm, we have a duty to rescue them if we can do so without causing serious injury to ourselves. I discuss the grounds and content of the duty to refugees further below.

What about cases in which prospective migrants are not at risk of serious harm? Such cases constitute *discretionary admissions*, where the decision to admit is not morally required (Blake 2002). There are at least two fundamental interests that underlie the state's right to control immigration and justify regulation of "discretionary admissions." One is the interest of *individuals* in being free from unwanted obligations. Membership in a political community is a source of special rights and obligations, and meeting the membership-based obligations imposes burdens on all members to do their part. As Blake has argued,

> The would-be immigrant who wants to cross into a given jurisdiction acts to impose a set of obligations upon that jurisdiction's current residents. That obligation limits the freedom of those residents by placing them under standing obligations to act in

particular ways in defense of that migrant's rights. In response to this, legitimate states may refuse to allow immigrants to come in, because the residents of those states have the right to refuse to become obligated to those would-be immigrants.

(2013, pp. 119–20)

In my view, a second fundamental interest grounding the state's right to control immigration is irreducibly *collective*, an interest in collective self-determination (Song 2018, 66). Collective self-determination enables a distinctive kind of freedom, what we might call political freedom and what Rousseau calls "moral liberty": "obedience to the law one has prescribed for oneself" (1987, 150–151). Collective self-determination is a form of political freedom that is only possible through membership in a collective. If a demagogue were to seize power without the support of the people he seeks to rule, he would not take something away from the individuals *qua* individuals; instead, he takes something from the group as a whole, the right to collective self-determination. If migrants are present in a state's territory without authorization, they sidestep the political process by which members of that political community can define who the collective self is. The right to collective self-determination includes the right to regulate migration and membership into the political community.

The collective self-determination argument offers a middle ground in highly polarized debates about migration: what is required is not a policy of "closed borders" or "open borders" but instead "controlled borders and open doors." In contrast to proponents of "open borders," it recognizes the moral significance of political membership as a source of special rights and obligations. A government may show some partiality toward the interests of its members. For example, a government is justified in excluding prospective migrants who want to migrate to pursue higher wages above an already decent level if doing so protects important interests such as sustaining social welfare programs that serve the less advantaged members of the political community. Yet, in contrast to those who favor "closed borders," it acknowledges the obligations of countries to open their doors to refugees and other migrants at risk of serious harm.

3.4 Qualifications on State Sovereignty Over Immigration

The right of collective self-determination grounds the right of states to control immigration, but this right is *qualified*, not absolute. Democratic states are constrained by moral principles that have found institutional expression in international and domestic law, including laws defining the responsibilities of states to refugees and unauthorized migrants.

The first moral qualification pertains to refugees and other migrants at risk of serious harm. Refugees are in urgent need of protection from persecution by their home state or the failure of their home state to protect them from violence by third parties. The UN Refugee Convention defines a refugee as someone who "owing to well-founded fear of being persecuted for reasons of race, religion, nationality, membership of a particular social group or political opinion, is outside the country of his nationality and is unable… or unwilling to avail himself of the protection of that country." The Convention definition, which has been incorporated into the domestic law of many states, does not include individuals who are forcibly displaced for other reasons, such as famine or environmental disasters, nor does it include those who remain inside their country of origin.

What is normatively significant about refugees is not simply that their basic needs are not being met but also that their basic needs can *only* be met by allowing them to enter a safe country and granting asylum. By contrast, asylum is not the only or best remedy for many people suffering environmental disasters. If the disaster is temporary, it is reasonable to expect people to return home after the danger has passed and communities have been rebuilt. Those displaced by environmental disasters may be entitled to refugee status if the displacement is indefinite, as in the case of island communities facing rising sea levels. Recognizing "climate change refugees" as refugees would be in keeping with the rationale of the Convention definition broadly understood.

In my view, instead of broadening the legal definition of "refugee" to include all migrants at risk of serious harm, the refugee category should continue to focus on people fleeing persecution, but international protection such as material assistance and asylum should also be extended to other *necessitous migrants* whose basic needs are not being met (Song 2018, 120). The appropriate form of assistance will depend on the particular circumstances of migrants and should be tailored to meet their particular needs. Sometimes the only remedy is to grant asylum; in other cases, they may be able to receive emergency assistance in their countries of origin and eventually return to their homes. In addition, refugee and migration policy must be a part of broader efforts to end the violence and deprivation that fuel migration, including peace-building efforts to help restore the rule of law and development assistance to create infrastructure, deliver public services, and support economic development. Establishing robust development programs rather than militarizing borders should be an essential component of any migration control program.

Another challenge pertaining to refugees is that even those who meet the legal definition of refugee are not receiving the assistance they need. The principle of *nonrefoulement*, which says that contracting states will not return refugees to the countries where their life or freedom would be threatened, has come to be widely recognized as an obligation with a legally binding character. By contrast, the *resettlement* of refugees from the country where they first found safety to a third country for permanent residence is not recognized as a binding obligation. In 2015, the UNHCR submitted 134,000 refugees to states for resettlement, and states admitted 107,100 refugees, but this was only 0.66 percent of the 16.1 million refugees under the UNHCR's mandate at the time (UNHCR 2015). There is enormous disparity in how the responsibility toward refugees is distributed among states: the vast majority of refugees reside in developing countries in refugee camps or in cities where they have limited opportunities for education and work, while developed countries have taken in only a tiny fraction of refugees. The dominant approach adopted by most developed states is one of deterrence and exclusion: interception on the high seas, erection of walls and fences, sanctions on airline carriers, and bilateral and regional agreements to prevent onward movement of migrants.

Yet, few of these developed states have directly challenged international law or taken steps to withdraw from the Refugee Convention or other human rights instruments. They recognize that international refugee law serves as an important tool to ensure the continued commitment of less developed states that host the vast majority of the world's refugees. States have a duty to cooperate in the international refugee-protection system, and this should include working with the UNHCR to determine a fair scheme of responsibility sharing. A fair scheme must take account of the integrative capabilities of states, including the size of the state's territory, its population, and GDP (Gibney 2015). It would be a huge step forward for democratic states to recognize they have a duty to take in refugees and develop mechanisms for determining and implementing a fair scheme of responsibility sharing.

A second qualification on state sovereignty over immigration applies to the treatment of unauthorized migrants by liberal democratic states. On the one hand, migrants who enter without authorization or overstay their temporary visas have violated immigration law. Some argue immigration law should be enforced and unauthorized migrants deported to their countries of origin. On the other hand, there are countervailing considerations of justice that support granting rights, including the right to stay, to unauthorized migrants. I consider three countervailing considerations, which have found some legal grounding in liberal democratic states.

First, the social membership principle says unauthorized migrants should be granted the right to stay because they have already become members in virtue of the social ties they have developed. As Carens puts it, "living within the territorial boundaries of a state makes one a member of society" and "this social membership gives rise to moral claims in relation to the political community" (2013, 158). When migrants have been settled for a period of time (Carens proposes five years), they become social members and are entitled to the right to stay and the opportunity to become citizens (147). The social membership principle is reflected in immigrant legalization and amnesty programs and in immigration proceedings in which a migrant's social ties play a role in canceling removal.

A second constraining principle is the principle of fair play. Most migrants contribute to the economy through their labor and support the government through their tax payments. They work in agricultural and construction jobs, clean people's houses and yards, and care for the young, the ill, and the elderly. These contributions are morally significant because they generate requirements of reciprocity and fairness: migrants contribute to the host society and are owed something in return (Hosein 2016, 167; Song 2018, 187). Reciprocity requires that migrants' contributions be rewarded with material benefits. The state could provide stronger labor and employment rights to ensure that migrants retain more of the productive surplus created by their work and fund health insurance to protect them from the risk of serious illness. Reciprocity can also be interpreted as requiring the right to stay.

A third constraining principle has to do with the vulnerability of migrants to exploitation. Equality is a core constitutional principle. In a society of equals, caste-like distinctions between groups, whether based on race, gender, or immigration status, are morally objectionable. Systematic inequality between groups renders some groups vulnerable to subordination at the hands of others. This concern animates Walzer's argument against the "permanent alienage" of migrants: "Men and women are either subject to the state's authority, or they are not; and if they are subject, they must be given a say, and ultimately an equal say, in what that authority does" (1986, 61). In *Plyler v. Doe* (1982), the U.S. Supreme Court identified unauthorized migrants as a potential "caste" in American society. The Court said that the U.S. government through "sheer incapability or lax enforcement of the laws" had created

> a substantial "shadow population" of illegal migrants. This situation raises the specter of a permanent caste of undocumented resident aliens, encouraged by some to remain here as a source of cheap labor, but nevertheless denied the benefits that our society makes available to citizens and lawful residents. The existence of such an underclass presents most difficult problems for a Nation that prides itself on adherence to principles of equality under law.
>
> *(202)*

Such anti-caste concerns ground Owen Fiss's argument for extending certain rights, including welfare rights, to unauthorized migrants (1999). Adam Hosein draws on them to argue for their right to stay (2016, 169–172).

In addition to these justice arguments, there are rule of law arguments for extending legal status and rights to unauthorized migrants (Song and Bloemraad 2022). First, it can promote consistency and predictability in a system of immigration enforcement that is highly discretionary. A second argument draws from the rationale behind statutes of limitations: it is wrong to make people live indefinitely with a looming threat of serious legal consequences for a past action, except for the most serious offenses. If the state is unable or unwilling to enforce immigration law in a timely and reasonably predictable manner, "the principle of legal certainty demands that the state cut its losses, so to speak, and recognize the right of individuals, to move on with their lives" (Ellermann 2014, 301). Third, legalization can provide a fresh start for the immigration system. The presence of large numbers of unauthorized migrants can undermine the credibility of the overall immigration system and divert resources needed for new policies. Legalization programs can promote the rule of law by clearing up a backlog of cases where the law has not been enforced. Legalization serves as a pragmatic response to administrative failure, bringing the law and actual behavior into closer alignment for the purposes of effective governance and systemic legitimacy (Bosniak 2013, 348).

3.5 Conclusion

This chapter has provided a critical survey of arguments for the intermediate ethical position of qualified state sovereignty and advanced an argument based on the value of collective self-determination for "controlled borders and open doors." On this account, states have the right to control immigration as part of the political community's right of collective self-determination, but this right is qualified by certain moral constraints, including the duty to open doors to refugees and other necessitous migrants and extend a path to residency and membership to unauthorized migrants.

References

Abizadeh, Arash. 2008. "Democratic Theory and Border Coercion: No Right to Unilaterally Control Your Own Borders." *Political Theory* 36 (1): 37–65.
Blake, Michael. 2002. "Discretionary Immigration." *Philosophical Topics* 30 (2): 273–289.
Blake, Michael. 2005. "Immigration." In *A Companion to Applied Ethics*, edited by R.G. Frey and Christopher Heath Wellman, 224–237. Malden, MA: Blackwell.
Blake, Michael. 2013. "Immigration, Jurisdiction, and Exclusion." *Philosophy & Public Affairs* 41 (2): 103–130.
Bosniak, Linda. 2013. "Amnesty in Immigration: Forgetting, Forgiving, Freedom." *Critical Review of International Social and Political Philosophy* 16 (3): 344–365.
Carens, Joseph H. 1987. "Aliens and Citizens: The Case for Open Borders." *Review of Politics* 49 (2): 251–273.
Carens, Joseph H. 1992. "Migration and Morality: A Liberal Egalitarian Perspective." In *Free Movement: Ethical Issues in the Transnational Migration of People and of Money*, edited by Brian Barry and Robert E. Goodin, 25–47. University Park, PA: University of Pennsylvania Press.
Carens, Joseph H. 2013. *The Ethics of Immigration*. Oxford: Oxford University Press.
Clemens, Michael. 2011. "Economics and Emigration: Trillion-Dollar Bills on the Sidewalk?" *Journal of Economic Perspectives* 25 (3): 83–106.
Cole, Phillip. 2000. *Philosophies of Exclusion: Liberal Political Theory and Immigration*. Edinburgh: Edinburgh University Press.
Ellermann, Antje. 2014. "The Rule of Law and the Right to Stay: The Moral Claims of Undocumented Migrants." *Politics & Society* 42 (3): 293–308.
Fine, Sarah. 2013. "The Ethics of Immigration: Self-Determination and the Right to Exclude." *Philosophy Compass* 8 (3): 254–268.

Fiss, Owen. 1999. *A Community of Equals: The Constitutional Protection of New Americans*, edited by Joshua Cohen and Joel Rogers. Boston: Beacon Press.
Gibney, Matthew. 2015. "Refugees and Justice between States." *European Journal of Political Theory* 14 (4): 448–463.
Hosein, Adam. 2016. "Arguments for Regularization." In *The Ethics and Politics of Immigration: Core Issues and Emerging Trends*, edited by Alex Sager, 159–179. New York: Rowman & Littlefield.
Locke, John. [1690] 1980. *Second Treatise of Government*, edited by C.B. Macpherson. Indianapolis, IN: Hackett Publishing Company.
Miller, David. 1995. *On Nationality*. Oxford: Oxford University Press.
Miller, David. 2014. "Immigration: The Case for Limits." In *Contemporary Debates in Applied Ethics*, edited by Andrew I. Cohen and Christopher Heath Wellman. Malden, MA: Wiley-Blackwell.
Miller, David. 2016. *Strangers in Our Midst: The Political Philosophy of Immigration*. Cambridge, MA: Harvard University Press.
Ngai, Mae M. 2004. *Impossible Subjects: Illegal Aliens and the Making of Modern America*. Princeton, NJ: Princeton University Press.
Oberman, Kieran. 2016. "Immigration as a Human Right." In *Migration in Political Theory: The Ethics of Movement and Membership*, edited by Sarah Fine and Lea Ypi, 32–56. Oxford: Oxford University Press.
Pevnick, Ryan. 2011. *Immigration and the Constraints of Justice: Between Open Borders and Absolute Sovereignty*. Cambridge: Cambridge University Press.
Rawls, John. 1971. *A Theory of Justice*. Cambridge, MA: Harvard University Press.
Renan, Ernest. [1882] 2018. *What Is a Nation? and Other Political Writings*. Translated by M.F.N. Giglioli. New York: Columbia University Press.
Rousseau, Jean-Jacques. [1762] 1987. *The Social Contract. Basic Political Writings*, edited by Donald A. Cress. Indianapolis, IN: Hackett Publishing Company.
Simmons, A. John. 1992. *The Lockean Theory of Rights*. Princeton, NJ: Princeton University Press.
Smith, Rogers M. 1997. *Civic Ideals: Conflicting Visions of Citizenship in U.S. History*. New Haven, CT: Yale University Press.
Song, Sarah. 2017. "Why Does the State Have the Right to Control Immigration?" In *NOMOS LVII: Migration, Emigration, and Immigration*, edited by Jack Knight, 3–50. New York: New York University Press.
Song, Sarah. 2018. *Immigration and the Limits of Democracy*. Oxford: Oxford University Press.
Song, Sarah, and Irene Bloemraad. 2022. "Immigrant Legalization: A Dilemma between Justice and the Rule of Law." *Migration Studies* 10 (3): 484–509.
Souter, James. 2014. "Towards a Theory of Asylum as Reparation for Past Injustice." *Political Studies* 62 (2): 326–342.
Steiner, Hillel. 1992. "Libertarianism and the Transnational Migration of People." In *Free Movement: Ethical Issues in the Transnational Migration of People and of Money*, edited by Brian Barry and Robert E. Goodin, 89–94. University Park, PA: Pennsylvania State University Press.
Stilz, Anna. 2013. "Occupancy Rights and the Wrong of Removal." *Philosophy & Public Affairs* 41 (4): 324–356.
United Nations. 1966. "International Covenant on Civil and Political Rights." Available at: www.ohchr.org/en/professionalinterest/pages/ccpr.aspx.
UNHCR. 2015. *Global Trends: Forced Displacement in 2015*. Geneva. https://www.unhcr.org/576408cd7.pdf. [Accessed November 27, 2022].
Waldron, Jeremy. 1992. "Superseding Historic Injustice." *Ethics* 103 (1): 4–28.
Walzer, Michael. 1983. *Spheres of Justice: A Defense of Pluralism and Equality*. New York: Basic Books.
Wellman, Christopher Heath. 2008. "Immigration and Freedom of Association." *Ethics* 119 (1): 109–141.
Wellman, Christopher H. 2011. "In Defense of the Right to Exclude." In *Debating the Ethics of Immigration: Is There a Right to Exclude?* edited by Christopher H. Wellman and Phillip Cole, 13–56. Oxford: Oxford University Press.
Young, Iris M. 2011. *Responsibility for Justice*. Oxford: Oxford University Press.

4
FREE MOVEMENT
A Human Right or a Citizenship Right?

Rainer Bauböck

4.1 Introduction

Should people be free to move across international borders? Since the 1980s, this question has been debated intensely by economists and political theorists. Many of the former defend universal freedom of movement as conducive to development and the reduction of global inequalities (e.g. Milanovic 2016), and many of the latter argue that it is entailed by a commitment to individual liberty and moral equality (e.g. Oberman 2016). From these perspectives, the main obstacle to free movement is state sovereignty, which includes the power of states to control immigration into their territory and admission to their citizenship. Theorists taking the other side in this debate have emphasized that these state prerogatives can be justified on grounds of democratic self-determination. In this view, being able to select new members is the essence of collective self-determination (Song 2019: 69; Walzer 1983: 38–39) and control over immigration is necessary to preserve solidarity and trust among citizens (Miller 1995, 2016).

In this chapter, I will argue for a perspective on free movement that combines the insights and transcends the antagonisms of these positions. In this view, free movement as a *human right* needs to be balanced against and constrained by the self-government rights of immigration-receiving societies. Taking free movement seriously as a human right implies, however, that liberal democratic states must justify their immigration control towards would-be immigrants by demonstrating that it is actually necessary for preserving their democratic self-government. At the same time, such states ought to promote free movement as a *citizenship right* for their own citizens and open their territory to other countries' citizens on a basis of reciprocity.

A second aim of this chapter is to narrow the gap between normative arguments about free movement derived from liberal principles and those applying to real-world contexts. The goal is not to discredit radical critiques of immigration control but to distinguish more clearly between the non-ideal features of the international state system, which prompt even liberal states to engage in deeply illiberal immigration policies, and the general requirements of democratic self-government in a world consisting of a plurality of bounded polities.

This chapter will first clarify what is meant by free movement (Section 2) and then discuss the conditions and limitations of a human right to free movement (Section 3). Section 4 considers whether alternatively free international movement could be promoted and expanded as a citizenship-based right and concludes that although free movement remains an important liberal ideal, the greatest challenges of social justice in the contemporary world require enhancing opportunities for regular migration that is subject to immigration control. Section 5 summarizes the argument and ends with sceptical reflections on future prospects for free international movement.

4.2 Conceptualizing Free Movement

In its most basic interpretation, free movement is the capacity of individuals to move their bodies in space as they intend without being obstructed. Since humans are animals that need to move in order to find food and partners for procreation, or escape from various dangers to their lives, free movement in this sense is a basic condition of human life. Being able to choose where to go is also an essential aspect of human freedom. Thomas Hobbes may have gone too far when he declared that 'Liberty, or Freedome, signifieth (properly) the absence of Opposition; (by Opposition I mean externall Impediments of motion)' and attributed such freedom even to the movement of inanimate objects (Hobbes 1651/1973: 110).

In a modern understanding, natural impediments to movement, such as mountains, rivers and seas, hardly count any more among the relevant obstacles that make people unfree in their movement. This may be partly due to technological progress in transportation, but it has even more to do with a modern world view that freedom is primarily curtailed (as well as enabled) by the coercive exercise of political power. What we mean when we call movement free is that it is based on a person's intentions and choices (including over when to leave and where to go) and has been authorized by political authorities. Movement becomes unfree when coercion overrules individual will at any point of the process.

By contrast, the common distinction between forced and voluntary migration refers mainly to the context of departure. Where people are pushed out of their homes – through direct use of force against them, through generalized violence that threatens their security, or through a lack of economic means for survival – their movement is forced. Where migration is motivated by a search of better opportunities, a wish to join family members elsewhere, or mere curiosity and a desire to experience life in a different place, we may call it voluntary. Yet voluntariness of departure is not sufficient to call movement free. For this, the individual must be in control also regarding her destination. Only where she can freely enter an intended destination and is authorized to stay there as long as she wishes is her movement fully free.

Free movement so defined can still be constrained and conditioned in various ways. First, it may be constrained spatially through the exclusion of certain destinations. If I can move freely within the territory of my country but can enter only those others with which mine has concluded admission agreements, then my freedom of movement is restricted to a certain space. If I can freely enter another country but can stay there only for a limited period, then it is limited in time. And if there are conditions attached to entering or staying, such as sufficient income or health insurance for non-economically active EU citizens migrating within the European Union, then freedom of movement is conditional. As long as movement remains free within such sufficiently wide constraints, it still makes sense to speak about limited forms of free movement.

In order to grasp better what it takes to turn free movement into a right, we need to take into account how the modern state system structures human migration and mobility. Over a long historical period, movement inside state borders was densely regulated – either at local level through autonomous municipalities exercising admission controls (Prak 2018), or through central state authorities' efforts to disperse ethnic minorities and prevent internal migrations of destitute groups. Even economic emigration from Europe was densely regulated until the late 19th century, as origin states were concerned about a loss of human resources needed for their economies and war efforts (Zolberg 2007). By comparison, until World War I, admission control was a much lesser concern, as the newly independent European settler colonies were desperate to promote immigration and European states often lacked both interest and capacity to enforce immigration control (Torpey 2000). It is only in the 20th century that a liberal norm of free internal movement and emigration emerged and was eventually enshrined in international human right law,[1] while immigration control became the main focus of regulatory efforts in democratic states.

Against this background, it makes sense to define free movement not just as individually intended and politically authorized movement in space but more specifically as the right to cross territorial borders. Free internal movement within independent states exists where authorities of substate jurisdictions, such as municipalities or autonomous provinces and regions, no longer enjoy any power to control emigration from or immigration into their territories and where central state authorities guarantee free movement rights within the country's borders. Free movement between independent states exists where countries of origin honour the universal human right of free emigration and where destination countries authorize free entry and stay within their territory.

Since all contemporary states claim and enjoy immigration control powers as an essential feature of their territorial sovereignty, free international movement does not exist in the current world as a universal human right, but only for the citizens of particular countries. Nevertheless, the number of countries involved in free movement arrangements and the number of individuals benefiting from these has greatly increased over the last fifty years. Regional unions of states have agreed to free movement rights for the nationals of their member states in Europe (the European Union, EFTA countries and Switzerland), in South America (the Mercosur and Andean Unions) and Africa (ECOWAS and the East African Union) (Acosta 2019; Nita et al. 2017). Some countries have concluded special bilateral or multilateral free movement agreements (the Nordic Passport Union after World War II, the British-Irish Common Travel Area, the Trans-Tasman Travel Arrangement between Australia and New Zealand). Most significantly, there has been a strong global trend towards accepting dual citizenship (Vink et al. 2019). The right to return to one's country of citizenship is one of the strongest individual rights enshrined in international law.[2] Multiple citizens enjoy this right in several countries and thus a right to move freely between them.

Free international movement, even in its conditional manifestations, needs to be distinguished from regular immigration. Whereas the former requires that countries waive their immigration control powers, the latter involves exercising them by selecting immigrants and determining the conditions under which they can apply for residence, enter the country and stay there. Canada admits large numbers of immigrants every year, and there is a broad political consensus on the benefits of immigration, but it subjects nearly all its immigrants (apart from returning Canadian citizens) to immigration control. By contrast, in the member states of the European Union, immigration is much more contested, but much of it is based on free movement rights of EU citizens who are not subjected to immigration control.

International refugee protection is also generally organized in such a way that states exercise their immigration control powers. Refugees resettled in liberal democracies of the Global North are individually selected by these. Asylum seekers do not enjoy a general legal right to enter a destination country, and their right to stay depends on filing an asylum claim and its acceptance by the host country. The admission of Ukrainian war refugees into the European Union since February 2022 represents a rare exception through which refugees enjoy something resembling free movement rights with no limits being placed on their admission, a right to choose their destination country within the EU, and access to employment. The main limitation is that the protection granted is temporary and its extension may depend on the further course of the war and return options for the several millions of internationally displaced persons.

Finally, there is also irregular migration through unauthorized border crossings or overstaying of visas and residence permits. Although one could say that irregular migration means states have failed to effectively exercise their immigration control powers, it is clear that, by definition, unauthorized immigration is not free if that requires having been authorized by the destination country.

4.3 Free Movement as a Human Right

After this brief sketch of human and citizenship rights to free movement codified in international law and emerging from the practice of liberal democratic states, let us now consider normative arguments for a more expansive conception that also includes a general right to immigration.

Human rights are meant to protect fundamental human interests. As already pointed out in Section 1, freedom of movement can plausibly be counted among these. We can regard free movement either as having intrinsic value as a core aspect of individual autonomy itself, or as instrumentally necessary in order to achieve other goals that individuals should be free to pursue.

An intrinsic-value view creates a strong presumption in favour of a general human right of free movement and a corresponding duty of political authorities to justify restrictions, for the same reasons as they have to justify restrictions on freedom of speech or association. As with these other freedoms, regarding free movement as having value in itself does not mean that it is a nearly absolute right of the same kind as those human rights the violation of which can never be justified, or only in the most extreme circumstances, such as the right not to be tortured or enslaved. The main question is for which reasons and in which ways a general human right to free movement may be legitimately restricted.

An instrumental view provides somewhat weaker foundations. David Miller argues that states have duties to provide individuals with an adequate range of resources and opportunities in their territory. If they succeed in this task, then their citizens cannot claim that other states have duties to admit them if they want to seek additional opportunities there (Miller 2007: 205–8). As Kieran Oberman (2016) points out, Miller's argument implies that there is also no human right to free movement within states, as long as people can find adequate opportunities within a part of the national territory. By contrast, on Oberman's view, human rights are meant to protect individuals' interests in access to the *full* range of existing life options and not only those that may be deemed adequate for a decent life. He concludes that there is no difference between the interests of citizens and foreigners in this regard. Both the intrinsic value and Oberman's expansive instrumental value view suggest that free movement should be regarded as a general human right, whereas Miller's narrow instrumental view does not. It supports instead regulated forms of refugee protection and immigrant admission that provide people who are deprived of basic security and resources in their countries of origin, and whose situation there cannot be improved through foreign assistance with admission opportunities in countries where they could lead a decent life. Migrants may, however, also pursue other kinds of interests that are not adequately captured by either of these arguments. For example, Sahar Akhtar argues for a conditional right to international relocation of persons who are seeking to live in a country where they can better pursue their preferred way of life. If immigrants join a society where a way of life that attracts them is already strongly practiced, this does not come at a high cost to the society. Nevertheless, such an interest may not be strong enough to ground either a right of free movement or a state duty of priority admission over other more needy migrants (Akhtar 2016).

Proclaiming a general human right to free movement does not amount to calling for open borders, since there may be legitimate reasons for restricting this liberty. There are several such grounds that have been widely discussed (Carens 2013: 255–287; Cassee 2016: 261–278; Oberman 2016: 45–52); they include the threat that free immigration may pose to cultural homogeneity, public security, and social welfare regimes. While these may look prima facie convincing, invoking them shifts the perspective from the universal one of human rights to the particular one of the interests of states and their citizens. When liberals consider permissible restrictions of free speech or association, they don't accept that particularistic state interests can be strong enough to justify general restrictions. For such basic liberties, only those restrictions are considered legitimate that are necessary to maintain the conditions under which all can enjoy the same freedom.[3] Invoking the particular interests of states and their citizens as a reason for restricting a universal liberty seems therefore prima facie inappropriate.

On the other hand, state interests are hard to ignore if in the modern world movement can only be free when it has been authorized by states. There are two ways how the particular interests of states and their citizens can be invoked in this debate. One is to regard states as ideally neutral arbiters between the universal interests of all humans in free movement and the particular interests of local populations that may be negatively affected by it. If one adopts this perspective, it seems impossible to understand and justify a categorical difference between freedom of internal movement within states and emigration from them, on the one hand, and immigration control, on the other hand. Internal free movement may greatly affect local populations, for example by jeopardizing the survival of regional ethnic and linguistic minorities. Freedom of emigration may severely undermine the provision of social services and especially of public health care in poorer countries. Only few authors (e.g. Ypi 2008) argue, however, that these widely recognized free movement rights could be restricted on such grounds in the same way as immigration across an international border.

A second way of factoring in interests of states is to regard them as human rights legislators that have agreed to abolish their powers of control over internal movement and emigration while retaining those over immigration. In order to better understand this asymmetry between restrictions on immigration and emigration or internal movement, we need to consider the context of a global political system composed of independent states. In the real world, this system is shaped by great inequalities of power and resources and by legacies of colonial domination. Many institutions of global governance reflect these inequalities. Yet in the realm of international human rights law, states are equally sovereign co-legislators of international norms enshrined in conventions or emerging from state practice. Human rights have not been declared by a global legislator or through doctrines developed by a global court. They have instead emerged from a consensus among states positioned as equal members of the international state system.

When reflecting on the moral bases of human rights, philosophers are not bound to adopt this perspective of states as members of an international political order. Yet when it comes to free movement, this seems necessary. In Section 1, we have defined free movement as involving the authorized crossing of borders of territorial jurisdictions. The bearers of duties corresponding to free movement rights are therefore territorial political authorities. And the activity of crossing borders itself creates a fundamental asymmetry between exit and entry.[4] The addressee of a right to emigration is the political authority of the territory where the individual currently resides. The same authority cannot, however, authorize an individual to enter another jurisdiction. In order to secure a negative liberty of emigration, all that is needed is that the government of the territory of origin does not prevent departure. If one conceives of free emigration as a more robust positive right that depends on opportunities to exercise it, then that government may have a positive duty to issue the departing citizen with travel documents, and there must be at least *one* other government that authorizes admission to its territory. Yet to make exit free, it does not matter how many other states are ready to admit an emigrant. By contrast, for universal free movement, the migrant must be able to choose her destination, and the corresponding duty to keep borders open for immigration falls then on *all* governments worldwide.

Defenders of universal freedom of movement could respond by insisting that territorial political authorities should not have the power to authorize or control the crossing of their borders in the first place, in which case exit and entry would be morally symmetric. They can point to the situation of municipalities or provinces that lack such powers, which enables free internal movement within a country's borders. The question that still needs to be addressed is then whether the fact that independent states have retained these powers in the current international political order can be justified or supported on normative grounds.

Joseph Carens has proposed a negative reply that relies on a 'cantilever' argument. In his view, the intrinsic and instrumental value of freedom of movement for individual autonomy, which supports a human right within state borders, and the countervailing reasons for legitimate restrictions apply equally to migration across international borders. Therefore, the right of states to control immigration appears to make a morally arbitrary distinction that is incompatible with the claim that internal free movement is a human right – rather than a special right of citizens (Carens 2013: 237–245).

This argument fails, however, to consider that free movement involves the crossing of political borders. The relevant question is whether the internal and external borders of states and the jurisdictions demarcated by them are sufficiently similar to sustain a cantilever argument that relies on an inference from internal to international free movement.

One objection against Carens' argument has been raised by Michael Blake (2013). Liberal states accept that they have special duties towards the people inside their jurisdiction to secure their rights, and these duties are quite costly (Holmes and Sunstein 1999). If immigrants can freely choose their destination and settle there, they are imposing additional duties and related costs on the current citizens and residents without their consent. As this seems unfair, the citizens of destination states can claim immigration control powers.

An empirical objection against this argument is that this is exactly the position in which municipalities and provinces find themselves. They have to provide public services for diverse populations whose size and composition depends to a significant extent on migration flows over which local governments have no control. These substate jurisdictions are, however, nested within a national territory, and most of their citizens are simultaneously citizens of the country. This is what enables them to rely on support by a national government when it comes to bearing the costs of rights provision to immigrants in their territory and, if that is no longer sufficient, also to demand that this government control immigration at the external borders in order to avoid that municipalities are overwhelmed. By contrast, independent states are not nested in a global polity on whose support they could count in this respect.

We have now again invoked an empirical argument about the international order that could be challenged by claiming that if this order – even in its ideal aspect as a system of equally sovereign states – creates a fundamental obstacle to realizing international free movement, then it ought to be transformed into a global polity that would 'internalize' all international migration by turning independent states into something like the provinces of a federation. Defenders of this utopia can suggest that this power in such a global polity could be widely dispersed and distributed across levels so that currently independent states still retain substantial powers of self-government, just as the provinces of contemporary federal states do (Höffe 1999).

One can raise several objections against this utopia, such as concerns about its feasibility starting from a system of independent states all of which would have to agree to abandon their external sovereignty. One can also be worried about its desirability given that enforcing open borders throughout the world and compensating countries that are disadvantaged through free migration flows may require a degree of centralization of power and resources at the global level that is dangerous for democracy. Yet all such reasons for scepticism seem misplaced as arguments against a free movement utopia, since its defenders can always fortify their vision through alternative empirical assumptions. For example, they could argue that in a less unequal world where states have roughly similar powers and their citizens roughly similar opportunities, incentives for international migration would be drastically reduced and states might be both ready to open their borders and able to bear the burdens of free movement with little need for global enforcement and redistribution. From a perspective of global justice, this argument seems to me coherent and convincing. It entails, however, that international freedom of movement as a universal human right is not an ideal for the near future but presupposes a very significant transformation of the global order (Bauböck 2009).

From a democratic viewpoint, however, the ideal of a global federal state looks much less attractive. This perspective warns us against making ideal-theory assumptions about benevolent governments that comply with their duties of justice. It puts an emphasis not only on internal checks and balances but also on the external dispersion of power across independent polities that divide humanity into distinct politically constituted societies, and it alerts us about the fragility of democratic polities that can all to easily degenerate into autocratic ones and that operate in a world large parts of which are governed by non-democratic regimes. Although a world consisting only of stable democratic states would certainly be ideal, the basic democratic norm of self-government itself inhibits efforts to bring about this ideal. Constitutions that could effectively prevent the rise of anti-democratic political parties would be themselves undemocratic. And foreign interventions that aim to replace non-democratic with democratic regimes violate the self-determination rights of another people. In other words, whereas the distinction between ideal and non-ideal theory introduced by John Rawls has been productive for theories of justice, it seems less so for normative theories of democracy. Given these inherent dangers to and limits of democracy, the ideal of a global federal polity as a precondition for achieving a universal right of free movement looks not only distant but also problematic.

If these arguments for accepting a plurality of independent states as a background condition for the flourishing of democracy in the current world are accepted, the next question is what justifies attributing to them immigration control powers. One argument is that states need to be able to defend themselves against external threats emerging from other states. If a militarily powerful state aims to colonize or annex another state, then denying the latter the right to control immigration might expose it to invasion.[5] If states lack such powers, then invasion need not follow a military occupation of territory but could also precede it in the form of massive settlement of populations in a territory that is subsequently claimed by the aggressor under the pretext of protecting its citizens there.

A second argument for preserving immigration control powers of independent states even under conditions where global disparities of economic resources and opportunities have been reduced is that – unlike local polities whose citizens share a national citizenship – independent states should be free to meet their domestic duties of social justice through adopting their own comprehensive welfare systems. Imagine a country that wants to experiment with a generous system of unconditional basic income when its neighbours retain social insurance-based systems supplemented by income-tested poverty relief. Free movement between these states would either quickly overwhelm the basic income reform or lead to a two-tiered system where only citizens and already established long-term residents receive the basic income, whereas newcomers have to fend for themselves, which contradicts the core rationale of an inclusive and egalitarian system of social citizenship.

4.4 Free Movement as a Citizenship Right

My preliminary conclusion is that a universal human right of free movement is not only a coherent and morally attractive ideal but also a rather distant one that presupposes a fundamental transformation of the international state system. Focusing instead on the conditions for democratic self-government suggests that a plurality of independent polities that guarantee freedom of emigration and internal movement but retain the power to control immigration might not be merely a more realistic scenario but also normatively defensible.

This does not mean, however, that we need to give up on international freedom of movement, as there is an alternative pathway towards that ideal that already exists in the real world but has been rarely considered by political theorists. Free movement rights between states emerge currently from the combination of two human rights: the right of everyone to freely leave any country and the right to return to one's country. While the former right is universal, the personal scope of the latter is restricted. It is mostly interpreted as a right of citizens to return to their country of nationality, although the UN Human Rights Committee has advocated a broader interpretation under which also long-term legal residents can claim readmission to their host country (Human Rights Committee 1999). Since all countries provide for transmission of their citizenship to at least the first generation born abroad to a citizen parent, the right to 'return' also covers large populations who have never before set foot in the country whose citizenship they have inherited.

The combination of free exit and return seems to yield only a right of one-way movement to one particular destination. Yet, as pointed out in Section 1, there are three constellations in which this combination creates genuine freedom of international movement, even if it remains limited in its personal and geographic scope. One is through explicit free movement agreements between states, the second through free movement rights for the citizens of regional unions of states, and the third through the acceptance of multiple citizenship. The second and third pathways to free movement have been opened by an ever-increasing number of states, which means that today more people enjoy free movement rights between more states than ever before.

How should one assess this progress from a normative perspective? Can it be justified to make free movement rights conditional on citizenship in these ways? Obviously not, if the distribution of citizenship itself is morally arbitrary, as many authors have claimed it is. Here again, answers will differ depending on whether we interpret the question as one about global distributive justice or as about the conditions for democratic self-government. From the former perspective, birthright citizenship looks, as Joseph Carens has famously put it, like a feudal status inherited at birth that largely determines people's opportunities in life, including those of improving their lot by moving to another country (Carens 1987; Milanovic 2016; Shachar 2009). From the latter perspective, citizenship has two essential functions: externally, it attributes responsibility for the protection of individuals' rights to particular states and, internally, it determines who are the members of a political community who have a claim to collective self-government. In an international system of independent states, these functions are indispensable for democracy. In order to counter the charge of moral arbitrariness, however, we also need a normative principle that ought to guide the allocation of citizenship.

This question conjures up the much-debated demos boundary problem. The problem is that any democratically legitimate decision on membership seems to presuppose a bounded demos that already includes all those with a legitimate claim to membership (Whelan 1983). There are three basic responses to this conundrum: one that clings to procedural solutions so that either the current members of the demos can legitimately decide on whom to admit (Schumpeter 1942/1976) or that potential future members have to be included in a special demos deciding on issues of citizenship and electoral rights (Ahlhaus 2020). A second approach is to acknowledge that democratic norms cannot resolve the issue and to refer instead to pre-politically given boundaries of a people based on a shared language, history and sense of common destiny, that is, on linking citizenship to national identity (Miller 2009). A third approach is to look for a substantive principle of democratic inclusion that can be applied to the problem (Dahl 1989). The two main candidates for such a principle have been that of including all whose interests are affected by decisions of a particular demos (Arrhenius 2005; Goodin 2007) or all who are subjected to or addressed by the coercive laws of such a demos (Abizadeh 2008; Beckman 2022; López-Guerra 2005; Owen 2012; Stilz 2011).

My position in this debate has been that procedural solutions remain stuck in the boundary paradox, that pre-political ones are damaging for democracy by justifying both illegitimate exclusion and problematic over-inclusion, and that the principles of including all affected interests and all subjected to coercion address the questions of whose interests should be taken into account and whose rights should be protected, but cannot determine who has a claim to be a member of a self-governing political community. As an alternative response to the latter question, I have defended a principle of including all citizenship stakeholders, defined as those individuals whose interests in autonomy and well-being are structurally linked to the collective self-government and flourishing of a particular polity (Bauböck 2018).

If we apply this principle to the contexts of international migration, it endorses that all permanent residents in a democratic country are given access to its citizenship while those who emigrate have a claim to retain their citizenship and pass it on to a first generation born abroad, but not beyond that. If all democratic states adopted such guidelines, then the right to return would be distributed in a non-arbitrary way to those individuals who have a sufficiently strong link to a country as its current or former residents or as the offspring of these. First- and second-generation migrants would generally qualify for dual citizenship and thus enjoy free movement rights between precisely those countries to which they have genuine biographical links.

Reciprocity-based and regional free movement regimes can also be endorsed normatively if the right to free emigration generates positive duties of states vis-à-vis their citizens. These include minimally the issuing of passports, but arguably also stronger duties to enable citizens' freedom by negotiating opportunities for entry (through visa waiver agreements) and immigration there. Other states cannot be normatively bound to waive their immigration control for the citizens of a country unless there are reciprocal rights for their own citizens. States can and should therefore meet their duties to promote their own citizens' free movement opportunities through bilateral and regional free movement agreements (Bauböck 2020).

In a final step, this normative case for free movement as a citizenship-based right could aim at the same goal of universal scope that we have previously characterized as the distant goal of a human rights approach. The crucial condition would be, once again, overcoming non-ideal features of the international state system, namely the excessive inequality of resources and opportunities, and of power asymmetries between independent states. Most political theorists agree that the exercise of immigration control powers through excluding would-be immigrants needs to be justified towards them. From a democratic perspective, the main justification is that open door immigration could overwhelm the stability of democracies and their capacity of self-government. Yet this fear is only rational under conditions of strong disparities between states. In a less unequal world, states would have little reason to refuse reciprocity-based free movement arrangements with most other states.

Although on this argument the human rights and the citizenship approach converge towards the same goal of universal free movement, they still differ in their presupposition. The former requires a global polity that internalizes all international migration and whose constituent states are thus deprived of immigration control powers, whereas the latter assumes a world of independent states that retain this power but have normative reasons to waive it in most cases. The latter assumption is also compatible with concerns about the inherent problems with stabilizing democracy internally and spreading it to other countries mentioned at the end of Section 3. By retaining immigration control powers as an element of their external sovereignty, democracies remain able to respond to a deteriorating environment.

So far, I have argued in this section that a citizenship-based right to free movement is not morally arbitrary if citizenship itself is allocated in non-arbitrary ways. This conclusion can still be challenged from a global justice perspective. One worry might be that the three pathways to free movement that I have sketched further enhance the opportunities of the already privileged citizens of wealthy countries, such as those in the European Union. However, as the South American and African examples demonstrate, the creation of regional unions with free movement rights does not depend on the wealth of its member states but on an absence of large economic disparities between them. Moreover, the global trend towards acceptance of dual citizenship has been mostly driven by the interests of sending countries, many of which are in the Global South. Dual citizenship provides migrants with free movement opportunities between poor and rich countries even if the former would not be accepted by the latter as members of reciprocity-based agreements covering all citizens.

A second and stronger objection is that regional unions may require reinforcing external borders of unions for the sake of protecting free movement within them. Yet, once again, this dynamic seems to be a particular European experience driven by the stark disparities between the EU and its southern neighbourhood that has not manifested itself in the same way in South American and African contexts (Acosta 2018; Geddes et al. 2019).

The third and strongest worry is that citizenship-based free movement will still exclude a large majority of individuals whose nationality does not offer chances to move to countries where they would find protection of their fundamental rights or better economic opportunities. Some advocates of universal free movement have defended it as a remedial right that responds to global distributive injustice between states by providing opportunities to those born as citizens of poor countries (Carens 2013) and by flattening the undeserved citizenship premium of the Global North through a more equal global distribution of income from labour (Milanovic 2016). Many authors, including this one, remain however sceptical (Bader 1997; Bauböck 2009; Seglow 2006). Unregulated movement from poor to rich countries is unlikely to benefit the worst off in the former who mostly lack the resources needed for emigration. Moreover, the price to be paid for a reduction of inequality between countries might be a huge increase of inequality within them. Most importantly, if a more equal distribution of opportunities in society depends on state regulation of capitalist market economies, then it seems naïve to expect this outcome from a global deregulation of migration – in the absence of a strong global political authority that could enforce a minimum of social rights worldwide.

While free movement is an implausible remedy for global disparities of income and wealth, regulated migration could be an important ingredient of a proper response (Niño Arnaiz 2022). This would require a combination of resource transfers to poor countries and of opportunities for migration from them that benefit not only the destination country but also the migrants themselves and their countries of origin. What is required for remedial migration to achieve its goal is not free movement and the abolishing of immigration control powers, but a transnational governance of regular migration that overcomes the unilateral dominance of receiving state interests (Bauböck and Ruhs 2022; Owen 2021).

4.5 Conclusion

This chapter started with a conception of free movement as the politically authorized crossing of territorial borders in which the individual is free to leave, to enter, to stay, and to return. Free movement is restricted in its personal or geographical scope if only certain groups enjoy it and if they can only choose certain destinations. Free movement so defined is different from both regular and irregular migration. In the former case, migration is authorized but subjected to regulation and control; in the latter case, it is unauthorized and thus also not free in the relevant sense.

The right to move freely within a state's territory, the right to leave freely any such territory, and the right to return to one's country have been recognized as human rights.

The only obstacle to a universal human right of free movement remains the power of independent states to control immigration into their territory. Justifications for this power have been hotly debated among political theorists. Those regarding free movement as having intrinsic value or as serving a wide range of goals that humans should be equally entitled to pursue tend to challenge this power.

I have distinguished between a human rights strategy that aims to replicate the conditions for free internal movement within states on a global scale and a democratic strategy that aims to expand reciprocity-based free movement channels for the citizens of particular countries. My conclusion is that the former is much more demanding because it presupposes a fundamental transformation of the international order, while the latter strategy can be pursued within that order and without challenging the power of states to control immigration. A global expansion of free movement along the citizenship path would, however, require a flattening of economic disparities and power asymmetries between states. Contrary to the view of authors who regard free movement also as a remedial right for overcoming global inequalities, I have suggested that transnational governance of regular migration is more likely to contribute to this goal.

Let me conclude on a sceptical note. In contrast to the human rights strategy, the citizenship strategy is 'realistic' in a broad sense, as it starts from real-world conditions present in the current international state system and aims to overcome its non-ideal features while retaining the equal sovereignty of independent states and their capacity as co-legislators of international law. It is, however, not meant to be 'realistic' in a narrow sense of prescribing a feasible course of action that builds on a prognosis of future developments. From the latter perspective, there is currently little reason for optimism. While opportunities for citizenship-based free movement have greatly expanded in a context of rapid globalization after the end of the Cold War, we have more recently seen the emergence of new border regimes with unprecedented efforts to seal land borders through walls and fences, the use of digital technologies for separating people entitled to cross-border mobility from those subjected to control, and the transformation of borders from geographic lines into extended zones of immigration control outside and inside states' territories (Mau 2022; Shachar 2020). Most importantly, in their efforts to deter unwanted immigration, also liberal democratic states are resorting to practices such as push-backs of asylum seekers, penalizing sea rescue efforts or creating inhumane conditions of detention and deportation that violate fundamental human rights. As Lukas Schmid has recently argued, the systematic violation of human rights in the exercise of immigration control undermines the legitimacy of that control quite independently of whether one believes it could be justified in principle on grounds of states' right to self-government (Schmid 2022, see also Bender and Silverman in this volume).

A second reason for scepticism about the prospects for free movement is the current polycrisis consisting of the decline of democracy in a growing number of states, the increased likelihood of military confrontation between nuclear powers, the prospect of new global pandemics and, most importantly, the looming climate disaster. None of these crises is conducive to a further opening of states for free movement. They are instead more likely to generate new waves of mass displacement and forced migration that are perceived by destination states as threats requiring a further fortification of immigration control.

Optimists may count on the unprecedented need for international collaboration and global governance to avert the worst scenarios of global warming, which could foster a transformation of the international order of the same magnitude as the human rights revolution and creation of the UN system after World War II. In such a scenario, expanding opportunities for both freedom of international movement and regular migration could be embraced as an important element of mitigation and accommodation responses to a hotter climate.

It is not the task of political theory to derive normative conclusions from speculations about the future. All it can do is clarify what justice and democracy demand from political institutions and decisions in our present world. In this respect, the case for universal freedom of movement is strong, even if the prospects for enhancing it in real world politics don't look bright.

Notes

1 See Article 13 of the 1948 Universal Declaration of Human Rights (UDHR) and Article 12 of the 1966 International Covenant on Civic and Political Rights (ICCPR).
2 See Article 13.2 of the UDHR and Art. 12.4 of the ICCPR.
3 For example, freedom of assembly may need to be regulated in order to avoid overcrowding and violence between rival groups that deter individuals from exercising their associative freedoms.
4 For discussion of this asymmetry see, amongst others Walzer (1983); Cole (2000, 2006); Miller (2007: 208–9).
5 The experience with European colonialism is invoked by Immanuel Kant as a reason for limiting a cosmopolitan right of free movement to a right to hospitality (Kant 1791/1991).

References

Abizadeh, Arash (2008), 'Democratic Theory and Border Coercion: No Right to Unilaterally Control Your Own Borders', *Political Theory*, 36 (1), 37–65.
Acosta, Diego Arcarazo (2018), *The National Versus the Foreigner in South America. 200 Years of Migration and Citizenship Law* (Cambridge: Cambridge University Press).
Acosta, Diego Arcarazo (2019), 'The Expansion of Regional Free Movement Regimes. Towards a Borderless World?', in Paul Minderhoud, Sandra Mantu, and Karin Zwaan (eds.), *Caught In Between Borders: Citizens, Migrants and Humans. Liber Amicorum in Honour of Prof. Dr. Elspeth Guild* (Oisterwijk, NL: Wolf Legal Publishers).
Ahlhaus, Svenja (2020), *Die Grenzen Des Demos. Mitgliedschaftspolitik Aus Postsouveräner Perspektive* (Frankfurt am Main: Campus).
Akhtar, Sahar (2016), 'Being at Home in the World: International Relocation (Not Open Borders)', *Public Affairs Quarterly*, 30 (2), 103–127.
Arrhenius, Gustaf (2005), 'The Boundary Problem in Democratic Theory', in Folke Tersman (ed.), *Democracy Unbound: Basic Explorations* (Stockholm: Filosofiska institutionen, Stockholms Universitet), 14–29.
Bader, Veit M (1997), 'Fairly Open Borders', in Veit M. Bader (ed.), *Citizenship and Exclusion* (London: Macmillan), 28–61.
Bauböck, Rainer (2009), 'Global Justice, Freedom of Movement and Democratic Citizenship', *European Journal of Sociology/Archives Européennes De Sociologie*, 50 (1), 1–31.
Bauböck, Rainer (2018), *Democratic Inclusion. Rainer Bauböck in Dialogue*. Manchester: Manchester University Press. https://manchesteruniversitypress.co.uk/9781526105233/
Bauböck, Rainer (2020), 'The Democratic Case for Immigration', *Politische Vierteljahresschrift/Political Science Quarterly*, 61 (2), 357–375.
Bauböck, Rainer and Ruhs, Martin (2022), 'The Elusive Triple Win: Addressing Temporary Labour Migration Dilemmas Through Fair Representation', *Migration Studies*, 10 (3), 528–52.
Beckman, Ludvig (2022), *The Boundaries of Democracy: A Theory of Inclusion* (Abingdon and New York: Routledge).
Bender, Felix and Silverman, Stephanie (2023) "The Urgency of Addressing Immigration Detention in Normative Political Theory", in Akhtar, Sahar (ed.) *Routledge Handbook on the Ethics of Immigration*. New York, Routledge.

Blake, Michael (2013), 'Immigration, Jurisdiction., and Exclusion', *Philosopy and Public Affairs*, 41 (2), 103–30.
Carens, Joseph H. (1987), 'Aliens and Citizens: The Case for Open Borders', *The Review of Politics*, 49 (2), 251–73.
Carens, Joseph H. (2013), *The Ethics of Immigration* (Oxford: Oxford University Press).
Cassee, Andreas (2016), *Globale Bewegungsfreiheit. Ein Philosophisches Plädoyer Für Offene Grenzen* (Berlin: Suhrkamp).
Cole, Phillip (2000), *Philosophies of Exclusion. Liberal Political Theory and Immigration* (Edinburgh: Edinburgh University Press).
Cole, Phillip (2006), 'Towards a Symmetrical World. Migration and International Law', *Ethics and Economics*, 4 (1).
Dahl, Robert (1989), *Democracy and Its Critics* (New Haven: Yale University Press).
Geddes, Andrew, et al. (eds.) (2019), *The Dynamics of Regional Migration Governance* (Aldershot: Edward Elgar).
Goodin, Robert (2007), 'Enfranchising All Affected Interests, and Its Alternatives', *Philosophy and Public Affairs*, 35 (1), 40–68.
Hobbes, Thomas (1651/1973), *Leviathan* (London: Everyman's Library).
Höffe, Otmar (1999), *Demokratie Im Zeitalter Der Globalisierung* (München: Beck).
Holmes, Stephen and Sunstein, Cass (1999), *The Cost of Rights. Why Liberty Depends on Taxes* (New York: Norton).
Human Rights Committee (1999), 'General Comment 27, Freedom of movement (Art.12)', UN. Doc CCPR/C/21/Rev.1/Add.9.
Kant, Immanuel (1795/1991), 'Perpetual Peace: A Philosophical Sketch', in Reiss, H. S. (ed.), *Kant: Political Writings*, 2 edn.; Cambridge: Cambridge University Press, 93–130.
López-Guerra, Claudio (2005), 'Should Expatriates Vote?, *The Journal of Political Philosophy*, 13 (2), 216–34.
Mau, Steffen (2022), *Sorting Machines: The Reinvention of the Border in the 21st Century* (London: Polity Press).
Milanovic, Branko (2016), *Global Inequality. A New Approach for the Age of Globalization* (Cambridge, MA: Harvard University Press).
Miller, David (1995), *On Nationality* (Oxford: Oxford University Press).
Miller, David (2007), *National Responsibility and Global Justice* (Oxford: Oxford University Press).
Miller, David (2009), 'Democracy's Domain', *Philosophy and Pulbic Affairs*, 37, 201–28.
Miller, David (2016), *Strangers in Our Midst. The Political Philosophy of Immigration* (Cambridge, MA: Harvard University Press).
Niño Arnaiz, Borja (2022), 'Should We Open Borders? Yes, But Not in the Name of Global Justice', *Ethics & Global Politics*, 15 (2, 3), 55–68(14). DOI:10.1080/16544951.2022.2081398
Nita, Sonja, et al. (eds.) (2017), *Migration, Free Movement and Regional Integration* (Paris: UNESCO and UNU-CRIS).
Oberman, Kieran (2016), 'Immigration as a Human Right', in Sarah Fine and Lea Ypi (eds.), *Migration in Political Theory* (Oxford: Oxford University Press), 32–56.
Owen, David (2012), 'Constituting the Polity, Constituting the Demos: on the Place of the All Affected Interests Principle in Democratic Theory and in Resolving the Democratic Boundary problem', *Ethics and Global Affairs*, 5 (3), 129–52.
Owen, David (2021), 'Global Justice and the Governance of Transnational Migration', in Leanne Weber and Claudia Tazreiter (eds.), *Handbook of Migration and Gobal Justice* (Cheltenham: Edward Elgar).
Prak, Maarten (2018), *Citizens Without Nations. Urban Citizenship in Europe and the World, c. 1000-1789* (Cambridge: Cambridge University Press).
Schmid, Lukas (2022), 'Saving Migrants' Basic Human Rights from Sovereign Rule', *American Political Science Review*, 116 (3), 954–67.
Schumpeter, Joseph (1942/1976), *Capitalism, Socialism, and Democracy* (London: Allen and Unwin).
Seglow, Jonathan (2006), 'Immigration, Justice and Borders: Towards a Global Agreement', *Contemporary Politics*, 12 (3-4), 233–46.
Shachar, Ayelet (2009), *The Birthright Lottery. Citizenship and Global Inequality* (Cambridge, MA: Harvard University Press).

Shachar, Ayelet (2020), *The Shifting Border. Legal Cartographies of Migration and Mobility. Ayelet Shachar in Dialogue*, eds Anthony Simon Laden, Peter Niessen, and David Owen (Critical Powers; Manchester: Manchester University Press).

Song, Sarah (2019), *Immigration and Democracy* (Oxford: Oxford University Press).

Stilz, Anna (2011), 'Nations, States, and Territory', *Ethics*, 121 (3), 572–601.

Torpey, John (2000), *The Invention of the Passport: Surveillance, Citizenship, and the State* (Cambridge: Cambridge University Press).

Vink, Maarten, et al. (2019), 'The International Diffusion of Expatriate Dual citizenship', *Migration Studies*, 7 (3), 362–83. https://doi.org/10.1093/migration/mnz011

Walzer, Michael (1983), *Spheres of Justice. A Defense of Pluralism and Equality* (New York: Basic Books).

Whelan, Frederick G (1983), 'Prologue: Democratic Theory and the Boundary Problem', in J.R. Pennock and J.W. Chapman (eds.), *NOMOS 25: Liberal Democracy* (New York: New York University), 13–47.

Ypi, Lea (2008), 'Justice in Migration. A Closed Borders Utopia?', *Journal of Political Philosophy*, 16 (4), 391–418.

Zolberg, Aristide (2007), 'The Exit Revolution', in Nancy L. Green and François Weil (eds.), *Citizenship and Those Who Leave. The Politics of Emigration and Expatriation* (Urbana and Chicago: University of Illinois Press), 33–60.

PART II

Open Borders or Right to Control

Practical Approaches

5
IMMIGRATION AND ECONOMIC FREEDOM

*Ilya Somin**

5.1 Introduction

Economic liberty plays an important role in debates over immigration restrictions. That is true of both "negative" economic freedom of the type traditionally valued by libertarians and classical liberals and "positive" freedom of the sort emphasized by left-liberal thinkers. Immigration restrictions severely undermine both types of economic liberty for both would-be immigrants and receiving-country natives.

It does not, by itself, prove that all such restrictions should be abolished. But it does strengthen the case for abolition, from the standpoint of a wide range of liberal and libertarian views. The issue is not just that migration restrictions reduce economic liberty but also that they do so on a vast scale – far more than is conventionally recognized, especially in the case of natives. It applies to both negative and positive economic freedom.

Immigration policy raises a wide range of normative considerations. In this chapter, I focus on dimensions related to negative and positive economic freedom and argue that both weigh heavily against migration restrictions, from the standpoint of any theory that assigns significant value to one or both of these types of liberty. Restrictions might still be justified on a variety of other grounds. But economic freedom is a crucial factor weighing against them.

I use "natives" to refer to all current citizens of receiving nations, which often includes many who were born elsewhere but acquired citizenship either by naturalization or by virtue of being foreign-born children of citizens.

Section 5.2 of the chapter focuses on libertarian "negative" economic freedom. It shows that migration restrictions severely restrict the negative economic liberty of both immigrants and natives. That is true both on libertarian views that value such freedom for its own sake[1] and on those that assign value to it for more instrumental reasons, such as promoting human autonomy and enabling individuals to realize their personal goals and projects.[2]

In Section 5.3, I take up left-liberal "positive" theories of economic freedom, which primarily focus on enhancing individuals' access to important goods and services and

DOI: 10.4324/9781003037309-8

enabling them to have the resources necessary to live an autonomous life.[3] Some also focus on expanding human capacities generally.[4] Many give special emphasis to enhancing the economic prospects of the poor. Here too, migration restrictions impose severe costs on both immigrants and natives. And those effects are enormous.

Section 5.4 briefly outlines a framework for considering possible negative side effects of migration on various types of economic liberty. I have developed that framework and its application to specific issues in greater detail in my book *Free to Move*.[5]

5.2 Immigration and Negative Economic Freedom

Prominent libertarian political philosopher Robert Nozick famously described economic freedom as "capitalist acts between consenting adults."[6] Economic liberty can be understood as the right to engage in consensual transactions involving the exchange of goods and services. Some libertarian theorists, including Nozick himself, value such liberty for its own sake.[7] Others support it for more instrumental reasons, such as the promotion of autonomy and empowering individuals to pursue their personal projects.[8]

It is easy to see how migration restrictions massively constrain the economic liberty of potential migrants. In many cases, they end up being cut off from a vast range of economic opportunities in freer, wealthier societies and thereby consigned to a lifetime of poverty and severely constrained options under repressive and corrupt governments.[9]

This is particularly true of those would-be migrants who end up trapped in socialist or otherwise severely statist societies that ban most forms of private property, severely restrict market transactions, and block private entrepreneurship. Socialist regimes such as the Soviet Union, Cuba, and – most recently – Venezuela have in fact generated vast numbers of migrants and refugees. Over the last decade, some 7 million refugees have fled the present socialist government of Venezuela – the biggest refugee crisis in the history of the Western Hemisphere.[10] The previous record was, of course, held by the massive outflow of refugees from Communist Cuba, with some 1.5 million fleeing (mostly to the United States),[11] out of a Cuban population that numbered only about 7.1 million in 1960, the year after Communists seized power in that country.[12]

More generally, immigrants tend to move toward countries with greater negative economic freedom, with destination countries usually ranking much higher on standard scales of both economic and personal freedom than countries of origin.[13] Even in cases where the regime migrants leave behind is not as statist as Cuba, Venezuela, or the USSR, migrant gains in negative economic freedom are often enormous.

Immigration restrictions constrain the negative economic liberty of natives as well.[14] If the government bars a potential immigrant from entering the country, thereby preventing her from starting a business, that restricts potential economic transactions by her employees and customers, many of whom would be natives. Similarly, if immigration restrictions bar migrant workers and renters, that reduces opportunities available to native employers, customers, and landlords, among others.

The issue is not simply that immigrants and natives have fewer economic opportunities than they would otherwise. At least from the standpoint of libertarian and other similar theories of negative liberty, a reduction in opportunities is not by itself a reduction in economic liberty. For example, if Jane rejects my offer to become my research assistant, there is no reduction in my negative economic freedom even though I lose the opportunity to have her as an employee.

Rather, negative economic liberty is restricted only when opportunities are barred through some sort of coercive action, either by the government or by some other entity. In the case of immigration restrictions, such coercion is very obviously present, as would-be migrants are literally forcibly prevented from entering the country in question and pursuing opportunities there.[15] If they choose to enter illegally, they risk being forcibly deported and even subjected to criminal penalties.[16] As Joseph Carens puts it, "[b]orders have guards and the guards have guns."[17] While those guns are usually trained at migrants, the coercion involved also restricts the liberty of natives.

In sum, coercive restrictions on migration are unavoidably also coercive restrictions on natives' rights to engage in economic transactions with potential immigrants. This is true even if the law only imposes direct penalties on migrants rather than natives. The latter are nonetheless affected by the former. But in fact, the law often directly coerces the natives as well, most obviously in the case of employers punished for hiring undocumented immigrants and also when it comes to laws punishing citizens who aid, harbor, employ, or abet illegal migrants in various ways.[18]

Less obvious than the brute fact that migration restrictions constrain the negative economic liberty of both immigrants and natives is the extraordinary extent of that constraint. Few, if any, current government policies in the United States and other liberal democracies constrain natives' economic freedom more. It is because immigration restrictions bar a truly enormous number of "capitalist acts between consenting adults," as Robert Nozick famously called them.[19]

Prior to the COVID-19 pandemic and cuts instituted by President Donald Trump, the United States usually took in some 1 million legal immigrants per year,[20] a figure that has recently been regained, after a steep decline.[21] Even a relatively modest 10% increase in that figure would mean an extra 100,000 immigrants each year, and 1 million more over a ten year period. If we assume, very conservatively, that each of these people – if allowed into the United States – engages in five economic transactions per year with natives, that means failure to increase the immigrant intake by 10% forestalls 500,000 such transactions in the first year alone, and 5 million transactions over ten years.

And that's just from the 100,000 people barred in the first year included in the analysis. If we expand our frame of reference to include the would-be migrants barred in year 2, year 3, and so on, we quickly end up with hundreds of millions of coercively prevented economic transactions with natives. And the figure increases even more once we compare the status quo not to the relatively modest reform of a 10% increase in legal migration but to the total abolition of immigration restrictions.

Economists estimate that the abolition of migration restrictions throughout the world would eventually double the world's gross domestic product (GDP).[22] That is because many millions of people are trapped in dysfunctional and oppressive political systems and could greatly increase their productivity if given the chance to move to freer, more prosperous societies. Upon integration into their new homes, they can take advantage of the "place premium" from working in a location with better economic and political institutions.[23]

If mainstream economists' estimates of the economic effects of free migration are even remotely accurate, this implies that migration restrictions forcibly block a truly enormous number of beneficial economic transactions between immigrants and natives.

Particularly in the United States, the scale of the effect is magnified by the fact that relative to natives, immigrants are more likely to engage in entrepreneurship, establish new businesses, and contribute to scientific innovation.[24] US immigration restrictions are particularly significant in reducing scientific innovation by immigrants and their children because the United States has so many of the world's most important research facilities.[25]

Barring people who contribute disproportionately to entrepreneurship, business formation, and scientific innovation likely blocks even more beneficial economic transactions than barring an equivalent number of statistically average people would. The former likely engage in more and larger transactions with more natives than the latter.

The enormous impact of migration restrictions on negative economic freedom holds true regardless of whether we assess it from the standpoint of deontological libertarian theory or under approaches where its primary value resides in its effects on autonomy or the pursuit of life plans and "projects."

From a libertarian deontological perspective, almost any coercive restriction on economic liberty is a significant rights violation.[26] Under this approach, it does not matter whether the next-best alternative to exclusion from a particular country is desirable or not. Some deontological viewpoints might downplay or even ignore the significance of very minimal restrictions on economic transactions. For example, if each such transaction is subject to a one-cent tax, it might be too petty to qualify as a meaningful constraint. But that surely is not true if the transactions are subject to heavy civil fines (as under current US law) or if they are prevented entirely because the person who might have entered into them with you has been deported or blocked from entering the country to begin with.

Any theory that assigns intrinsic value to negative economic liberty at all would have to count such constraints as at least somewhat significant. And even if each individual blocked transaction is only a small restriction on economic liberty, the aggregate impact of many millions of them still adds up to a massive effect.

From a more instrumental standpoint, some blocked transactions are more significant than others. For example, blocking a transaction that opens up a rewarding new career may impact autonomy or project pursuit more than stopping some minor exchange.[27]

But whether we value all voluntary economic transactions more or less equally or give special priority to some, migration restrictions block a truly vast number of them, for natives as well as for potential migrants themselves. Thanks to migration restrictions, many thousands, perhaps even millions, of natives are cut off from careers that might otherwise open up to them, thanks to immigrant entrepreneurs. Others are barred from opportunities that would be created by scientific and technological innovations immigrants disproportionately facilitate. And all of these effects are on a vast, almost unimaginable scale.

The massive scale of immigration restrictions reduces the significance of debates over how morally significant each individual blocked transaction is. Even if each individual instance is of only minor significance, the cumulative impact of millions of such cases is still great. If only a small proportion of the transactions (e.g., 1% or 10%) have high importance (e.g., those that involve innovations or those that help people start a new and more rewarding career), it still translates to a huge aggregate number of high-value transactions blocked – many thousands every year.

The question of how to measure negative liberty is a disputed one, and there is no consensus on the subject.[28] But the effects of immigration restrictions on it are gargantuan under any plausible approach to measurement. Whether we weight each transaction equally or emphasize more far-reaching ones more; whether we take a deontological approach to liberty or a more consequentialist one, the impact is enormous.

The direct effects of immigration restrictions on economic liberty are very great. But restrictions also have a number of significant indirect effects that are also substantial.

Immigration restrictions almost always require an extensive enforcement apparatus to make them effective. That, in turn, requires significant restrictions on the economic liberty of both immigrants and natives. It is virtually impossible to restrict the latter, without also regulating the former. Such indirect effects of migration restrictions on natives can have a big effect on economic liberty.

Perhaps the most striking example is the way in which many US citizens are caught up in the machinery of detention and deportation established to apprehend and expel illegal migrants. In the 1930s, the US government deported some 600,000 American citizens to Mexico, mostly Mexican-Americans whom the authorities mistook for undocumented migrants.[29] Such practices persist on a smaller, but still substantial scale, today.

Political scientist Jacqueline Stevens estimates that the federal government detained or deported some 4,000 American citizens in 2010 alone, with a total of 20,000 between 2003 and 2010.[30] These abuses are rooted in the extremely low levels of due process afforded in immigration detention and deportation proceedings, compared most other severe restrictions on liberty.[31] In principle, these practices can be reformed and stronger protections against mistaken detention and deportation introduced. But doing so would make it difficult to quickly deport large numbers of migrants, to begin with. Between 2007 and 2018, the United States deported well over 300,000 migrants every year, except one (295,000 in 2017), a staggering number that would be difficult to handle if extensive due process protections were required.[32]

In addition to infringing liberty more generally, detention and deportation are severe constraints on economic liberty, specifically. People who are detained or deported are rarely able to engage in much in the way of "capitalist acts between consenting adults."

While not as drastic in their impact as detention and deportation, other aspects of migration restriction policy also indirectly restrict the economic liberty of natives. For example, efforts to regulate employers to prevent them from hiring illegal migrants also raise the cost of hiring other workers, by requiring ID and background checks that create new expenses and often lead to "false positives" (misidentifying US citizens as undocumented migrants).[33] Similarly, the construction of walls and other barriers in order to keep out migrants along land frontiers such as the US border with Mexico often requires the use of eminent domain to seize private property, which in turn greatly impedes the economic liberty of owners.[34]

Some argue that theories of negative freedom can justify immigration restrictions on the grounds that governments have a right to exclude migrants at will for the same reasons that private property owners have the right to exclude trespassers, and members of private clubs can bar new members.[35] I have criticized such theories in detail elsewhere.[36] Here, I will only reiterate the point that acceptance of the idea that national governments are entitled to the same sorts of powers over their territories as homeowners and club members would entail the near-total destruction of liberty for natives, no less than immigrants.[37]

5.3 Immigration and Positive Economic Freedom

Positive theories of economic freedom, advanced primarily by left-liberals, have a very different focus from negative ones defended by libertarians. Broadly speaking, theories of positive economic liberty can be divided into two categories. Some focus generally on expanding access to economic resources and transactions, so as to widen the range of choice available to people, and increase their capacities.[38]

Others place special emphasis on ensuring access to resources and opportunities for the poor and disadvantaged, most notably in the case of John Rawls' famous "difference principle," which requires economic inequalities to be structured in ways that maximize the benefit to the least well-off group within a society.[39] Still, other theories combine these two themes in various ways, emphasizing both the need to prioritize the poor and to ensure the generally widespread expansion of economic choice and autonomy.[40]

Unlike negative-liberty theorists, positive-economic liberty advocates do not necessarily assign any inherent value to economic market transactions. They value them, if at all, only in so far as such transactions enhance human choices and capabilities and improve the lot of the disadvantaged. If these goals are better achieved through government intervention that limits market transactions, than by more laissez-faire policies, positive liberty advocates have good reason to support the former at the expense of the latter. Nonetheless, it turns out that migration restrictions are a serious threat to positive economic liberty, just as they also undermine the negative kind. They do so not because of the intrinsic value of economic transactions blocked by immigration restrictions but because of their instrumental effects.

In the case of would-be migrants, those effects are staggeringly enormous. Freedom to migrate can expand positive economic freedom for millions of people around the world, whose options are now severely limited. Moreover, many of them are among the world's poorest and most oppressed people. Enabling them to move to wealthier and freer societies would simultaneously vastly expand economic freedom conceived of as increased autonomy, choice, and capability and *also* disproportionately benefit the poor, thereby greatly reducing economic inequality.[41] Simply by moving to the United States or another relatively affluent society, migrants from poor nations can increase their incomes and productivity severalfold.[42] And that does not consider the potential impact of increases in their skills, which are usually easier to achieve in the destination country.

Things are more complicated if the focus is limited to natives of the receiving country, as demanded by some political theorists who argue that governments have a right to exclude migrants in order to benefit the former, or that principles of equal opportunity and distributive justice apply primarily within national borders, not across them.[43]

However, there is strong reason to conclude that open migration will also greatly expand the positive economic freedom of natives. As already noted, eliminating migration restrictions would create vast new wealth, potentially doubling world GDP. Such an enormous expansion of productivity and resources could hardly avoid creating enormous benefits for natives, as well as immigrants. Even if the former captured "only," say, 20% of the new wealth, it would still be a dramatic improvement in their position relative to the status quo. And that is likely to be the case whether the freedom in question is defined as access to resources, opportunities to improve human capacities, or some combination of both.

Moreover, some of the new wealth is likely to be used in ways that create especially large benefits in expanding positive economic liberty for natives (as well as migrants themselves). As discussed in Part I, immigrants disproportionately contribute to scientific and medical innovation. Many such innovations create literally life-saving benefits. A dramatic recent example highlights this point.

Both of the two most successful COVID-19 vaccines developed so far – those produced by Pfizer, BioNTech, and Moderna – were produced in large part by immigrants from poor nations, or children thereof, who could not have made these pathbreaking contributions had they or their parents been forced to remain in their countries of origin.[44] These vaccines have saved many millions of lives around the world. And immigration made them possible.

It is also obvious that in the process, they have greatly expanded positive economic freedom for both immigrants and natives. It is difficult or impossible to exercise any such freedom if you are dead or seriously ill from COVID-19 and also hard to do so in an economy that remains paralyzed by the pandemic, as many would have been for much longer, absent vaccination.

Perhaps one can argue that these benefits of migration will be captured so long as potential innovators can migrate to *some* nation where they can reach their potential, even if many doors remain closed to them. But the more are closed, the more such people will be excluded from the place where they could be at their *most* productive, even if there are still opportunities available to them better than those in their countries of origin.

More broadly, technological and scientific innovation is crucial to expanding positive freedom over time. It is central to the expansion of positive economic freedom over time, by any measure.[45] To the extent that free migration increases the pace of such progress, it dramatically contributes to the expansion of positive economic liberty.

Moreover, scientific and technological progress, in most cases, disproportionately benefits the poor and disadvantaged, thus satisfying the concerns of those who believe the latter deserve special consideration in theories of economic freedom and distributive justice. The wealthy can, to some extent, use access to labor and capital to substitute for technology. As Milton and Rose Friedman famously put it, "[t]he rich in Ancient Greece would have benefited hardly at all from modern plumbing: running servants replaced running water."[46] This probably understates the benefits of plumbing for the wealthy. But there is little doubt that plumbing – and other similar innovations – benefited the poor to a greater degree than the rich.

The poor also benefit disproportionately from medical innovations, such as the COVID-19 vaccines. They have a higher mortality rate from COVID-19 and other contagious diseases due to tighter living conditions and being more likely to have to work in person among other factors.[47]

The contribution of immigrants to scientific and other innovation is so great that it by itself likely outweighs any negative effects of immigration on the positive liberty of natives, including the native-born poor. Massive reductions in disease and mortality and increases in standards of living caused by technological improvements easily outweigh such possible negative effects as wage competition in some industries. The same goes for potential negative side effects of outmigration on the economies of the nations left behind by migrants. These latter are also in large part offset by the large remittances migrants from poor nations often send back to their countries of origin.[48]

Despite the major economic advantages of freedom of movement, it is arguable that some native workers are net losers from migration because migrants compete with them for jobs, thereby reducing their wages. In the United States, studies suggest this effect is largely limited to native-born high school dropouts.[49] Even so, it could be argued that from the standpoint of theories prioritizing the economic freedom of the native-born poor, such immigrants must be excluded.

However, even if some small subset of native workers are net economic losers from immigration, there are ways to address this issue without actually excluding migrants. The most obvious solution is to tap – through taxation – some of the vast wealth created by immigration and use it to subsidize the wages of whatever group of native workers we believe are unfairly disadvantaged.[50]

In this way, we can simultaneously retain the economic benefits created by migration – including those that expand positive economic freedom – and mitigate possible downsides for the native poor. Moreover, this can easily be achieved simply by utilizing existing wage subsidy programs, such as the US earned income tax credit.[51] It does not require any major institutional innovations. There are, however, a number of other possible mechanisms by which migrants or those who employ them and consume their products could be incentivized to pay for such programs.[52]

I do not necessarily endorse such discriminatory taxes and wage subsidies. Here, I merely contend that – from the standpoint of theories of positive economic freedom that prioritize the needs of the native-born – they are preferable to the exclusion of immigrants, including "low-skill" ones. The latter can still make important contributions to economic growth and development that expand positive liberty for natives (as well as themselves). This is especially true when we recall that those who arrive as low-skill workers need not remain so, nor is it likely to be true of many of their children.[53] And wage subsidies for natives can offset the possible negative effect of competition for jobs within particular industries.

As with the impact on negative freedom, the effect of immigration restrictions on natives' positive freedom can be gauged to some degree by analogy with the effects of deporting native-born workers. It is difficult to deny that expelling, say, 1 million of the latter from the United States would have a hugely negative impact on the positive liberty of those who remain, even if some might benefit from a reduction in job competition. By the same token, we can expect effects of comparable magnitude from barring equivalent numbers of migrants, especially if the latter are, on average, more likely than natives to engage in innovation and entrepreneurship.

Like negative economic liberty, the positive liberty of both immigrants and natives is also undermined by the indirect effects of the enforcement system for migration restrictions. For example, when natives end up getting detained or deported by government agencies tasked with expelling illegal migrants, that very obviously reduces their positive liberty.[54]

5.4 Potential Negative Side Effects of Migration on Economic Liberty

Immigration restrictionists have outlined a variety of potential negative effects of migration, including ones that might undermine either negative or positive liberty. Such scenarios include overburdening the welfare state, lowering the wages of native workers, damage to political and economic institutions (including by immigrant voters who make bad choices at the ballot box), and a variety of others. I have addressed these and other potential negative side effects of migration in much greater detail in my book *Free to Move: Foot Voting, Migration, and Political Freedom*.[55] Here, I merely summarize my general framework for dealing with them.

It is based on a three-part test for assessing consequentialist objections to migration rights. Before concluding that restrictions are justified, we must answer three questions in ways that rule out alternative approaches to dealing with the issue at hand.

First, we should ask whether the harm in question is real. Many of the standard objections to expanding migration rights are greatly overblown, including those relevant to questions of economic liberty. For example, extensive evidence indicates that immigration generally does not increase burdens on the welfare state and that the vast majority of immigrants are net contributors to the public fisc.[56]

Second, where migration creates genuine problems, we should ask whether it is possible to deal with the issue by using "keyhole solutions" that minimize the risk without barring migrants.[57] For example, if it turns out that immigrants unduly increase welfare burdens, the obvious keyhole solution is eligibility for various welfare benefits – as already occurs under the Welfare Reform Act of 1996 and similar legislation in other nations.[58]

Finally, where keyhole solutions are inadequate, we should ask whether tapping the vast wealth created by expanded migration to mitigate negative side effects that cannot be addressed in other ways. For example, if – contrary to most social science research – it turns out that immigration lowers the wages of native workers (thereby potentially constraining their positive freedom), then policymakers can tap some of the wealth generated by immigration to increase wage subsidies to whichever groups are adversely affected in ways we conclude are unjust.[59]

5.5 Conclusion

Economic liberty is far from the only issue at stake in debates over migration rights. There is a variety of other justifications for migration restrictions. But theories of economic liberty are nonetheless crucial elements of the debate. And whether we focus on negative liberties or positive ones, migrants or natives, the enormous scale of the impact of migration restrictions on economic freedom strengthens the case for dropping barriers to international freedom of movement.

Notes

[*] Professor of Law, George Mason University. Parts of this chapter are adapted, with permission, from Ilya Somin, "Immigration and the Economic Freedom of Natives," *Public Affairs Quarterly* (forthcoming).
1 See, e.g., Robert Nozick, *Anarchy, the State and Utopia* (New York: Basic Books, 1974).
2 See, e.g., Loren Lomasky, *Rights, Persons, and the Moral Community* (Oxford: Clarendon Press, 1987); John Tomasi, *Free Market Fairness* (Princeton: Princeton University Press, 2012).
3 See, e.g., Charles Taylor, "What's Wrong with Negative Liberty," in *The Idea of Freedom*, ed. Alan Ryan (Oxford: Oxford University Press, 1979); Ronald Dworkin, *Taking Rights Seriously* (Cambridge: Harvard University Press, 1977); Phillippe Van Parijs, *Real Freedom for All* (Oxford: Oxford University Press, 1995).
4 See, e.g., Amartya K. Sen, *Development as Freedom* (New York: Knopf, 1999).
5 Ilya Somin, *Free to Move: Foot Voting, Migration, and Political Freedom* (New York: Oxford University Press, rev. ed. 2022), ch. 6.
6 Nozick, *Anarchy, the State and Utopia*, 163.
7 See works cited above. For overviews of different libertarian theories of economic liberty, see Eric Mack, *Libertarianism* (Medford: Polity, 2018), ch. 4, and Jason Brennan, *Libertarianism: What Everyone Needs to Know*, (New York: Oxford University Press 2012), ch. 6.
8 See, e.g., Lomasky, *Rights, Persons, and the Moral Community*; Tomasi, *Free Market Fairness*.
9 See, e.g., Joseph A. Carens, *The Ethics of Immigration* (New York: Oxford University Press, 2012); Carens, "Aliens and Citizens: The Case for Open Borders," *Review of Politics* 49 (1987): 249–72; Somin *Free to Move* ch. 3; Bas Van der Vossen and Jason Brennan, *In Defense of Openness: Why Global Freedom Is the Humane Solution to Global Poverty* (New York: Oxford University Press, 2018), ch. 2; Michael Huemer, "Is There a Right to Immigrate?" *Social Theory and Practice* 36 (2010): 29–61; Bryan D. Caplan, *Open Borders: The Science and Ethics of Immigration* (2019), chs. 1–2.
10 United Nations High Commissioner for Refugees, "Venezuela Situation" (accessed Mar. 25, 2023), available at https://www.unhcr.org/en-us/venezuela-emergency.html.
11 Brittany Blizzard and Jeanne Batalova, "Cuban Immigrants in the United States," Migration Policy Institute, June 11, 2020, available at https://www.migrationpolicy.org/article/cuban-immigrants-united-states.
12 World Bank, "Population Total – Cuba," available at https://data.worldbank.org/indicator/SP.POP.TOTL?locations=CU.

13 Somin, *Free to Move*, 69–70; David Bier, "187 Million Immigrants Have Moved to Freer Countries," Cato at Liberty, May 3, 2021, available at https://www.cato.org/blog/187-million-immigrants-have-moved-freer-countries.
14 For an extensive overview, see Somin, "Immigration and the Economic Liberty of Natives."
15 For a helpful, more detailed exposition of why immigration restrictions are unavoidably coercive, see Huemer, "Is there a Right to Immigrate?"
16 See, e.g., 8 USC § 1325 (outlining criminal penalties for illegal entry into the United States).
17 Carens, "Aliens and Citizens," 251.
18 See 8 U.S.C. § 1324(a)(1)(i)-(v) (outlining penalties for a variety of such offenses).
19 Nozick, *Anarchy, the State, and Utopia*, 163.
20 Somin, *Free to Move*, 202
21 See Ilya Somin, "US Regains Pre-Trump, Pre-Pandemic Levels of Migration, *Reason*, Apr. 19, 2023, available at https://reason.com/volokh/2023/04/19/us-regains-pre-trump-pre-pandemic-immigration-levels/
22 See Michael Clemens, "Economics and Emigration: Trillion-Dollar Bills Left on the Sidewalk?" *Journal of Economic Perspectives* 25 (2011): 83–106; cf. Philippe Legrain, *Them and Us: How Migrants and Locals Can Thrive Together* (London: OneWorld, 2020), 69-73 (citing additional literature on this point); Somin, *Free to Move*, 71–73 (assessing this estimate and addressing some criticisms of it).
23 For overviews, see Michael A. Clemens, Claudio Montenegro, and Lant Pritchett, "The Place Premium: Bounding the Price Equivalent of Migration Barriers," *Review of Economics and Statistics* 101 (2019): 201–13; Michael A. Clemens, Claudio Montenegro, and Lant Pritchett, "The Place Premium: Wage Differences for Identical Workers across the US Border," Center for Global Development Working Paper No. 148 (2009); Michael A. Clemens and Lant Pritchett, "Income Per Natural: Measuring Development for People Rather than Places," *Population and Development Review* 34 (2008) 395–434.
24 For a recent overview and citations to data, see Ilya Somin, "How Immigration Restrictions Harm U.S. Citizens, Too," *Regulatory Review*, Dec. 15, 2020, available at https://www.theregreview.org/2020/12/15/somin-immigration-restrictions-harm-citizens/; See also Sari Pekkala Kerr and William R. Kerr, "Immigrant Entrepreneurship in America: Evidence from the Survey of Business Owners, 2007 and 2012." *Research Policy*. 49 (2020); 1–18; Robert Krol, "Effects of Immigration on Innovation and Entrepreneurship," *Cato Journal* 41 (2021): 551–69.
25 Ruchir Agarwal, et al., "Why U.S. Immigration Barriers Matter for the Global Advancement of Science," IZA Discussion Paper No. 14016 (2021), available at https://privpapers.ssrn.com/sol3/papers.cfm?abstract_id=3762886; see also Jennifer Hunt and Marjolaine Gauthier-Loiselle, "How Much Does Immigration Boost Innovation? *American Economic Journal: Macroeconomics*, 2 (2010):31–56 (finding that 1 point increase in the percentage of immigrant college graduates increases the per capita number of patents in the United States by 9–18 percent).
26 See, e.g., Nozick, *Anarchy, the State, and Utopia*.
27 For a discussion of the relative importance of different types of economic transactions from such a standpoint, see, e.g., Tomasi, *Free Market Fairness*, 76–79, 188–92.
28 See, e.g., Ian Carter, "The Measurement of Pure Negative Freedom," *Political Studies* 40 (1992):.38-50; Hillel Steiner, "How Free: Computing Personal Liberty," *Royal Institute of Philosophy Supplements* 15 (1983): 73–89.
29 Francisco Balderrama and Raymond Rodriguez, *Decade of Betrayal: Mexican Repatriation in the 1930s* (Santa Fe: University of New Mexico Press, 2006).
30 Jacqueline Stevens, "US Government Unlawfully Detaining and Deporting US Citizens as Aliens," *Virginia Journal of Social Policy and the Law*, 18 (2011): 606–720, 608.
31 For an overview, see Ilya Somin, "Immigration Law Defies the American Constitution," *The Atlantic*, Oct. 3, 2019.
32 Abby Budiman, "Key Findings About US Immigrants," Pew Research Center, Aug. 20, 2020, available at https://www.pewresearch.org/fact-tank/2020/08/20/key-findings-about-u-s-immigrants/.
33 See, e.g., Alex Nowrasteh and Jim Harper, "Checking E-Verify: The Costs and Consequences of a National Worker Screening Mandate," Cato Institute Policy Analysis No. 775 (2015), available at https://www.cato.org/policy-analysis/checking-e-verify-costs-consequences-national-worker-screening-mandate#.

34 See, e.g., Ilya Somin, "To Build the Wall, Trump Might Make Thousands of Americans Suffer," *Washington Post*, Jan. 19, 2019, available at https://www.washingtonpost.com/opinions/to-build-the-wall-trump-might-make-thousands-of-americans-suffer/2019/01/19/fd39abe6-150e-11e9-b6ad-9cfd62dbb0a8_story.html; Gerald Dickinson, "Property Musings at the US-Mexican Border," *Maryland Journal of International Law* 33 (2018): 162–82.
35 See, e.g., Christopher Heath Wellman, "Freedom of Movement and the Right to Enter and Exit," in *Migration in Political Theory: The Ethics of Movement and Membership*, ed. Sarah Fine and Leah Ypi (New York: Oxford University Press, 2016), 83, 87; and Christopher Heath Wellman, "Immigration and Freedom of Association," *Ethics* 119 (2008): 109–141.
36 Somin, *Free to Move*, 110–15. See also critique in Huemer, "Is there a Right to Immigrate?"
37 For a detailed discussion of this point, see Somin, *Free to Move*, 111–13.
38 See, e.g., Sen, *Development as Freedom*; Isaiah Berlin, *Four Essays on Liberty* (New York: Oxford University Press, 1958).
39 John Rawls, *Theory of Justice* (Cambridge: Harvard University Press, 1971).
40 See, e.g., Samuel Freeman, *Liberalism and Distributive Justice* (New York: Oxford University Press, 2018); Kai Nielsen, *Equality and Liberty* (New York: Rowman & Littlefield, 1985).
41 For recent overviews of some of the relevant evidence on these points, See Somin, *Free to Move*, ch. 3; Van der Vossen and Brennan, *In Defense of Openness*), ch. 2; and Caplan, *Open Borders*, chs. 1-2.
42 For an overview, see Somin, *Free to Move*, 71-72; for a summary of the enormous "place premiums" that accrue to migrants to the United States from a variety of poor nations, see Michael A. Clemens, Claudio Montenegro, and Lant Pritchett, "The Place Premium: Bounding the Price Equivalent of Migration Barriers," *Review of Economics and Statistics* 101 (2019): 201–13; cf. Michael A. Clemens and Lant Pritchett, "Income Per Natural: Measuring Development for People Rather than Places," *Population and Development Review* 34 (2008) 395–434.
43 See, e.g., Rawls, *Theory of Justice*; Rawls, *The Law of Peoples* (Cambridge: Harvard University Press, 1999); Freeman, *Liberalism and Distributive Justice*, chs., 4, 8; Stephen Macedo, "The Moral Dilemma of US Immigration Policy: Open Borders vs. Social Justice," in *Debating Immigration Policy*, ed. Carol Swain (Princeton. NJ: Princeton University Press, 2007).
44 See Ilya Somin, "Thank Immigration for the New Covid-19 Vaccines," *Reason*, Nov. 22, 2020, available at https://reason.com/volokh/2020/11/22/thank-immigration-for-the-new-covid-19-vaccines/.
45 For important overviews, see, e.g., Johan Norberg, *Open: The Story of Economic Progress* (New York: Atlantic Books, 2020); Joel Mokyr, *The Lever of Riches: Technological Creativity and Economic Progress* (New York: Oxford University Press, 1990).
46 Milton Friedman and Rose D. Friedman, *Free to Choose* (New York: Harcourt Brace Jovanovich, 1980), 147.
47 See, e.g., Juergen Jung, et al., "Coronavirus Infections and Deaths by Poverty Status: The Effects of Social Distancing," *Journal of Economic Behavior and Organization* 182: 311–30 (2021).
48 Somin, *Free to Move*, 79–80.
49 For a review of the evidence, see Somin, *Free to Move*, 149–50.
50 For this "keyhole solution," see Somin, *Free to Move*, 149–50, Bryan Caplan, "Why Should We Restrict Immigration?," *Cato Journal* 32 (2012): 5–21.
51 Somin, *Free to Move*, 150.
52 See discussion of various mechanisms for increasing fiscal contributions of immigration in ibid., 140–41.
53 See Somin, "Immigration and the Economic Liberty of Natives."
54 See discussion of this phenomenon in Part I.
55 Somin, *Free to Move*, ch. 6.
56 Somin, *Free to Move*, 138–40.
57 On the concept of keyhole solutions, see Somin, *Free to Move*, 128-29; and Bryan Caplan, "Why Should We Restrict Immigration?," *Cato Journal* 32 (2012): 5–21. The phrase "keyhole solution" seems to have been first introduced by Tim Harford, *The Undercover Economist* (New York: Oxford University Press, 2005), 130–31.
58 On this keyhole and other ones relevant to the issue of overburdening the welfare state, see Somin, *Free to Move*, 139–40.
59 For a discussion of a number of such proposals, see Somin, *Free to Move*, 149–50.

6
THE ECONOMIC CASE FOR LIBERALIZED IMMIGRATION POLICIES

Howard F. Chang

6.1 Introduction

In this chapter, I will review and draw upon my prior work to outline the economic case for liberalized immigration policies. The case that I set forth is economic insofar as I adopt the consequentialist normative framework typically assumed by economists who seek to derive policy prescriptions from economic analysis. In particular, I take the objective to be the maximization of social welfare, understood to be a function of the satisfaction of the preferences of individuals.

This objective begs the question of which individuals are the objects of concern for public policy: Is the objective to maximize global welfare, extending equal concern to all persons, or is the objective of immigration policies to pursue only the national interest, understood to give priority to the welfare of natives in the country of immigration? In my prior work, I have argued that the appropriate objective under an ideal theory of justice would be the pursuit of global welfare, understood to give equal weight to the interests of all persons. See, e.g., Chang (2008a; 2011). I will not defend cosmopolitan welfarism in this chapter; instead, I will begin this chapter by assuming this objective in Section 6.2, but I will relax this assumption later.

In some of my prior work, I assume instead that the objective is to promote the national interest, for the sake of argument, simply because this objective is commonly assumed by those who defend restrictive immigration policies. See, e.g., Chang (1998; 2018). Given that concerns about the national interest are likely to dominate policy debates and the determination of policies in the real world, the analysis of national economic welfare will be relevant for policy prescriptions even for those who believe in cosmopolitan welfarism as a matter of ideal moral theory, as long as political constraints remain relevant as a practical matter. With these considerations in mind, I turn to the question of national economic welfare in Section 6.3 of this chapter.

6.2 Global Social Welfare

On their face, immigration restrictions are costly because they prevent people from migrating to a country where they would prefer to live. In particular, this chapter will focus on the migration of workers who move in pursuit of higher wages. The output of the world economy grows when workers migrate from a country with low wages to a country with higher wages because those wages indicate that the worker produces more value in the country of immigration than that worker produced in the country of emigration. Labor migration increases global wealth by allowing labor to move to a more valuable use. For this reason, basic economic theory raises a presumption in favor of the free movement of labor. Both the migrating worker and the economy employing that worker enjoy the gains produced by their transactions in the labor market, and immigration restrictions reduce global wealth by preventing these gains from trade, distorting the global labor market, and causing a misallocation of labor that wastes human resources and creates needless poverty in countries of emigration.

The greater the inequality in wages between countries, the more the world gains from labor migration, and the greater the costs imposed by restrictions preventing this migration. Given the magnitude of wage inequality observed in the world today, many economists infer that the potential gains from liberalizing migration are huge. For surveys of this literature, see Clemens (2011), Chang (2008a, pp. 4–6), and Chang (2015, pp. xii–xiv). Clemens et al. (2019) study 42 source countries for immigration to the United States, for example, and find that a male worker in his late thirties with 9–12 years of education from the median country would raise his real earnings by a factor greater than 3.95, implying that migration barriers cost the global economy trillions of dollars per year. Estimates produced by Hamilton and Whalley (1984, pp. 70–74) suggest that the elimination of immigration restrictions could more than double gross national product (GNP) worldwide and would reduce international income inequality by raising wages dramatically in poor countries left behind by migrating workers. Hanson (2007, p. 325) studies the effects of a decade of Mexican emigration to the United States and finds empirical evidence of a positive impact on wages in Mexico in the range of 6–9 percent.

Even modest liberalization of migration would bring substantial increases in income and improvements in income distribution: The World Bank (2006, pp. 25–35) finds that liberalization of migration from "developing" countries to "high-income countries" sufficient to increase the labor force in high-income countries by 3 percent would generate large gains in global welfare, with gains going to the migrants, the destination countries, and those left behind in source countries (who would receive an increased flow of remittances sent home by migrants). Under this scenario, developing country households, including the migrants themselves, would enjoy the greatest gains, thereby reducing international income inequality. Given these benefits of liberalized migration and the costs of migration restrictions, how can one justify restrictive policies within a cosmopolitan consequentialist framework?

6.2.1 *Environmental Protection*

Some defend immigration restrictions in terms of the effects of migration on the environment. I survey and discuss these environmental concerns in Chang (2010, pp. 349–56). Some of these restrictionists suggest that emigration will undermine incentives for citizens of source countries to restrain population growth or protect their local environment from pollution. To the extent that a larger world population places greater demands on natural resources in the global commons, any tendency to undermine population control would harm the global environment. One must weigh these conjectures, however, against the empirical evidence that migration would have salutary effects on population growth and environmental protection.

This evidence indicates that a world of liberalized migration would be a world with a smaller population rather than a larger population. First, migrants moving from developing countries with high fertility rates to destination countries with lower fertility rates tend to reduce their own fertility to the lower rates found in destination countries. Immigration restrictions force prospective migrants to remain in source countries where they are likely to have more children than they would if they were allowed to migrate. Second, immigration restrictions increase the incentive for destination countries to adopt fertility policies to increase their population growth rates. As these countries shrink in population and grow older, they find they have fewer workers to support the retired, and they respond to this demographic problem with policies to encourage natives to have more children. Liberalized immigration would be an alternative response to this demographic problem because immigrants tend to be young workers with many years of work still ahead of them and thus the most to gain from migration. Third, liberalized migration would allow incomes to rise in poor countries, not only by reducing the abundance of labor and increasing wages but also by increasing the flow of remittances from workers abroad. This improvement in the standard of living in poor countries seems likely to reduce birth rates there toward the lower levels observed in wealthier countries. Thus, the net effect of liberalized migration on fertility would probably be a decline in world population growth.

Furthermore, empirical evidence also provides some reasons to think that liberalized migration would promote environmental protection through other channels. First, by improving the standard of living in developing countries, liberalized immigration would also increase the demand for environmental protection. As incomes rise in those countries, the political pressure for more pollution control also increases, as residents become more able to afford the costs of environmental protection. The available evidence supports the hypothesis that protection of the local environment improves once incomes rise above a sufficient level, at least for some pollutants. See, e.g., Grossman and Krueger (1995) (studying panel data collected across different countries and finding improved air and water quality when income per capita rises above $8,000 in 1985 dollars). Second, even if migration had no effect on environmental policies, the movement of people from poor countries to wealthy countries would tend to move them into jurisdictions with more stringent pollution controls. Any comprehensive evaluation of the environmental impact of liberalized migration would have to take all of these environmental benefits into account.

Yet some environmentalists defend immigration restrictions precisely because international migration would increase incomes for the poor. These restrictionists fear that immigrants who enjoy higher incomes as a result of migration would adopt the consumption patterns observed in wealthier countries and thereby cause greater harm to the environment than they would if they remained poor in their home countries. In particular, residents of wealthy countries consume more fossil fuels and other natural resources per capita than residents of poor countries, generating more emissions of carbon dioxide and other greenhouse gases per capita and thereby contributing more to climate change. These environmentalists urge governments to restrict immigration precisely because these restrictions trap prospective migrants in the poverty that they seek to escape through emigration. This deliberate embrace of poverty as an environmental policy is an especially ugly brand of environmentalism that neglects the availability of more efficient, more equitable, and more humane alternative policies.

To the extent that migration increases environmental harm, the best response would be an environmental policy tailored to address the specific environmental problem at issue. For example, pollution taxes, such as a carbon tax on fossil fuels, can deter both immigrants and natives from the specific activities that generate harmful emissions rather than placing a disproportionate share of the burden of pollution control on the poor in developing countries. Immigration restrictions are relatively clumsy and wasteful instruments for environmental protection because they needlessly sacrifice the benefits of migration, including the gains from trade in the labor market that immigrant workers and the employing economy would both otherwise enjoy. Environmental policies for environmental problems would avoid the collateral damage that immigration restrictions cause, including the poverty that would be mitigated by liberalized migration.

6.2.2 *Segregation of Cultural Communities*

Others defend immigration restrictions as necessary to preserve distinctive cultural communities that people value. The communitarian political theorist Michael Walzer (1983) is the leading proponent of this defense of immigration restrictions. In Chang (2007), I subject Walzer's claims to an economic analysis and offer a critique within a cosmopolitan consequentialist framework, drawing upon insights from the economic literature.

In the first part of my critique, I assume that Walzer is correct to value the segregation of people into distinctive cultural communities and consider whether the satisfaction of people's preferences for this segregation justifies immigration restrictions. Both economic theory and empirical evidence raise doubts about Walzer's empirical claim that nations must restrict immigration to ensure the distinctiveness of cultural groups in the world. Instead, freely mobile individuals with heterogeneous preferences would be expected to sort themselves voluntarily into distinct communities. Tiebout (1956) suggests the classic model of this process, in which individuals who desire different bundles of local public goods move into different communities so that they can enjoy the bundles that they prefer. Consistent with this theory, empirical evidence reveals patterns of segregation in which diverse populations sort themselves into diverse sets of more homogeneous communities at the local level.

Walzer acknowledges the alternative of voluntary segregation at the local level rather than immigration restriction at the national level, but he rejects this alternative based on two claims. First, Walzer (p. 39) insists that in order to ensure distinctive communities, immigration controls, or "closure" as he puts it, "must be permitted somewhere," that is, "[a]t some level of political organization." Second, he asserts that we should prefer "closure" at the national level rather than the local level because "individual choice is most dependent upon local mobility."

The Tiebout model and the evidence of the Tiebout process in the real world, however, cast doubt on both of these claims. The Tiebout model suggests that voluntary residential segregation at the local level would satisfy preferences more efficiently because it allows people to enjoy living in a distinctive community that matches their preferences while still maintaining access to labor markets in nearby communities within commuting distance. Immigration restrictions at the national level are relatively costly as a means of segregation because they sacrifice gains from trade in the labor market. Furthermore, the social benefit of immigration restrictions at the national level seems less weighty, given their remote and attenuated effects on the associational interests of individuals, compared to segregation at the local level, which has a more obvious and direct impact on daily life in an individual's immediate neighborhood.

Walzer (p. 39) is not satisfied with the segregation that emerges through voluntary choices, however, insisting that "closure" is necessary to maintain distinctive communities as "a stable feature of human life." In part, Walzer (p. 37) may perceive a need for segregation maintained through the coercive power of the state because he may value "communal cohesion" in "non-utilitarian terms" so that he may attach more value to the segregation of communities than the residents of those communities themselves do. Even if decentralized voluntary choices fail to produce the degree of segregation that people desire, however, society has the option of using zoning ordinances or restrictive covenants to segregate people based on their national origin at the local level, much like those used in the United States in the past to maintain racial segregation, which would at least preserve the option of trade in local labor markets.

Societies like the United States that espouse liberal ideals of equality, however, now reject segregation imposed by law at the local level. This hostility to de jure segregation at the local level should raise questions regarding the legitimacy of segregationist preferences as a justification for immigration restrictions at the national level. In some of my prior work, I argue that liberal ideals may constrain the objectives that society may pursue through the state and its laws and therefore may require a theory of social welfare that excludes the satisfaction of preferences that are objectionable from a liberal perspective. See Chang (2000, pp. 179–96). In Chang (2007, pp. 120–30), I suggest that these moral constraints apply not only to de jure segregation at the local level but also to immigration restriction at the national level, which only broadens the geographic scope of the community from which we exclude the victims of segregationist policies and thereby expands the range of opportunities denied to them. Therefore, in the second part of my critique of Walzer's defense of immigration restrictions, I relax the assumption that the satisfaction of segregationist preferences is a legitimate element of social welfare, argue that segregationist policies are unfair to those who are excluded from important opportunities on that basis, and conclude that "liberal states should seek to liberalize their immigration policies, thereby reducing global inequalities in economic opportunity" (p. 130).

6.3 The National Interest

In political debates over immigration policies, those who urge immigration restriction typically invoke the national interest rather than considerations of global welfare. Given the dominant role played by concerns about the national interest in public debates, I now turn to the case for liberalized immigration framed in terms of national economic welfare. In particular, I focus on the economic interest of natives, which is commonly thought to justify immigration restrictions.

The gains from trade in the labor market would flow not only to the immigrants who receive higher wages but also to the natives in the economy employing the immigrant workers. While some native workers may compete with immigrant workers in the labor market and see their wages fall, that loss would merely be a transfer among natives: Those who employ those native workers, and ultimately the consumers who enjoy the goods produced and services provided by those workers, would enjoy a gain that exactly offsets any loss to those workers. Moreover, those who would benefit also enjoy an additional gain by employing immigrants: They gain value from immigrant workers that exceeds the wages paid to immigrants for their labor. Thus, natives as a group enjoy a net gain from immigration in the form of this surplus from employing immigrant workers. In the United States, for example, Borjas (2014, pp. 151–58) attempts a crude calculation of this immigration surplus using a variety of assumptions and derives estimates ranging from 0.24 percent to 1.35 percent of gross domestic product (GDP), which comes to an extra $35.6 billion to $201.8 billion in income every year in a $15 trillion economy.

Furthermore, a country can increase the immigration surplus substantially by liberalizing immigration. As the labor force becomes increasingly immigrant, more of any decline in wages would fall on immigrant workers rather than on any native workers. Therefore, an increase in the immigrant workforce would cause more than a proportionate increase in the immigration surplus. See Chang (2015, p. xv). Liberalized immigration would not only promote the economic welfare of natives as a group but also yield increasing returns.

6.3.1 Income Distribution Among Natives

While economists agree that the effects of immigrant workers through the labor market are on balance positive for the real income of natives as a group, immigration may nevertheless have an adverse effect on the distribution of that income among natives. Proponents of immigration restrictions often claim that these restrictions serve to protect native workers from foreign competition in the labor market. The magnitude of any adverse effect of immigration on native workers is an empirical question that has spawned a vast literature. For a survey of this literature, see Chang (2015, pp. xv–xxvii). When the National Academies of Sciences, Engineering, and Medicine (hereinafter National Academies) (2017, p. 267) surveyed the literature studying the wage effects of immigration in the United States, however, it concluded that "when measured over a period of more than 10 years, the impact of immigration on the wages of natives overall is very small," and "[e]stimated negative effects tend to be smaller (or even positive) over longer periods of time (10 years or more)."

One reason that immigration has so little adverse impact on the wages of natives is the effect of immigration on the demand for labor. When immigrants enter an economy, they expand not only the supply of labor but also the demand for goods and services. As consumers, they generate more demand for labor, including the labor supplied by native workers. Moreover, the entry of immigrant workers increases profits in the sectors of the economy that employ those workers, which stimulates more investment in those sectors. This influx of capital will expand the sectors employing immigrant workers, expanding the demand for labor in those sectors, which tends to offset the wage impact of the expanded supply of labor.

Most important, the empirical evidence indicates that immigrants and natives have different skills, so they are imperfect substitutes in the labor market and often do not compete for the same jobs. For example, immigrants are likely to have different language skills than natives, so employers are likely to find natives better suited for some tasks while immigrants concentrate on others. Thus, Peri and Sparber (2009) find that natives and immigrants in the United States tend to specialize in different occupations based on the comparative advantage that natives enjoy in the English language. As a result, immigrant workers compete with one another far more than they compete with native workers. Immigrant labor may even complement native labor so that the net effect of an immigrant influx may be to stimulate demand for native labor and thereby raise wages for natives.

To the extent that economists find any evidence of a negative impact of immigration on native workers in the United States, this effect seems limited to the shrinking minority of natives with less than a high school education. See National Academies (2017, p. 267) and National Research Council (1997, p. 228). This evidence suggests that immigration restrictions might at best serve to protect the least educated native workers from the adverse effects of immigrant competition. Given the small adverse effects of immigration on native wages, however, these protectionist policies seem especially misguided. Immigration restrictions sacrifice gains from trade and reduce the income of natives as a group. If these restrictions confer any benefit on any native worker, they do so by imposing a larger cost on all the other natives who gain from the participation of immigrants in the labor market. Thus, protectionist restrictions amount to a costly policy to transfer wealth from most natives to other natives.

As long as natives care about the distribution of wealth among natives and not just the total wealth of natives as a group, of course, the government might be willing to sacrifice some wealth to achieve a more equitable distribution. To the extent that a country of immigration seeks to reduce after-tax income inequality, however, the government could probably do more good at a lower cost through progressive tax policies than through immigration restrictions. As I suggest in Chang (2009; 2015, pp. xxvii–xxx; 2018, pp. 131–33), making the same transfer of wealth through the tax system rather than through protectionist immigration restrictions could make all income classes of natives better off because protectionism sacrifices the gains natives would enjoy from employing immigrants.

Redistribution through the tax system, of course, is not costless: Higher taxes on those with more income to benefit those with less income will reduce incentives to earn income by working, saving, and investing. These distortions, however, result from any redistribution of income from the rich to the poor, whether the redistribution is achieved through the tax system or through immigration restrictions. For example, if protectionist immigration restrictions reduce the return to capital or increase the cost of services used by the wealthy by reducing the supply of immigrant workers, then this implicit tax reduces the incentives to save, invest, or become wealthy. If protectionist restrictions raise the real wages of high school dropouts relative to those of more educated workers, then this protectionism reduces the incentives for students to finish high school and invest in their own human capital. Immigration restrictions impose the same costly distortions as those imposed by progressive taxes, but these restrictions also sacrifice gains from trade in the labor market and thereby needlessly introduce a second distortion on top of the distortions inherent in income redistribution.

This type of double distortion need not increase the cost of redistribution, however, if the two distortions happen to counteract one another. In theory, one distortion could operate to mitigate the other, thereby reducing rather than increasing the costs of redistribution through the policy in question. In the case of immigration, however, the empirical evidence indicates that protectionist restrictions add distortions that aggravate rather than mitigate the distortions in work incentives associated with redistribution. In particular, immigration restrictions drive up the cost of services consumed disproportionately by households in which both spouses work, such as child care, food preparation, and housekeeping. This disparate impact on these households is especially likely to discourage work. Studies in various economies receiving immigrants, including the United States, Italy, Spain, and Hong Kong, confirm this hypothesis, finding that immigration increases the supply of female labor among natives. See Chang (2015, pp. xxix–xxx; 2018, p. 132 n.107). Thus, distortions specific to immigration restrictions aggravate the distortions in income redistribution, supplying even more reasons to favor redistribution through the tax system instead.

6.3.2 *Fiscal Concerns*

Even if natives enjoy a net benefit from immigration in the labor market, immigrants could still impose costs on natives through the public sector. In particular, restrictionists often raise concerns about the impact of immigrants on the public treasury. At least in the United States, however, the empirical evidence suggests that immigration confers a net fiscal benefit on natives, as discussed in Chang (2015, pp. xxx–xxxiii; 2018, pp. 117–25).

The National Research Council (NRC) (1997) provides a comprehensive calculation of the fiscal impact of immigration in the United States, including the tax revenue generated and the costs imposed on the public treasury not only by the immigrants themselves but also by all of their descendants. The NRC calculates a range of estimates for the total fiscal impact, including the effects at not only the federal level but also the state level, using various sets of assumptions. Using the most plausible set of assumptions for its "baseline" scenario, the NRC (pp. 325–26, 336–37) finds that the average recent immigrant in 1996 has a positive fiscal impact of $80,000 in net present value in 1996 dollars.

The National Academies (2017, pp. 359–493) provide an updated set of estimates that account for changes in government budgets and in the composition of the immigrant flow, again using various sets of assumptions. Under the set of assumptions that correspond most closely to the NRC baseline scenario, the National Academies (p. 446) find that the average recent immigrant has a positive fiscal impact of $279,000 in net present value in 2012 dollars. Even accounting for inflation, this estimate implies that the fiscal benefit generated by the average immigrant has more than doubled in the 20 years since the NRC performed its calculation. See Chang (2018, p. 118). Furthermore, for reasons explained in Chang (2018, pp. 117–25), even this estimate by the National Academies is based on unduly conservative assumptions that introduce a bias in favor of a negative impact. Thus, a calculation more faithful to the NRC baseline scenario would imply an even larger fiscal benefit than that estimated by the National Academies.

Even the NRC baseline scenario, however, suggests some basis for concerns about the fiscal impact of the least educated immigrants, who are often the focus of restrictionist complaints about immigration. Because immigrants with less education tend to have lower incomes, they tend to pay less in taxes and are more likely to use means-tested public benefits. Although more educated immigrants have a positive fiscal impact, the NRC (p. 334) estimates that the average immigrant with less than a high school education imposes a modest net fiscal cost of $13,000 in net present value in 1996 dollars.

Even if the least educated immigrants pose some risk of a fiscal burden for natives, natives would still benefit from their participation in the labor market. From the perspective of the economic welfare of natives, the best response to fiscal concerns would not be to exclude these immigrants from the country but to admit them subject to restrictions on access to means-tested public benefits. This response would improve the fiscal impact of immigrants without sacrificing the gains from trade in the labor market that would raise standards of living for both immigrant workers and natives.

Welfare reform legislation enacted in the United States in 1996 adopted this strategy in response to fiscal concerns about immigration. An alien admitted for permanent residence after this law took effect is ineligible for "any Federal means-tested public benefit" for the first five years after entry, with only narrow exceptions. See Chang (1998, p. 392). Assuming that this law would exclude immigrants from only seven specified means-tested programs (including welfare, food stamps, and nonemergency Medicaid) for the first five years after arrival, the NRC (p. 339) estimates that the 1996 legislation would improve the fiscal impact of the average immigrant by $8,000 in net present value. If the fiscal impact of the average immigrant with less than a high school education improved by this amount, for example, then under the NRC's baseline scenario, that immigrant would now impose an even smaller fiscal cost of only $5,000 in net present value in 1996 dollars.

To ensure that the least educated immigrants impose no net fiscal burden in expected value, a government concerned only about the economic welfare of natives might exclude the immigrants in question from a larger set of programs or delay their access to such programs for a longer period of time. In the United States, a longer delay would also require delayed access to citizenship because all citizens enjoy access to these programs on an equal basis. The United States could pursue this policy by admitting the least educated migrants on "nonimmigrant" visas for temporary workers rather than immigrant visas. Unlike immigrants, nonimmigrants are not admitted as permanent residents and are thus not eligible for most public benefits and not eligible to naturalize as citizens. Under the 1996 welfare legislation, both nonimmigrants and unauthorized immigrants are ineligible for "any Federal public benefit." See Chang (1998, pp. 391, 395). Thus, the United States can liberalize access to its labor market for even the least educated workers without imposing a burden on the public treasury by admitting them on nonimmigrant visas and by restricting access to public benefits for as long as necessary to address fiscal concerns.

If one were to define the national interest exclusively in terms of the economic interest of natives, then this strictly nativist notion of the social welfare objective might imply the admission of the least educated migrants as guest workers without any access to citizenship and public benefits. A broader notion of the welfare objective, however, might give natives priority but also give some weight to the interest of others. This broader notion of the national interest might allow a guest worker to gain permanent residence and ultimately naturalize as a citizen but only after generating enough of a net fiscal benefit while paying taxes as a guest worker to cover the net fiscal cost expected to follow from permanent residence, citizenship, and access to public benefits. This criterion would require less educated immigrants to earn access to public benefits by "paying their own way" first, which in turn would allow liberalized admissions without imposing a net fiscal burden on natives.

A more relaxed criterion might allow less educated immigrants to impose some fiscal burden as long as more educated immigrants confer enough of a fiscal benefit to cover the costs imposed by less educated immigrants. This criterion, however, would impose a budget constraint that could limit the number of less educated immigrants who could gain admission. This budget constraint would impose a tradeoff between the number of less educated immigrants who could enter and their access to citizenship and public benefits.

Under either criterion, admission as a guest worker on a nonimmigrant visa need not imply either a temporary stay or permanent status as an alien. Proposals for immigration reform in the United States have included programs to liberalize access to nonimmigrant visas for temporary workers with a limited path to citizenship for those who work for a long enough period as nonimmigrants. The proposal for comprehensive immigration reform passed by the Senate in 2013, for example, would have created a new program for guest workers that would allow them to apply for permanent residence through a merit-based points system that would award points for each year working lawfully in the United States up to a limit of twenty points. See Chang (2018, pp. 140–42).

Restrictions on access for guest workers to citizenship and public benefits would not be consistent with liberal ideals of equality. Walzer (1983, pp. 52, 58, 60), for example, claims that a society that relies on guest workers for labor is "a little tyranny" in which the guest workers are ruled by "a band of citizen-tyrants," violating principles of "political justice" in a "democratic state." I have argued in Chang (2002; 2008b), however, that liberals should tolerate guest worker programs as second-best policies that would promote the interests of those workers better than the alternatives of exclusion or entry as unauthorized immigrants. As long as the self-interest of natives imposes constraints of political feasibility on the liberalization of admissions for less educated workers, guest worker programs may be necessary to relax those constraints by addressing concerns about the fiscal impact of citizenship for these workers.

Political and economic circumstances may vary from country to country. A country with more progressive policies for the redistribution of wealth, for example, may have greater concerns about the fiscal impact of less educated immigrants and greater demand for restrictions on access to citizenship and public benefits. Programs for guest workers may vary accordingly: Some countries might allow guest workers to become citizens only after a relatively short period, whereas others might require a long period or impose other demanding requirements that restrict access. This access is a matter of degree, and programs for guest workers may adopt any point along this continuum to satisfy critics concerned about the political or fiscal effects of citizenship for less educated immigrants.

Restrictionists who adopt a strictly nativist notion of the national interest may oppose any path to citizenship for guest workers. While liberal ideals may call for quick and easy access to citizenship, as long as the economic interest of natives remains a dominant consideration in debates over immigration policy, liberals should be prepared to accept restrictions on access to citizenship in order to make liberalized admissions politically feasible. Given the gains in global welfare generated by liberalized access to labor markets in wealthy countries, liberals should give priority to liberalized admissions and accept political compromises that may sacrifice easy access to citizenship and public benefits.

6.4 Conclusion

Liberalized admissions improve social welfare by allowing immigrant workers and the economies that employ them to enjoy gains from trade in the labor market. These gains promote global welfare and advance the economic interests of natives in the country of immigration, but they benefit the migrants themselves most of all. To the extent that immigration raises concerns about environmental protection, the segregation of cultural communities, the distribution of income among natives, or fiscal concerns, there are less restrictive alternatives to immigration restriction that are more narrowly tailored to the problems in question. These less restrictive alternatives do not sacrifice gains from trade in the labor market and thus avoid the collateral damage caused by immigration restrictions.

Although this chapter has focused on gains from trade in the labor market, the case for liberalized admissions is more general than the immigration of workers. Immigrants may enjoy other important gains from migration, including freedom from persecution or family reunification. Natives enjoy other gains from trade with immigrants, such as when natives sell goods or services to immigrant consumers, sell or rent homes to immigrant residents, buy goods or services from immigrant vendors, or work for immigrant entrepreneurs. All these benefits from migration contribute to global social welfare, producing gains for natives in the country of immigration as well as for the immigrants. This chapter has focused on only one component of the harm inflicted by immigration restrictions.

Gains from trade militate in favor of liberalized admissions, whether from the perspective of global social welfare or from the perspective of the economic welfare of natives in the country of immigration. The main tension between the liberal cosmopolitan and nativist welfare objectives lies in the appropriate treatment of less educated immigrants. While the nativist would prefer restrictions on their access to citizenship and public benefits, the liberal would favor policies more generous to these immigrants. On this question, liberals should accept political compromises that may include programs for guest workers, as a concession that would allow the greatest possible liberalization of admissions within the constraints of political feasibility. While such a compromise may not be ideal from a liberal perspective, it would be misguided to forego worthwhile reforms because they fall short of the ideal.

References

Borjas, George J. (2014), *Immigration Economics*, Cambridge, MA: Harvard University Press.
Chang, Howard F. (1998), "Migration as International Trade: The Economic Gains from the Liberalized Movement of Labor", *UCLA Journal of International and Foreign Affairs*, 3 (2), Fall/Winter, 371–414.
Chang, Howard F. (2000), "A Liberal Theory of Social Welfare: Fairness, Utility, and the Pareto Principle", *Yale Law Journal*, 110 (2), November, 173–235.
Chang, Howard F. (2002), "Liberal Ideals and Political Feasibility: Guest-Worker Programs as Second-Best Policies", *North Carolina Journal of International Law and Commercial Regulation*, 27 (3), 465–81.
Chang, Howard F. (2007), "Cultural Communities in a Global Labor Market: Immigration Restrictions as Residential Segregation", *University of Chicago Legal Forum*, 2007, 93–130.
Chang, Howard F. (2008a), "The Economics of International Labor Migration and the Case for Global Distributive Justice in Liberal Political Theory", *Cornell International Law Journal*, 41 (1), 1–25.
Chang, Howard F. (2008b), "Guest Workers and Justice in a Second-Best World", *University of Dayton Law Review*, 34 (1), 3–14.
Chang, Howard F. (2009), "Immigration Restriction as Redistributive Taxation: Working Women and the Costs of Protectionism in the Labor Market", *Journal of Law, Economics & Policy*, 5 (1), 1–29.
Chang, Howard F. (2010), "The Environment and Climate Change: Is International Migration Part of the Problem or Part of the Solution?, *Fordham Environmental Law Review*, 20 (2 & 3), Winter, 341–56.
Chang, Howard F. (2011), "The Immigration Paradox: Alien Workers and Distributive Justice", in Rogers M. Smith (ed.), *Citizenship, Borders, and Human Needs*, Philadelphia, PA: University of Pennsylvania Press, 92–114.
Chang, Howard F. (2015), "Introduction", in Howard F. Chang (ed.), *Law and Economics of Immigration*, Northampton, MA: Edward Elgar Publishing, xi–xlv.
Chang, Howard F. (2018), "The Economics of Immigration Reform", *UC Davis Law Review*, 52 (1), November, 111–44.
Clemens, Michael A. (2011), "Economics and Emigration: Trillion-Dollar Bills on the Sidewalk?", *Journal of Economic Perspectives*, 25 (3), 83–106.
Clemens, Michael A., Montenegro, Claudio E., and Pritchett, Lant (2019), "The Place Premium: Bounding the Price Equivalent of Migration Barriers", *Review of Economics and Statistics*, 101 (2), 201–13.
Grossman, Gene M. and Alan B. Krueger (1995), "Economic Growth and the Environment," *Quarterly Journal of Economics*, 110 (2), May, 353–77.
Hamilton, Bob and Whalley, John (1984), "Efficiency and Distributional Implications of Global Restrictions on Labour Mobility", *Journal of Development Economics*, 14 (1), January–February, 61–75.
Hanson, Gordon H. (2007), "Emigration, Labor Supply, and Earning in Mexico," in George J. Borjas, *Mexican Immigration to the United States*, Chicago, IL: University of Chicago Press.
National Academies of Sciences, Engineering, and Medicine (2017), Francine D. Blau and Christopher Mackie (eds.), *The Economic and Fiscal Consequences of Immigration*, Washington, DC: National Academy Press.
National Research Council (1997), "The Future Fiscal Impacts of Current Immigrants," in James P. Smith and Barry Edmonston (eds.), *The New Americans: Economic, Demographic, and Fiscal Effects of Immigration*, Washington, DC: National Academy Press, 297–362.
Peri, Giovanni and Sparber, Chad (2009), "Task Specialization, Immigration, and Wages", *American Economic Journal: Applied Economics*, 1 (3), 135–69.
Tiebout, Charles M. (1956), "A Pure Theory of Local Expenditures", *Journal of Political Economy*, 64 (5), October, 416–24.
Walzer, Michael (1983), *Spheres of Justice: A Defense of Pluralism and Equality*, New York, NY: Basic Books, Inc.
World Bank (2006), *Global Economic Prospects 2006: Economic Implications of Remittances and Migration*, Washington, DC: International Bank for Reconstruction and Development.

7
IMMIGRATION
Some Arguments for Limits

Hrishikesh Joshi

7.1 Introduction

Over the past few decades, several philosophers, political theorists, and economists have defended a presumptive case for open borders. They have then argued that this presumptive case is undefeated by the purported countervailing considerations. Further, some contend that the reasons given for immigration restrictions, if successful, would also justify *internal* movement restrictions as well as limits on other important freedoms we take for granted within liberal democracy.

With a few exceptions, the open borders view seems to enjoy a privileged position in the literature. Ryan Pevnick (2011, 79), for instance, writes: "it is no exaggeration to describe open borders as the dominant position among academics writing about justice and immigration. Indeed, here it is any non-open border position that is seen as so much fanciful provocation." The purpose of this essay is to discuss some arguments against this orthodoxy on two broad fronts. First, once we take a broader view of the costs and benefits of unrestricted migration, it is not obvious that the open borders considerations robustly win out. Second, given what we consider to be the proper function of liberal democratic governments in other, non-migration-related domains, it's not obvious why such governments may not legitimately control their borders in most ordinary circumstances.

In what follows, I will first outline the presumptive case for open borders on both rights-based and utility-based fronts (Section 7.2). Then, I will suggest some reasons to think that the rights-based argument is not decisive, once we take a broader picture of the relevant rights involved (Section 7.3). In Section 7.4, I draw on some of the new literature on migration and institutional change to offer reasons to think that the utility calculus for unrestricted migration is not obviously in the positive. Section 7.5 concludes.

7.2 The Presumptive Case for Open Borders

As a resident of the state of Arizona in the United States, I am free to travel to California or Maine. I am also free to move there permanently if I want and seek employment, no questions asked. Not so if I wanted to move to Turkey or Japan. Visiting is one thing, but permanently settling there will involve many bureaucratic obstacles. In general, moving to a new country usually means meeting very specific requirements—one must be employed in specific sectors, have immediate family, or demonstrate that one meets the conditions required for refugee status. Further, mere travel across certain borders, even for the purpose of temporary visiting, requires visas. Open borders theorists find these asymmetries troublesome. In their ideal regime, people would be able to move across countries just as they are able to move across states (perhaps with exceptions for fugitives or terrorists).

The issue then is this: there are many people who, if given the opportunity, would move across international borders to seek a better life, as they see it, elsewhere. However, they are stopped from doing so by a coercive system of border controls. This, as many writers have rightly noted, cries out for justification. "Borders have guards and the guards have guns," writes Joseph Carens (1987, 251). And most prospective immigrants are not armed invaders or the like. Rather, "they are ordinary, peaceful people, seeking only the opportunity to build decent, secure lives for themselves and their families. On what moral grounds can these sorts of people be kept out? What gives anyone the right to point guns at *them*?"

In a similar vein, Michael Huemer (2010) presents us with a hypothetical scenario. Marvin, who is out of food, seeks to go to the marketplace to trade something he has for some bread. However, Sam, who is armed, stops Marvin from entering with a threat of force. This seems, *prima facie*, like a rights violation—a severe one at that. The analogies are then straightforward: Marvin is like the prospective immigrant who would like to trade his labor for material goods and opportunities, while Sam is like the government and its authorized agents who prevent this trade from taking place. Kieran Oberman (2016) argues that people have a deep interest in making personal decisions about where to live and work, as well as how, when, and where to engage politically. These interests ground the right to free movement—and this right is infringed by most border control policies.

Some writers have emphasized that it's not only the prospective immigrants whose rights are violated. Chandran Kukathas (2021) has recently argued that immigration restrictions limit the freedom of natives as well—they limit who current residents can employ, befriend, rent to, and so on. Carens (1987) likewise notes that a prospective employer, who would like to, say, employ foreigners to work on his farm, is restricted in his actions by immigration policy. From a libertarian perspective especially, this looks like a rights violation—namely, of the right to invite people onto one's property as one sees fit and to exchange in ways consented to by both parties.

Besides the rights-based presumptive case for open borders, there is also the welfarist case. The thought here is that free movement across borders would substantially increase global welfare. Free movement would allow people to seek employment where their skills and talents are best used. Imagine first a within-country case. Suppose an individual has the desire and talent to become a neurosurgeon. But she happens to be born in a small rural town, where the constraints on the division of labor mean that she cannot specialize to that extent. At most, she can go to the local nursing school and become a general-purpose nurse. Forbidding her to move to the city would be a great loss on two fronts. First, her desire to become a neurosurgeon (and we might add, her desire to live and work in a big city) would be frustrated. Second, given her drive and talents, she could help many people who need brain surgery—but if she is not allowed to relocate to train and practice, this potential welfare gain is forgone.

Of course, this sort of reasoning applies across borders as well. While the advent of remote work has allowed many people to cooperate across international borders, many jobs require physical presence. Some have argued that the free movement of people would dramatically increase world GDP (Caplan and Weinersmith 2019; Clemens 2011; Kennan 2013). The basic idea is that countries differ drastically in the amount of productivity they facilitate. Countries with good infrastructure, rule of law, robust markets, and stable political institutions facilitate much more productivity than countries where these features are lacking. Under a regime of open borders, individuals would generally move to places where they would be more productive and thereby enjoy a higher standard of living. This would benefit not only the people who move but also the world at large, given that the size of the economic "pie" would increase.

Of course, there might be some people who "lose out" in this process. Particularly, it might be the case that workers in some industries within the developed world (fast food, factory work, etc.) would see their wages depressed (Borjas 2016). Nonetheless, the thought is, that given the enormous aggregate gains in global productivity, these workers could be compensated such that open borders would be a win for all parties. In other words, an open-borders regime would be *Kaldor-Hicks superior*, even if not *Pareto superior* to the status quo.[1]

7.3 Reconsidering the Rights-Based Argument

Freedom of movement is limited by international border controls. This, as noted above, is considered a rights violation by many theorists. However, freedom of movement is limited in all sorts of ways within modern liberal democracies, and typically we don't consider these to be rights violations (Joshi 2018; 2020; Steinhoff 2022). Most obviously, our property rights limit the rights of others to move freely. But it's not only private property that sets these limits. We are typically not free to enter a boarding area within an airport without proper documentation and security checks. Certain areas of government buildings or military facilities are also off-bounds to those without specific privileges and documents. National parks and wilderness areas likewise place limits and restrictions on where we may move or live.

These types of restrictions will strike most readers as justified. What justifies such limits? If we like the methodology of tying rights to important interests, we can ask: What interests of ours are protected by certain limits on others' movement? When you own a house or rent an apartment, others are not permitted to enter without your consent. Even agents of the government must typically obtain a warrant before they can legally enter. In the case of one's living quarters, it is easy to see the (very weighty) interests that are protected by these rules. First, there is the interest in privacy. We have a strong interest in having a sphere of our lives that is not easily accessible to others. Second, there is an interest in a sort of self-determination within a specific sphere. We want to be able to arrange our furniture as we see fit, sleep without disturbance after a specific time, and so on. Third, there are reasons concerning safety—knowing that others must obtain our consent before entering puts us at some peace (though not perfect peace) about our security. Likewise in the case of airports, military facilities, and so on, restrictions are justified on grounds of public safety. Limits on who can stay in which parts of a national park in what season can be justified on the basis of a collective interest we have in natural preservation. An even more obvious case is that of our interest in bodily integrity. If rights to such integrity are to mean anything, they must set limits to others' freedom of movement, given that we are physical, materially extended creatures. And finally, property rights can be defended on the grounds that we have an interest in securing the fruits of our labor, or alternatively, operating within a system that makes positive sum games possible via division of labor and trade (Schmidtz 1994; Smith 1776).

The point is not that these specific rationales will carry over to justifying border controls. Rather, these cases are illustrative of a more general point: if we can identify important interests that hinge on our ability to set limits on others' movement, then that can go some way in justifying those limits—as we see in these other, presumably less controversial, cases of property, airports, and the like.

What might these interests be in the case of political associations like countries? We can get some traction on this question by looking at other sorts of associations (cf. Wellman 2008). Consider, for example, one's housemates. We often have a significant interest in determining who our fellow housemates will be—for who is part of this association will determine in large part what the norms around the house will look like. Will there be frequent parties, or will it be a quiet house? Will people cook together or separately? And so on. Similar points can be made about a host of other associations. Anyone who has been part of a co-op will recognize that it matters quite a bit who the other members are, where their priorities lie, what norms they accept, and so on.

Of course, one might say that the relation of compatriot is much less intimate than that of a housemate. But though it is less intimate, in other ways, it is more significant. Within a democratic society, our fellow citizens have *coercive control* over us.[2] And so, their perspectives, their moral viewpoints, and the norms they accept can have a deep influence on the structure of our lives and the opportunities we enjoy. Within constitutional limits, our fellow citizens decide (albeit indirectly in a representative democracy) what is criminally punishable, how much taxes we ought to pay, where those taxes ought to go, and so on. And constitutional matters themselves are often open to interpretation. Because the judges who are tasked with such interpretation are in turn appointed by democratically elected officials, even the constitutional rules of the game are sensitive to the composition of the demos. Furthermore, admission is often permanent or indefinite. If you don't like your roommates, it's relatively easy to move out. But once you and I are co-citizens, we're usually stuck with each other (for better or for worse) indefinitely.

The Nobel Prize-winning economist James Buchanan emphasized that this power that comes with joining the demos complicates the immigration debate in underappreciated ways. He wrote:

> The entry of an immigrant into an ongoing social-political-legal-economic order, with a defined membership, an experienced history, and a set of informal conventions, necessarily modifies the structure of "the game itself"... Membership involves more than a joining of the economic exchange network. Membership carries with it the power and authority, even if small, to modify the political-legal-constitutional parameters within which the economic game is played.
>
> (Buchanan 2007, 62)

In the abstract, at least, it is plain to see why we might have an interest in who else is admitted into the demos—given the coercive power that is granted upon entry. I say in the abstract because this interest might turn out to be, for all practical purposes, unaffected by immigration policy if it turns out either that cultures do not differ significantly enough or that assimilation occurs at a fast enough rate. In other words, if it turns out, as an empirical matter, that the "game" Buchanan refers to would not be substantially altered due to an open immigration policy, then limits on entry would not in fact protect our interest in maintaining and living within a particular set of laws, norms, and institutions—though they might in distant possible worlds.

The relevant empirical question then becomes: (to what extent) are social and political institutions (construed broadly) robust to significant inflows of people? Another Nobel Prize-winning economist, Elinor Ostrom, known for her work on the commons problems, noted that the sorts of informal rules and norms that enable cooperation are *fragile*. They can be destroyed in a number of ways, including the external imposition of rules not endorsed by the community and the growth of corruption, among other things. Most importantly for our purposes, Ostrom (2000, 153) writes:

> All economic and political organizations are vulnerable to threats, and self-organized resource-governance regimes are no exception. Both exogenous and endogenous factors challenge their long-term viability. Major migration (out of or into an area) is always a threat that may or may not be countered effectively...In-migration may bring new participants who do not trust others and do not rapidly learn social norms that have been established over a long period of time. Since collective action is largely based on mutual trust, some self-organized resource regimes that are in areas of rapid settlement have disintegrated within relatively short times.

The deep point here is that institutions should not be treated as an *exogenous* variable when it comes to immigration policy—rather, they are *endogenous*. That is, immigration policy can change the institutions we live under (whether for better or for worse).

A wide range of empirical work supports the claim that institutions change due to the movement of people. This is by no means an exhaustive survey, but I want to briefly note some of the relevant findings.[3] To begin, a recent article examines how southern whites changed the political and cultural landscape as they moved to other states during the 20th century (Bazzi et al. 2023). Among other things, they influenced their neighbors to adopt more conservative religious norms and increased the national partisan realignment by supporting a "New Right" coalition. Assimilation, this would suggest, is a two-way street. Another relevant question is whether norms of corruption tend to migrate as people do—an important factor to consider given that corruption levels can greatly affect government efficacy and living standards. Dimant et al. (2015) find that movement from countries with high levels of corruption tends to robustly increase corruption within receiving OECD countries. That said, the finding is perhaps inconclusive, as Bologna Pavlik et al. (2019) have recently disputed this effect.

One potential upshot of the Dimant et al. (2015) paper is that the cultural norms of the countries of origin of would-be immigrants can matter for the potential consequences of immigration policy. A related recent finding by Berggren et al. (2023) is that immigrants whose countries of origin have more tolerant cultures tend to integrate more into European societies. They write: "Our main finding is that tolerance plays a positive role for integration. The more tolerant the background culture, the higher the individual degree of economic, civic-political, and cultural integration" (Berggren, Ljunge, and Nilsson 2023, 1096). According to the authors, this relationship is quite robust. Building on a wide-ranging survey of the literature on the topic, the economist Garett Jones (2023) defends the thesis that, in general, immigration from country A to country B tends to change the institutions of country B in the direction of those of country A. Relatedly, Alesina and Giuliano

(2015, 938) conclude, based on their survey of the extant literature on the topic, that "[c]ulture and institutions interact and evolve in a complementary way, with mutual feedback effects. Thus, the same institutions may function differently in different cultures, but culture may evolve in differing ways depending on the type of institutions."

If we think of culture in a deeper sense, as involving complex norms, expectations, and normative perspectives (as opposed to shallower differences in, say, food or dress conventions), it is plausible that people have an interest in the preservation of culture (De Clercq 2017). But could this interest ground a *right* to limit immigration? Some philosophers will doubt this based on a "cantilever" argument. Thus Carens (2014, 237) contends that "treating the freedom to move across state borders as a human right is a logical extension of the well-established democratic practice of treating freedom of movement within state borders as a human right." The thought then is that if considerations of cultural change were legitimate grounds on which to restrict movement, then they could also be grounds to restrict *internal* movement—say from Arizona to Maine. However, it would be illegitimate and illiberal for the government to allow such internal restrictions; therefore, it is also illegitimate and illiberal for the government to restrict movement across its borders (cf. Freiman and Hidalgo 2016).

While more needs to be said to defend the point in detail, I want to briefly note one problem with this approach. The problem is that such arguments would overgeneralize in implausible ways to other domains. Thus, suppose a couple owns a house jointly. Given this, it would be wrong (barring unusual circumstances) for one partner to prevent the other from moving from the kitchen to the living room. But it does not follow that it would be wrong for either of them to try to prevent an uninvited stranger from entering their house. The very same grounds that would be sufficient for either of them to take this action against the stranger (say, that they do not want company at the moment), would not be sufficient for either of them to take that very action against the other partner.

Furthermore, it is possible to suggest different grounds on which internal freedom of movement is justified that do not carry over to the international case. Sarah Song (2019) has recently argued that the former is necessary to promote social cohesion and that this justification does not extend to movement across international borders. Besides, she argues, it is implausible that internal cultural distance is likely to be as great as cross-border cultural distance in most cases. The cultural distance between the average resident of Georgia and New York is plausibly much smaller than that between, say, the median residents of Japan and Ethiopia or Mexico and Egypt.

Some have argued that liberalism itself is committed to open borders (Freiman and Hidalgo 2016). In a previous article (Joshi 2018), I noted that this putative commitment would put liberalism in a troubling dilemma, depending on the empirical facts of the matter. Thus suppose Country A in general has liberal norms, endorsed by most of the population. Country B, however, is an illiberal theocracy—most residents support strictly different rules for men and women, death penalties for apostasy, persecution of religious minorities or atheists, and so on. However, suppose that due to its economic success, Country A is an attractive destination. Suppose further that the norms held by people in Country B are "sticky"—they take a long time to change if they do at all. Country B, in addition, has a much larger population than Country A. What is liberalism committed to in this case? Should Country A adopt open borders, even if, foreseeably, this would mean the eventual end of liberalism in Country A?

Perhaps from a particular sort of anarcho-libertarian premise, coupled with strict deontic, or rights-based, constraints, one might say that despite the potential consequences, limits to free movement (unless excluded by private property rights) are simply wrong. Kant (1996) famously thought that it is wrong to lie even if doing so would foreseeably prevent a murder. Thus, one might think, border controls are wrong irrespective of the forecasted consequences. However, this move would saddle the open borders position with commitments that many do not share. To illustrate, Huemer thinks that it's wrong for Sam to prevent Marvin from entering the marketplace. But he also also thinks that governments act wrongly in collecting taxes because they lack the authority to do so (Huemer 2012). Most readers, I assume, would reject this view. In a recent paper, Freiman and Hidalgo (2022) accept the consequence that a robust open borders position requires specific libertarian assumptions—but that means, for the non-libertarians among us, where we end up on the issue might depend on a complex weighing of a range of different considerations. And it's not clear that the open borders position will win out.

7.4 Consequentialist Considerations

As noted in Section 7.2, the economic case for open borders relies on the productivity differential across countries. Global free movement of labor, the thought goes, would allow people to move to places where they could be more productive, and hence dramatically increase global GDP. This increase in the economic pie then would come with an increase in average welfare.

However, the case is less clear-cut if the institutions that enable productivity could themselves change significantly as a result of migration. As Buchanan brings out in the quote from Section 7.3, migration of people is different from trade of commodities—for the simple reason that people are not commodities. Thus, the economic arguments for free trade of goods—so as to allow commodities to find the most efficient uses and to allow for more division of labor—are of limited applicability in the case of migration. That is because, as discussed in the previous section, the institutions that allow for high levels of productivity are themselves sensitive to the composition of the demos.

In his new book, Jones (2023) argues, using a range of case studies and data, that as people move, so do economic institutions—in general, for the most part.[4] Jones further argues that this has been the historical norm for centuries. Relatedly, there is recent literature on the "deep roots" of economic development. Spolaore and Wacziarg (2013, 325) write that in this area, the "evidence suggests that economic development is affected by traits that have been transmitted across generations over the very long run."[5] That said, however, it's not immediately obvious still that open borders would not increase aggregate welfare. For, even if it turns out that developed countries would lose some institutional quality, that may well be outweighed by the welfare gains accrued to individuals who would be free to move. The utilitarian cost-benefit calculus might thus still favor open borders, even granting the endogeneity assumption regarding economic institutions.

However, Jones contends, the entire world has a strong interest in preserving the institutional quality of the developed countries that produce the most scientific innovation. It is common to point out the negative externalities that developed countries have imposed on the rest of the world—particularly pollution and the resulting climate change. It is less common to note the *positive* externalities. Jones notes that much of the world's technological, medical, and scientific innovations—vaccines, aircraft, electronics, surgical treatments, solar panels, and so on—originate from just seven countries he calls the I-7. These are: South Korea, Japan, China, the U.K., France, Germany, and the U.S. Given how much scientific innovation promotes welfare—think of the lives saved by vaccines or the vastly increased food supply enabled by fertilizers—the entire world has an interest in the economic institutions of these seven countries. Jones then argues that even a small decline in the institutional quality of these countries would have a dramatic negative impact on the welfare of the rest of the world. It is therefore not clear, even from a purely utilitarian or effective altruist perspective, that open borders policies would be best.

This debate is by no means settled. Some economists have contested the idea that institutions would be negatively affected by migration in the way discussed above (Nowrasteh and Powell 2020). But even uncertainty in this regard might plausibly trigger a precautionary principle. Insofar as innovation is important for humanity's future flourishing, as a whole (including, for example, innovation aimed at reducing climate-related risks), the burden of proof might shift toward the defenders of open borders.

7.5 Conclusion

Nothing I've said in this essay supports a policy of total restriction. Surely there are many cases where immigration benefits everyone. In the U.S., for example, a large proportion of innovators have immigrant backgrounds (Bernstein et al. 2022). But a lot more work needs to be done to defend the *right* to migrate across any international border. Insofar as the initial arguments made by philosophers like Carens and Huemer offer a *prima facie* case for open borders, the arguments discussed in this essay might be seen as attempts to meet the burden on the other side. Importantly, while freedom of movement is an important right, we readily acknowledge limits to this right in a range of domains. These limits are indispensable for human flourishing in a range of ways. There is no reason to think the case of immigration is any different.[6]

Notes

1 A distribution D_2 is Pareto superior to D_1 if at least one person is better off in D_2 and nobody is worse off. A distribution D_3 is Kaldor-Hicks superior to D_1 if transfers could be made relative to D_3 so as to achieve a Pareto superior outcome, D_2. See Gaus and Thrasher (2021) for further illustration.
2 In a similar vein, Michael Blake (2020) defends the right to exclude on the basis that newcomers impose weighty *obligations* on existing members. Those obligations entail working to support institutions that secure the moral rights of the newcomer within the jurisdiction. For Blake, the imposition of a new obligation of this sort impinges on one's freedom in an important sense, such that one is (often) within one's rights to refuse to take on the obligation. Blake's claim about obligations is distinct from the above point about coercion, but it serves to highlight in a different way why we are often right to care about policies for admission into the jurisdiction where we live.
3 For a much more comprehensive discussion of the literature and its potential upshots see Jones's (2024) contribution to this volume.
4 For a shorter summary of some of the main relevant points from the book, see Jones's essay in this collection.
5 See also Comin, Easterly, and Gong (2010) and Ang (2013).
6 Thanks to Sahar Akhtar for helpful comments on an earlier version of this essay.

References

Alesina, Alberto, and Paola Giuliano. 2015. "Culture and Institutions." *Journal of Economic Literature* 53 (4): 898–944.

Ang, James. 2013. "Institutions and the Long-Run Impact of Early Development." *Journal of Development Economics* 105: 1–18.

Bazzi, Samuel, Andreas Ferrara, Martin Fiszbein, Thomas Pearson, and Patrick A Testa. 2023. "The Other Great Migration: Southern Whites and the New Right." *The Quarterly Journal of Economics* 138 (3): 1577–1647. https://doi.org/10.1093/qje/qjad014.

Berggren, Nicolas, Martin Ljunge, and Therese Nilsson. 2023. "Immigrants from More Tolerant Cultures Integrate Deeper into Destination Countries." *Journal of Comparative Economics* 51 (4): 1095–1108.

Bernstein, Shai, Rebecca Diamond, Abhisit Jiranaphawiboon, Timothy McQuade, and Beatriz Pousada. 2022. "The Contribution of High-Skilled Immigrants to Innovation in the United States." *NBER Working Paper 30797*. https://doi.org/10.3386/w30797.

Blake, Michael. 2020. *Justice, Migration, and Mercy*. New York: Oxford University Press.

Bologna Pavlik, Jamie, Estefania Lujan Padilla, and Benjamin Powell. 2019. "Cultural Baggage: Do Immigrants Import Corruption?" *Southern Economic Journal* 85 (4): 1243–61.

Borjas, George J. 2016. *We Wanted Workers: Unravelling the Immigration Narrative*. New York, NY: W.W. Norton.

Buchanan, James M. 2007. "A Two Country Parable." In *Justice in Immigration*, edited by Warren F. Schwartz. Cambridge University Press.

Caplan, Bryan, and Zach Weinersmith. 2019. *Open Borders: The Science and Ethics of Immigration*. New York: First Second.

Carens, Joseph H. 1987. "Aliens and Citizens." *Review of Politics* 49 (2): 251–73.

Carens, Joseph H. 2014. *The Ethics of Immigration*. New York: Oxford University Press.

Clemens, Michael A. 2011. "Economics and Emigration: Trillion-Dollar Bills on the Sidewalk?" *Journal of Economic Perspectives* 25 (3): 83–106.

Comin, Diego, William Easterly, and Erick Gong. 2010. "Was the Wealth of Nations Determined in 1000 BC?" *American Economic Journal: Macroeconomics* 2 (3): 65–97.

De Clercq, Rafael. 2017. "Huemer on Immigration and the Preservation of Culture." *Philosophia* 45: 1091–98. https://doi.org/10.1007/s11406-017-9830-3.

Dimant, Eugen, Tim Krieger, and Margarete Redlin. 2015. "A Crook Is a Crook ... But Is He Still a Crook Abroad? On the Effect of Immigration on Destination-Country Corruption." *German Economic Review* 16 (4): 464–89.

Freiman, Christopher, and Javier Hidalgo. 2016. "Liberalism or Immigration Restrictions, but Not Both." *Journal of Ethics and Social Philosophy* 10 (2): 1–23. https://doi.org/10.26556/jesp.v10i2.99.

Freiman, Christopher, and Javier Hidalgo. 2022. "Only Libertarianism Can Provide a Robust Justification for Open Borders." *Politics, Philosophy & Economics*. https://doi.org/10.1177/1470594X221091278.

Gaus, Gerald, and John Thrasher. 2021. *Philosophy, Politics, and Economics: An Introduction*. Princeton, NJ: Princeton University Press.

Huemer, Michael. 2010. "Is There a Right to Immigrate?" *Social Theory and Practice* 36 (3): 429–61.

Huemer, Michael. 2012. *The Problem of Political Authority*. New York: Palgrave Macmillan.

Jones, Garett. 2023. *The Culture Transplant: How Migrants Make the Economies They Move to a Lot Like the Ones They Left*. Stanford, CA: Stanford University Press.

Jones, Garett. 2024. "Migration as a Culture Transplant: Neoclassical and Institutional Channels." In *The Routledge Handbook of the Ethics and Economics of Immigration*, edited by Sahar Akhtar. New York: Routledge.

Joshi, Hrishikesh. 2018. "Is Liberalism Committed to Its Own Demise?" *Journal of Ethics and Social Philosophy* 13 (3): 259–67. https://doi.org/10.26556/jesp.v13i3.367.

Joshi, Hrishikesh. 2020. "For (Some) Immigration Restrictions." In *Ethics: Left and Right*, edited by Bob Fischer, 191–99. New York: Oxford University Press.

Kant, Immanuel. 1996. *Practical Philosophy*. Edited by Mary J. Gregor. Cambridge: Cambridge University Press.

Kennan, John. 2013. "Open Borders." *Review of Economic Dynamics* 16: L1–13.

Kukathas, Chandran. 2021. *Immigration and Freedom*. Princeton, NJ: Princeton University Press.
Nowrasteh, Alex, and Benjamin Powell. 2020. *Wretched Refuse? The Political Economy of Immigration and Institutions*. New York: Cambridge University Press.
Oberman, Kieran. 2016. "Immigration as a Human Right." In *Migration in Political Theory: The Ethics of Movement and Membership*, edited by Sarah Fine and Lea Ypi, 32–56. Oxford: Oxford University Press.
Ostrom, Elinor. 2000. "Collective Action and the Evolution of Social Norms." *Journal of Economic Perspectives* 14 (3): 137–58.
Pevnick, Ryan. 2011. *Immigration and the Constraints of Justice: Between Open Borders and Absolute Sovereignty*. New York: Cambridge University Press.
Schmidtz, David. 1994. "The Institution of Property." *Social Philosophy and Policy* 11 (2): 42–62.
Smith, Adam. 1776. *An Inquiry into the Nature and Causes of the Wealth of Nations*. 3rd (1871). London: Alex Murray & Son.
Song, Sarah. 2019. *Immigration and Democracy*. New York: Oxford University Press.
Spolaore, Enrico, and Romain Wacziarg. 2013. "How Deep Are the Roots of Economic Development?" *Journal of Economic Literature* 51 (2): 325–69.
Steinhoff, Uwe. 2022. *Freedom, Culture, and the Right to Exclude: On the Permissibility and Necessity of Immigration Restrictions*. New York: Routledge.
Wellman, Cristopher Heath. 2008. "Immigration and Freedom of Association." *Ethics* 119 (1): 109–41.

PART III

Culture, Language, and Institutions

8
MIGRATION AS A CULTURE TRANSPLANT
Neoclassical and Institutional Channels

Garett Jones

8.1 Introduction

Do migrants make the economies they move to a lot like the ones they left? At least in some cases, the answer must be an emphatic yes. When Acemoglu, Johnson, and Robinson (2001) refer to the U.S., Canada, Australia, and New Zealand as "Neo-Europes," we intuitively know the meaning of that term: after 1500, migrants from Europe moved in their millions to these nations, and imposed European-style institutions upon them with violent force. And so it is little surprise that the economies of these Neo-Europes are at least as productive today as Western European economies—they're close cousins, after all.

An important question for social scientists is whether such migration-driven "culture transplants" have occurred, on average and in the long run, beyond this handful of Neo-Europes. And it's particularly important to know whether such culture transplants are likely to occur in the 21st century as well: perhaps culture transplants happened in the past, but perhaps now migrants rapidly and quickly assimilate to their new homes, having negligible effects on the institutions of the countries they move to. Alternatively, maybe migrants and their descendants import new attitudes, but perhaps government institutions and national productivity are overwhelmingly unresponsive to the views and behaviors of these new citizens, so perhaps there's no important link from changes in the views of voters to changes in institutional outcomes.

Moral consequentialists—utilitarians in particular—should be deeply interested in whether migration to the world's rich countries is likely to either improve or worsen institutional quality in the nations that migrants move to. That's because the vast majority of the world's innovation, the world's research and development (R&D), occurs in just seven countries: Japan, China, South Korea, the U.S., Germany, Japan, and France. These nations, which I've called the I-7, produce pharmaceutical research, electronics innovation, and engineering marvels that, eventually, improve lives in nearly every nation on Earth (Jones, 2022). These nations are the research and development labs for the entire planet, and since a nation's level of R&D is highly sensitive to the quality of that nation's government institutions, any decline in institutional quality in the I-7 places future improvements in well-being for the global poor at risk.

DOI: 10.4324/9781003037309-12

The traditional view of the cruel tradeoffs of migration is captured by the works of Borjas (1994, 2003) and Clemens (2011). Clemens correctly notes that the benefits of migration to migrants from poor countries are absolutely massive—his "trillion dollar bills on the sidewalk." And Borjas notes that lower-skilled previous residents of the nation—so-called "natives"–likely suffer small wage declines due to competition from immigrants. The conventional way to evaluate the utilitarian or consequentialist merits of freer migration to rich countries is then to compare the massive benefits to the migrants against the apparently smaller costs to the so-called native-born. It's a comparison of a benefit going to people currently living in poor countries against a cost to people currently living in rich countries.

But once we turn our attention to the I-7's crucial role in globally shared innovation, we realize that there may be a new, far crueler tradeoff: the benefits of migration to people moving from poor countries to rich countries versus the possible long-run impact of that migration on global innovation and on productivity in the world's poorest countries. If migration to rich countries hurts institutional quality in those rich countries, then the migrating poor may pick up their trillion-dollar bills today at the expense of generations of future poor people around the world, who may thereby lose the equivalent of many more trillions of dollars worth of future live-improving innovations. Whether migration to rich countries shapes government quality and economic innovation in those rich countries is thus a question of first-order importance for anyone interested in the overall effects of migration on human well-being. The cruel tradeoffs of migration policy may well be global in scope and may extend across many generations.

Two vast empirical literatures have proven indispensable in shaping answers to the question of whether migrants—and importantly, their descendants—import cultural norms that shape government institutions and productivity. The first is known, regrettably, as the "epidemiological approach" to cultural transmission, and the method is simple. Investigators draw upon modern surveys like the World Values Survey (WVS), the General Social Survey (GSS), and the European Values Study, and check to see if, for example, today's second-generation Italian-Americans hold social and policy views a lot like people in Italy today (*inter alia*, e.g., Giavazzi et al., 2019; Borrell-Porta et al., 2017).

The research is valuable because it easily and repeatedly demonstrates that second-generation migrants whose ancestors came from different countries really do hold different attitudes, on average, depending on where their ancestors came from. In some cases, researchers look beyond the second-generation to the third- and fourth-generation—the grandchildren and great-grandchildren of migrants, and they generally find substantial persistence, even with their noisy proxies for ancestry. This stylized fact makes belief in full, rapid assimilation untenable. To be sure, the relationship is stronger for some views than others, and for some survey questions, full assimilation really does appear to happen. But for savings behaviors, views on the role of government, and generalized trust, this "epidemiological approach," which I'll instead call the attitude migration approach, finds strong evidence of multi-generational persistence among migrants. Since, particularly in democracies, governments tend to move in the direction of voter attitudes (Caplan, 2007), this offers a plausible mechanism for the theory that the descendants of migrants would make the countries they go to at least somewhat like the ones they left.

The second relevant scholarly literature is the Deep Roots literature, sometimes known as the persistence literature. The portion of this literature relevant to our question—the migration-adjusted Deep Roots literature—grew out of a paper by Putterman and Weil (2010) that focuses on the role of migration in explaining modern differences in productivity across countries. They showed that on average, regions of the Old World where there was long experience living under organized states or long experience with settled agriculture tend to be more prosperous today, and tend to have better institutions; the past was prologue.

And that relationship held strongly when they included the New World as well—but only when they adjusted for migration. In other words, it only held strongly when Putterman and Weil took account of the fact that many people moved, both voluntarily and all too often involuntarily, from places with differing lengths of experience with states and agriculture. When people—particularly people from Western Europe and China—moved from places with longer experiences with statehood and settled agriculture to places where the residents had much less such experience, these migrants' new homelands ultimately became a lot like the places they'd left. These migrants did not fully assimilate to the local norms. Many scholars have built on the Putterman and Weil migration-adjustment approach, and the evidence thus far is compelling: if one wants to use data from the distant past to predict a nation's prosperity today, one should always "adjust for migration."

The remainder of this paper draws out the methods and messages of these two literatures in greater detail, drawing in part on (and occasionally drawing verbatim from) my recent book with Stanford University Press, *The Culture Transplant* (2022). Section 2 reviews the attitude migration literature, which finds that many important attitudes appear to migrate and are transmitted in large part to at least the second generation. Those attitudes include views on the role of government, the role of women in society, and views toward generalized trust. A smaller literature looks at actual behaviors, in particular, whether savings behaviors are partly transmitted to the children and even grandchildren of migrants. Section 2 concludes by reviewing the political economy evidence that democracies are responsive to changes in the electorate, so new people, on average, create new policies.

Section 3 reviews the migration-adjusted Deep Roots literature, looking in particular at three well-studied measures: ancestral experience living under organized states (S), settled agriculture (A), and ancestral experience in the year 1500 using the world's frontier technology (T). Together, I informally denote these as a nation's SAT score.

Section 4 applies these literatures to the important test case of Southeast Asia, a region that has been heavily shaped by overwhelmingly peaceful migration from people from China over the last few centuries. Singapore stands out as a strong illustration of cultural transplant theory, but Malaysia, Thailand, Indonesia, and the Philippines all have Chinese ethnic minorities who continue to pass along, to some degree, the deep roots of Chinese culture. The Southeast Asian experience is particularly important for illustrating how peaceful, voluntary migration can shape institutional quality.

Section 5 addresses some of the criticisms of cultural transplant theory that have arisen in recent years, and Section 6 concludes.

8.2 Attitude Migration

A continuing stream of empirical papers shows that, as Alesina et al. (2015) put it:

> Cultural values are relatively slow to evolve, as a vast literature on the behavior of immigrants to other countries, mainly the United States, shows.

Much of the attitude migration literature—but as we'll see, by no means all—checks to see whether second-generation immigrants hold views a lot like those in their parent's country of birth. As a reminder, a second-generation immigrant is a child of immigrants, someone whose parents were born in a different country than she was. Why study the second-generation? In part, because first-generation immigrants are largely self-selected, they're quite likely to be quite different from the average citizen back in their country of origin. A first-generation immigrant to France may have chosen to go to France because she knew she had a set of cultural, linguistic, or economic preferences and skills that made France a good fit for her; she may have chosen France precisely because she thought she could assimilate quickly. Second-generation immigrants, by contrast, didn't get to decide where they were born, so national self-selection can't be driving the results.

8.2.1 *Neoclassical Examples*

The earliest paper of which I am aware to use the methodological approach discussed here doesn't look at attitudes at all; it looks at concrete behaviors. Fernández (2011) notes that an influential paper by Antecol (2000) used male and female labor force participation…

> in the country of ancestry to examine whether culture plays a role…in the inter-ethnic gender gap in labor force participation rates in the United States.

Indeed, Antecol found evidence that home-country gender gaps in labor force participation were partly transplanted to the U.S. in the second generation. This paper was the start of the "vast literature" that Alesina et al. mentioned above.

Fuchs-Schündeln et al. (2020) use country-of-origin data from the WVS to predict the savings behaviors of second-generation migrants to Germany; they find that a one standard deviation increase across countries in whether children should be taught the value of thrift predicts a rise in the second-generation migrant's savings rate by between 0.8 and 1.6 percentage points. A one standard deviation increase is, informally, comparable to the average difference you'd find between any two countries in the researcher's sample. The range of estimates arises from differences in the statistical specification—in what the researcher "controls for" or attempts to hold constant when making comparisons across people whose parents came from different countries.[1] [Costa-Font et al. (2018) find broadly similar results for migrants to the U.K., extending results to the third generation.]

The numbers from the Fuchs-Schündeln paper may sound small except for the fact that the mean savings rate in their sample is 7.7%. That means they're reporting between a 10% and a 21% increase in the savings rate. For comparison, William Gale of Brookings long ago reported that shifting to a flat-rate income tax would plausibly raise the U.S. savings rate by half a percent to 1% of GDP, a 10% to 20% rise in total savings (Gale, 1996). Thus, a one-standard-deviation rise in thrift in a second-generation migrant's nation of origin is comparable, per person, to the plausible effect of one of the most widely discussed pro-savings tax reforms. The narrow neoclassical effects of migration policy on national productivity appear too big to ignore.

8.2.2 *The Migration of Familism*

Alesina et al. (2015) investigate a more conventional form of attitude migration: not attitudes toward frugality but attitudes toward the proper role of government. They only look at second-generation migrants to the U.S., and find, as so often, that attitudes partly migrate from the country of origin to the U.S. Their particular interest is in how family-based or "familistic" cultures (Banfield (1967))— i.e., cultures with strong family values, including a preference to live close to one's immediate family—can create demand for stringent labor market regulation.

What do they find?

US [second-generation] immigrants coming from countries with strong family ties tend to consider job security as...important... They are more likely to believe that the government should save jobs or directly intervene to regulate wages.

Alesina and Giuliano (2015) find a similar relationship when making cross-country comparisons: people who live in countries with strong family values are more likely to demand stronger government regulation of the labor market, whether the country itself is rich or poor.

Strong family values appear, on average, to create a demand for labor market regulation, and the alternative, weaker family values—greater individualism—appear to increase demand for laissez-faire labor market policies.

8.2.3 Proxies for Ancestry

How do scholars determine the migrant's nation of ancestry? They use two methods: asking a generic question about where one's ancestors came from or just asking directly where one's mother and father were born. When studies of U.S. populations use the GSS, as Alesina et al. did above, the approach is to draw on a question that asks merely where one's ancestors came from—and respondents are allowed to give up to three answers in order of personal importance. But since second- and third-generation Americans frequently have ancestors who came from multiple countries, and since the regression estimates typically treat the top country of origin as the sole country of origin, scholars are likely underestimating the effect of ancestry.

Consider this analogy: If researchers running a double-blind study of a new medicine's effectiveness mistakenly gave all the test subjects only a half dose instead of the full dose of the medicine, then if we found out that the medicine improved patient health in a small but real way, then we should conclude, probably but not certainly, that a correctly run study that gave all patients a full dose would have yielded an even larger effect. Noise-laden proxies for explanatory variables tend to bias coefficients toward zero in simple cases, as Durbin noted (1954). Thus, proxies that are systematically noisy, like the GSS ancestry proxy, are nearly guaranteed to make any reported effects of ancestry appear artificially small.

However, as mentioned above, some studies of second-generation immigrants do directly ask respondents where their parents were born, a question that few respondents are unlikely to know the answer to. Thus, many studies of second-generation attitude migration have quite precise information about cultural ancestry. Both methods—the noisier question about general ancestry and the more precise question about where one's parents were born—routinely find evidence that attitudes migrate.

8.2.4 Intra-European Attitude Migration[2]

An alternative to the WVS and GSS is the European Values Study (EVS). Borrell-Porta et al. (2017) used the EVS to create a nearly encyclopedic paper that tested out cultural transplant theory by looking at over a dozen survey questions. This team, based at the London School of Economics, looked at attitude persistence among immigrants who moved from one European country to another. In the second generation, ancestral-country attitudes on three questions were very persistent, heavily transplanted from the ancestral country to the new home, with correlations greater than 0.5. Speaking informally, that means that over half of the differences in answers to these questions in the ancestral country appear to be transmitted to second-generation migrants in the new country.[3] Paraphrasing, the questions were these:

If people don't work, do they turn lazy?
Who is responsible for taking care of a person: the individual or the state?
Does a preschool child suffer if the mother works outside the home?

On four more questions, ancestral-country attitudes were moderately persistent into the second generation but showed more fade-out than the above three, with correlations ranging from 0.25 to 0.5, so home-country attitudes predicted about one-fourth to one-half of differences in destination-country attitudes. These cultural transplants were real, but nowhere close to complete. Again paraphrasing:

Do you trust the European Union government?
Do you think most people can be trusted?
How important is family to you?
How important is God to you?

There were quite a few questions where fade-out was essentially complete, where ancestral-country attitudes had little to no bite at all, with correlations between home country average views and the views of second-generation migrants of less than 0.25 (with some even slightly negative). These cultural transplants failed almost completely. A few examples:

Is it bad for women to work outside the home?
Can the police be trusted?
Are you religious?
Are immigrants a strain on the welfare system?

Intra-European migration gives us a chance to test for full migrant assimilation, and at least in the second generation, the outcome is diverse: some attitudes converge to local norms (on average) and some don't. But note that among the most persistent is one question explicitly about the role of the state—whether it should take care of a person—and another is plausibly related to preferences for redistribution and labor market regulation—whether non-workers turn lazy. Trust in the EU is also moderately persistent in the second generation. Politically relevant attitudes clearly can persist among intra-European migrants.

Giavazzi et al. (2019) found broadly similar results when looking at second-generation U.S. immigrants. They separately looked at fourth-generation immigrants. Under a lax measure of assimilation—checking to see what percentage of respondents closed more than half the opinion gap between first-generation migrants from their country of origin and the U.S. average—they found that when it came to views on cooperation, 81% of fourth-generation migrants assimilated, but when it came to views on government, only 38% assimilated. I should emphasize the laxness of the assimilation measure: closing half the gap by the 4th generation. Even when grading on a curve, it's hard to find evidence of full assimilation. Of course, to the extent that migrants are bringing productivity-boosting opinions and behaviors, that "failure" of assimilation could of course give a great boost to productivity.

8.2.5 Generalized Trust: Attitude Migration and Experimental Correlates

The most-studied question in the attitude migration literature is this one:

> Generally speaking, would you say that most people can be trusted or that you need to be very careful in dealing with people?

This question, known as the generalized trust question, has been a staple of social science research for decades, and its national, international, and experimental correlates have been documented and debated in great detail. This short review can of course only touch on this range of literatures; in *Why Trust Matters* (2021), economic theorist Ben Ho offers an excellent nontechnical survey of the trust literature.

At least one empirical finding regarding trust is unambiguous: answers to the generalized trust question migrate from one country to another, and are routinely transmitted to the second generation to a sizable degree. In *The Culture Transplant* I look across a variety of trust migration studies: Canada, Australia, the U.S., and the above-mentioned pan-European study all find that trust migrates and persists to some degree in second-generation migrants. Notably, these results from different countries generally use different datasets, so this is not a one-dataset result. Even among studies that draw upon the widely used WVS, different studies include datasets from differing sets of years. The persistence percentage differs from study to study, country to country, specification to specification, and includes a high value like 71%, and a low value like 17%. I take 40% trust migration as an informal central tendency; a little less than half but a lot more than zero.

Müller et al. (2012), taking a critical approach to trust migration, looked across waves of the WVS to see if the moderate trust migration to the U.S. documented in one influential paper, Algan and Cahuc (2010), was a fragile result that depended on the precise wave (year) of the WVS data. In one set of results, they used a multi-generation adaptation of the measure emphasized here: they included second-generation migrants born between 1910 and 1975, third-generation migrants born after 1935, and fourth-generation migrants born after 1960. Algan and Cahuc called this "Inherited Trust in 2000." Müller et al. compared results across the 2005, 1995, 1990, and 1981 waves of the WVS, in addition to the 2000 survey used by Algan and Cahuc. Algan and Cahuc reported 46% trust migration with this multi-generation measure, and across the four other waves, Müller et al. found three higher rates of trust migration (56%, 52%, 47%) and one lower (33%). The median of these four values is thus 50% and the mean is 47%, a confirmation of the Algan and Cahuc result.

Müller et al. then check two more measures that Algan and Cahuc use, both of which downweight more recent waves of immigrants. One just looks at fourth-generation migrants—the great-grandchildren of the original migrants. Another measure, which Algan and Cahuc called "Inherited Trust in 1935," looks only at second-generation Americans born *before* 1910, third-generation Americans born *before* 1935, and fourth-generation Americans born *before* 1960. This measure thus puts more weight on the distant past ancestry of survey respondents compared to the Inherited Trust in the 2000 measure; the respondents are also an average of 15 years older in the 1935 Trust sample.

Out of these eight longer-run estimates, three are larger than the aforementioned 46% (72%, 53%, 61%), and five are smaller, with three much smaller: 37%, 29% 12%, 10%, 5%.). These eight estimates are statistically less precise overall—half lack the asterisks that researchers mistakenly (McCloskey and Ziliak (2010)) place excessive weight upon—so the true values could plausibly be much larger or much smaller than the estimated values. But with a median across the eight of 34% and a mean of 33% across these eight estimates, and even higher estimates for the 2000 Trust measure above, there's good reason to treat the Müller et al. study as a confirmation of the attitude migration literature, even if the authors themselves treat it as a critique.

With trust migration well-established by the standards of modern empirical research, one wonders whether such survey responses translate into real-world behavior, as we saw with savings or labor force decisions earlier. Experimental economists have used the famed Berg et al. (1995) trust game to see whether people who say they think people can be trusted are themselves more trusting (investing some experimentally-provided cash to a stranger's project in hopes of getting some money back), more trustworthy (actually returning some discretionary amount of money back to the investor after the project turns a profit) or neither. In a typical game, an "Investor" is handed five one-dollar bills, and chooses whether to keep them all, send them all over to an anonymous partner, or keep some and send the rest to that anonymous partner. The partner—whom I'll call the "Returner," finds that when the money arrives, it has doubled: so $2 sent over becomes $4, for example. The Returner then makes a decision a lot like that of the original investor: does she keep all $4, send back all $4 to the Investor, or keep some and send back some?

So, do trust attitudes predict the behavior of either the Investors or the Returners? In particular, in countries where the WVS reports that people are more trusting, do Investors in this game act in a more trusting manner? Do they send more money over? Johnson and Mislin (2011, 2012) investigated this question. They collected data from trust game experiments run around the world on a total of 23,000 subjects: this led to 152 experimental results from 30 countries that reported the "trust" result (what fraction of the money the Investor sends over). They summarize a key finding in their 2012 paper:

> a one standard deviation increase in the percent of survey respondents who answer 'yes' to the WVS Trust Question is associated with an increase in a country's experimentally measured trust of about 28% of a standard deviation.

They found statistically imprecise and quantitatively much smaller relationships between national trust and experimental trustworthiness (Returner's fraction sent back). The corresponding coefficients, two with negative signs, were one-third or less the size of the trust (Investor) coefficients.

The 2012 paper is, to my knowledge, still the only cross-country comparison of trust game results against WVS trust measures, but it offers a signal of external validity of this simple survey question: and it suggests that in countries with high levels of survey trust, experimental subjects are, on average, more trusting in the lab. Within-country trust game experiments have a more contested set of results, but the heart of the debate is not over whether the generalized trust question captures anything at all, but whether the trust question captures the respondent's level of *trustworthiness* rather than the respondent's level of trust. Glaeser et al. (2000) famously find that in their Harvard-run trust game,

> [s]tandard attitudinal survey questions about trust predict trustworthy behavior in our experiments much better than they predict trusting behavior.

Notably, the Glaeser et al. "trust predicts trustworthiness" result has been replicated sufficiently—including in rural Bangladesh by Johansson-Stenman et al. (2013), among Peruvian microfinance participants by Karlan (2005), and among Emory University students Capra et al. (2008), that even though the finding is not universal, Rick Wilson (2018) looks at the literature and concludes:

> It would seem that the attitudinal measures [of trust] from the GSS and WVS are correlated, in some manner, with trustworthiness.

One well-known counterexample to these results is Fehr et al. (2003) which instead found in a large sample of the general German population—not just college students—that the survey trust measure predicted trusting behavior by the Investor rather than trustworthy behavior by the Returner.

A literature that dives more deeply into the microfoundations of trust continues to interpret the results of these and other studies. One important possibility is that answers to the generalized trust question may capture *preferences* toward cooperative behavior rather than *beliefs* about the likelihood of trustworthy actions by others. For example, Thöni (2017) investigated another canonical experimental setting—a public goods game. In the public goods game, a small number of players are each given, say, the same five $1 bills. Those players then simultaneously, independently, and anonymously decide how many of those dollar bills to place in a metaphorical pot rather than just keep it; all the money placed in the pot instantly doubles and is then divided equally among all players.

A rational, selfish player would hope that everyone else contributes to the pot, but will choose to "free ride" by putting in nothing. A pure altruist might well contribute everything in order to help the strangers playing the game. In real life, it's common for about 1/3 of the money to be put in the metaphorical pot, though there is wide variation (Ostrom 2000). Based on Thöni's experience in running versions of this public goods game, he concludes that the generalized trust survey question appears to capture a generalized preference for cooperation. As he put it:

> The prominent and widely used TRUST question seems to be a measure for preferences for cooperative behavior, i.e., the willingness to take a leap of faith when entering a social dilemma.

This literature has not settled on a complete explanation for these varied results, and none may be forthcoming. To my knowledge, there's been no systematic effort to integrate the default within-country "trust predicts trustworthiness" result with the Johnson/Mislin cross-country "trust predicts trust" result. But if the answer to this simple survey question usually predicts some form of pro-social behavior in the lab, whether that means more trusting behaviors from the Investor or more trustworthiness from the Returner, then social scientists should consider a high-trust answer to the WVS trust question to be a statistical signal of higher social capital.

8.2.6 From Attitudes to Policy to Institutions

If multi-generational migrants import new (and potentially better) attitudes, will these attitudes change government in important ways? In democracies, can migration shift the political views of citizens sufficiently to lead to broadly based institutional change?

The most direct mechanism for such change would be if elected politicians responded to voters. One important example: Calderon et al. (2023) found that the Great Migration of African-Americans was a notable force in somewhat improving America's institutions surrounding racial equality. When African-Americans moved from the Jim Crow South, where it was nearly impossible for the vast majority of African-Americans to vote, to the North, where it was easier for African-Americans to vote, local politicians in the North became highly responsive to the views of these new voters, and overall pushed harder for civil rights legislation as a result. Indeed, the authors find evidence that white voters in states that had more African-American migrants shifted their political views toward racial equality—so the migrants changed the views of the previous residents. I've referred to this reverse assimilation phenomenon as "The Spaghetti Theory of Cultural Change," since the arrival of Italian-Americans to the U.S. obviously increased the likelihood that other Americans ate Italian food. Assimilation is often a two-way street—where migrants change the views of previous residents and previous residents also change the views of migrants.

Likewise, the scholarly literature on women's suffrage finds strong evidence that U.S. states and nations around the world that gave women the right to vote saw policy changes so widespread that one can only think of them as "institutional" in scope (*inter alia*, Lott and Kenny (1999), Doepke et al. (2012)). Both of these cases—women's suffrage and the Great Migration—are consistent with the predictions of the median voter theorem: When new voters arrive with new views, whether literally in the case of African-Americans moving northward or metaphorically in the case of women arriving to the world of suffrage, politicians who want to win elections will have a strong incentive to move in the direction of those new views. New people create new policies. A second more speculative possibility builds upon Acemoglu's "Why Not a Political Coase Theorem?" (2003) and Olson's Roving and Stationary Bandits model (1993). Even autocratic governments have some incentive to maximize their tax revenue. That means that if a highly productive "market-dominant minority" (Chua (2004)) could become even more productive under better economic institutions, then autocrats have an incentive to improve institutional quality, since such institutional improvements could substantially boost the autocrat's tax revenue. Institutional reform efforts are costly, difficult, and risky, so autocrats and democrats alike are more likely to make the effort when the potential return is highest. And the presence of a market-dominant minority in a country may increase that potential return to reform just enough to spur that reform effort.

8.3 The Deep Roots of Economic Development

Putterman and Weil's (2010) Global Migration Matrix belongs at the beginning of any discussion of the migration-adjusted Deep Roots literature. They estimated which fractions of which populations had moved where since 1500, whether their movements were voluntary or forced. They chose 1500 since, after that time, the age of European migration and conquest shifted the world's population massively. Where feasible, Putterman and Weil used modern genetic measures to inform their migration estimates. The result of their effort is that economists now have credible estimates of which fraction of each country's population originally hails from China, sub-Saharan Africa, or Western Europe, and so on. This is particularly useful in the New World but is also important when looking across the modern nations of Southeast Asia.

Putterman and Weil also created estimates of the number of millennia (before 1500) that a nation's residents practiced settled agriculture and created a more complicated index that estimates how much ancestral experience living under organized governments a nation's ancestors had. These "Agricultural History" and "State History" scores predict modern income levels, but they do far better when one adjusts for post-1500 migration. For example, the R^2 of the correlation between migration-*unadjusted* Agriculture and State History scores versus modern log GDP per capita are merely 8% and 6%, respectively. However, the R^2 of the correlation between migration-*adjusted* Agriculture and State History scores versus modern log GDP per capita are 22% and 24%, respectively.

One immediately wonders whether this increase in predictive power is merely driven by the "Neo-Europes" mentioned earlier, and so the authors run two-control regressions that include both a simple migration-adjusted measure and a migration-adjusted measure interacted with a dummy for the Neo-Europes. The Neo-Europes have (statistically significant) *negative* signs, a signal that they're underperforming, though the net migration-adjusted Deep Roots coefficient is still positive. A separate two-control horse race between the migration-adjusted measures and fraction of European descent finds positive coefficients on the European descent coefficient but also finds the coefficients of the original migration-adjusted State and Agricultural History measures little-changed from their original values. The "Deep Roots" result that migration has shaped long-run national productivity is thus not overwhelmingly driven by Europe or by the descendants of Europeans. Many people outside of Europe contribute to the statistical explanatory power of the migration-adjusted Deep Roots literature.

These results document clearly that, as many in the literature have put it at one time or another, the history of peoples matters more for the wealth of nations than the history of places. But Putterman and Weil went further, trying out different Deep Roots measures, indexes of the past, to see how they performed when adjusted for migration. One measure they use stands out: Comin, Easterly and Gong's (2010) Technological History index for the year 1500 AD. Comin et al. had a team of researchers dive into reference works in the history of technology in order to create an index of what fraction of the world's technology each nation was using in the year 1500. Their Technological History index outperformed Putterman and Weil's own indices, with migration unadjusted and adjusted R^2 against modern log GDP per capita of 18% and an exceptionally high 53% [see Figure 8.1].

Going beyond the migration-adjusted Deep Roots as predictors of output per person, James T. Ang (2013) made a thorough investigation of whether these three measures—migration-adjusted State, Agricultural, and Tech history (SAT)—could predict modern institutional quality [see Figure 8.2]. Indeed they did, and in all three cases, the migration-adjusted measures outperformed the migration-unadjusted measures. When it comes to institutional quality, the migration-adjusted past is prologue. This isn't just a generic story of persistence, a story that nothing much changes; it's instead a story of *migration-adjusted* persistence, a story that things are quite likely to change in a land when new people move to that land.

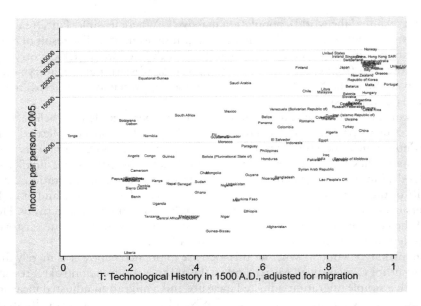

Figure 8.1 Comin, Easterly, Gong (2010) Technological History Score in 1500, Adjusted for Migration vs. GDP per Capita, 2005.

Sources: X-axis is from Comin, Easterly, Gong (2010); the log-scaled Y-axis is from the Penn World Tables. The Pearson correlation is 0.63 in GDP levels; 0.69 when GDP is logged.

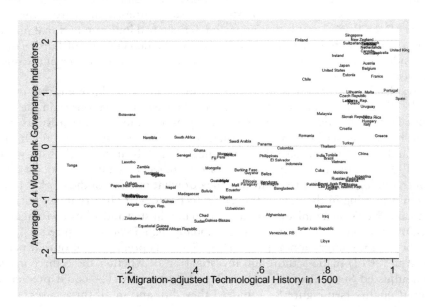

Figure 8.2 Comin, Easterly, Gong (2010) Technological History Score in 1500, Adjusted for Migration vs. World Bank Governance Indicators.

Sources: Comin, Easterly, and Gong (2010); Kaufmann and Kraay (2021). The four averaged governance indicators are Control of Corruption, Rule of Law, Government Effectiveness, and Regulatory Quality. The Pearson correlation is 0.59.

8.4 A Test Case: Southeast Asia[4]

> The Chinese diaspora has ... certain unique cultural characteristics that potentially could be conducive to economic growth.
>
> —*Jan Priebe and Robert Rudolf (2015)*

Across the nations of Southeast Asia, there is a strong relationship between the percentage of a nation that is of Chinese ancestry and current GDP per person; given the relatively low Deep Roots scores in the region before the arrival of Chinese migrants, and given the relatively high Deep Roots scores for China in 1500, the Deep Roots theory would predict that, other things equal, a rise in Chinese migration would raise productivity and institutional quality.

The data are generally consistent with that claim. In Malaysia, 33% of the population was reported to be of Chinese descent in a 2002 study by Rauch and Trinidade; 10% in Thailand, 4% in Indonesia, and 2% in the Philippines. GDP per capita in those four countries is $30,000, $19,000, $12,000, and $9,000 respectively. Singapore, vastly richer per capita than these countries, is estimated to have an ethnically Chinese community that makes up 76% of its population. The well-documented "market-dominant minority" phenomenon is clearly visible across Southeast Asia in the Chinese community. Of course, this doesn't mean that all ethnically Chinese residents are rich or even middle-class, but it does mean, in part, that the nation's large, profitable companies are disproportionately run and owned by families of Chinese descent. On average, there is a positive relationship between the Chinese proportion of a Southeast Asian country's population and conventional measures of institutional quality.

Priebe and Rudolf made a more systematic estimate of the economic role of the Chinese diaspora in their 2015 paper, "Does the Chinese Diaspora Speed Up Economic Growth in Host Countries?" Their question is an important one: "We examine whether countries grow faster if their population comprises a larger share of overseas Chinese." After controlling for geography, starting levels of education, and so on, what do they find? A "country's initial [number of] overseas Chinese is positively related to subsequent growth."

Priebe and Rudolf went further and checked to see how economies with large Chinese migrant populations differed from other statistically similar economies: "The presence of overseas Chinese contributes to a country's participation in international trade, [faster growth in machines, equipment, and factories], and increased ... productivity, which in turn all stimulate growth." The authors, like many who study Southeast Asia, draw on the evidence for cultural differences as well:

> According to some scholars overseas Chinese are characterized by a comparatively strong emphasis on family economic success, including long working hours, thrifty and dynamic family businesses, and a high emphasis on educating the next generation. These cultural traits, if large enough to leave their footprint on a whole society, might have repercussions for ... a country's economy.

So how much do overseas Chinese citizens appear to matter for a nation's economy? Using cross-country data from 1970 to 2010, Priebe and Rudolf find that a 10 percentage point increase in a nation's Chinese share of the population predicts that the nation would grow 0.7% faster per year. Because of compounding, that would mean a nation where

10% of the population had Chinese ancestors would be 10% richer in a decade compared to a similar nation that had zero citizens with Chinese ancestry. And if, hypothetically, these numbers were taken literally, it would mean that China itself should grow 7% faster per year than otherwise similar nations without any Chinese immigrants—countries with the same education level, the fraction that is immigrants, same population density, similar geography, etc. That might sound unrealistically high until you realize that from the death of Mao until 2010, incomes per person in China grew about 8.5% per year according to the World Bank, an astonishingly high rate, especially for such a long period. During that same time, the average income in the typical country grew 2% per year—a 6.5% annual gap—so China's experience isn't that far from what one would predict from Priebe and Rudolf's research.

You might ask yourself whether they found such a strong link because their statistical analysis includes China itself in the average. But it doesn't. The authors intentionally omitted China, Taiwan, Hong Kong, and Macau. This is a study of the Chinese diaspora that includes data from 147 countries but includes only one majority-Chinese country (Singapore), so there's no way for Chinese-majority countries to skew the results. Both casual empiricism and sophisticated cross-country statistical analyses find evidence that the Chinese Diaspora is transplanting the migration-adjusted Deep Roots of prosperity across Southeast Asia.

8.5 Critiques of Culture Transplant Theory

Four prominent writers have critiqued some version of cultural transplant theory: Bryan Caplan (2019; 2022), Alex Nowrasteh (2022), and Clemens and Pritchett (2019). I consider them in turn. Caplan argues that "the biggest flaw" (2019, p. 125) with the Deep Roots literature is that it is ostensibly not robust to population-weighting. Of course, development and growth economists almost never population-weight their samples, in part because economists believe that the actions of governments appear to be central to productivity—nations, not individuals, are the quantitative focus when studying the Wealth of Nations. But consider his statistical critique: Caplan reports that State (S) and Agricultural History (A) Deep Roots scores become small and statistically insignificant predictors of modern GDP per capita when the global sample is population-weighted. That happens largely because the U.S., China, and India are sufficiently big outliers.

But his critique omits Tech History (T), which has long been known to be the most robust of the three SAT scores. Since T proxies 1500 AD technology, while S and A each measure outcomes going back thousands of years, it's unsurprising that T does the best job predicting modern GDP per capita: it's the most recent measure of the three. In any case, when one runs simple population-weighted cross-country regressions of current log GDP per capita on the Tech history measure (T in the SAT score), T is once again a statistically significant predictor of prosperity with a large coefficient (Jones, 2023). Further, running conventional growth regressions rather than level regressions makes all three of S, A, and T statistically significant with sizable coefficients even when population-weighted: China and India may be Deep Roots outliers to some degree, but both are growing quickly, and neither are substantial outliers when it comes to Tech History.

Nowrasteh's critique of cultural transplant theory focuses on a critique of the trust literature. He makes two notable assertions: the first is a claim that the evidence for the multigenerational migration of trust attitudes is fragile, and perhaps an artifact of the WVS wave that Algan and Cahuc used. We've already seen that's not true, and we've seen that the migration-of-trust result has been replicated with intra-European migration data as well. A second claim is that, as Nowrasteh (2022) alleges:

> [R]esponses to the trust question generally don't predict trusting behavior in real-world micro-level experiments, trust games, or investment games (Algan and Cahuc, 2013…)

Nowrasteh includes many citations beyond this Algan and Cahuc citation, all to support his assertion about that the survey trust question doesn't predict experimental behavior, but that is the first paper he lists. However, consider this quote from the very Algan and Cahuc (2013) essay in *Annual Reviews* that Nowrasteh is referring to:

> But it is worth noting that there is a strong correlation between trust as declared in surveys and levels of cooperation and reciprocity observed in laboratory experiments.

This citation from Nowrasteh thus does not support his claim about the views of Algan and Cahuc. More importantly, as we've seen, the scholarly literature routinely (but not universally) finds an experimental relationship between the survey measure of generalized trust and *either* trusting or trustworthy behavior in experiments, so responses to the trust question appear to be a reasonable proxy for social capital.

Clemens and Pritchett (2019) agree that "[c]ulture and norms have been shown to be transmissible by migrants," and cite key papers in the area. However, they argue that the connection from culture and norms to institutions and productivity is too hazy to build a case for immigration restrictions upon. They do not discuss the Deep Roots evidence for a link between migration and institutional quality (Ang, 2013; Putterman and Weil, 2010), nor do they consider the possible role of the median voter theorem (Caplan 2007) or the lessons one could draw from the Great Migration of African Americans from the South to the North. They thus turn to a model that assumes that there is no permanent effect of migration on institutions or productivity, whether positive or negative.

In their model, they assume that migrants come from a country with a different productivity level than that prevailing in the destination country, and they assume that when migrants arrive, they start off with their old, different productivity level. But Clemens and Pritchett assume full productivity assimilation of those migrants in the long run (at a constant rate a per year, $0 < a < 1$). Their assumption stands in contrast to the real-world experiences of, *inter alia*, Chinese migrants across Southeast Asia, who on average have not assimilated to the productivity norms of their fellow citizens in countries like Indonesia, Thailand, and Malaysia. It's also in at least severe tension with James T. Ang's findings that migration-adjusted Deep Roots measures predict institutional quality better than migration-unadjusted measures. Full long-run productivity assimilation is a difficult assumption to maintain in light of existing evidence, and it erases the experience of Chinese migrants. I hope that future work on the effects of migration on productivity can take into account the cross-country, multi-generational persistence of success, on average, among the Chinese diaspora across Southeast Asia.

8.6 Conclusion and Future Work

The cultural transplant literature focuses on the multi-generational effects of migration on the destination country's institutions and productivity. The attitude migration literature finds that savings and labor market behaviors, views on the proper role of government, and views toward trust all persist to a notable degree until at least the second generation and often beyond. Future work, perhaps using more accurate genetic or archival proxies for ancestry rather than mere survey questions, will, one hopes, be able to more accurately document the blend of cultural persistence and two-way assimilation surely occurs in the real world.

Future work can also document how and to what extent multi-generational migrants, once assimilated into the political systems of their new homes, shape future economic policies. Is the median voter theorem the most important mechanism? Is political representation by the children and grandchildren of migrants an important channel for shaping institutions? Do leaders in non-democracies respond less than leaders of democracies to the migration-induced shifts in citizen preferences? If so, how much less? Do non-citizens or temporary migrants have negligible effects on institutions and total factor productivity in all, most, or some cases? Again, what mechanisms create these outcomes?

Putterman and Weil's 2010 migration matrix can also be updated with the latest information, including more recent genetic data on ancestry. Above all, I hope that the people of the Chinese diaspora, with their example of large-scale, overwhelmingly peaceful migration that appears to have increased total factor productivity and institutional quality across Southeast Asia over the last two centuries, will receive scholarly attention from economists that they deserve.

Cultural transplant theory suggests that there is likely to be a global tradeoff between helping the world's poor by massively opening up migration to rich countries versus helping the world's poor by treating those same rich countries—particularly the highly innovative I-7—as our planet's great research facility. If an I-7 nation chose a migration policy that substantially lowered its Tech History score or its tendencies toward frugality, trust, or trustworthiness, that could jeopardize national productivity in that country. Such a policy could also potentially impose costs on the entire planet for generations to come. As I show in *The Culture Transplant*, a nation's research efforts are highly sensitive to its institutional quality, so any policy reform that reduces that nation's government quality would jeopardize the entire planet's growth rate of scientific and engineering excellence. Further research, of course, is needed to understand how likely such an outcome is and whether skill-based or points-based immigration policies in the I-7 could overcome the risks to long-run global productivity growth documented by cultural transplant research.

It is premature to offer concrete policy recommendations, but consider this proposal: for countries that use points-based migration systems, like Canada, Australia, New Zealand, or Japan, governments could give a small positive weight to applicants from countries where the non-natural resource GDP per capita or national savings rate is higher. This would slightly encourage migration from countries where people tend to have better government quality, higher rates of thrift, and a greater ability to cooperate productively on large, complex tasks. If even a small portion of those traits are imported into the I-7, then those new migrants can offer a gift to their new homelands that may well persist across the generations.

This short essay has necessarily omitted much relevant literature—my omissions of Collier (2013) and Borjas (2015) are especially regrettable—but I close with a quote from Putterman and Weil (2010). Looking across multiple Deep Roots measures of past proxies for productivity, and checking to see how those proxies predict modern GDP per capita, they report their finding, which has been replicated in many forms many times since:

> The most notable finding of the table is that, as expected, adjusting for migration substantially improves the predictive power of any of the alternative measures of early development that we consider.

Past is prologue—a statement that, as Putterman and Weil found, is particularly true when one adjusts for migration.

Notes

1 Since this attempt to hold "other things equal" in empirical comparisons is so common in empirical research and so difficult to do properly, let's discuss this particular example: when comparing across survey respondents who had the same age and gender as each other, those whose parents came from moderately thriftier countries typically saved 1.6 percentage points more of their income compared to those whose parents came from less thrifty countries. But if instead of making that simple comparison, one instead compared people with not only the same age and gender, but also those with similar incomes, similar employment status, similar education levels, and so on, then those with parents from thriftier countries typically saved only 0.8 percentage points more of their income.

If we wanted to know whether second generation migrants from thrifty countries are higher savers, which is the better comparison? The first estimate, the 1.6 percentage point effect. Why? In part, because it's comparing two features that are extremely unlikely to be affected, either directly or indirectly, by the level of thriftiness in the country of origin—just age and gender. The second, bulkier comparison looks at savings differences between people who are also similar in income, employment, and education—traits that are themselves plausibly influenced by the thriftiness of the culture one's grandparents were raised in.

We want to know what "the typical migrant whose parents came from France" is like, not what "the typical migrant whose parents came from France and who earns just as much as the average immigrant whose parents came from the USA" is like. That extra "control," that extra attempt to "hold other things equal" ends up bringing a quite unrepresentative hypothetical person into our comparison, and that hypothetical person probably has a different and quite uninteresting savings rate than the first person we were looking at.

There is a broader lesson here: this problem of possible overcontrol bias [trying to hold the "wrong things equal"] in multivariate regressions is real, and it's important not to presume that more controls are better, as Julia Rohrer (2018) has recently emphasized.

2 This subsection draws language verbatim from *The Culture Transplant* (2022).
3 Correlation coefficients are the square root of the R^2 of a bivariate regression as well as the regression coefficient from *any* bivariate regression where both left- and right-hand side variables have been transformed to have mean zero and standard deviation of unity. Since R^2 is the "percent of variance explained," and variance is itself a sum of *squared* differences across the observations on the left-hand side, then it is both natural and wise to interpret the correlation coefficient, R, as the percent of differences in the Y (left-hand side) variable that can be predicted by the X (right-hand side) variable. For estimates that aren't driven by outliers, R is usually quite close to the sum of absolute deviations in the Y variable that can be predicted solely by deviations in the X variable.
4 This subsection draws language directly from *The Culture Transplant* (2022).

References

Acemoglu, Daron. "Why not a political Coase theorem? Social conflict, commitment, and politics." *Journal of Comparative Economics* 31, no. 4 (2003): 620–652.

Acemoglu, Daron, Simon Johnson, and James A. Robinson. "The colonial origins of comparative development: An empirical investigation." *American Economic Review* 91, no. 5 (2001): 1369–1401.

Alesina, Alberto, Yann Algan, Pierre Cahuc, and Paola Giuliano. "Family values and the regulation of labor." *Journal of the European Economic Association* 13, no. 4 (2015): 599–630.

Alesina, Alberto, and Paola Giuliano. "Culture and Institutions." *Journal of Economic Literature* 53, no. 4 (2015): 898–944.

Algan, Yann, and Pierre Cahuc. "Inherited trust and growth." *American Economic Review* 100, no. 5 (2010): 2060–2092.

Algan, Yann, and Pierre Cahuc. "Trust and growth." *Annual Reviews of Economics* 5, no. 1 (2013): 521–549.

Ang, James B. "Institutions and the long-run impact of early development." *Journal of Development Economics* 105 (2013): 1–18.
Antecol, Heather. "An examination of cross-country differences in the gender gap in labor force participation rates." *Labour Economics* 7, no. 4 (2000): 409–426.
Berg, Joyce, John Dickhaut, and Kevin McCabe. "Trust, reciprocity, and social history." *Games and Economic Behavior* 10, no. 1 (1995): 122–142.
Borjas, George J. "The Economics of Immigration." *Journal of Economic Literature* 32, no. 4 (1994): 1667–1717.
Borjas, George J. "The Labor Demand Curve is Downward Sloping: Reexamining the impact of immigration on the labor market." *Quarterly Journal of Economics* 118, no. 4 (2003): 1335–1374.
Borjas, George J. "Immigration and globalization: A review essay." *Journal of Economic Literature* 53, no. 4 (2015): 961–974.
Borrell-Porta, Mireia, Joan Costa-Font, and Azusa Sato. "Changing Culture to Change Society?" In *Social Economics: Current and Emerging Avenues*, edited by Joan Costa-Font and Mario Macis. Cambridge, MA: MIT Press, 2017.
Calderon, Alvaro, Vasiliki Fouka, and Marco Tabellini. "Racial diversity and racial policy preferences: The great migration and civil rights." *Review of Economic Studies* 90, no. 1 (2023): 165–200.
Caplan, Bryan. *The Myth of the Rational Voter: Why Democracies Choose Bad Policies*. Princeton University Press, 2007.
Caplan, Bryan. *Open borders: The science and ethics of immigration*. First Second, 2019.
Caplan, Bryan. "The Case for 50 Percent Open Borders." *Reason*. November 15, 2022.
Capra, C. Mónica, Kelli Lanier, and Shireen Meer. "Attitudinal and behavioral measures of trust: A new comparison." SSRN Working Paper, 2008.
Chua, Amy. *World on fire: How exporting free market democracy breeds ethnic hatred and global instability*. Anchor, 2004.
Clemens, Michael A. "Economics and emigration: Trillion-dollar bills on the sidewalk?" *Journal of Economic Perspectives* 25, no. 3 (2011): 83–106.
Clemens, Michael A., and Lant Pritchett. "The new economic case for migration restrictions: an assessment." *Journal of Development Economics* 138 (2019): 153–164.
Collier, Paul. *Exodus: How Migration Is Changing Our World*. Oxford: Oxford University Press, 2013.
Comin, Diego, William Easterly, and Erick Gong. "Was the wealth of nations determined in 1000 BC?" *American Economic Journal: Macroeconomics* 2, no. 3 (2010): 65–97.
Costa-Font, Joan, Paola Giuliano, and Berkay Ozcan. "The cultural origin of saving behavior." *PloS one* 13, no. 9 (2018): e0202290.
Doepke, Matthias, Michele Tertilt, and Alessandra Voena. "The economics and politics of women's rights." *Annu. Rev. Econ.* 4, no. 1 (2012): 339–372.
Durbin, James. "Errors in variables." *Revue de l'institut International de Statistique* (1954): 23–32.
Fehr, Ernst, Urs Fischbacher, Bernhard von Rosenblatt, Jürgen Schupp, and Gert G. Wagner. "A Nation-Wide Laboratory: Examining Trust and Trustworthiness by Integrating Behavioral Experiments into Representative Surveys." Working Paper (2003).
Fernández, Raquel. "Does culture matter?" *Handbook of Social Economics* 1 (2011): 481–510.
Fuchs-Schündeln, Nicola, Paolo Masella, and Hannah Paule-Paludkiewicz. "Cultural determinants of household saving behavior." *Journal of Money, Credit and Banking* 52, no. 5 (2020): 1035–1070.
Gale, William G. "Flat Tax Impact on Saving and the Economy," Brookings Institution, February 19, 1996.
Giavazzi, Francesco, Ivan Petkov, and Fabio Schiantarelli. "Culture: Persistence and Evolution." *Journal of Economic Growth* 24 (2019): 117–154.
Glaeser, Edward L., David I. Laibson, Jose A. Scheinkman, and Christine L. Soutter. "Measuring trust." *Quarterly Journal of Economics* 115, no. 3 (2000): 811–846.
Ho, Benjamin. *Why Trust Matters: An Economist's Guide to the Ties That Bind Us*. Columbia University Press, 2021.
Johansson-Stenman, Olof, Minhaj Mahmud, and Peter Martinsson. "Trust, trust games and stated trust: Evidence from rural Bangladesh." *Journal of Economic Behavior & Organization* 95 (2013): 286–298.

Johnson, Noel D., and Alexandra A. Mislin. "Trust games: A meta-analysis." *Journal of Economic Psychology* 32, no. 5 (2011): 865–889.

Johnson, Noel D., and Alexandra Mislin. "How much should we trust the World Values Survey trust question?" *Economics Letters* 116, no. 2 (2012): 210–212.

Jones, Garett. *The Culture Transplant*. Stanford, CA: Stanford University Press, 2022.

Jones, Garett. "China Grew Fast and other Econometric Critiques of *Open Borders: The Science and Ethics of Immigration*." Working paper, 2023.

Karlan, Dean S. "Using experimental economics to measure social capital and predict financial decisions." *American Economic Review* 95, no. 5 (2005): 1688–1699.

Kaufmann, Daniel, and Aart Kraay. *Worldwide Governance Indicators*. Washington, DC: World Bank, 2021.

Lott, Jr, John R., and Lawrence W. Kenny. "Did women's suffrage change the size and scope of government?" *Journal of Political Economy* 107, no. 6 (1999): 1163–1198.

McCloskey, Deirdre Nansen, and Steve Ziliak. *The Cult of Statistical Significance: How the Standard Error Costs us Jobs, Justice, and Lives*. University of Michigan Press, 2010.

Müller, Daniel, Benno Torgler, and Eric Uslaner. "A comment on 'Inherited trust and growth'." *Economics Bulletin* 32, no. 2 (2012): 1481–1488.

Nowrasteh, Alex. "Review of The Culture Transplant, Part I." *Deep Dives*, (2022), https://anowrasteh.substack.com/p/review-of-the-culture-transplant

Olson, Mancur. "Dictatorship, Democracy, and Development." *American Political Science Review* 87, no. 3 (1993): 567–576.

Ostrom, Elinor. "Collective Action and the Evolution of Social Norms." *Journal of Economic Perspectives* 14, no. 3 (2000): 137–158.

Priebe, Jan, and Robert Rudolf. "Does the Chinese diaspora speed up growth in host countries?" *World Development* 76 (2015): 249–262.

Putterman, Louis, and David N. Weil. "Post-1500 population flows and the long-run determinants of economic growth and inequality." *Quarterly Journal of Economics* 125, no. 4 (2010): 1627–1682.

Rauch, James E., and Vitor Trindade. "Ethnic Chinese networks in international trade." *Review of Economics and Statistics* 84, no. 1 (2002): 116–130.

Rohrer, Julia M. "Thinking clearly about correlations and causation: Graphical causal models for observational data." Advances in methods and practices in psychological science 1, no. 1 (2018): 27–42.

Thöni, Christian. "Trust and Cooperation: Survey Evidence and Behavioral Experiments," in *Social Dilemmas: New Perspectives on Trust*, Paul AM Van Lange, Bettina Rockenbach, and Toshio Yamagishi, eds. Oxford University Press, 2017.

Wilson, Rick K. "Trust experiments, trust games, and surveys." *Oxford Handbook of Social and Political Trust*, E. M. Uslaner ed., (2018): 279–304.

9
LANGUAGE AS A CRITERION OF IMMIGRANT SELECTION

Daniel M. Weinstock

9.1 Introduction

I want in this paper to explore the ethical issues involved in the use of language as a criterion of immigrant selection. I will be asking the question: under what circumstances, if any, is it acceptable for a country to admit immigrants on the basis of their capacity to speak the language of the receiving society? I will proceed as follows. First, I will engage in some conceptual ground clearing aimed at elucidating the notion of *discretionary immigration*, that is, immigration that is not in fulfilment of a country's obligations with respect to migration, most notably its obligations to admit legitimate refugees and asylum claimants. I will show that to the extent that we admit of the possibility for a country to engage in discretionary immigration, this does not imply that it can deploy just *any* criteria in selecting immigrants. Discretionary immigration places us in a decision space in which countries *may* deploy certain criteria in selecting immigrants (or not select any immigrants at all), but this does not mean that there are not certain criteria that it is disallowed from deploying. Second, I will discuss the question of whether *linguistic competence*, in a sense that I will define below, falls within the range of morally permissible criteria. I will suggest that linguistic competence may not be as clearly permissible as may seem at first glance, a fact that becomes apparent once we distinguish criteria relevant to *admission*, and those that are relevant to *integration*. Third, and finally, I will suggest some conditions that might make it permissible for some societies (but not others) to select for immigration on the basis of linguistic competence. The conditions have to do with the linguistic vulnerability that some linguistic majorities find themselves in, which might require that they erect bulwarks not available to other societies against internal threats to linguistic assimilation.

9.2 Discretionary Immigration Policy and Its Limits

For the purposes of the present paper, I will assume, *arguendo*, that countries have the right to exercise some control over their borders, in the sense that it is permissible for them to engage in the selection of new members.[1] In other words, I will assume for present purposes the falsity of the "open borders" thesis. Note, however, that to deny the open borders thesis is not to affirm an unlimited prerogative on the part of states to select whomever they want. Most obviously, all states have a moral responsibility to take in a number of refugee claimants that are compatible with their receiving capacity (Owen 2020). They also have obligations of family reunification. Given the number of people in the world who meet relevant criteria for admissibility as refugees (a number that is set to increase with the explosion in the number of climate refugees (Lister 2014)), it is possible that discretionary immigration is a purely *theoretical* possibility.

Once a country has met its moral obligations with respect to migration, it may, though it need not, take in immigration claimants that it is not required to take in. It may in other words engage in *discretionary immigration*.

Now, to say that a country can take in immigration claimants that it is not morally required to take in does not mean that it can exercise an unrestricted prerogative in this domain (Carens 2003, Carens 2013). There may be some criteria that it would be morally noxious for it to employ in exercising its discretion. Societies of immigration such as Australia and Canada used to privilege white immigration, a practice that is now universally seen as morally condemnable. Though some may still argue that it is acceptable for "Judeo-Christian" countries to select on the basis of religion, it seems fairly plain that this is a veiled way to engage in Islamophobic immigration practices.[2]

On the other hand, some criteria seem morally unobjectionable, though they may not be morally admirable. For example, countries often use immigration as an economic tool. Most uncontroversially, at least on the face of it, immigration is sometimes used as a way of filling gaps in a country's labour market. If Canada has a shortfall of optometrists, it seems acceptable, all things being equal, for it to favour immigrants who have the requisite professional qualifications. Now, all things are not always equal, and it seems clear that in using immigration as a way of filling labour market gaps it must avoid engaging in "brain drain", that is in recruitment that depletes less advantaged countries of essential human resources (Brock and Blake 2014). But once these side constraints on the exercise of the prerogative to select immigrants have been satisfied, it does not seem morally abhorrent to use labour market considerations to exercise a country's morally permissible discretion with respect to migration.

More controversial might be the willingness of prospective migrants to make significant financial investments in the country to which they purport to migrate (Shachar and Hirshl 2014). On the one hand, there seems something crass in allowing some people to buy themselves into citizenship in a country. On the other hand, it is possible that part of our intuitive moral objections to this practice stems from the assumption that rich potential investors are being preferred to applicants who should be admitted on humanitarian grounds. While this may be true in the real world, we are operating here on the assumption that countries have fulfilled their moral obligations with respect to refugee claimants, asylum seekers, and candidates for family reunification. In such a context, admitting immigrants who are capable of making a significant financial investment in the prospective country of immigration seems less morally problematic.

Why is it morally objectionable for countries to use race and religion as criteria to fill the discretionary portion of their overall intake of immigrants? To ask the question in a philosophically more perspicuous manner: can the wrongness of selecting on the basis of race or religion be identified in a manner that would allow us to pick out other morally condemnable criteria as well? Racism is wrong because it is, well, racist. While this is importantly true, and while it is important for us to be able to say that racism is wrong irreducibly, there may be other things that are wrong with racist or religiously intolerant grounds of selection that do allow for the kind of generalization we are looking for. Is there some kind of underlying moral consideration that allows to pick out religion and race as an inadmissible criterion, and that could also help us to identify *other* excluded criteria?

The problem with finding a moral principle that might allow us to distinguish between morally admissible and inadmissible principles of selection is that once we have accepted a morally acceptable category of discretionary immigration, we are in so doing accepting that host countries can admit immigrants on self-serving grounds. And on an intuitive conception of what morality requires, self-servingness and morality are at odds with one another. But this would be to take too limited a conception of how morality affects our reasoning, both as individuals and as collective entities. Moral considerations provide us with grounds for taking up certain ends, but it also indicates side-constraints that should be observed in the pursuit of ends not themselves required by morality. We have already suggested in the context of this short discussion that discretionary immigration is impermissible in the case of states that have not fully satisfied their obligations with respect to those persons who cannot reasonably be expected to remain in their country of residence, because, for example, of war, persecution, or environmental collapse.

But I would suggest that those who are able to exercise coercion and the denial of resources on others through border control (Abizadeh 2008) owe each other a certain kind of moral justification (Forst 2014). Though I clearly do not have enough space to do anything more than gesture towards the kind of justification that I think is required, let me at least suggest the following. I would argue that the justifications offered for various selection principles must meet two conditions. First, it must be sincerely expressed. That is, the grounds that are actually operative in selecting immigrants must be the ones actually stated. Hypocrisy, it is said, is the tribute that vice pays to virtue. It could be that certain grounds may simply not be publicly affirmable on the part of agents who are concerned with their moral standing among peers. Second, it must be morally intelligible to those to whom it is addressed, and in particular, to those who are excluded by the operation of the principle in question. It would clearly be too much to ask that those who are rejected as claimants *agree* with the principle on the basis of which they have been rejected. But they must be able to recognize these principles as valid prudential principles, that is, as principles that validly structure a polity's pursuit of its own good (Cf. Miller 2016).

It seems quite clear that racist and religiously intolerant grounds could not pass this rough and ready test. On the other hand, it also seems that the kind of criteria I adduced above, economic and labour market considerations, could be presented as admissible grounds of collective prudence.

9.3 Is Language an Admissible Criterion?

How does language fare with respect to the criterion I have briefly suggested above? *Prima facie*, it would seem to pass muster. There are solid prudential reasons for states to want its citizens to share a public language. A shared language allows people to work together, and to achieve a degree of mobility within the country that they hope to live in. It allows them to deliberate democratically over the important issues about which they will have to make collective decisions. It allows governments to communicate efficiently with their citizens about the myriad range of issues about which they legitimately want to be able to communicate. It would seem, therefore, that language is a perfectly acceptable criterion on the basis of which to choose putative immigrants within the discretionary segment of a country's overall intake.

Things may not, however, be as simple as I have made them seem in the foregoing paragraph. For there seem to be alternatives to requiring prior language proficiency as a condition of admission. Consider: a state that takes in immigrants has control over the educational system that is in place on its territory. It can therefore require of immigrants that they send their children to school in the public language. It can, in other words, integrate future members in such a way that their children reach a high level of fluency by adolescence. As for adult immigrants themselves, states possess a wide range of ways in which to incentivize them to learn the public language of the country to which they are immigrating quite quickly. They can, for example, impose intensive language training upon them upon arrival, as Israel does with its "ulpan" system, and make the receipt of certain benefits conditional upon linguistic proficiency. For example, Flanders has a policy that makes eligibility for social housing conditional in this way,[3] and the Canadian province of Quebec has recently passed legislation that requires that immigrants be able to receive social services in French no more than 6 months after their arrival. These policies, and others like them, are instantiations of the prescription that Philippe Van Parijs has put forward to linguistic groups aiming to secure their languages in the face of myriad assimilative regional and global pressures, including immigration, namely, that they should "grab a territory" and enact legislation upon it aimed at offsetting these pressures (Van Parijs 2011). Now, as I have argued elsewhere (Weinstock 2015), some of these measures may be objectionable on broad liberal-democratic grounds (Weinstock 2015). The limited point I want to make here is that states have tools at their disposal to facilitate the linguistic integration of immigrants.

Given these facts about the linguistic control that states can have over prospective immigrants, the preference for candidates for immigration who already speak the public language in question starts looking more ethically problematic. Consider two prospective immigrants, Alex and Brenda, who are similar in all respects in terms of their attractiveness as immigrants. The only salient difference is that Alex speaks the public language of the polity to which he purports to move, whereas Brenda does not, though, as a candidate for immigration, she is aware of the fact that upon arrival she will be subjected to a host of incentives and constraints that will make it the case that she (and presumably her children) will gain proficiency in the language in short order.

What could justify a systematic preference for applicants like Alex, as opposed to ones that resemble Brenda? After all, the legitimate reasons that states have to ensure that as many of its citizens as possible, and ideally all of them, speak the public language have to do with conditions on *integration* rather than on *admission*. In virtue of the multiple dimensions of public communication that we have pointed to above, it might even make sense to speak of a moral *obligation* on the part of those who purport to be admitted to full membership in the society in question that they learn the *lingua franca*, which will most often be the language of the majority (Hoesch 2022). But on the face of it, the need for linguistic integration does not tell in a clear manner between those who are already speakers of the language in question and those who will be made to acquire it as a condition of admission to full membership.

If this is the case, returning to our earlier discussion of the criteria that can legitimately be invoked by host societies in selecting immigrants, it seems that insisting upon prior language competence violates the principle distinguishing between permissible and impermissible criteria. Absent very special circumstances, it is not beyond the ability of any prospective immigrant to learn the language of the society to which they plan to move. The conditions of linguistic integration can thus be met equally well by prior speakers and by prospective speakers. Preference for prior speakers thus falls foul of the principle according to which the coercion that border control exerts upon individuals should be based on criteria the relevance of which they could reasonably accept. Consider Brenda. It is hard to think of any way that she could be addressed by the society that has rejected her as a prospective new member on the basis of linguistic considerations that would not end up treating her in a manner that violated the principles of public justification briefly described above. "We know that you and your children could learn our language to a high level of proficiency", we can imagine an immigration official saying to Brenda, "and that you could therefore meet the conditions of linguistic integration just as well as Alex, but we nonetheless prefer to admit Alex because of his prior proficiency". Brenda could justly respond that there is no reason, relative to the purposes that the possession of a common public language serves, to prefer Alex over her.

An obvious answer on the part of my hypothetical immigration official adjudicating between Alex and Brenda would be to claim that there is a way of distinguishing between them that does speak to the ability of the society in question to function linguistically. This answer would be to the effect that it would be costless to integrate Alex into the public language, whereas the linguistic integration of Brenda would involve costs that, *ex hypothesi*, could be avoided.

This response would not be convincing. Indeed, the children of immigrants are typically integrated linguistically by attending a society's schools. This involves costs that are, as it were, already on the ledger. What's more, language training could be a net economic benefit, to the extent that it creates employment. Funds invested in language training are typically returned into the economy through the greater purchasing power afforded to those tasked with the linguistic integration of immigrants. Investment in language training can thus be seen, in broadly Keynesian spirit, as part and parcel of the state's responsibility to create jobs and to stimulate the economy. Finally, those prospective immigrants who possess fluency in another language or languages upon arrival increase the overall linguistic capacity of the society that they aspire to become members of, and thereby confer an economic benefit upon the society that would likely offset any costs involved in language training.

Despite initial appearances, therefore, there is something morally problematic, at least at first glance, with using prior language competence as a criterion for the selection of immigrants. Those who possess such prior competence should obviously not be penalized because of their language skills, but to the extent that prospective immigrants can all acquire the public language of the society to which they hope to be admitted, there seems to be no reason to prefer prior competence that does not fall foul of the principle distinguishing morally permissible from morally impermissible criteria for immigrant selection that we have established above. If the hypothetical state we are considering can admit either Alex or Brenda, but not both, maybe the fairest choice procedure is to flip a coin.

9.4 The Case of Vulnerable Languages

Are there any circumstances under which the previous conclusion does not obtain? Do certain host societies present features that make it the case that it would be morally allowable to use prior competence in the public language as a criterion for selection? I want in this final section to suggest that there are. Prior language competence can be used when the public language of the receiving society is *vulnerable*.

The public languages of some host societies are subject to political and sociolinguistic forces that exercise considerable assimilative pressure upon them. Consider the cases of French in the Canadian province of Quebec, or of Flemish in Flanders, of Catalan in Spain, Breton in France, or of Welsh in the United Kingdom. These languages exist in politically and sociolinguistically highly unfavourable circumstances. First, they are spoken in polities that encompass minority nations that, in many cases, possess considerable powers of self-government within federal or quasi-federal structures (including, in some cases such as Quebec's, powers over immigration), but which are nonetheless subject to political decisions taken by majorities in the larger states to which they belong. Even when these majorities evince "benign neglect" towards minority nations rather than outright hostility, these political decisions rarely take the conditions that would sustain minority languages and cultures into account (Kymlicka 1995).

Second, the languages with which these linguistically distinct minority nations coexist within plurilingual and multinational political contexts are more powerful in at least three ways. First, and most obviously, they are spoken by more people. Second, in virtue of the fact that they are majority languages, they tend to dominate the larger polity's main institutions – political, economic, cultural, and academic. Third, in many cases, they are not just dominant in the larger polity, but regionally, and sometimes even globally. This is especially true of those minority nations that coexist with an English majority, as English has achieved the status of a global *lingua franca*.

The combination of these factors makes it the case that the languages in question have to face the assimilative pressure exercised upon them by nationally, regionally, or globally more "attractive" languages (Weinstock 2020). Sociolinguists have shown that, all things equal, there is a tendency for people to choose languages that allow them to access broader linguistic networks, as this increases the range of people with whom they can come into contact in order to form commercial, cultural, intellectual, and even romantic links. Left to their own devices, people will tend to make linguistic decisions in the direction of the larger, and therefore more powerful languages, both with respect to macro-level decisions (what language will they educate their children in?) and in micro-level contexts (what language should be spoken during a particular gathering?). Asymmetrical bilingualism is therefore dangerous for smaller languages, in that there is always an incentive for immigrants to go towards the larger, and therefore more communicatively effective, language. What's more, this pressure is felt by speakers of the smaller language themselves, who may be tempted to defect to the larger language (for example, in the education of their children) in order to provide themselves and their children with broader ranges of opportunities of all kinds (Laponce 1974).

In such sets of circumstances, speakers of the smaller language find themselves in a collective action problem. Let's assume that they would rather, all things equal, be able to continue to live in their own language. That is, they would rather that their language be the public language of their national territory. All things are, however, not always equal. Indeed, their preference might quite rationally be conditional upon a sufficient number of their fellows also choosing to conduct their affairs in the smaller language. If this condition is not fulfilled, then the language in question ceases to be a viable vehicle for them, and for their children. And thus, the pressure to defect to the larger language exists even among those for whom the smaller language is a mother tongue. It is in this sense that some languages are *vulnerable*. Powerful incentives exist for immigrants, but also for native speakers, to defect from it (Patten 2019).

The examples of linguistic vulnerability that I have thus far adduced concern a small but not insignificant set of cases, those of minority nations whose linguistic fate is at least in part due to the fact that they do not possess full sovereignty, but rather share political institutions with the members of a larger linguistic group. But it is at least arguable that the linguistic vulnerability that I have just described characterizes language groups that do possess their own sovereign state. The linguistic globalization which has in large measure placed English in the position of global *lingua franca* has modified the linguistic behaviour of important actors within sovereign states as well. To cite but one example, English is now commonly used as the language of academic interchange in a wide set of countries, where academic institutions have reached the conclusion that it was in the interest of individual researchers but also of academic institutions as a whole that the results of their research be made available to the scholarly community in the language that allows these results to have the broadest influence, namely, English. A similar story could be told across a wide range of central areas of human endeavour. Increasingly, globalization makes it the case that statehood does not represent an impregnable bulwark against linguistic erosion (Da Silva and Weinstock 2022).

The societies whose languages are vulnerable in the manner just described thus face a pair of apparently legitimate linguistic objectives. The first is shared with all societies, namely, the possession by all citizens of a *lingua franca* facilitating democratic deliberation, commercial and economic interaction, and political communication. Obviously, the attainment of this objective is threatened by linguistic erosion resulting from the operation of the sociolinguistic and political forces that have just been described.

The second objective is that these linguistic activities be carried out not just in *any* language, but in *their* language. For this to occur, the collective action problem that these forces place smaller language groups in needs to be addressed through appropriate policies. As we have seen, some of these policies are moderately coercive in nature. They involve requiring that the instruction of children be carried out in the language that needs to be protected, requiring of businesses at least of a certain size that they carry out their internal communications in the language in question. They make the receipt of certain benefits, including citizenship status, conditional upon a sufficient mastery of the language. And so on.

Arguably, however, the stability of a vulnerable language cannot rely entirely upon coercive measures. Clearly, measures aimed at erecting bulwarks against linguistic erosion are only justifiable, if they are, to the extent that the speakers of the language in question actually want to continue using their language in public settings. This will typically be the case to the extent that language constitutes part of the *identity* of those speakers. For them, threats to language are considered not only, and perhaps not even principally as instrumental, cost-benefit matters, but as going to the very core of who they are. They may thus be inclined to accept a certain degree of disadvantage relative to the kinds of benefits that might accrue to them by being full participants in larger language networks. To the extent that they experience this identity link with their language, they will support self-binding measures that prevent them from fully accessing these networks to the extent that they may under certain circumstances be tempted to.

Other factors may contribute to speakers of a vulnerable language being at least to some degree immune from the full force of the collective action problem that was described above. For example, speakers of a vulnerable language may, aside from the identity stake just mentioned, have slightly lesser fluency in the larger language that poses a sociolinguistic threat. If this is the case, they may not view it as a fully adequate vehicle with which to engage in (commercial, academic, interpersonal) linguistic exchange. Speaking in game-theoretical terms, they may not be as inclined to defect from the collaborative option that the choice of their mother tongue represents as they might be if they were to have equal fluency in both languages.

Thus, though smaller languages of the kind that we have been concerned with in this essay are rendered vulnerable by their coexistence with larger, more sociolinguistically powerful language, their vulnerability can be offset at least to some degree not just by mildly coercive legislation, but also by the motivational support that comes from the identity stake that speakers of the vulnerable language have in the survival of the language, and also by the instrumental preference that they might have for it to the degree that they are more fluent in it than they are in the larger and all things equal more powerful language with which they coexist.

This somewhat long exposition hopefully makes clear the contribution that immigration can make to stabilizing a vulnerable language. In a context of vulnerability such as I have described, it might make sense to select immigrants who share the profile that I have just ascribed to domestic native speakers of the language. That is, it might make sense to recruit immigrants who have an identity stake in the language, and who therefore are more likely to freely make use of it in public settings, and to support mildly coercive legislation one of the principal aims of which is to take the non-cooperative option off the table for native speakers who may be tempted to defect if not provided with the assurance that others will also behave linguistically so as to maintain the status of the language as a viable public language. These immigrants with prior competence in the language are also statistically more likely to find the language in question to be a more adequate vehicle for communication given greater fluency in it.

It is on the other hand plausible to suppose that immigrants who are not prior speakers of the vulnerable language will have less of an identity stake in it, and may be inclined to regard questions of language choice from a more instrumental point of view. To the extent that they are fluent speakers of the larger language, it will also likely be the case that they will often find it to be a more convenient and efficient vehicle for linguistic exchange.

Note moreover that the "message" that would be sent out to prospective immigrants who were disfavoured for admission relative to immigrants with other language profiles would not be the same as that which would be manifested in circumstances in which linguistic vulnerability was not an issue. In the case we are presently considering, there is an avowable purpose served by the selection of speakers with prior competence that does not obtain in the case of host societies whose language is not vulnerable in the manner that we have been describing. The question that we imagined Brenda putting to a hypothetical immigration official would now have a publicly affirmable answer: it is possible that, as a speaker with prior competence, Alex's membership will offset the vulnerability that characterizes the state's public language more effectively than Brenda's would.

9.5 Conclusion

The moral dimensions of public policy questions constitute complex webs. Attempting to answer certain moral questions sometimes requires that other questions be set aside for the sake of argument. Not all questions can be answered all at once.

The foregoing discussion makes two moral presuppositions that can all be questioned. The first, which has already been made explicit, is that some segment of a country's overall immigration intake is discretionary, that is, it is not entirely taken up by its obligations towards persons with morally urgent claims to admission.

The second is that language preservation is a morally valid policy goal, one that can in certain circumstances justify the use of mildly coercive legislation that would in other contexts be morally suspect, such as limiting the choices that people make in a number of domains, such as the language in which they educate their children. This question, or rather set of interlocked questions, are obviously up for debate. For some, language is too protean a phenomenon for talk of preservation to make much sense (Wee 2010). Theorists who agree that language is in principle worthy of protection will disagree about what derogations from standard liberal norms can be justified by appeal to this goal. Where in the pursuit of this objective is the line separating proportionate and disproportionate abridgements of individual rights (Weinstock 2015)?

This paper has obviously not provided any answers to these associated questions. It has set itself the more limited task of determining whether, if at all, it is morally permissible to use prior language competence as a criterion of immigrant selection. My argument has been that this is problematic in cases in which the language of the host society is not vulnerable. Joseph Carens has argued that the use of prior competence in *either* English or French was an unobjectionable criterion for immigrant selection in Canada (Carens 2003). My argument would allow to distinguish more perspicuously between the case of English Canada, and that of Quebec. Whereas the latter may be justified in according preference to candidates with prior knowledge of French, there seems no reason to give priority to English-speakers for admission to Canada, given the fact that the incentive structure that they will find themselves upon arrival will exercise great pressure towards their gaining fluency in the public language without the need either for the prior selection of anglophones, or indeed for the implementation of coercive legislation aimed to ensure that immigrants will learn English.

Notes

1 The classic case for the right to member selection is Walzer 1984. For a recent case for open borders, see Van der Sossen and Brennan 2018.
2 The case of Israel, and of its Law of Return, represents a special case, discussion of which lies beyond the scope of this paper.
3 https://www.brusselstimes.com/38236/flanders-a-person-s-knowledge-of-dutch-will-need-to-be-checked-for-them-to-keep-social-housing

References

Abizadeh, Arash (2008). "Democratic Theory and Border Coercion: No Right to Unilaterally Control Your Own Borders", *Political Theory*, vol. 36, no. 1, pp. 37–65.
Brock, Gillian, and Michael Blake (2014). *Debating Brain Drain. May Governments Restrict Emigration?* Oxford: Oxford University Press.
Carens, Joseph (2003). "Who Should Get In? The Ethics of Immigration Admissions", *Ethics and International Affairs*, vol. 17, no. 1, pp. 95–110.
Carens, Joseph (2013). *The Ethics of Immigration*. Oxford: Oxford University Press.
Da Silva, Michael and Daniel Weinstock (2022). "Reconciling the Cultural Claims of Majorities and Minorities", in R. Koopman and L. Orgad (eds.), *Majorities, Minorities, and the Future of Nationhood*. Cambridge: Cambridge University Press, pp. 129–150.
Forst, Rainer (2014). *The Right to Justification*. New York: Columbia University Press.
Hoesch, Matthias (2022). "Do Immigrants Have a Moral Duty to Learn the Host Society's Language?", *Res Publica*, vol. 29, no. 1, pp. 23–40.

Kymlicka, Will (1995). *Multicultural Citizenship*, Oxford: Oxford University Press.
Laponce, Jean (1974). *Language and Territory*. Ottawa: University of Ottawa Press.
Lister, Matthew (2014). "Climate Change Refugees", *Critical Review of International Social and Political Philosophy*, vol. 17, no. 5, pp. 618–634.
Miller, David (2016). *Strangers in our Midst: The Political Philosophy of Immigration*. Oxford: Oxford University Press.
Owen, David (2020). *What Do We Owe to Refugees?*. Oxford: Polity Press.
Patten, Alan (2019). "Protecting Vulnerable Languages: The Public Good Argument", *Oxford Studies in Political Philosophy*, vol. 5, pp. 147–170.
Shachar, Ayelet and Ram Hirshl (2014), "On Citizenship, States, and Markets", *Journal of Political Philosophy*, vol. 22, pp. 231–257.
Van der Sossen, Bas, and Jason Brennan (2018). *In Defense of Openness. Why Global Freedom is the Humane Solution to Global Poverty*. Oxford: Oxford University Press.
Van Parijs, Philippe (2011). *Linguistic Justice for Europe and for the World*. Oxford: Oxford University Press.
Walzer, Michael (1984). *Sphere of Justice. A Defense of Pluralism and Equality*. Basic Books.
Wee, Lionel (2010). *Language without Rights*. Cambridge: Cambridge University Press.
Weinstock, Daniel (2015). "Can Parity of Self-Esteem Serve as the Basis for the Principle of Linguistic Territoriality?", *Res Publica*, vol. 21, no. 2, pp. 171–183.
Weinstock, Daniel (2020). "Language Justice and the Case of "Mere Numbers"", in Y. Peled and D. Weinstock (eds.), *Language Ethics*, Montreal: McGill-Queens Press.

10
ON MIGRATION AND BACKLASH

Michael Blake

10.1 Introduction

There is a curious disconnect between the public debates about migration, and the philosophical debates about that topic. In contemporary politics, migration as a topic has been used to motivate the populist and authoritarian challenges to democratic political institutions. Democracy has, for the past two decades, been in open retreat from anti-democratic forces; Freedom House has recorded over twenty straight years in which the number of democratic societies in the world has fallen (Repucci and Slipowitz, 2021). Increasingly, too, recent years have brought a rise in the open willingness of authoritarian regimes to disdain not only the practice, but even the *theory*, of democratic governance; democracy has fallen in perceived importance, so much so that despotic regimes no longer feel compelled to pretend that they are democratic (Csaky, 2021). Democratic norms have been placed under threat by any number of factors, but one significant one seems to be the rise of populist resistance to democratic norms; populist parties have been able to harness a resentment on the part of many citizens against the perceived illegitimate power of global institutions and global elites (Müller, 2020). The populist gains political power by telling the local citizens that their wisdom – and their rightful power – have been stolen by the unrighteous outsiders, who have captured the corrupt and weak institutions of domestic politics. This resentment of the outsider, naturally, has led to a politics in which migration is positioned as a key means by which the outsider has taken what is not rightly his. In 2019, for instance, more than eighty percent of self-described conservative voters described undocumented migration as a "significant problem" for the United States – with an equal number approving of an expansion of the wall between Mexico and the United States (Pew Research Center, 2019). It is worth noting that two-thirds of these voters thought that current circumstances required a President strong enough to "break the rules," if needed, to vindicate the rights of American citizens (Cox and Jones, 2016).

If current political discourse focuses on whether or not migration rights ought to be reduced or eliminated, modern political philosophy about migration tends to focus on whether or not those rights ought to be radically increased. Within the recent literature on the morality of migration, the most prominent debate is over whether or not *any* restrictions on the free movement of individuals across borders can be made coherent with liberal politics. The debate is divided between those who would regard any curtailing of the right to migrate as fundamentally illiberal (Carens, 2013; Hidalgo, 2018; Oberman, 2016) and those who are willing to countenance some restrictions on the part of states to exclude the unwanted would-be migrant (Blake, 2020a; Miller, 1995; Miller, 2016; Song, 2018). Even among this latter set, however, the broad conclusion is that much modern control of migration – including the exclusion of so-called "economic migrants," who are seeking forms of poverty and marginalization but do not qualify as refugees under international law – is morally unjustifiable. If the modern political debate is about whether or not a radically *reduced* flow of migration is a moral imperative, the modern philosophical debate tends to agree with the proposition that a significantly *increased* right to migrate ought to be asserted.

In itself, this disagreement might tell us nothing of interest; it is entirely possible for political philosophy about justice to be done in an unjust world, or a world full of people with unjust preferences, and for the writings of philosophers to therefore have only tangential and theoretical application to the political discourse of that world. It is, however, somewhat awkward that philosophy has so little to say to or about the populist and the anti-migration politician. Joseph Carens has usefully distinguished between a realistic and idealistic ethics of migration (Carens, 2013); on the former, but not the latter, facts about the real world of political institutions and agents can enter into our moral conversations. Carens has rightly endorsed the relevance of both forms of theorizing – and we have recently seen a rise in non-ideal theorizing about migration (Reed-Sandoval, 2020; Mendoza, 2015). Political philosophers have not, however, tended to spend much time thinking about those agents whose anti-migrant policies are so fundamentally alien to the ideal theories with which those philosophers tend to begin. Thinking about these agents, however, seems to be an important philosophical task – if only because how liberal politics ought to *respond* to these agents may be an important question. The response to anti-migrant political agents represents, I have argued, a sort of tragic dilemma for the liberal, in that acting on her first-order political preference (a more open migratory regime) may end up undermining support for, and the stability of, the liberal institutions through which liberal justice is guaranteed. As such, the liberal political agent may have two options, each deeply unpalatable:

1 She may push for the opening of the border, which does justice towards those who have a right in justice to migrate; but, in so doing, she may undermine the liberal institutions by which rights more generally are maintained, and puts the stability of her liberal state at risk in the long run; or
2 She may help perpetuate liberal rights within the state, by continuing the current unjustifiable regime of migratory rights – or even restricting those rights; in so doing, however, she is complicit in a politics in which those migrants are not provided with those rights that she herself understands liberalism to provide them.

She may, in short, do justice at the border, and risk the undermining or collapse of justice within; or she may do what helps to preserve justice within the state, but only at the cost of doing wrong at the border.

I have termed this dilemma the Bigot's Veto, and I believe the dilemma it poses to be a genuine and genuinely tragic one – tragic, that is, in the sense that there is no option here but to engage in significant wrongdoing; whatever one does, in face of this dilemma, one has done something wrong, and indeed something for which one might rightly feel something approaching moral shame (Blake, 2020a). This dilemma is an empirical one, in that it holds true only in those circumstances in which no option is available that protects rights in both the short run and in the long run; it is, however, a dilemma whose circumstances may resemble those in which we ourselves currently find ourselves. In the present chapter, I want to explore this dilemma, and examine some ways in which that dilemma might be made less wrenching. I will examine two distinct means by which the conflict might be evaded. On the first, we can avoid the dilemma, because justice itself means something other than what the dilemma takes it to mean. This is what I will describe as a *theoretical* response to the dilemma, on which liberal theory itself can continue to provide idealized moral guidance, and the theory itself does not stand impugned by the dilemma as posed. On the second, we cannot solve the dilemma, but we can – in Wittgenstein's sense – sometimes *dissolve* that dilemma, or at least find means by which we might in practice make it possible for us to make the choice it demands less horrifying. I will argue that there are some significant difficulties with the theoretical replies to the dilemma. I do not claim that these difficulties cannot be overcome; they might, and indeed the moral frameworks giving rise to these difficulties are somewhat in conflict, such that not all of these apparent difficulties can be real simultaneously. There is, however, no *easy* way to dispel these difficulties; or so, at any rate, it seems to me. I will argue, however, that there might be practices – some of which can be brought about by political tools, and some of which cannot – that might blunt the effects of that dilemma. Even here, however, my conclusions will be tentative and partial; we may hope that the Bigot's Veto becomes a less pressing concern in our shared political future, but we do not have the tools needed by which we might ensure this dilemma is avoided.

10.2 Migration and Backlash in Liberal Theory

It is worth pausing, for a moment, to be precise about what it is that the practice of justice demands. I follow John Rawls in thinking that stability is a requirement for any theory of justice; while Rawls might have been optimistic in his thought that a just society would produce its own forms of support, he was not wrong to think that *some* form of support would be a necessary part of a plausible theory of political justice (Blake, 2020b). A theory of justice, then, must be specific about how it is that it gives the citizens of a society a reason to abide by the norms and institutions of that society. It must also, of course, be capable of providing some normative guidance about those norms and institutions; one primary role of a theory of justice, after all, is to provide some critical response to existing forms of political authority, by telling us what that authority must do to be justified. There are, then, two things that are required by any theory of justice; it must tell us what justice *requires*, and it must tell us how those requirements can be brought into institutional *reality*.

We can begin our analysis of the theoretical response to the Bigot's Veto, then, by dividing between two different sorts of theoretical replies. On the first, we might moderate the force of this dilemma by arguing that it represents only a temporary and local worry about the institutional realization of the liberal ideal; the supposed tragic dilemma is not a deep worry about the instantiation of liberalism, but instead is a merely *transitional* issue with the movement from illiberalism to liberalism. On this reply, we might simply differentiate between what stability requires in the short term, and what it requires in the longer term – and preserve liberalism, by situating the compromises demanded by the Bigot's Veto as temporary and (in the sense used by economists) frictional. On the second, we might focus instead on the nature of the norm defended by liberalism, and seek to redescribe that norm so that the rights of migrants are not necessarily those defended by liberals as the presentation given above might imagine. We can preserve liberalism, on this conception, by regarding it as less prone to expanding the rights of would-be migrants as current liberal theorists tend to believe. Each of these methods focuses on one of the two aspects of liberal theorizing described above. The first seeks to preserve liberal theory, by making the backlash against liberalism a (merely) temporary and irrational response to the doing of justice; it is, instead of a challenge to liberal theory, at most a technical problem for the one charged with the design of liberal policy. The second seeks, instead, to preserve liberalism by redescribing its normative guidance. We can reaffirm liberalism's coherence, on this view, by redescribing liberalism so as to alter its seemingly radical conclusions about migration.

We can consider these two options in turn. The first response, as above, seeks to overcome the Bigot's Veto as a problem, by reducing that problem to something like a temporary and local problem in the process of moving from injustice to justice. Carens's distinction between the realistic and idealistic ethics of migration is, of course, a key example of how this might be done. For Carens, it is true that liberalism as a theory demands that borders be, as a matter of principle, made open to those who wish to cross them; but it is also true that liberal states should not, as a matter of political practice, open these borders *immediately* (Carens, 2013). Radical change away from injustice must be managed, on Carens's realistic ethics, so that the transition minimizes the violence and injustice that any radical change – even one demanded by justice – often entails. Carens's own examples include the political process of reconstructing South Africa after the abolition of Apartheid, and the elimination of the slave trade in Britain and in the United States; both of these sorts of transitions were required by justice, and both require skilful practice on the part of politicians, so as to manage the ways in which new political realities were brought into being against the wishes of at least some political agents. These ideas are buttressed by Lorenzo Del Savio, who argues in a recent paper that the binary distinction between a realistic and an idealistic ethic of migration ought to be replaced with a continuum, representing our best understanding of what is feasibly accomplished by politics at the present (Del Savio, 2020). Importantly, however, both of these theorists regard those opposed to justice in migration as being, in themselves, not important sources of moral reasoning; Del Savio argues that we cannot take the ideas or attitudes of those engaging in anti-immigration backlash seriously "in normative discussions regarding migration," since the legitimacy of these ideas or attitudes is itself up for normative analysis – and since, if these attitudes are "unjust, harmful, or both," then what they recommend is likely to be "morally reprehensible" (Del Savio, 2020, at 210). We have the same attitude towards those engaging in illiberal backlash, that is, that John Rawls argues we ought to have towards racists or theocrats within liberal society; we do not analyse their reasons of theories, but instead simply hope that their regrettable attitudes do not become popular (Rawls, 1971).

The second response, in opposition to the first, takes the populist attitude towards migration seriously, and seeks to adjust the content of liberal theorizing in response. There are several ways in which this might be done – only two of which I will consider here. The first mode of limitation is to take liberalism itself as having an implicit set of background conditions. On this view, liberalism's guarantees apply within the state – but some more restricted set of rights might be taken to apply outside that state's borders, so that perhaps liberalism does not have the radical implications for migration that it seems recently to have had. It is not true, of course, that all theorists who differentiate between what is owed to the citizen and to the would-be migrant thereby derive conservative implications about migration; David Miller, for example, argues that social trust requires the right to limit migration – but arrives, nonetheless, at conclusions about migratory rights that seem considerably more expansive than those currently defended by most wealthy states (Miller, 2016; see also Blake, 2020a). But it is possible for a liberal theory to defend something like the present set of migratory rights, by means of a theoretical restriction on the application of liberal rights to those who share a particular history and vocabulary *about* those rights. Michael Walzer's view, most centrally, has this implication; he is able to defend robust rights to exclude the outsider, because those rights make sense within – and are understood by – only a particular cultural community of character, which maintains and preserves the right to preserve itself as such (Walzer, 1986). A liberalism derived from Walzer's methodology might overcome the dilemma described, simply by giving those who are opposed to migration a home within liberal theory itself. A liberal polity that excluded the unwanted outsider would no longer, on this view, be illiberal in its refusal to open its borders; it would, instead, be capable of preserving its ability to pursue liberalism, precisely because it preserved the distinctiveness without which the practice of liberal politics is impossible.

The second mode by which liberal ideals might be moderated, in contrast, does not presume to undermine the demands of liberal ideals – but seeks to return the notion of *compromise* to a prime place within liberal theorizing. Thorben Knobloch and Corinna Mieth have recently proposed a means by which the idea of compromise might be brought to bear on practical politics about migration, by regarding those whose views on migration are disfavoured by liberal ideals as having a legitimate right to have those views heard through and in political processes. On this account, the need for political compromise demands that citizens attracted to the liberal ideal of migration, and those who believe in a more restricted vision of politics on which migratory rights are less robust, have reason to seek to do politics together – in a *modus vivendi* that has the potential to become itself a source of reasons for political negotiation, as the fact of shared social cooperation might give rise to a stable practice of political negotiation and compromise (Knobloch and Mieth, 2021). In this analysis, the concerns of those who are inclined towards populist anti-migration backlash might be brought back into the democratic conversation. The conversation, moreover, represents a morally appealing vision of mutual respect and accommodation between citizens who disagree about political reality – a vision that, in some respects, echoes the concerns behind Rawls's own development of public reason (Rawls, 1989). In a related vision, Stephen Macedo argues that liberals who disagree with populist anti-migration rhetoric must nonetheless seek compromise with their fellow citizens who are attracted by such rhetoric – and must, in particular, seek first to understand how such rhetoric might have become so attractive, and what epistemic blind spots have developed amongst educated liberals (Macedo, 2021). These methods, again, do not necessarily negate the existence of a tragic choice, but they do demonstrate a mode by which that choice might be overcome – not by privileging liberal conclusions over populist ones, but by extending the reach of democratic conversation, and by demonstrating to those attracted to populism that they have a place within that conversation going forward.

These visions are powerful and attractive, and I do not claim here to have presented them in adequate detail; nonetheless, I want here to describe some difficulties these methods might encounter in replying to these worries about backlash. We can begin by examining the response, which sees the backlash as a merely temporary or frictional response to the doing of justice. This response is, I think, not obviously wrong – and, certainly, represents one possible outcome for our shared political future; we might come to accept that constraints on migration are as obviously wrong as chattel slavery, and look back to resistance to open borders as morally retrograde in a similar way. But I am not convinced that this is the only future – nor even that this is the only future for which we might rightly hope. There are two broad families of reasons for this: the first of which focuses on the moral importance of democratic reasoning, and the second of which focuses on the complexity – and difficulty – of moral motivation.

We can begin with the former, and note that our best theorizing about liberalism tends to give some space over for democratic deliberation – and that democratic deliberation requires, at least sometimes, for *bad* reasons to be given moral importance. What I mean by this is that, in contrast to Del Savio, there are occasions on which we might rightly insist on the moral authority of policy that is best justified with reference to a flawed, or wrongful, account of justice. This is morally unexceptional, I think, within much liberal practice; if I am convinced that justice within the state of Washington requires an income tax, and you (wrongly) think that justice is compatible with Washington's reliance on sales taxes, I cannot simply ignore your preference and impose a sales tax if I were somehow to acquire the power to do so. It would be undemocratic – and, therefore, *unjust* – for me to do so, even if I happen to have incontrovertible moral evidence (that you, foolishly, fail to find motivating) that a reliance on sales tax is regressive. The analysis given by such philosophers as Del Savio and Carens supposes that opposition to migratory rights is not only wrongful, but wrongful in such a way that it ought to be regarded as an exception to the general presumption that democracy allows even wrongful answers to a certain degree of deference. This supposition might be correct; but it is not, yet, clear why it *must* be correct. It is, further, entirely likely that – as Macedo notes – those academics who take populism to be appealing only to racists are displaying their own class biases, more than anything else. As Macedo notes, the past few decades have been devastating to the economic chances of poorly educated white Americans – and those arguing against restrictions on migration have tended to ignore or minimize the effects of migration upon the rural and the poorly-educated (Macedo, 2021). Carens and Del Savio, in short, seem to regard anti-migration backlash as something that brings no particular rational content – populist voters are wrong, and we have no need to listen to them; we can simply hope that they, like hurricanes or earthquakes, are as few in number as possible. This solution, however, runs the risk of treating fellow citizens as morally irrelevant, simply because they are morally wrong – and as morally ignorant, even when they might be reacting to moral facts we have reason to take seriously.

The second worry about this solution begins with the thought that liberal democracy requires the will to do politics with particular others – and that the motivation to do politics in that way is not a limitless resource. The thought that our motivation to treat others well is limited is, as it were, baked into liberal politics, which seeks – in Rousseau's phrase – to take laws as they might be, but men as they are. This idea is echoed in Rawls's concept of the burdens of judgement, on which the capacity of being motivated by the ends of others is not infinite – indeed, our limited capacity for identification with the other is at the heart of Rawls's rejection of consequentialist political theorizing (Rawls, 1989). For Rawls, as for most liberals, good citizens need not display angelic levels of altruism; they are limited in their capacity to be morally motivated by the goods of others. This is relevant to the populist, though, because if the one engaging in anti-migration backlash is morally wrong – as I think she is – it cannot be simply because she is limited in her will to do politics with, and therefore be motivated by the goods of, some particular set of others. We are *all* limited in that way, except perhaps some small set of saints or heroes. The populist might be mistaken in an empirical way, about the true effects of migration upon her interests – although, as I have noted, we need not assume she is always so mistaken. The populist undoubtedly makes a moral error when she advocates for authoritarian or anti-democratic modes of politics. But we cannot assert, without more, that she is making a moral error in refusing to take the good of a particular other as a moral reason to accept a lowered outcome for her own good. As Rawls and others have emphasized, there is nothing in this sort of selfishness that is inherently illiberal; such moral limits are, instead, part of the factual background with which liberalism begins.

We might, further, note that there are similar considerations that might apply to the national identities on which the exclusion is predicated. The fact of preferring the goods of insiders to outsiders is wrong in many contexts; but it cannot be taken to be wrongful in all contexts – or, at least, some theorists, not themselves populists or authoritarians, have felt the preservation of a moral distinction between insiders and outsiders as important enough to merit preservation. Anna Stilz notes, for one, that the abstract propositions of liberalism are only comprehensible in the distinctive linguistic and cultural forms that exist within particular nations; the defence of the nation, then, might stand with liberalism – rather than against it (Stilz, 2009). Yael Tamir notes that the thin and formal rights of liberalism are poorly able to motivate significant moral sacrifices such as military service and redistributive initiatives – and that a thick national identity has often been used to ground egalitarian liberalism (Tamir, 2020). Similar ideas might be found in any number of theorists, including Ryan Pevnick, Sarah Song, and Will Kymlicka. If this is right, though, then the one who is attracted to populism is not reflecting a momentary and aberrant immoral preference, as Carens and Del Savio might imagine; instead, it is possible that what she feels is a comprehensible and morally defensible impulse, directed here towards an immoral and unjust plan of action.

We can see this worry, finally, by looking at a site of migration worry not often considered by philosophers – the migration of American citizens to Mexico. In recent years, American citizens have settled in significant numbers in Mexico City, drawn by its cosmopolitan atmosphere, relatively cheap cost of living, and the newly available freedoms provided by digital and long-distance careers. The response to these newcomers by those already present within Mexico City has been, predictably, less than uniformly positive. Flyers were recently distributed in districts popular with newly arrived digital nomads, which read: "New to the City? Working Remotely? You're a f__ing plague and the locals f__ing hate you. Leave." More moderately, Fernando Bustos Gorozpe, a Professor of Philosophy, recounts looking around a restaurant and noticing that every party there except his own was speaking English; he posted a widely read critique of the demographic changes in Mexico City, noting that the demographic changes they brought made things worse for those who were born in Mexico (Linthicum, 2022). The structure of these complaints – these outsiders are bringing changes with them, including linguistic change, and that is making things worse for those of us already here – should be familiar to anyone who has paid attention to the rise of populism. In both cases, the fact of demographic change, ascribed to migration, is felt as a sort of displacement and alienation from one's place of origin. In the United States, voters who described themselves as feeling like "strangers in their own land" were three and a half times more likely to vote for Donald Trump than those voters who did not feel that way.

My point here is emphatically *not* that Americans voting for Trump are morally akin to Mexicans displeased by wealthy Americans moving to Mexico City. There are any number of means by which moral distinctions might be drawn between the two – starting, of course, with the profound privileges held by such digital nomads, in terms of linguistic power in the world economy, holdings of wealth, and (quite often) racial privilege. The phrase "these foreigners are taking over" has a morally different valence, depending upon where it is spoken and who it is that is speaking. The problem, though, is that precisely because the expression of antipathy towards newcomers derives its moral significance from these local and complex facts, it is all too easy for those who are already somewhat privileged to regard themselves as subject to a unique and unjust form of humiliation when some of that privilege is removed. The moral phenomenology of displacement, I would suggest, is the same both for the one who is unjustly displaced, and the one who is (merely) lowered in his unjust privilege. There are two facts that follow from this. The first is that the moral condemnation of the one attracted to the populism must proceed slowly and carefully; the feelings on which that attraction begins have roots that are not in themselves morally wrongful. The ones attracted by the populist message may be morally wrong in the politics they endorse, but they are not uniquely malignant people in finding themselves susceptible to worries about alienation and displacement. The second is that recognition that one is *not* morally akin to the residents of Mexico City under consideration – that one is a recipient of privilege, instead of a subject of colonial violence – requires a tremendous amount of moral strength, and an exceptional will to be honest with one's self about the world and one's place within it. It is all too easy for those who are born into privilege to think that such privilege is either non-existent or natural; moral corruption is a standing risk in moral self-examination. Precisely because of this, however, it is all too easy for moral entrepreneurs such as populist politicians to provide easy answers to such morally complex questions; and we should be as heartened by the fact that many resist the populist, as disheartened by the fact that many do not.

At this point, however, we might proceed to an examination of the second way of responding to the Bigot's Veto – by looking at those who would redefine the concept of justice, so as to make it more capable of evading the dilemma in question. We can deal fairly quickly with the issue of a range limitation on liberalism, since there are familiar problems with any such range limitation; to place a boundary on the reach of the most basic terms of liberal equality seems to stand in some tension with the moral universalism that makes liberalism appealing. Even if a given liberalism emerges from a particular context, that is, it is far from clear that we can arbitrarily limit its application to that context. The recognition of such arbitrary line-drawing, moreover, has been the source of enormous moral progress – as the arbitrary exclusion of women, people of colour, and atheists from political voice has gradually and imperfectly been removed from existing liberal institutions. A more moderated attempt at boundary-drawing, such as those discussed above, might have some more ability to present itself as tenable liberalism – but it is telling that these liberalisms, such as those described by Stilz and Tamir, tend to have conclusions in the realm of migration that would not please those attracted by populism; once some significant sort of liberal rights is given over to would-be migrants, those migrants tend to acquire more title to move than contemporary states would like to give them.

A liberalism of compromise – the second mode by which we might redescribe liberalism's core theoretical vision – seems potentially more tenable. Rawls's revision of his own theory, after all, was intended to provide space within liberal politics for both comprehensive liberals and reasonable adherents of other doctrines to do politics together fairly. If we were, with Knobloch and Mieth, to provide space for (some) populists to negotiate with liberals committed to more open borders, we might extend the political conversation – and gain the advantages, moral and structural, of a liberal sort of political community.

I am convinced that such a vision of compromise and negotiation holds the best chance of being successful in practice. I am not, however, entirely convinced – in large part because of a problem in the logic of compromise, which we might call the problem of recursion. Any attempt to tolerate that which is contrary to the conclusions of liberal theory must identify a limit to that which is tolerable; there are compromises, in short, that cannot be made, and cannot be made because they are too far from liberalism itself. We need, that is, some theory that is distinct from liberalism about how far liberalism must extend itself – to what set of populists, that is, that must be included. Knobloch and Mieth are aware of this, and offer a reply – the compromise must be focused on maintaining a "compromising mindset," which would include the commitment to the ongoing development of a liberal political community as a site of democratic contestation (Knobloch and Mieth, 2021, at ck 263). My worry is, however, that this idea is itself subject to interpretive differences – indeed, it may be as difficult to interpret as the underlying ideals of liberal equality themselves. If this is so, then we might face differences between parties not only about when to exclude migrants from the polity, but also about which parties to the discourse are fairly included within that discourse. Liberals will disagree with reasonable non-liberals about migration, that is – but they are also likely to disagree, between themselves and with others, about which non-liberal agents are in fact behaving reasonably, and so are entitled to participation within the liberal conversation.

I think this problem – which is recursive since it demands a sort of meta-theory, to solve the disputes about the political methods by which we solve first-order disputes of politics – is one that is likely made worse by our tendency to moral corruption. As discussed above, it is all too easy for us to reinterpret facts and ideals in a manner that demonstrates our own moral adequacy; and this, I think, is likely to be a particularly worrying fact in democratic communities, in which migrants are striking because of their procedural absence. Citizens, after all, vote; would-be migrants do not. This structural fact is enough to ensure that most politicians will be more careful in their moral attention directed towards citizens than towards would-be citizens. Once again, unless we are careful in institutional design or exceptional in moral strength, we are all too predictably able to fall into delusion about the circumstances, needs, and interests of those who are other than ourselves.

The final worry with this solution, however, is the most basic: the alienation and resentment of many of those who are attracted to populism are only contingently directed at the migrant. The migrant is a convenient focus for those who feel economically and culturally irrelevant within a given society; but if the populist is given the right to exclude the migrant, it is far from clear that the populist message would lose its power. That power is derived from the normative power of the scapegoat – and any number of scapegoats might be found, from the welfare queens of Ronald Reagan to the current hysteria surrounding drag queens. Peter Glick's analysis of scapegoating posits that a group can gain unity and pride from a shared condemnation of others; those others must be viewed as simultaneously powerful, alien, malignant, and defeasible (Glick, 2005). The migrant is a prime candidate for this role; but if the populist succeeds in taking the migrant off the political board, there is no limit to the number of other pieces that might be used in the migrant's stead. What this means, though, is that the compromising mindset defended by Knobloch and Mieth may not be enough to solve the issue of backlash – for, even if a compromise is reached in one area of political life, the alienation and resentment that led to such backlash might simply be redeployed by a political agent somewhere else. What is required for the backlash to be eliminated, then, might be something more difficult than even the will to compromise; we might require the will to abandon our felt alienation and grievance, even when politicians exist who continue to nurture that grievance and keep it fresh.

10.3 Migration and Backlash in Political Practice

I think we might then turn from theoretical solutions to the Bigot's Veto, to political responses to this dilemma that do not propose to eliminate it. There are, I think, some political problems that do not have political solutions – or, at any rate, solutions that sit comfortably within ideal theory. John Rawls describes the family as one such problem. So long as people are raised within families that differ in their attentiveness or interest in child-rearing, perfect equality of opportunity will never exist; some parents will give their children more than other parents, and children will therefore come into their lives with undeserved forms of advantage. We cannot effectively eliminate this injustice, however, without making things considerably worse for all humans; a world without parents and children would be unlike any world we know, and would be even less likely to instantiate justice and equality in any form we value (Rawls, 1971).

If this is right, though, then the best we can hope for is not a clear set of instructions from liberal theory, but instead a piecemeal set of ideas about what sorts of facts in the world could make this necessary injustice as small as possible. To borrow an idea from Wittgenstein, we might describe this as seeking – in the limit case – to *dissolve* the problem, instead of solving it. Wittgenstein's problems were logical and linguistic, of course, and he sought to dissolve them by demonstrating that they need not continue to be held by us *as* problems. In the political analogue, we might instead seek the circumstances under which the problem we discuss no longer requires as much of our moral attention; it may never fully disappear, as Wittgenstein thought philosophical pseudo-problems might, but would might nonetheless imagine a world in which this problem ceased to cause as much consternation.

The circumstances that might dissolve the problem of backlash, I think, include some that are open to some degree of political control, and others that are only indirectly and imperfectly subject to collective alteration – if at all. There are any number of means by which we might hope for this outcome; at present, I will discuss only three.

The first might be the thought that some populist politics is amplified not simply by ideas and arguments, but by emotions and more psychological facts. Many of the worst forms of backlash might depend upon the ability to see the migrant not as fully human, but as something akin to a pestilence – as vermin, as a plague, or as any of the other metaphors traditionally used by fascist authors and politicians. The response to this sort of dehumanization, however, is often best made not through philosophy, but through proximity. Having contact with migrants is potentially a mode by which the opposition to migration itself might be made less extreme. This proposition is made more plausible, moreover, from the fact that the most vociferous opposition to migration – and the most felt attraction to the populist politics of Donald Trump – emerged in the United States in those counties that themselves had the fewest migrants. This suggests, perhaps, that there may be some mode by which the opposition to migration might be dissolved by the fact of migration itself, so long as this migration is done in such a way as to gradually acclimatize the native-born to the reality and moral humanity of the migrant herself. It also might suggest, more controversially, that there are reasons to seek to avoid the geographic concentration of migrants, given the ways in which the current political differences between urban and rural populations are often combined with anti-migrant politics – both in the United States and elsewhere (Gest, 2016).

The second mode by which the backlash might be dispelled would involve the revitalization of forms of identity-creation that cross national boundaries. With the decline in American public life of civic associations, identity as an American has taken on a disproportionately large role in self-description (Putnam, 2020). Were these other forms of association – including union membership, membership in trade associations, membership in organized affinity groups, and so on – made more regular, people would have more frequent opportunities to recognize the similarity and common humanity across national and cultural groups. There is, of course, very little ability on the part of any political group to directly bring this sort of identification about; but it is nonetheless to be hoped that a more complex vision of moral identity might give rise to a less simplistic view of the outsider to the nation. There is, indeed, some experimental evidence that such a complex view of the self might give rise to political benefits; Moses Shayo has demonstrated that redistributive politics are more likely to emerge when citizens identify by class as much as by nation (Shayo, 2009). We might think, in short, that individuals inclined towards solidarity and membership across national boundaries would be less likely to see those national boundaries as indicating a moral chasm – or taking such a chasm to be worth sacrificing liberal politics for.

The final mode by which we might seek to dissolve this problem is, in the end, the negative mode – by which I mean we might have reason to remind those inclined towards authoritarian politics about the *disadvantages* of authoritarianism. Academics, I think, have spent too little time engaging in the project of rehearsing why it is that democratic rule tends to be more predictable and safe than autocratic rule – and we might be of some use in the project of reminding ourselves, and our fellow citizens, about the risks of arbitrary power. Those who justify abrogating democratic norms tend to imagine that anti-democratic power will be used *by* them, rather than brought to bear *against* them. We might avoid the politics of backlash, in short, by focusing not simply on the moral reality of the migrant, but the empirical reality of a world after democracy's erosion.

None of these, of course, is akin to solving the problem entirely; none of these is enough, in other words, to fully demonstrate how liberalism can avoid the dilemma posed by the Bigot's Veto, and hence the wrenching moral choice of doing justice within the state or at the border. But we can hope that these modes, or some others like them, will at least make this dilemma less wrenching in years to come. Given the gradual decline of respect for liberal democracy as both practice and as ideal, these gradual and partial improvements might be sufficient to be worth celebrating.

References

Blake, Michael. 2020a. *Justice, Migration, and Mercy*. New York: Oxford University Press.
Blake, Michael. 2020b. "Right-Wing Populism and Noncoercive Injustice: On the Limits of the Law of Peoples." In Jon Mandle and Sarah Roberts-Cady, eds., *John Rawls: Debating the Major Questions*. Oxford: Oxford University Press, 2020.
Carens, Joseph. 2013. *The Ethics of Immigration*. New York: Oxford University Press.
Cox, Daniel, and Robert P Jones. 2016. "Two-Thirds of Trump Supporters Say Nation Needs a Leader Willing to Break the Rules." PRRI/The Atlantic Poll, March 7, 2016. Available at: https://www.prri.org/research/prri-atlantic-poll-republican-democratic-primary-trump-supporters/

Csaky, Zselyke. 2021. "Nations in Transit 2021: The Antidemocratic Turn." Freedom House Reports. Available at: https://freedomhouse.org/report/nations-transit/2021/antidemocratic-turn

Del Savio, Lorenzo. 2020. "Anti-Immigration Backlashes as Constraints." *Ethical Theory and Moral Practice*, 23(1): 201–222.

Gest, Justin. 2016. *The New Minority: White Working Class Politics in an Age of Immigration and Inequality*. Oxford: Oxford University Press.

Glick, Peter. 2005. "Choice of Scapegoats." In John F. Dovidio et al., eds., *On the Nature of Prejudice: Fifty Years After Allport*. London: Blackwell Publishing.

Hidalgo, Javier. 2018. *Unjust Borders: Individuals and the Ethics of Immigration*. London: Routledge Press.

Knobloch, Thorben, and Corinna Mieth. 2021. "Migration, Democratic Stability, and Compromising Mindsets." In Corinna Mieth and Wolfram Cremer, eds., *Migration, Stability, and Solidarity*. Baden-Baden: Nomos Verlagesellschaft.

Linthicum, Kate. 2022. "Americans are Flooding Mexico City. Some Want Them Gone." The Los Angeles Times, July 27, 2022. C

Macedo, Stephen. 2021. "Populism, Localism, and Democratic Citizenship." *Philosophy and Social Criticism*, 47(4).

Mendoza, José. 2015. "Enforcement Matters: Reframing the Philosophical Debate Over Immigration." *Journal of Speculative Philosophy*, 29(1): 73–90.

Miller, David. 1995. *On Nationality*. New York: Oxford University Press.

Miller, David. 2016. *Strangers in Our Midst: The Political Philosophy of Immigration*. Cambridge: Harvard University Press.

Müller, Jan-Werner. 2020. *Democracy Rules*. New York: Farrar, Straus, and Giroux.

Oberman, Kieran. 2016. "Immigration as a Human Right." In Sara Fine and Lea Ypi, eds., *Migration in Political Theory: The Ethics of Movement and Membership*. New York: Oxford University Press.

Pew Research Center. 2019. "Most Border Wall Opponents, Supporters Say Shutdown Concessions Are Unacceptable." January 16, 2019. Available at https://www.pewresearch.org/politics/2019/01/16/most-border-wall-opponents-supporters-say-shutdown-concessions-are-unacceptable/

Putnam, Robert. 2020. *Bowling Alone: The Collapse and Revival of American Community*. New York: Simon and Schuster.

Rawls, John. 1971. *A Theory of Justice*. Cambridge: Belknap Press.

Rawls, John. 1989. *Political Liberalism*. New York: Columbia University Press.

Reed-Sandoval. 2020. *Socially Undocumented: Identity and Immigration Justice*. New York: Oxford University Press.

Repucci, Sarah, and Amy Slipowitz. 2021. "Freedom in the World 2021: The Global Expansion of Authoritarian Rule." Freedom House Reports. Available at https://freedomhouse.org/report/freedom-world/2019/democracy-retreat

Shayo, Moses. 2009. "A Model of Social Identity With an Application to Political Economy: Nation, Class and Redistribution". *American Political Science Review*, 103(2): 147–174.

Song, Sarah. 2018. *Immigration and Democracy*. New York: Oxford University Press.

Stilz, Anna. 2009. *Liberal Loyalty: Freedom, Obligation, and the State*. Princeton: Princeton University Press.

Tamir, Yael. 2020. *Why Nationalism*. Princeton: Princeton University Press.

Walzer, Michael. 1986. *Spheres of Justice*. New York: Basic Books.

11
THE NATION, THE STATE, AND THE FOREIGNER
Rethinking the Place of Nationalism in the Ethics of Immigration

Lior Erez

11.1 Introduction

It is often said that the reports of nationalism's death have been greatly exaggerated. In recent years, we have seen a resurgence of nationalist sentiments around the world, from the Trump administration's Muslim Ban in the US to the UK's decision to leave the European Union (Brexit) to India's Citizenship Registration Act. These developments have been described as the new "Global Divide" of the twenty-first century, with immigration policies serving as a major flashpoint for the ideological clash between nationalism and globalism. Empirical research has indicated that nationalist politics is a significant factor in explaining why states turn to stricter immigration controls (Ko and Choi, 2022). Given its centrality in the real-world politics of immigration, one can hardly be surprised by a surge of academic interest in the topic (Mylonas and Tudor 2021). However, political philosophy's engagement with the nation remains a confusing endeavor. This may be because the subject matter itself resists precise definitions, as the contours of the nation and its accompanying ideology – nationalism – evolve and change in different historical and geographical contexts. This is true for most political ideologies; but as noted nationalism scholar Benedict Anderson once wrote, "unlike most other isms, nationalism has never produced its own grand thinkers: no Hobbeses, Tocquevilles, Marxes, or Webers" (Anderson 2006). Thus, even at the definitional stage, thinking about the nation philosophically is off to a rocky start.

Ethical theories of nationalism face several additional challenges beyond the issue of definition. The first of these challenges is the enduring suspicion within political philosophy that nationalism is inherently irrational, immoral, and dangerous. In the words of political theorist John Dunn, nationalism is "the starkest political shame of the twentieth century, the deepest, most intractable, and yet most unanticipated blot on the political history of the world since the year 1900" (Dunn 1979, 57). From this perspective, nationalism is exclusionary, tribalist, and narrow-minded, akin to racism. It is incompatible with the foundational belief in the moral equality of all persons, and is therefore not suitable for serious ethical consideration but rather for ideological or conceptual analysis.

In response to this challenge, several notable efforts have been made in recent decades to defend a more respectable version of nationalism that can be compatible with, or even necessary for, liberal and democratic politics (Gans 2003; Gustavsson and Miller 2020; Miller 1995; Moore 2001; Tamir 1993). In the ethics of immigration, this could be interpreted as finding a version of nationalism that could be compatible with the view that immigrants are morally equal (Miller 2016b). However, this raises a new theoretical challenge: can the claims of nationalism be properly tamed by liberal political morality without becoming indistinguishable from liberalism? In the ethics of immigration, specifically, this becomes an urgent question if we keep in mind the distinction between the *nation* as a cultural and identity group, and the *state* as a politico-legal institution. After all, the literature is rife with arguments defending the liberal state's right to control its own borders, or the duties and rights of immigrants in a liberal state. Given that it is the state, and not the nation, that determines and enforces immigration policy, what does "the nation" add to liberal statism? If "nation-state" is not a redundancy, then the nationalist should be able to provide reasons and justifications not available to the non-nationalist, and it is unclear that the tamed versions of nationalism are able to do so (Lægaard 2009).

In addition to the definitional and conceptual challenges, there is also a methodological challenge in ethical theorizing about nationalism: how can we ask normative questions about nationalism without buying into the ideological premises of nationalism? In other words, how can we theorize *about* nationalism without *doing* nationalism? This is a difficult task, as nationalism is an ideology that is deeply embedded in the political, cultural, and social fabric of many societies. In the social sciences (Wimmer and Glick Schiller 2002), and more recently in the normative political philosophy of migration (Sager 2016), this tendency is referred to as "methodological nationalism." As Sager argues, methodological nationalism comes in different variants: political theorists often employ supposedly value-neutral ideas and categories ("citizen," "immigrant"), treat the nation-state as a natural and unproblematic assumption (for example, in its right to control its borders), or assume a territorial limitation for their theories and concepts (for example, assuming that a "societal culture" ends at the border). My aim in this chapter will be to resist these methodological fallacies, albeit with a more precise focus on the nation rather than the composite nation-state.

In this chapter, I aim to provide a normative framework for thinking about the relationship between nationalism and immigration. Despite the fact that most real-world politics of immigration is deeply informed by nationalism, normative theorists of immigration are reluctant to discuss nationalism as a potentially legitimate position. This, in my view, is a mistake. Despite the often unsavory nature of actually-existing nationalism, I believe that the arguments motivating it deserve serious ethical consideration, even if only to be rejected all things considered. To this end, I will structure the chapter around three prominent argumentative narratives of nationalism, which I refer to as the Propertarian Account, the Functionalist Account, and the Majority Rights Account. These argumentative narratives can be found both in "the wild" and, in their more moderate form, in academic philosophical writing defending "liberal nationalism." The purpose of this structure is to show that each line of nationalist argument is distinctive in its justification for the regulation of immigration, both in regards to questions of admission and to questions of immigrant integration, and explain this through the different ways they conceptualize the relationship between the nation and the state.

While the different lines of argument proposed by the three accounts are often conflated or used interchangeably by the same authors, it is analytically useful to study them independently, to identify their drawbacks and limitations, and to consider their implications for the ethics of immigration policy. In addition, I will also suggest ways in which each argumentative narrative could be "moderated" – that is, how it could be made more compatible with liberal and democratic values, and specifically with the belief in the moral equality of persons. This chapter therefore offers an argumentative map of nationalism's distinct contribution to the ethics of immigration, and a framework for thinking about how to approach this complex and contentious issue.

11.2 The Propertarian Account: The Nation Owns the State

In the more traditional, and perhaps commonplace, view of the nation and its relationship to the state, this relationship is defined in terms of ownership. Following philosopher Chaim Gans and historian Oded Steinberg, I will refer to this narrative as the "Propertarian Account" (Gans and Steinberg 2023). The way this account makes sense of the term "nation-state" is in viewing it in the possessive – the nation's state – with the state as the property of the nation. The nation is, in this view, a collective agent with its own values, interests, and ends, and the state is the instrument through which this agent advances these ends, claims its rights, and fulfills its duties. As Samuel Fleischacker describes this position:

> "Nations ought to own a state; the state ought to own a certain territory; and the relationship between the nation and the territory will then be much like the one between an individual property-owner and his things: an opportunity for the nation to express its character or interests or beliefs in the shaping of the material world".
>
> *(Fleischacker 2013)*

Two questions immediately arise: what is it precisely that the nation "owns" when it is imagined to own the state? And how did it come to own it? One possible answer, as was suggested by the quote from Fleischacker above, is to describe this connection in terms of territorial rights. As David Miller describes this position in his defense of the nationalist theory of territory, "states can claim territorial rights when they represent groups with legitimate claims to the land over which the state exercises jurisdiction" (Miller 2019, 330). These groups have a legitimate claim to the land if they have occupied it for a long time, if their actions endowed the land with value, or if the land has an important symbolic significance in the group's culture. A second possible answer is that, in a similarly Lockean fashion, nations become owners of institutions and thus deserving of the benefits of these institutions when they create them or endow them with value. Members of the nation own the political institutions of the state and the goods produced by these institutions (cf. Pevnick 2011 (a non-nationalist version of this argument)).

The Propertarian Account has immediate implications for two central questions in the ethics of migration: the question of exclusion and the question of integration. First, if I own something, I get to decide who has access to it. In an infamous speech, Australian politician Pauline Hanson revealingly draws the following analogy, claiming that "if I can invite whom I want into my home, then I *should have the right to have a say in who comes into my country*" (emphasis added). One of the basic rights associated with property ownership, arguably the most important right associated with it (Penner 2000), is the right to exclude.

If the state is the nation's property, it would follow that the nation has the right to exclude non-members from the state: either excluding them from the territory or excluding them from benefiting from the state's institutions. Second, the propertarian account suggests that if owners do permit the use of their property, they have the right to set the conditions for this use. In the analogous case of the ethics of immigration, this suggests that the nation has the right to set the terms for immigrant integration.

The propertarian account may succeed in providing a version of the nationalist argument that is compatible with the moral equality of outsiders. On a basic level, the propertarian claim to private property is justified in universal terms, allowing nationalists to accept that their nation owns the state and can make exclusionary claims regarding outsiders. Interpreted through the territory or institutional line of argument, the propertarian account identifies a morally relevant distinction between co-nationals and outsiders, justifying differential treatment from a moral perspective. However, the plausibility of this argument depends on the acceptance of a controversial view of "the nation" as a collective agent capable of endowing value and making claims of ownership. On most theories of collective agency, this is a questionable claim. Given the scope of this chapter, we'll assume that the nation could be this kind of agent at least under some circumstances.

There are two further objections to this view, however. The first is that it is a mistake to conflate property rights with state sovereignty, what Fleischacker (2013) calls the common mistake of nationalism. On this objection, to conceptualize the relationship between the nation and the state as one of ownership is to accept that the sovereign has full discretion over what policy to pursue in the name of the "nation" (Ripstein 2017). If the classic view on property is of a "sole and despotic dominion," then this view is objectionably authoritarian regardless of whether the dictator is an individual tyrant or the national community. For the ethics of immigration, this is particularly concerning, as it seems to imply that the nation-state would be permitted to adopt the most exclusionary and discriminatory policies.

The second objection is that this account relies on a "sleight of hand" by conflating the nation as a cultural and historical group, and the people understood as the citizens of the state (Breuilly 1993, 62, 390; cf. Yack 2001). The worry here is that, while in democratic polities it is legitimate to view the people as sovereign, tying this power to the nation is exclusionary and dangerous, especially given that most societies are culturally heterogeneous.[1] As Rainer Bauböck argues, "[t]he conflation between national and democratic majorities is therefore not merely a conceptual mistake but has all too often been an institutionalized reality. Where national majorities claim ownership of the state and deny minorities equal citizenship, democracy becomes indeed the rule of ethno-cultural majorities over minorities" (Bauböck 2022, 42). Immigration policy would therefore illegitimately favor the interests of the dominant cultural group over minority groups. Gans and Steinberg cite as an example the former Malaysian Prime Minister Mahathirbin Mohamad, arguing that "[…T]he Malays are the rightful owners of Malaya[…].," and therefore "[I]f citizenship [in Malaysia] is conferred on races other than the Malays, it is because the Malays consent to this." (Gans and Steinberg 2023).

Defenders of the Propertarian view have at their disposal different responses to these objections. One immediate response is to relax the assumption regarding ownership rights and replace despotic decisionism with ethical content. In this view, nations are ethical communities where members have special obligations to one another, which justifies giving their interests more weight in comparison to those of non-members. But that does not necessarily entail that the interests of outsiders are simply disregarded, and the nationalists may well concede that in some cases (for example, of people in dire need), the lesser interests of co-nationals are overridden. Miller usefully describes this view as "quasi-contractual," seeking to find a fair balance between the rights and obligations of the immigrants and the receiving society (Miller 2008). Note, however, that in order for this response to still be recognizably one of property ownership, the bar for overriding the nation's right to the state should be relatively high. Otherwise, the argument turns into a comparative assessment of competing interests, which, as we shall see in the following sections, is a much weaker account.

A second response available to the nationalists is to render the nation itself more inclusive, making it easier to become part of the national "self" who is the owner of the state. A typical liberal answer to the challenge of exclusivity is trying to frame national identity around purely political values, thus rendering the connection between national identity and the majority culture weaker. With regards to questions of immigration, this approach presents two attractive features. The first is that "the nation" will now include all of the state's citizens, mitigating the danger of domination by the national majority. The second is that while newly arrived immigrants would still be required to accept national values, these would be defined in universal, unobjectionable terms – tolerance, the rule of law, and civic equality. This purely political approach to the "civic nation" has been criticized as overly abstract and unrealistic (Canovan 2001; Yack 2012). Many scholars of nationalism, moreover, are skeptical of the possibility of hermetically separating the people and the nation. "Bring the people into political life," writes Michael Walzer, "and they arrive marching in tribal ranks and orders, carrying with them their own language, historical memories, customs, beliefs, and commitments" (Walzer 1999, 206).

An alternative to this approach is to retain the cultural elements of national belonging, but to argue that newcomers can become integrated into the national community by accepting the public elements of the national culture. Kymlicka (1995, 96) claimed that "In deciding to uproot themselves, immigrants voluntarily relinquish some of the rights that go along with their original national membership." Nationalists still maintain that the nation has the right to require the immigrant to integrate into the national culture. As Miller writes (Miller 2016a, 449), immigrants cannot "expect to be able to reproduce the inclusive 'societal culture' … of the place they have left. They have joined a society with an existing public culture, and although they can reasonably expect that the culture will over time adjust in ways that recognize their presence, for the moment they must acknowledge its precedence in some domains." But unlike racial markers, cultural markers such as "a shared literary and artistic tradition, key political moments, food and leisure, preferences, and national jokes" (Lenard and Miller 2018) are learnable and therefore not as objectionably exclusionary. These kinds of cultural markers do not require the immigrant to abandon her original cultural identity in order to become a member of the nation. I can learn the significance of hockey in Canadian culture without abandoning my passion for American football. Unlike political ideology, cultural identity is more a matter of family resemblance than a set of necessary commitments; Apple pie may be American, but, as Miller writes, "You do not have to enjoy apple pie in order to be an American" (Miller 2017). In this way, the demands of integration toward minorities and immigrants do not seem overly demanding.

Since in the actual world, some nations exist across state borders, some national policies of immigration may be extremely open toward those that they perceive as external members of the nation. Israel's Law of Return is perhaps one of the more famous examples of this kind of policy, as it grants members of the Jewish nation (who are not necessarily Jewish by religion) the right to immigrate, and to receive automatic citizenship upon arrival. But this of course assumes that the nation predates the state, and, interestingly, this line of argument could be subverted to extend the boundaries of the nation beyond the state borders. Rogers Smith, for example, has argued that even if we assume that the desires of those in such national communities to extend membership only to those with whom share identity characteristics should be respected, this entails an obligation to offer membership to those whose identity was coercively constructed by the actions of the state – for example, the colonized (Smith 2011). Alasia Nuti and Sara Amighetti advance a more radical version of this argument, claiming that the formerly colonized constitute an inseparable element of the national identity, and so nationalists cannot justify the restriction on the entrance of members of the nation's former colonies by resorting to an argument about the preservation of national identity (Amighetti and Nuti 2016).

In summary, the Propertarian Account posits that the nation owns the state and therefore has the right to exclude non-members from the state's territory or institutions. While this argument may be compatible with the moral equality of outsiders, it is limited in its ability to address issues of inclusion and integration. Furthermore, its reliance on the concept of national ownership raises questions about the moral legitimacy of such ownership and about the potential for conflict between different nations' claims to ownership. As such, while the Propertarian Account may provide an internally coherent account of the relationship between the nation and the state, its usefulness in justifying the right to exclude remains limited.

11.3 The Functionalist Account: The Nation as the Instrument of the State

The problems with the Propertarian Account suggest that the instrumental approach to nationalism may provide a more helpful framework for thinking about the relationship between the nation and the state in the ethics of immigration. In this view, the nation serves as an instrument for the state, providing the necessary social, cultural, and psychological preconditions for the state to effectively and reliably achieve its goals. Older functionalist theories viewed national identity as valuable for the state in terms of maintaining stability and providing social cohesion in an industrialized, large-scale society. Already in the nineteenth century, in Chapter 16 of his *Considerations on Representative Government,* John Stuart Mill famously argued that "Free institutions are next to impossible in a country made up of different nationalities" (Mill 1861). More recently, nationalism scholar Ernst Gellner argued that nationalism serves a number of important functions in industrial society, including providing a sense of identity and belonging for individuals, facilitating social mobility and integration, and promoting economic growth and development (Gellner 1983).

More contemporary versions of the argument justify the instrumental value of nationalism in terms of desirable ethical ends that are considered legitimate goals of a just liberal state. In some of its versions, the Functionalist Account appeals to the value of individual autonomy, and asserts that individuals can only exercise this autonomy against a stable cultural background that provides them with a range of options from which they can freely choose, as well as a context for the meaning of their choices. Liberal nationalists argue that a stable national culture is important for the autonomy of the nation's members, and that co-nationals (as well as the state in which they live) have a duty to maintain this culture (Kymlicka 1995, 80; Miller 1995, 85–86; Tamir 1993, 84). The

Functionalist Account also asserts that the kind of institutions required for the implementation of liberal ends require a widespread attitude of solidarity and trust for their stable functioning (Miller 1995, 92–94; Tamir 1993, 82; Moore 2001, 80–101), and that a shared national identity is the primary (and perhaps sole) source of this motivational precondition in modern states. This is because a shared national identity grounds associative duties of solidarity toward co-nationals. In her recent book, for example, Yael Tamir argues that nationalism fosters a cross-class coalition, without which the wealthy and powerful will seek to opt out of the institutions of the welfare state (Tamir 2019). Finally, liberal nationalists argue that only by referring to the pre-political community of the nation can the boundaries of the demos – that is, those who are both the authors and subjects of political power – be determined in a non-circular manner (Miller 2009; Moore 2001; cf. Abizadeh 2012; Kymlicka 2022).

If a national identity is needed for a society to be stable and to foster trust, solidarity, and cohesion among different groups, then the state has a responsibility to regulate actions and behaviors that could potentially harm that national identity. In the case of immigration policy, this means that policies about who is allowed to enter the country and how they are integrated into society should be based on how those decisions will affect the national identity's sustainability, even if this leads to frustrating the interests and rights of prospective and existing immigrants. For example, if we consider welfare institutions, the argument is that unrestricted immigration can lead to excessive diversity, which in turn can reduce trust and solidarity and undermine the social foundation for policies that aim to reduce economic inequality. This trade-off between the ability to sustain socially egalitarian institutions and respect for immigrants' rights is known as the "progressive dilemma," an unsavory choice between neoliberal multiculturalism and an exclusionary welfare state (Kymlicka 2015). Analogous arguments could be made about the harmful effects of immigration on political polarization, on the ability to sustain the necessary conditions for cultural autonomy, or civic motivation more generally (Banting and Kymlicka 2017; Blake 2020; Holtug 2022; Tamir 2019).[2]

The force of this argument largely depends on the validity of the empirical claims it is based on. If these claims are true and we accept that preserving stable institutions of liberal democracy and the welfare state are within the state's remit, then the state can use this argument to justify regulating admission and implementing stricter integration policies. From a moral standpoint, this argument is consistent with the moral equality of immigrants, and provides public reasons for these policies that they cannot reasonably reject: it appeals not to some arbitrary whim of the state or its self-interest, but to objectively valuable ends. Furthermore, unlike the Propertarian Account, which assumes that the immigrants' home state must have an equal right to exclude in order to be justifiable, the Functionalist Account suggests that regulating immigration may be in the best interest of the immigrants themselves; if their motivation for immigrating to a particular state is its stable and well-ordered institutions, then they have a vested interest in preserving these institutions.

However, the empirical evidence for the Functionalist Account is, at best, inconclusive. For example, it is unclear whether diversity has a negative impact on social cohesion. Nils Holtug's book on this topic cites a meta-study of 90 studies on the subject, with over half of them offering mixed results (Meer and Tolsma 2014 cited in; Holtug 2022). Furthermore, even if excessive diversity (defined in cultural or ethnic terms) harms social cohesion, trust, or solidarity, it does not necessarily mean that a shared national identity is the only or best solution to this problem. Since the Functionalist Account values national identity only instrumentally, as a way to provide the necessary cultural backdrop for individual autonomy or to generate socially beneficial attitudes, it remains unclear whether preserving national identity is the optimal policy in all national contexts, especially if the trade-offs suggested by the progressive dilemma are to be considered. It is also possible that some conceptions of nationalism may be more suitable for this purpose than others (Miller and Ali 2014). As previously discussed, some liberal nationalists argue for a cultural form of nationalism in which belonging to the nation is based on sharing cultural norms, allowing for more diversity. But as critics of this argument have pointed out, the effects on the social trust of even moderate forms of national identity are not necessarily positive (Erez 2019; Pevnick 2011).

From a more conceptual perspective, a major weakness of this argument in comparison to the Propertarian Account is that, even if the empirical claims are true, they fall short of establishing a right to regulate immigration, either through excluding potential migrants or through strict integration policy. The Propertarian Account relies on the idea of ownership rights, which, importantly, assumes at least some scope of permission to act in less than optimal ways. I have the right, for example, to never use the spare bedroom in my house, even if someone else could have used it more efficiently. But this response is not available to the Functionalist Account. As Michael Blake formulates this point, "[a]t most, it has identified something useful, something good – and those things must be made to stand up against other goods, to see which is more important" (Blake 2014, 528–29). Even if we suppose that a widespread national identity is necessary for sustaining, say, a stable civic motivation in support of the welfare state, and that immigration undermines this widespread national identity, this merely means that there is a reason to preserve national identity, not that it will necessarily be the right thing to do all things considered. It is possible that sacrificing the efficiency of the welfare state, for example, would be a price worth paying for protecting the basic rights of prospective immigrants (Sandelind 2019).

An additional, normative problem with the Functionalist Account is the assumption that immigration undermines social trust and solidarity. This raises questions about the underlying mechanism behind this effect, and whether it is the result of legitimate concerns or objectionable bigotry (Erez 2019). If the former, then the progressive dilemma presents a genuine clash between values. However, even if we view mistrust of immigrants as morally objectionable, it is still unclear what place these attitudes should have in normative theory. This raises the question of how to approach non-ideal attitudes in normative political philosophy, and whether we should accept them as face value, take them into account as background conditions, or exclude them altogether (Enoch 2018; Erez 2015; Estlund 2011). Michael Blake (Blake 2020) argues that allowing bigoted attitudes to influence immigration policy presents policymakers with a tragic choice, which is reflected in many real-world political arguments by liberal politicians (Wintour 2018). Therefore, it is crucial to consider this distinction in order to better understand the normative justification of nationalism (Lægaard 2006).

The Functionalist Account is a prominent view among liberal nationalists, for obvious reasons: it offers a useful framework for thinking about the relationship between the nation and the state without assuming the problematic ontology of the nation as the owner of the state. This view is also seen as compatible with the moral equality of immigrants. However, there are several criticisms of the Functionalist Account. Firstly, it is questionable whether a shared national identity is necessary for fostering trust, solidarity, and cohesion among different groups in society. Secondly, this view could potentially lead to exclusionary and discriminatory policies toward immigrants and minority groups, which can undermine trust and cohesion (Erez 2020). Given these criticisms, the instrumental value of nationality only provides a *pro tanto* reason for regulating immigration and is insufficient in itself for a right to regulate immigration. The instrumental value of nationality alone does not provide a strong enough justification for regulating immigration.

11.4 The Majority Rights Account: The State as a Neutral Arbiter between Groups

Let us take stock. Considering the Propertarian and Functionalist Accounts, we can see that the argument from nationalism faces what we might call a "Goldilocks" problem. The Functionalist account, as we've seen, is compatible with the moral equality of immigrants and could, arguably, be based solely on legitimate and universally acceptable reasons, but its reliance on contestable empirical and causal facts makes it too weak to support a right to control immigration. Conversely, the Propertarian account – if successful – would provide a strong foundation for such a right, analogous to the right of property ownership. But it relies on a questionable social ontology – the state as the instrument of the nation – and possibly illiberal assumptions about property and duties to non-members. These render it problematic for liberal nationalists, and attempts to moderate the account are successful only at the cost of making it useless. To get an account that is "just right", in other words, nationalists need an argument that establishes a right to restrict immigration or demand stricter immigration policies, without the burden of the Propertarian Account's questionable assumption.

The Majority Rights Account is used to justify protecting the cultural identity and values of the majority group by restricting immigration and imposing stricter integration policies on immigrants and minority groups. According to Liav Orgad (2015, 197), majority rights are the cultural interests of the majority that are protected by law and grant privileges to the majority that must be respected by others. While not explicitly about national groups, I follow Da Silva and Weinstock (2022) in arguing that this argument, more often than not, is one of "majority nationalism," establishing the claim of the cultural majority to shape state policies, the public sphere, and national symbols according to its interests. This argument is sometimes presented in the language of functionalism, claiming that diluting the widespread cultural identity through immigration would be detrimental to civic virtue, solidarity, and trust. However, it is important to recognize that the Majority Rights Account presents the problem as a violation of the cultural rights of the majority group, regardless of these external, negative effects. In addition, this is viewed as a legitimate claim right, not as an unfortunate fact about the majority's bias or irrational fears.

Interestingly, in recent years we have seen an increasing number of scholarly works advancing this line of argument through a liberal-democratic framework. In political discourse, demands to restrict immigration to protect the majority culture are often identified with right-wing populism, if not explicit racism. A notorious example is Enoch Powell's so-called "Rivers of Blood" speech, in which he lamented the predicament of White Britons who, "[f]or reasons which they could not comprehend, and in pursuance of a decision by default, on which they were never consulted... found themselves made strangers in their own country" (Powell 1968). Contemporary proponents of this line of argument are, naturally, wary about the racial undertones of this kind of language and the implication that the rights of the majority trump those of vulnerable minorities.[3] They seek, instead, to advance it through more reasonable and acceptable frameworks. One such prominent framework, is, surprisingly enough, liberal equality and multiculturalism.

From liberal equality, the Majority Right Account borrows the idea that the state should be a neutral arbiter of claims between citizens. From multiculturalism, it takes the idea that groups have rights, namely rights to preserve and protect their culture. In essence, the Majority Rights Account accepts both of these claims, but maintains that multicultural theory is applying the principle in a way that is inconsistent with the neutrality of the state: it only grants cultural group rights to minority groups, but not to the majority groups. This "asymmetrical multiculturalism" (Kaufmann 2018) is problematic, since, in cases where there is tension or a conflict, it will always favor the interests of the minorities over those of the majorities. Liav Orgad and Ruud Koopmans argue that this bias against the majority group was seen as acceptable to liberals and multicultural theorists since they assumed that the majority group would be able to protect its interests through majoritarian politics, but that this assumption can no longer hold. "A majority rights debate is emerging," they write "because, in an increasing number of cases concerning immigration, cultural, and identity issues, clear numerical majorities do not translate into concomitant political decisions." (Orgad and Koopmans 2022, 7). In brief, the argument claims that if a just state should be protecting minority rights, it should also be protecting majority rights.

To better illustrate this argument, I turn to its most sophisticated exemplar, Orgad and Koopmans' "Intergroup Differentiation Approach" (Orgad and Koopmans 2022). Building on Kymlicka's (1995) typology of three types of ethnocultural minority group – indigenous people, national minorities, and migrant groups – Orgad and Koopmans develop a relational theory of minority-majority constellations, allowing for the possibility that the majority group could also be indigenous or migratory, and assigning greater weight to the claims of indigenous, "homeland" groups against those of "migratory" ones. Against the supposed assumption that majorities require no protection from the state, they argue that the majority group is entitled to the protection of its cultural rights where political or demographic factors render them vulnerable. Majorities could be vulnerable to threats from immigration in four distinct scenarios (Orgad 2015, 189–95): where large-scale immigration could lead to the loss of their majority status (for example, in the case of Polynesian Fijians); where the national majority is a regional minority, threatened by a more powerful and culturally imperialistic neighbor (for example, Estonians in regards to Russia); where the majority group has a history of being persecuted or victimized (for example, Jews in Israel), and where the majority displays the "state of mind" of a threatened minority (for example, Croats in relation to the Serbian minority in Croatia). In each of these cases, the majority group has a legitimate claim for state protection of its cultural rights, and it is possible (especially if the majority is "indigenous" and the minority is "migratory") that this would require the restriction and regulation of immigration by the minority group.

We can see, therefore, why this line of argument is attractive for nationalists who wish to regulate and restrict immigration. Working within the language of liberalism and multiculturalism, and not making dubious claims about one national group owning the state, the Majority Rights Account can arguably be seen as redeeming nationalism while remaining compatible with a commitment to universal moral equality. Indeed, the main move of this argument is presented in the language of equality, demanding equal treatment of all cultural groups within the state. That said, the Majority Rights account is not without its critics. A primary worry by some is that, despite its authors' best intentions, this account risks legitimizing a dangerous form of nativism, exaggerating the threat of immigration to the integrity of the majority culture and downplaying the myriad ways in which the majority culture is already promoted and defended (Eisenberg 2020; de Waal and Duyvendak 2022). As in the Functionalist Account, we may well worry that the majority's fear is a self-fulfilling prophecy that merely reflects an unjustified bias. Others are concerned that the argument relies on an essentialized account of the cultural majority, which conflates the idea of (substantive) majority culture with the (procedural) democratic majority (Bauböck 2022). Some critics deny that the concept of "majority cultural rights" is necessary or useful (Bauböck 2022; Kymlicka 2022), while others concede that majority groups might have cultural rights, but that cases in which these need the kind of protection Majority Rights theorists defend are much more specific and rare (Da Silva and Weinstock 2022; Patten 2020).

As this debate is still in its early days, we can expect the arguments for and against to become more nuanced and sophisticated. The significance of the Majority Rights Account, for now, is in its return to the language of rights, formerly associated with the Propertarians and then largely abandoned by the Functionalists. Unlike the functional argument, it is able to frame the demand to restrict and regulate immigration in the language of rights, and not merely utility or instrumental value. If successful, the Majority Rights Account is capable of delivering the desired result of the Propertarian Account – grounding the right to control and regulate immigration – without the latter's problematic assumptions. Whether it will be successful remains, for now, an open question.

11.5 Conclusion

The Propertarian, Functionalist, and Majority Rights Accounts provide distinct rationales for a nationalist argument on the ethics of immigration, largely driven by their different conceptualization of the relationship between the nation and the state. For the Propertarian, the relationship is one of ownership; as the state is the property and instrument of the self-determining nation, the latter retains the right to decide who to admit, and on what conditions. For the Functionalist, the nation is the instrument of the state, providing the cultural, sociological, and psychological preconditions for pursuing the state's interests and fulfilling its obligations. This justifies state action toward maintaining a preserving national identity for its instrumental value, and that includes regulating immigration and requiring immigrants to integrate into the national culture. Finally, for the Majority Right Theorist, "the nation" is the majority cultural group within a state, which like all other groups has a right to cultural protection and preservation. The state has an obligation to protect and fulfill this group against potential threats, among others the threat of large-scale immigration. The different positions are summarized in the table below.

	Propertarian	*Functionalist*	*Majority Rights*
State-Nation Relationship	The nation owns the state; the state is an instrument of the nation	The nation is an instrument of the state; the nation provides the preconditions for the state's institutions	The nation is one of several different cultural groups within the state, each with collective rights against the state

(Continued)

	Propertarian	*Functionalist*	*Majority Rights*
Main argument for regulating immigration	The right to exclude; self-determination	Maintaining the positive effects of national identity (trust, solidarity, social cohesion)	Protecting the culture of the majority nation group
How to make compatible with moral equality	Less absolute property rights; A more porous nation	Cultural accounts of the nation	Balance of interests between majority and minority

Given the importance of nationalism in the real-world politics of migration, I argue that those interested in the ethics of immigration should make it a central focus of our analysis. In the introduction to this chapter, I highlighted three general challenges for an ethical analysis of nationalism. Considering the moral challenge, I have demonstrated that, while controversial, all three accounts can be made compatible with the moral equality of immigrants and could be justified through plausible liberal-democratic frameworks. It is a different question, of course, whether they can achieve that while also supporting restrictive policies on immigration, as I have argued throughout the chapter. Considering the challenge that moderate versions of nationalism are indistinguishable from liberal statism, I hope it is now clear that taking the distinction between the nation and the state seriously, and considering the possible accounts of how the two relate, provides fertile ground for normative arguments not otherwise available. This has the added value of addressing the methodological challenge: using the framework I employed in this chapter, seeing the state and the nation as distinct, allows us to theorize both without accepting either the boundaries of the nation or the borders of the state as natural. Thus, I hope that this framework will provide a useful starting point for future analyses of nationalism in the ethics of immigration.

Acknowledgments

I benefitted from the comments and suggestions of Sahar Akhtar, Steven Klein, Nick Martin, Nathan Milikowsky, David Miller, Liav Orgad, Clara Sandelind and Or Rosenboim. Many thanks as well to Chaim Gans who generously shared with me a copy of his work in progress.

Notes

1. For a rejection of the conflation between national self-determination and the state in the context of immigration, see (Gans 1998).
2. Note that I am not talking here about the economic version of this argument, according to which "extensive welfare states tend to attract low-skilled migrants who stand to benefit from high minimum wages, high-level social services and free health care, but who are a net economic burden to the state." (Holtug 2022). This may or may not effect solidarity, trust, etc., which is the effect the on which the functionalist account focuses.
3. Although some are, let us say, less careful than others (for example, Kaufmann 2018; Huntington and Dunn 2004; Eatwell and Goodwin 2018).

References

Abizadeh, Arash. 2012. 'On the Demos and Its Kin: Nationalism, Democracy, and the Boundary Problem.' *American Political Science Review* 106 (4): 867–82. https://doi.org/10.1017/S0003055412000421.

Amighetti, Sara, and Alasia Nuti. 2016. 'A Nation's Right to Exclude and the Colonies.' *Political Theory* 44 (4): 541–66. https://doi.org/10.1177/0090591715589764.

Anderson, Benedict. 2006. *Imagined Communities: Reflections on the Origin and Spread of Nationalism*. Verso.

Banting, Keith, and Will Kymlicka, eds. 2017. *The Strains of Commitment: The Political Sources of Solidarity in Diverse Societies*. Oxford University Press.

Bauböck, Rainer. 2022. 'Are There Any Cultural Majority Rights?' In *Majorities, Minorities, and the Future of Nationhood*, edited by Liav Orgad and Ruud Koopmans, 35–62. Cambridge University Press.

Blake, Michael. 2014. 'The Right to Exclude.' *Critical Review of International Social and Political Philosophy* 17 (5): 521–37. https://doi.org/10.1080/13698230.2014.919056.

Blake, Michael. 2020. *Justice, Migration, and Mercy*. Oxford University Press.

Breuilly, John. 1993. *Nationalism and the State*. Manchester University Press.

Canovan, Margaret. 2001. 'Sleeping Dogs, Prowling Cats and Soaring Doves: Three Paradoxes in the Political Theory of Nationhood.' *Political Studies* 49 (2): 203–15. https://doi.org/10.1111/1467-9248.00309.

Da Silva, Michael, and Daniel Weinstock. 2022. 'Reconciling the Cultural Claims of Majorities and Minorities.' In *Majorities, Minorities, and the Future of Nationhood*, edited by Liav Orgad and Ruud Koopmans, 129–50. Cambridge University Press.

Dunn, John. 1979. *Western Political Theory in the Face of the Future*. Cambridge University Press.

Eatwell, Roger, and Matthew Goodwin. 2018. *National Populism: The Revolt Against Liberal Democracy*. Pelican.

Eisenberg, Avigail. 2020. 'The Rights of National Majorities: Toxic Discourse or Democratic Catharsis?' *Ethnicities* 20 (2): 312–30. https://doi.org/10.1177/1468796819866488.

Enoch, David. 2018. 'Against Utopianism: Noncompliance and Multiple Agents'. *Philosopher's Imprint* 18 (16). http://hdl.handle.net/2027/spo.3521354.0018.016.

Erez, Lior. 2015. 'Cosmopolitanism, Motivation, and Normative Feasibility.' *Ethics & Global Politics* 8 (1): 26347. https://doi.org/10.3402/egp.v8.26347.

Erez, Lior. 2019. 'Where the Heart Is: Liberal Nationalism, Social Trust, and Multiple National Belongings'. In *Liberal Nationalism and Its Critics: Normative and Empirical Questions*, edited by Gina Gustavsson and David Miller. Oxford University Press. https://doi.org/10.1093/oso/9780198842545.003.0014.

Erez, Lior. 2020. 'Liberal Nationalism, Immigration, and the Problem of Multiple National Identities.' *Critical Review of International Social and Political Philosophy* 23 (4): 495–517. https://doi.org/10.1080/13698230.2018.1479816.

Estlund, David. 2011. 'Human Nature and the Limits (If Any) of Political Philosophy.' *Philosophy & Public Affairs* 39 (3): 207–37. https://doi.org/10.1111/j.1088-4963.2011.01207.x.

Fleischacker, Sam. 2013. 'Owning Land Versus Governing a Land: Property, Sovereignty, and Nationalism.' *Social Philosophy and Policy* 30 (1–2): 373–403. https://doi.org/10.1017/S0265052513000186.

Gans, Chaim. 1998. 'Nationalism and Immigration.' *Ethical Theory and Moral Practice* 1 (2): 159–80.

Gans, Chaim. 2003. *The Limits of Nationalism*. Cambridge University Press.

Gans, Chaim, and Oded Steinberg. 2023. 'Liberationist Nationalism V. Proprietary Nationalism'. With Authors [Unpublished Manuscript].

Gellner, Ernest. 1983. *Nations and Nationalism*. Cornell University Press.

Gustavsson, Gina, and David Miller. 2020. *Liberal Nationalism and Its Critics: Normative and Empirical Questions*. Oxford University Press.

Holtug, Nils. 2022. *The Politics of Social Cohesion: Immigration, Community, and Justice*. Oxford University Press.

Huntington, Samuel P., and Steve Dunn. 2004. *Who Are We?: The Challenges to America's National Identity*. Simon and Schuster.

Kaufmann, Eric. 2018. *Whiteshift: Populism, Immigration and the Future of White Majorities*. Allen Lane.
Ko, Jiyoung, and Seung-Whan Choi. 2022 'Nationalism and Immigration Control' *Nations and Nationallism* 28 (1): 12. https://doi.org/10.1111/nana.12801
Kymlicka, Will. 1995. *Multicultural Citizenship: A Liberal Theory of Minority Rights*. Clarendon Press.
Kymlicka, Will. 2015. 'Solidarity in Diverse Societies: Beyond Neoliberal Multiculturalism and Welfare Chauvinism.' *Comparative Migration Studies* 3 (1): 17. https://doi.org/10.1186/s40878-015-0017-4.
Kymlicka, Will. 2022. 'Nationhood, Multiculturalism, and the Ethics of Membership.' In *Majorities, Minorities, and the Future of Nationhood*, edited by Liav Orgad and Ruud Koopmans, 87–128. Cambridge University Press.
Lægaard, Sune. 2006. 'Feasibility and Stability in Normative Political Philosophy: The Case of Liberal Nationalism.' *Ethical Theory and Moral Practice* 9 (4): 399–416. https://doi.org/10.1007/s10677-006-9048-0.
Lægaard, Sune. 2009. 'Liberal Nationalism on Immigration'. In *Nationalism and Multiculturalism in a World of Immigration*, edited by Nils Holtug, Kasper Lippert-Rasmussen, and Sune Lægaard, 1–20. Palgrave Macmillan UK. https://doi.org/10.1057/9780230377776_1.
Lenard, Patti Tamara, and David Miller. 2018. 'Trust and National Identity'. In *The Oxford Handbook of Social and Political Trust*, edited by Eric Uslaner.
Meer, Tom van der, and Jochem Tolsma. 2014. 'Ethnic Diversity and Its Effects on Social Cohesion.' *Annual Review of Sociology* 40 (1): 459–78. https://doi.org/10.1146/annurev-soc-071913-043309.
Mill, John Stuart. 1861. *Considerations on Representative Government*.
Miller, David. 1995. *On Nationality*. Oxford University Press.
Miller, David. 2008. 'Immigrants, Nations, and Citizenship.' *Journal of Political Philosophy* 16 (4): 371–90. https://doi.org/10.1111/j.1467-9760.2007.00295.x.
Miller, David. 2009. 'Republicanism, National Identity, and Europe.' In *Republicanism and Political Theory*, edited by Cecile Laborde and John Maynor, 133–58. John Wiley & Sons.
Miller, David. 2016a. 'Majorities and Minarets: Religious Freedom and Public Space.' *British Journal of Political Science* 46 (2): 437–56. https://doi.org/10.1017/S0007123414000131.
Miller, David. 2016b. *Strangers in Our Midst*.
Miller, David. 2017. *Solidarity and Its Sources*. Oxford University Press. http://www.oxfordscholarship.com/view/10.1093/acprof:oso/9780198795452.001.0001/acprof-9780198795452-chapter-2.
Miller, David. 2019. 'Lockeans Versus Nationalists on Territorial Rights.' *Politics, Philosophy & Economics* 18 (4): 323–35. https://doi.org/10.1177/1470594X18779147.
Miller, David, and Sundas Ali. 2014. 'Testing the National Identity Argument.' *European Political Science Review* 6 (02): 237–59. https://doi.org/10.1017/S1755773913000088.
Moore, Margaret. 2001. *The Ethics of Nationalism*. OUP Oxford.
Mylonas, Harris, and Maya Tudor. 2021. 'Nationalism: What We Know and What We Still Need to Know.' *Annual Review of Political Science* 24: 109–32.
Orgad, Liav. 2015. *The Cultural Defense of Nations: A Liberal Theory of Majority Rights*. Oxford University Press.
Orgad, Liav, and Ruud Koopmans. 2022. 'Majority–Minority Constellations: Toward a Group-Differentiated Approach.' In *Majorities, Minorities, and the Future of Nationhood*, edited by Liav Orgad and Ruud Koopmans, 1–34. Cambridge University Press.
Patten, Alan. 2020. 'Populist Multiculturalism: Are There Majority Cultural Rights?' *Philosophy & Social Criticism* 46 (5): 539–52. https://doi.org/10.1177/0191453720903486.
Penner, James. 2000. *The Idea of Property in Law. The Idea of Property in Law*. Oxford University Press.
Pevnick, Ryan. 2011. *Immigration and the Constraints of Justice: Between Open Borders and Absolute Sovereignty*.
Powell, Enoch. 1968. 'Speech at Birmingham'. 20 April 1968. https://www.telegraph.co.uk/comment/3643823/Enoch-Powells-Rivers-of-Blood-speech.html.
Ripstein, Arthur. 2017. 'Property and Sovereignty: How to Tell the Difference.' *Theoretical Inquiries in Law* 18 (2): 243–68. https://doi.org/10.1515/til-2017-0013.
Sager, Alex. 2016. 'Methodological Nationalism, Migration and Political Theory.' *Political Studies* 64 (1): 42–59. https://doi.org/10.1111/1467-9248.12167.

Sandelind, Clara. 2019. 'Can the Welfare State Justify Restrictive Asylum Policies? A Critical Approach.' *Ethical Theory and Moral Practice* 22 (2): 331–46. https://doi.org/10.1007/s10677-019-09989-3.

Smith, Rogers M. 2011. 'Living in a Promiseland?1: Mexican Immigration and American Obligations.' *Perspectives on Politics* 9 (3): 545–57. https://doi.org/10.1017/S153759271100274X.

Tamir, Yael. 1993. *Liberal Nationalism*. Princeton University Press.

Tamir, Yael. 2019. *Why Nationalism*. Princeton University Press.

Waal, Tamar de, and Jan Willem Duyvendak. 2022. 'The Majority Oppressed? On Asymmetrical Multiculturalism and Majority Rights.' *Comparative Migration Studies* 10 (1): 42. https://doi.org/10.1186/s40878-022-00319-8.

Walzer, Michael. 1999. 'The New Tribalism: Notes on a Difficult Problem.' In *Theorizing Nationalism*, edited by Ronald Beiner, 205–18. State University of New York Press.

Wimmer, Andreas, and Nina Glick Schiller. 2002. 'Methodological Nationalism and Beyond: Nation-State Building, Migration and the Social Sciences.' *Global Networks* 2 (4): 301–34. https://doi.org/10.1111/1471-0374.00043.

Wintour, Patrick. 2018. 'Hillary Clinton: Europe Must Curb Immigration to Stop Rightwing Populists'. *The Guardian*, 22 November 2018, sec. World news. https://www.theguardian.com/world/2018/nov/22/hillary-clinton-europe-must-curb-immigration-stop-populists-trump-brexit.

Yack, Bernard. 2001. 'Popular Sovereignty and Nationalism.' *Political Theory* 29 (4): 517–36.

Yack, Bernard. 2012. 'The Myth of the Civic Nation'. In *Nationalism and the Moral Psychology of Community*, 23–44. The University of Chicago Press.

PART IV

Immigration and Discrimination

12
EXCLUDING BY RACE, ETHNICITY, AND RELIGION

Sahar Akhtar

12.1 Introduction

In almost all scholarly discussions, any linkage between immigration restrictions and factors like race, ethnicity, or religion is widely criticized. But is it always wrong for a state to base its admissions policies on race, ethnicity, or religion? In this chapter, I offer one way to try to address this question. I will start by explaining the basic framework that I employ, which is grounded in the idea of wrongful discrimination. In particular, I will focus on a growing class of views that argue that discrimination is wrong when it degrades a group. Then, I will discuss different considerations that determine whether racial, ethnic, or religious immigration policies degrade a group or not and offer examples. Contrary to what most commentators maintain, I will argue that not all cases of excluding by race, ethnicity, or religion are in fact morally wrong.[1]

12.2 Immigration and Its Ties to Race, Ethnicity, and Religion

Immigration policies have often intersected with considerations of race, ethnicity, and religion.[2] Perhaps the most infamous and offensive measures are now relics of the past. These include policies such as the 1882 Chinese Exclusion Act in the United States, which prohibited the entry of Chinese laborers[3]; Australia's 1901 Immigration Restriction Act, famously known as the White Australia Policy, aiming to bar non-white people from entering the country[4]; and Uganda's sudden expulsion of South Asians, primarily Indians, in 1972 during President Idi Amin's rule.[5] There are also numerous recent examples. For instance, Kiribati, a nation made up of three small Pacific Island groups that is projected to be the first to lose its land due to shifting climate patterns, has granted citizenship since 1979 to anyone with ties to the I-Kiribati people.[6] Since 1986, Liberia has exclusively granted citizenship to individuals of Black African origin.[7] Though no longer in effect, Japan's 1990 policy favored the admission of people of Japanese descent from countries like Brazil and Peru.[8] Furthermore, Israel's Law of Return, established in 1950, continues to provide automatic admission and citizenship exclusively to the people of Jewish heritage. While many such recent policies might be less objectionable and might not suggest animosity towards specific groups than those of the deeper past, many still raise ethical concerns.

Among normative scholars of immigration, there is near-universal agreement that racial, ethnic, and religious immigration criteria are almost always, if not always, morally wrong.[9] The primary exception is Michael Walzer. While Walzer suggests that the use of such criteria might be unfortunate, he does not altogether condemn even some notoriously problematic policies, including the White Australia Policy, which was rooted in the belief that whites are superior to other races. Moreover, he implied that policies such as White Australia may be employed to preserve a state's dominant culture. It seems that for him, the moral limits on any such policy come only from considerations related to people with urgent admission needs, including refugees, as he claims that such policies are morally permissible if the state in question cedes some territory to provide refuge to people fleeing oppression and the like.[10] Outside of such urgent cases, Walzer suggests that using racial criteria even in the manner of a White Australia Policy is not wrong.[11]

As with Walzer's view, under the brief analysis that follows, racial, ethnic, and religious immigration criteria are not always wrong. However, the analysis also departs from Walzer's diagnosis of cases like that of White Australia and his more general claim that such criteria may be permissible whenever they protect the state's dominant culture. Based in an increasingly accepted understanding of wrongful discrimination, we will see that the analysis here allows us to easily reject cases like White Australia while retaining the idea that, in many other cases, racial, ethnic, and religious criteria are not morally wrong.

12.3 Discrimination and Degradation

Broadly speaking, wrongful discrimination concerns differential treatment that disadvantages people because of their socially salient, identity-constitutive characteristics, or treats them in an inferior manner.[12] These notions describe characteristics, such as race, ethnicity, religion, and gender, which shape interaction across a wide range of social contexts,[13] and can influence how one is regarded and treated by others. Additionally, such characteristics are partly constituted by how people sharing the characteristic, or the group's members, self-understand the trait, which can often be in response to how others have perceived, interacted with, and treated the group in the past.[14]

There are a variety of differentiating acts that could count as discrimination, but since we are discussing immigration, what is important here is the differential admission or exclusion of people on the basis of people's identities—which I will call "selective exclusion". Reasons why selectively excluding people from any association on the basis of their race, ethnicity, or religion is considered wrong vary and include the views that such characteristics are beyond the group's control,[15] that they are normatively irrelevant,[16] or that such selection would undermine one's freedom to deny that their race or ethnicity plays a central role in their life or conception of themselves.[17] But here I will focus on a growing set of views which are concerned with what we might call the social structure and expression of degradation. This family of views is concerned with whether exclusion expresses a demeaning or denigrating message about a group or sends the message that they are morally inferior,[18] (further) undermines the group's social bases of self-respect,[19] or perpetuates certain social meanings, or stigmas, against the group.[20]

Whether any of these forms of degradation occurs in any given case will depend on a complex variety of both empirical and normative judgments, and I will certainly not be able to get to most of the relevant issues in this short chapter.[21] But a central issue that must be attended to is, in the context of global social relations and institutions, the group's social status, or, whether the group is comparatively vulnerable or whether it is comparatively secure or powerful. I define vulnerable groups as those which face substantial disadvantages in material, political, or cultural terms, or even in terms of self-respect, in comparison to more globally secure or powerful groups.[22] For instance, these groups might have comparatively little power to affect international interactions—including political relationships that occur from membership in international bodies (e.g., the United Nations, International Monetary Fund [IMF], and World Bank), climate agreements, treaty negotiations, trade, and economic associations, war and armed conflict, as well as immigration—or comparatively little power to gain international economic, social, and political goods (e.g., territory, natural resources, and recognition of sovereignty). Alternatively, they might face a way of life that is substantially threatened, including central aspects of the way of life such as its dominant language. Finally, whether because of one of the former or because a group has experienced, say, alienation, marginalization, or oppression, it might (also) encounter disadvantages in the social bases of self-respect.

For each of these related ways that selective exclusion can degrade a racial, ethnic, or religious group, global social status matters. That is, whether selective exclusion expresses a demeaning or denigrating message about the disfavored group or sends the message that the group is morally inferior, erodes the social bases of the group's self-respect, or perpetuates stigmas against the group depends on, among other issues we explore below, whether the excluded group is vulnerable, as well as whether there are any differences in (dis)advantages between the admitting group and excluded group. It's important to clarify that social status is a continuum notion—as there isn't a hard line between a globally secure and a globally vulnerable group (though we can often identify clear cases of each), and that even vulnerable groups can vary in the degree and type of disadvantages that they experience. Moreover, to say that a group is vulnerable does not mean it is vulnerable in comparison with every other group and with respect to every region of the world or every social context. These qualifications will be important for exploring how global status is relevant for whether selective exclusion on the basis of race, ethnicity, or religion degrades others.

12.4 When Does Selective Exclusion Wrong Others?

In this section, I will try to illustrate the broad approach described in the previous section by exploring a number of actual and hypothetical examples. It's important to emphasize from the start that the analysis I provide here will be inconclusive. Particularly in instances in which a group's global status varies, whether over type, region, or both, whether its selective exclusion degrades others in any specific case will depend on a variety of both empirical and normative issues, and we will only get to some of the more central ones here. More than providing definitive answers, what I hope to do is show how the normative ideas provided by the basic approach can assist in thinking through complex immigration cases.

Both explicitly disfavoring and explicitly favoring others on the basis of race, ethnicity, or religion involves selecting against or selectively excluding some group (or groups). But though there might not always be a clear distinction between the two sorts of stances,[23] explicitly disfavoring a group or a few groups will almost always raise greater moral concerns, especially when the latter are vulnerable. In fact, aside from possible rare exceptions,[24] it seems that explicitly excluding a vulnerable group always degrades people in the group even when the admitting group is also highly vulnerable and, moreover, does not seem to depend on either type or region of disadvantage. To see this, consider Polynesians, an ethnolinguistic group that has historically had exceedingly little power in global interactions and now faces significant climate-related obstacles,[25] including significant health concerns.[26] If Polynesians in some state, such as Tuvalu, were to have an immigration policy explicitly disfavoring the admission of Muslims, it would seem that Polynesians' own significant global vulnerability would bear little on whether the policy wrongs Muslims. Taken as a group, Muslims have experienced varying forms of marginalization and prejudice, especially since the terrorist acts committed in the United States on September 11, 2001, which have contributed to violence and attacks against them in many states around the world.[27] Because of this background, it is plausible to interpret criteria that single them out for a disadvantage as reflecting, say, unwarranted fear and as expressing a demeaning message about them.[28]

In contrast, determining whether explicitly favoring one's own group for admission degrades any group is far more complicated, requiring attention to comparative (dis)advantage differences between admitting and excluded groups and region and type of disadvantage. Let's begin examining policies which favor one's own group by focusing on the type of disadvantage. A good example concerns the world's Jewish population. As a result of the lasting effects of the Holocaust and other forms of persecution and racism experienced by the Jewish people, they arguably face substantial disadvantages in terms of the global social bases of their self-respect. At the same time, they experience considerable advantages in global economic, political, and military terms.[29] Moreover, they have access to valuable life opportunities in a variety of wealthy states, including Israel.[30] Because of these kinds of significant advantages, if an admitting group were to favor its own group members, thereby selectively excluding Jewish people, among others, this might not wrong them. An illustrative case is if India were to have a policy preferring the admission of Hindu Indians. Hindu Indians enjoy a relatively secure status around the world, including in terms of how they are regarded by others (India's economic growth may certainly be either an indication or a cause of this).[31] Moreover, a significant number of Hindu Indians residing outside of India assume leadership roles within affluent nations' business and political spheres (including the United States, the UK, and Australia), and generally seem to enjoy a considerably higher status than many other racial and ethnic minorities in those states.[32] To clarify, as a result of their comparatively powerful global status, the selective favoring of Hindus in an admission policy would likely degrade specific vulnerable groups, such as the Bengalis, owing to the historical and current context of Hindu–Muslim relations, particularly the strained relations with the Bengali population in India.[33] However, as there appears to be no contentious history between Hindus and Jews, India's policy would unlikely degrade Jewish people. Conversely, if a European nation were to have a policy preferring the admission of Christians over other groups, the situation would differ. Given the history and societal backdrop of substantial injustices perpetrated against Jewish people in specific parts of Europe, such a policy would undoubtedly demean them or further erode the social bases of their self-respect.

Let me show now how the fact that a group's (dis)advantages are largely only regional might play a role. Consider Christians living in the Middle and Near East. They are disadvantaged in relation to that region (and North Africa[34]) but not in other areas, including

Europe, North and South America, and parts of Asia. An implication of their vulnerability being primarily regional is that while it would seem to clearly degrade Christians if countries in the region, such as Pakistan, Jordan, or Bahrain, were to favor the admission of their dominant religious group (Muslims), if, say, Japan were to favor the admission of practitioners of Shinto or Buddhism, that would likely not degrade Christians.[35] In large part, this is because there do not seem to be any sustained patterns of viewing Christians with prejudice or disdain in that region of Asia, and so there is little if anything to support interpreting their selective exclusion as treating or regarding them as inferior. But that is not true of the Middle East and nearby regions.[36]

Sometimes, region and type of (dis)advantage can interact in ways that also have consequences for whether exclusion can degrade a group. Take again Polynesians and consider the history of policies such as White Australia, which was designed to exclude nonwhites from Australia.[37] Against this sort of background, Polynesians' disadvantages in terms of self-respect are likely considerably amplified in the context of social relations in the South Pacific area.[38] Thus, if, say, New Zealanders, were to explicitly favor members of their own racial or ethnic group, it would almost certainly degrade Polynesians. It would be far less clear, however, if, say, Brazilians favoring the admission of their own racial or ethnic group would degrade Polynesians.

If the admitting group's vulnerability varies either regionally or according to the type of (dis)advantage, this can also affect whether its selectively favoring its own group degrades others. Consider, first, the type of (dis)advantage an admitting group faces. Though it might be unlikely that a group would experience only material disadvantages—that is, apart from any other disadvantage—if any group were in such a situation, it is far from clear how their vulnerability would be reduced or meaningfully addressed by selective immigration favoring their group.[39] Because of this, any rationale for immigration favoring their group would likely be unsupported and would more likely reflect some sort of attempt to selectively exclude a particular group or groups.

In contrast to material disadvantages, disadvantages in the social bases of self-respect and in way-of-life terms, especially in combination, appear to present the clearest rationales for selective immigration. For instance, in light of the significant injustices Jewish people have experienced, Israel's favoring of the admission of Jews would seem to support the idea of a place where Jews always have secure membership, and it isn't obvious that there are plausible alternative routes to selective immigration for effectively addressing these disadvantages. As a result, we can imagine certain immigration policies favoring the admission of Jews that would not degrade others. However, just because there is a clear rationale supporting immigration favoring one's group does not mean that any immigration policy doing so avoids wronging others. Indeed, it seems that Israel's current such effort, the Law of Return, which again grants automatic admission and citizenship to all and only Jewish people, does wrong others, especially Palestinians, given a contentious and violent history between Jews and Palestinians, with Palestinians being vulnerable along multiple dimensions, including that they themselves lack secure membership.

I've just explored how a combination of disadvantages in self-respect and way-of-life factors can provide a clear justification for favoring immigrants from within one's own group (though not necessarily any policy designed to do so). To emphasize the significance of these dual disadvantages, let's examine the situation of Arabs. Primarily identified as Muslims, they have been disadvantaged in terms of self-respect, particularly in the aftermath of September 11, 2001. However, Arabs also undoubtedly have significant global economic and political power and access to numerous important opportunities in a variety of states, thereby enjoying a secure way of life.[40] And the latter certainly matters. Imagine if the United Arab Emirates, for instance, were to enact a policy prioritizing the admission of Arabs solely due to their Arab identity. Given that Arabs are the majority groups within several prosperous states and consequently do not experience a vulnerable way of life,[41] it becomes implausible to interpret the policy as an effort to safeguard their status in any manner. Since there appears to be insufficient support for any rationale aimed at securing their status, the policy would surely degrade certain vulnerable groups, particularly those with a history of severe injustices in the region, such as the Kurds.[42]

Now, let's turn our attention to Japan's policy implemented in 1990, favoring the entry of other Japanese descendants applying for immigration.[43] While the Japanese populace might face global disadvantages due to a rapidly declining population, potentially impacting their way of life, they have substantial power in global economic terms and do not seem disadvantaged in self-respect terms.[44] Though it might make sense to interpret the immigration policy as an attempt to safeguard their way of life, the policy might still degrade specific groups, including Filipinos, due to the historical and current context of Japanese-Filipino relations. This context includes Japan's previous wartime offenses and atrocities committed against Filipinos.[45]

On the other hand, the immigration policy of Kiribati looks very different. Since gaining independence in 1979, it has favored the admission of those whose ancestry is linked to the I-Kiribati people, automatically conferring them citizenship.[46] The I-Kiribati face a significant climate-related threat to their dominant way of life and, additionally, are globally disadvantaged in economic and political terms.[47] Given all of this, Kiribati's immigration policy seems clearly aimed at securing its way of life and would be difficult to view as degrading any who are excluded.[48]

12.5 Conclusion

In closing this chapter, I want to note again that what I have just discussed is not exhaustive or definitive. For many of the cases examined, there may be other morally and empirically relevant issues that, if considered, would alter the normative evaluation of some case. More than providing definitive answers, I hope to have provided a general framework, based in a dominant conception of the wrong of discrimination, for examining racial, ethnic, and religious immigration policies. In contrast to the many views that either suggest that all (or virtually all) racial, ethnic, and religious immigration criteria are wrong and in contrast to views, including Walzer's, that suggest that such criteria are always morally permissible if tied to protecting a way of life, the framework here suggests that the moral status of cases varies greatly.

Notes

1 Parts of this chapter were adapted from Akhtar, Sahar. *Immigration and Discrimination: (Un) welcoming Others*, Oxford: Oxford University Press, 2024.
2 For some of this work, see: Lake and Reynolds, *Global Colour Line*; Givens, Terri E. 2007. "Immigration and Immigrant Integration"; d'Appollonia and Reich, "Immigration, Integration and Security"; Fine, "Immigration and Discrimination"; Song, *Immigration and Democracy*, 34; Akhtar, Sahar. "Race beyond our Borders: Is Racial and Ethnic Immigration Selection Always Morally Wrong?" *Ethics* 132, no. 2 (2022): 322–51; Akhtar, Sahar. *Immigration and Discrimination*.
3 "Chinese Exclusion Act: Primary Documents in American History", Library of Congress, https://guides.loc.gov/chinese-exclusion-act.

4 "The Immigration Restriction Act 1901", National Archives of Australia, Australian Government, https://www.naa.gov.au/explore-collection/immigration-and-citizenship/immigration-restriction-act-1901.
5 Segawa, "Tension between Indians".
6 See the Constitution of Kiribati, Articles 19 and 23.
7 See Tannenbaum, et al., "Aliens and Nationality Law". The authors note that Article 27(b) of the constitution limits citizenship to "a person who is a Negro, or of Negro descent, born in Liberia and subject to the jurisdiction thereof" or "a person born outside Liberia whose father (i) was born a citizen of Liberia; (ii) was a citizen of Liberia at the time of the birth of such child, and (iii) had resided in Liberia prior to the birth of such child". p. 13.
8 Chung, *Immigration and Citizenship*.
9 See (for example) Carens, *Ethics of Immigration*, 174, 179, 182; Miller, *Strangers in Our Midst*, 102,103. David Miller, "Immigrants, Nations, and Citizenship", 389; Fine, "Immigration and Discrimination", 146; Blake, *Justice, Migration, and Mercy*; Wellman, "Freedom of Association"; Lim, "Selecting Immigrants by Skill"; Mendoza, " Presumptive Rights of Immigrants"; Blake, "Immigration, Association, and Antidiscrimination". Song, *Immigration and Democracy*, 34–35.
10 Walzer, 46–48.
11 Walzer, 46–48.
12 See Khaitan, Tarunabh. 2015. *A Theory of Discrimination Law*. Oxford: Oxford University Press, pp. 49–56.
13 This aspect of nondiscrimination is, it seems, critical. See the valuable work by Kasper Lippert-Rasmussen, "The Badness of Discrimination", *Ethical Theory and Moral Practice*, 9(2006):167–85,169; 2014. *Born Free and Equal: A Philosophical Inquiry into the Nature of Discrimination*. New York: Oxford University Press.
14 Iris Marion Young, *Justice and the Politics of Difference* (Princeton, NJ: Princeton University Press, 1990), especially pp. 43–48. Owen Fiss, "Groups and the Equal Protection Clause", *Philosophy and Public Affairs* 5, no. 2 (1976): 107–177, pp. 148–149.
15 For instance, see Richard Kahlenberg's discussion suggesting that this is why racial discrimination is wrong (Kahlenberg, Richard, 1996. *The Remedy*, New York: Basic Books, 54–55.)
16 Moreau, Sophia, 2010. "What is Discrimination?" *Philosophy and Public Affairs*, 38: 143–179, 147.
17 See the discussion by Julie C. Suk "Quotas and Consequences: A Transnational Re-evaluation", in *Philosophical Foundations of Discrimination Law*, ed. Deborah Hellman and Sophia Moreau, New York: Oxford University Press, 2018; pp. 228–249.
18 Anderson, Elizabeth and Richard Pildes, Expressive Theories of Law: A General Restatement", *University of Pennsylvania Law Review* 148/5(2000):1503–76; Hellman, Deborah. 2008. *When Is Discrimination Wrong?* Cambridge, MA: Harvard University Press; and Shin, Patrick, 2009. "The Substantive Principle of Equal Treatment", *Legal Theory*, 15: 149–172. Stuart White can be partly interpreted along these lines as well; see "Freedom of Association and The Right to Exclude", *Journal of Political Philosophy* 5/4(1997): 373–391, esp. 384–385.
19 Sunstein (1994) stresses such issues. Also see White's concerns about dignity interests (1997: 384–85). Moreau brings our attention to how certain "structures" (institutions, policies, and physical structures) can implicitly accommodate the interests and concerns of the advantaged group(s) and, in this way, can sometimes condition self-respect (or its relative absence) for more vulnerable groups. An example concerns how buildings with wheelchair ramps in the back might make people using wheelchairs feel that they should "not to be seen" or that they should be "out of sight". (See: Sophia Moreau, "Equality and Discrimination", in Cambridge Companion to the Law, 2020, John Tasioulas (ed), Cambridge: Cambridge University Press, pp. 171–190.
20 See Loury, Glenn C. *The Anatomy of Racial Inequality*. Harvard University Press, 2002, pp. 60–67.
21 For a more extensive examination of these issues, see Akhtar, *Immigration and Discrimination*.
22 See Khaitan, 2015, 54–56; Amartya Sen, *Inequality Reexamined* (Clarendon Press, 1992); 28–30. By including cultural disadvantage, this may be a broader understanding of vulnerability than discussed by antidiscrimination theorists. But my emphasis on culture is inspired by both Iris Marion Young's discussion of cultural imperialism (1990, pp. 59–61) and Will Kymlicka's argument that certain cultures should have special group-differentiated rights (See Kymlicka, *Multicultural Citizenship: A Liberal Theory of Minority Rights* [Oxford, UK: Clarendon Press, 1995], 108–113.) I believe cultural disadvantage has not received adequate attention in the antidiscrimination

literature, perhaps because the other forms of disadvantage are considered to overlap significantly with cultural disadvantage. But as we will see in the global context, this is not always the case. For instance, we will see that a group might have a vulnerable global status in light of its substantial population decline and consequent damage to its way of life but not experience significant material or political disadvantages.

23 For instance, if an immigration policy explicitly states a preference for every race in the world except for one that is not mentioned, it looks like a clear case of disfavoring.
24 Consider a group that is significantly disadvantaged in terms of its distinct way of life and some other disadvantaged group that is an existential threat to it because of a history of violent conflict between the groups. It may be permissible for the first group to explicitly exclude the second (and vice versa) (but notice how tentative this seems and how rare the scenario is).
25 On the relation between Polynesians' global disadvantages and climate change risks, see Lallemant-Moe, "Polynesian Political Awakening". The World Risk Index 2019 ranks several Polynesian-majority states among the top twenty most at-risk countries for extreme natural events (leading to water scarcity). For instance, Vanuatu and Tonga are ranked first and third respectively. Bündnis Entwicklung Hilft, *WorldRiskReport 2019*, 7, 47, 56.
26 World Health Organization, *Human Health*.
27 "Violence Against Muslims: 2008 Hate Crime Survey", *Human Rights First*; Carr, James (ed.). 2015. *Experiences of Islamophobia: Living with Racism in the Neoliberal Era*. New York: Routledge; Ma, Haiyun. 2019. "The Anti-Islamic Movement in China". *Hudson Institute*.
28 Though we may not know for sure whether any such attitude is behind an immigration policy, it is nevertheless hard to imagine any case of explicitly disfavoring as not involving some such attitude. At the very least, it seems to suggest a failure to consider the interests of the members of the selectively excluded group, or, put differently an "absence of appropriate recognition of someone's personhood, whether that absence comes about willfully or by neglect" (Eidelson, 2015, p. 75).
29 Since the majority of the world's Jewish population lives in Israel (which is 73.9 percent Jewish) (https://www.jewishvirtuallibrary.org/latest-population-statistics-for-israel), measures of Israel's advantages in these terms may be sufficient to illustrate the point. For instance, it has about the thirtieth largest economy in the world (https://databank.worldbank.org/data/download/GDP.pdf). Considering its size of less than eight million people (https://www.worldometers.info/world-population/israel-population/), this ranking is significant. And it is ranked thirtieth for its overall prosperity (https://www.prosperity.com/globe/israel). Additionally, it ranks tenth for longest lifespan (https://knoema.com/atlas/ranks/Life-expectancy). According to one ranking that compiles information based on sources such as the *CIA World Factbook*, Israel is among the top twenty states worldwide in terms of the military's strength and size (https://www.globalfirepower.com/country-military-strength-detail.php?country_id=israel#:~:text=For%202021%2C%20Israel%20is%20ranked,on%2003%2F03%2F2021).
30 See previous note. Outside of Israel, the great majority of the world's Jewish population lives in the United States (38.8 percent), followed distantly by France (3.1 percent), Canada (2.7 percent), and the UK (2.0 percent) (https://www.jewishvirtuallibrary.org/jewish-population-of-the-world#region).
31 For instance, India is one of the fastest-growing economies in the world. As of 2018, it ranked seventh among states globally in share of world GDP (https://www.theglobaleconomy.com/rankings/gdp_share/) and thirteenth in share of total world exports (https://www.theglobaleconomy.com/rankings/share_world_exports/). Its 2019 GDP was calculated to be 2.871 trillion U.S. dollars (https://data.worldbank.org/indicator/NY.GDP.MKTP.KD.ZG?locations=IN), and, in recent years, it has enjoyed a roughly 7–8 percent rate of growth (https://data.worldbank.org/indicator/NY.GDP.MKTP.KD.ZG?locations=IN&most_recent_year_desc=true). Additionally, it has made substantial progress in combatting absolute poverty, lifting more than ninety million people out of extreme poverty during the period 2011–2015 and shrinking the extremely poor's population share from 21.6 percent in 2011 to 13.4 percent in 2015 (https://www.worldbank.org/en/country/india/overview).
32 Consider their success in the US, for instance. In 2021, the most popular and successful start-ups are Robinhood, Clubhouse, and Instacart, all of which were founded by Indian Americans (https://www.businessinsider.in/business/startups/news/indian-americans-behind-some-of-the-most-popular-startups-and-technology-firms-in-the-us/slidelist/81884255.cms). The number of billion-dollar startups founded by Indian Americans is considerably higher than that for any

other non-native group (fourteen in comparison to eight for Canadian Americans, the next-highest-ranked group) (https://theatlas.com/charts/Hy3DRvRwg; https://www.vox.com/world/2017/2/8/14547212/trump-executive-order-h1b-silicon-valley). Also see Vucetic, Srdjan. 2011.*The Anglosphere: A Genealogy of a Racialized Identity in International Relations*. Stanford: Stanford University Press, Ch.3 and 147–148; https://www.pewresearch.org/global/2016/09/19/3-how-indians-see-their-place-in-the-world/

33 See, for instance, https://www.nytimes.com/2019/08/31/world/asia/india-muslim-citizen-list.html and https://www.bbc.co.uk/newsround/45007750 on the recent citizenship tests implemented in India's Assam state, which is heavily populated by Bengali Muslims.

34 For a recent overview of some of these issues, see Patrick Wintour, "Persecution of Christians 'coming close to genocide' in Middle East – report", The Guardian, May 2, 2019. https://www.theguardian.com/world/2019/may/02/persecution-driving-christians-out-of-middle-east-report. Also, see discussion in *Immigration and Discrimination*, Chapter 3, section 3.

35 Concerns about discrimination in some domestic contexts also seem responsive to regional differences. For instance, consider Appalachian whites in the United States, who (because of a perceived dialect) are stereotyped as lazy and inbred by others in surrounding regions. Many outside these areas may be unable to identify Appalachians on the basis of their perceived characteristics, making their salience as a social group mostly regional, and thus there are laws forbidding discrimination against Appalachian whites in the region, such as in Cincinnati, but not in other parts of the United States. Of course, laws should not determine how we think about the ethics of discrimination, but it's worth noting how regional variation matters for discrimination norms even domestically. For valuable discussion, see William Rhee & Stephen C. Scott, 2018.

36 Christians experience widespread discrimination and persecution in the area. According to one report, their treatment in countries such as Algeria, Iran, Iraq, Syria, and Saudi Arabia has reached an alarming stage, with numerous reports of attacks on churches, confiscation of property, and arrests. (Aid to the Church in Need. *Religious Freedom in the World 2018*, 2018. https://www.churchinneed.org/wp-content/uploads/2018/11/RFR-2018-Exec-Summary-Web-version.pdf.)

37 See Wellman, 2008: 140.

38 See further discussion in *Immigration and Discrimination*, Chapter 3, section 4.

39 There are likely numerous alternative strategies for bolstering a group's material position in the world, including engaging in global trade, developing the sorts of domestic institutions that reduce poverty (stable property rights, legally enforced trade, and commerce (See: Douglass North, *Institutions, Institutional Change, and Economic Performance* (Cambridge, UK: Cambridge University Press, 1990); Daron Acemoglu and James A. Robinson, "Unbundling Institutions", *Journal of Political Economy* 113 (2005): 949–995; Acemoglu and Robinson, *Why Nations Fail* (New York: Crown Business, 2013).

40 See further discussion in *Immigration and Discrimination*, Chapter 3, especially section 3.

41 For instance, six Arab-majority states count among the thirty richest states in the world in per capita terms, with Qatar the single richest (https://www.gfmag.com/global-data/economic-data/richest-countries-in-the-world). And, in total, Arabs constitute the majority in twenty-two states around the world (https://data.worldbank.org/indicator/SP.POP.TOTL?locations=1A&most_recent_value_desc=false).

42 As with Polynesians, it's likely that Kurds' disadvantages in terms of self-respect are considerably more compromised in the region, considering the background of injustice against Kurds by other groups in the region. https://www.hrw.org/report/2009/11/26/group-denial/repression-kurdish-political-and-cultural-rights-syria; https://www.reuters.com/article/us-syria-security-kurds-factbox/factbox-the-kurdish-struggle-for-rights-and-land-idUSKBN1WO19X. Additionally, though Kurds make up the fourth-largest ethnic group in the Middle East, they do not have their own state (https://www.bbc.com/news/world-middle-east-29702440).

43 Chung, *Immigration and Citizenship*.

44 For instance, Japan's per capita wealth is among the top thirty in the world, making the average Japanese person relatively prosperous (https://statisticstimes.com/economy/projected-world-gdp-ranking.php; https://www.statista.com/statistics/684329/japan-population-distribution-by-wealth-range/). After the United States and China, Japan has the largest share of millionaires in the world (https://www.economist.com/graphic-detail/2019/10/22/millions-of-millionaires). Japanese people enjoy success in many wealthy states apart from Japan. For instance, the 2018 annual

median income for Japanese Americans was $74,000, while the national average was $63,100 (https://ncrc.org/wp-content/uploads/2020/05/Racial-Wealth-Snapshot_Asian-American.pdf). And in 2018, Asians had the highest SAT scores (https://nces.ed.gov/fastfacts/display.asp?id=171). Japan also has one of the best health care systems in the world (second best, according to one ranking: https://docs.prosperity.com/9016/0508/7373/Japan_2020_PIcountryprofile.pdf) and the second- or third-longest lifespan (https://www.macrotrends.net/countries/JPN/japan/life-expectancy). Finally, it has an equitable and highly respectable education system (https://docs.prosperity.com/9016/0508/7373/Japan_2020_PIcountryprofile.pdf, p. 13).

45 See https://www.nytimes.com/2001/09/02/world/japanese-veteran-writes-of-brutal-philippine-war.html; https://www.npr.org/sections/goatsandsoda/2020/12/04/940819094/photos-there-still-is-no-comfort-for-the-comfort-women-of-the-philippines.
46 Constitution of Kiribati, Articles 19 and 23.
47 https://www.countryreports.org/country/Kiribati/economy.htm; https://data.worldbank.org/country/KI
48 Even under Carens's open-borders view, it at most seems pro tanto wrong [see (e.g.) 1992, p. 40].

13
NATIONALITY AND IMMIGRATION RESTRICTIONS

Rufaida Al Hashmi

13.1 Introduction

States have long excluded would-be immigrants on the basis of nationality. For example, the United States passed the Chinese Exclusion Act of 1882, which prohibited all immigration of Chinese labourers, and the 1924 National Origins Act, which limited the immigration of southern and eastern European immigrants. One of Australia's very first laws was the White Australia Policy, which effectively excluded all non-European migrants.

Selection on the basis of nationality is not a thing of the past.[1] One recent and notorious example is Trump's Muslim ban, which banned would-be immigrants from several Muslim-majority countries. Before that, the United States had the National Security Entry-Exit Registration System, which placed additional requirements on travellers from several Middle Eastern countries. The selection of would-be immigrants on the basis of nationality also occurs in more indirect ways. For example, the Netherlands arguably introduced pre-entry tests for family immigration in order to deter migrants from Turkey and Morocco (Ellermann and Goenaga, 2019).

This chapter focuses on the selection of would-be immigrants on the basis of nationality. I refer to these as nationality-based immigration restrictions. The chapter proceeds as follows. In the first section, I examine whether these restrictions are morally wrong on the grounds that they track selection on the basis of ethnicity or race. In the second section, I consider whether nationality-based immigration restrictions are wrong because they track another clearly problematic selection criterion, which is religion. In the third section, I explore whether some forms of nationality-based immigration restrictions are wrong for reasons other than tracking clearly morally wrong criteria. In particular, I consider whether some of these restrictions are wrong because they rely on statistical generalisations. In the fourth section, I consider the indirect selection of would-be immigrants on the basis of nationality.

13.2 Nationality, Race, and Ethnicity

One worry with nationality-based immigration restrictions is that they can track clearly problematic criteria, such as race or ethnicity. This was the case, for example, with the 1924 National

Origins Act, which limited the visas offered to each nationality on the basis of how many people of that nationality were in the United States. One of the main goals of the policy, however, was to exclude eastern and south Europeans. As Mae Ngai (1999, p. 69) points out, "the central theme of that [legislative] process was a race-based nativism, which favored the 'Nordics' of northern and western Europe over the 'undesirable races' of eastern and southern Europe."

Political theorists generally assume that it is always wrong to exclude would-be immigrants by race or ethnicity. So, if nationality tracks race or ethnicity, exclusion on the basis of nationality could perhaps be wrong for the same reason as exclusion on the basis of race or ethnicity. So, what makes the exclusion of would-be immigrants by race or ethnicity morally wrong? It is worth noting that this presents a difficult challenge to defences of a state's right to exclude (Fine, 2016). If we accept that a state has a right to exclude, then it seems that states are morally permitted to select immigrants on whatever grounds they like, including race and ethnicity. This is a problem for proponents of a state's right to exclude, as they want to reject such exclusion as morally wrong. By contrast, the problem does not arise for proponents of open borders, as they take almost all exclusion to be morally wrong.

Proponents of a state's right to exclude have offered different accounts of the wrongness of exclusion by race or ethnicity. Their aim is to show that it is consistent to defend a state's right to exclude and to simultaneously condemn the exclusion of would-be immigrants by race and ethnicity. Consider first Michael Blake's response to this issue. He argues that exclusion on the basis of race or ethnicity is morally wrong because it is demeaning to citizens who belong to the targeted groups. Blake (2002, p. 284) argues "the state making a statement of racial preference in immigration necessarily makes a statement of racial preference domestically as well." So, for example, the 1924 National Origins Act would have been demeaning to southern and eastern Europeans who were already members of the United States.

As many have pointed out, the problem with Blake's account is that it implies that states are morally permitted to exclude would-be immigrants by race or ethnicity if there were no members of the targeted groups living in the receiving state (Wellman, 2011). For example, if there were no southern or eastern Europeans in the United States, then there would be no members of the targeted groups in the United States who would be demeaned by the 1924 National Origins Act. Similarly, Sarah Fine (2016, p. 147) notes that Blake's argument implies that a state that has expelled its ethnic and racial minorities is morally permitted to exclude would-be immigrants who belong to these groups. Blake's argument therefore fails to explain why it would be wrong for a racially or ethnically homogenous state to exclude would-be immigrants by race or ethnicity.

A second argument is that excluding would-be immigrants by race or ethnicity is morally wrong because it is insulting to the would-be immigrants themselves. Unlike Blake's argument, this argument locates the wrong of exclusion in what is done to the immigrant rather than the citizens or residents. In his earlier work, David Miller (2005) endorses such a view. Miller (2005, p. 204) claims that "to be told that they belong to the wrong race, or sex (or have hair of the wrong colour) is insulting, given that these features do not connect to anything of real significance to the society they want to join."[2]

Luara Ferracioli (2022) takes issue with this insult line of reasoning. She argues that a policy can be insulting but not morally wrong. One case that Ferracioli (2022, p. 54) discusses is that of a state that places an age limit of fifty for its skilled worker visas on the grounds that those above fifty will not be net contributors to its economy. Ferracioli grants that this policy might communicate an insulting message to would-be immigrants and citizens over the age of fifty. However, she argues that a state has good reasons for selecting immigrants that can be net positive contributors to its economy, and these reasons do not seem to be undermined by people's emotional responses to the policy. Ferracioli concludes that we need a different account of the wrong of exclusion on the basis of ethnicity or race.

There is, however, a third view that is not insult-based. This is one that Blake (2008) and Miller (2015) more recently have defended. On Miller's view, states can exclude would-be immigrants – and in turn, set back their interests – only on the basis of reasons that the would-be immigrants would be able to accept. According to Miller, these are reasons that show that exclusion connects to a morally legitimate aim of a political community. Miller argues that there can be no reason for excluding would-be immigrants by race or ethnicity that the excluded would-be immigrant would be able to accept. This is because "the use of such criteria cannot be linked in any remotely plausible way to the values that a political community may wish to pursue" (Miller, 2015, p. 400).[3]

But this account also seems to run into some troubles. Consider the White Australia Policy, which as its name suggests aimed to excluded non-white immigrants. The White Australia Policy was often justified on the grounds of preserving a hegemonic national culture (Stratton and Ang, 1994, p. 141). Some political theorists, including Miller himself, maintain that the preservation of national culture is a morally legitimate aim of a political community that can justify a state's right to exclude. With such a view of what counts as a morally legitimate aim of a political community, it is unclear how Miller's account can explain the wrongness of policies such as the White Australia Policy.[4]

As I mentioned earlier, political theorists generally assume it is always wrong to exclude would-be immigrants by race or ethnicity. Since I am applying these accounts to nationality-based restrictions, this would imply that such restrictions that track ethnicity or race would also always be morally wrong. However, Sahar Akhtar (2022) challenges this assumption. Akhtar maintains that it might be permissible for group with a vulnerable social status to exclude others. Akhtar's (2022, p. 330) argument is that it can be "permissible for vulnerable groups to selectively favor the admission of their own group membership since such differential selection may ... [help] secure the conditions of their own equality." For example, she considers that Japan's immigration policies that favour Japanese descendants might be justified in light of Japan's rapid population decline. In light of this, it is important to consider whether nationality-based restrictions are *always* wrong if they track race or ethnicity.

Much of this debate refers to historical cases of nationality-based restrictions that tracked race or ethnicity, such as the White Australia Policy or the National Origins Act of 1924. As we have seen, these cases are important because they can help explain the wrongness of nationality-based restrictions today that also track race or ethnicity. But these historical cases can be important for other reasons too. Policies such as the White Australia Policy or the National Origins Act are seen as paradigmatic cases of wrongful discrimination in the history of immigration policy. Now notice that if these policies were not enacted, the excluded would-be immigrants and their descendants would have lived in a place with presumably better opportunities for them.[5] They might therefore have a claim to compensation, as they likely would have been better off. More broadly, this highlights the ways in which states might have to reckon with the history of racism and discrimination in immigration policy.[6]

13.3 Nationality and Religion

Nationality-based restrictions can also track another clearly morally problematic criterion, which is religion. This is especially true of immigration policy in the United States after the terrorist attacks of September 11, 2001. Created shortly after 9/11, the National Security Entry-Exit Registration System placed additional requirements on travellers from predominantly Muslim-majority states. More recently, former president Trump banned would-be immigrants from several Muslim-majority states. Trump's comments made it clear that Muslims were the target. For example, he called for "a total and complete shutdown of Muslims entering the United States" (Taylor, 2015).

It is important to note that many of these policies that target religious extremism are based on an extremely tenuous link between these nationalities and a threat to national security (Brock, 2020). For example, since the 9/11, not one person has been killed in the United States by someone whose parents came from the countries included in Trump's Muslim ban (Shane, 2017). Many have nevertheless continued to maintain that these nationality-based immigration restrictions are justified on national security grounds. In order to rebut this argument, we might say that this kind of nationality-based immigration restrictions is morally wrong because it tracks religion.

So, what makes excluding would-be immigrants on the basis of religion wrong? Gillian Brock (2020) focuses specifically on the Muslim ban and argues that it violates the requirements of a state's claim to legitimacy. I will focus on one of these conditions, namely the internal requirement. According to this requirement, states must protect the human rights of their citizens. Brock argues that the Muslim ban violates this requirement by undermining rights such as the right to freedom of religion and the right to nondiscrimination.[7] It is plausible that, as a result of the Muslim ban, Muslim Americans may face further discrimination and even violence in various contexts.

However, such an argument implies that the Muslim ban wrongs members of the United States rather than the would-be immigrants who are excluded by such a policy. It is odd to say that the Muslim ban is wrong because it stifles the human rights of Americans rather than it is wrong because it wrongs the excluded would-immigrants. It is after all the excluded would-be immigrants who are clearly the most impacted group. To avoid this implication,[8] we might want to cash out the wrong of a Muslim ban in terms of what is done to the would-be immigrants themselves.

There are several options on how to proceed here. For example, we might follow Michael Blake (2020, p. 130) in taking Trump's Muslim ban to be wrong partly because "the ban would likely be experienced by Muslim migrants themselves as containing a statement of their own moral infirmity." This would be unsurprising, especially given Trump's comments about Muslims. However, as we have seen, this insult line of reasoning has its problems. Adam Hosein (2019) instead argues against Trump's Muslim ban on the grounds that it exacerbates problematic global relations. Hosein (2019, p. 92) notes that the United States already exerts power over various Muslim-majority countries, and so, a Muslim ban would contribute to a "*global* order in which some people and some nations stand above each other."

So far, I have been assuming that nationality-based restrictions are morally wrong only insofar as they track other criteria on the basis of which it would be clearly morally wrong to select would-be immigrants. This also seems to be tacitly assumed by both sides in the debate on Trump's Muslim ban. Defenders of the ban argue that it did not target Muslims, and Trump went so far as to include non-Muslim-majority countries to the list, such as Venezuela, arguably in order to avoid this charge. Critics of the ban respond to this by arguing that the ban was really motivated by Islamophobia. Both sides then took issue with it not necessarily because it excluded would-be immigrants on the basis of nationality but because it indirectly excluded would-be immigrants by religion. But it is important to consider whether a nationality-based restriction could be wrong in and of itself.

13.4 Statistical Generalisations

I suggested that it might be fruitful to look at the wrongs of nationality-based restrictions independently of whether they track other criteria. I will explore this by focusing on two aspects of nationality-based restrictions that Antje Ellerman and Agustín Goenaga (2019) highlight. In this section, I consider how some nationality-based restrictions rely on statistical generalisations. Consider the United States visa waiver programme, which allows nationals of many countries to travel to the United States without a visa. As Ellermann and Goenaga (2019, p. 106) explain, "visa waiver policies are typically based on low 'disqualification rates,' that is, they are conditioned on a low proportion of national passport holders having violated the conditions of their admission." So, this kind of nationality-based restriction is based on statistics about the national group of the individual would-be immigrant.

What should we think of this kind of nationality-based restriction? Could it be morally wrong because of its use of statistical generalisations? We might think that it is wrong to treat people on the basis of what others similar to them are like rather than on the basis of what they are like as individuals. It does seem intuitively wrong to burden individuals on account of what others similar to them have done. We might conclude that would-be immigrants should be judged on the basis of their own individual characteristics and personal background rather than what others similar to them are like.

However, it is not always morally wrong to rely on statistical generalisations. For example, it seems completely uncontroversial for a school to hire a teacher with a teaching certificate over one without one on the basis of the statistical fact that those with a teaching certificate tend to be better teachers. The use of statistical generalisations is often both inevitable and morally unproblematic.[9]

Perhaps here we can draw on some of the arguments made against racial profiling. As Adam Hosein (2018, p. e3–e4) explains, the standard case for racial profiling "assumes that there is currently a statistical correlation in our society between membership in particular racial groups and committing certain kinds of crimes." Similarly, the case for the visa waiver program also assumes that nationality is statistically correlated with violating the conditions of admission. And importantly in both cases, the statistical correlation is very often dubious.[10] It is nevertheless important to show that this argument is morally wrong for reasons "that go beyond the possibility that it would be ineffective at exposing crime" (Hosein, 2019, e4) or, in the case of visa waiver programs, ineffective at preventing violations of visa conditions. It would be a strong case against visa waiver policies if it can be shown that they are wrong, regardless of their effectiveness.

It is often said that racial profiling seems more morally problematic when the profiled group suffers from background injustice (Bou-Habib, 2011). We are more likely to oppose the racial profiling of a group that "has been, or is, systematically or unjustly disadvantaged in the distribution of significant goods, such as housing, education, or jobs, and/or if it has been or is subjected to widespread and persistent racism" (Bou-Habib, 2011, p. 34). The racial profiling of a privileged group is not seen as morally problematic as the racial profiling of a marginalised group.

Perhaps visa waiver policies are also wrong because the statistical generalisation targets groups that suffer from background injustice. Indeed, these kinds of visa systems tend to favour those from wealthy countries: "in 2010, nationals of OECD countries could travel visa free to seventy-four countries, compared to twenty-two countries for non-OECD nationals" (Ellermann & Goenaga, 2019, p. 105). Against a background of unequal global relations between OECD and non-OECD, it might be morally problematic for OECD countries to use statistical generalisations to further disadvantage the position of non-OECD countries. As in the case of racial profiling, background injustice can make the use of statistical generalisations morally problematic.

Yet, this argument might be more complicated in the immigration context for several reasons. First, there could be cases in which the excluding state has a weak, even non-existent, relationship with the country whose nationals it excludes. In this case, background injustice cannot make the use of statistical generalisations wrong, as there would be no background context to begin with. But even if there is a context of background injustice, more needs to be said on the grounds on which the background injustice undermines this use of statistical generalisations. The reasons offered in justification of this idea in the domestic context – such as Kasper Lippert-Rasmussen's (2006) argument that the non-profiled groups are sometimes responsible for the factors that lead to the higher offender rate – might not apply so well in the immigration context.

In this section, I explored how nationality-based restrictions can be wrong for reasons other than that they track clearly morally wrong criteria. I focused on visa waiver programs, which select immigrants for admission by nationality. But there are many other nationality-based restrictions that are also widely accepted. Think of, for example, freedom of movement within the European Union. This is obviously nationality-based: France grants free entry to, for example, Germans but not to, for example, Canadians. This raises the more general question of why nationality-based restrictions are accepted when selection on the basis of other criteria is not. For example, some argue that discrimination is morally wrong because it selects people on the basis of traits that are beyond their control.[11] The nationality one is born into is also largely beyond one's control. We might therefore argue that nationality-based restrictions are wrong because would-be immigrants are excluded on the basis of what is beyond their control. It is worth further exploring the wrongs of nationality-based restrictions separately from other criteria they might track.

13.5 Indirect Selection

So far, I have only considered policies that *directly* select would-be immigrants on the basis of nationality. Policies such as Trump's Muslim ban or the 1924 National Origins Act explicitly excluded certain nationalities. By contrast, some policies could be said to *unintentionally* adversely impact would-be immigrants of certain nationalities. I follow Kasper Lippert-Rasmussen (2013, p. 61) in taking "unintentional" to mean that "it reflects no bias on part of the discriminator against members of G on account of their being members of G."

Consider the income requirements that family sponsors must meet in order to bring family members to the United Kingdom. The increased income threshold of 2012 has been said to disadvantage would-be immigrants from the Global South. To take a concrete example, "whereas the median annual income of a white British man is well above the threshold (£24,000), the median income of a woman of Pakistani origin is half that required for sponsoring a spouse (£9,700)" (Ellermann & Goenaga, 2019, p. 100). This means that it is less likely that a woman of Pakistani origin living in the United Kingdom will meet the income requirement to be able to bring her family member from, say, Pakistan. The family reunification policies of other countries such as Germany have also been said to unintentionally adversely impacted those from the Global South (Ellermann and Goenaga, 2019).

There are very good reasons to be sceptical that these policies *unintentionally* disadvantage would-be immigrants of certain nationalities. For example, Germany introduced language requirements for family reunification applicants supposedly in order to promote socioeconomic integration, but the real aim was to deter Muslim women coming to Turkey (Ellermann and Goenaga, 2019). And, as I mentioned at the start, the Netherlands introduced pre-entry tests for family unification arguably in order to make it more difficult for those from Turkey and Morocco to immigrate (Ellermann and Goenaga, 2019).[1] Many ostensibly neutral selection criteria are not in fact neutral.

It is nevertheless important to consider whether such policies would be morally problematic, *even* in the absence of any bias. As Kasper Lippert-Rasmussen (2013, p. 55) notes, this is because "biases and intentions are often hard to prove, whereas it is easy to show that a certain group is 'excluded' or suffers from 'disproportionately prejudicial effects.'" In the immigration context too, politicians might deny that policies are motivated by prejudice or bias, or they might reject that biased comments are relevant to the justification of the policy. This is why it is important to show that these policies might be wrong, even if we grant that these policies do not reflect any bias.

Notice, however, that an adverse impact on its own is not sufficient to make an immigrant selection policy wrong. Almost any immigrant selection policy will adversely impact *some* group. For example, Canada's English and French language requirements in its points system might disadvantage, say, Swedes. But it's far from clear that this means that Swedes are wrongfully excluded.

It is helpful here to draw on the literature on indirect discrimination, as it grapples with very similar issues. According to Equality Act 2000 of the United Kingdom, for example, a policy that unintentionally adversely impacts a group only counts as indirect discrimination if the policy is a *disproportionate* means of achieving a legitimate aim. This is similar to how indirect discrimination is defined in many legal systems (Collins and Khaitan, 2018). Two elements tend to be important for the proportionality test. First, do the discriminatory effects outweigh the aim of the policy? And second, are there non-discriminatory means that achieve the same benefit?[12]

To illustrate, consider the famous 1971 U.S. Supreme Court case, Griggs v. Duke Power Co. The case focused on a company's requirement that employees pass a specific test in order to transfer between departments. While these tests did not explicitly disadvantage any particular group, "black applicants performed worse than white applicants on the test, a disparity that almost certainly reflected their different educational opportunities within a segregated school system" (Collins and Khaitan, 2018, p. 1). Importantly, it was decided that the test counts as indirect discrimination not purely because black applicants were adversely impacted but also because the test "seemed to be unrelated to good performance on the job" (Collins and Khaitan, 2018, p.1).

Should an immigration policy that unintentionally adversely impacts a group count as indirect discrimination only if it is a *disproportionate* means of achieving a legitimate aim? Recall, one part of the proportionality test is whether the interests of the discriminatees are outweighed by the interests of the discriminators. This might be more difficult to apply

---

1 I discuss many of these policies elsewhere. See (Al Hashmi, 2024)

in the immigration context. For example, Désirée Lim (2019, p. 914) argues we cannot straightforwardly balance the interests of the state against the interests of would-be immigrants as "the comparativeness weightiness of these interests rest on our views about more fundamental questions." That is, some will maintain that would-be immigrants have very strong interests in migrating, while others will contend that states have even stronger interests in setting their own immigration policy. We might therefore conclude that the proportionality condition cannot help us determine which immigration policies count as indirect discrimination.

However, it is worth noting that similar concerns have been raised with how the proportionality test is applied within the state. For example, some argue that not enough weight is in practice given to the discriminatory effects of adverse impact in the proportionality test.[13] The solution, however, has not been to remove the proportionality test but to improve its application. Second and more importantly, we should consider *why* there is a proportionality test for indirect discrimination before we dismiss its relevance for the immigration context. For example, John Gardner (1996) suggests that the proportionality condition is necessary, as it prevents overly demanding burdens on employers to equalise opportunities.[14] Similarly, we might well ask whether there is a reason to limit how demanding duties against indirect discrimination can be in the immigration context.[15]

13.6 Conclusion

This chapter considered the selection of would-be immigrants on the basis of nationality. This, as we have seen, intersects with other important issues, such as religious discrimination, historical injustice, and the use of statistical generalisations. The first two sections considered whether nationality-based restrictions are morally wrong because they track other clearly morally problematic criteria. The third section examined whether some nationality-based restrictions could be morally wrong because they rely on statistical generalisations rather than because they track other criteria. The final section explored immigration restrictions that indirectly exclude would-be immigrants on the basis of nationality. The chapter shows that, despite how commonplace and widely accepted nationality-based immigration restrictions are, they need to be subject to critical scrutiny.

Notes

1. For more on this, see Liav Orgad and Theodore Ruthizer (2010).
2. Wellman (2008, p. 139) also argues that would-be immigrants do not have a right not to be insulted by admission decisions.
3. Blake reaches a similar conclusion in a slightly different way. Blake (2008, p. 971) argues that since there is a coercive relationship between the immigrant and the state they wish to enter, states must treat would-be immigrants as moral equals: "when the state selects only some prospective immigrants for admission, it must rely upon reasons that reflect the moral equality of all prospective immigrants—reasons that ought to be accepted in the end even by those excluded."
4. While I do not further explore this here, Miller could respond in several ways. He could, for example, argue that not any means can be used to achieve a legitimate goal or that we need to be careful about what counts as an acceptable national culture. It is also worth noting that Sarah Fine (2016) makes a similar criticism but in response to Miller's insult-based argument. Fine (2016, p. 144) notes that it seems to follow from Miller's argument that "if race, for example, did connect to something "of real significance" to the receiving country, then the would-be immigrant's complaint would lose its force."

5 I make this argument elsewhere. See Al Hashmi (2021).
6 For a discussion of related issues, see Fine (2016) and Lim (2021).
7 Jesse Tomalty (2021) proposes a revision of Brock's argument to deal with the problems that she raises.
8 It is worth noting that this implication may not follow from Brock's other legitimacy requirements.
9 For more on statistical discrimination, see Kasper Lippert-Rasmussen (2007).
10 Ellerman and Goenaga make this point about visa waiver programs. While "Canadians, for example, account for the majority of visa overstays in the United States and, moreover, have the highest overstay rate of all nationalities," they nevertheless "continue to enjoy not only visa-free travel but also remain exempt from US-VISIT controls" (Ellermann & Goenaga, 2019, p. 107).
11 For a discussion of these views, see Altman (2020).
12 The second stage captures the point that "the test of proportionality often includes the additional element that the rule will not be justified if there were other ways of achieving the same aim that would have had a lesser adverse impact on a disadvantaged group" (Collins, 2018, p. 253).
13 For example, see Lane and Ingleby (2018).
14 For more on this view indirect discrimination law as a redistributive program, see Eidelson (2015, p. 48–51).
15 For a further discussion of indirect discrimination in immigration policy, see Mendoza (2018).

Bibliography

Akhtar, S., 2022. Race beyond Our Borders: Is Racial and Ethnic Immigration Selection Always Morally Wrong? Ethics 132, 322–351.
Al Hashmi, R., 2021. Historical Injustice in Immigration Policy. Political Studies.
Al Hashmi, R., 2024. Cultural Injustice and Refugee Discrimination, Law and Philosophy.
Altman, Andrew, "Discrimination", The Stanford Encyclopedia of Philosophy (Winter 2020 Edition), Edward N. Zalta (ed.). <https://plato.stanford.edu/archives/win2020/entries/discrimination/>.
Blake, M., 2002. Discretionary Immigration. Philosophical Topics 30, 273–289.
Blake, M., 2008. Immigration and Political Equality. San Diego Law Review 45, 963–980.
Blake, M., 2020. Justice, Migration, and Mercy. Oxford University Press, Oxford.
Bou-Habib, P., 2011. Racial Profiling and Background Injustice. The Journal of Ethics 15, 33–46.
Brock, G., 2020. Justice for People on the Move: Migration in Challenging Times. Cambridge University Press, Cambridge.
Collins, H., 2018. Justification of Indirect Discrimination. In: Collins, H., Khaitain, T. (Eds.), Foundations of Indirect Discrimination Law. Hart Publishing, Oxford, pp. 249–278.
Collins, H., Khaitan, T., 2018. Indirect Discrimination Law: Controversies and Critical Questions. In: Collins, H., Khaitan, T. (Eds.), Foundations of Indirect Discrimination Law. Hart Publishing, Oxford, pp. 1–30.
Eidelson, B., 2015. Discrimination and Disrespect. Oxford University Press, Oxford.
Ellermann, A., Goenaga, A., 2019. Discrimination and Policies of Immigrant Selection in Liberal States: Politics & Society 47, 87–116.
Ferracioli, L., 2022. Liberal Self-Determination in a World of Migration. Oxford University Press, Oxford.
Fine, S., 2016. Immigration and Discrimination. In: Fine, S., Ypi, L. (Eds.), Migration in Political Theory: The Ethics of Movement and Membership. Oxford University Press, Oxford, pp. 126–149.
Gardner, J., 1996. Discrimination as Injustice. Oxford Journal of Legal Studies 16, 353–368.
Hosein, A., 2018. Racial Profiling and a Reasonable Sense of Inferior Political Status. Journal of Political Philosophy 26, 1–20.
Hosein, A., 2019. The Ethics of Migration: An Introduction. Routledge, Abingdon, Oxon.
Lane, J., Ingleby, R., 2018. Indirect Discrimination, Justification and Proportionality: Are UK Claimants at a Disadvantage? Industrial Law Journal 47, 531–552.
Lim, D., 2019. The Indirect Gender Discrimination of Skill-Selective Immigration Policies. Critical Review of International Social and Political Philosophy 22, 906–928.
Lim, D., 2021. Low-Skilled Migrants and the Historical Reproduction of Immigration Injustice. Ethical Theory and Moral Practice 24, 1229–1244.

Lippert-Rasmussen, K., 2006. Racial Profiling Versus Community. Journal of Applied Philosophy 23, 191–205.
Lippert-Rasmussen, K., 2007. Nothing Personal: On Statistical Discrimination. Journal of Political Philosophy 15, 385–403.
Lippert-Rasmussen, K., 2013. Born Free and Equal? A Philosophical Inquiry into the Nature of Discrimination. Oxford University Press, Oxford.
Mendoza, J., 2018. Discrimination and Immigration. In: Lippert-Rasmussen, K. (Ed.), The Routledge Handbook of the Ethics of Discrimination. Routledge, Abingdon, Oxon, pp. 254–264.
Miller, D., 2005. Immigration: The Case for Limits. In: Cohen, A., Wellman, C. (Eds.), Contemporary Debates in Applied Ethics. Blackwell, Oxford, pp. 193–206.
Miller, D., 2015. Justice in Immigration. European Journal of Political Theory 14, 391–408.
Ngai, M., 1999. The Architecture of Race in American Immigration Law: A Reexamination of the Immigration Act of 1924. The Journal of American History 86, 67–92.
Orgad, L., Ruthizer, T., 2010. Race, Religion and Nationality in Immigration Selection: 120 Years After the Chinese Exclusion Race. Constitutional Commentary 22, 237–296.
Shane, S., 2017. Immigration Ban Is Unlikely to Reduce Terrorist Threat, Experts Say [WWW Document]. The New York Times. URL https://www.nytimes.com/2017/01/28/us/politics/a-sweeping-order-unlikely-to-reduce-terrorist-threat.html (accessed 5.28.22).
Stratton, J., Ang, I., 1994. Multicultural Imagined communities: Cultural Difference and National Identity in Australia and the USA. Journal of Media & Cultural Studies 8, 124–158.
Taylor, J., 2015. Trump Calls For "Total and Complete Shutdown of Muslims Entering" U.S.: NPR [WWW Document]. NPR. https://www.npr.org/2015/12/07/458836388/trump-calls-for-total-and-complete-shutdown-of-muslims-entering-u-s?t=1648911644632&t=1653759264382 (Accessed May 28, 2022).
Tomalty, J., 2021. Religious Discrimination at the Border. Ethical Perspectives 28, 362–373.
Wellman, C.H., 2008. Immigration and Freedom of Association. Ethics 119, 109–141.
Wellman, C.H., 2011. Selection Criteria. In: Wellman, C.H., Cole, P. (Eds.), Debating the Ethics of Immigration: Is There a Right to Exclude? Oxford University Press, Oxford, pp. 143–154.

14
IMMIGRATION AND SOCIAL IDENTITY FORMATION

Amy Reed-Sandoval

14.1 Introduction

Something happens to our social identities when we migrate and cross borders. Most obviously, perhaps, we cross international barriers as a member of a designated national group: for example, *as a Canadian, as an Ecuadorian, as a South African*, etc. Some border-crossers may experience this with ambivalence or amusement. Others may "feel" their national identities strongly upon being identified along nationalistic lines at border checkpoints, such as Iroquois/Haudenosaunee border-crossers who, in Audra Simpson's words, feel *especially* Indigenous as they cross settler state borders with their Haudenosaunee passports.[1] Our sense of ascribed national identity may also be underscored upon migrating to a new state—especially if the majority of the new state's members speak a language and participate in social customs and political practices that strike us as "foreign."

Additionally, migrants and border-crossers may be oppressed or "outed" on the basis of their social identities due to immigration enforcement and expulsion strategies that are either explicitly discriminatory or applied in a discriminatory fashion. On a very basic level, passports immediately identity individuals to immigration agents in terms of their ages, genders, and places of birth, foregrounding these aspects of social identities at borders whether they like it or not. More worryingly, as explored in Latinx philosophies of migration, regardless of whether a passport is ever requested or shown, Latin American and Latinx migrants (along with other migrants of color) are unduly targeted by immigration enforcement strategies within the United States.[2] Meanwhile, pregnant women/people who cross borders for abortion care are often made to feel that they are doing something morally wrong—like the pregnant woman in the United Sates who had to travel out of state for legal abortion care, and said that she felt she was doing so "under the cover of night."[3] The so-called "Public Charge Rule" is also wielded against pregnant people as well as people with disabilities who attempt to migrate and border-cross—many of whom find their disabilities highlighted, publicly scrutinized, and sometimes used to deny them entry.[4] Refugees of color are also routinely discriminated against in refugee protection regimes, as the world has seen as Africans fleeing Ukraine following the Russian invasion of that country have been refused protections more readily granted to their European counterparts.[5]

DOI: 10.4324/9781003037309-19

Furthermore, those who migrate and cross borders may be forced to not only reveal, but also to in fact *discuss*, aspects of their social identities that they do not feel comfortable disclosing to strangers, such as their sexual identities (for instance, LGBTQ migrants are particularly vulnerable to "demands for sexual confession" from border agents).[6]

Finally, as I shall explore in this chapter, immigration systems also *create* social identities. I understand "immigration systems" in terms of what Eduardo Bonilla-Silva has called a "racialized social system"—though I hasten to add that immigration systems are also sexist, ableist, homophobic, classist, and otherwise oppressive (Bonilla-Silva, too, acknowledges the intersection of racialized social systems with other axes of oppression). He argues that "once a racial system roots, we all become habituated by its norms, culture, and collective practices,"[7] and that "actors tend to follow [racial systems] which reproduces racial domination."[8] Since racism is systemic, he argues, *everyone* is incorporated into its "game," both consciously and unconsciously. If we understand immigration systems as racialized social systems, I maintain, we come to perceive how racist social injustice in immigration is produced not only by immigration laws that may or may not be explicitly racist but also by social attitudes about immigration and the uneven ways in which immigration laws are enforced. Indeed, as Bonilla-Silva argues, "what is needed is a concerted effort to eliminate the racial practices and culture that reproduce white advantage and non-white disadvantage at *all levels.*"[9]

In this chapter, I shall explore how immigration systems—understood as racialized social systems involving both immigration laws and related social attitudes about immigration—not only underscore and oppress but also *create* social identities that are vulnerable to oppression. The idea that immigration creates social identities is at the core of the expression "we didn't cross the border, the border crossed us!"—a phrase that was popularized in the United States following the U.S.-Mexican war, when the United States violently seized a hefty portion of Mexico's land and thus "made" U.S. citizens out of Mexicans. Similarly, immigration systems *created* social identities when the violent remapping of the Americas and Africa during colonialism's first and second waves generated new borders and, along with them, new national identities with which citizens often did not identify. Imposed borders can, and often do, impact the selfhood and self-development of those who feel their presence most deeply—as illustrated by Gloria Anzaldúa's famous descriptions of the U.S.-Mexico border that she experiences in terms of the grating of her skin and the generation of a "mestiza consciousness"—a pluralistic consciousness and self who simultaneously occupies multiple "worlds"[10]—and corresponding identity.[11]

The idea that migration systems create social identities is a motivating concern in my book *Socially Undocumented: Identity and Immigration Justice*. Therein, I argue that being "undocumented"—or, to invoke the more common slurring term, "illegal"—is not necessarily a matter of lacking legal permission to live and work in the society in which one currently lives. To be socially undocumented, I argue, is to possess an ethnoracial and class-based identity that causes one to be *perceived* as undocumented, and consequently rendered vulnerable to forms of migration-related oppression. It is not only a socially constructed identity, but also real, and it is the source of systemic immigration injustice, particularly in the United States.

In this chapter, I will explore how immigration systems create social identities by outlining, first of all, three aspects of my argument in *Socially Undocumented*: (1) the distinction I draw out between being legally and socially undocumented; (2) my working, philosophical understanding of what a "social identity" is; and (3) my presentation of socially undocumented identity as a source of immigration injustice. My goal, however, is not simply to

Immigration and Social Identity Formation

rehash these arguments (which can be found in the book) but to show how this identity-based approach to pursuing immigration injustice in the case of socially undocumented oppression can be used methodologically to reveal and combat other forms of identity-based oppression in the realm of immigration.

To exemplify this, I shall then explore one additional way in which immigration policies create social identities-namely, through the creation by immigration systems of "fallen women." I shall also point out, if only in passing, how immigration systems create social identities by (1) creating adults out of children; and (2) creating "borderlands identities." Note that for considerations of space, most of my cited examples involve immigration-related discrimination in the United States; however, immigration systems produce oppressed social identities on a global scale. In my conclusion, I argue that when crafting immigration policies, state actors must constantly ask themselves: *will this policy create or underscore oppressed social identities*? And *how can otherwise combat identity-based oppression in the sphere of migration*?

14.2 Socially Undocumented Oppression

14.2.1 *Socially versus Legally Undocumented*

In *Socially Undocumented*, I ask the reader to imagine two people: Gary and Alicia. Gary is a white, male citizen of the United Kingdom who strives to become a punk rock star. He believes that he will achieve the success of which he dreams upon relocating to Washington, D.C., as he senses the "punk scene" there is far better. He initially comes to the United States on a tourist visa and plays as many gigs as he can get. Still, fame eludes him. Eventually, his tourist visa runs out, but he continues to live and work as a musician in the United States without legal permission. Gary begins to feel frustrated by his situation: he believes that he is being denied professional opportunities because of his legally undocumented status, and he is underpaid by some club managers following his performances. Years go by, and Gary also begins to wish that he could vote in U.S. elections; he wants to make his voice heard. More time goes by, and Gary, now more frustrated than ever, returns to the United Kingdom.

I then ask the reader to envision another legally undocumented person: Alicia. Alicia is originally from Mexico, and she has spent a year working as a housecleaner for several wealthy families in Los Angeles, California. She made the decision to leave Mexico after her husband (a farmer displaced by NAFTA) was killed while attempting his own unauthorized U.S.-Mexico border-crossing. Alicia lives in a cramped apartment with several other migrant families from Mexico and Central America, from which she must travel for several hours by bus to reach her employers' houses. While some of her employers are nice, others force her to work in unsafe conditions, and even threaten to notify immigration enforcement of her unauthorized status if she fails to work extra, unpaid hours. About a year after her arrival, Alicia is deported back to Mexico after a police officer collaborating with immigration enforcement demands that she "show her papers" on the street, and she fails to do so.

Now let us consider the similarities and differences between Gary and Alicia. Both individuals lived and worked in the United States without legal permission (though the circumstances of their respective entries were vastly different)—that is, they were both legally undocumented. Both experienced disadvantages associated with their respective legal statuses.

And, finally, both Gary and Alicia eventually returned to their countries of origin. Beyond this, though, their experiences were radically dissimilar, and these differences, I argue, are indicative of how immigration systems create social identities and associated oppression.

Though both stories are hypothetical, it does not require a great deal of imaginative work to get a clear sense of how the experiences of someone "positioned" like Gary, and those of someone "positioned" as Alicia, would differ. We can easily imagine Alicia navigating Los Angeles with fear, and perhaps even shame. When she spots a police officer, her heartbeat and blood pressure rise. Many of her employers look down on her, and she has likely been targeted by racial slurs, such as people calling her an "illegal." Despite her incredibly hard work that causes her to end each day with swollen feet and a sore back, she earns very little money and can barely send anything home to her family that depends on her. Alicia tells herself that she is doing right by her family, but a part of her feels that she is doing something very wrong.

We can easily imagine Gary, on the other hand, moving about D.C. relatively fearlessly. In addition to his public performances as a punk rocker, he frequents bars and cafes, and he takes in the sights of the city without giving much thought to a possible police encounter—even when sporting a spiky collar and black sweater with the words *God Is Dead*! sprawled across the front in blood-red letters. Though he cannot achieve the level of success that would await him were he to become a legal U.S. resident, Gary often earns handsome sums of money for his gigs and is able to live alone in a small, but pleasant, apartment. When he leaves the United States, it is on his own terms.

Given Gary and Alicia are both legally undocumented, why are their lived experiences so different? The answer, I argue, is that though they are both legally undocumented, Alicia, but not Gary, is *socially undocumented*. A socially undocumented person, I argue, is a person who is "perceived to be undocumented on the mere basis of their appearance, and subjected to demeaning, immigration-related constraints on that basis."[12] Crucially, socially undocumented identity, which I explain in greater detail below, does not always "track" legal status—though many people are, like Alicia, both socially and legally undocumented. One can, in fact, *have* legal permission to be in the United States and elsewhere, and still be socially undocumented, as we saw in the context of the Bracero Program—a temporary guest worker program that ran from 1942 to 1963, through which Mexican agricultural laborers were brought to the United States to do field work, generally under highly exploitative conditions–and the mass deportations of scape-goated, Mexican-origin U.S. citizens during and immediately after the Great Depression.[13]

The sort of "unjust, immigration-related constraints" to which socially undocumented people are regularly subjected include, for instance, being targeted by police officers working for immigration enforcement, and by immigration enforcement officials themselves. We saw that Alicia is thus targeted, but Gary is not—despite the fact that they are both legally undocumented. Being called an "illegal" is another immigration-related constraint that socially undocumented people uniquely face (this is why it is not only easy for us to imagine Alicia being denigrated with such language but also easy for us to imagine that Gary *never* gets targeted in this way).

Additionally, socially undocumented people tend to get hired for underpaid, exploitative, dangerous jobs such as housecleaning, work in meatpacking plants, and day labor (or *jornalero*).[14] While Gary certainly sometimes gets "stiffed" by his employers and gets denied certain professional opportunities, he is paid better, and treated with considerably more respect, than Alicia. Indeed, Gary would likely struggle to get hired as a housecleaner or a factory work at a meat packing plant if he tried.

This means, I submit, that we cannot diagnose the poor treatment that Alicia receives in the United States's immigration *system* in terms of her legally undocumented status—for in that case, Gary would be fairing equally, or at least similarly to Alicia. The problem is that Alicia is *perceived* as undocumented—or as an "illegal"—and that makes her vulnerable to oppression. Furthermore, this oppression is distinctively connected to immigration policies and attitudes about immigration. Alicia has an "illegal" *identity*, or, to use my preferred term, a socially undocumented identity: one that is connected to her race, gender, and class, and also to immigration law, immigration histories, and immigration discourses in the United States. The immigration system, broadly understood, *made* socially undocumented identity, and people like Alicia are compelled to bear the associated burdens.

14.2.2 Social Identity

When I say that the U.S. "immigration system" makes socially undocumented identity—and, more broadly, that immigration systems create social identities—just what to I mean by "social identity"? Social identities take many forms, and can include, for instance, one's political party affiliation, one's membership in recreational clubs, and one's nationality. Through immigration processes, one may change one's nationality, and one may also experience changes in one's political and recreational preferences. Unless these changes are forced and/or leave one vulnerable to oppression, they are not, *prima facie*, morally concerning. They constitute, instead, what Kieran Oberman describes as "life options" that are sometimes enhanced or made available through immigration, such as "friends, family, civic associations, expressive opportunities, religions, jobs, and marriage partners."[15]

In contrast, when immigration systems create oppressed social identities such as socially undocumented identity—the sorts of identities that concern us from a social justice perspective—they create what Linda Martín Alcoff calls "visible identities." *Visible identities*, Alcoff argues, function as "horizons" or "perspectival locations" from which those who possess them perceive and comprehend the world. Visible identities are also embodied, she maintains, in at least two senses: *first*, as horizons and perspectival locations, they are situated within a human body—a body that sees, feels, and thinks. Second, visible identities are situated in bodies that are visibly sexed and racialized. Visible identities emerge from the interface between systemic social responses to bodies that are ascribed a particular race and gender, on the one hand, and the ways in which those who are thus ascribed interpret their social worlds (including themselves), one the other. This brings about what Alcoff calls "one's particular substantive position,"[16] which is also the content of one's (visible) social identity. As Alcoff explains, "knowing is a kind of immanent engagement, in which one's own self is engaged by the world—touched, felt, and seen—rather than standing above. One not only changes but is changed as well."[17]

Visible social identities are, therefore, both real and socially constructed. They develop in response to real histories and patterns of social relations that impact how "one's own self is engaged by the world," and changed by it. We construct our self-understanding, and our "vantage point" on the world, within functioning social systems that position us in certain ways in relation to others. Additionally, the way in which our self is "engaged by the world" changes not only our hermeneutic horizon, but also, our very embodiment. As

Alcoff explains, "racial and sexual difference is manifest precisely in bodily comportment, in habit, in feeling, and perceptual orientation. These make a part of what appears to me as the natural setting of all my thoughts."[18] One famous illustration of how sexual difference (for example) is manifested in bodily comportment comes from Iris Marion Young in her essay "Throwing Like A Girl," in which she explores how women generally take up less space with their bodies, proportionally speaking, than men, and how they often neglect to employ their full body strength when engaged in activities like throwing balls. In turn, this embodied sexual difference often impacts how women and girls perceive the world and their place in it.[19]

It is within this framework of social identity that I argue that to be "socially undocumented" is to have a social identity that does not necessarily correspond with unauthorized status in the United States or elsewhere. Socially undocumented people are systematically treated "as illegals"—that is, they are *called* "illegals," told to go back to their countries, hired for exploitative jobs that tend to be associated with unauthorized immigrant labor, targeted by police and immigration enforcement at borders and state interiors, and more. This generates a "socially undocumented embodiment," which may be manifested in terms of a tendency to physically hide from immigration enforcement and police officers, general unease in public spaces, and more. It also generates a socially undocumented horizon, which includes a sophisticated understanding of immigration (in)justice that is sometimes manifested in the form of art and activism.

In sum, I have outlined two central features of my argument to the effect that immigration systems such as that of the United States *create* socially undocumented identity. When such social identities are vulnerable to oppression, as is socially undocumented identity, then justice demands that we seek out information about how immigration systems are complicit in unjust social identity development. This will, in turn, require complex policy responses to migration injustice. In the case of socially undocumented identity, it entails recognizing that putting legally undocumented migrants on a path to citizenship is a very important policy goal—but insufficient for the purpose of diminishing *social* illegality. In Bonilla-Silva's words, we need reform at *all levels*.

14.2.3 Social Justice

More specifically, combatting unjust social identity formation in the realm of immigration (and elsewhere) requires us to work toward what Elizabeth Anderson has called a "community of equals" and "democratic equality," which "integrates principles of distribution with the expressive demands of equal respect."[20] The expressive demands of equal respect demand major structural changes in terms of how people with oppressed identities are spoken about, treated, and conceived—and in terms of how they are conditioned to conceive themselves. In Iris Marion Young's words, such an approach requires us to consider not just "justice toward issues concerning wealth, income, and other material goods,"[21] but also "decision-making power and procedures, division of labor, and culture."[22] Combatting unjust social identity formation also requires understanding of the facts that, as Alcoff maintains, social identities are constantly influx, and that their meanings can sometimes be powerfully shifted by those who have them.

With this in mind, I devote the rest of this chapter to two goals. *First*, I briefly explore additional ways in which social identities are shaped and sometimes created by immigration policies—focusing, in the main, on how immigration systems create "fallen women."

Second, I outline ways in which immigration policy can be productively reoriented to combat unjust social identity formation.

14.3 More Oppressive Social Identity Formation

Immigration systems do not merely produce social undocumented identity. They also frequently produce "fallen women": a broad term that I use to refer to women and girls who are taken to stray from patriarchal gender norms that oppress women, and who are therefore socially sanctioned. The idea of the "fallen women" can be traced to the Old Testament, where Eve, along with Adam, is exiled from the Garden of Eden after sampling the forbidden fruit that gives her forms of knowledge that serve to deprive her of her innocence. "Fallen women" like Eve are understood to have lost God's grace. Victorian society was particularly obsessed with "fallen women" as an explicit social problem stemming from a failure to express (or repress) one's feminine sexuality in socially mandated ways. As Nina Auerbach argues, in Victorian novels such as those penned by Browning and Tennyson, the "fallen woman" "becomes the abased figurehead of a fallen culture."[23] Auerbach explains that "then and now, she seems to enlightened minds a pitiable monster, created by the neurosis of a culture that feared female sexuality and aggression and so enshrined a respectability sadistic cautionary tale punishing them both."[24]

Immigration systems, I submit, are complicit in creating "fallen women" out of women and girls: they generate, therefore, yet another oppressive social identity. Here are some examples of this phenomenon in the United States and Mexico: (1) at nation-state borders across the globe, women and girls who attempt to migrate have historically been subjected to interrogation about their pregnancies and romantic relationships at borders. Eithne Luibhéid, in her book *Entry Denied: Controlling Sexuality at the Border*, narrates the story of Catherine Dolan, an Irish migrant who was humiliated by a panel of medical professionals collaborating with immigration enforcement for attempting to enter the United States after becoming pregnant out of wedlock in the context of an affair with a married man.[25] (Dolan was denied entry to the United States.) As noted previously, pregnant people may be denied entry to the United States if a CBP (Customs and Border Protection) officer deems them "liable to become a public charge."

Another example of how immigration systems create "fallen women": in the United States, the Page Act of 1875 effectively deemed Asian women who attempted to enter the United States were labeled "prostitutes," and thus denied entry on that basis. Meanwhile, as noted in the Introduction, abortion seekers who must cross borders for abortion care have reported feeling as if they are doing something terribly wrong.[26] In Mexico, meanwhile, many Indigenous women who migrate internally, from places like rural Oaxaca to Mexico City, report being chastised for violating feminine norms upon returning to their villages of origin.[27]

In sum, the act of migration on the part of many women constitutes a "fall" from grace and deviation from ascribed norms. This often serves to situate women and pregnant people who cross borders and migrate within a new social category that leaves them highly vulnerable to oppression. As we saw in the case of socially undocumented oppression, this is sometimes, but not always, the result of specific immigration policies. While the sexist components of the Page Act and the Public Charge Rule are, indeed, immigration polices that target or have targeted women, the experiences of pregnant people crossing borders for abortion care, or those of some Indigenous Oaxacan women (for example) who receive social condemnation upon their return to their villages of origin, are not. This shows, once again, that our efforts at immigration reform need to be informed by a philosophical account of social identity formation in connection to immigration systems.

For example, we should explore how immigration systems sometimes compel children who cross borders to "become adults" and "lose their childhoods," given associations between border-crossing and the loss of innocence.[28] For example, in "Criminals in Our Land! Border Movement and Apprehension of Children from Bangladesh Within the Juvenile Justice System in India," Chandi Basu argues that for Bangladeshi children in India, border-crossing is considered "non-normative"—that is, it is at odds with the behavior of well-behaved children. Crossing the border into India as a Bangladeshi child threatens the vision of childhood as "innocence" within the Indian juvenile justice system, leaving Bangladeshi children particularly vulnerable to sanction and detention "Second, we must explore, as a matter of immigration policy and associated social attitudes and practices, how "borderlands" identities are generated by borders and their enforcement." As Anzaldúa and countless other borderlands scholars have shown, being physically situated near a state border, particularly as a person of color, leaves one vulnerable to oppression as an inhabitant of the borderlands.[29] She explains that "*los atravesados* live here: the squint-eyed, the perverse, the queer, the troublesome, the mongrel, the mulatto, the half breed, the half-dead; in short, those who cross over, pass over, or go through the confines of 'the normal'."[30] In Anzalduan spirit, we need a careful, multi-disciplinary analysis of how immigration systems create new social identities that leave people vulnerable to injustice.

14.4 Conclusion: Future Directions

In this chapter, I have argued that immigration systems create social identities that are vulnerable to oppression and social injustice. I have made this argument, in the main, by showing how the U.S. immigration system has produced socially undocumented identity, through which one is perceived to be undocumented on the basis of their appearance and subjected to demeaning-immigration related constraints on that basis. Beyond this, I have claimed that immigration systems produce "fallen women," created adults out of children, and created borderlands identities that are vulnerable to oppression.

This has serious implications for immigration justice. It means, I submit, that we must go beyond questioning whether individual immigration policies are just and unjust—and even whether their enforcement is uneven and discriminatory. While these questions are terribly important, we must also study how immigration systems impact our perceptions of human beings who migrate and border-cross, and of how people who migrate and border-cross perceive themselves. What is at stake here is our collective way of understanding social relationships and their potential—and of whose "hermeneutic horizons," bodies, and very "selves" are socially validated. We need to bring to our immigration policy discussions a clear understanding of the metaphysics of social identity; indeed, we will not achieve justice in immigration until we understand how immigration systems in the modern world are central to who we all are. This means, furthermore, that every immigration policy that is proposed ought to be scrutinized to see if it will oppress minority groups or create new, oppressed identities. Finally, we must also consider how immigration policy can be used to undermine oppressed social identities that our system has already brought into existence.

Notes

1. Audra Simpson, *Mohawk Interruptus: Political Life Across the Borders of Settler States*, Durham, NC: Duke University Press, 2014.
2. For an overview of this literature, see José Jorge Mendoza, "Latinx Philosophy and the Ethics of Migration," in *Latin American and Latinx Philosophy: A Collaborative Introduction*, ed. By Robert Eli Sanchez, (New York: Routledge, 2018), pp. 198–219.
3. Carmen Landau and Lisa Long, "Under the Cover of Night: Abortion Across Borders," in *MEDICC Review*, vol. 17 no. 4 (2015), page 60.
4. For further discussion, see Douglas C. Baynton, "Defectives in the Land: Disability and American Immigration Policy, 1882–1924," in *Journal of American Ethnic History*, vol. 24 no. 3 (Spring 2005), pp. 31–44.
5. See Sunday Israel Oyebamiji et al, "Echoes of Color Discrimination in Refugee Protection Regime: The Experience of Africans Feeling the Russian-Ukrainian War," in *Migration Letters* vol 19 no. 5 (September 2022), pp. 697–707.
6. See Eithne Luibheid, "Looking Like a Lesbian: The Organization of Sexual Monitoring at the United States-Mexico Border," in *Journal of the History of Sexuality*, vol. 8 no. 3, pp. 477–506.
7. Eduardo Bonilla-Silva, "What Makes Systemic Racism Systemic," in *Sociological Inquiry* vol. 93 no. 1 (2021), p. 519.
8. Bonilla-Silva, page 519.
9. Bonilla-Silva, 524.
10. For further discussion of "mestiza consciousness" and related concepts in Latina feminist literature, see Mariana Ortega, "'New Mestizas', '"World-Travelers"', and Dasein: Phenomenology in the Multi-Voiced, Multi-Cultural Self," in *Hypatia* vol. 16 no. 3 (2011), pp. 1–29.
11. See Gloria Anzaldua, *Borderlands/La Frontera: The New Mestiza*, Fifth Edition (San Francisco, CA: Aunt Lute Books, 2022), especially chapter 1
12. Amy Reed-Sandoval, *Socially Undocumented: Identity and Immigration Justice* (New York: Oxford University Press, 2023).
13. For further information about the Bracero Program and Repatriation of U.S. citizens and legal residents of Mexican origin, see Mae Ngai, *Impossible Subjects: Illegal Aliens and the Making of Modern America* (Princeton, NJ: Princeton University Press, 2004, and Francisco E. Balderrama and Raymond Rodriguez, *Decade of Betrayal* (Albuquerque: University of New Mexico Press, 1999).
14. For further discussion see Juan Thomas Ordoñez, *Jornalero: Being A Day Laborer in the USA* (Oakland, CA: University of California Press, 2015).
15. Kieran Oberman, "Immigration as a Human Right," in *Migration in Political Theory: The Ethics of Movement and Membership*, Sarah Fine and Lea Ypi, eds. (Oxford: Oxford University Press, 2016), page 38
16. Alcoff, *Visible Identities: Race, Gender, and the Self* (New York: Oxford University Press, 2005), page 96
17. Alcoff, p. 112
18. Alcoff, p. 126
19. See Iris Marion Young, "Throwing Like a Girl," in *On Female Body Experience: Throwing Like a Girl and Other Essays* (New York: Oxford University Press, 2015, pp. 27–45.
20. Elizabeth Anderson, "What Is the Point of Equality," in *Ethics* vol. 109 no. 2 (1999), page 289.
21. Iris Marion Young, *Justice and the Politics of Difference* (Princeton: Princeton University Press, 2011), page 16
22. Young (2011), page 15.
23. Nina Auerbach, "The Rise of the Fallen Woman," *Nineteenth Century Fiction*, vol. 35, no. 1 (1980), page 31.
24. Nina Auerbach, "The Rise of the Fallen Woman," *Nineteenth Century Fiction*, vol. 35, no. 1 (1980), page 31.
25. See Eithne Luibheid, *Entry Denied: Controlling Sexuality at the Border* (Minneapolis: University of Minnesota Press, 2015).
26. I discuss this in "Crossing Borders for Abortion: A Feminist Challenge to Border Theory," in *Journal of Social Philosophy* vol. 53 (2022).

27 See Iván Sandoval Cervantes, *Oaxaca In Motion: An Ethnography of Internal, Transnational, and Return Migration* (Austin: University of Texas Press, 2022).
28 For further discussion, see various chapters of *Children and Borders*, edited by Spyrous Spyrou and Miranda Christou (Palgrave MacMillan: Hampshire, 2014).
29 For further details, see, once again, Mendoza (2018).
30 Anzaldúa, page 3.

References

Amy Reed-Sandoval. 2020. *Socially Undocumented: Identity and Immigration Justice* (New York: Oxford University Press).
Amy Reed-Sandoval. 2022. "Crossing Borders for Abortion: A Feminist Challenge to Border Theory," in *Journal of Social Philosophy* vol. 53, pp. 296–316.
Audra Simpson 2014. *Mohawk Interruptus: Political Life Across the Borders of Settler States*, Durham, NC: Duke University Press.
Carmen Landau and Lisa Long. 2015. "Under the Cover of Night: Abortion Across Borders." in *MEDICC Review*, vol. 17 no. 4, p. 60.
Douglas C. Baynton. 2015. "Defectives in the Land: Disability and American Immigration Policy, 1882-1924," in *Journal of American Ethnic History*, vol. 24 no. 3, pp. 31–44.
Eduardo Bonilla-Silva. 2021. "What Makes Systemic Racism *Systemic?*" in *Sociological Inquiry* vol. 93 no. 1, p. 513–533.
Eithne Luibheid. 1998. "Looking Like a Lesbian: The Organization of Sexual Monitoring at the United States-Mexico Border," in *Journal of the History of Sexuality*, vol. 8 no. 3, pp. 477–506.
Eithne Luibheid. 2015. *Entry Denied: Controlling Sexuality at the Border* (Minneapolis: University of Minnesota Press).
Elizabeth Anderson. 1999. "What Is the Point of Equality?" in *Ethics* vol. 109 no. 2, pp. 287–337.
Francisco E. Balderrama and Raymond Rodriguez. 1999. *Decade of Betrayal* (Albuquerque: University of New Mexico Press).
Gloria Anzaldúa. 2022. *Borderlands/La Frontera: The New Mestiza*, Fifth Edition (San Francisco, CA: Aunt Lute Books).
Nina Auerbach. 1980. "The Rise of the Fallen Woman." in *Nineteenth Century Fiction*, vol. 35, no. 1, pp. 29–52.
Iris Marion Young. 2005. "Throwing Like a Girl," in *On Female Body Experience: Throwing Like a Girl and Other Essays* (New York: Oxford University Press).
Iris Marion Young. 2011. *Justice and the Politics of Difference* (Princeton: Princeton University Press).
Israel Oyebamiji et al. 2022. "Echoes of Color Discrimination in Refugee Protection Regime: The Experience of Africans Feeling the Russian-Ukrainian War." in *Migration Letters* vol 19 no. 5, pp. 697–707.
José Jorge Mendoza. 2018. "Latinx Philosophy and the Ethics of Migration." In *Latin American and Latinx Philosophy: A Collaborative Introduction*, ed. By Robert Eli Sanchez, (New York: Routledge), pp. 198–219.
Juan Thomas Ordoñoez. 2015. *Jornalero: Being A Day Laborer in the USA* (Oakland, CA: University of California Press).
Kieran Oberman. 2016. "Immigration as a Human Right." *Migration in Political Theory: The Ethics of Movement and Membership*, Sarah Fine and Lea Ypi, eds. (Oxford: Oxford University Press).
Mae Ngai. 2004. *Impossible Subjects: Illegal Aliens and the Making of Modern America* (Princeton, NJ: Princeton University Press).
Mariana Ortega. 2011. "'New Mestizas', '"World-Travelers"', and Dasein: Phenomenology in the Multi-Voiced, Multi-Cultural Self," in *Hypatia* vol. 16 no. 3, pp. 1–29.
Linda Martín Alcoff, 2005. *Visible Identities: Race, Gender, and the Self* (New York: Oxford University Press).

15
THE ETHICS OF SKILL-SELECTIVE IMMIGRATION POLICIES

Désirée Lim

15.1 Introduction

Assuming the states have the right to exclude migrants, as many immigration theorists conventionally take for granted, a crucial component of states' right to exclude is their ability to exercise discretion over which non-citizens that they *do* choose to include. Inclusion may take the form of giving non-citizens permission to live and work in the receiving state or the willingness to place them on the path to future citizenship. While I do not seek to challenge this assumption,[1] in order to speak to a broader audience, I focus on how states may permissibly exercise this *prima facie* right. In practice, states have used selection criteria that many believe to be morally wrong. Historically, they have introduced immigration policies that express a preference for certain migrants over others on the basis of race, ethnicity, or religious identity, sometimes to the degree that migrants who are non-members of the preferred groups have been automatically excluded from consideration. The United States's Nationality Act of 1790, for example, limited eligibility for citizenship by naturalization to "free white persons" (Immigration History 2023). While there are some exceptions to the rule,[2] many philosophers regard racial preferences as morally impermissible. Preferring migrants of a certain race over others may be perceived as wrongful because it is unfair, arbitrary, or reflects an attitude of racial animus that would be harmful to the equal status of citizens who belong to dispreferred groups.

Considerably less disputed is states' selection of migrants on the basis of *skill*, which has been largely left unchallenged because, unlike selection on the basis of race, it seems to serve a legitimate and useful goal. Countries are assumed to have an interest in recruiting talented non-citizens, who are often described as the world's "best and brightest", to take up sought-after occupations in the receiving state. To be clear, states that are encountering labor shortages in much-needed fields may show preference for migrants with specific skill sets, such as New Zealand's prioritization of nurses and other medical workers during the COVID-19 pandemic. However, this chapter focuses on a more general definition of skill-based selection, wherein states commonly express their preference for *highly skilled migrants* (such as doctors, scientists, and software engineers) over *low-skilled migrants* (such as cleaners, servers, or agricultural workers).

DOI: 10.4324/9781003037309-20

Furthermore, it is important to see that states do not just prefer highly skilled migrants in the sense of prioritizing their admission over low-skilled migrants under circumstances where only a limited number of migrants can be feasibly included. Rather, many states harbor an explicitly contemptuous and demeaning attitude toward low-skilled migrants, who are framed as undesirable populations who need to be "kept out". Anti-immigration political discourse often draws attention to their purported criminality, alongside their tendency to drain welfare resources, and the potential economic threat they may pose to low-skilled citizens. Consequently, immigration can be understood as a "bifurcated regime of scrutiny and restriction on the one hand, and proactive recruitment on the other" (Shachar and Hirschl 2014). That said, there is an obvious disconnect between xenophobic rhetoric and the reality of states' reliance on low-skilled migrants, who *are* usually willfully admitted in large numbers – without legal documentation to boot – due to the essential labor they provide under deeply disadvantageous, exploitative, and often dangerous conditions. Any meaningful discussion of skill-selective immigration policies, I think, must take stock of hierarchical systems of admission.

This chapter on the ethics of skill-selective immigration policies will proceed in this order. First, I describe skill-selective immigration policies and how they operate in practice. Next, focusing on the issue of wrongful discrimination and whether preferential treatment on the grounds of skill ought to be regarded as such, I will explain more conventional stances on skill-selective immigration policies: chiefly those that view skill-selection as desirable and morally neutral. After this, using the wrongfulness of racial selection as a guiding point, I turn to more critical analyses of skill-selection.

15.2 Skill-selective Immigration Policies and Present-Day Examples

In this section, following the work of Ayelet Shachar and Ran Hirschl, I explain the global significance of skill-selective immigration policies and, thus, their theoretical relevance for the ethics of immigration. From there, I elaborate in more detail on three present-day forms of skill-selective immigration policies.

In order to secure their own power and superiority in a "pantheon of excellence", states have come to believe that they must boast the "ability to draw human capital, to become an 'IQ magnet'" (Shachar and Hirschl 2013). As Shachar and Hirschl continue:

> Just as they introduce restrictions on most other categories of entrants, governments are proactively "picking winners" who are fast-tracked to citizenship based on their skills, innovation, and potential contribution to the country's stature, economic growth, and international reputation. From the wealthy and highly educated, to top scientists, elite athletes, world-class artists, and successful entrepreneurs and innovators, a citizenship-for-talent exchange – what we might call *Olympic citizenship* – is on the rise.
>
> *(2013)*

States' decision to select migrants on the basis of skill, then, must be understood against a backdrop of steep competition in a knowledge-based global economy, where countries are continually seeking to maintain or gain relative advantages over each other (Shachar and Hirschl 2014). To wit, if it is not already clear enough, states' drive to recruit highly skilled migrants does not spring out of their desire to cultivate the talents of skilled individuals, regardless of their birthplace or origin, as valuable ends in themselves. Rather, skilled non-citizens are *instrumentally* granted the opportunity to migrate as a means of bolstering receiving states' prestige and cachet in a cut-throat "race for talent".

Shachar and Hirschl draw attention to instances where those regarded as extraordinarily talented – including opera stars, superstar athletes, and other individuals who have received internationally recognized prizes or awards like a "Pulitzer, Oscar, [or] Olympic Medal" – have been granted preferential admission under, for example, the United States's O-1 visa, which is reserved for "Individuals with Extraordinary Ability or Achievement" and their assistants or immediate family members. These examples are certainly paradigmatic cases of skill-selection in play. Nevertheless, Shachar and Hirschl's analysis extends to states' preference for "highly skilled" migration writ large. In a similar spirit, my chapter will pay close attention to states' preference for "skilled" and "talented" migrants who *need not* be deemed extraordinary or exceptional, but rather, come from educated, accredited, and professionally experienced (hence "skilled") backgrounds. I outline three examples of skill-selective immigration policies below. First, states may create visa categories that are targeted at taking in highly skilled migrants. For example, the United States offers the "H1-B" visa category. According to the American Immigration Council:

> The H1-B is a temporary (nonimmigrant) visa category that allows employers to petition for highly educated foreign professionals to work in "specialty occupations" that require at least a bachelor's degree or the equivalent. Jobs in fields such as mathematics, engineering, technology, and medical sciences often qualify.
>
> *(2022)*

Currently, the annual statutory cap on H1-B visas is 65,000, with 20,000 additional visas for foreign professionals who have graduated with a master's degree or a doctorate from a US higher education institution. Similarly, the United Kingdom offers "Skilled Worker" visas, which targeted at highly skilled migrants who must have received a job offer that corresponds to a list of recognized occupations, including "chief executives and senior officials", "social and humanities scientists", "electrical engineers", and "barristers and judges" (GOV.UK 2023a). Quite pointedly, the government's website on the Skilled Worker visa notes that "[c]hefs are eligible for a Skilled Worker visa, but cooks are not" (GOV.UK 2023b).

Second, states may utilize "points-based" admissions systems that favor the admission of highly skilled workers. Points-based systems are currently operational in countries like the United Kingdom, Canada, Australia, and New Zealand. For greater ease, Canada, "choose[s] skilled workers based on their skills and ability to contribute to Canada's economy" (Government of Canada 2023), allows skilled workers to apply through a special "Express Entry" online system that unskilled workers do not have access to. Through "Express Entry", skilled workers are assessed, scored, and ranked through a points-based "Comprehensive Ranking System" (CRS) on the basis of their skills, education, language ability, and work experience. Australia's Department of Home Affairs website also provides a calculator tool that would-be skilled migrants can use to measure their eligibility – similarly, points are assigned based on qualities like age, language skills, skilled employment experience, educational qualifications, and specialist education qualifications (Australian Government Department of Home Affairs 2020).

Third, states have implemented guest worker programs that are intended to admit low-skilled workers on a temporary basis, with no option for a path toward citizenship. While guest worker programs concern the treatment of low-skilled migrants and need not be tethered to a preference for highly skilled workers, the preference for skilled migrants cannot be disambiguated from states' *dis*preference for low-skilled migrants, and by extension, a tendency to subject them to comparatively unfavorable treatment. Consider the US's H2-A visa program for temporary agricultural workers, as well as its H2-B program, which is intended to bring foreign nationals to take up temporary non-agricultural jobs. The leading industries that employ H-2B workers roughly correspond to the low-skill service industries with the highest prevalence of migrant workers in the United States, including Administrative and Support Services (especially groundskeeping and landscaping), Forestry, Fishing and Hunting, and Construction. Saliently, the H-2B visa is the "only employment-based visa available to foreign workers without a college education working outside agriculture, with immaterial exceptions" (Clemens and Lewis 2022). As Clemens and Lewis state, demand for H2-B visas far outstrips its statutory cap of 66,000 workers a year, to the extent that the Department of Labor (which is required to process firms' petitions for H-2B visas) processes firms' petitions in randomized order (2022).

The key difference between the US's visa programs for high and low-skilled workers, as I have alluded to earlier, is that H1-category visas typically allow for a path toward permanent residency and, from there, citizenship. At the same time, although both H1 and H2 programs may tie migrants' right to stay in the United States to their employment status, therefore rendering them deportable if they lose their jobs, given the low-skilled (and less prestigious) nature of H2 migrants' work, which affords them far less workplace authority and autonomy, H2 migrants are far more vulnerable to abuse and exploitation that they are unable to speak up about, such as workplace abuse, wage theft, and other working conditions like substandard health and safety procedures. The magnitude of these problems, of course, radically increases when low-skilled migrants are undocumented and are therefore more directly vulnerable to deportation.

The extraordinarily poor working conditions of low-skilled migrants were exposed soon after the outbreak of the COVID-19 pandemic, where meatpacking companies like Tyson Foods, JBS, Smithfield Foods, Cargill, and National Beef were slow to implement protections for workers early on in the pandemic, with recent data showing 86,000 meatpacking workers – who predominantly consisted of migrant workers – tested positive and that 423 had died (Chadde 2022). These numbers stand alongside reports that the meat industry dismissed government warnings to stockpile masks and develop plans to socially distance workers on processing lines, and allegations by families of deceased workers that meatpacking companies tried to hide cases by instructing plant nurses to record COVID-related absences as "flu-like symptoms" (Grabell 2020). As Daniel Costa writes,

> The specter of retaliation makes it understandably difficult for temporary migrant workers to complain to their employers and government agencies about unpaid wages and substandard working conditions. Private lawsuits against employers who break the law are also an unrealistic avenue for not enforcing rights, for two reasons: First, most temporary migrant workers are not eligible for federally funded legal services under US law, and second, those who have been fired are unlikely to have a valid immigration status permitting them to stay in the United States long enough to pursue their claims in court.
>
> *(2022)*

Further issues disproportionately experienced by low-skilled migrants, again due to their relative lack of power and much higher likelihood of originating from impoverished backgrounds, include illegal recruitment fees and debt bondage to third-party labor recruiters who secure their employment opportunities in the United States. In more extreme cases, temporary migrant workers have found out, upon arrival, that the jobs they were promised do not actually exist (Costa 2022).

15.3 Ethical Analyses of Skill-Selective Immigration Policies

In this section, I turn to philosophical accounts of the ethical permissibility of skill-selective immigration policies. To be sure, skill-selective immigration policies turn up a considerable number of ethical questions. One of these concerns, raised by Shachar and Hirschl, relate to the fundamental relationship between states and their members: the unequivocal valuing of "talent" may "pose serious moral hazards to liberal-democratic and egalitarian notions which at least formally assign to membership *irrespective* of how innovative, talented or accomplished they are" (Shachar and Hirschl 2014). Relatedly, the fact that membership is being increasingly used as a "recruitment tool" to out-compete other countries may erode more traditional understandings of political membership as a sacred bond between members of a specific sociopolitical community, allowing treasured notions of belonging and community to be overshadowed by economically driven motives. My chapter, however, centers on the question of *when* selection, or *which* forms of it are morally wrongful. This is because the ethical permissibility of skill-selection has largely turned on whether skill-selective immigration policies – like racially selective immigration policies – constitute a form of wrongful discrimination. As I will show, whether we should regard them as such will depend on the theory of wrongful discrimination in play.

15.3.1 The Moral Arbitrariness View of Discrimination

On a popular theory of wrongful discrimination, discrimination is wrongful when it leads to differential treatment on the basis of a morally arbitrary property – that is, one that is irrelevant to the goals and purposes of the selection at hand. Call this the Moral Arbitrariness view of wrongful discrimination. Suppose that I am deemed ineligible for a job on the grounds of my race. According to the Moral Arbitrariness view, such discrimination is wrongful because I am excluded from applying for a reason that has (as in the vast majority of employment-based discrimination cases) nothing to do with my ability to perform the job effectively. Alternatively, suppose that I am deemed ineligible for a job that requires me to speak Spanish – for example, the position of tour guide to an exclusively Spanish-speaking group of vacationers – simply because I do not speak the language. Unlike in the former case, it seems that my ineligibility would *not* count as an instance of wrongful discrimination, because the language that I cannot speak is directly relevant to the basic tasks I am required to perform on the job.

This is where views on the wrongfulness of racial and skill-selective immigration policies start to come apart. David Miller, for instance, states that "discrimination on grounds of race, sex, or instances, religion" is indefensible because "these features do not connect to anything of real significance to the society they want to join" (Miller 2005). Here, Miller seems to be evincing the moral arbitrariness view of discrimination. Applying the moral arbitrariness view to skill, on the contrary, seems to render skill-selective immigration policies permissible to the degree that skill *is* relevant to migrant selection. Following its logic, the public endorsement of skill as a favorable factor need not be any more objectionable than state policies that promote adult enrolment in post-secondary education, or state employers' propensity to favor skilled citizens in making hiring decisions (MacKay 2016). The reason for this is that states have a *legitimate purpose* in selecting immigrants on the basis of skill. Going back to Shachar and Hirschl's observations about why states primarily engage in skill-selection, "retaining economic competitiveness" may well be the "legitimate purpose" that states act upon. Similarly, Caleb Yong remarks that states may permissibly design labor policies that are driven by generating a higher level of economic resources, as "greater access to economic resources generally facilitates the pursuit of various personal ends", including the freedom, health, and well-being of their citizens (2016). Presumably, we would not be able to say the same of racially selective immigration policies.

It is nevertheless worth putting some pressure on the moral arbitrariness view of wrongful discrimination. There is a real worry, I think, that vague and abstract terms like "moral relevance" and "legitimate purpose" may be able to accommodate the invidious attitudes that underlie racist immigration policies. Think, here, of the notorious "White Australia" policy that began to exclude persons of non-European origin from migrating to Australia in 1901 and was only comprehensively dismantled by 1973. John Curtin, Australia's Prime Minister between 1941 and 1945, insisted that White Australia was not motivated by racial antagonism:

> Our laws have proclaimed the principle of a White Australia, we do not intend that to be, and it never was, *an affront to other races*. It was devised for economic and *sound human reasons*.
>
> *(National Archives of Australia 2010, my emphasis)*

As Curtin later remarked, continuing to defend Australia's racially exclusionary policy:

> …this country shall remain forever the home of the descendants of those people who came here in peace in order to establish in the South Seas an outpost of the British race.
>
> *(Rajan 2017)*

Keeping these quotes in mind, it does not require much stretch of the imagination to see how justifications for White Australia could be phrased as "legitimate purposes" that are *relevant* to the social goals of the nation. Curtin's reasoning (and that of many other Australian politicians who supported the policy) might be summed up as such: Australia harbored a strong desire to preserve its predominantly Anglo cultural heritage, which would have been watered down by the presence of non-white migrants with very different cultural backgrounds that made it difficult for them to assimilate into the dominant culture. While Curtin's remarks may have been disingenuous, putting his true intent aside, it is difficult to argue for why "cultural preservation" could not serve a legitimate purpose *in theory*. Additionally, going back to the moral arbitrariness view of wrongful discrimination, racial exclusion need not be justified by the desire to "preserve culture" for race to plausibly count as a relevant criterion. Race may, after all, be strongly *relevant* to citizens who strongly prefer to only live among people of the same race and do not wish to receive immigrants from other backgrounds.

15.3.2 Self-determination and the Right to Discriminate

Assuming that we continue judging racial selection to be impermissible even if they may indeed serve a "legitimate purpose", how else might we develop an objection to racially discriminatory immigration policies? Furthermore, what ethical ramifications might an altogether different theory of wrongful discrimination have for skill-selective immigration policies?

One possible response is to abandon the assumption that racial selection is impermissible in the first place. We see this in the work of Michael Walzer, who seems to *prima facie* accept "White Australia" as a policy that, drawing on the words of an Australian minister of immigration, cannot be reasonably be objected to because it is the "elementary right of every government" to "decide the composition of the nation" (1984). Yet, as Walzer continues:

> Assuming, then, that there actually is superfluous land, the claim of necessity would force a political community like that of White Australia to confront a radical choice. Its members could yield land for the sake of homogeneity, or they could give up homogeneity (agree to the creation of a multiracial society) for the sake of the land. And those would be their only choices. White Australia could survive only as Little Australia.
> *(1984)*

The crux of Walzer's stance, as I read the passage above, is that states *ought* to have the right to determine the composition of their members, even if this means engaging in discrimination through selecting immigrants on unsavory grounds like race, but only to a point. In a world of scarce resources, where basic goods like land are necessary to the "bare requirements of physical survival" (Walzer 1984), states can be fully self-determining only if they are *not* hoarding necessary resources for a select group of people (i.e. white Australians) while leaving others in desperate need. In this way, while Walzer does not object to states' right to engage in racial discrimination *in principle*, he demarcates the moral limits of their right to prefer certain migrants over others.

For those who remain opposed to racial or skill-based selection, Walzer's position may be friendlier to their stance than it appears at first blush. For instance, extending his approach to skill-selective immigration policies, one possible takeaway could be that skill-selective immigration policies are permissible *up to a stage* that many states have long surpassed. States may serve as exclusive fortresses for the educated, skilled, and wealthy if, and only if, they are not hoarding resources that are necessary for the bare survival of the poor and unskilled. Arguably, given the sheer numbers of would-be migrants who are desperately trying to escape conditions of poverty, danger, and destitution, we may have already reached the point where states in the Global North *must* rein in their skill-selective policies, or else find some other way of redistributing opportunities and resources.

15.3.3 The Status-Harming View of Wrongful Discrimination

Unexpectedly, another theorist who places great stock in states' right to self-determination offers us a reason for why racial selection may be wrongful, and from there, a starting point from which we may criticize skill-selective immigration policies. While Christopher Heath Wellman does not explicitly discuss skill-selective immigration policies, accepting his view of states' right to exclude non-citizens would likely render the question a non-starter. This is because Wellman locates the right to exclude in states' right to *freedom of association* (2008) –

that is, their ability to associate with, or disassociate from, non-citizens of their choice. The collective right to freedom of association, as Wellman characterizes it, is not at all dissimilar from our individual right to freedom of association, including our recognized and protected freedom to marry (or not marry) individuals of our choice. Consequently, while Wellman is careful to qualify that he does not condone racism, he expresses some ambivalence as to whether states reserve the right to engage in racial selection. Again, treating freedom of association as the focal point, much like how individuals *do* reserve the right to choose their marriage partners on the basis of race, even if we may judge them to have acted with morally undesirable or wrongful attitudes. In the end, Wellman concludes that selecting immigrants on the basis of race would only be wrongful if it means excluding members of racial groups who are presently already citizens, which would violate our special duties to "respect our fellow citizens as equal partners in the political cooperative" (2008). In contrast, while racially based exclusion would surely be insulting to non-citizens, it is unclear for Wellman that the non-citizen has a "right not to be insulted in this way" (2008). This leaves open the possibility that a racially homogenous state could permissibly select non-citizens on the basis of race, because no existing citizens would be disrespected.

While other philosophers have mounted strong objections to Wellman's account of the right to exclude,[3] I do not discuss them here. Rather, I am interested in a question that springs out of the exception that Wellman is willing to make for the case of race-based selection. Suppose he is correct that fellow citizens have a right not to be insulted and disrespected that non-citizens do not have. Other than race, could there be examples of selection that are similarly insulting to non-citizens – and could skill be one of them? For Michael Ball-Blakely, generalized skill-selection is pro tanto unjust in part because it reinforces existing biases, worsening status-harms for residents of low-socioeconomic status (SES). As he observes:

> The claim that we prefer the skilled to the unskilled, the educated to the uneducated, and the financially secure to the insecure is also heard by members of receiving countries. And there is considerable overlap between this message and the stereotypes and biases that set the social status of low-SES residents.
>
> *(Ball-Blakely 2022)*

The "overlap" that Ball-Blakely has in mind includes the widespread belief that the poor are commonly seen as responsible for their own poverty, due to individualistic or internal causes like being lazy, not putting in enough effort, or substance abuse, as well as the belief that the poorly educated are "blamed and held responsible for their own education, overall leading to social circumstances where those with low-SES persons view themselves, and are viewed in turn, as "less developed, intelligent, morally upstanding, or even attractive" (Ball-Blakely 2022). As a result, implicit and explicit biases against low-SES persons may serve to further undermine their equality of opportunity. The problem with skill-selective immigration policies for Ball-Blakely, then, is how they can *also* denigrate the social status of low-SES residents by expressing the attitude that their skills, education, and salaries render them substantially less desirable in the eyes of the state. This argument runs parallel to Wellman's comments on the circumstances under which race-based selection is morally impermissible: that is, when discriminatory immigration policies undermine the equal status of fellow citizens who belong to the "undesirable" group.

Apart from the status-harms that skill-selective immigration policies may inflict on citizens, in my own work, I have argued that status-harms to non-citizens are also of serious normative concern. It is necessary to state, here, that I reject Wellman's premise that it is only members of the same cooperative who owe special duties of respect to one another. Rather, my stance is that all persons, by virtue of their humanity, have a right not to be subject to demeaning and inferiorizing treatment. To see the basic difference: unlike Wellman, I think it would be wrong for a state to exclude migrants on the basis of racist beliefs and attitudes *even if* the state is racially homogenous at that very moment. It is counter-intuitive, in my view, to say that racially discriminatory immigration policies are *only* wrongful because they violate certain citizens' right to equal respect, while *not* violating any right of the would-be migrants who have been excluded because of their racial identity. Equal respect, at least on my view, is something that is owed to *all persons* and not just fellow members of one own state. To clarify, I do not mean here that all would-be migrants have a right to inclusion in the receiving state; they may not. Rather, I believe that they have a *global* right – as do all human beings – not to be excluded or dismissed from acquiring meaningful opportunities on the basis of noxious stereotypes and biases, as in the case of stigmatic attitudes and beliefs about inferiority on grounds of race or skill.[4]

While Ball-Blakely delves into the considerable overlap between stigmatizing stereotypes about low-SES residents and low-SES migrants, such as the tendency toward criminality or being responsible for their own poverty, here, I pay closer attention to the stereotypes that pertain more particularly to low-skilled migrants (Lim 2023). I am referring, here, to stereotypes and assumptions about low-skilled migrants that are brought up ubiquitously as talking points by anti-immigrant lobby groups. For example, it is often claimed that the presence of low-skilled migrants is harmful for citizens because they adversely affect the earnings of low-skilled American workers or compete with them for jobs (or, as it is typically put more crudely, "steal" jobs from citizens). It is also routinely claimed that low-skilled migrants place a heavy strain on welfare systems, disproportionately taking up resources that are intended for citizens' use. Yet, the preponderance of these beliefs, which have been heavily contested in the empirical literature, seems far more attributable to xenophobic stereotypes about low-skilled migrants as particular kinds of undesirable people, than to well-grounded, soundly-proven facts about their impact on receiving states (Lim 2023).

To the contrary, low-skilled workers make up an essential component of states' economies, with the value and necessity of their labor going largely unrecognized. More than this, recalling my discussion of guest worker programs and the relative disadvantages that are experienced by low-skilled migrants, immigration laws have been described as "misaligned with the reality of migrant flows and labor needs" (Golash-Boza 2009). Especially in the case of the United States, it is likely that numerical caps on low-skilled migrants are kept artificially low in order to sustain a relatively powerless workforce comprised of people who find it difficult to exercise their labor rights. Comparing states' treatment of highly skilled and low-skilled migrants, skill-selective immigration policies *on the whole*, then, may be far better understood as potent tools of oppression rather than a morally neutral form of selection.

15.4 Conclusion

In my chapter, I have sought to accomplish a number of goals. First, I have provided an overview of the structure of skill-selective immigration policies, alongside the motivations that may underlie them. While states are invested in recruiting highly skilled migrants as a means of remaining economically competitive, I have also suggested that their preference for highly skilled migrants cannot be disentangled from demeaning and contemptuous attitudes toward low-skilled migrants, who experience obvious dispreferential treatment. Second, while ethical concerns about skill-selective immigration policies do not completely reduce to questions of wrongful discrimination, I have covered a range of perspectives on why skill-selective immigration policies may or may not constitute a form of wrongful discrimination. On one hand, it is possible to treat states' preference for skilled migrants as a legitimate and non-arbitrary practice; on the other, we must take seriously the possibility that skill-selection may wrongfully demean low-SES citizens *and* low-skilled migrants.

Notes

1 For an influential defense of an "open borders" position that challenges states' right to exclude, see Joseph Carens's "The Ethics of Immigration" (New York: Oxford University Press, 2015.)
2 Michael Walzer can be read as one interesting exception. I discuss his work in more detail in Section III. More recently, Sahar Akhtar has argued that racial and ethnic immigration selection is not always morally wrong in certain cases (2022).
3 For example, see Fine 2010.
4 It is important to clarify that not *all* race-based immigration preferences may be racist in character, in the sense of imputing racial inferiority to migrants of particular races from a position of racial superiority. I take it that at least some race-based immigration preferences may be justified on other grounds.

Bibliography

Akhtar, S. (2022) 'Race Beyond our Borders: Is Racial and Ethnic Immigration Selection Always Morally Wrong?', *Ethics* 132.2, pp. 322–351.
American Immigration Council (2022), *The H1-B Visa Program and Its Impact on the U.S. Economy*. Available at: https://www.americanimmigrationcouncil.org/research/h1b-visa-program-fact-sheet (Accessed April 16 2023).
Australian Government Department of Home Affairs (2020), *Points table for Skilled Independent visa (subclass 189)*. Available at: https://immi.homeaffairs.gov.au/visas/getting-a-visa/visa-listing/skilled-independent-189/points-table (Accessed April 16, 2023).
Ball-Blakely, M. (2022) 'Skill-selection and Socioeconomic Status: An Analysis of Migration and Domestic Justice', *Journal of Social Philosophy* 53.4, pp. 595–613.
Carens, J. (2015) *The Ethics of Immigration*. New York: Oxford University Press.
Chadde, S. (2022) 'COVID-19 cases, deaths in meatpacking industry were much higher than previously known, congressional investigation shows', *MidWest Center for Investigative Reporting*, October 28. Available at: https://investigatemidwest.org/2021/10/28/covid-19-cases-deaths-in-meatpacking-industry-were-much-higher-than-previously-known-congressional-investigation-shows (Accessed April 16, 2023).
Clemens, M. and Lewis, E. G. (2022) 'The Effect of Low-Skill Immigration Restrictions on US Firms and Workers: Evidence From A Randomized Lottery', *National Bureau of Economic Research* Working Paper 30589, pp.12.
Costa, D. (2022) 'Second-class workers: Assessing H-2 visa programs' impact on workers', *Economic Policy Institute*, July 20. Available at: https://www.epi.org/publication/second-class-workers-assessing-h2-visa-programs-impact-on-workers (Accessed April 16, 2023).
Fine, S. (2010) 'Freedom of Association Is Not The Answer', *Ethics* 120.12, pp. 338–356.
Golash-Boza, T. (2009) 'The Immigration Industrial Complex: Why We Enforce Immigration Policies Destined to Fail', *Sociology Compass* 3.2, pp. 295–309.
GOV.UK (2023a), *Skilled Worker visa: eligible occupations and codes*. Available at: https://www.gov.uk/government/publications/skilled-worker-visa-eligible-occupations/skilled-worker-visa-eligible-occupations-and-codes (Accessed April 16, 2023).
GOV.UK (2023b), *Skilled Worker visa*. Available at: https://www.gov.uk/skilled-worker-visa/your-job (Accessed 16 April 2023).

Government of Canada (2023), *Eligibility for Express Entry programs*. Available at: https://www.canada.ca/en/immigration-refugees-citizenship/services/immigrate-canada/express-entry/eligibility.html (Accessed April 16, 2023).

Grabell, M. (2020), 'The Plot to Keep Meatpacking Plants Open During Covid-19', *Propublica*, May 13. Available at: https://www.propublica.org/article/documents-covid-meatpacking-tyson-smithfield-trump (Accessed April 16 2023).

Immigration History (2023), *Nationality Act of 1790*. Available at: https://immigrationhistory.org/item/1790-nationality-act (Accessed April 16 2023)

Lim, D. (2023) *Immigration and Social Equality: The Ethics of Skill-Selective Immigration Policies*. New York: Oxford University Press.

MacKay, D. (2016) 'Are Skill-Selective Immigration Policies Just?', *Social Theory and Practice* 42.1, pp. 123–153.

Miller, D. (2005) "Immigration: The Case for Limits" in Cohen, A. I. and Wellman, C. H. (eds.) *Contemporary Debates in Applied Ethics*. Oxford: Blackwell, pp. 193–206.

National Archives of Australia (2010), *White Australia to be defended against Japan – extract from speech by Prime Minister John Curtin*. Available at: https://www.naa.gov.au/learn/learning-resources/learning-resource-themes/war/world-war-ii/white-australia-be-defended-against-japan-extract-speech-prime-minister-john-curtin (Accessed April 16, 2023).

Rajan, S. (2017) 'Stumbling on from the White Australia Policy', *The Stringer: Independent News*, October 10. Available at: https://thestringer.com.au/stumbling-on-from-the-white-australia-policy-12641 (Accessed April 16, 2023).

Shachar, A., and Hirschl, R. (2013) 'Recruiting 'Super Talent': The New World of Selective Migration Regimes', *Indiana Journal of Global Legal Studies* 20.1, pp. 71–107.

Shachar, A., and Hirschl, R. (2014) 'On Citizenship, States, and Markets', *Journal of Political Philosophy* 22.2, pp. 231–257.

Walzer, M. (1984) *Spheres of Justice: A Defense of Pluralism and Equality*. Oxford: Martin Robertson.

Wellman, C. H. (2008) 'Immigration and Freedom of Association', *Ethics* 119.1, pp. 109–141.

Yong, C. (2016) 'Justice in Labor Immigration Policy', *Social Theory and Practice* 42.4, pp. 817–844.

PART V

Entry, Exit, and Exploitation

16
CITIZENSHIP TESTS

Thom Brooks

16.1 Introduction

Most individuals acquire citizenship at birth. This may be on account of where they were born or the citizenship of their parents. But others choose to acquire citizenship through naturalization in a different country. No country provided exam-like tests for anyone seeking to naturalize a century ago. However, this has become increasingly common over the last few decades. This raises the issue of how these tests are designed and implemented.

This chapter surveys different models for how citizenship tests are run. These include the United States, Australia, the European model, and the United Kingdom. Each has contrasting expectations for new citizens and how they are assessed. After surveying the different models, the chapter will conclude with some general observations about how tests for citizenship should be administered and delivered better.

16.2 The United States

The first standardized citizenship test originated in the United States of America in 1986. The "civics" test's primary purpose was mostly symbolic. Applicants for citizenship must answer correctly at least six of ten questions to pass. There is no multiple choice. But if a test is failed, it may be sat again for free a second time. All who pass can then swear an oath and swiftly become American citizens (USCIS 2008).

The American government does not keep secret what might be asked of applicants. Border agents ask ten questions from a free and easily accessible list of 100 possible questions that includes their answers (USCIS 2019). This is admirably accountable and transparent. Anyone can see what might be asked and what must be answered – whether or not they are American or wish to become American. The US government has a Citizenship and Integration Grant Program providing preparation resources, support, and information for immigrants and organizations. There is also a learning-together toolkit for parents to use in exploring civics and citizenship education with their children. There is also an Outstanding Americans by Choice Initiative celebrating immigrants who have become naturalized Americans, which showcases new citizens making positive contributions to the US culture and society.

Its factual contents can be safely described as non-partisan and uncontested. For example, US tests might ask for the name of the first American President (George Washington) or who was President during the US Civil War (Abraham Lincoln). Test questions ask for the name of the institution at the top of each of the three branches of American government: the President, Congress, and the Supreme Court. There are questions of geography like naming either of the two longest rivers (Mississippi and Missouri) or anyone of the over 2000 Native American tribes, such as the Apache, Iroquois, Mohawk, Pequot, or Sioux.

Things were not always this way. Shortly after the test was originally launched, it included several areas of relatively trivial information seemingly unessential for citizenship. One such question was to accurately know the height of the Bunker Hill Monument. A second and more problematic example was a question about how many stars are on a quarter. The problem with this was that more than one quarter was in circulation and they had different numbers of stars on them. These questions have all since been removed (Romero and Jordan 2020).

More recently, the US test was changed albeit briefly during the last days of former President Donald J. Trump's term of office. He wished to make the test far more difficult for the individuals to pass. The test was doubled in size asking twenty questions (instead of ten) with the same requirement that 60% of the questions are answered correctly. The correct answer was changed for questions. The previously right answer for who Senators represent was changed from "all people of the state" to "citizens in their state" highlighting that not all people in a state were citizens and were excluded. Instead of needing to name one of three branches of government, applicants now needed to name all three to get a single question correct.

The US Citizenship and Immigration Services agency accepted that these changes created potential barriers for individuals in the process of naturalization. Despite this partisan effort to make more people fail, pass rates remained high at 94% mitigating the impact of these changes (Kwok 2021). Nevertheless, there were growing concerns that most US citizens could not pass the test themselves (CBS News 2021). Shortly after his election, President Joe Biden reversed Trump's changes and reverted the test to its previous shorter, uncontroversial and non-partisan content and format as was set out in 2008 (Sands 2021).

The US citizenship test is popular with many American lawmakers. Almost half of all US states require students to learn about the citizenship test as part of their studies for a high school diploma. This is useful in demonstrating that information about good citizenship is for all citizens – and not only migrants seeking to naturalize.

The test has not been popular with everyone. Sometimes criticized for measuring "rote memorization" rather than inculcation of civic values, a regular complaint is no particular knowledge about American citizenship is necessary because most Americans acquire nationality at birth (Spiro 2008:43). There is also the essentially contested nature of American identity.

Tests are often thought to be exclusive by their nature. Some will fail and so be excluded from the full rights and responsibilities of citizenship. But the American citizenship test is not designed as a last barricade to naturalization. Its role remains largely symbolic. The main obstacles are all overcome by the time that someone is able to take the test, such as fulfilling residency and good moral character requirements. A substantial effort is made to support applicants accessing the information in a clear and transparent way with grants and funded programs to provide added support and signposting role model naturalized citizens to send a message of inspiration and welcome.

The US test is a bridge, not a barrier, to acquiring US citizenship. The pass rate of more than 94% emphasizes this important point. But, as we shall see, not all forms of testing follow the American model.

16.3 Australia

The origins of the Australian citizenship test are in a report, *Australian Citizenship for a New Citizenship*, by the Australian Citizenship Council (2000) and led by Sir Ninian Stephen. This work was launched in 2000 after a public consultation and reported in May 2001. The report recommended affirmation ceremonies to welcome new Australian citizens. This report introduced the idea of launching a new citizenship test, and it recommended that the government encourages non-Australians to pursue naturalization.

The Australian citizenship test was aimed at demonstrating knowledge of the responsibilities and privileges that citizens enjoy (Australian Government 2001). Successful applicants would take part in new citizenship ceremonies as well – and these reforms were to prove influential elsewhere, notably in the United Kingdom. However, the new Australian citizenship test did not appear for several years later. Australia used the teething problems of the November 2005 launch of the UK's citizenship test – originally inspired by Australia's plans for a test – as an occasion to learn lessons for introducing the Australian test.

There was a review conducted on how the test would be delivered in 2006 (Australian Government 2006). In a Parliamentary Library note, it was observed that the rollout of the test was delayed somewhat, in part, to review the implementation of the UK's citizenship test launched in 2005. The Australian review noted that UK adopted what was seen as a high-brow approach to British life with the citizenship test's focus on traditional institutions like the courts, the church, and the Crown to the relative exclusion of the workplace and everyday life.

Their test was introduced through the Australian Citizenship Amendment (Citizenship Testing) Act 2007. The Australian test handbook is free to download online and easy to locate. The test's contents include information about the meaning of Australian citizenship, such as noting the duty to vote, to work in the defense force or public service, and serving on juries. All test applicants are asked about Australian values like freedom of speech and of religion, support for democracy, and the rule of law.

At first, there was some mockery of its contents. For example, Sue Harris Rimmer (2007:5) noted that some humorists claimed it asked questions akin to "is it best to take a sick day on: (a) when the cricket's on, (b) when the cricket's on or (c) when's the cricket on?" but the actual test is very different. However, it did include information about cricketeer Sir Donald Bradman. The test handbook noted that "he was small and slight but amazingly quick on his feet, playing his shots almost like a machine" (Reuters 2008). While there is no doubt that Bradman is one of Australia's most celebrated sportsmen, it is highly questionable why it is essential for Australian citizenship that someone know he was "small and slight" and bat "like a machine." While this information has been in the official test handbook for all applicants to memorize, former Prime Minister Kevin Rudd confirmed that no one had ever been asked about Bradman on any test.[1] This raises concerns about why it was included in the test handbook for memorization if never actually used in any test. This is because all test handbook information is presented as important and testable, but clearly not all facts are sufficiently notable to warrant testing which somewhat undermines the use of the test.

The current edition of the test has since removed this description of Bradman and his cricket batting style. Entitled *Our Common Bond*, the test handbook is about fifty pages long. Launched in November 2020, its main focus is on national values. This is done through five multiple-choice questions about the values of mutual respect, equality, and democracy that must all be answered correctly – as a part of correctly answering 75% of the full set of twenty test questions.

The Australian model is a test centered on essential values. It is virtually alone in requiring not only a pass, but that questions about specific issues are passed, too. This raises barriers making it more difficult for individuals to pass than the less complex and more generalized American test. But the Australian test's contents have remained controlled and revised to ensure focus on values and everyday information needed for good citizenship. Its aim is more of a bridge than a barrier to citizenship in its pursuit of ensuring new citizens know about Australian values and specific issues.

16.4 The European Model

The description of a "European model" refers to the use of the test in European countries, such as France, Germany, and the Netherlands, but not limited to these three. The test has operated as an obstacle to obtaining citizenship. One consequence is its use has reduced naturalization applications in these countries (van Oers 2013:276). However, what distinguishes the European model to citizenship tests is its combining the learning of citizenship with the learning of a national language (Joppke 2010).

For example, in France, individuals who apply for citizenship are interviewed. The purpose of the interview is to "verify, pursuant to Article 21-24 of the Civil Code, that the applicant has in particular sufficient knowledge of French history, culture and society" (French Government 2022). French citizenship tests cover information in a 28-page *Citizens' Handbook* (French Ministry 2015).

Of course, the French citizenship test is taken only in French. A part of the test's design is that applicants who successfully answer enough questions correctly are held to also be demonstrating a sufficient grasp of the French language. Both basic knowledge about France and the French language are seen as essential for citizenship.

Individuals seeking to become German citizens can apply after eight years. Each must renounce their current nationality because Germany does not recognize dual nationality. Germany's citizenship test has thirty-three questions. Individuals must get seventeen or more correct to pass. Three of the correct answers must relate to questions about whichever German state the applicant lives in. The German citizenship test covers subjects such as Germany's legal system, society, and living conditions (German Federal Ministry 2022).

Like with France, the German citizenship test is about more than citizenship. The test is taken only in German, and part of its purpose is to ensure new prospective citizens have an adequate understanding of German citizenship and of German language. This dual aim is held to support integration.

Similarly to France and Germany, the Netherlands has a citizenship test that applicants take in Dutch. This is delivered in the form of a civic integration diploma (Dutch Ministry 2022). The awarding of a diploma provides a kind of unique qualification for new citizens.

However, the main hurdle is not proving knowledge of Dutch politics, history, or culture, but demonstrating sufficient Dutch language skills.

While each administers the test in different ways, the European model has in common the view that citizenship is about learning key facts across social and political areas with an emphasis on sufficient language of the national language – in a kind of language test examined through questions about mostly politics, history, and culture. All of the information about becoming a citizen is generally freely available. While the essential requirements around language may cause the primary difficulty for some candidates, it is clear the model is intended to support learning about citizenship integrated with language courses where prospective citizens learn and engage with others also going through the process. Again, the process is generally more of a bridge than a barrier although language may pose a significant obstacle for some. While the process may be difficult to pass, there is additional support – and not only for language acquisition – to mitigate the more robust approach.

16.5 The United Kingdom

The origins of the UK's citizenship test are found in a specific event. In May 2001, there was rioting in areas such as Burnley and Oldham. The government became concerned about communities of citizens old and new living side by side with parallel lives. The terrorist attacks in the United States on 9/11 only made the government more resolute to act, but a decision was made to create a citizenship test to ensure new citizens knew of and adopted shared fundamental British values, understood public institutions, and understood how to make a life in the UK.

The British Nationality Act 1981 introduced a requirement that anyone applying for naturalization must have "sufficient knowledge about *life in the United Kingdom,*" although it did not specify how this should be done (emphasis added). But it was not until the Nationality, Immigration and Asylum Act 2002 that Parliament formally mandated that this knowledge about life in the United Kingdom must be evidenced through a "life in the United Kingdom" citizenship test – named for the requirement in primary legislation.

The main question concerned what the test's content should be. This was influenced heavily by the Commission on the Future of Multi-Ethnic Britain chaired by Lord (Bhikhu) Parekh in 2000. Parekh's Commission rejected the view of the UK as a single, fixed idea of the community in favor of a "community of communities" (Parekh 2000). This was followed by a review led by John Denham MP that found that "it is…essential to establish a greater sense (?) of citizenship based on common principles that are shared by all sections of the community". (Home Office 2001).

However, a key group here was the "Life in the UK" Advisory Group run by Sir Bernard Crick. This was a group of mostly educationalists, including Crick, that conducted the first – and thus far the last – public consultation into what a test for British citizenship test should be about. The consultation led to much feedback from various areas about how they were uniquely different – often focusing on regional customs and culture from national dishes to patron saints – rather than what made all British citizens *British*. The Group noted:

> To be British…mean[s] that we respect the laws, the elected parliamentary and democratic political structures, traditional values of mutual tolerance, respect for equal rights and mutual concerns, and that we give our allegiance to the state (as commonly

symbolized in the Crown) in return for protection. To be British is to respect those over-arching specific institutions, values, beliefs and traditions that bind us all, the different nations and cultures together in peace and in a legal order.

(Home Office 2003:8)

The result was a citizenship test based around shared values and public institutions that relate to all citizens in common.

The UK's test launched on 1 November 2005. It required applicants to answer correctly 18 or more of 24 multiple-choice questions in 45 minutes. And then the problems begin. The first edition of the test handbook needed to be purchased. It gave no examples of what kinds of questions someone might expect.

Worse, there were factual errors throughout. There were problems of historical fact. For example, the test got wrong where King Charles II lived in exile saying he was in France when he was in Holland, instead (Home Office 2005:28). The test got wrong a quotation from Sir Winston Churchill and, curiously, the test wrongly claims Northern Ireland is a part of Great Britain, when Great Britain is only composed of England, Scotland, and Wales (Home Office 2005: 57, 17). Perhaps worst of all, the original test got wrong the number of Members of Parliament. It claimed there were only 645 when there were 646 (Home Office 2005:61). When Crick was asked why the test contained so many errors, he replied frankly: "there are errors in it because it was done fairly quickly because we didn't want to keep immigrants waiting for citizenship" (Glendinning 2006).

Two years after its launch, the UK government published a second edition in 2007. This version aimed to correct the original test's mistakes but went much further in the number of public programs and other information required for study. The problem with this was that many of these programs changed after the test handbook was published and left uncorrected. My research confirmed it was possible to sit for a citizenship test where every correct answer was factually untrue – mostly because departments had changed name, merged, or were closed (Brooks 2012, Brooks 2013). For these reasons, the problem of MP numbers was revived. After the second edition corrected its error and confirmed there were 646 Members of Parliament, Parliament voted to change the number of constituencies to 650 in 2010.

Moreover, the test asked questions about how to access programs that applicants could not use. Part of the issue here was the UK had changed the use of the test to a requirement for *both* citizenship *and* permanent residency (Indefinite Leave to Remain). Unlike other countries, the UK's *citizenship* test had effectively become a *residency* test. This meant applicants had to pass the test earlier in their naturalization journey than before. Normally, individuals naturalizing must wait a year before they can apply for citizenship – and this can take at least another six months. It is often about two years from passing the citizenship test to acquiring citizenship.

The second test edition introduced a for-purchase official practice book of questions to study in preparing for the test. However, the book is clear that none of its questions appear worded in the same way on the test. This claim has not been supported by interview with applicants (Brooks 2016). Either way, the UK test material is not as accessible or transparent as other citizenship tests found elsewhere. All materials must be purchased. The official guide lacks full information about the test format with all actual questions hidden from applicants that might be asked.

It is a setting up of barriers designed to make more fail. This seems borne out by some of the data. For example, the most test attempts before passing is 118 times in 2015 and 2016 (Foster 2021). At £50 per test sitting, this would have cost £5900 in total before paying any application fees for permanent residency or citizenship. It is noteworthy that the Home Office guidance since the test was launched made clear that tests cannot be taken more than once every seven days, and yet here was someone taking the test 118 times in 104 weeks in an apparent breach of the Home Office's own guidance on how tests should be administered.

One curiosity of the UK test is it can be taken in multiple languages. While virtually all take the test in English, it can be taken in Welsh or Scots Gaelic. However, the test handbook is only published in English. This raises questions about why the test would be available to take in languages that have no test handbook for applicants to study in these languages. There is a further issue that Cornish was recognized about a decade ago as having the same protected minority status as the Welsh and Scots. While ministers have recognized that there must be some inclusion of Cornish history and culture in the test – as well as a test available to sit in Cornish – nothing has been done.

The third and current edition of the test was published in 2013. It continues to contain factual errors, such as claiming the largest monetary denomination is the £50 note when there are £100 in circulation (Home Office 2013:74). Again, many of its problems since relate to its being a handbook published in 2013, and much of its contents have become out of date. Most notably, Her Late Majesty The Queen had died. The government later decided this information would be removed but not replaced. Also removed is any mention of MP numbers, as the government plans to reduce them, but applicants must know the number of members in the Welsh Assembly, Scottish Parliament, and Northern Ireland Assembly at Stormont. Applicants must know the basics about the court system, but there is no mention of the UK Supreme Court which is the lead body. And so, the UK test does not currently ask anyone seeking British citizenship to know who is the head of state, how many sit in the mother of all parliaments nor which court is supreme in a test described as moving from trivia to the trivial "like a bad pub quiz" (Brooks 2022).

While there is certainly information of practical use included such as where to pay tax and information about shared fundamental British values, what stands out most is all the practical information removed in the current edition that had been a part of the earlier two editions. Applicants need not know any longer how to report a crime, how to contact emergency services nor register with a doctor. But there are questions about how many feet tall is the London Eye, the approximate age of Big Ben, and the name of Britain's first curry restaurant, which had only operated for a couple of years.

The UK test is unique among those models considered. Its official information is hidden behind a paywall and test questions are kept secret. The test's contents are too often impractical and out of date. The test can be taken in multiple languages, but only one has a test handbook. This is not a program for supporting migrants to naturalize and integrate like seen with the other models. For this reason, I have argued that a fundamental reform should happen. It is a test for British citizenship that few British citizens can pass. In written and oral evidence to several Parliamentary committees, my recommendations for making the test fit for purpose have been accepted although we await for the government to act (Brooks 2022). One crucial aspect of this is that while the UK's test has had the aim and purpose of fostering integration, there has never been any official consultation into whether this has been achieved. This is alarming given that over two million have taken the test with many reporting the test and the naturalization process has not always been positive in supporting integration (Brooks 2016). It suggests a carelessness – or even insincerity – in delivering on the test's aims and purposes, as otherwise there would be greater attention to accuracy, providing support and evidence-based analysis.

16.6 Conclusion

Citizenship tests are becoming increasingly popular. More countries are enacting them, and there are different models to choose from. This chapter has surveyed some of the key models. There are some broad similarities in the topics covered with all including history and government, and others noting public institutions and shared values. Most make information about their test easy to find and free to access, but there is the notable exception of the UK. Most focus on civics, although the European model gives strong emphasis on language acquisition. Finally, the process of naturalization is often an isolating experience faced by individuals alone, although the American and European models offer some exceptions.

Nevertheless, it might be considered whether a written or multiple-choice exam is the best way to ascertain whether someone possesses the requisite knowledge for being a citizen. As the political theorist Joseph Carens (2013:59) has observed, "tests of civil competence never actually test civic competence. The tests that assess a person's knowledge of various facts about the history and institutions of the country tell us nothing about a person's civic capacities." It could be argued that living within a new country for a period of time without engaging in any criminal activity, paying all taxes owed, and making some positive contribution is fundamentally what we might wish from future fellow citizens.

The different ways of using citizenship tests share in common the view that there is information – whether about values or a collective narrative – that is centrally important and helps forge communal ties. Passing tests is meant to show new citizens have the capacity to connect in some meaningful way with existing citizens. This approach presupposes some view around what should serve as relevant values and other information for such an exercise. But, notably, it ought to include the involvement in citizens in drawing up some bottom-up approach (Brooks 2023). However, too often this is a top-down policy area where government sets out what it thinks is most relevant but raises serious risks that a noble effort of aiming to bring diverse people together might end up driving them further apart. It matters that those passing citizenship tests can participate fully in collective life like any other citizen. If not, the aim and purposes of the enterprise are lost.

Moreover, it is also important that the best way to confirm where the aims and purposes are met is through an exam and not some alternative. If another way was better, we might fulfil the same aims and purposes through different means.

In any event, the use of citizenship tests continues to grow and expand. This chapter has highlighted that there are different models for how this might work – and how these tests might be reformed and improved.

Note

1 News.com.au. 2009. "Don Bradman was never in Australian citizenship test" (21 October).

Bibliography

Australian Citizenship Amendment (Citizenship Testing) Act. 2007.
Australian Citizenship Council. 2000. *Australian Citizenship for a New Century*. Canberra: Australian Citizenship Council.
Australian Government. 2001. *Australian Citizenship...A Common Bond: Government Response to the Report of the Australian Citizenship Council*. Canberra: Commonwealth of Australia.
Australian Government. 2006. *Australian Citizenship: Much More Than a Ceremony*. Canberra: Department of Immigration and Multicultural Affairs.
British Nationality Act. 1981.
Brooks, Thom. 2012. "The British Citizenship Test: The Case for Reform," *Political Quarterly* 83: 560–566.
Brooks, Thom. 2013. *The 'Life in the United Kingdom' Citizenship Test: Is It Unfit for Purpose?* Durham: Durham University.
Brooks, Thom. 2016. *Becoming British: UK Citizenship Examined*. London: Biteback Publishing.
Brooks, Thom. 2022. *Reforming the UK's Citizenship Test: Building Bridges, Not Barriers*. Bristol: Bristol University Press.
Brooks, Thom. 2023. *Global Justice: An Introduction*. Oxford: Blackwell.
Carens, Joseph. 2013. *The Ethics of Immigration*. Oxford: Oxford University Press.
CBS News. 2021. "Most Americans could not pass a citizenship test, a major issue for the country" (19 January).
Dutch Ministry of Justice and Security. 2022. *Civic Integration for More Secure Residence Permit and Naturalization*. Url: https://ind.nl/en/Pages/Integration-in-the-netherlands.aspx.
Foster, Kevin. 2021. House of Commons Debate: British Nationality, Assessments (Question 144733) (8 February).
French Government. 2022. Naturalisation. Url: https://www.service-public.fr/particuliers/vosdroits/F2213.
French Ministery de l'Interieur. 2015. *Livret du Citoyen*. Url: https://www.immigration.interieur.gouv.fr/content/download/79473/584355/file/Livret-du-citoyen_pageapage_5mars2015.pdf.
German Federal Ministry of the Interior and Community. 2022. *Naturalization*. https://www.bmi.bund.de/EN/topics/migration/naturalization/naturalization-node.html.
Glendinning, Lee. 2006. "Citizenship guide fails its history exam," *The Guardian* (29 April).
Home Office. 2001. *Building Cohesive Communities: A Report of the Ministerial Group on Public Order and Community Cohesion*. London: Home Office.
Home Office. 2003. *The New and the Old: The report of the 'Life in the United Kingdom' Advisory Group*. London: Home Office Communications Directorate.
Home Office. 2005. *Life in the United Kingdom: A Journey to Citizenship*. London: The Stationary Office.
Home Office. 2007. *Life in the United Kingdom: A Journey to Citizenship*, 2nd edition. London: The Stationary Office.
Home Office. 2013. *Life in the United Kingdom: A Guide for New Residents*, 3rd edition. London: The Stationary Office.
Kwok, Abe. 2021. "In the end, Trump's tougher citizenship test had no impact on immigrants," *Arizona Republic* (14 June).
Nationality, Immigration and Asylum Act. 2002.
News.com.au. 2009. "Don Bradman was never in Australian citizenship test" (21 October).
Parekh, Bhikhu, ed. 2000. *The Future of Multi-Ethnic Britain: Report of the Commission on the Future of Multi-Ethnic Britain*. London: Profile.
Reuters. 2008. "Strewth! Australia drops cricket from citizenship test" (22 November).
Rimmer, Sue Harris. 2007. *Bills Digest: Australian Citizenship Amendment (Citizenship Testing) Bill 2007*. Canberra: Australian Parliament.
Romero, Simon and Miriam Jordan. 2020. "New U.S. citizenship test is longer and more difficult," *New York Times* (3 December).
Sands, Geneva. 2021. "Biden administration rolls back Trump-era citizenship civics test," *CNN* (22 February).

Spiro, Peter J. 2008. *Beyond Citizenship: American Identity After Globalization*. Oxford: Oxford University Press.
United States Citizenship and Immigration Services (USCIS). 2008. "Study for the test (2008 version)."
United States Citizenship and Immigration Services (USCIS). 2019. "Civics (History and Government) Questions for the Naturalization Test," url: https://www.uscis.gov/sites/default/files/document/questions-and-answers/100q.pdf (accessed 16 March 2023),
van Oers, Ricky. 2013. *Deserving Citizenship: Citizenship Tess in Germany, the Netherlands and the United Kingdom*. Leiden: Martinus Nijhoff Publishers.

17
TEMPORARY MIGRATION AND WORKER EXPLOITATION

Michael Kates

17.1 Introduction

One of the most widely known facts among economists and political scientists studying immigration is the "Rights-Numbers Tradeoff": there is a negative correlation between the rights temporary workers enjoy and the overall number of them that states are willing to admit inside their borders (Pritchett, 2006; Ruhs and Martin, 2008; Rodrik, 2011; Ruhs, 2013; Posner and Weyl, 2014, 2018; Milanovic, 2016). In other words, the more open a country is to migrant workers, the less extensive are their rights in comparison to citizens and permanent residents.

By way of example, consider the so-called "Kafala system" used by states in the Gulf Cooperation Council. Countries like Bahrain, Kuwait, Qatar, and Saudi Arabia admit many foreign workers in the construction sector, but they also sharply curtail their rights in exchange for temporary access to the labor market. Under this system, migrant workers are forced to rely on the sponsorship of a single employer and need their permission to transfer jobs, end an employment contract, and even enter or exit the country. A less extreme but still illustrative example can be found in countries like Hong Kong and Singapore. Both admit a relatively high number of low-skilled migrant workers, but they are required to waive certain rights as a condition of employment. Domestic workers are not protected by local labor laws, and migrant workers in Singapore are legally prohibited from either living with or marrying citizens. By contrast, although Western democracies grant migrant workers an extensive set of rights vis-à-vis citizens and permanent residents, they admit relatively fewer of them on a per capita basis.

My aim in this chapter is to assess the moral significance of this fact. Is it morally permissible for states to grant temporary workers a less extensive set of rights than citizens and permanent residents? Or would doing so be wrongfully exploitative?[1] In answering these questions, I have three main goals. First, I want to reconstruct the case for limiting the rights of temporary workers in the strongest possible terms. I do so out of the conviction that an argument is not fully defeated unless it's criticized in its most compelling form. Second, I want to show that one of the most powerful defenses of equal rights for temporary workers in the literature is unsound. Finally, I want to briefly sketch a novel argument for why limiting the rights of temporary works would be exploitative.

Before proceeding further, two clarifications are in order. First, there are at least three kinds of rights at issue in this discussion. In exchange for granting migrant workers temporary access to their labor market, states may choose to limit (1) their *membership* rights, i.e., the rights that migrants are typically granted after a certain period of time in a country such as the right to vote or the right to obtain citizenship; (2) their *social* rights, i.e., the rights that normally accompany permanent residency in a given jurisdiction such as the right to access social programs and welfare benefits like health insurance or old age and disability pensions; or (3) their *labor* rights, i.e., the rights that migrant workers are morally entitled to claim against their employers such as the right to a minimum wage or decent working conditions.[2]

I will focus on (3) for two main reasons. First, the vast majority of discussion on this issue has focused on (1) and (2). By contrast, very little has been written on (3). It is thus worth examining a relatively unexplored issue. Second, and related to the above point, there is widespread agreement that the case for restricting membership rights on a permanent basis seems difficult to sustain (see, e.g., Walzer, 1983; Lenard and Straehle, 2011; Carens, 2013), whereas the case for restricting at least some types of social rights, e.g., non-contributory welfare rights, seems far more plausible (see, e.g., Stilz, 2010; Ruhs, 2013; Bertram, 2019). There is, however, little agreement on the question of whether it's morally permissible for states to restrict the labor rights of migrant workers. *Prima facie*, however, the case for restricting (3) seems much stronger. Although the decision to pay temporary workers a sub-minimum wage or subject them to a less stringent set of workplace standards is obviously morally significant, it doesn't necessarily raise deeper questions about their moral status. What's more, the goods being exchanged—restrictions on wages and working conditions, on the one hand, and access to a country's labor market, on the other—seem far more commensurable and so it seems easier to believe that there can be legitimate tradeoffs among them. Accordingly, if I can show that there's no good reason to restrict the labor rights of temporary workers, then that will significantly advance the debate on this topic.

Finally, I will assume that states have the right to control their borders, i.e., a right to decide how many migrants, if any, they wish to enter. Like others in the literature, I adopt this assumption merely for the sake of argument and not because I believe it's the correct position in the ethics of immigration. In any event, it seems clear that if individuals had a right to migrate to any country of their choosing, then it would be wrong for states to attach conditions to their entrance (Oberman, 2017). Proceeding on the basis of the opposite assumption helps me to avoid this issue.

17.2 The Case for Limiting the Labor Rights of Temporary Workers

To see the force of the argument for limiting the labor rights of temporary workers, consider the following facts. First, one of the most significant influences on a person's life prospects is their *place* of birth. Other things being equal, a person born in the United States has a much higher lifetime expectation of economic resources than a person born in, say, Uganda. Economist Branko Milanovic calls this the "citizenship premium," and, according to his calculations, it accounts for about two-thirds of a person's income over the course of their life. As Milanovic puts it:

> The world is unequal in a very particular way: most of the inequality, when we break it down into inequality within countries and among countries, is due to the latter. When income differences among countries are large, then a person's income depends

significantly on where they live, or indeed where they were born, since 97 percent of the world's population live in the countries where they were born.

(2016, p. 132)

Second, and related to the above point, there are enormous *wage differentials* between workers in different countries. That is, the price that workers can fetch on the labor market varies greatly from one place to another. In fact, studies have shown that workers in the exact same occupation can command vastly different wages depending on *where* they are working. For example, according to a survey compiled by Freeman and Oostendorp (2000), a typical construction worker in India earned about $48 per month during a five-year period, whereas one in Sweden earned $2481 per month. Moving from the former to the latter country would thus substantially improve their welfare. Indeed, not only would migrant workers themselves benefit from these jobs, but if they sent back part of their wages to their home country in the form of remittances, then that would substantially reduce global poverty. It is not surprising, therefore, that many people in low-income countries are eager to work abroad. Faced with the choice between staying at home and moving to a high-income country, thousands of workers choose the latter option.

The problem, of course, is that since states have a right to control their borders, they may only be willing to admit migrant workers on their own terms. In exchange for the right to enter, they may demand that temporary workers accept a sub-minimum wage or be willing to work under sub-standard conditions. The price of admittance may come, therefore, at a steep moral cost. Indeed, it's precisely for that reason that many philosophers have criticized the practice. For example, in the words of Michael Walzer:

> As a group, [temporary workers] constitute a disenfranchised class. They are typically an exploited or oppressed class as well, and they are exploited or oppressed at least in part because they are disenfranchised, incapable of organizing effectively for self-defense. Their material condition is unlikely to be improved except by altering their political status. Indeed, the purpose of their status is to prevent them from improving their condition; for if they could do that, they would soon be like domestic workers, unwilling to take on hard and degrading work or accept low rates of pay.
>
> *(1983, p. 59)*

In short, many people believe that if temporary workers are forced to accept a less extensive set of labor rights than citizens and permanent residents to gain access to a country's labor market, then they are being exploited.

But despite the intuitive appeal of this conviction, it's actually quite puzzling.[3] To see why, note that high-income countries have three different options in response to the claims of migrant workers:

1 *No entrance*: They can decide not to admit any migrant workers inside their jurisdiction.
2 *Entrance on unequal terms*: They can decide to admit a large number of migrant workers on unequal terms, i.e., with a less extensive set of labor rights than citizens and permanent residents.
3 *Entrance on equal terms*: They can decide to admit a small number of migrant workers on equal terms, i.e., with the exact same set of labor rights as citizens and permanent residents.[4]

The puzzle arises because there's a conflict between how defenders of equal rights for migrant workers rank these options and their actual impact on the welfare of migrant workers. That is, defenders of equal rights for migrant workers believe that although both (1) and (3) are morally permissible, (2) is not. If they assume, moreover, that helping a greater number of migrant workers is, other things being equal, better than helping fewer of them, then we can generate the following ranking of these options:

(3) > (1) > (2)

By contrast, if we classify these options in terms of how they actually impact the welfare of migrant workers, then we get the following ranking:

(2) > (3) > (1)

That is, even though the overall gains in welfare generated by admitting a large number of migrant workers on unequal terms outweigh the overall gains in welfare generated by admitting a small number of migrant workers on equal terms, it still seems better for states to admit *some* migrant workers on equal terms than to admit *no* migrant workers.

The problem, however, is that these rankings are in tension with each other. In particular, notice that even though (3) > (1) in both rankings, (1) > (2) in the first ranking and (2) > (1) in the second ranking. But there are two reasons why this seems puzzling. First, it's not entirely clear why defenders of equal rights for migrant workers believe that it's morally better to admit no migrant workers than to admit a large number of migrant workers on unequal terms. How can (1) > (2) when (2) is *better* for some migrant workers (indeed, a great many of them), and *worse* for no one? This seems to violate the principle that if it's possible to make at least one person better off, without at the same time making anyone worse off, then it seems *prima facie* morally permissible to do so.[5] Second, and to make matters even worse, how can defenders of equal rights for migrant workers believe that (2) is morally impermissible when they believe that (1) is morally permissible, and yet (2) is better than (1) for the welfare of migrant workers? Or, to put the point another way, how can an option be better for migrant workers than a morally permissible alternative and yet itself be morally impermissible? This seems to violate the intuition that if an act is wrong, then it must wrong *someone*.

Notice that this way of framing the problem is different, and, in my view, much stronger, than how it's typically portrayed in the literature. On the one hand, some have argued that defenders of unequal rights for temporary workers can simply appeal to the *volenti* principle: to a willing person, no wrong is done (Bell and Piper, 2006; Miller, 2008; Oberman, 2017; Wellman, 2022). That is, if temporary workers consent to an offer of less extensive labor rights in exchange for greater access to a country's labor market, then they have no legitimate grounds of complaint against it. But that's false. There are many examples of offers that are wrongful despite being consensual. Consider

Rescue: B falls into a very deep pit. A is the only one that's able to rescue her. In exchange for doing so, he offers B the following labor contract: "I will rescue you only if you agree to be my servant for the remainder of your existence."

A's offer is clearly unethical. Part of the reason, I submit, is that he's violating his pre-existing duty of rescue. A has an obligation to help B if he can do so at a reasonable cost to himself, but he is instead proposing to discharge his duty only if B is willing to accept extremely degrading conditions. The state's offer, by contrast, is fundamentally different. They do *not* have a pre-existing duty to help migrant workers. To the contrary, they have a right not to admit any migrant workers if they so choose. But if states have a right not to admit any migrant workers, and their offer is mutually beneficial, then how can it be morally wrong of them to pay temporary workers a sub-minimum wage if the latter voluntarily accepts it?

On the other hand, others have argued that if states are justified in restricting the rights of temporary workers, then that's only because they're being forced to make a "compromise" with injustice (Bertram 2019). That is, the only reason why it would be permissible to grant temporary workers a less extensive set of labor rights than citizens and permanent residents is that the latter are simply unwilling to act justly. After all, they're perfectly able to admit temporary workers on equal terms; they simply choose not to. Accordingly, it might be wise or prudent for temporary workers to accede to the demands of high-income countries, but we shouldn't confuse that with justice. As Christopher Bertram puts it, "it distorts our moral understanding, specifically, our understanding of justice, to represent a pragmatic compromise with unjust attitudes as exemplifying what justice itself demands" (2019, p. 290).

Although I am sympathetic to this line of argument, it overlooks the fact that states are morally permitted not to admit *any* migrant workers. Indeed, Bertram accepts that states have a right to control their borders and so may decide who is and who isn't allowed to enter. But if it's morally permissible for high-income countries to close their borders and thus effectively deny people from low-income countries the opportunity to receive any work-related benefits, then how can it be morally wrong of them to pay migrant workers a sub-minimum wage simply because that's less than what citizens and permanent residents are making? Without a compelling answer to these questions, the puzzle remains.[6]

17.3 The Case Against Limiting the Labor Rights of Temporary Workers

To make progress on this issue, consider Joseph Carens' argument against limiting the labor rights of temporary workers (Carens, 2013, ch. 6).[7] According to Carens, it's morally impermissible for states to provide one set of labor rights for citizens and permanent residents, on the one hand, and another set of labor rights for temporary workers, on the other. States must pay temporary workers the same minimum wage as citizens and permanent residents and impose the same set of health and safety standards on the workplaces that employ them. Why? The reason is that "the purpose of these regulations is to establish minimum standards for economic activity, thus limiting the terms to which workers can agree and the risks to which they can be exposed within a given jurisdiction" (Carens, 2013, p. 115). Accordingly, if it is morally impermissible to employ citizens and permanent residents on terms *below* that minimum standard, then it should also be morally impermissible to do the same for temporary workers.

To be sure, Carens does recognize the obvious fact that "the rules regulating working conditions vary between states" (2013, p. 115). For example, some states have higher or lower minimum wages than others. But that fact is not, by itself, a sufficient justification for providing temporary workers with a weaker set of minimum standards than citizens and permanent residents. For, according to Carens, "every state is responsible for what goes on inside its own jurisdiction" (2013, p. 115). And since temporary workers "are people working within the state's jurisdiction," its judgment about what constitute an acceptable minimum standard should also apply to them. In the words of Carens:

> A state has to make a judgment about acceptable health and safety standards and other minimum working conditions within its own territory. Temporary workers are people working within the state's jurisdiction. It makes no sense to say that conditions that are deemed to be unsafe or unhealthy for citizens and residents are fine for temporary workers.
>
> *(2013, p. 115)*

The minimum standards that govern workplace relations should thus not be contingent on a worker's membership status. To the contrary, they should apply equally to *all* workers inside a state's jurisdiction.

At the core of Carens' argument, therefore, are two claims:

The Minimum Standards Claim: states should provide the same set of minimum labor standards to all workers.

and

The Responsibility Claim: states are morally responsible for the economic activity that occurs inside its jurisdiction.

Indeed, these claims are mutually supporting. The Minimum Standards Claim explains *what* obligations states have to temporary workers and The Responsibility Claim explains *why* states have them. Critically evaluating Carens' argument thus requires that we answer two questions. First, are these claims plausible? Second, do they support Carens' conclusion that it's morally impermissible to provide temporary workers with a different set of labor rights than citizens and permanent residents? I will argue that although there are plausible interpretations of both of these claims, they do not necessarily support the conclusion that the same set of labor rights should be provided to all workers inside a state's jurisdiction. If we want to reach that conclusion, then we must look elsewhere.

Let's begin our analysis with The Minimum Standards Claim. At first glance, it seems hard to deny that states have a moral obligation to provide the same set of minimum labor standards to *all* workers. After all, if it's morally *impermissible* to pay one set of workers a sub-minimum wage, then how can it be morally *permissible* to do so for another set of workers? Since a minimum wage sets a threshold below which workers may not be paid, states should be forbidden from establishing two different sets of minimum labor standards. Temporary workers should thus be paid the same minimum wage as citizens and permanent residents.[8]

But the problem with this claim is that it's ambiguous between two different interpretations of what a "minimum labor standard" is. On the one hand, Carens might be arguing that states should apply the same set of minimum *moral* standards to all workers inside its jurisdiction. For example, if a certain wage is required to meet the basic needs of workers, i.e., a "living wage," then it would represent the minimum wage below which all workers may not be paid from a *moral* perspective.[9] On the other hand, Carens might be arguing that states should apply the same set of minimum *legal* standards to all workers inside its jurisdiction. For example, if a government establishes a "statutory minimum wage," then it would represent the minimum wage below which workers may not be paid from a *legal* perspective. These two interpretations can come apart because the statutory minimum wage can be set at whichever level the relevant governmental authority chooses and so is not necessarily tied to an account of the basket of goods and services that are required to meet a worker's basic needs. In some jurisdictions, it may be lower than a living wage (LW); in other jurisdictions, it may not be.

Given this ambiguity, how should we assess the Minimum Standards Claim? The first thing to notice is that it's correct under the first interpretation. Indeed, on this construal, the Minimum Standards Claim almost seems true by definition. For how can one believe that it's morally permissible to pay workers less than the *moral* minimum? Note, however, that the truth of that claim does *not* imply that temporary workers must be paid the same *legal* minimum wage as citizens and permanent residents. To see why, suppose that the LW is 10 and the statutory minimum wage is 20.[10] Under these circumstances, it's unclear why it would be morally impermissible to pay temporary workers a wage that's higher than 10 but lower than 20, e.g., 15. Although temporary workers would receive a different wage than citizens and permanent residents, they would still be paid more than what's required from a moral perspective[11] (see Figure 17.1 for an illustration).

If Carens wishes to deny that possibility, then he would have to show that any wage less than the legal minimum wage was itself morally impermissible. But it's not obvious what the argument for that conclusion would be. If the statutory minimum wage can be set at any level the relevant governmental authority chooses, then circumstances may arise in which it's fixed at a rate that is higher than the moral minimum.[12] And since the moral minimum establishes a *floor* below which workers may not be paid, not a ceiling, it's difficult to see why it would be wrong to pay temporary workers a wage that's more than 10 but less than 20. In fact, not only does Carens seem to recognize this possibility when he grants that it's moral permissible for different states to have different minimum labor standards, but he also provisionally accepts that states have a right to control their borders. But if that's the case, then how can it be wrong for states to pay temporary workers less than the legal minimum wage when they're already permitted to provide them with *no* benefits?

In response to this objection, Carens can invoke The Responsibility Claim. On his view, the reason why it's morally impermissible to pay temporary workers less than the statutory minimum wage is that states have a *special* responsibility to all workers inside its jurisdiction, that is, an obligation to treat them in a morally permissible way. They must ensure, for example, that each and every worker is paid a fair or non-exploitative wage. For that reason, it's morally irrelevant that temporary workers can voluntarily accept a wage that's less than the legal minimum. Since states have a special obligation to all workers inside its

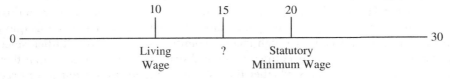

Figure 17.1 Statutory minimum wage is greater than a living wage.

jurisdiction, "the policies that regulate working conditions for citizens and permanent residents should apply to temporary workers as well" (Carens, 2013, p. 115).

The problem with this response, however, is that it begs the question. Carens assumes that the only way that states can fulfill their special responsibility to temporary workers is by paying them the same statutory minimum wage as citizens and permanent residents, but it's precisely the content of that responsibility that requires explanation. After all, one can accept the claim that states have a special responsibility to all workers inside its jurisdiction and yet deny that it's morally impermissible to pay temporary workers less than the legal minimum. For example, if temporary workers are paid a LW, then it's not obvious why states would be abdicating their special responsibility to those workers. Indeed, one might even argue that it's unfair to require high-income countries to pay temporary workers the same minimum wage as citizens and permanent residents since states that admit migrant workers are already doing more than anyone else to help people in low-income countries. Given that Carens doesn't have a clear response to these objections, he fails to adequately explain why it's wrong to pay temporary workers less than citizens and permanent residents.

17.4 A Fair Wage for Temporary Workers

We can make progress on these questions by looking at the problem from a different perspective. Instead of focusing on the special responsibility that *states* have to workers inside its jurisdiction, we should concentrate on the special responsibility that *employers* have to employees inside their workplace. After all, even if states set the minimum wage for temporary workers, employers are the ones that will ultimately be paying it. By shifting our focus from states to employers, we will be in a better position to explain what's a fair wage for temporary workers.

To see why, recall the puzzle with which we began. The puzzle, roughly speaking, was that if it's morally permissible for high-income countries *not* to benefit people in the developing world by closing their borders, then how can it morally impermissible of them to pay migrant workers a sub-minimum wage simply because that's *less* than what citizens and permanent residents are making? But as soon as we turn our attention to the relationship between employers and employees, the puzzle becomes easier to handle.[13]

Consider in this regard the relationship between A, an employer, and B, a temporary worker. Suppose A offers B a job at his factory for a sub-minimum wage, and B voluntary accepts it. At first glance, it seems that B has no complaint against A in this scenario because her wage is higher than the one she would have been paid in her home country. She thus has a good reason to prefer A's offer to the available alternatives. But that ignores a crucial aspect of their relationship. For when A hires B, their transaction generates a social surplus. That is, they jointly produce benefits that exist only *because* of their relationship. And so that raises the question as to how those benefits should be distributed. What, in other words, is a fair distribution of the social surplus between A and B? Seen in this light, it's irrelevant that temporary workers gain relative to the pre-transaction status quo under which they are denied access to a high-income country's labor market. Rather, since each party to a transaction is morally entitled to a fair distribution of the benefits that they produced together, what matters is whether their share of it is *disproportionate* or *excessive*. Is either A or B getting too much or too little in comparison with the other? The answer to this question is provided by an account of a fair wage.

Broadly speaking, there are two dominant accounts of a fair wage for temporary workers in the literature. On the one hand, Daniel Attas (2000) has put forward an account of a fair wage based on the standard of free market competition. On his view, temporary workers receive an unfair distribution of the gains of social cooperation just in case the wage that they're offered is less than the one they would have received under conditions of perfect market competition. Indeed, given the nature of most guest worker programs, Attas believes that's a very likely possibility. Since temporary workers typically face a range of labor market restrictions that constrain their ability to freely move between occupations, employers can use their market power to pay them significantly less than they would otherwise have to. According to Attas, therefore, most temporary workers are exploited.

On the other hand, Robert Mayer (2005) has argued that temporary workers are exploited just in case they are paid less than a "living wage," i.e., a wage that enables them to meet their basic needs. Indeed, Mayer believes that the only reason why temporary workers would accept a wage that falls below that threshold is that they are trying to escape a desperate situation. Accordingly, one reliable way of determining whether employers are taking unfair advantage of the vulnerability of temporary workers is by looking at the latter's employment options. If temporary workers lack any decent alternatives to choose from, then the offer they receive from employers will likely fall below a LW and thus be exploitative.

Which one of these accounts (if any) is correct? How do we know what's a fair wage for temporary workers? These are difficult questions. I suspect that different people have different intuitions on this issue, and both of the accounts we've surveyed seem to be vulnerable to powerful objections. For example, it's not obvious why the market-clearing wage (MCW) is the correct standard of a fair wage *in general*. The market for sweatshop labor is an extremely competitive one, but most people think that sweatshops are the paradigmatic case of exploitation. Similarly, if workers are exploited just in case they're not paid a LW, then that seems to imply that it's *impossible* to exploit someone whose basic needs are met. But many people believe that adjunct lecturers are exploited and the vast majority of them are able to purchase food, clothing, shelter, etc. Faced with these problems, it's not clear how we can make progress on this issue.

In what follows I outline a general framework for determining a fair wage for temporary workers. The framework is modeled on a modified version of John Rawls' (1999) original position and veil of ignorance. The basic idea is that we are to imagine a bargaining situation between an employer and a temporary worker, but with the important qualification that neither party knows who he or she is. This will ensure that no one can propose a solution to the bargaining problem that is biased in their favor and so the resulting agreement between them will be fair. Now, this framework will, of course, be controversial, and I cannot fully defend it here.[14] But I do hope to show that it provides a more compelling account of a fair wage than existing approaches in the literature.

With these points as background, consider the parameters of the bargaining problem itself. To fix ideas, start with the concept of a *reservation price* (RP). A reservation price is the price that a party must receive if they are to agree to a transaction in the first place. In the case of employers (EM), it is the *maximum* they are willing to pay temporary workers. By contrast, in the case of temporary workers (TW), it is the *minimum* wage they are willing to accept from employers. Indeed, given the subject matter, we can be reasonably precise here. For example, we know that the *most* employers would be willing to pay temporary workers is the statutory minimum wage. After all, what reason would they have to hire temporary workers if they were paid more than citizens and permanent residents? Additionally, we know that the *least* temporary workers would be willing to accept from employers is the value of the best available alternative in their home country plus the cost of relocation. For why would temporary workers be willing to migrate to a different country if they lacked a clear financial incentive?

Thus, suppose that RPEM = 20 and RPTW = 10. From this it follows that the bargaining range will be located between these two points and that any point within that range will be beneficial to both parties. That is, each one of them will prefer a transaction at any point within the bargaining range to no transaction. And so, this raises the question: if both parties know the bargaining range but neither one of them knows whether they are an employer or a temporary worker, then where exactly will their transaction point be located? What's the distribution of wages such that, once the veil of ignorance is lifted, it will be acceptable to them no matter who they turn out to be? I submit that, in line with Rawls' original reasoning for his theory of justice, both parties would select the point within the bargaining range that corresponds to the *maximin* (MM) solution concept, i.e., the point that maximizes the gains for the worst off, or 20 (see Figure 17.2 for an illustration). Temporary workers should thus be paid the statutory minimum wage—the same as citizens and permanent residents. My argument for this conclusion proceeds in three steps.

First, it seems hard to deny that both parties would initially select 15, i.e., the point of equal division (ED). Why? The basic reason is that, under the veil of ignorance, they have no grounds for privileging one party over the other. There is, in other words, no basis, at this stage of the bargaining problem, for assuming that either one of them has a greater initial claim to the social surplus. To the contrary, both parties have an equal *conditional* claim to the benefits that they produced together.

But even though their deliberation would begin at 15, there are two reasons why it wouldn't end there. First, all points > 15 and ≤ 20 are in the bargaining range and thus beneficial to both parties. And so even if a move away from the point of ED would benefit one of them more than the other, that would still not be sufficient grounds to reject it. Second, and more importantly, since neither one of them knows, once the veil of ignorance is lifted, who they will turn out to be, they both have a strong incentive to maximize the gains to the least well-off party, i.e., choose 20. After all, if they turned out to be an employer, then the worst that would happen is they would lose out on a certain amount of additional revenue. By contrast, if they turned out to be a temporary worker, then the consequences of not being paid the statutory minimum wage would potentially be disastrous. It would thus be prudent of them to err on the side of caution and act as if they were the latter instead.

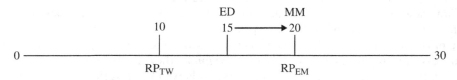

Figure 17.2 Why parties in the original position would choose MM.

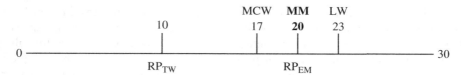

Figure 17.3 Why parties in the original position would choose MM over MCW and LW.

Finally, consider why the parties in the original position would choose MM over both the MCW and the LW (see Figure 17.3 for an illustration). On the one hand, the parties would choose MM over MCW because, in virtually all high-income countries, the statutory minimum wage (20) is higher than the wage that low-wage workers can fetch on the market (say, 17). Indeed, the reason why governments adopt the statutory minimum wage in the first place is that, on its own, the MCW is insufficient; it fails to provide low-wage workers with even the most basic necessities. Parties in the original position would, therefore, have a decisive reason to reject it. On the other hand, a LW faces the exact opposite problem. Although I considered the possibility that it might be lower than the statutory minimum wage, in the real world it's typically much higher (say, 23). At first glance, then, it seems that the parties in the original position would have strong grounds to select it. The problem, however, is that it would likely exceed the reservation price of employers and thus fall outside the bargaining range. But if employers don't have a financial incentive to hire temporary workers, then paying them a LW would be counterproductive. It would, in other words, harm the very people it was meant to help. And so, the upshot is that MM would be chosen over both MCW and LW behind the veil of ignorance. The statutory minimum wage is a fair wage for temporary workers.

17.5 Conclusion

In this chapter, I have argued that it would be wrong for states to restrict the labor rights of temporary workers. Instead, they must employ them on the same terms as citizens and permanent residents. But even though states have an obligation to provide equal rights for temporary workers, several important questions remain. Before concluding, let me briefly highlight two of them.

First, can temporary workers *waive* the labor rights to which they are morally entitled? That is, suppose employers have an obligation to pay temporary workers the same minimum wage as citizens and permanent residents, but, other things being equal, they prefer to hire fellow nationals. Assuming that it's not wrong to have such a preference, would it be permissible for temporary workers to voluntarily accept a sub-minimum wage if doing so was the only way to incentivize firms to hire them? Answering this question requires an account of the conditions, if any, under which individuals can waive their rights in general. Surprisingly, there are few systematic treatments of this issue in the literature.[15] Intuitively, some rights can be waived (e.g., the right to privacy), whereas others cannot be (e.g., the right against selling oneself into slavery). It's not clear, however, where labor rights fall on this spectrum. More work needs to be done, therefore, on this question.

Second, how *stringent* are the labor rights of temporary workers? By that I mean, is the right to a minimum wage or decent working conditions absolute? Or are there circumstances in which it would be all things considered justifiable to override them?

Presumably, the answer is the latter. Very few rights, if any, are absolute, and it's not obvious why labor rights would be one of them. But that still leaves open the question as to how much weight to assign labor rights in our moral calculus. This is a difficult question. Philosophers have made a lot of progress in determining what rights people have, but very little progress in determining how to balance rights against other values. Practically speaking, however, that is what ultimately matters. Hopefully, there will be more research on this question in the future.

Notes

1 For the purpose of this chapter, I will assume that to exploit someone is to take *unfair* advantage of their vulnerability or desperate situation. But beyond this truism, substantial disagreement remains. Different theorists of exploitation have different accounts about what it means to treat some "unfairly," and I will defend my own view on this issue in Sec. 17.4 below. The basic idea underlying all such accounts, however, is that exploitation involves an unfair distribution of the benefits and burdens of social cooperation.
2 Notice that if the labor rights of migrant workers are restricted, then, unlike their membership or social rights, they would be restricted *immediately*. Temporary migrants would, for example, be paid a sub-minimum wage from the very moment they started working. This makes the practical effect of labor rights restrictions unique.
3 This puzzle is a modified version of the "nonworseness claim" first formulated by Wertheimer (1996, 2011).
4 Of course, states can also admit a *large* number of migrant workers on *equal* terms, but the Rights-Numbers Tradeoff shows why that's not a live option.
5 This is a version of the so-called "Pareto principle."
6 Indeed, the puzzle is further compounded by the fact that many people believe that it's morally permissible for firms in high-income countries to outsource production to workers in low-income countries even if a sub-minimum wage in the former country is *higher* than a fair wage in the latter country.
7 I focus on Carens' argument for two reasons. First, his views on the ethics of immigration are extremely influential. Second, his case against limiting the labor rights of temporary workers is one of the most systematic in the literature.
8 One further objection to paying migrant workers a sub-minimum wage is that doing so would have negative effects on citizens and permanent residents. For example, if this policy were implemented, then it might push down the latter's wages and incentivize firms to hire less of them. It is thus not clear that states even have a self-interested reason to adopt it. Although this is ultimately an empirical matter, I have two brief points in response to this objection. First, this proposal can be targeted at industries that only attract migrant workers (including ones that are undocumented). This would ensure that citizens and permanent residents are not exposed to increased labor market competition (Stilz, 2010). Second, even if states have a self-interested reason not to adopt this policy, it's still worth asking whether doing so would be morally permissible. Accordingly, I will morally evaluate this policy on the assumption that paying temporary workers a sub-minimum wage is *not* harmful to citizens and permanent residents.
9 For the sake of argument, I provisionally assume that it's morally impermissible to pay workers less than a living wage. In the next section, I question that assumption.
10 The currency doesn't matter for our purposes.
11 Abizadeh (2014) raises a similar objection.
12 Although Carens might object that the legal minimum rarely, if ever, exceeds the moral minimum in the real world, that's irrelevant. His argument is meant to show that it's not morally permissible for temporary workers to be paid less than citizens and permanent residents, and this counterexample disproves that proposition.
13 For a more comprehensive solution to this puzzle, see Kates (2023).
14 I defend this account at greater length in Kates (2019).
15 The lone exception, to my knowledge, is McConnell (2000).

References

Abizadeh, A. (2014) 'Review of Joseph H. Carens, *The Ethics of Immigration*', *Notre Dame Philosophical Review* [online]. Available at: https://ndpr.nd.edu/reviews/the-ethics-of-immigration/ (Accessed August 1, 2022)

Attas, D. (2000) 'The case of guest workers: exploitation, citizenship, and economic rights', *Res Publica*, 6(1), pp. 73–92.

Bell, D.A. and Piper, N. (2006) 'Justice for migrant workers? The case of foreign domestic workers in Hong Kong and Singapore' in Kymlicka, W. (ed) *Multiculturalism in Asia*. Oxford: Oxford University Press, pp. 196–222.

Bertram, C. (2019) 'The openness-rights trade-off in labour migration, claims to membership, and justice, *Ethical Theory and Moral Practice*, 22(2), pp. 283–296.

Carens, J.H. (2013) *The ethics of immigration*. Oxford: Oxford University Press.

Freeman, R.B. and Oostendorp, R.H. (2000) 'Wages from around the world: pay across occupations and countries', *NBER Working Paper*, No. 8058.

Kates, M. (2019) 'Sweatshops, exploitation, and the case for a fair wage', *Journal of Political Philosophy*, 27(1), pp. 26–47.

Kates, M. (2023) 'Sweatshops, exploitation, and the nonworseness claim', *Business Ethics Quarterly*, 33(4), pp. 682–703.

Lenard, P.T. and Straehle. C. (2011) 'Temporary labour migration, global redistribution, and democratic justice', *Politics, Philosophy & Econ*, 11(2), pp. 206–230.

Mayer, R. (2005) 'Guestworkers and exploitation', *The Review of Politics*, 67(2), pp. 311–334.

McConnell, T. (2000) *Inalienable Rights*. New York: Oxford University Press.

Milanovic, B. (2016) *Global Inequality*. Cambridge, MA: Harvard University Press.

Miller, D. (2008) 'Irregular migrants: an alternative perspective', *Ethics and International Affairs*, 22(2), pp. 193–198.

Oberman, K. (2017) 'Immigration, citizenship, and consent: what is wrong with permanent alienage?' *Journal of Political Philosophy*, 25(1), pp. 91–107.

Posner, E. A. and Weyl, E.G. (2014) 'A radical solution to global income inequality: make the US more like Qatar', *The New Republic* [online]. Available at: https://newrepublic.com/article/120179/how-reduce-global-income-inequality-open-immigration-policies (Accessed August 1, 2022)

Posner, E. A. and Weyl, E.G. (2018) *Radical Markets: Uprooting Capitalism and Democracy for a Just Society*. Princeton: Princeton University press.

Pritchett, L. (2006) *Let Their People Come: Breaking the Gridlock on International Labor Mobility*. Washington, DC: for Global Development.

Rawls, J. (1999) *A Theory of Justice*, revised edition. Cambridge, MA: Harvard University Press.

Rodrik, D. (2011) *The Globalization Paradox: Why Global Markets, States, and Democracy can't Coexist*. Oxford: Oxford University Press.

Ruhs, M. (2013) *The Price of Rights: Regulating International Labor Migration*. Princeton: Princeton University Press.

Ruhs, M. and Martin, P. (2008) 'Numbers vs. rights: trade-offs and guest worker programs', *International Migration Review*, 42 (1), pp. 249–265.

Stilz, A. (2010) 'Guestworkers and second-class citizenship', *Policy and Society*, 29(4), pp. 295–307.

Walzer, M. (1983) *Spheres of justice*. New York: Basic Books.

Wellman, C. H. (2022) 'Immigration', in Zalta, E.N. (ed) *The Stanford Encyclopedia of Philosophy* (Fall 2002 Edition). Available at: https://plato.stanford.edu/archives/fall2022/entries/immigration/>. (Accessed August 1, 2022)

18

TREATING PEOPLE AS RESOURCES

Emigration and the Brain Drain

Bas van der Vossen

The ethics of migration is often divided into two questions: the ethics of immigration and the ethics of emigration. The two are commonly treated as separate issues. Compare international law. While countries are given almost complete discretion to set their own immigration policies, limits to emigration are considered human rights violations. Article 13(2) of the Universal Declaration of Human Rights provides that "everyone has the right to leave any country, including his own".[1]

Nevertheless, some have argued that countries can justifiably, and perhaps should, limit emigration. In particular, these authors argue that emigration should be limited to stop or reduce a so-called *brain drain*. A brain drain occurs when highly skilled or educated people leave a country, thus "draining" its existing human capital.

I believe that the common assumption about immigration (i.e. that it can be justifiably restricted for almost any reason) is deeply and horribly wrong. I believe that the common assumption about emigration (that restricting it is horribly wrong, the hallmark of tyranny) is correct. The purpose of this chapter is to make clear why, despite people's worries about the brain drain, this is the case. People have a right to emigrate whenever and for whatever reason they choose.

This, then, is not merely a chapter offering an overview of the different perspectives people have taken on this issue. I do aim to provide such an overview, but this chapter aims at something more. In my view, restrictions on emigration (proposed or existing) are among the gravest injustices that occur around the world. It's a part of the goal of this chapter to convince you of this fact.

This injustice takes form in two ways. The first is the most obvious: countries putting restrictions on *emigration*. The second is more common, and less obvious: receiving countries putting restrictions on *immigration* to "help" sending countries achieve the same outcome. As it will become clear, both are deeply and seriously wrong.[2]

How to Argue for Migration Restrictions

To think about the ethics of restrictions to migration, we first need to see such restrictions for what they are. Restrictions of migration constitute coercive restrictions to people's freedom. While such restrictions aren't necessarily unjust, they do call for justification. The purpose of this section is to establish this point.

Let's approach the matter by considering a number of simple thought examples, as thought-experiments that involve inter-personal restrictions to freedom. Such thought-experiments are a good way to think through the moral issues here because they help elucidate that, at least *absent some good justification*, restrictions to people's freedom of movement are morally wrong.

So, consider the following example, offered by Michael Huemer:

Starvin' Marvin

Starvin' Marvin heads to the market looking for food. Marvin has little to trade. However, suppose there are people at the market willing to trade food for whatever Marvin has. Unless someone stops him, Marvin will get to the market, make the trade, and eat. Imagine, however, that Donald forcibly prevents Marvin from getting to the market. Donald posts guards to keep him out. The guards continually capture Marvin and turn him away. As a result, Marvin can't barter for food, starves and dies.[3]

It's clear, Huemer writes, that Donald did something morally wrong. He did not simply *fail to help* Marvin, he *actively hurt* Marvin, using violence, by preventing him from making a trade with a willing partner. Our intuitions aren't particularly conflicted about this. It's very clear that, unless Donald had some really good reason on his side, he seriously wronged Marvin.

Of course, there can be such reasons. Perhaps Marvin has a dangerous, communicable disease. In that case, the need to protect the people on the marketplace could justify Donald in restricting Marvin's freedom. Similarly, if Marvin is planning to set off a bomb in the marketplace. But that's the point. Unless there *is* such a reason, Donald cannot prevent Marvin from getting to the market. And the reason is equally clear: Donald cannot coercively limit Marvin's freedom. At least not without some compelling reason.

Restrictions to migration seem analogous to the case of Marvin. When countries keep emigrants in or immigrants out, they are not just failing to help them but refusing to do them a favor. People in rich countries want to hire poor foreigners, and the foreigners want the jobs. They want them enough to uproot their lives and travel across the world. But governments stop them, using coercive measures like armed sentries, fences, and so on. They thus use force to stop those foreigners from making lifesaving or life-changing trades with willing partners. Again, unless they have some very good justification, these interferences seem equally wrong.

Perhaps you object to the use of this analogy. Perhaps you think the fact that Marvin is *starving* does all the work here. But if Marvin weren't starving, the same call for justification would arise. It might be less poignant, but it would be there. Or you might think that the fact that Donald is a private person matters. If Donald represented an entire community or nation, say, things might be different? But, again, this is not the case. To see this, consider the following, alternative scenario, not involving poverty or a sole individual restrictor.

Group Restrictions

Jane lives in rural Montana. She wants to leave as she is poor and there are not many jobs around. After careful consideration, Jane decides to move to Texas. A willing landlord in Texas is happy to rent her an apartment, and some employers in Texas want to interview her. Jim, who has lived in Texas his whole life, suspected that Jane might come and notified his neighbors. They took a vote and the majority agreed that Jane needs to go home. Together they meet her at the border, tell her they don't want her there, and pull their guns when Jane tries to enter anyway.

Again, it's plain that the restriction remains wrong, even though it is carried out by a group that is deciding things democratically, and even though Jane is not starving. The problem remains the same: Jim and his neighbors simply lack the *right* to tell Jane where she can go. The fact that Jim brought a group adds nothing to the case. If the individuals in that group lack the right to make that decision, them showing up together doesn't make a difference. Nor does the fact that they took a vote matter. If the group lacks the right to make this decision, then its deciding in a particular (democratic) way doesn't help either. Again, Jane can move about freely *unless* there is some good, independent justification for preventing her.

None of this proves that all migration restrictions are unjust, of course. Perhaps countries can limit people's freedom to move not merely because they are groupish or democratic but because of some other (related?) feature. Or perhaps there is some other reason. But that isn't quite the point here. The point, rather, is that such a reason needs to be established. And so, the burden of proof rests with the person defending migration restrictions. They need to convince us that such restrictions are, despite initial appearances, justifiable from an ethical point of view. Those who simply want to let people be free face no such burden.

So, what would a good justification look like? At least two things need to be shown. First, the defender of migration restrictions needs to show that there will be actual harm from people having the freedom to migrate where they want. And second, the defender needs to show that this harm is sufficiently serious to justify coercive interference with people's liberty. Only if both these steps can be completed, will an argument to restrict migration succeed.

Arguments like this aren't hard to imagine. People's freedom to move may justifiably be limited in order to quarantine them, as happened during the COVID-19 pandemic. Perhaps it may also be done during periods of extreme civil disorder. And, obviously, criminals completing a prison sentence can be denied the freedom to leave the country. But these are not the kinds of arguments offered by proponents of emigration restrictions.

Brain Drain Arguments

Most popular, at least among philosophers, is the argument that people's freedom to emigrate can be limited in order to avoid a so-called brain drain, the departing of skilled or educated people from a country. The argument is primarily meant to apply to poor or developing countries (more on this in a bit).

Let's review how David Miller, the leading philosopher defending migration restrictions, makes the case. Miller offers several reasons why people's freedom needs to be coercively limited.[4] One of these goes as follows:

> [Free] migration is damaging to the human rights of those left behind, who are deprived of health workers and, looking beyond health, of other professionals such as engineers who might make an important contribution to development goals if they stayed at home.

The argument goes roughly as follows: since people "at home" need those health care workers and engineers, their decision to leave constitutes a serious *harm* to others. And generally, people can be forced not to harm others. Thus, forceable emigration restrictions can be justified. Call this the *harm-argument*.

A second argument holds that people "have special obligations to their compatriots, which they can best discharge by using their skills in a way that ministers to basic needs". Authors offer various reasons for this conclusion, but one prominent one has to do with the kinds of special obligations that are said to follow from benefitting from tax-funded services. Thus, writes Miller:

> [People] have been educated at public expense to equip them with skills which, it is reasonable to assume, were intended to be used for the benefit of the citizens who have paid for their education.

People who wish to emigrate have enjoyed tax-funded benefits. Since they've received such benefits, they owe a debt to their fellow citizens. Since one can in general be forced to repay one's debts, forcible restrictions to emigration can be justified, too. Call this the *debt-argument*.

These arguments are among the most widely shared or put forward justifications for limiting people's right to emigration.[5] Let's go through each of them to see how they hold up under scrutiny.

The Harm-Argument

The harm-argument is a popular one. Miller has made it in several places, as have others.[6] But there is much wrong with it. Most importantly, it simply gets the facts wrong. Social scientists have studied what happens when people are allowed to leave poor countries, and the claim that they are thereby harming others turns out to be plainly false. The truth is that the opposite policy, forcing people to stay, in fact has negative effects. The fact that authors like Miller (continue to) ignore it, is quite frankly bizarre.

The reason why limiting emigration harms countries is not hard to see. When you remove people's option to leave to other places, especially places where they might find a better life, you discourage them to invest in their own education and other forms of human capital.[7] Most people who want to leave their homes do so because they cannot find adequate or fulfilling work there. Forcing doctors and nurses to remain in Ghana, say, does not automatically create more health sector jobs there. It just forces them to accept different jobs, typically jobs that are below their skill level.

The option of emigrating thus incentivizes people to invest in themselves. Because they know that, even though chances might be small of finding work at home, there's always the possibility to move elsewhere. However, only small numbers of those who invest in themselves actually do end up leaving. And countries generally are much better off when people invest in their human capital.

Second, and more obviously, those who leave end up sending money back home through remittances. This can amount to significant sums and actively helps those who stayed behind, including the very poor.[8] One study found that a 10% increase in a country's share of emigrants leading to a 2.1% decline of people living on less than $1 a day, and a 10%

increase in remittances leading to a 3.5% decrease in the poverty rate.[9] Over time, the largest share of remittances is sent to poorer families.[10]

Opponents of free emigration often either deny or make light of these facts. Thomas Pogge, for example, writes that remittances will not help the poorest, and thus that helping "needy foreigners", requires a commitment "*not* to the struggle to get more of them admitted into the rich countries, but *rather* to the struggle to institute an effective programme of global poverty eradication".[11]

If things were different, would that matter? Suppose emigration *did* hurt a society, would that justify limiting people's freedom? It's not obvious why this would be the case. After all, it's not as if our societies in general have a claim to our services. Suppose a Ghanaian doctor chooses not to emigrate but to stay put and pursue her passion, say, for woodworking instead. The doctor would still be depriving other Ghanaians of her medical services, thus constituting the same harm Miller and others are worried about. But plainly, that would *not* justify sending the police over to our doctor to force her to remain a doctor. Such an interference would be much too intrusive, and much too coercive, to pass moral muster. We all get to live our own lives, and that includes doctors, too. (How many would continue to train to become a doctor, if it didn't?)

Of course, this doesn't mean we don't have to help anyone else. It just means that there are important limits to what we can be *made* to provide, including help. The fact that Ghanaian people are harmed by an absence of enough good doctors no more justifies forcing Ghanaian doctors to remain there than it justifies forcing Canadian doctors, say, to move to Ghana.[12]

The Debt-Argument

The debt-argument holds that people can be coercively prevented from leaving their country because they owe a kind of debt to it. The general thought is that people have special ties or obligations that they owe to their fellow countrymen. Why? The most popular and clear reason offered has to do with the tax money that the country has invested in people.

Above, we saw Miller make this argument. Gillian Brock agrees. According to her:

> there is a deep unfairness in allowing those who have been trained by an impoverished state to simply leave that state and sell their talents to the highest bidder; those who have sacrificed to train that individual deserve some reasonable return on their investment.[13]

It's true, of course, that people can be justifiably forced to repay their debts. The question is whether Miller, Brock, and others are correct in claiming that people receiving tax-funded benefits thereby incur an enforceable debt. And this, unfortunately, is simply false.

The clearest cases in which obligations of repayment can arise involve agreements or contracts. Suppose some generous philanthropist had offered our Ghanaian doctor a scholarship to get through medical school. And suppose that one of the conditions of accepting the scholarship had been that, after graduating, the recipient remains in Ghana for three years to work as a doctor. If our doctor had indeed (knowingly and voluntarily) accepted the scholarship, it seems plausible to say that she ought to stay in Ghana for three years and practice medicine after graduation.

But is this the same issue as Miller and Brock have in mind? It depends on whether tax-funded benefits are like contracts in the relevant sense. More precisely, it depends on whether the people who receive them are accepting them in ways similar to the agreement above. Perhaps if our doctor really had a choice, was told what the expectations are, and would *not* be forced to stay in Ghana had she decided (in that case) to study medicine abroad – perhaps then, Miller and Brock would be right.

Miller and Brock, however, do not wish to make emigration restrictions depend on people's *choices*. Their idea is that people who live in a country enjoy a wide array of public services, and this suffices for the debt. As a result, everyone in a country has the same burden of repayment. And so, in principle, everyone could be stopped from leaving. It's just that emigrating doctors so valuable to raise the question of restricting their freedom.

But this really is unacceptable. Perhaps it's possible that having benefits just foisted upon us, without us having a choice in the matter, can make us indebted in certain ways. Perhaps, for example, we might owe a debt of gratitude for those benefits. But what's decidedly *not* possible is that we can become indebted in a way that can justify serious and coercive limits to our freedom, without us having any choice in the matter. For such a possibility would make us all extremely vulnerable.

Consider the following example:

Coercive Philanthropist

You receive an email from someone, calling himself a philanthropist. The email tells you he will pay 50% of your bills moving forward. In return, you will be forced to work for his company for three years. You can't refuse the offer.

Suppose you do refuse. And suppose the "philanthropist" sends the cops to your home. Clearly, it's them who are in the wrong, not you. And that's clear, despite the fact that you *did* enjoy a serious benefit. The benefit as such simply does not justify the coercion. That requires something more: it requires that you accept the benefit, on those terms, knowingly and voluntarily. But, contrary to Miller's and Brock's arguments, that simply not what's going on here. The requirement to stay they defend *is* merely foisted on people, and it's foisted in the name of some other foisted benefits.

What, then, of the debt of gratitude? Doesn't allowing free emigration allow people like our Ghanaian doctor to simply avoid repaying what they owe (as a matter of gratitude)? Perhaps. But note what's allegedly owed here: repayment on an investment. And there is a much easier way to repay that, one that avoids the draconian measure of trapping innocent people in their countries. Countries could simply hold their citizens tax liable when abroad for whatever amount represents a fair return. But this, of course, is radically different from what's being proposed. And it doesn't get Miller and Brock what they seem to want.

Miller offers one more argument, saying that people can be made to stay because they can best repay their debts by staying and working. It's questionable whether this is true. The best way to repay would seem to be to repay. But even if Miller is right, the argument goes nowhere. No one has a right that you repay them in the most efficient or optimal way. They don't even have a right that you repay them in the most *desired* way. The conclusion thus remains in place: people who want to leave their countries should be free to do so.

Treating People as Resources

If you're like me, the arguments above make you very uncomfortable. To me, there is something off-putting, something deeply amiss, with picturing people as primarily investments, financial layouts to which some return needs to be recovered. These are *people* first, and as such are owed their freedom, rights, and respect. Describing them as, quite literally, "public investments", entities representing a dollar figure lost, something to be recouped, forcibly if need be, is to objectify them in a really problematic way. To put it bluntly, it simply dehumanizes people.

Treating people as people might sometimes mean that those who receive benefits don't repay them. But perhaps that's just the price of being a decent society. At other times, treating people as people might mean that those they've benefitted won't have to repay them either. It's not the worst thing in the world. And it definitely doesn't call for the kinds of measures we really only see in the worst kinds of countries.

Just as people aren't resources, they aren't owned by their societies either. We are born in societies, true. And perhaps this means we are born with ties and allegiances. But whatever those ties and allegiance amount to, they must be such as to not sacrifice individuals at the altar of the collective. Justice does not call for suffocating swaths of people. Nor does it mean turning societies into prisons.

A healthy society would be the kind of place that attracts people who are willing to benefit that society, without asking for every dollar back. Such a society will have to make sure that it treats its contributors well. Telling people that if they invest in human capital, and become potential contributors, they will be forfeiting important freedoms, is not a recipe for such a society. It's a recipe for poverty and oppression.

It's striking, then, that authors like Miller and Brock take their aim at poor and developing countries. Brock writes that she's worried about "emigrants departing from developing countries, because this is where vulnerabilities and losses are most pressing".[14] But this just adds injury upon injury. If there is something perverse about treating people as resources, there is something even more perverse about treating them as resources in response to the "vulnerabilities and losses" that they already experience. People who are vulnerable and suffering don't need *additional* burdens on top of what they're already unfortunate enough to bear.

Notes

1 *Universal Declaration of Human Rights* (1948). Available at: https://www.un.org/en/universal-declaration-human-rights/. The right is inscribed in most major human rights documents. See, e.g., Article 2 of Protocol No. 4 to the *European Convention on Human Rights*. Available at: https://www.echr.coe.int/Documents/Convention_ENG.pdf.
2 The arguments of this chapter closely follow and develop the account offered in B. van der Vossen & J. Brennan, *In Defense of Openness*, (Oxford: Oxford University Press, 2018), ch. 2.
3 This paraphrases M. Huemer, "Is There a Right to Immigrate?" *Social Theory and Practice* 36 (2010): 429–461.
4 All quoted arguments are from D. Miller, *Strangers in Our Midst*, (Cambridge, MA: Harvard University Press, 2016), p. 109.
5 For similar arguments, see K. Oberman, "Can Brain Drain Justify Immigration Restrictions?," *Ethics* 123 (2013): 434–437; G. Brock & M. Blake, *Debating Brain Drain: May Governments Restrict Emigration?* (Oxford: Oxford University Press, 2015), chap. 4; and T. Pogge, "Migration and Poverty," in *Citizenship and Exclusion*, ed. V. Bader. (Basingstoke: Macmillan, 1997).
6 See e.g.: "[migration] will do little to help the very poor, who are unlikely to have the resources to move to a richer country. Indeed, a policy of open migration may make such people worse off still

if it allows doctors, engineers, and other professionals to move from economically undeveloped to economically developed societies in search of higher incomes, thereby depriving their countries of origin of vital skills". D. Miller, "Immigration: The Case for Limits", in: *Contemporary Debates in Applied Ethics*, eds. Andrew I. Cohen and Christopher H. Wellman. (Oxford: Blackwell, 2005), p. 198. Compare Pogge, "Migration and Poverty", pp. 14–15.
7 Easterly and Nyarko 2009.
8 This is extremely well documented. See, among many others, P. Acosta, C. Calderon, P. Fajnzylber, and H. Lopez, "What is the Impact of International Remittances on Poverty and Inequality in Latin America?," *World Development* 36 (2008): 89–114; S. Gupta, C. Pattillo, S. Wagh, "Effect of Remittances on Poverty and Financial Development in Sub-Saharan Africa", *World Development* 37 (2009): 104–115; H. de Haas, "International Migration, Remittances and Development: Myths and Facts", *Third World Quarterly* 26 (2005): 1269–1284; L. Pritchett, *Let Their People Come: Breaking the Gridlock on International Labor Mobility*, (Washington, DC: Center for Global Development, 2006).
9 R. Adams and J. Page, "Do International Migration and Remittances Reduce Poverty in Developing Countries?," *World Development* 33 (2005): 1645–1669.
10 See O. Stark, E. Taylor, and S. Yitzhaki, "Remittances and Inequality", *The Economic Journal* 96 (1986): 722–740; V. Koechlin and G. Leon, "International Remittances and Income Inequality: An Empirical Investigation", *Journal of Economic Policy Reform* 10 (2007): 123–141; D. McKenzie and H. Rapoport, "Network Effects and The Dynamics Of Migration and Inequality: Theory and Evidence From Mexico", *Journal of Development Economics* 84 (2008): 1–24.
11 See Pogge, "Migration and Poverty", pp. 14–5. For similar remarks, see Brock and Blake, *Debating Brain Drain: May Governments Restrict Emigration?*, pp. 205–6.
12 Miller tries to avoid this implication by saying that "the wider duty toward compatriots must by qualified by a personal prerogative to pursue goals of one's own. So on the one hand, a trained doctor who loses her vocation and comes to detest medical practice cannot be required to continue working in that field; and on the other hand, if it is simply impossible to lead a decent life within her country of origin, for what ever reason, the doctor is entitled to find a way out" (Miller, *Strangers in Our Midst*, p. 109). However, this is plainly *ad hoc*, and Miller offers no argument for why the qualification applies to Canadians or Ghanaian woodworkers, but not Ghanaian doctors.
13 Brock and Blake, *Debating Brain Drain: May Governments Restrict Emigration?*, p. 5. Similarly, Kieran Oberman writes: "An obligation of repayment is owed by skilled workers who have acquired skills, during their adult life, at the poor state's expense. It obliges them to repay the costs of their training either with money or with their labor." Oberman, "Can Brain Drain Justify Immigration Restrictions?," *Ethics 123* (2013).
14 Brock and Blake, *Debating Brain Drain: May Governments Restrict Emigration?*, p. 14.

PART VI

Climate, Refugees, and Protection

19
CLIMATE MIGRANTS ARE NOT REFUGEES

Max Gabriel Cherem

19.1 Introduction

People use the phrase *climate refugee* to convey the similarity between those fleeing their country to escape persecution and those fleeing climate change induced "natural" disasters or environmental degradation. Indeed, both refugees and climate migrants are forced to move by factors beyond their control. Many who speak in this way want to expand the legal definition of a refugee or its scope of application. They claim there is no *normative* difference between refugees and (all or some) climate migrants. As such, either refugee law itself or the way it is applied should expand to cover climate migrants. I disagree. There are always practical and normative differences between refugees and climate migrants.[1] Even in cases when climate change renders an entire state uninhabitable, those displaced are not "refugees", and there are good reasons why the remedies of refugee law are inapposite.

Moreover, the strategy of assimilating climate migrants to refugees is not risk free. Many theorists apparently think that, by assimilating "climate migrant" to "refugee" and emphasizing the similarities, we can help more people by extending refugee protections to climate migrants. One obvious problem with this strategy has been repeatedly raised by the Office of the United Nations High Commissioner for Refugees: as "the terminology and notion of environmental refugees or climate refugees…ha[s] *no basis* in international law" UNHCR has "serious reservations" about such advocacy (UNHCR 2009). For example, if such advocacy ends up assimilating "refugee" to "climate migrant", then this would "undermine the international protection regime" (UNHCR 2012).

My objections to such advocacy are not just pragmatic ones about the smartest tactics for feasibly protecting climate migrants nor about the possible devaluing effects of inflationary rhetoric[2]. They are also theoretical. The colloquial "climate refugee" trope obscures more than it illuminates. The label does not refer to a cohesive underlying group because climate change is a complex and heterogeneous phenomenon (Draper 2024). Moreover, even if we narrowly define the category so that the group makes coherent sense (e.g. by limiting ourselves to those whose entire state is made uninhabitable by anthropogenic climate change), then these people would simply be stateless but not necessarily refugees (Alexander and Simon 2014)[3]. Taking climate migrants to be the same as refugees would flatten and expunge certain normative distinctions.

To preview where I am headed: the *way* people are harmed or wronged has implications for the corrective justice measures they are owed, and such measures differ between refugees, climate migrants, and natural disaster victims. For example, while we may appropriately appeal to charity or general humanitarian aid to assist victims of purely natural disasters (e.g. earthquakes or volcanic eruptions), human-induced climate disasters often call for responses involving collective liability (e.g. of high-emitting countries). Furthermore, climate change disasters that specifically *force* people to *flee* their country raise unique questions about responsibility and repair that are themselves normatively distinct from the questions raised by refugees fleeing persecution (Nine 2010; Kolers 2012; Eckersley 2015; Buxton 2019; Morrow 2020; Wilcox 2021; Brock 2021). Moreover, while human rights are in some way involved in aiding both refugees and climate migrants, there are serious problems with either reductively subsuming these groups to each other or exclusively analyzing them with the lens of some generalized notion of "human rights". This is perhaps unsurprising since a global justice framework only *partly* captures some of the normative terrain for refugee issues and is even less helpful for climate change (Jamieson 2014, 193–200). Yet many theorists continue to overuse a human rights frame of analysis for migration.[4] In contrast, I argue that both climate migrants and refugees are normatively distinct from each other, and that each should be helped separately rather than lumped together.

19.2 The Definition of a Refugee

The concept of a "refugee" is quite old. The modern legal definition in the 1951 Refugee Convention and 1967 Protocol grew out of prior attempts at a definition. The League of Nations in the Interwar period had numerous treaties that defined refugees in a group-by-group, geographic, or piecemeal fashion (Skran 1995). There were *Russian* and *Armenian* refugees, refugees from *the Saar* or *Germany*, etc. After WWII, Allied authorities and non-governmental agencies resettled millions of "displaced persons" who didn't wish to return to their pre-war homes. The International Refugee Organization (1947–51) used its own rather amorphous but, nevertheless, more individual and universal refugee definition (Ballinger 2012).

This older approach was even used in the early days of the UN. For instance, Palestinians and Koreans each had their own UN agencies (UNRWA and UNKRA)[5] that, among other tasks, assisted refugees. Since such agencies predated UNHCR and the Refugee Convention, they were not absorbed into modern refugee law; UNRWA continues today.[6] Yet, apart from this *one* exception, all other early refugee concepts and institutions were replaced or subsumed by today's individualized and universal[7] conception of a refugee. Older notions proved too weak and ineffectual, or their group and place-based nature created unintended negative side effects.[8]

The 1951 Refugee Convention defines a refugee as "any person who: owing to a *well-founded fear of being persecuted* for reasons of race, religion, nationality, membership of a particular social group, or political opinion, is *outside the country of his nationality*, and is unable to or, owing to such fear, is unwilling to avail himself of the protection of that country".[9] This definition has persecution and location criteria. Most[10] climate migrants meet neither. As the Israeli delegate to the Convention observed with respect to persecution:

> [the refugee definition] obviously did not refer to refugees from natural disasters, for it was difficult to imagine that fires, floods, earthquakes or volcanic eruptions, for instance, differentiated between their victims on the grounds of race, religion or political opinion. *Nor did that text* [the definition] *cover all man-made events.*[11]

Even if we focus on "natural" disasters that *are* "man-made" (e.g. via climate change), it still seems a stretch to say, as some do, that such people are *persecuted* or otherwise intentionally targeted (Cooper 1998; Kozoll 2004; Duong 2010; see Gardiner 2011 on the related defense of a state "political responsibility" lens for climate issues). And, persecution aside, most people who move due to climate change can do so *in* their country. They therefore don't trigger the alienage criterion. Even *if* they cross borders, they can return (at least to another area) amid the disaster or after it.

Despite this apparent clarity from the very start of the modern legal definition of a refugee, the notion of "climate refugees" has stubbornly endured. Most scholars trace the first formal definition to Essam El-Hinnawi, who was commissioned to compose a 1985 report on the topic for the United Nations Environment Program. He came up with the following:

> Environmental refugees are defined as those people who have been forced to leave their traditional habitat, temporarily or permanently, because of a marked environmental disruption (natural and/or triggered by people) that jeopardized their existence and/or seriously affected the quality of their life. By "environmental disruption" in this definition is meant any physical, chemical and/or biological changes in the ecosystem (or the resource base) that render it, temporarily or permanently, unsuitable to support human life.[12]

There are now many definitions of climate change "refugees",[13] but this one is a good start.

Scholars across various disciplines argue we should recognize all or some climate migrants as refugees entitled to new membership in other states (Cooper 1998; Kozoll 2004; Bell 2004; Biermann and Boas 2008; Westra 2009; Byravan and Rajan 2010; Gemenne 2015, 2017; Rosignoli 2022; Kent and Behrman 2018; Behrman and Kent 2018; Biermann 2018). Consultants for various NGOs and the United Nations have also forwarded this basic claim (El-Hinnawi 1985; Jacobson 1988; Myers 2002; Conisbee and Simms 2003). While philosophers and political theorists have not been as invested in defending this claim, those who wish to challenge the refugee definition have nevertheless been surprisingly ready to assert that at least some of those fleeing climate change should be "refugees" covered under refugee law.

Among migration theorists, there are two main lines of thought: (1) we should expand the definition of a refugee itself so as to better align with its *moral* underpinnings; (2) we should keep the current legal definition but expand its application to better align with the spirit or *internal normative logic* of the refugee regime. A third strategy advocates a new treaty or status for climate change exiles (Falstrom 2002; Docherty and Gianni 2009; for criticism see McAdam 2011), or a new protocol to the UNFCC (Biermann and Boas 2008; 2010; Williams 2008; Byravan and Rajan 2015) or the refugee convention (below). If such proposals are truly new, then they create something *different* than refugee status, and it is unclear why we should use the term "refugee"; if they link up with or expand existing refugee law, then many of the critiques I survey with the first two approaches apply. I therefore largely set this third strategy aside.

The first line of thought is found within broader arguments to abolish or expand the refugee definition itself. While these theorists do not centrally focus on "climate refugees", each arrives at the conclusion that all or some of those fleeing climate change and/or natural disasters should be refugees (Shacknove 1985; Pogge 1997; Gibney 2004; Carens 2013; Dummett 2001; Miller 2016; Boom 2018; Kukathas 2004, 2016; Beaton 2020a, 2020b).

Other scholars who *do* focus on climate migrants have made more systematic claims within the second line of argument (Cooper 1998; Kälin 2010; Duong 2010; Lister 2014; Pellegrino 2015; Byravan and Rajan 2010).[14] They think the refugee definition makes sense and is largely correct, but that it has an underlying, internal normative logic that can and should be applied to the most extreme cases of climate migration—e.g., those fleeing small island states submerged by rising sea levels.

I am more sympathetic to this latter position. But I fear folding even this small subset of climate migrants into refugee law is conceptually unjustified, driven by (understandable) advocacy, and may ironically yield the opposite outcome as intended. Ultimately, I show that it is conceptually confused to see any climate migrants as refugees. With that said, the issue of what we rhetorically *call* this smaller subset of climate migrants is steeped in strategic concerns that reach beyond clarifying the underlying concepts or political philosophy.[15]

19.3 Expanding or Abolishing the Definition

The first argumentative strategy is the most common yet least systematic. A variety of scholars challenge the tenability of the refugee definition itself. They argue either that the definitional dividing-line between refugees and other needy migrants is unjustified (Kukathas 2004, 2016; Pogge 1997), or that one or both of the refugee definition's two main criteria—persecution and alienage—need to be relaxed or abolished (Carens 2013; Dummett 2001; Miller 2016; Boom 2018; Beaton 2020a, 2020b;). In making their arguments, they claim—often as an obvious and positive aside—that, on their views, many climate migrants would now qualify as refugees.

Advocates of open borders think the line between refugees and other needy outsiders is untenable. For example, Kukathas rejects the standard assumption that legitimate sovereign states have the right to control immigration. He claims (with over-simplicity) that "the invention of the passport" in WWI was "precisely to control refugee flows" and that "the category of refugee was created by states not so much to enable us to fulfill our duties to the distressed and unfortunate as to make it easier for us to avoid them" (Kukathas 2004; 2016). He is skeptical about the refugee definition since he is skeptical about immigration controls. As the general rule cannot stand, neither can the exception.

The specific way Kukathas dismisses the refugee definition illustrates a mistake: the assumption that refugee status tracks some purely *moral* underlying category defined in terms of generalized need. He notes, "making a moral distinction between refugees and immigrants" is problematic since it "suggests that we draw a line distinguishing our obligations in a way that may not make much sense, morally speaking" (Kukathas 2016, 254–255). He holds this view since he incorrectly thinks the distinction is, "motivated by…a concern to address the needs of those who are most vulnerable or suffer most". He argues that realizing this motivation is impossible since there are "many…economic migrants who face greater threats to their well-being than do some refugees" (Kukathas 2016, 258). Against the backdrop of such assumptions, he speaks disapprovingly of the current "narrow definition" excluding "people fleeing war, natural disaster, or famine" (Kukathas 2004, 217). Similarly, Thomas Pogge claims it is false that "there is small class of *needy foreigners* whose admission is of much greater importance than that of the desperately poor…[:] political refugees fleeing persecution" (Pogge 1997, 15). Like Kukathas, he argues with his own assumption that neediness underlies the refugee regime. *If* refugee status were meant to track generalized need, then it would do a poor job of it, and we would do better to shift our energies to some other metric (e.g. poverty) or to open borders. But these arguments dissolve once we realize that refugee status was never meant to be a proxy for generalized need.

Others are more cautious. They argue that one or both of the definition's criteria should be expanded. This would include more people, like climate migrants, and supposedly better reflect the underlying *moral rationale* for the category of a refugee. For instance, Andrew Shacknove famously argued we should relax both the persecution and alienage criteria.[16] For him, citizens of legitimate states have a "moral...claim" to a "normal, minimal relation of rights and duties between the citizen and state, the negation of which engenders refugees". He thinks we can unpack the rights on the citizen-side of this bond in terms of basic *needs*, and that "absence of state protection of the citizen's basic needs"[17] is what matters. This absence or negation arises not only with "tyrannical" or "predatory" regimes who *persecute* but also with corrupt or feckless governments who allow such "chaos" that "government (or society)...cease[s] to exist".

Accordingly, Shacknove's refugee is "a person whose government fails to protect his basic needs, who has no remaining recourse than to seek international restitution of those needs, and who is so situated that international assistance is possible". The references to someone's government and "no remaining recourse" jointly refer to Shacknove's social contractualism and his focus on the citizen-state relationship. For Shacknove, *how* a basic needs shortfall came about is indeed relevant. He notes, "it would be incongruently illogical to expect social institutions to contend with sources of vulnerability beyond human control" and that "the legitimacy of the state resets exclusively on its control of human actions rather than on its control of natural forces". This means that if a basic needs shortfall arose via an unforeseeable natural disaster outside the control of one's government, it would not create refugees since "the bonds uniting citizen and state...[can] endure even when the infrastructure or harvest of a region is obliterated" by nature. Several prominent contemporary defenders of "climate refugees" agree with this point, and accordingly distinguish them from natural disaster victims.[18]

Theorists like Carens and Dummett disagree. They set aside questions like whether threats are targeted (Dummett 2001, 37) or whether they are of such a nature as to be subject to the control of a refugee's government. They instead claim that "the severity of the threat to basic human rights and the degree of risk" is what matters rather than "the source or character of the threat" (Carens 2013, 201). Reinterpreting persecution as severity of risk to basic human rights would clearly include many more climate migrants in the refugee definition. Unlike Shacknove's focus on whether we can realistically see the institutions of a person's state as responsible for a threat,[19] Carens and Dummett are more interested in the bare fact *that* a threat to basic human rights exists and that many host countries are in a position to fix this by offering surrogate protection and new membership.

Interestingly, while Carens' capacious definition of a refugee doesn't require a person's country of origin to be causally responsible for the situation they are fleeing, he postulates that those potential host countries most responsible for global warming have the strongest obligation to admit "environmental refugees". Since "causal connections can generate moral duties" and there is a connection (albeit "diffuse and contested") between the emissions of the rich, industrialized countries and the effects of climate change on poorer countries, "we should already be starting to think about environmental refugees—people forced to flee their homes because of global warming and the resulting changes in the physical environment" (Carens 2013, 195; 330, fn11; Gardiner 2011, esp. section III). On such an account, a person can be a refugee even when internal relocation is possible and their government committed no wrong.

Miller, Boom, and Beaton would all concur that it doesn't matter whether threats are subject to the control of a refugee's government and that we need to move beyond a strict reliance on persecution. Miller, for example, "understand[s] refugees to be people whose human rights cannot be protected except by moving across a border, whether the reason is state persecution, state incapacity, or prolonged natural disaster" (Miller 2016, 83). Similarly, Boom thinks being "recognized under international law as a refugee...should... depend only on the severity of the threat he or she flees and the likelihood the threat will materialize if he or she returns" (Boom 2018, 526)[20]. His proposal extends to "outbreaks of fatal diseases" as well as "people fleeing catastrophic natural hazards...[that] meet...some threshold of severity...[like] "a major hurricane or tsunami [that] directly hits...the entirety of a small island nation" (530). Yet, in contrast to Carens or Dummett, all three *do* think it matters whether someone can be helped *in situ* and at home, or if they can "only avoid this threat [to their basic human rights] by migrating" (Miller 2016). Indeed, Beaton cautions, "refugeehood should be reserved for those individuals who require refuge *in particular* in order for their fundamental human rights to be guaranteed". Yet, she thinks this description captures many fleeing risks that cannot be fixed on their home territory, including some climate refugees.

I disagree with all these theorists in one way or another. We cannot set aside either the issue of whether a threat is within the control of a refugee's government or whether someone can be helped either in-country or otherwise apart from refugee law. Doing so creates numerous practical and theoretical issues. The practical issues have received the most attention in the literature, and so, I simply flag them here (also see Shahar in the present volume).

One obvious issue with many expansionist accounts is the concern with inflationary rhetoric mentioned at the start. For example, if we "conflate...the idea of disaster victim and refugee", then "the key features of refuge protection" would potentially be lost and "the lowest common denominator adopted" (McGregor 1993, 162); legal obligation might be replaced with discretionary charity. Another related issue is of misleading connotations: the term "climate refugee" might illicitly suggest that environmental or even specifically anthropogenic climate change "can be meaningfully separated from political and economic changes" when, in all but the clearest (sinking island) cases, they are inextricably intertwined (McGregor 1993, 158; Draper 2024). This might in turn give the impression that the chances of folding "climate refugees" into existing law are better than they really are—since it severely downplays the challenges of "sorting" those displaced by environmental versus other factors. In this same vein, by "highlight[ing] one forcer of displacement", the "climate refugee" category "underplay[s] what may be more proximate causes—such as repressive governments, poor policies, failing economies, complicated colonial and cold war legacies, uneven levels of economic development, and civil strife" (White 2019, 133). This can serve a "de-politicizing" ideological function that "may suit [powerful] political actors to lay the blame for displacement on climate change" (Draper 2024, 9; Kibreab 1997; Betts and Pilath 2017).

Yet another practical concern with the "climate refugee" category is that it is often used alongside dire warnings about the disastrous consequences of climate change. Climate change is spoken about as "a threat multiplier that will produce 'climate refugees'", and the specter of such refugees swamping "our" borders is supposed to make us "take climate change seriously". But this rhetorical coupling may only "further...an agenda focused on militarized border security" and "distract...attention from more fruitful policy responses" (White 2016). It may be counterproductive insofar as it "can also reinforce images of a Malthusian squeeze" and "contributes to the paranoia of 'Fortress Europe' and...restrictive asylum policies". This would inaccurately present our situation "as a battle between increased population and available land, rather than a negotiated, and often conflictual, partitioning of resources between different groups" (McGregor 1993, 163).

Indeed, as odd as it may seem, this ideological Malthusian mis-framing may already be bearing rotten fruit in the form of strange political bedfellows: governing coalitions made up of far-right ultra-nationalists and traditionally left green parties. Despite popular assumptions, there is nothing inherently progressive about caring for the environment. Indeed, "while the rhetoric of 'environmental emergency' may inspire efforts to protect broad-based populations, it may also drive hoarding by the powerful and the exclusion of out-groups". This should not be surprising: such catastrophizing rhetoric "has deep roots on the Right and has very often been invoked to justify profoundly illiberal policies" (Gilman 2020).

Most of these concerns are decently well known. But they are largely pragmatic worries about possible unintended effects of rhetorical advocacy that doesn't take conceptual clarity seriously. The specifically *theoretical* concerns with the category of "climate refuge" will become clearer after I summarize and critique the second inclusionary strategy.

19.4 Keep the Definition but Expand Its Application?

The second argumentative strategy is to keep the refugee definition but highlight how refugee law has an internal normative "logic" that can and should be applied to cover a subset of climate migrants: those whose homelands are uninhabitable due to climate change. The clearest example is small island states (predicted to eventually be) submerged by rising sea levels (e.g. Kiribati, Tuvalu, the Maldives, the Soloman Islands). Depending on what "uninhabitability" means, this may also include states with sharp decreases in freshwater access, that become too hot for habitation, or that fail when densely populated and economically important river deltas flood (e.g. Egypt, Vietnam, Guyana, Bangladesh). Lister and Pellegrino follow this second general approach. Each articulates an underlying normative logic in the law that nevertheless goes beyond it. Duong and Cooper do the same but stay squarely in the law. They argue that refugee status should cover those fleeing disappearing small islands states given that refugee law was developed alongside human rights law and is properly interpreted in light of it.[21] Byravan and Rajan argue for the similar notion of "climate exiles" and, at least at times, note a protocol to the refugee convention would be one way forward; Kincaid follows a similar logic[22]. I have much greater sympathy for this general tack but still disagree that even this smaller subset of climate migrants should be folded into refugee law. For clarity, I focus on Lister and Pellegrino.

Lister's approach is to answer the question of "What...makes refugees a normatively distinct group"? by focusing on what they are owed. Using this approach, he concludes refugees are "normatively distinct...because such people could only, or at least could best, be helped by providing them the particular remedy of asylum, understood as including both non-refoulement and a "durable solution"". If this is the *sine qua non* of a refugee, then there are people the law excludes who could "only or best" be helped in this way. Thus, following refugee law's logic, Lister thinks asylum is *also* owed to "the subset of those displaced by climate change or other environmental disruptions" when three conditions are met: "expected indefinite duration, where international movement is necessitated, and where the threat is not just to a favored or traditional way of life, but to the possibility of a decent life at all".

For Lister, these criteria jointly identify the correct subset of those who could and should be easily included. Indefiniteness means that the threat causing people to flee is "not short term" and requires a "permanent solution". The "role of international or cross-border movement" is key because if "internal relocation will not be a plausible option" he claims we are then "faced with a group of people who can *only* be helped by granting them residence in a safe, new, state". Lastly, a partial "corollary" is that this group faces threats "to the possibility of living a decent life at all, not merely to a favored or traditional way of life". This is crucial since he wants to establish that "providing relief to individuals" (not collectives) is all that is really needed.

Pellegrino reaches the same conclusion—"climate migrants fleeing from sinking islands…are climate refugees…entitled to [refugee convention] protection"—but gets there another way. For him, refugees are distinctive because of five conditions in the legal definition. He asks whether there is "a unifying factor" across these that "makes refugees the holders of a specific *right*…to be admitted on a durable basis". His answer is refugees "suffer a further wrong" beyond "persecution, deprivation, or lack of state protection": "the wrong of forced displacement". On his view, "forced displacement is a wrong because living in a place is a right of any individual, as permanent occupancy of a place is needed to cultivate morally essential plans, relationships, and projects, as well as to enjoy State protection". For Pellegrino, if people's "right to occupy a territory is violated, they should be compensated". This points toward questions of what counts as "proper" compensation (though he does not elaborate).

The differences here are instructive. In essence, Lister starts with the central objects of a refugee's right (asylum understood as non-refoulement and a durable solution) and then works backwards by seeing who else, beyond current refugees, might be especially helped by these objects. Pellegrino starts with a right and right-holder and asks what might be distinctive about the position of the right-holder such that it generates an entitlement to the right. While Lister establishes that those with literally "no choice but to enter another country" should be given a "decent life" elsewhere, Pellegrino establishes that they are entitled to "proper" compensation for the specific reason that their right of territorial occupancy was violated by forced displacement traceable to human actions. Lister's view covers both a "subset of those displaced by climate change" (e.g. those fleeing sinking small islands states) *and* some of those fleeing "environmental disruptions of…indefinite duration" (e.g. the Montserrat eruption). Pellegrino's view only covers the former. Finally, Lister exclusively endorses extending the remedies of refugee law, whereas it is unclear if Pellegrino sees this as the only or best solution.

19.5 Theoretical Issues

While the second inclusionary approach is better than the first, they both raise not only practical but also theoretical problems. Moreover, the conclusion that we should cover even a limited set of climate migrants under specifically refugee law is not justified. I focus on two main critiques of the second approach that reveal theoretical issues. I engage Lister's view, as it is not only the most well developed defense of this claim[23] but also because I take it to be representative of frameworks and assumptions shared by migration theorists who see climate migrants as refugees.

First: it seems misplaced to take either the *objects* of rights or the "only or best" *remedies* for violated rights as our point of departure. Doing so downplays the role of entitlements and overlooks the need for a "fit" between wrongs and remedies. Second and relatedly: since human agency need not be behind a threat, there is less of a role for state responsibility to direct duties or for remedies to be impacted by *how* people were wronged. I'll explain these in order.

While the objects of refugees' rights are certainly *part* of what makes refugees into a distinctive group, it is worth asking whether this choice of frame reveals the full normative story. One basic point to remember is that whether someone *can* be helped by something is different from whether they are *entitled* to it.[24] It is also important to recall that this is a specific framing choice. We could just as easily investigate the normative distinctiveness of refugees as Pellegrino does: by looking at the unique underlying entitlement structure they possess.

The attempt to derive refugees' distinctiveness from possible remedies creates an ambiguity as to whether asylum for each displaced individual is the "only", "best" or just a sufficient remedy. Lister claims, "temporary protection will not suffice" if the threat is of indefinite duration. He repeatedly says asylum is the "only or best"[25] way to help refugees and a subset of climate migrants. Yet, when talking about how internal relocation is "not... plausible" for those fleeing sinking island states, he claims they "can *only* be helped by granting them" asylum in a new state. Since he goes on to consider and reject other possible remedies, he must mean that, from his perspective, asylum is the "best" remedy in the sense of most feasible.[26]

One would therefore expect a strong and principled rejection of other possible remedies such as a system of rolling, auto-renewed "temporary" protection visas (like erstwhile Nansen passports; see Heyward and Ödalen (2016)), ceding or creating territory so that displacees may once again self-govern (Nine 2010; Kolers 2012; Buxton 2019), or affording them the option of collective resettlement and quasi-autonomy rights on ceded land, which may, over time, become ceded territory (Angell 2021; Dietrich and Wündisch 2015; Wündisch 2022). Yet, Lister spends most of his argument focusing on "pragmatic concerns" like "problems of implementation" and fears of public "backlash" (which, he admits, "do not settle the conceptual or moral issue"). This likely follows from his understanding of the methodology of "progressive conservativism".[27]

As for a *principled* rejection of other remedies, he only engages two rather strong views on directly ceding territory. He takes these views to claim that "there is a right to self-determination, held by groups, that ought to be enforceable against the international community". He notes that the claim that rights can be held by groups is "highly controversial" and, anyways, an entitlement to new territory depends on an "implausible account of responsibility", as it fits neither a criminal nor a tort model of responsibility.[28] He concludes, "individual remedies *can satisfy* our moral duties" and "providing relief to individuals, as individuals, *suffices* to meet our moral duties" (my emphasis; notice the slide from "only or best" to "sufficient").

While Lister's focus on feasibility is admirable, my worry is his argument and others in the literature lean far too heavily on speculation about "realistic" institutional possibilities. The problem here is that the apparently "best" remedy we can *pragmatically* hope for is quite different from the "best" remedy from a conceptual standpoint. Let me explain.

In discussions of justice, it is widely believed that there needs to be a certain degree of fit between remedies and wrongs. Certainly, theorists dispute the exact nature of and reasons for this fit: it could be that remedies must "reference...the fundamental interest" behind the violated right (Wündisch 2022); it could be "a desideratum of egalitarian theory...[that] the form of remedy...match the type of injustice it addresses" (Anderson 1999, 304); it could be that in cases of non-accidental harm, we must focus on reparations for unjust harms instead of compensation for losses (Buxton 2019); it could be that "even if *the actual remedy* is not determined by the nature of the wrong, *the form of the remedy* is" (Cornell 2020, 215)[29]. The general point is nicely expressed via example: if a person's *right to vote* were violated, then it would be an ill-fitting and inappropriate response for their government to just pay them money (Dietrich and Wündisch 2015).

From the perspective of ensuring this "fit", the remedy of collective resettlement on new land so as to reestablish *collective political* self-determination seems superior to Lister's remedy of each climate exile having a separate "opportunity...to be part of a self-determining group" such that their "basic needs...are met, and the[ir] life is normally free of danger and persecution". For, *that* bundle of goods could be secured for each individual if they were scattered amongst the states of the world, or even for each individual of the group if they were all together in an ideally administered camp (presuming they had more say than refugees in current camps).[30] But, what they would still lack is the collective political self-determination that was lost when their land had been submerged by global collective irresponsibility. Put differently, Lister's solution doesn't seem to care much about a key "difference between" refugees and those fleeing sinking island states: whether we can assume state authorities "are unwilling to protect" people or whether they are willing "to provide protection and assistance" but simply unable to and in need of some external help or adaptation (Kälin 2010; Beitz 2009, 39–40).

Moreover, insofar as *responsibility* necessarily drops out of accounts that lump together refugees, climate exiles, and those fleeing certain "environmental disruptions" (e.g. volcanic eruptions like in Montserrat), we lose sight of the distinction between harms and wrongs; between compensation and reparation. This gets at the "supply side", so to speak, of the relationship of fit. Just as it would be inappropriate to be paid money when one's right to vote were violated, so too it would be inappropriate if the remedy (whatever it was) was provided by a private foundation or a neighboring government—presumably they are not the party responsible. While we might say it is a good thing that a remedy is provided (and it may be all we can reasonably expect in certain circumstances), this does not erase the fact that—at least with respect to both refugees and climate exiles—the victim has a specific complaint against a specific actor (or group of actors). This is important for a number of reasons.

As environmental ethicists have noted, "climate change is both an issue of harmful impacts and a question of wrongdoing", and the "tools of philosophy go beyond harms accounting" (Lee and Kincaid 2016, 141). While "harm is often hitched to wrongdoing", they do come apart and are not always addressed together. The "harms [that] actually manifest" from climate change "will be important factors in determining the specific content of remediation....[but] justifying remediative obligation does not itself hinge on whether harms can be avoided or undone" (Lee and Kincaid 2016, 143). Even if we put things back the way they were for climate exiles, that is not the end of the moral story. We cannot *simply* see "the wrong [a]s a void that must be filled...as though a piece of a puzzle has been removed and needs to be put back" in by anyone (Cornell 2020, 224). Here is why this matters for the issue at hand.

Typically, "compensation aims to remedy accidental damage or harm, whereas reparations aim to rectify injustice". As such, "compensation may be given to a victim by a third party" while "reparations...can only be successfully offered by those responsible for the harm" (Buxton 2019, 199). This is why it is appropriate to help the victims of genuinely natural disasters through humanitarian aid no matter which state or group gives it. Yet, with refugees, we *do know* exactly who is responsible: the state of origin—whether it directly persecuted or stood idly by while some of its citizens persecuted others. Even if it is unlikely that a persecuting state will mend its ways and atone for its sins by facilitating return and offering reparations, the durable solution of "voluntary repatriation" seems to at least hold that possibility (partly) open. And, of course, the need for the responsible party to pay is what underlies proposals that seize and use the assets of mass refugee-producing states to help refugees transitioning to new states.

Climate exiles are an intermediate case between victims of natural disasters and refugees. They are produced by the foreseeable harms of (at least "luxury") greenhouse gas emissions that lack an adequate justification. This is unjust. Such harms "are not exactly deliberate—we are not emitting greenhouse gases *for the purpose* of harming others". This differs from the persecution that creates refugees. Yet, it is also true that these harms "are also not accidental" in the sense that we could plausibly say "we did not expect the harms to occur" (Morrow 2020, 96; Broome 2012). These harms arise collectively instead of being created by targeted persecution or pure accident. In addition to the point from above about the remedy itself seeming to call for (at least the option of) regaining collective political self-determination, some sort of collective liability would also seem to be a fitting and essential part of the remedy.

In the eyes of those who would redefine the category of a refugee to include climate exiles and those fleeing (some) natural disasters, all this likely seems too picky. For them, it really doesn't matter *who* helps these people only *that* they are in desperate need and should be helped. At some level, this is of course precisely the right response. Any other response in some ways misses the urgency of their claim. But my only point is that there is a moral remainder left over when people who are unjustly wronged and harmed are helped by the (contingent and discretionary) goodwill of others, while the responsible party is never made to acknowledge their wrongdoing or pay for what they've done.

This theoretical issue directly translates into an issue of implementation. While the "distinctive questions of responsibility" that arise with respect to climate exiles may or "may not bear directly on the first-order question of what we owe to particular displaced persons", they certainly *do* "have an important bearing on the second-order question of how the costs of protection should be distributed" (Draper 2024, 8). With respect to refugees, we are pretty certain as to who *should* shoulder the burden—the state of origin—even if *forcing* them to do so is impossible due to power dynamics. In political philosophy, there are all sorts of debates about a fair and equitable distribution of costs *given this non-ideal reality* and, in other disciplines, debates about how we might creatively use institutional innovations to force the actual offenders to pay (Lee 1986; Sazak 2015; Blocher and Gulati 2016; Goodwin-Gil and Sazak 2015). Yet, with respect to climate refugees, these second-order questions of burden sharing are totally different. The answers to these second-order burden sharing questions that we come up with will largely depend on something like a centralized losses and damages fund, as well as where we come down with respect to debates about the "polluter pays" or "beneficiary pays" principles, or various states' "luxury" versus subsistence emissions.

One final theoretical reason I don't think it makes sense to lump together refugees with even Lister and Pellegrino's smaller subset of climate exiles from sinking small island states is that doing so erases the fact that refugees and climate migrants each have distinct *complaint* against different actors and, since the distinctiveness of this complaint will very likely impact how they perceive the specific wrong that they have suffered, this may impact the content of what they are owed. Briefly, the point is that "the appropriate remedy depends on the perspective of the victim ex post". Nicolas Cornell gives the following example:

> Imagine that an employee comes up with an innovative idea while not clearly operating within the scope of her employment contract. Nonetheless, the employer promptly patents the innovation. We can imagine the employee seeking either compensation for her uncompensated labor or seeking ownership of the patent. These represent different forms of complaint against the employer. One is a complaint that one didn't get paid for one's work; the other is a complaint that one's idea was stolen. The same set of facts could be basis for either grievance, but not both.

In short, *how* a victim themselves sees the wrong that they have experienced is one important factor in determining remedies since this will yield a different grievance pressed against the offender(s). And, how victims see that wrong will depend on things like "how much harm was done, how much value or disvalue was generated, and how…the victim regard[s] the injury" (Cornell 2020, 230).

Now, it is certainly possible that a climate exile from a sinking island state might see the wrong that they have suffered along Lister's lines: as the loss of their own individual "opportunity to be part of a self-determining group". But it seems equally plausible that they might interpret the loss as of losing final collective political self-determination with other members of their community. If so, then instead of opting for resettlement in an entirely different state, they might choose to press for ceded land or territory with others from their society.[31] Lister acknowledges that this sort of arrangement can and has happened—for instance, as with the bilateral agreement between New Zealand and Tuvalu (Lister 2014, fn. 33). If that is so, then I fail to see why we *must* (either logically or realistically) opt for folding climate exiles into refugee law (e.g. why this is the "only or best" remedy) rather than by exploring innovative institutional possibilities whose remedies may actually serve them far better. While options like directly ceding territory or creating artificial floating islands may seem fairly unrealistic, I do think that there are less dramatic proposals and multiple "tracks" of possible remedies that would not involve expanding refugee law and which would avoid the practical and theoretical challenges surveyed above.

Indeed, refugee law already has three tracks—the durable solutions—that in some vague sense acknowledge that refugees might see the wrong they have suffered differently. Apart from asking for (often far-away or overseas) resettlement, claimants might opt to try for voluntary repatriation (typically mediated by another state or UNHCR), or "local resettlement" in a neighboring state, or (what some call the "fourth solution") just by establishing their lives in another state that (merely) respects their rights to be there and live in exile—perhaps until the danger passes. I fail to see why a similar suite of "durable solutions" could not be offered to climate exiles. I also fail to see what is really gained by referring to climate exiles as "refugees", whereas the risks of such rhetorical advocacy are crystal clear. At least theoretically, there are good reasons to keep climate migrants and refugees conceptually distinct. I leave questions of rhetoric and strategic political advocacy to others.

Notes

1 Climate and environmental factors can be one (or even *a* core) element in a refugee claim. Burson (2010) and Scott (2021) identify cases where a natural disaster plus subsequent discriminatory government or social (in-) action can *together* meet the refugee definition. I fail to see why such people are not just refugees. Regardless, these cases do not pick out those that "climate refugee" advocates want to include.
2 The worry about inflationary rhetoric is common in the human rights literature. See O'Neill (1996, 2000). I just flag it here, especially for proposals for a "climate *refugee*" protocol establishing competing refugee definitions.
3 I agree more with the UNHCR expert panel in Prato over a similar panel in Bellagio. See Alexander and Simon (2014), fns. 4–6 as well as Kälin (2010) 101–103.
4 My complaint is not with a human rights lens for refugee issues. Such a lens is preferable to, for example, a humanitarian lens. Indeed, I generally endorse the "human rights" approach to interpreting refugee law pioneered by James Hathaway and fleshed out by subsequent scholars like Michelle Foster. My complaint is with how political philosophers and theorists straightforwardly conflate refugee rights with either human rights or with an approach informed by "new", "integrated", or "Wilsonian" humanitarianism; Leebaw (2007) fns. 56–58.
5 The United Nations Relief and Works Agency for Palestine Refugees in the Near East and the United Nations Korean Reconstruction Agency. Each had a humanitarian mandate and was complimented by a parallel agency with a "political" mandate to settle the conflict: the UN Conciliation Commission for Palestine (UNCCP) and the UN Commission for the Unification and Rehabilitation of Korea (UNCURK). Other conflicts at the time, particularly those the UN was thought to have a role in creating or exacerbating, were met with this two-track model (though, I'm unsure if this model was a conscious choice). Regardless, it presents an alternative for securing impartiality apart from the impartiality of (classical or "new") humanitarianism or human rights; see Leebaw (2007).
6 Pre-Convention "refugees" were absorbed (Article 1A(1)) or else otherwise provided for. A case of alternate provision: Article 1D excludes those with their own UN agency until their situation is resolved or the agencies are shut down (according to some, they could then choose their signatory asylum state as no more individual assessment is needed). Art. 1D is thus sometimes called the "suspended inclusion" clause. This deflates Kent and Behrman's point, noted by Rosignoli (2022), that there have been and (the mistake) currently are *competing* refugee definitions.
7 Here, I ignore issues related to Art. 41, as well as the positions of Turkey and Congo as signatories that did not lift their 1951 restrictions (though, see RRIL p. 36). For the time being, I will also ignore how the OAU convention and Kampala Declaration do recognize, within Africa, some people as refugees apart from individualized criteria. Those definitions are in addition to the standard definition rather than in competition with it.
8 I don't have space here, but the problems of UNRWA and its special "zone of operation" in the geographic vicinity are well known.
9 1951 Convention on the Status of Refugees Article 1A(2). Hereinafter, "Convention" refers to the convention as amended by the 1967 Protocol.
10 *Supra* fn. 1.
11 Conference of the Plenipotentiaries on the Status of Refugees and Stateless Persons, "Summary Record of the Twenty Second Meeting" (26 November 1951).
12 El-Hinnawi (1985).
13 Rosignoli (2022) catalogs about 20 definitions.
14 Byravan and Rajan mention a Protocol to the Refugee Convention as one way of operationalizing their notion of "climate exiles" (see fn. 7). In later work they are *explicit* that a protocol to the UNFCC is preferable. Kälin 2010 pp. 96-103 is similar to yet ultimately unlike these others. He discusses how people fleeing sinking small island states might be fruitfully analyzed with an approach "that takes inspiration from three elements of the refugee definition" while *resisting* fully assimilating such a case to refugee law due to a key "difference between the two situations".
15 I'm open to persuasion on this count. But I also think, apart from theoretical concerns, I make a strong case as to why practically or strategically speaking we ought not *call* climate migrants "refugees". Scholars like Gemenne (2015) argue that the rhetorical pull of the label "climate refugees"

may justify ignoring or downplaying any conceptual differences. Mayer (2018) gives a persuasive counterargument.
16 I focus here on persecution, as his expansion of alienage is more stipulation than argument.
17 Curiously, he says "in refugee policy circles, basic threats to the individual are usually divided into three categories: persecution, vital (economic) subsistence, and natural calamities" and seeks to show how "each of these three categories of deprivation…can…violate the citizen's…rationale for entering society" and thereby "constitute a sufficient condition for refugeehood". He cites Grahl-Madsen's commentary on refugee law for this claim, but there is no mention of it on the relevant cited pages nor, as far as I can tell, anywhere else in that two-volume text or in any other text Shacknove cites. It is also odd that, in considering these three categories of basic threats, "natural calamities" simply drops out of his discussion after brief consideration of Sen and Lofchie's work on the political causes of famines. By the end of the article Shacknove comes to rely on Henry Shue's account of the relevant basic rights as those to "physical security, vital subsistence, and liberty". Clearly, only the first two nicely match his first two "categories of deprivation" or "basic threats". Now, in the 1980s, US refugee scholars *did* speak of persecution, subsistence, and natural calamities since the Refugee Act was being revised at the time and there was debate about how to do so. The prior US definition was in (only) some ways more inclusive than the international definition as it theoretically allowed refugees from "natural calamities" (this was never successfully used, then removed).
18 See, for example, Kent and Behrman (2018), 59.
19 This is ironic since it seems to be tacitly born out of an assumption that the threats generating refugees will originate from within (rather than from outside) a particular state, but the OAU definition he ultimately endorses explicitly includes threats created by *other* states that impact a refugee's state.
20 I cannot square this with his stipulation at the start that "nothing of consequence turns on the use of" the term "refugee" and that readers "can substitute [their] label of choosing…in evaluating [his]…argument".
21 Indeed, these authors miss an easy opportunity. There are two main interpretive schools for refugee law: that of Hathaway and Foster and that of Goodwin-Gil and McAdam (Lister 2014 signals his reliance on the latter at fn. 8). The first view is known as the "Human Rights" approach to refugee law, and is highly influential. Neither Cooper nor Duong develops their argument from this angle, but they surely could have done so with more persuasive power. Yet, it is unclear if doing so would have yielded the conclusions that they wanted or if, instead, it would've yielded the view (which I largely *do* endorse) noted in fn. 1 above. Kälin does seem to say that the internal normative logic of the refugee regime essentially applies to those fleeing sinking island states, but he perceptively notes a key difference and so stops short of saying we should necessarily fold such people into refugee law.
22 Kincaid (2019 PhD dissertation)—which specifically links up with refugee law but, in distinction to others in this section, is about "climate refugees" more broadly.
23 The version of Pellegrino's view I engage with was published as a brief piece in a policy journal. He published a contemporaneous chapter in a political philosophy-oriented anthology that makes a similar claim in the first part. But he then asserts that this challenges the territorial rights of states—a conclusion that seems to indicate we are *not* simply folding this group into *existing* refugee law. This means I either do not fully understand his view or have noticed that his view holds space open for solutions beyond refugee law. As such, I simply reference the more concise "policy" version of Pellegrino above, and then engage Lister's more thoroughly developed account.
24 See Jack Donnelly (2003, 8–10): "Rights are not…reducible to enjoying a benefit" and "a human [or refugee] right…should not be confused with…enjoyment of the object of the right".
25 Beaton (2020 b) uses the same locution when defining refugees as people "whose interests can *only or best* be satisfied by means of refuge" [my emphasis].
26 He cannot be using "best" to mean morally best. It is not clear that when we have a duty to aid, we always and necessarily have a duty to aid in the way that is optimal or "best" for the recipient of the aid, or even all things considered. Wellman (2011, 68) correctly flags but does not engage with "the normative question as to whether", even when wealthy states are required to help those seeking admission, they "are morally required to help in the *optimal* fashion". In a similar vein, Sreenivasan (2010, 479) discusses how deontological liberty rights shield one from the demands of a best-case "all things considered" consequentialist morality.

27 Ironically, I agree that this is the right approach for the topic at hand. As he aptly puts it, this approach thinks, "more "ideal" proposals are often worse than useless…[since] they may lead to greater injustice". But, I simply disagree that all alternative remedies lack "feasibility and likelihood of successful adoption". Moreover, I take to heart Hourdequin's point that dominant institutions and practices can impoverish our imagination for how the world might be different (chapter 5).
28 While I will not get into this, one obvious alternative is the insurance model of responsibility. See Draper (2019) for how this would explicitly work and make sense applied to climate migrants.
29 He summarizes a position he does not fully endorse—for, "determined by" doesn't mean *fully* "determined by".
30 One way to understand the difference between Lister and Pellegrino is through the lens of an old, technical debate in refugee law: whether asylum refers to mere protection (e.g. against refoulement) or to a *place* of (presumably state) protection; see Kimminich (1968, 7, 33). With respect to the ideally administered camp idea above: in his Tanner lectures, Walzer noted how hotels *do* offer protection and a "decent life" (for a time) for asylum applicants awaiting a determination of their claim, but presumably applicants need something more. On how the remedy of an individual right of migration for climate exiles misses the importance of *place* see Buxton (2019) 215. The only instance I am aware of where refugees in a camp actually exercised final ("verdictive") collective political self-determination was when, in 1975, around 1500 Vietnamese evacuated to the US territory of Guam demanded to go back, eventually convincing US authorities and UNHCR to let them to sail back on a boat they manned themselves.
31 They may also see the claim as properly addressed to the top emitters of greenhouse gases (or, in special circumstances, one polluter in particular), or they may think that the claim is redeemable in the currency of either new membership or internal relocation and job skill retraining monies. The point is not that *everything* hinges on how a victim sees things, but just that how they see things cannot be ignored.

Bibliography

Alexander, Heather and Jonathan Simon. "Sinking into Statelessness," *Tilburg Law Review*. 20–25. 2014.
Anderson, Elizabeth. "What Is the Point of Equality?," *Ethics*. 109 (2): 287–337. 1999.
Angell, Kim. "New Territorial Rights for Sinking Island States," *European Journal of Philosophy*. 20 (1): 95–115. 2021.
Ballinger, Pamela. "Entangled or 'Extruded' Histories? Displacement, National Refugees and Repatriation after the Second World War," *Journal of Refugee Studies*. 25 (3): 366–386. 2012.
Beaton, Eilidh. "Replacing the Persecution Condition of Refugeehood," *Archiv fur Rechts- Und Sozialphilosophie*. 106 (1): 4–18. 2020a.
Beaton, Eilidh. "Against the Alienage Condition for Refugeehood," *Law and Philosophy*. 39 (2) 147–176. 2020b.
Behrman, Simon and Avidan Kent (eds.) *Climate Refugees: Beyond the Legal Impasse?* (London: Routledge, 2018).
Beitz, Charles. *The Idea of Human Rights* (Oxford University Press, 2009).
Bell, Derek. "Environmental Refugees: What Rights Which Duties," *Res Publica*. 10: 135–52. 2004.
Betts, Alexander and A. Pilath. "The Politics of Causal Claims: the Case of Environmental Migration," *Journal of International Relations and Development*. 20 (4): 782–804. 2017.
Biermann, Frank. "Global Governance to Protect Future Climate Refugees" in *Climate Refugees: Beyond the Legal Impasse?* Behrman and Kent (eds.) (London: Routledge, 2018)
Biermann, Frank and Ingrid Boas. "Protecting Climate Refugees: The case for a Global Protocol," *Environment*. 50(6): 8–17. 2008.
Biermann, Frank and Ingrid Boas. "Preparing for a warmer world: Towards a Global Governance System to Protect Climate Refugees," *Global Environmental Politics*. 10(1): 291–300. 2010.
Black, Richard. "Environmental Refugees—Myth or Reality?" New Issues in Refugee Research UNHCR Working Paper no. 34.
Blocher, Joseph and Mitu Gulati. "Competing for Refugees: a Market-Based Solution to a Humanitarian Crisis," *Columbia Human Rights Law Review*. 48 (1): 53–111. 2016.

Boom, CD. "Beyond Persecution: a Moral Defense of Expanding Refugee Status," *International Journal of Refugee Law*. 30 (3): 512–531. 2018.

Brock, Gillian. "Travel Bans, Climate Change, Refugees and Human Rights: a Response to My Critics," *Ethics and Global Politics*. 14 (2): 110–125. 2021.

Broome, John. *Climate Matters: Ethics in a Warming World* (New York: Norton, 2012).

Burson, Bruce. "Environmentally Induced Displacement and the 1951 Refugee Convention: Pathways to Recognition," in *Environment, Forced Migration, and Social Mobility*. Afifi, Tamer and Jill Jäger (eds.) (Berlin: Springer, 2010)

Buxton, Rebecca. "Reparative Justice for Climate Refugees," *Philosophy*. 94 (2): 193–219. 2019.

Byravan, Sujatha and Sudhir Rajan. "The Ethical implications of Sea-Level Rise due to Climate Change," *Ethics and International Affairs*. 24(3): 236–260. 2010.

Byravan, Sujatha and Sudhir Rajan. "Sea-Level Rise and Climate Change Exiles: A possible Solution," *Bulletin of the Atomic Scientists*. 71(2): 21–28. 2015.

Carens, Joseph. *The Ethics of Immigration* (New York: Oxford University Press, 2013)

Conisbee, Molly and Andrew Simms. *Environmental Refugees: The Case for Recognition* (London: New Economics Foundation, 2003).

Cooper, Jessica. "Environmental Refugees: Meeting the Requirements of the Refugee Convention," *New York University Environmental Law Journal*. 6 (3): 480–529. 1998.

Cornell, Nicolas. "What Do We Remedy?" in *Civil Wrongs and Justice in Private Law*. Paul B. Miller and John Oberdiek (eds.) (New York: Oxford University Press, 2020).

Dietrich, Frank and Joachim Wündisch. "Territory Lost—Climate Change and the Violation of Self-Determination Rights," *Moral Philosophy and Politics*. 2 (1): 83–105. 2015.

Docherty, Bonnie and Tyler Giannini. "Confronting a Rising Tide: A Proposal for a Convention on Climate Change Refugees," *The Harvard Environmental Law Review*. 33(2): 349–403. 2009.

Donnelly, Jack. *Universal Human Rights in Theory and Practice, 2nd edition* (Ithaca: Cornell University Press, 2002).

Draper, Jamie. "Responsibility and Climate Induced Displacement," *Global Justice: Theory, Practice, Rhetoric*. 11 (2): 59–80. 2019.

Draper, Jamie. "Climate Change and Displacement: Towards a Pluralist Approach," *European Journal of Political Theory*. 23 (1): 44–64. 2024.

Dummett, Michael. *On Immigration and Refugees*. (Routledge, 2001)

Duong, T.T. "When Islands Drown: the Plight of 'climate Change refugees' and Recourse to International Human Rights Law," *University of Pennsylvania Journal of International Law*. 31 (4): 1239–1266. 2010.

Eckersley, Robyn. "The Common but Differentiated Responsibilities of States to Assist and Receive 'Climate Refugees," *European Journal of Political Theory*. 14 (4). 2015.

El-Hinnawi, E. *Environmental Refugees* (Nairobi: United Nations Environment Program, 1985).

Falstrom, Dana Zartner. "Perspective: Stemming the Flow of Environmental Displacement: Creating a Convention to Protect Persons and Preserve the Environment," *Colorado Journal of International Environmental Law and Policy Year Book*. 13 (1): 1–30. 2002.

Gardiner, Steve. "Is No One Responsible for Global Environmental Tragedy? Climate Change as a Challenge to Our Ethical Concepts," in *The Ethics of Global Climate Change*. Denis G. Arnold (ed.) (New York: Cambridge University Press, 2011).

Gemenne, Francois. "One Good Reason to Speak of Climate Refugees," *Forced Migration Review*. 49 (1): 70–71. 2015.

Gemenne, Francois. "The Refugees of the Anthropocene," in *Research Handbook on Climate Change, Migration and the Law*. (Northampton, MA: Elgar 2017)

Gibney, Matthew. *The Ethics and Politics of Asylum* (Cambridge: Cambridge University Press, 2004).

Gilman, Nils. "The Coming Avocado Politics: What Happens When the Ethno-Nationalist Right Gets Serious About the Climate Emergency?" *Breakthrough Journal*, 12. Winter 2020.

Goodwin-Gil, Guy and Selim Can Sazak, 2015. "Footing the Bill: Refugee Creating States' Responsibility to Pay," *Foreign Affairs* (July)

Heyward, Clare and Jorgen Ödalen. "A Free Movement Passport for the Territorially Dispossessed" in *Climate Justice in a Non-Ideal World*. (Oxford: Oxford University Press, 2016)

Hiraide, LA. "Climate Refugees: A Useful Concept? Towards an Alternative Vocabulary of Ecological Displacement," *Politics*.

Hourdequin, Marion. *Environmental Ethics: From Theory to Practice* (London: Bloomsbury, 2015).

Jamieson, Dale. *Reason in a Dark Time* (New York: Oxford University Press, 2014).

Kaduuli, Stephen. "Canada has a Moral Obligation to Accept Climate Migrants," *Policy Options*. February 5th, 2020.

Kälin, Walter. "Conceptualizing Climate Induced Displacement," in *Climate Change and Displacement: Multidisciplinary Perspectives*. Jane McAdam (ed.) (Oxford: Oxford University Press, 2010).

Kent, Avidan and Simon Behrman. *Facilitating the Resettlement and Rights of Climate Refugees: An Argument for Developing Existing Principles and Practices*. (Abingdon: Routledge, 2018).

Kibreab, Gaim. "Environmental Causes and Impacts of Refugee Movements: a Critique of the Current Debate," *Disasters*. 21 (1): 20–38. 1997.

Kincaid, Jordan. Help or High Water: On the Moral Entitlements of and State Responsibilities to Climate Refugees (University of Colorado PhD dissertation)

Kimminich, Otto. *Asylrecht* (Berlin: Luchterhand, 1968).

Kolers, Avery. "Floating Provisos and Sinking Islands," *Journal of Applied Philosophy*. 29 (4): 333–343. 2012.

Kozoll, Christopher M. "Poisoning the Well: Persecution, the Environment, and Refugee Status", *Colorado Journal of International Environmental Law and Policy*. 15 (2): 271–307. 2004.

Kukathas, Chandran. "The Case for Open Immigration" in *Contemporary Debates in Applied Ethics* (Malden, MA: Wiley-Blackwell, 2004).

Kukathas, Chandran. "Are Refugees Special?" in *Migration in Political Theory*. Fine, Sarah and Lea Ypi (eds.). (New York, Oxford University Press, 2016).

Lassily-Jacob, Veronique. and Michael Zmoleck. "Environmental Refugees," *Refuge*. 12 (1): 1–4 1992.

Lister, Matthew. "Climate Change Refugees," *Critical Review of International Social and Political Philosophy*. 17 (5): 618–634. 2014.

Lee, Alexander and Jordan Kincaid. "Two Problems of Climate Ethics: Can We Lose the Planet but Save Ourselves?," *Ethics, Policy and Environment*. 19 (2): 141–144. 2016.

Lee, Luke T. "The Right To Compensation: Refugees and Countries of Asylum," *The American Journal of International Law* 80 (3): 532–567. 1986.

Leebaw, Bronwyn. "The Politics of Impartiality: Human Rights and Humanitarianism," *Perspectives in Politics*. 5 (2): 223–238. 2007.

Mayer, Benoit. "The Arbitrary Project of Protecting Environmental Migrants," in *Environmental Migration and Social Inequality*. Robert McLeman, Jeanette Schade, and Thomas Faist (eds.) (New York: Springer, 2015).

Mayer, Benoit. "Who Are "Climate Refugees"? An Inquiry into Post-Truth Academic Politics," in *Climate Refugees: Beyond the Legal Impasse?* Avidan Kent and Simon Behrman (ed.) (London: Routledge, 2018).

Mayer, Benoit. "Environmental Migration" as Advocacy: Is It Going to Work?" *Refuge*. 29(2): 27–41. 2014

McAdam, Jane. *Climate Change, Forced Migration, and International Law*. 2012

McAdam, Jane. "Swimming Against the Tide: Why a Climate Change Displacement Treaty Is Not the Answer," *International Journal of Refugee Law*. 23 (1): 2–27. 2011.

McGregor, JoAnn. "Refugees and the environment," in Black, R. and Robinson V. (eds.) *Geography and Refugees: Patterns and Processes of Change* (London: Belhaven, 1993).

Miller, David. *Strangers in our Midst* (Cambridge, MA: Harvard University Press, 2016).

Moberg, Kara. "Extending Refugee Definitions to Cover Environmentally Displaced Persons Displaces Necessary Protection," *Iowa Law Review*. 94 (3): 1107–1137. 2009.

Morrow, David. *Values in Climate Policy* (New York: Rowman and Littlefield, 2020).

Myers, Norman. "Environmental Refugees: A Growing Phenomenon of the 21st Century," *Philosophical Transactions of the Royal Society London*. 357: 609–613. 2002

Nine, Cara. "Ecological Refugees, State Borders, and the Lockean Proviso," *Journal of Applied Philosophy*. 2010.

O'Neill, Onora. *Towards Justice and Virtue* (New York: Cambridge University Press, 1996).
O'Neill, Onora. *Bounds of Justice* (New York: Cambridge University Press, 2000).
Pellegrino, Gianfranco. "Climate Refugees: a Case for Protection" in *Canned Heat: Ethics and Politics of Global Climate Change* Di Paola, Marcello and Gianfranco Pellegrino (eds.) (London: Routledge, 2014).
Pellegrino, Gianfranco. "Climate Refugees and their Right to Occupancy" *Global Policy*. 2015.
Pogge, Thomas. "Migration and Poverty" in *Citizenship and Exclusion*, ed. Viet Bader (Houndmills: Palgrave Macmillan 1997).
Rosignoli, Francesca. *Environmental Justice for Climate Refugees* (Abingdon: Routledge, 2022)
Sazak, Selim Can. "An Argument for Using Frozen Assets for Humanitarian Assistance in Refugee Situations," *Journal of International Affairs*. 68 (2): 305–318. 2015.
Scott, Matthew. *Climate Change, Disasters, and the Refugee Convention* (New York: Cambridge University Press, 2021).
Shacknove, Andrew. "Who is a Refugee?" *Ethics*. 95 (2): 274–284. 1985.
Skran, Claudena. *Refugees in Interwar Europe The Emergence of a Regime*. (New York: Oxford University Press, 1995)
Sreenivasan, Gopal. "Duties and Their Direction," *Ethics*. 120 (3): 465–494. 2010.
UNHCR. 2009. *Climate Change, Natural Disasters and Human Displacement: a UNHCR perspective*
UNHCR. *The State of the World's Refugees: in Search of Solidarity* (Oxford: Oxford University Press, 2012).
Wellman, Christopher Heath. "Freedom of Association and the Right to Exclude," in *Debating the Ethics of Immigration: Is There a Right to Exclude?* Christopher Heath Wellman and Phillip Cole (ed.) (New York: Cambridge University Press, 2011).
Westra, Laura. *Environmental Justice and the Rights of Ecological Refugees* (London: Routledge, 2009).
White, Gregory. "The Specter of Climate Refugees: Why Invoking Refugees as a Reason to 'Take Climate Change Seriously' Is Troubling" *Migration and Citizenship Newsletter of the American Political Science Association*. 4 (2): 38–44. 2016.
White, Gregory. "Climate Refugees: A Useful Concept?" *Global Environmental Politics*. 19 (4): 133-138. 2019.
Wilcox, Shelly. "Does Brock's Theory of Migration Justice Adequately Account for Climate Refugees?" *Ethics and Global Politics*. 14 (2): 75–85. 2021.
Williams, Angela. "Turning the Tide: Recognizing Climate Change Refugees in International Law," *Law and Policy*. 30 (4): 502–529. 2008.
Wündisch, Joachim. "Towards a Non-Ideal Theory of Climate Migration," *Critical Review of International Social and Political Philosophy*. 25 (4): 496–527. 2022.

20
IMMIGRATION AND CLIMATE CHANGE

Dan C. Shahar

20.1 Introduction

In the public mind, one of climate change's gravest threats is its potential to displace people across international borders as domestic environmental conditions become untenable.[1] Some forecasts of these movements' magnitude are staggering, such as Norman Myers' oft-repeated figure of 200 million people displaced by 2050.[2] Particularly salient are the plights of low-lying island nations, whose residents seem threatened with statelessness as sea levels rise. The international community's history of serving refugees and other displaced persons makes it difficult to imagine a graceful response to an ongoing flood of millions of involuntary climate emigrants.[3] Thus, it is unsurprising that media coverage of so-called "climate refugees" has often adopted the tone of a developing global catastrophe.[4]

Digging into these concerns' substance reveals this common way of framing the issue of climate-induced migration is misleading. As we will see, most experts do not anticipate that climate change will drive unprecedented levels of urgent, forced emigration. In part, this is because they expect people displaced by environmental forces to relocate primarily *within* national borders rather than across them. However, even residents of existentially threatened nations are expected to retain considerable discretion over when and how they emigrate. Thus, the deluge of "climate refugees" is unlikely to materialize in the form some have envisioned. Climate change undoubtedly will shape countless location decisions in the coming decades, but the resulting movements will not manifest as millions of people throwing themselves at foreigners' feet due to suddenly untenable ecological conditions at home.

In one sense, this is good news, at least from the perspective of exploring the ethical and economic dimensions of immigration. However, just because climate change's impacts will not create certain specific problems some anticipate, this does not lessen the gravity of the harms that will occur. Nor does it obviate the need to consider international migration as a mechanism for helping victims protect themselves. On the contrary, crossboundary mobility will be pivotal in shaping both the magnitude of climate change's impacts and the moral significance of its harms. By clarifying our understanding of how

DOI: 10.4324/9781003037309-27

climate change likely will influence migration, we can position ourselves better to navigate the challenges a warming world will bring.

20.2 Beyond "Climate Refugees"

The stylized "climate refugee" has become a media mainstay as climate change's "human face."[5] If we take term "climate refugee" at face value, it denotes an individual who must seek asylum in a foreign country because climate change has made it unfeasible to remain or return home.[6] However, there are at least four drawbacks to using the concept of "refugees" to structure our thinking about climate-induced migration. (For further development of the case against extending the concept of "refugees" to cover climate change victims, see Max Gabriel Cherem's chapter in this volume.)

The first drawback to using this concept is a technical feature of the international human rights laws that govern refugees. The United Nations High Commissioner for Refugees (UNHCR) defines refugees as people who have fled their home countries "owing to a well-founded fear of being persecuted for reasons of race, religion, nationality, membership of a particular social group, or political opinion."[7] Since climate change does not constitute "persecution," individuals it displaces are not "refugees" in the eyes of international law.[8] This exclusion from refugee status is not merely an artifact of international negotiators' failure to consider environmental displacement when formulating the 1951 Convention Relating to the Status of Refugees. It also reflects the fact that international norms have traditionally placed the responsibility to care for victims of environmental stressors on those individuals' home countries.[9]

Because many countries cannot mobilize effective humanitarian relief, there are valid questions about climate victims' prospects under the prevailing regime. But this problem is not unique to the climate change domain. Many people worldwide face hardships because their governments fail to care for them adequately. Yet, international norms generally do not require foreign countries to take responsibility for these individuals. Refugees' special status comes from the recognition that persecution victims *must* seek help from foreign governments in foreign territories to escape further victimization.[10] Except in cases where environmental harms combine with other more deliberate forms of targeting, there is no equivalent need to serve climate victims this way.

The official distinction between "refugees" and so-called "internally displaced persons" reflects different ways of assigning legal responsibility for meeting victims' needs. But it also illuminates a second, more fundamental issue with using the idea of "climate refugees" to frame discussions of climate-induced migration. Talk of "refugees" implies movement across national borders. However, historical experience shows most people displaced by environmental factors (e.g., droughts, floods, hurricanes) relocate domestically—especially into cities from rural areas.[11] People who respond by crossing into other countries often do so because they have contacts (e.g., family members) or opportunities in the receiving country, not because circumstances strictly force them to emigrate.[12] Although climate change may alter some of these dynamics, most experts project future movements will continue to occur primarily within national borders.[13]

High rates of domestic movement will cause significant difficulties for migrants and their sending and receiving communities.[14] Depopulation (and its economic ramifications) may multiply the challenges confronting regions that are hard-hit by ecological changes. Meanwhile, urban areas may struggle to absorb influxes of displaced rural poor without experiencing increases in homelessness, crime, and other social ills. In regions with communal property regimes (including many Pacific Islands), displaced individuals may struggle to settle in new areas without upsetting others' ties to their land.[15] These will be daunting problems in the coming decades. But they primarily will involve citizens of the countries where they occur, and their solutions will come from *domestic* planning, policymaking, and entrepreneurship—not immigration arrangements.[16] Except in unusual cases, it will be unhelpful to analogize these frictions to the intergroup political conflicts that produce refugees of the traditional kind. Plausibly, industrialization, urbanization, and economic disruption will provide better templates for thinking through these challenges.

A third problem with talk of "climate refugees" comes from its implication that climate stressors will cause people to flee urgently, without planning, and in reaction to specific precipitating events. There is little doubt a warming world will experience migration episodes of this kind, as these have occurred throughout history, climate change aside.[17] But climate-induced migration will not consist only of exigent relocation. Many impacts will emerge gradually, giving victims discretion over when, how, where, and even whether to leave.[18] Moreover, environmental conditions often will play only a partial role in explaining individuals' choices to move.[19] Residents of a warming world will consider economic opportunities and challenges, family needs, and many other factors when making location decisions. Hence, people facing similar environmental circumstances often will make very different choices.[20] Unlike people displaced by war—or even a natural disaster—most climate migrants will be unable to say they had no choice but to move immediately, especially to a foreign country.[21] Again, the more faithful analog to many of these displacements may be economic dislocation (e.g., from a significant local industry's decline) rather than violent conflict presenting immediate dangers to life and limb.

An additional problem with the "climate refugee" narrative is that emigration is costly, and people capable of bearing these costs tend to be privileged by global standards. Many of those whom climate change will hit hardest will be too poor to consider international relocation as a feasible response. Even when facing significant hardships, they either will move domestically or will submit to dealing with hazards in place.[22] Given this, emigration in a warming world often will signal *empowerment* and not only desperation.

Together, these issues suggest talk of an imminent flood of "climate refugees" is misleading. Individuals who relocate in response to climate change generally will not be "refugees" in the eyes of international law. They will move primarily within national borders, and responsibility for ensuring their welfare will fall on domestic authorities rather than foreign governments. Individuals who choose to relocate to other countries will do so primarily in response to specific opportunities and connections abroad. Rarely will these individuals' circumstances compel them to rely on protection and aid from other countries in a manner analogous to traditional refugees. More typically, they will emigrate in an orderly, deliberate way to pursue the best opportunities for themselves and their families.

At first glance, residents of low-lying island nations may seem to represent a significant class of exceptions to these generalizations. Insofar as climate change could cause some of these people's countries to disappear or become uninhabitable, the resulting hardships might seem analogous to those refugees endure. Although victims might not be targets of persecution, climate change still could force them to leave their country and preclude them from relying on their government for aid. Even if the term "refugee" *legally* would not apply to such people, this might seem to be a technical or semantic point rather than a substantive one.[23]

Granting this exception would require noting that the population threatened by such a fate is dramatically smaller than the figures commonly reported in discussions of "climate refugees." One reason for this is that many island communities are linked politically to countries that face no threat of disappearance, offering escape routes for citizens who need them. For example, the approximately 1500 residents of Tokelau all live on land within 5 m of sea level. However, Tokelau is a dependent territory of New Zealand, and Tokelauans enjoy full citizenship rights as New Zealanders.[24] Thus, there is no threat climate change will force Tokelauans to emigrate (as opposed to relocating somewhere within New Zealand's territory). Meanwhile, the Marshall Islands' approximately 58,000 residents enjoy national independence, but a Compact of Free Association with the United States allows Marshallese citizens to live, work, and study within U.S. borders without a visa indefinitely.[25] The list of islands that climate change could plausibly render uninhabitable with no connection to a "mainland" territory is limited to just a few countries: the Maldives (pop. 541,000), Kiribati (pop. 123,000), Tuvalu (pop. 12,000), and Nauru (pop. 11,000).[26] Although the numbers of people living in these countries are substantial, they do not portend an ongoing flood of millions of displaced persons at a time.

Matters are complicated further by the difficulty of assessing how changing sea levels will impact island nations' viability. It may seem intuitive that as sea levels rise, the habitable and arable portions of low-lying islands will shrink accordingly. However, the physical dynamics that shape island structures are complex. There are natural processes (e.g., related to sediment deposition and reef-building) by which islands can rise in step with changing sea levels. Island communities can also alter their coastlines deliberately through infrastructure investments. These dynamics explain how long-term observations of islands in the Pacific Ocean can show no consistent relationship between sea level and island size.[27] Although experts anticipate sea levels will continue to rise, they remain uncertain about whether climate change will cause low-lying island nations to disappear and, if so, which ones.[28]

Even if climate change eventually will make some countries uninhabitable, this does not imply the primary threat these nations' citizens face is one of sudden displacement. Sea level rise is a gradual process. Long before citizens face engulfment, they will confront other challenges that make relocation progressively salient.[29] Flooding may become increasingly common and burdensome during exceptionally high tides or extreme weather events.[30] Seawater may intrude into already limited freshwater resources and make farmland unproductive.[31] Ocean acidification, rising water temperatures, and sea level changes may make fish and other vital goods less available.[32] Decreased local food production may increase dependency on expensive and highly processed imports. A need for costly infrastructure projects may result in tax increases and construction-related inconveniences. When some citizens respond to these hardships by moving away, their departures may make it increasingly difficult for others not to follow suit.[33]

These compounding challenges will push island residents to make difficult choices about whether to remain in their home communities long before environmental circumstances make them *uninhabitable*. For those who choose to delay relocation, the hardships may become considerable. However, unlike the persecuted individuals who become "refugees" in the traditional sense, most residents of disappearing nations will retain substantial discretion over precisely when and how to move. Indeed, individuals who wish not to leave their homes often will have options to remain even after local conditions have become inviable. For example, even today, it is common for island families to send members to mainland economic centers to take advantage of superior economic opportunities.[34] Migrants' remittances may enable families to delay relocation even when their home communities have become incapable of supporting them.[35]

For all these reasons, the "climate refugee" lens remains misleading even when applied to the citizens of low-lying island nations. Climate change eventually may force some individuals in these nations to emigrate (unlike in most other climate change victimization cases). However, although climate change may impose significant pressure on these individuals, they typically will still have meaningful choices about when and how they move. Their movements are unlikely to manifest the deluge of urgently displaced victims many proponents of the "climate refugee" narrative envision. This image is even less fitting for the millions of others who will navigate climate challenges in the decades ahead.

20.3 Three Functions of International Mobility

Characterizing climate change's future victims as "refugees" is unhelpful. However, this does not imply we should ignore these victims' hardships or immigration's potential to alleviate them. Even without a flood of "climate refugees," international mobility can serve vital functions in a warming world. For instance, one crucial role is to enhance people's discretion over what climatic burdens and risks they will bear. Although climate change likely will expose everyone to some hardships and dangers, many of its impacts will vary in kind and magnitude across space.[36] Thus, people often will find it easier to cope with climate change's manifestations in some places over others. Since national borders affect whether specific options are open to people, immigration policies will affect how well individuals can protect themselves in a warming world.

The value of immigration options will be most apparent when individuals use them to leave high-risk areas for safer alternatives. However, even when people choose not to relocate, the availability of *options* to do so remains morally significant. To see this, consider that many people in a warming world will prefer to live in vulnerable areas because of countervailing benefits these locations offer. Some even may pay a premium for these risky options. For instance, people may continue to demand luxurious beachfront condominiums despite the availability of safer, less expensive alternatives inland. When individuals *freely assume* such risks, it is reasonable to regard them as bearing substantial responsibility for resulting burdens. By contrast, hardships will have greater moral gravity when people have few or no meaningful options to escape from harm's way.[37] To the extent emigration options empower people to mitigate climate risks, they can reduce climate change's moral badness even if many decline these options. (Of course, empowering people to move requires much more than opening borders. Emigration is infeasible for many of climate change's most vulnerable victims. Even so, removing legal barriers to immigration is a vital element of broader efforts to empower people to protect themselves from climate change.)[38]

Our earlier discussion of economic migration illuminates a second crucial function cross-boundary movements can play in alleviating climate harm. As we have seen, permanent relocation is not the only way people can use mobility to protect themselves. Another strategy is to move temporarily to capitalize on economic opportunities abroad. Migrants who do this can accumulate resources to bring home or send to relatives as remittances. People in hard-hit areas may use these resources to support livelihoods beyond what local conditions can sustain. Thus, opportunities for economic migration can provide a vital adaptation pathway even when primary residences remain unchanged.[39]

When migrants take advantage of international options (whether permanently or for temporary work), the foreign footholds they establish also can fulfill a third function. I noted earlier that when environmental stressors displace people, the resulting movements occur primarily within national borders. A principal class of exceptions to this are people who have contacts in other countries. It is hardly surprising that individuals who face relocation are more likely to consider international options when they expect to be welcomed by people they know. Along similar line, even the presence of an established expatriate community can offer a link home that makes emigration less daunting.[40]

Creating expatriate communities is another domain where emigration options' value extends beyond those who choose to move. These communities assure threatened residents that if local conditions became untenable, other places could offer meaningful opportunities to preserve their identities and traditions. Thus, even small numbers of early immigrants can play a pivotal role in lowering barriers to movement for others.

Considering these functions reinforces why the "climate refugee" lens is unhelpful for thinking about immigration in a warming world. The imperative to facilitate international movements does not come primarily from a need to accommodate individuals who are displaced suddenly from their homes and require urgent refuge abroad. Most people who consider international relocation in response to environmental stressors will have substantial discretion over when, how, where, and often even whether to move. In this context, immigration's significance will come from its value as an *option*. International relocation can empower individuals to exchange local hazards and hardships for alternative conditions or use foreign markets to accumulate resources to sustain life at home. People who capitalize on such opportunities can establish footholds in foreign countries, lowering barriers for others to follow them. Even if many residents of threatened areas choose not to pursue these options, open pathways across international borders will remain morally pivotal.

Before moving on, it will be useful to mention a potential fourth function for immigration that concerns the translocation of entire communities. In line with our discussion of the importance of cultural ties, some have looked toward community-scale resettlement as a strategy for enabling people to relocate *together*, potentially averting some of climate change's worst impacts by preserving groups' cohesion. If successful, such efforts could yield vital benefits that are difficult to replicate through piecemeal movements of individuals or families. However, historical attempts at international community relocation have faced significant challenges, and some climate-threatened communities have expressed resistance toward embarking on these experiments.[41]

For purposes of tractability, I will not try to settle whether international community resettlement is practically viable or attractive. However, in the present context, it is noteworthy that successful community resettlement is a complex undertaking that requires careful long-term planning and negotiation by both emigrants and receiving nations. Given its connotations of urgent and unplanned exodus by desperate victims, the "refugee" metaphor is distinctly ill-suited to guide our thinking about such delicate processes. In practice, attempts at international community resettlement sometimes fail precisely because threatened communities *are not* like refugees: despite the threats they face, they can reject arrangements they find unattractive and hold out for better deals.[42] By moving beyond talk of "climate refugees" and emphasizing translocation's value as an *option*, we can approach community resettlement with a better appreciation for groups' retained agency over their collective fates.

20.4 Common but Differentiated Responsibilities

Climate victims' agency has significant upshots for what emigration options they likely will pursue. For example, we can anticipate people will prefer destinations they can easily access that offer appealing economic opportunities.[43] Correspondingly, far-off countries with weak economies will attract little interest.[44]

Countries with attractive destinations for climate victims can significantly reduce climate change's moral gravity by facilitating migration from vulnerable areas. As we have discussed, acting on these opportunities may not always require accepting large influxes of permanent residents. For example, granting temporary work visas sometimes may be just as important as allowing longer-term relocation.[45] Permitting even small numbers of migrants to begin forging new expatriate communities also can significantly alter numerous other potential victims' prospects. It sometimes may be possible to create bilateral arrangements between specific sending and receiving communities instead of opening borders to all comers.[46] Capitalizing on possibilities like these may be especially vital in countries where political realities prevent broader easing of border restrictions.

These observations notwithstanding, empowering climate victims to get out of harm's way will require at least some desirable destination countries to accept significant numbers of newcomers. Although there is considerable evidence that immigrants benefit their receiving communities[47]—and although there are powerful ethical arguments for relaxing immigration barriers in general[48]—reluctance to welcoming large influxes of migrants is widespread. Frequent sources of resistance include concerns about cultural or political assimilation, public safety, labor market competition, and impacts on social programs, among other anxieties.[49] Whether or not these apprehensions are empirically valid, they may be sufficiently widespread to render climate victims' relocation options inadequate.[50]

One potential strategy for addressing this problem is to treat welcoming immigrants as a valid contribution to global climate efforts.[51] The United Nations Framework Convention on Climate Change (UNFCCC) has long recognized countries can help fight climate change in diverse ways. The UNFCCC's principle of "common but differentiated responsibilities" formalizes this idea.[52] To date, discussions of this principle typically have revolved around countries' differing development levels, administrative capacities, and financial assets. However, the underlying notion of common but differentiated responsibilities is well-suited to recognizing diverse roles in facilitating mobility in a warming world.[53] Some attractive destination countries may provide more value to international climate efforts by accepting immigrants than by fighting climate change in other ways (e.g., by mitigating greenhouse gases, transferring technologies, or funding adaptation projects). On the other hand, it may be appropriate to expect countries unwilling or unable to provide meaningful migration pathways to contribute more along alternative dimensions.

Accepting this view would have significant ramifications for climate politics. For instance, one storyline in recent climate negotiations has been India's unwillingness to pledge substantial reductions in national greenhouse gas emissions.[54] With one of the world's largest populations of citizens living in poverty, India understandably has been reluctant to make commitments that could impair its economic growth. India's limited bureaucratic capacity also makes domestic monitoring and enforcement of emissions reductions a challenge. Yet, because India is one of the world's top-three greenhouse gas emitters,[55] its hesitance has enabled other nations to dodge accountability for acting themselves.

This section's analysis suggests that instead of fixating on India's greenhouse gas emissions, it may be wiser to emphasize relaxing border restrictions as an alternative contribution. India's borders virtually envelop Bangladesh, one of the most vulnerable countries to climate change's impacts. When Bangladeshi citizens have sought refuge in other countries following past environmental crises, India typically has been the destination of choice.[56] India stands to make a vital contribution to global climate efforts by facilitating these movements and helping migrants assimilate. By treating such actions as commensurable with emissions reductions, the international community could enable India to become an ambitious contributor to the fight against climate change without threatening its path to prosperity.

Along very different lines, the United States also has presented a roadblock to global climate efforts due to its reluctance to bear costs without corresponding sacrifices by other nations.[57] Unlike India, the United States' resistance does not come from concerns about meeting its citizens' basic needs. The sources are complex, including ideological opposition to environmentalists' left-leaning orientation, desires to preserve America's position as the world's preeminent superpower, leaders' unwillingness to alienate politically powerful interests, and so on. Some of these motivations are more sympathetic than others. But regardless of whether we endorse these reasons, the U.S.'s foot-dragging has played a central role in paralyzing global climate negotiations.

Yet, like India, the United States is distinctly positioned to contribute to climate efforts by facilitating migration. Because of its west coast's proximity to Pacific Island communities, the United States long has been an attractive destination from many climate-threatened locales.[58] However, most foreign nationals hoping to dodge climate perils in the United States face formidable legal obstacles.[59] The U.S.'s relationship with the Marshall Islands illustrates how relaxing these hurdles could provide escape routes to citizens who otherwise might face grave climate threats. Recognizing such arrangements as valid contributions to global climate efforts could enable the U.S. to display climate leadership without needing to make certain sacrifices it historically has rejected.

Highlighting immigration's potential to fulfill countries' "common but differentiated responsibilities" should not blind us to the difficulties of lowering barriers to foreign entrants. In practice, we may find that even holdouts like India and the United States would sooner slash their emissions than help vulnerable foreigners escape from harm's way. However, if the opposite proved true, the reforms imagined here could facilitate progress on climate change that has proven elusive thus far.

20.5 Conclusion

Climate change will shape countless location decisions in the coming decades. As we have seen, experts project most environmentally induced movements will occur within national borders. Still, opportunities to emigrate to other countries will play a crucial role in determining climate change's severity and moral significance.

Sensationalist narratives about "climate refugees" misrepresent immigration's likely place in a warming world. A more sophisticated outlook would focus less on episodes of urgent displacement and more on mundane relocation decisions by individuals who retain agency. By exploring creative ways to facilitate these movements and rewarding nations that welcome immigrants, the global community can alleviate some of climate change's gravest threats.

Notes

1. See, e.g., Michael P. Nash, *Climate Refugees* (Beverly Hills, CA: Beverly Hills Productions, 2010); Jon Shenk, *The Island President* (San Francisco, CA: Actual Films, 2011); Jared P. Scott, *The Age of Consequences* (El Segundo, CA: Gravitas Ventures, 2017).
2. Norman Myers, "Environmental Refugees: A Growing Phenomenon of the 21st Century," *Philosophical Transactions of the Royal Society of London B* 357, no. 1420 (2002): 609–613.
3. Throughout this chapter, I use the phrase "climate migrant" as a shorthand way to refer to people who migrate in response to climate change. This mode of expression is imprecise since not all movements in response to climatic (or environmental) factors reflect responses to climate *change*. On this point, see John R. Campbell, "Climate-Change Migration in the Pacific," *The Contemporary Pacific* 26, no. 1 (2015): 1–28, at 9. By way of illustration, people often choose to retire in areas with more comfortable weather. These people may move *because of the climate*, but not (necessarily) because it is *changing*. My references to "climate migration" will not address such cases.
4. For discussion, see Carol Farbotko, "Tuvalu and Climate Change: Constructions of Environmental Displacement in the *Sydney Morning Herald*," *Geografiska Annaler: Series B, Human Geography* 87, no. 4 (2005): 279–293; Anne Chambers and Keith S. Chambers, "Five Takes on Climate and Cultural Change in Tuvalu," *The Contemporary Pacific* 19, no. 1 (2007): 294–306.
5. For instance, the website for Michael Nash's *Climate Refugees* (http://www.climaterefugees.com/home.html) explicitly markets the feature as "A multi-award winning documentary film about 'the human face of climate change.'"
6. It bears noting that many who speak of "climate refugees" do so loosely, drawing on the term's emotional appeal without committing to a robust analogy between climate victims and refugees. Although such commentators can plausibly claim their arguments dodge the criticisms I raise below, this is only because they are engaging in hyperbole or, worse, rhetorical sleight of hand. (At the extreme, we may note the possibility of using the term "refugee" to refer to anyone who would face a hardship if they didn't move somewhere else—a usage that would severely underrepresent the challenges actual refugees face.)
7. United Nations High Commissioner for Refugees, *Convention and Protocol Relating to the Status of Refugees* (Geneva: UNHCR, 2010), 14.
8. For discussion, see Jane McAdam, *Climate Change, Forced Migration, and International Law* (New York: Oxford University Press, 2012), 42–48.
9. Walter Kälin, "Conceptualising Climate-Induced Displacement," in *Climate Change and Displacement: Multidisciplinary Perspectives*, edited by Jane McAdam, 81–103 (Portland, OR: Hart Publishing, 2010). The United Nations articulates its standards for serving such victims in a separate set of Guiding Principles on Internal Displacement. See United Nations Office for the Coordination of Humanitarian Affairs, *Guiding Principles on Internal Displacement* (New York: United Nations, 2001).
10. For further exploration of the subtleties involved in distinguishing threats to basic interests from specific rights to international relocation, see Sahar Akhtar, "Being at Home in the World: International Relocation (Not Open Borders)," *Public Affairs Quarterly* 30, no. 2 (2016): 103–127 at 116–117.
11. McAdam, *Climate Change, Forced Migration, and International Law*, ch. 6; Intergovernmental Panel on Climate Change (IPCC), *Climate Change 2022: Impacts, Adaptation, and Vulnerability* (New York: Cambridge University Press, 2022), 1079–1083.
12. Jon Barnett and Michael Webber, "Accommodating Migration to Promote Adaptation to Climate Change," *Policy Research Working Paper* 5270 (Washington, D.C.: World Bank, 2010), 7; McAdam, *Climate Change, Forced Migration, and International Law*, 170–171; Jane McAdam, "Swimming against the Tide: Why a Climate Change Displacement Treaty is Not *the* Answer," *International Journal of Refugee Law* 23, no. 1 (2011): 2–27, 12.

13 Foresight, *Migration and Global Environmental Change: Future Challenges and Opportunities* (London: Government Office for Science, 2011); Kanta Kumari Rigaud, Alex de Sherbinin, Bryan Jones, Jonas Bergmann, Viviane Clement, Kayly Ober, Jacob Schewe, Susana Adamo, Brent McCusker, Silke Heuser, and Amelia Midgley, *Groundswell: Preparing for Internal Climate Migration* (Washington, D.C.: World Bank, 2018).
14 For discussion of these and other challenges, see Foresight, *Migration and Global Environmental Change*, ch. 4; Rigaud et al., *Groundswell*.
15 John Campbell and Richard Bedford, "Migration and Climate Change in Oceania," in *People on the Move in a Changing Climate: The Regional Impact of Environmental Change on Migration*, edited by Etienne Piguet and Frank Laczko, 177–204 (New York: Springer, 2014); Dalila Gharbaoui and Julia Blocher, "The Reason Land Matters: Relocation as Adaptation to Climate Change in Fiji Islands," in *Migration, Risk Management and Climate Change: Evidence and Policy Responses*, edited by A. Milan, B. Schraven, K. Warner, and N. Cascone, 149–173 (Cham: Springer, 2016).
16 One likely exception will come in the form of a "domino effect" where influxes of displaced individuals induce others in the receiving communities to relocate. See McAdam, *Climate Change, Forced Migration, and International Law*, 171–172; Luca Marchiori, Jean-François Maystadt, and Ingmar Schmumacher, "The Impact of Weather Anomalies on Migration in Sub-Saharan Africa," *Journal of Environmental Economics and Management* 63, no. 3 (2021): 355–374; Mathilde Maurel and Michele Tuccio, "Climate Instability, Urbanisation and International Migration," *The Journal of Development Studies* 52, no. 5 (2016): 735–752. Insofar as the people emigrating under such scenarios would not be the ones directly impacted by climate change, it would seem especially questionable to characterize them as "climate refugees."
17 United Nations Office for Disaster Risk Reduction, *Sendai Framework for Disaster Risk Reduction* (Geneva: United Nations, 2015). For specific discussion of such displacements in Bangladesh, see McAdam, *Climate Change, Forced Migration, and International Law*, ch. 6.
18 McAdam, *Climate Change, Forced Migration, and International Law*.
19 Colette Mortreaux and Jon Barnett, "Climate Change, Migration, and Adaptation in Funafuti, Tuvalu," *Global Environmental Change* 19, no. 1 (2009): 105–112, at 106–107; McAdam, *Climate Change, Forced Migration, and International Law*, 20–24; McAdam, "Swimming against the Tide"; Richard Black, "Environmental Refugees: Myth or Reality?" *New Issues in Refugee Research Working Paper* 34 (Geneva: United Nations High Commissioner for Refugees, 2001); Richard Black, W. Neil Adger, Nigel W. Arnell, Stefan Dercon, Andrew Geddes, and David S.G. Thomas, "The Effect of Environmental Change on Human Migration," *Global Environmental Change* 21S (2011): S3–S11; IPCC, *Impacts, Adaptation, and Vulnerability*, 1079, 2067–2068.
20 Barnett and Webber, "Accommodating Migration to Promote Adaptation," 13; Foresight, *Migration and Global Environmental Change: Future Challenges and Opportunities* (London: Government Office for Science, 2011); Frank Laczko and Etienne Piguet, "Regional Perspectives on Migration, the Environment and Climate Change," in *People on the Move in a Changing Climate*, 1–20, at 2.
21 Graeme Hugo, "Climate Change-Induced Mobility and the Existing Migration Regime in Asia and the Pacific," in *Climate Change and Displacement: Multidisciplinary Perspectives*, edited by Jane McAdam, 9–35 (Portland, OR: Hart Publishing, 2010), helpfully frames this point by distinguishing movements that constitute "adaptation"—i.e., occurring when it is still tenable to remain—from those that constitute "displacement"—i.e., occurring when it is untenable to remain. This distinction cannot be applied cleanly in practice, partly because what counts as "tenable" is a matter of judgment and partly also because individuals for whom it is *currently* tenable to remain may sensibly view relocation as mandatory if they judge conditions will *soon* become untenable. Hugo is thus correct to describe a continuum between fully voluntary and fully involuntary relocation, in "Environmental Concerns and International Migration," *The International Migration Review* 30, no. 1 (1996): 105–131.
22 Foresight, *Migration and Global Environmental Change*; Jon Barnett and Natasha Chamberlain, "Migration as Climate Change Adaptation: Implications for the Pacific," in *Climate Change and Migration: South Pacific Perspectives*, edited by Bruce Burson, 51–60 (Wellington: Institute of Policy Studies, 2010), 54; Barnett and Weber, "Accommodating Migration to Promote Adaptation," 8–9. Helen Adams, in "Why Populations Persist: Mobility, Place Attachment and Climate Change," *Population and Environment* 37, no. 4 (2016): 429–448, notes individuals' place attachments can play a similar role in immobilizing people independent of resource constraints.

23 See on this point Kälin, "Conceptualising Climate-Induced Displacement," 96–98; Matthew Lister, "Who Are Refugees?" *Law and Philosophy* 32, no. 5 (2013): 645–671; Matthew Lister, "Climate Change Refugees," *Critical Review of International Social and Political Philosophy* 17, no. 5 (2014): 618–634.
24 New Zealand Foreign Affairs & Trade, "Our Aid Partnerships in the Pacific: About Tokelau" (2023), available online at https://www.mfat.govt.nz/en/aid-and-development/our-aid-partnerships-in-the-pacific/tokelau/about-tokelau/.
25 U.S. Department of State Bureau of East Asian and Pacific Affairs, "U.S. Relations with Marshall Islands: Bilateral Relations Fact Sheet" (2021), available online at https://www.state.gov/u-s-relations-with-marshall-islands/. The United States has similar relationships with the Federated States of Micronesia and Palau. See U.S. Department of State Bureau of East Asian and Pacific Affairs, "U.S. Relations with the Federated States of Micronesia: Bilateral Relations Fact Sheet" (2021), available online at https://www.state.gov/u-s-relations-with-the-federated-states-of-micronesia/; "U.S. Relations with Palau: Bilateral Relations Fact Sheet" (2022), available online at https://www.state.gov/u-s-relations-with-palau/.
26 List of threatened nations from Etienne Piguet, "Climatic Statelessness: Risk Assessment and Policy Options," *Population and Development Review* 45, no. 4 (2019): 865–883. Population estimates for 2022 from World Bank, "Population Estimates and Projections," *Databank* (2022), available online at https://databank.worldbank.org/source/population-estimates-and-projections.
27 McLean, Roger and Paul Kench, "Destruction or Persistence of Coral Atoll Islands in the Face of 20th and 21st Century Sea-Level Rise?" *Wiley Interdisciplinary Reviews: Climate Change* 6, no. 5 (2015): 445–463; Virginie K.E. Duvat, "A Global Assessment of Atoll Island Planform Changes over the Past Decades," *Wiley Interdisciplinary Reviews: Climate Change* 10, no. 1 (2018): e557; IPCC, *Impacts, Adaptation, and Vulnerability*, 2055–2056; Paul Kench, Murray R. Ford, and Susan D. Owen, "Patterns of Island Change and Persistence Offer Alternate Adaptation Pathways for Atoll Nations," *Nature Communications* 9 (2018): art. 605.
28 McLean and Kench, "Destruction or Persistence of Coral Atoll Islands"; Virginie K.E. Duvat, Alexandre K. Magnan, Chris T. Perry, Tom Spencer, Johann D. Bell, Colette C.C. Wabnitz, Arthur P. Webb, Ian White, Kathleen L. McInnes, Jean-Pierre Gattuso, Nicholas A.J. Graham, Patrick D. Nunn, and Gonéri Le Cozannet, "Risks to Future Atoll Habitability from Climate-Driven Environmental Changes," *Wiley Interdisciplinary Reviews: Climate Change* 12, no. 3 (2021): e700.
29 For discussion of these and other challenges, see Jane McAdam, "'Disappearing States,' Statelessness and the Boundaries of International Law," in *Climate Change and Displacement*, 105–129 (Portland, OR: Hart Publishing, 2010). It bears noting some island communities face similar challenges due to factors other than climate change. See, e.g., John Connell, "Last Days in the Carteret Islands," *Asia Pacific Viewpoint* 57, no. 1 (2014): 3–15.
30 IPCC, *Impacts, Adaptation, and Vulnerability*, 2053–2055.
31 Ibid., 2058–2060, 2065.
32 Ibid., 2058, 2065–2066.
33 Jon Barnett, "On the Risks of Engineering Mobility to Reduce Vulnerability to Climate Change: Insights from a Small Island State," in *Climate Change and Human Mobility: Global Challenges to the Social Sciences*, edited by Kirsten Hastrup and Karen Fog Olwig, 169–189 (New York: Cambridge University Press, 2012); Piguet, "Climatic Statelessness," 874.
34 John Connell and Richard P.C. Brown, *Remittances in the Pacific: An Overview* (Manila: Asian Development Bank, 2005); Richard Bedford and Graeme Hugo, *Population Movement in the Pacific: A Perspective on Future Prospects* (Wellington, New Zealand: Labour & Immigration Research Centre, 2012), 32–36.
35 Piguet, "Climatic Statelessness," 873–874; IPCC, *Impacts, Adaptation, and Vulnerability*, 2076–2077. Notably, some commentators view the possibility of remittance-funded attachment to place as a perversity to be avoided—see, e.g., Rigaud et al., *Groundswell*, xxii. I make no such judgment here.
36 For discussion of regional variations in climate change's impacts, see IPCC, *Impacts, Adaptation, and Vulnerability*, chs. 9–16; Rigaud et al., *Groundswell*, ch. 4.
37 In practice, delineating between these categories may be difficult. For an illustration of some of these complexities, see A.R. Bell, D.J. Wrathall, V. Mueller, J. Chen, M. Oppenheimer, M. Hauer, H. Adams, S. Kulp, P.U. Clark, E. Fussell, N. Magliocca, T. Xiao, E.A. Gilmore, K. Abel, M. Call,

and A.B.A. Slangen, "Migration Towards Bangladesh Coastlines Projected to Increase with Sea-level Rise through 2100," *Environmental Research Letters* 16, no. 2 (2021): art. 024045.
38 For further discussion, see Dan C. Shahar, "Harm, Responsibility, and the Far-off Impacts of Climate Change," *Environmental Ethics* 43, no. 1 (2021): 3–20.
39 Barnett and Chamberlain, "Migration as Climate Change Adaptation"; IPCC, *Impacts, Adaptation, and Vulnerability*, 2076–2077.
40 Mortreaux and Barnett, "Climate Change, Migration, and Adaptation," 107; Barnett and Chamberlain, "Migration as Climate Change Adaptation"; Michael Beine, Frédéric Docquier, and Çağlar Özden, "Diasporas," *Journal of Development Economics* 95, no. 1 (2011): 30–41; McAdam, *Climate Change, Forced Migration, and International Law*, 202–205. For discussion of the importance of cultural connections in the context of Pacific Islander migration, see A. Ravuvu, "Security and Confidence as Basic Factors in Pacific Islanders' Migration," *Journal of the Polynesian Society* 101, no. 4 (1992): 329–341. For discussion of the role of "host family" arrangements for supporting new migrants, see Deborah McLeod, "Potential Impacts of Climate Change Migration on Pacific Families Living in New Zealand," in Burson (ed.), *Climate Change and Migration*, 135–157.
41 For discussion, see McAdam, "'Disappearing States'"; Campbell and Bedford, "Migration and Climate Change in Oceania"; Simon D. Donner, "The Legacy of Migration in Response to Climate Stress," *Natural Resources Forum* 39, nos. 3–4 (2015): 191–201; IPCC, *Impacts, Adaptation, and Vulnerability*, 2076.
42 See, e.g., McAdam, "'Disappearing States.'"
43 Barnett and Weber, "Accommodating Migration to Promote Adaptation," 36. Michael Beine and Christopher R. Parsons, in "Climatic Factors as Determinants of International Migration: Redux," *CESifo Economic Studies* 63, no. 4 (2017): 386–402, show former colonial powers can serve as especially salient destinations for citizens of their former colonies.
44 Barnett and Chamberlain, "Migration as Climate Change Adaptation," 52–53. Along similar lines, Hugh B. Roland and Katherine J. Curtis argue we should expect geographically isolated nations to exhibit lower rates of international migration due the sheer cost of relocation, in "The Differential Influence of Geographic Isolation on Environmental Migration: A Study of Internal Migration amidst Degrading Conditions in the Central Pacific," *Population and Environment* 42, no. 2 (2020): 161–182. Cristina Cattaneo and Giovanni Peri, in "The Migration Response to Increasing Temperatures," *Journal of Development Economics* 122 (2016): 127–146, argue even strong economies do not induce people to undertake long-distance emigration in significant numbers.
45 Barnett and Webber, "Accommodating Migration to Promote Adaptation," 18. New Zealand provides one illustration of how countries can welcome temporary migrants while maintaining tight restrictions on longer-term immigration. As of 2023, New Zealand grants visas to just 150 Kiribati citizens and 150 Tuvaluan citizens per year to relocate to within its borders indefinitely. These levels are double what they were just two years prior. See New Zealand Immigration, "Information about Pacific Access Category Resident Visa" (2023), available online at https://www.immigration.govt.nz/new-zealand-visas/apply-for-a-visa/about-visa/pacific-access-category-resident-visa. However, citizens from these countries are also eligible to apply for one of 19,000 openings for temporary work under New Zealand's Recognised Seasonal Employer scheme. See New Zealand Immigration, "Recognised Seasonal Employer (RSE) Scheme Research" (2023), available online at https://www.immigration.govt.nz/about-us/research-and-statistics/research-reports/recognised-seasonal-employer-rse-scheme.
46 McAdam, "Swimming against the Tide."
47 E.g., Jean-Christophe Dumont and Thomas Liebig, "Is Migration Good for the Economy?" *OECD Migration Policy Debates* (2014).
48 See, e.g., Joseph H. Carens, "Aliens and Citizens: The Case for Open Borders," *The Review of Politics* 49, no. 2 (1987): 251–273; Michael Huemer, "Is There a Right to Immigrate?" *Social Theory & Practice* 36, no. 3 (2010): 429–461; Kieran Oberman, "Immigration as a Human Right," in *Migration and Political Theory: The Ethics of Movement and Membership*, edited by Sarah Fine and Lea Ypi, 32–56 (New York: Oxford University Press); Javier S. Hidalgo, *Unjust Borders: Individuals and the Ethics of Immigration* (New York: Routledge, 2019).

49 See, e.g., Hrishikesh Joshi, "For (Some) Immigration Restrictions," in *Ethics, Left and Right: The Moral Issues That Divide Us*, edited by Bob Fischer, 191–198 (New York: Oxford University Press, 2020).
50 For discussion, see Robert McLeman, "International Migration and Climate Adaptation in an Era of Hardening Borders," *Nature Climate Change* 9, no. 12 (2019): 911–918.
51 Piguet, "Climatic Statelessness," 874.
52 United Nations General Assembly, *United Nations Framework Convention on Climate Change*, FCCC/INFORMAL/84 GE.05-62220 (E) 200705 (New York: United Nations, 1992).
53 Note that my way of adapting the idea of "common but differentiated responsibilities" to this context is not the only interpretation available. Robyn Eckersley, in "The Common but Differentiated Responsibilities of States to Assist and Receive 'Climate Refugees,'" *European Journal of Political Theory* 14, no. 4 (2015): 481–500, argues *all* countries should be treated as responsible for participating in efforts to aid climate migrants. In my view, it's preferable to urge countries that cannot offer migrants attractive destinations to contribute to climate change efforts in other ways.
54 E.g., Victor Mallet, "COP21 Paris Climate Talks: India Looms as Obstacle to Deal," *Financial Times* (Nov. 29, 2015), available online at https://www.ft.com/content/bfb36a16-94e5-11e5-bd82-c1fb87bef7af.
55 Hannah Ritchie and Max Roser, "CO_2 and Greenhouse Gas Emissions," *Our World in Data* (2020), https://ourworldindata.org/co2-and-other-greenhouse-gas-emissions. Note that if the European Union is considered as a single entity rather than as a union of separate countries, it qualifies as the third largest emitter, moving India into fourth place.
56 Sarfaraz Alam, "Environmentally Induced Migration from Bangladesh to India," *Strategic Analysis* 27, no. 3 (2003): 422–438.
57 E.g., U.S. Department of State, "COP21 Press Availability with Special Envoy Todd Stern" (Dec. 2, 2015), available online at https://2009-2017.state.gov/s/climate/releases/2015/250305.htm.
58 Bedford and Hugo, *Population Movement in the Pacific*, 50.
59 David J. Bier, "'Why Don't They Just Get in Line?' Barriers to Legal Immigration," *Cato Institute* (2021), available online at https://www.cato.org/testimony/why-dont-they-just-get-line-barriers-legal-immigration.

21
REFUGEES AND THE POLITICS OF (IN) HUMANITARIANISM

David Owen

21.1 Introduction

This chapter addresses the ethics of refugee protection in its contemporary context by focusing on the way in which the dominant humanitarian framing of refugees in popular and political discourse is constitutively open to exploitation by state's pursuing (what they take to be) their interests. Humanitarianism 'has become a language that inextricably links values and affects, and serves both to define and to justify discourses and practices of the government of human beings' (Fassin, 2011: 2), and this chapter traces the development of a strategy of exploiting humanitarian reasons to legitimate inhumane policies that are aimed at limiting state's exposure to obligations of protection (and whose effect is undermining of the institution of refugee protection) within the broader context of attempts at governing refugee movements through externalization policies and 'remote control' techniques.

It begins by sketching the features of 'humanitarian reason' before exploring how the operation of the international refugee regime has supported the rise of the humanitarian framing of refugees, where

> humanitarian' should be taken in an extended meaning, as connoting both dimensions encompassed by the concept of humanity: on the one hand the generality of human beings who share a similar condition (mankind), and on the other an affective movement drawing humans toward their fellows (humaneness).
>
> *(Fassin, 2011: 2)*

It then turns to examine the way in which internal features of 'humanitarian reason' provide opportunities for states to exploit humanitarian arguments to support inhumane policies. I will refer to this as 'politics of inhumanitarianism'. Having developed and illustrated this argument, I conclude by considering its implications for the future of global refugee protection and what alternative form of reason is required to resist it.

21.2 On Humanitarian Reason

How should we think about humanitarianism? As Fassin remarks:

> Humanitarian reason, by instituting the equivalence of lives and the equivalence of suffering, allows us to continue believing—contrary to the daily evidence of the realities that we encounter—in this concept of humanity which presupposes that all human beings are of equal value because they belong to one moral community. Thus humanitarian government has a salutary power for us because by saving lives, it saves something of our idea of ourselves, and because by relieving suffering, it also relieves the burden of this unequal world order.
>
> *(2011: 252)*

Humanitarianism seen as a natural expression of an ethics of empathy and politics of compassion towards the suffering of others thus affirms a form of global solidarity – precisely the kind of moral solidarity towards our fellows as vulnerable natural creatures that is often called for in relation to refugees. However, as Fassin notes, this politics of compassion is also 'a politics of inequality' in which those who offer assistance stand in an unequal political relation to those to whom aid is offered and this 'tension between inequality and solidarity, between a relation of domination and a relation of assistance, is constitutive of all humanitarian government' (2011: 3). Moreover, precisely because of the relations of equivalence that humanitarianism enacts:

> Humanitarian reason pays more attention to the biological life of the destitute and unfortunate, the life in the name of which they are given aid, than to their biographical life, the life through which they could, independently, give a meaning to their own existence.
>
> *(Fassin, 2011: 254)*

The relationship of domination within the relationship of assistance between those who save and those who suffer is a relationship between different orders of humanity, one cast in terms of leading a life and the other cast in terms of simply living. Refugees are not unaware of this difference. On the contrary, the emergence of the humanitarian picture of the refugee in the First World War was accompanied by the recognition of the cost of such a status:

> To be labelled a refugee had demeaning consequences, stripping away attributes of social distinction and class to leave oneself exposed to a sense of pure deprivation. The consequences of this silencing are eerily familiar to the modern reader. A Belgian refugee spoke from the heart when he summed up his feeling: 'One was always a refugee – that's the name one was given, a sort of nickname (sobriquet). One was left with nothing, ruined, and that's how people carried on talking about "the refugee". We weren't real people anymore.
>
> *(Gatrell, 2013: 49–50)*

In this context, we might suspect that there is a certain potential for inhumanity contained within humanitarian government or, perhaps better, that it is necessarily insufficient as an acknowledgment of the humanity of the other (think, for example, of those warehoused for years in refugee camps). This is not to condemn humanitarian practices and acts as such but to highlight the point that a politics of compassion cannot amount to a politics of dignity and, hence, that a critically self-reflective humanitarianism necessarily calls for its own transcendence.

Yet, the prevalence of the language, practices, and agents of humanitarianism in the contemporary field of refugee protection (and elsewhere) also raises another possibility, namely, the co-option of humanitarianism as a medium through which to enact and perform forms of inhumane treatment of asylum seekers and refugees – what I will call 'the politics of inhumanitarianism'. We can start to address this phenomenon by sketching the context within which this mode of politics emerges before turning to analyze the way in which its justificatory form takes advantage of a central tension within humanitarianism.

21.3 On the Politics of Inhumanitarianism

Consider three features of the contemporary refugee regime. The first is that the international refugee regime provides no mechanism for determining fair responsibility sharing among members of the international community. Rather it is limited to being organized around the strong norm of non-refoulement. The general upshot is, first, that while states, collectively, have an interest in the provision of the refugee protection (in some form), each state has an interest in being able to regulate (and this often means minimize) its own exposure to responsibilities of refugee protection and, second, states that border refugee-producing states are bound by the norm of non-refoulement to admit refugees, while distant states may enjoy considerable discretion over whether, to what extent, and in what ways to contribute to refugee protection. Of course, this might not be such a problem if the chances of being a state subject to spontaneous refugee flows from neighbors were evenly distributed, but they are not. Rather proximity to refugee-production, like refugee-production itself, is typically a product of durable patterns of global domination and disadvantage that are part of the continuing after-lives of European imperialisms. Consequently, for the most part, those states who produce, are in close proximity to, and bear the burdens of, significant refugee flows are postcolonial states.

The second feature is that the international response to refugees, significantly shaped by the history of UNHCR practice, has increasingly taken up a humanitarian picture of refugee protection. This decenters the focus on persecution in favor of a wider construal of forced displacement and hence of those for whom protection is required but, simultaneously, has involved a shift of focus from the refugee as a political subject of rights to the refugee as a humanitarian subject of needs. This is a shift not unrelated to the spread of the scope of refugeehood from Europe to encompass Asia and Africa, and, after 1969, to have global scope. This shift toward humanitarian reasons is further demonstrated by the expansion of the UNHCR's role in relation to displaced persons who remain inside their states of nationality – so-called 'internally displaced persons' (IDPs) – and, more recently, to address persons who are displaced by natural disasters (an issue that assumes increasing large proportions in the context of climate change). These are significant in practical terms with global numbers of IDPs being typically at least double those of refugees. What is important for our purposes, however, is that from the humanitarian standpoint, it is relatively straightforward to see why not only the situation of people who have crossed borders to flee generalized conditions of violence but also that of those who remain within a state characterized by such conditions demand our aid as long as it is not unreasonably burdensome for us to provide it. Just as the differentiation of those whose lives are endangered by persecution and those whose lives are endangered by the breakdown of public order appears morally arbitrary from a humanitarian perspective, so too does the differential treatment of either those outside and inside the state in question or those whose lives are threatened by natural disasters rather than human ones. Moral solidarity demands that we approach all of these persons as having the same kind of claim on us, and while there may be salient differences in terms of addressing those claims (for example, the dangers of trying to protect persons inside a state engaged in civil war), these are matters relating to the different burdens that may arise in the different situations rather than differences in the kinds of claim made on us.

The third feature is the development of the interaction of human rights law and the international refugee regime through the expanded principle of non-refoulement in which the norm of non-refoulement established in the Convention is extended to cover persons who do not fall under the Convention criteria of refugeehood but have human rights-based grounds not to be returned to their home state. Such 'complementary protection' is 'typically granted where the treatment feared does not reach the level of severity of "persecution," or where there is a risk of persecution but it is not linked to one of the Refugee Convention grounds' (McAdam, 2014: 204–205).

The interaction of these three features has given rise to a regime of refugee protection characterized by, first, the spread and intensification of externalization policies and techniques of remote-control by advantaged polities such as, for example, the USA, Australia, UK, and the EU; second, a de facto bargain in which states of the Global South take the vast majority of refugees in so long as states of the Global North provide (albeit inadequate) financial support and don't press human rights concerns; and, third, the confrontation of refugees with a limited and increasingly bad set of choices.

The point of externalization and remote-control practices on the part of advantaged states is to prevent or limit the access of asylum seekers to their territory since territorial presence is typically taken as the key trigger for the legal operation of the norm of non-refoulement in relation to claimants. Consider the EU for example:

> The system as currently devised appears to imply that, while pre-entry controls can operate extraterritorially, protection obligations arise only if potential beneficiaries present themselves at the (physical) borders of the EU and that no distinction is necessary at the pre-border stage between refugees and other migrants. It seems to be understood that pre-entry controls can be conducted independently from their (differential) impact on protection seeker rights. In this line, Hailbronner has argued that 'it is doubtful whether the principle of non-refoulement implies … a general duty of States to organize their entry and immigration, visa and transport legislation in such a way that potential political refugees may use their right to seek and enjoy asylum effectively'. He opines that '[a] legal duty arises only when and in so far as a potential refugee … has come within the scope of territorial jurisdiction of a State …'.
>
> *(Moreno-Lax, 2017: 247–8)*

This interpretation of the norm of non-refoulment can, and should, be contested (Moreno-Lax, 2017), but its current operational sway underwrites the political logic of externalization and the use of remote-control techniques to maintain the discretionary power of advantaged states and to limit their potential exposure with respect to asylum admissions. (The UK's current Illegal Migration Bill's proposals to make irregular entry a categorical reason, with very few exceptions, for transferring entrants to Rwanda for protection there and denying them any right to enter the UK in the future may be seen as an attempt to navigate even this constraint.) This political strategy is justified on the basis that humanitarian protection is available in the home region of refugees.

Of course, this might be less politically significant if opportunities for resettlement from states of initial refuge were widely available to refugees. However, given that they are not (and they currently run at around 1% of need), refugees are confronted with a situation in which safe legal routes to advantaged states are almost entirely denied to them. The immediate upshot of this situation is that the realistic choice set of refugees, as Serena Parekh (2020) has highlighted, is composed of three options:

1. Typically long-term residence in a refugee camp with very limited opportunities for shaping one's life.
2. Precarious lives in urban or peri-urban settings with a potentially wider range of opportunities but significant risks of exploitation, domination, and marginalization.
3. Dangerous journeys to advantaged states.

There are two points to notice about this condition.

The first is that it is inhuman in the dual sense of inhumanity (i.e., denying recognition of the other) and inhumane (i.e., an attitude expressing lack of compassion for the other) precisely because the options it offers make enjoying the ability to shape one's life conditional on risking that ability (up to and including risking one's life). The second is that it is unsurprising, given these circumstances, that some take up the third option and it is equally unsurprising, given the emergence of this travel market, that providers of border-crossing services arise to meet the demand. The rise of the smuggling industry is best seen as a response to the failure of the refugee protection regime to provide access to forms of protection in which refugees can coherently understand themselves as effective social and political agents able to navigate their environment and shape the development of their lives without incurring unreasonable risks.

The tragic irony of this development is not only that it increases the dangers of refugee journeys given that the illegality of border-crossing services means their supply is most likely (in many but not all contexts) to draw in providers already operating in zones of criminality, but also that this fact is, in turn, taken up and mobilized as a humanitarian reason for further intensification of externalization policies and technologies of remote-control. It is here that we enter the realm of the politics of inhumanitarianism.

An exemplary articulation of this politics is provided by the Australian Prime Minister Tony Abbot in 2015 as a part of his response to the charge by the UN special rapporteur on torture that Australia's refugee policy was in breach of its international commitments:

> The most humanitarian, the most decent, the most compassionate thing you can do is stop these boats because hundreds, we think about 1200 in fact, drowned at sea during the flourishing of the people smuggling trade under the former government.
> *(https://www.smh.com.au/politics/federal/tony-abbott-australians-sick-of-being-lectured-to-by-united-nations-after-report-finds-antitorture-breach-20150309-13z3j0.html)*

This rationale is one that has been embraced more recently by the EU in relation to Mediterranean sea crossings and by the UK in relation to boats crossing the Channel. Now, we may well wish to dismiss the use of this rationale as hypocritical, indeed cynical, political rhetoric, and no doubt there is much in favor of such a judgment, but to do so as if that were all that needs to be said would be to miss the significance of the fact that it is the language of humanitarianism that is used here and to occlude the character of the phenomenon in play. Let us then turn to address this phenomenon.

21.4 Exploiting Humanitarian Reason

We can start which what I will call 'justificatory inhumanitarianism': the rhetorical appeal to the language of humanitarianism to provide reasons (e.g., saving people from drowning) to support policies in which the exposure or subjection of those seeking irregular entry to inhumane treatment is presented as an unfortunate byproduct of the justified pursuit of humanitarian ends.

To explore the character of inhumanitarianism in this justificatory mode, we can begin by noting that humanitarian reason is situated within, and involves the negotiation of the tension between, two distinct justificatory poles, which we can gloss as a commitment to the view that humanitarianism means acknowledging that the suffering of each and every person matters in and of itself, and a commitment to the view that humanitarianism means aiming at the reduction of overall suffering. We might see the former commitment as one that pictures the humanitarian ideal as a constraint on action and that latter commitment as one that pictures the humanitarian ideal as a goal to which action is oriented.

A first feature of justificatory inhumanitarianism is its ability to take advantage of the tension within humanitarianism that arises with the recognition that a form of humanitarian government operating under the picture of the humanitarian ideal as constraint (i.e., addressing the distinct suffering of each and every life as mattering equally) may generate outcomes that are, in terms of the picture of the humanitarian ideal as a goal, bad. One way of negotiating this tension is to construct a distinction between 'naïve' and 'realistic' modes of humanitarianism – or, to borrow and adapt Weber's terms, a humanitarianism of conviction and a humanitarianism of responsibility. This distinction makes available a form of argument in which certain kinds of humanitarian practices can be represented as self-defeating. In the context of refugees, this takes the form of the argument that, for example, the operation of humanitarian search-and-rescue operations in the Mediterranean serves as a 'pull' factor that increases the numbers of people who are willing to undertake the journey with all the suffering and risks of death that it involves, and hence is liable to increase overall suffering and deaths. This was an objection already raised in relation to the Italian Mare Nostrum policy of 2013–2014 and following the withdrawal of state-based SAR activities has been extended to humanitarian NGOs. Thus, for example, as Cusumano and Villa note:

> As stated by the European Border and Coast Guard (still better known as Frontex), "SAR missions close to, or within, the 12-mile territorial waters of Libya ... influence smugglers' planning and act as a pull factor". Such operations may "unintentionally help criminals achieve their objectives at minimum cost, strengthening their business

model by increasing the chances of success. Migrants and refugees… attempt the dangerous crossing since they are aware of and rely on humanitarian assistance to reach the EU".

(Cusumano and Villa, 2019: 4)

The implication is that this kind of humanitarian conduct, while in one respect no doubt ethically admirable in its motivations is, in the overall context, ethically irresponsible.

A second feature of justificatory inhumanitarianism is its ability to take advantage of the tension within humanitarianism that arises with the recognition that a form of humanitarian government directed solely toward the goal of reducing overall suffering fails to acknowledge the importance of the distinction between persons, that is, that the suffering of each matters. Hence, it is liable to produce outcomes that are, from the standpoint of the picture of the humanitarian ideal as constraint, wrongful. One way of negotiating this tension is the construction of justifications for why some should be treated differently to others, that is, drawing a set of normative distinctions designed to distinguish those seeking irregular entry from the wider population of refugees and offering a moral justification of differential treatment in the service of reducing overall suffering.

An early example of this practice is the Australian introduction of the term 'queue-jumper' to describe those arriving by boat. The context here is that Australia operates an annual refugee resettlement quota (which was over 21,000 in 2016–2017 but down to under 14,000 in 2020–2021) and, given its geographical distance from refugee-producing states as well as its established visa regime, was historically reasonably well isolated from the issue of 'spontaneous arrivals'. Against this background, the Australian government was able, by presenting its contribution to refugee protection as fixed, to cast those asylum seekers aiming to arrive at its shores without humanitarian visas as cheating, attempting to queue jump rather than playing by the rules and, hence, as seeking to steal the place of more worthy refugees who are more worthy just in virtue of their respect for fair play.

In the case of the UK, a primary argument has concerned the fact that travel to the British Isles involves passing through EU states, most obviously France from where irregular Channel crossings, whether by boat or train, embark, and hence that those seeking irregular entry could and should have already claimed asylum in these safe states (an argument typically bolstered by a hyperlegal and obfuscatory reading of Art.31 of the Refugee Convention to support the claim that refugees should seek asylum in the first safe country they reach, an argument itself predicated on a humanitarian picture of refugees that stresses the biological over the biographical.) The normative work being done here is the suggestion that those seeking irregular entry are deliberately exploiting the refugee protection system for reasons that are unrelated to humanitarian protection and hence, in this respect, are akin to illegal economic migrants.

In these two cases, then a key part of the strategy is to introduce a hierarchy into the field of refugee protection that distinguishes those who conduct themselves appropriately according to what are presented as the relevant norms and those who's conduct breaches such norms. In neither case does this hierarchy simply deny that the latter are entitled to humanitarian protection, rather it exploits it as a reason for the denial of protection *here* by presenting 'protection here' as a rewarding wrongful conduct and doing so in a way that is encouraging others to imitate it, where this increase the risks of outcomes that are bad from a humanitarian perspective.

Justificatory inhumanitarianism thus deploys not just a humanitarian rhetoric but a form of argumentation that exploits tensions within the discourse of humanitarianism in order to legitimate its actions. We can also see elements of justificatory inhumanitarianism in EU policy with respect to Libya, but the overall legitimation strategy adopted here includes a further mode of humanitarian government in that it operates by outsourcing responsibility to, on the one hand, the Libyan coastguard with respect to search-and-rescue and, on the other hand, international humanitarian agencies with respect to protection of asylum seekers and refugees. This strategy shares the supply-side focus on 'stopping the boats' by disrupting the smuggler's model that also characterizes Australian and UK policy, but it combines this with directed funding to humanitarian agencies (rather than governments such as Nauru and Rwanda). Let us call this 'purposive inhumanitarianism', that is, the engagement of 'humanitarian' actors as a legitimation strategy. Thus, primarily through the EU Emergency Trust Fund for Africa, the EU has devoted approaching €500 million since 2015 to addressing migration-related issues in Libya, funding action by UNHCR, IOM, and a number of other humanitarian IOs and NGOs that have contributed substantially to the voluntary return of over 56,500 migrants to their countries of origin with reintegration support and the evacuation of more than 7,500 refugees and asylum seekers out of Libya. By outsourcing responsibility for humanitarian protection to agencies such as UNHCR that are largely dependent for their funding on the states that are asking them to take up this role, the EU can present itself as both committed to humanitarian protection and as standing at a distance from direct responsibility for the conditions confronted by asylum seekers and refugees.

Now we may, as I indicated earlier, be justifiably skeptical about just how much these governments care about the humanitarian protection of those seeking asylum compared to their main goal of sustaining their ability to exercise discretionary control over entry and hence limiting potential exposure to the triggering of non-refoulement obligations. On the contrary, we might reasonably see the inhumanity that asylum seekers and refugees experience as a product of these policies as part of their point. Thus, for example, Liz Thompson, a former migration agent involved in refugee-assessment interviews on Manus described the process as a 'farce', saying, 'Manus Island is an experiment in the ultimate logic of deterrence, designed to frustrate the hell out of people and terrify them so that they go home' (https://www.smh.com.au/politics/federal/riot-flared-as-manus-island-refugees-realised-lies-were-told-20140225-33ft3.html). The testimony of the poet-journalist Behrouz Boochani, who was interred on Manus Island for six years, in his memoir *No Friend But the Mountain* only reinforces this view. Similarly, we might think the sheer horror of the conditions of detained asylum seekers and refugees in Libya exposed by Sally Hayden's journalistic tour de force *My Fourth Time, We Drowned* aligns with the EU's focus via UNHCR and IOM of encouraging assisted voluntary returns or relocations to other African states such as Niger and Rwanda. Moreover, we might note that there is no empirically supported reason to believe that SAR NGO's act as a pull factor or that the continuing focus on supply-side interventions designed to disrupt the smuggler's business model has had, or is likely to have, any significant effect.

However, whether critics see the outcome-inhumanity of these policies as integral to them or as an unfortunate byproduct of them, and charge that the policies use of the language, practices, and agents of humanitarianism is cynical or hypocritical, the rhetoric that they deploy serves to channel the debate into, and reinforces, the humanitarian framework for the perception of refugee protection, mobilizing moral sentiments around the suffering of asylum seekers. In doing so, however, it serves to obstruct critical reflection on humanitarian reason itself.

21.4.1 Conclusion: Beyond Humanitarian Reason

Earlier I noted that a politics of compassion cannot amount to a politics of dignity and, hence, that a critically self-reflective humanitarianism necessarily calls for its own transcendence. Moreover, we may have reason to think that while, as Fassin (2011) argues, humanitarian reason has become a prevalent language for relating value and affect, we can also see what may be called 'dignitary reason' as an alternative way of linking value and affect in which it is not compassion for the suffering of another but rather indignation at the treatment of another that is the main driver of action. It is perhaps unsurprising that humanitarianism as a language of the advantaged should confront dignity as a language of the disadvantaged. Recall that it is a feature of humanitarian government that it is characterizes by an internal tension between a relation of inequality/domination and a relation of solidarity/assistance, and hence may itself be a target of indignation on the part of those positioned as beneficiaries of humanitarian policies precisely because they are not recognized as dignitary equals. A political ethics of refugee protection cannot simply challenge the forms of inhumanity currently being given expression within the terms of humanitarian reason; it must challenge this form of reasoning by building acknowledgment of human dignity into refugee protection.

Acknowledgments

My thanks to Sahar Akhtar for the invitation and editorial comments. A draft version of this chapter was presented as the Centre for Political Philosophy Annual Lecture at the University of Leiden in April 2023, and I am grateful to all present for their comments and questions.

References

Cusumano, E. & Villa, M., Sea rescue NGOs: a pull factor of irregular migration?, Policy Briefs, 2019/22, Migration Policy Centre - https://hdl.handle.net/1814/65024
Fassin, D. (2011) *Humanitarian Reason: A Moral History of the Present*, Berkeley: University of California Press.
Gatrell, P. (2013) *The Making of the Modern Refugee*. Oxford: Oxford University Press.
McAdam, J. 2014. 'Human Rights and Forced Migration'. In *The Oxford Handbook of Refugee and Forced Migration Studies* edited by E. Fiddian-Qasmiyeh, G. Loescher, K. Long & N. Sigona. Oxford: Oxford University Press, 203–214.
Moreno-Lax V (2017). The EU Humanitarian Border and the Securitization of Human Rights: The 'Rescue-Through-Interdiction/Rescue-Without-Protection' Paradigm. *Journal of Common Market Studies* 56,(1): 119–140. 10.1111/jcms.12651
Parekh, S (2020) No Refuge, Oxford: Oxford University Press.

PART VII
Immigration Enforcement

22
SHINING A LIGHT IN THE DARK
The Urgency of Addressing Immigration Detention in Normative Political Theory

Felix Bender and Stephanie J. Silverman

22.1 Introduction

Immigration detention presents core moral issues in the ethics of immigration to liberal, democratic countries. Detention of non-citizens for immigration-related purposes seems to have cemented into an integral part of the immigration control regime. It is a lynchpin in removal, settlement, admissions, and other practices that normative theorists take more seriously. But its mere presence does not make it *de facto* defensible. It is possible that many normative theorists are unaware of its violence; they would likely reject detention *if* they were more aware. Taking detention seriously matters for social and political thought, and for liberal life more generally.

This chapter focuses on Canada as a "best case" country. Canada boasts a limited and mostly rights-respecting detention system. Yet, this chapter also shows how this "best case" system presents cascading problems for migrant, racial, procedural, and fundamental justice. Canada, like other liberal democracies, keeps a relatively open hand to legalize and enact detention's violence, like separating children from their parents, incarcerating individuals without allowing them to exercise their basic rights, and deepening mental health issues and vulnerabilities (see Matthew Lister's chapter in this volume, "Children, Families, and Immigration Enforcement").

Normative theorists of immigration and citizenship pay insufficient attention to the time and space of borders and immigration enforcement mechanisms, and their impacts on individuals (Little 2015; McNevin 2011; Silverman 2014). Likewise, policies and laws create the nuts and bolts of detention, while normative theorists rarely devote the time to drilling down into the mechanics (see Sager 2016 and Lister 2023 for exceptions). As we shall see, if we want to know whether immigration detention can be defensible from a "deterrent" perspective or within an all-things-considered framework, we must look at "who" is subjected to detention. As soon as we do, we find that a racialized form of discrimination sits at the center of such practices.

We begin this chapter by providing an overview of immigration detention in Canada. This case study shows how even the "best" system is violent, causes great harm, fails to reach stated immigration policy goals, and is not morally defensible. We then discuss how detention figures within normative political theory and why it matters to studying immigration from a theoretical lens. Finally, we offer pathways to advance discussion on the roles of detention in normative political theory, thereby enhancing public and social thought and potentially creating more ethical immigration policymaking.

22.2 Legislating and Governing Immigration Detention

Detention policies, laws, and practices materialize in both dense and porous ways, making it tricky to study. Lacking a legal definition, we can understand immigration detention as incarcerating noncitizens for immigration-related reasons or to otherwise hasten the resolution of their immigration statuses. Detention's purported goals are by and large to enable removals of people with no right to remain, and to fortify the border against new arrivals; interdict overseas, or contract other states or offshore border agents to intercept migrants in transit; and hold and sort newcomers while their identities and claims are determined.

International instruments affirm the primacy of liberty rights for all humans regardless of citizenship, nationality, or migratory status. The Magna Carta, the Habeas Corpus Acts of England, and the French Declaration of the Rights of Man and the Citizen inscribe the right to liberty.[1] International human rights law, customary norms, and other legal instruments set guardrails on detention; since detention is an administrative, federal power, and seen as a sovereign prerogative, however, international standards are difficult to enforce in practice (Wilsher 2012).

The Canadian detention system is comprised of an amalgam of laws and legislation, internal guidance, jurisprudence, and norm-setting rules. Immigration law is housed in administrative law, and administrative law "sees" immigration detention as "holding" noncitizens. As such, detention policymaking professes no rehabilitative, integrative, or other social betterment purpose beyond preventing someone from absconding or otherwise avoiding a deportation. Most liberal countries approach asylum seekers and other migrants as threats to national security and governance and not as potential community members, with detention purposely resembling or mimicking criminal imprisonment (Mainwaring and Cook 2018).

In Canada, the federal Canada Border Services Agency (CBSA) oversees the architecture of the detention system. CBSA's responsibilities include arresting, holding, and recommending the release of noncitizens at the ports of entry and inside the territory. During the 2018-2019 fiscal year, before the COVID-19 pandemic, CBSA officials detained 8781 foreign nationals, with an average of 342 people detained each day who spent an average of 13.8 days in detention (CBSA 2020). Most longer-term detention in Canada occurs at the "back-end" or pre-deportation. In this way, the Canadian system deviates from the "front-end" detention made notorious through Donald Trump's "Zero Tolerance" policy of separating and detaining families seeking asylum at the US southern border. CBSA works in partnership with the local and provincial police, and the federal Royal Canadian Mounted Police. Adjudication or quasi-judicial oversight is the purview of the adjudicators at the Immigration Division of the Immigration and Refugee Board (IRB) tribunal.

Since 2000, at least sixteen immigration detainees have died while in custody and the number of deaths climbs even higher if you account for deaths after release from detention. On December 8, 2011, Jan Szamko became the first immigration detainee to die in a Canadian facility. A 31-year-old Romani national from the Czech Republic, Mr. Szamko came to Canada in November 2008 to join his wife and their 9-year-old daughter. Upon arrival, Mr.

Szamko claimed refugee status based on persecution by Neo-Nazis in the Czech Republic. After learning that his mother had fallen gravely ill, Mr. Szamko abandoned his refugee claim intending to return to the Czech Republic to see her, but his mother died before he could make arrangements to leave Canada. Although he re-applied soon after, the IRB refused his asylum claim and he was summoned for deportation. CBSA arrested and detained Mr. Szamko after missing two appointments. Canada detained Mr. Szamko for 11 days before his death in the Toronto West Detention Centre from an undiagnosed fluid buildup that compressed his heart, lowered his blood pressure, and shut down his bodily functions. During his last three days in detention, Mr. Szamko was in extreme physical distress. Guards noted that he was lying on the floor, and often covered in urine and feces. While in detention, nurses, two family physicians, and a psychiatrist evaluated his condition but did not find any acute medical issues. Instead, Mr. Szamko was deemed to be uncooperative, "good to fly," and faking illness. He died in his segregation cell in still covered in his own feces and urine (See Razack 2021; Silverman 2013; Silverman and Molnar 2016).

More recently, on January 28, 2022, Bryan Arthur Stone, a 56-year-old American citizen and father, died by suicide in detention at the Quebec IHC. While CBSA refused to release details about the case, the media accessed the Quebec coroner's investigation. The report stated that a "stressed and sad" Mr. Stone warned he would kill himself if he were deported and separated from his son. He had attempted suicide four days earlier, and in response, CBSA placed him in solitary confinement. The report concludes that "this death could have been avoidable." A long-time Quebec resident, Mr. Stone had been in immigration detention for 53 days at the time of his death (Fortier 2023).

Canada does not observe a legal time limit on individual periods of detention.[2] Instead, Canadian legislation sets out a system of statutory bail hearings, known as detention reviews or hearings, which is unique in the world. The hearings take place after 48 hours in immigration custody, then 7 days, and then every 30 days until release or removal. An IRB member presides over the hearings. In 2018-2019, 85% of detainees were held because CBSA deemed them unlikely to appear for an immigration or admissibility hearing (Durrani 2020). The average length of detention increased during the first period of COVID19 lockdowns (April–September 2020), more than doubling to 29 days compared with that period in the previous year. Of these, at least 85 people were detained for 100 days or more (Shantz 2023). Detention usually leads to release back into Canada, or removal from Canada.

CBSA detains people in its own designated medium-security facilities, known as immigration holding centers (IHCs), as well as in subcontracted police cells and provincial prisons. The IHCs are found near international airports in Toronto, Montreal, and Surrey, British Columbia (near Vancouver). IHCs feature barbed-wire fences, CCTV surveillance, and uniformed guards who survey and control detainees' movements. IHCs tend to have poor ventilation, lack hygiene products, and supply limited access to medical care (Gros and Muscati 2020). Detainees share rooms and eat meals together.

CBSA transfers about 20% to one-third of detainees to provincial prisons. Between April 2017 and March 2020, roughly 20% of detainees were incarcerated in 78 provincial jails across Canada. During the first months of the COVID19 pandemic (April–September 2020), this proportion *increased* to 50% of the detainee population while the overall population decreased (Shantz 2023). Most long-term detention cases of +99 days take place in Ontario prisons, and they are male and minority-identified (Silverman 2021: 174–175). CBSA pays provincial correctional authorities a daily cost per person ranging from $184

CDN in Quebec to $258 in Ontario to $448.69 in New Brunswick. Immigration detainees must wear prison garb, abide by prison policies, and endure overcrowding, lockdowns, restraints, inadequate mental health care, limited access to counsel, and barriers to outside family contact. People "routinely have their bodies and cells searched by guards, may be reliant on problematic videoconferencing technologies to 'link' to their in-person detention hearings, and are usually re-located further away from their networks of support than the IHCs" (Silverman and Kaytaz 2022: 5).

Detainees describe prisons and IHCs as sites where overcrowding and abysmal conditions ease the spread of disease and viruses (Jeovany 2018; Gros and Muscati 2020; Gros and van Groll 2015; Leung et al. 2019; Trovall 2019). Detainees in Canada and elsewhere consistently describe their confinements as stigmatizing and traumatic events (Abji 2020; Gros and Muscati 2020; Gros and van Groll 2015; Kennedy 2017; Keung 2017; Kronick, Rousseau, and Cleveland 2016). Mental health issues negatively affect detainees long after their custodial periods have ended (Cleveland, Rousseau, and Kronick 2012; Cleveland and Rousseau 2013). One teenager recounted her weeklong detention in Canada as follows: "It's not just that week. It stays with you all your life. It is horrible. I don't think anyone deserves to be in a holding centre. It is jail ... I am still very scared when I see a police officer. I hear someone knocking really hard and I think of what happened. I have flashbacks." (PressProgress 2018). Families report ongoing emotional distress, such as separation anxiety, selective mutism, sleep difficulties, and post-traumatic symptoms in their children after release from detention (Kronick, Rousseau, and Cleveland 2011, 2016). Staff testify to the trauma and emotional damage from working "on the inside" of immigration detention facilities (Anonymous 2016; Bosworth and Slade 2014; Conlon, Hiemstra, and Mountz 2017; Hall 2012; Hasham 2016; Ugelvik 2016).

Detainees have organized hunger strikes and other events across Canadian and other sites; they are drawing focus away from their presumed criminality and onto the inhumane conditions and procedural and natural injustices that typify their – and other prisoners' – plights. In 2016, for example, about 50 detainees at two Ontario correctional centers went on a hunger strike. They were demanding a meeting with the CBSA head to press their case for a 90-day time limit on detention. The strike lasted at least 2 weeks. At the time, Mr. Richard Abuwa had been detained for 27 months awaiting removal to Nigeria. He had immigrated to Canada as a child but repeated run-ins with the law triggered withdrawal of his residency status, rendering him ineligible for Canadian citizenship and legally removable. The CBSA deemed him a flight risk and detained him in a provincial jail: "It's a jail. No jails are fun. To me, it feels like I'm in segregation and living in a cage like an animal, treated like an animal, and then they expect me to behave rationally. It's not right. It's not fair" (CBC News 2016).

22.3 An Intersectional and Settler Colonial Analysis of Who Becomes "detainable"

Critical migration scholarship shows how countries in North America and Europe limit or curtail access to citizenship and belonging for people marginalized as Others (Bashford and Strange 2002; Chan 2005; de Noronha 2019; Silverman and Kaytaz 2022). Raced, classed, gendered, ableist, neoliberal, and post/neo-colonial biases feed into constructs of who deserves settlement and citizenship, and, conversely, who can be arrested, detained, and deported from the state's territory (Bosworth and Turnbull 2014; Gibney 2013; Mainwaring and Silverman 2017; Mountz 2020). Procedural and natural justice barriers impede equality and fairness for current and former detainees in North America (Goldring, Berinstein, and Bernhard 2009; Silverman and Kaytaz 2022) as in Europe (Bhatia 2020; Bosworth 2014). The association between more immigrants and crime has persisted despite the conclusions of numerous North American studies demonstrating that immigrants are significantly less likely to be involved in criminal behavior (Alladin and Hummer 2022; Jung 2020p; Orrenius and Zavodny 2019). Detention blurs or confuses the normative binaries separating immigration and criminal justice, leading to a moral acquiescence toward criminalizing low-income and minoritized populations.

An intersectional and settler colonial analysis reveals how racism, sexism, ableism, and heteronormativity insidiously order detention. Black feminist legal scholar Kimberlé Williams Crenshaw (1991, 1245) offers the term "intersectionality" to capture "the need to account for multiple grounds of identity when considering how the social world is constructed." An intersectional framework can connect groups and causes without dominating or occluding important differences. Intersectional frameworks create spaces to negotiate "tensions between assertions of multiple [identities] and the ongoing necessity of group politics" (Crenshaw 1991, 1296). An intersectional focus reveals how laws, policies, regulations, and practices understand and discipline racialized and immigrant bodies and identities. People experience immigration control and citizenship allocation mechanisms differentially across axes of identities, particularly during the neoliberal epoch.

In Canada, it is the "settler community that shapes the nation by enacting immigration policy that selects newcomers with particular attributes, while the longer-established Aboriginal community has no say in who is selected" (Aiken and Silverman 2022). Following Patrick Wolfe's (1999) framework, settler colonialism is not a historic event or occurrence but a condition of structural violence shaping race, gender, class, and sexual formations (see, also, Bhungalia 2018; Glenn 2015). Under the banners of nationhood and law, settler colonialism works with racial capitalism to legitimate and unjustly apportion access to land, property, human rights, and citizenship. Glenn argues that "colonial projects simultaneously structure, race, class and sexual relations between colonists and the colonized." The settler colonial framework both complements and deepens intersectional methodologies or standpoints (Glenn 2015, 55). Nation-building projects instrumentalize immigrants to further oppress Indigenous peoples. Laws and policies have long cast out racialized members from the rights of citizenship (Ngai 2004). Detention and its earlier incarnations of quarantine, residential schools, and internments played important roles of de-mobilization, arrest, isolation, stigmatization, criminalization, and banishment from the social and legal community. An intersectional and settler colonial framework makes clear that supposedly neutral immigration and citizenship policies – like who is "detainable" – embed violence into supposedly neutral programs.

Immigration detention ensures the "centrality of criminalization in the process of racially organizing society" (Escobar 2016: 59–60; see also Alexander 2012; Chan 2005; Golash-Boza 2016; Silverman and Kaytaz 2022). Detention laws and policies intertwine illegality and criminality with poverty and racialization (Benslimane and Moffette 2019; Dauvergne 2013; Stumpf 2006). An intersectional standpoint also forces the recognition that policing, detention, and deportation apparatuses support a settler colonial vision of citizenship and belonging in Canada. It also reveals that abuses, experiences of criminalization and stigmatization, and even death are not aberrations but part and parcel of how prisons are supposed to work (Aiken and Silverman 2022; Lydon 2016; Ware and Dias 2014).

Put simply, acquiescence to the harmful conditions of detention would not be acceptable if they were occurring to citizens in prisons. As Chacón (2017: p. 252) argues, "Conduct that gets a warning on college campuses can get you arrested, convicted, and deported [especially] in heavily policed, low-income neighborhoods." The cascading harms of indefinite detention far outweigh the administrative law infractions for which they are being inflicted. Detention creates "perpetual foreigners, as outside the 'we' of the 'imagined community' of the nation". An extremely harmful tautology emerges: immigrants are detainable because they are less rights-bearing than citizens; since immigrants are less rights-bearing, they become always-detainable and their abuse at the hands of the state matters less.

Related to the removed positionality adopted by many normative theorists, theorists need to address immigrants' rights and immigration justice alongside racial justice. A prime illustration is the tendency for normative theorists to refer to "the migrant" when discussing personal and ground rights [see, e.g., Miller (2016: 57) on "selecting some migrants and excluding others"; or Rajendra (2015) on "the migrant" and "migrant networks"]. Such facially neutral characterizations are political choices that obscure lived realities of racism and discriminate enforcement. Canada shows this well: while Black people (people of African descent) amount to around 8% of Toronto's population and 2% of the Canadian population, they fit the profile of almost all high-profile detainees in Canada. Police agencies consistently subject Black communities to high levels of social scrutiny, securitization, and surveillance (Berns-McGown 2013; Meng, Giwa, and Anucha 2015; Silverman 2021). As discursive links in a chain connecting immigration to criminality, the hyper-surveillance of racialized communities connects to anti-immigrant and tough-on-crime populism in Canada (e.g., Benslimane and Moffette 2019; Silverman 2021; Walia and Chu 2015). Racial, immigration, and prison justice are in fact deeply intertwined (e.g., Aiken and Silverman 2022), and normative theorists must go much further in disassembling and reassembling the intersections in their own studies.

22.4 The False Deterrent

Many normative political theorists do not rule out the admissibility of more closed borders. Some argue for it more directly than others, and many for different reasons, ranging from the preservation of cultural identity to the preservation of democratic rule and decision-making, all the way to the defense of individual rights and national economic safeguards at the expense of the economic wellbeing of non-nationals (For a small selection, see: Macedo 2007; Miller 2005; 2016; Walzer 1983; Wellman 2008; Whelan 1988). What the moral defense for possibly more closed borders does have in common is its seeming acceptance of detention. This group might be inclined to advocate for a more measured form of detention but not its elimination. They might maintain that the immigration enforcement bureaucracy should not subject detainees to prison's inevitable structural harms;[3] but detention could deter future (unwanted) migrants. Some policymakers likewise "assume detention deters future migration by projecting a transnational message of non-welcome via the bodies of detained and deported migrants" (Conlon et al. 2017: p. 148; see, also, Mainwaring and Silverman 2017). In the Canadian context, the Conservative Government of Stephen Harper repeatedly stoked the flames of fear that two boats ferrying Sri Lankan refugees to Canada would usher in draconian mandatory detention laws as a "deterrent" for future refugees coming to Canada (Mountz 2020: Chapter 5; Silverman 2013; Taylor 2015).

There is a subclass of deterrent justifications that may also appeal to normative theorists. We call this the "leaky boats" argument: in their searches for a better life, people are sometimes compelled to resort to contracting with traffickers and smugglers[4] or otherwise entering a "leaky boat" to undertake perilous journeys in unsafe vessels; some policymakers propose that it is their (or our?) duty in the Global North to discourage or protect these faceless masses of people hailing from the Global South from boarding leaky boats (or overcrowded trains, the backs of lorries, etc.). One means to discourage people from taking these routes is deploying the threat of mandatory detention.

Using detention to deter people from seeking asylum, however, is illegal and ineffective, no matter the concern for the dangers along the route. This is because the border is the only place to request asylum outside of an embassy or through the under-resourced UNHCR. Further, deterring people from reaching the border by threatening detention infringes their basic rights, including to self-determination and to seek asylum (Sampson 2015; Silverman and Molnar 2019). In line with Kantian principles of respect for individual human dignity, detention cannot be used as an unproven mechanism to dissuade future or would-be migrants from coming (Sampson 2015).

Moreover, and put plainly, this normative defense falls apart because detention does *not* work to deter inflows, decrease permanent settlement, or increase "voluntary" deportations (Alden 2017; Czaika and De Haas 2013; Golash-Boza 2015; Massey and Pren 2012*)*. Walls, fences, closed borders, and mandatory detention regimes are "known to lead to greater permanence in migration, as the possibility of 'circular migration' which enables people to move back and forth and retain strong links with their families, is removed" (Crawley et al. 2016: 73). Detention centers cannot and do not promote safety and security in local communities (Branche 2011; Guttin 2010; Hansen and Papademetriou 2014). While punitive border control measures like detention may be correlated to short-term decreases in inflows, such temporary abeyance is not a stoppage but a re-routing along more dangerous corridors that are often controlled by smugglers or traffickers. These corridors also lie along natural danger zones, such as the deserts, the mountains, the rivers, or the seas. These "natural perils" veil the complicity of the Global North: when a person dies from thirst in the desert, border guards do not bear the burden of justifying the suffering *en route* to the border (see, e.g., Amnesty International 2015; Kaytaz 2021; Last et al. 2017; Missbach 2021; Reitano, Adal, and Shaw 2014; Williams and Mountz 2016). Detention will fail as a deterrent mechanism because migration, particularly forced migration, is a complex, multi-level, natural phenomenon whose social, economic, and political determinants far outweigh any domestic immigration policy.

22.5 Discussion: Where Does Detention Fit into Normative Theory?

One normative interpretation of the Canadian "best case" would understand detention as obviously wrong. As a form of incarceration, detention violates fundamental human rights of prisoners and all people seeking asylum. These scholars would likely argue that no form of migration should be illegalized. Transnational borders should be open for anyone who wants to cross them and settle (Oberman 2017; Sager 2018). Since any form of state exclusion is wrong, detention is obviously wrong.

A second normative interpretation is what, exactly, the state owes to people making special claims for refugee protection. Some normative arguments for a right to exclude noncitizens flow from grounding sovereignty in territoriality and the moral worth of nationally delineated community (Miller 2016; Stilz 2011; see, also, Fine 2013). This position excepts temporary protection within the territory (e.g., Abizadeh 2016; Brock 2020; Walzer 1983). These theorists are parsing out who is "the refugee" from the much larger category of "the migrant." The intention is that the community *should* allow some refugees to enter, and eventually allow this minority-within-the-minority to apply for permanent membership in the nation (see, e.g., Kukathas 2016; Lister 2012, 2014). The act of distinguishing the refugee from the migrant mob is imbued with moral worth. Thus, justifying checks on who someone is to determine if they can enter, would flow from this position.

Yet, the paucity of attention to detention demonstrates that normative theorists focus too much on parsing the refugee from the migrant: theorists assume wrongly that identity checks are a normatively defensible *means* to get to the defensible *end* of admitting the refugees. Normative theory focuses on who gets in, not what happens to people who are waiting in spaces like detention centers to find out if they pass the test. This line of argument has, by and large, sidestepped the practicalities of what happens during key decision-making processes that take place in time and space.

A third normative interpretation is that detention is *not* wrong. By this, we do not mean that scholars endorse imprisonment of innocent people. We are saying that such theories *interpret* detention as an unfortunate cog in the larger wheel of immigration governance systems. Normative theorists stay silent because they see the *moral* problems as lying elsewhere, above, or before detention occurs. Without touching on detention, these theories probe the ethics of how much or how far to support states that guard, defend, and regulate their borders (Blake 2013; Wellman 2011, 2014; Miller 2007, 2013). With their minds focused on the question of rightness, these theorists support a moral right to exclude but fail to reckon with the violence needed to realize that right. Accordingly, they glide over the technicalities of what it means to grant states a right to remove people from their territories (see, e.g., Fine 2017). The dictum of the state's right to exclude requires a deportation machine and its handmaiden, detention. Yet, such theories depend on the idea that detention is a morally regrettable thing only IF it is also proportional.

If normative theorists' answer is not to ignore the existence of detention, how else can the two be combined into a less problematic normative framework? One argument would lead in the direction of more diverse forms of control. The state, if not allowed to detain those it wishes to exclude, will work toward innovating other forms of control over noncitizens. Only the frontiers of technological progress can limit such an imaginary of control. Indeed, the Canadian state is already using electronic monitoring, regular visits by the police, and voice-recognition software to track noncitizens. Whether such measures are not in themselves morally problematic is highly questionable. If detention is morally wrong because it unduly restricts human rights in a disproportionate way to their actions (of movement), then it seems hard to justify the state's large-scale and longer-term surveillance. This would involve unprecedented intrusions into the private sphere, implying monitoring not only movement but also social and political association of citizens and migrants.

This is exactly the wrong direction. The problem of detention as an amoral reaction to immigration decision-making must not be resolved by adding and justifying added layers of control and monitoring. A better reaction to the problem of detention is demanding that the state retreat. If forms of state control in these cases lead to harms, discrimination, and so forth, then perhaps the answer is that the state should not have such formidable powers to regulate admissions. This would open the door to a liberal reaction to immigration control: The idea is that there are hard limits to the degree of control the states can exert over individuals. Law or other forces must curtail the state's power where it leads to undue infringement on individual rights. Non-citizenship ought not to sway a liberal account. From a human rights framework, the "price tag" for a strategic retreat and toward a more morally defensible framework is not high: fewer controls would mean a less effective deportation machine.

Another way that taking detention more seriously could improve the normative political theory of immigration is by changing the theory's points of departure. Many theories on territory, nationalism, and immigration control are rooted in methodological nationalism – the idea that one should begin with thinking through the lens of the nation-state. This viewpoint or method takes the nation-state as the primary social and political unit of relevance. Such theories operate almost exclusively at the ontological and methodological level of the territorial state (as opposed to the individual, the family, the kinship network, the nomadic clan, etc.). Such a boundary limits scholars to thinking from the state's point of view (and not, to underline, from the views of people on the move). A starting point rooted in methodological nationalism prioritizes who gets in, whose movements are criminalized, and how best to discipline migrant bodies. Focusing on detention would require a more nuanced evaluation of migrants and immigration, asking not only what is just for states but what is just for migrants as well.

22.6 Conclusions

Immigration detention is inherently harmful, with lifetime pains germinating from brief periods of incarceration. Detention is not a proportional reaction to the transgression of irregular forms of immigration. Detention bears the mark of arbitrary discrimination. Detention has calcified into a cog in the misshapen wheel of contemporary immigration enforcement *and* yet it is morally wrong.

Normative theorists need to correct their blind spots on detention and its place in immigration ethics. As this study shows, even the "best-case" detaining state of Canada is normatively indefensible. There can be no such thing as an ideal form of detention that avoids being morally wrong. Ingrained in the very functioning and idea of detention is the harm of its subjects, the disproportionality to infractions of the law (which are only administrative and not criminal in nature), and a racialized form of discrimination. Whatever conflict occurs between rights on paper versus rights in practice, detention exemplifies how the outcome skews in favor of the community of citizens in morally abhorrent and indefensible ways.

By deleting detention from the calculus of moral acceptability of immigration control and borders, normative theory scholarship diminishes or removes from sight the pressing harms and violence of detention. When the leading intellectual lights are dark on a topic, the implication is that it is not worthy of time and attention. Fewer students will learn about detention. Detention will not be featured in books or textbooks, public opinion pieces or philosophical debates. The insight revealed by the intersectional and settler colonial lens is that the violence of detention is meted out to Others cast out from the community of citizens, and illuminates how policy, law, practice, scholarship, and the wider Anglo-American political and philosophical culture are soaking in a misunderstanding about the appropriateness of detention in liberal societies. It is time for normative theorists to turn the lights back on and take detention seriously when discussing the ethics of immigration control.

Notes

1 Modern international law promulgated the right to liberty in Article 9 of the Universal Declaration of Human Rights, and Article 9 of the International Covenant on Civil and Political Rights. Soft law and many treaties and conventions subsequently inscribed the right to be free from arbitrary incarceration, including but not exclusive to noncitizens. Silverman and Molnar (2019) cite the following documents: Universal Declaration of Human Rights, Articles 3, 7, and 9. Online. Available at www.un.org/en/universal-declaration-human-rights; International Covenant on Civil and Political Rights, Article 9(1). Online. Available at www.ohchr.org/en/professionalinterest/pages/ccpr.aspx; UN Human Rights Committee's General Comment 35. Online. Available at www.ohchr.org/EN/HRBodies/CCPR/Pages/GC35-Article9LibertyandSecurityofperson.aspx; UN General Assembly's Body of Principles for the Protection of All Persons under Any Form of Detention or Imprisonment, Principle 2. Online. Available at www.ohchr.org/Documents/ProfessionalInterest/bodyprinciples.pdf; European Convention on Human Rights, Article 5(1); UN Refugee Convention, Article 31. Online. Available at www.ohchr.org/en/professionalinterest/pages/statusofrefugees.aspx; Migrant Worker Convention, Article 16(1) Online. Available at www.ohchr.org/en/professionalinterest/pages/cmw.aspx; UN Declaration on the Human Rights of Individuals Who Are Not Nationals of the Country in Which They Live, Article 5(1)(a). Online. Available at www.un.org/documents/ga/res/40/a40r144.htm; Organization of African Unity, African Charter on Human and Peoples' Rights, also known as the Banjul Charter, Article 6. Online. Available at www.achpr.org/instruments/achpr; Organization of American States, American Convention on Human Rights, Article 7(1). Online. Available at www.cidh.oas.org/basicos/english/basic3.american%20convention.htm; Organization of American States, American Declaration on the Rights and Duties of Man, Article 1. Online. Available at www.cidh.oas.org/Basicos/English/Basic2.american%20Declaration.htm; Council of the League of Arab States, Arab Charter on Human Rights, Article 14. Online. Available at http://hrlibrary.umn.edu/instree/loas2005.html; UN High Commissioner for Refugees, Detention Guidelines, "Introduction." Online. Available at www.unhcr.org/en-us/publications/legal/505b10ee9/unhcr-detention-guidelines.html. See also Amnesty International UK Section, "A Matter of Routine: The Use of Immigration Detention in the UK," 2017. Available at www.amnesty.org.uk/files/2017-2/A%20Matter%20Of%20Routine%20ADVANCE%20COPY.PDF?ya06n1Z2uH6J0bP8HmO7R2Pn7nabDymO= (all accessed 22 December 2018).
2 The problem of indefinite detention is not unique to Canada. Australia, too, can keep foreigners locked up under immigration powers indefinitely and tends to hold people for many years while processing their refugee claims. In the US, immigration authorities can continually extend the period of confinement, so long as they bring it back to court.
3 As Scott (2015: p. 59) puts it in a discussion of prison violence,

> Rather than a perverse or pathological aberration, institutionally structured violence is an inevitable everyday feature of prison life. Permanent, ubiquitous, and operating independently of direct human action or intention, institutionally structured violence slowly but surely eats into people "from their insides out" and forms the bedrock upon which physical violence takes root.

4 In a June 2020 speech, for example, US President Donald J. Trump linked the migrants' own security to that of citizens and public confidence in the border wall, the detention system, and interdiction agreements in the Northern Triangle. President Trump's speech reads, in part: "we are also closing loopholes that have served as magnets over the last three years, enticing migrants to take a very dangerous journey north to the U.S. and enter our country illegally. We have entered into a number of game-changing agreements with our Northern Triangle partners to stem the flow of illegal migrants as well… we're seeing more and more migrants being turned around at Mexico's southern border before they reach our own. We're also addressing abuse. of the asylum system, clamping down on the use of frivolous asylum claims to illegally obtain work authorization here in the U.S. And we're also disrupting and dismantling dangerous cartels by using the unique capabilities of the United States Coast Guard as well as the United States Navy. And we're attacking these criminals where they're most vulnerable, and that's at the sea." (White House Briefings 2020)

References

Abizadeh, Arash. 2016. "The Special-Obligations Challenge to More Open Borders." In *Migration in Political Theory*, edited by S Fine and L Ypi, 105–124. Oxford: Oxford University Press.

Abji, Salina. 2020. "Punishing Survivors and Criminalizing Survivorship: A Feminist Intersectional Approach to Migrant Justice in the Crimmigration System." *Studies in Social Justice* 14 (01): 67–89.

Aiken, Sharry, and Stephanie J. Silverman, eds. 2022. *A World Without Cages: Bridging Immigration and Prison Justice*. Routledge.

Alden, Edward. 2017. "Is Border Enforcement Effective? What We Know and What It Means." *Journal on Migration and Human Security* 5 (02): 481–490.

Alexander, Michelle. 2012. *The New Jim Crow: Mass Incarceration in the Age of Colorblindness*. New York City: New Press.

Alladin, Terrence A., and Don Hummer. 2022. "Immigrant and Citizen Reincarceration in Pennsylvania." *American Journal of Criminal Justice* 47: 547–566.

Amnesty International. 2015. *Europe's Gatekeeper: Unlawful Detention and Deportation of Refugees from Turkey*. London: Amnesty International.

Anonymous. 2016. "I wish I'd never decided to work in an immigration detention centre." Last Modified 14 March, Accessed 17 March. https://www.politics.co.uk/blog/2016/03/14/i-wish-id-never-decided-to-work-in-an-immigration-detention-centre/.

Bashford, Alison, and Carolyn Strange. 2002. "Asylum-Seekers and National Histories of Detention." *Australian Journal of Politics and History* 48 (4): 19.

Bauder, Harald. 2016. "Possibilities of Urban Belonging." *Antipode* 48 (2): 252–271. doi:10.1111/anti.12174.

Benslimane, Souheil, and David Moffette. 2019. "The Double Punishment of Criminal Inadmissibility for Immigrants." *Journal of Prisoners on Prisons* 28: 1–22.

Berns-McGown, Rima. 2013. "I Am Canadian": Challenging Stereotypes About Young Somali Canadians. In *IRPP Study No. 38*. Montreal: Institute for Research on Public Policy.

Bhatia, Monish. 2020. "Crimmigration, Imprisonment and Racist Violence: Narratives of People Seeking Asylum in Great Britain." *Journal of Sociology* 56 (1): 36–52.

Bhungalia, L. 2018. "Governing Banishment: Settler Colonialism, Territory, and Life in an Econ-Omy of Death." In *Handbook on the Geographies of Power*, edited by M. Coleman and J. Agnew, 313–331. London: Edward Elgar Publishing.

Blake, Michael. 2013. "Immigration, Jurisdiction, and Exclusion." *Philosophy and Public Affairs* 41 (02): 103–130.

Bosworth, Mary, and Gavin Slade. 2014. "In Search of Recognition: Gender and Staff–Detainee Relations in a British Immigration Removal Centre." *Punishment & Society* 16 (02): 169–186.

Bosworth, Mary, and Sarah Turnbull. 2014. "Immigration Detention, Punishment, and the Criminalization of Migration." In *The Routledge Handbook on Crime and International Migration*, edited by Sarah Pickering and Julie Hamm. Aldershot: Routledge.

Bosworth, Mary. 2014. *Inside Immigration Detention*. Oxford: Oxford University Press.

Branche, Afton. 2011. *The Cost of Failure: The Burden of Immigration Enforcement in America's Cities*. Washington, DC: The Drum Major Institute for Public Policy.

Brock, Gillian. 2020. *Justice for People on the Move: Migration in Challenging Times*. Cambridge: Cambridge University Press.

Canadian Red Cross. 2019. Annual Monitoring Activity Report: Monitoring Period - September 2017 to March 2018. In *Immigration Detention Monitoring Program (IDMP)*.

CBC News. 2016. "Immigration detainee held in Ontario jail 'treated like an animal'" *As It Happens*. https://www.cbc.ca/radio/asithappens/as-it-happens-friday-edition-1.3691294/updated-immigration-detainee-held-in-ontario-jail-treated-like-an-animal-1.3691298. Accessed 02 January 2022.

Chacon, Jennifer M. 2017. "Immigration and the Bully Pulpit." *Immigration and Nationality Law Review*, 130: 243–268.

Chan, Wendy. 2005. "Crime, Deportation and the Regulation of Immigrants in Canada." *Crime, Law & Social Change* 44: 153–180.

Chimni, B.S. 2000. "Globalization, Humanitarianism and the Erosion of Refugee Protection." *Journal of Refugee Studies* 11 (03): 243–263.

Cleveland, Janet, and Cécile Rousseau. 2013. "Psychiatric Symptoms Associated With Brief Detention of Adult Asylum Seekers in Canada." *Canadian Journal of Psychiatry* 57 (07): 409–416.

Cleveland, Janet, Cécile Rousseau, and Rachel Kronick. 2012. "The harmful effects of detention and family separation on asylum seekers' mental health in the context of Bill C-31." Last Modified April, accessed January. http://www.csssdelamontagne.qc.ca/fileadmin/csss_dlm/Publications/Publications_CRF/brief_c31_final.pdf.

Conlon, Deirdre, Nancy Hiemstra, and Alison Mountz. 2017. "Geographical Perspectives on Detention: Spatial Control and Its Contestation." In *Challenging Immigration Detention: Academics, Activists and Policymakers*, edited by Michael J. Flynn and Matthew B. Flynn, 141–159. Northampton, MA: Edward Elgar Publishing.

Crawley, Heaven, Franck Düvell, Katharine Jones, Simon McMahon, and Nando Sigona. 2016. Destination Europe? Understanding the Dynamics and Drivers of Mediterranean Migration in 2015. *In MEDMIG Final Report*.

Crenshaw, K. W. 1991. "Mapping the Margins: Intersectionality, Identity Politics, and Violence Against Women of Color." *Stanford Law Review* 43 (6): 1241–1299. doi:10.2307/1229039.

Czaika, Mathias, and Hein De Haas. 2013. "The Effectiveness of Immigration Policies." *Population and Development Review* 39 (03): 487–508.

Dauvergne, Catherine. 2013. "The Troublesome Intersections of Refugee Law and Criminal Law." In *The Borders of Punishment: Migration, Citizenship, and Social Exclusion*, edited by Katja Franko Aas and Mary Bosworth. Oxford: Oxford University Press.

De Genova, Nicholas P. 2004. "The Legal Production of Mexican/Migrant "Illegality."" *Latino Studies* 2 (2): 160–185.

de Noronha, Luke. 2019. "Deportation, Racism and Multi-Status Britain: Immigration Control and the Production of Race in the Present." *Ethnic and Racial Studies* 1–18.

Durrani, Tebasum. 2020. "Why immigration holding centres could become COVID-19 hot spots." *TVO*. Last Modified 30 March, accessed 05 April. https://www.tvo.org/article/why-immigration-holding-centres-could-become-covid-19-hot-spots.

Escobar, Martha D. 2016. *Captivity Beyond Prisons: Criminalization Experiences of Latina (im) migrants*. Austin: University of Texas Press.

Fine, Sarah. 2013. "The Ethics of Immigration: Self-Determination and the Right to Exclude." *Philosophy Compass* 8 (03): 254–68.

Fine, Sarah. 2017. "Migration, Political Philosophy, and the Real World." *Critical Review of International Social and Political Philosophy* 20 (6): 719–25.

Fortier, Marco. 2023. « Une mort qui 'aurait pu être évitée' dans un centre de détention de migrants ». Le Devoir. Acessed online 08 May 2023 from https://www.ledevoir.com/societe/777864/immigration-une-mort-qui-aurait-pu-etre-evitee-dans-un-centre-de-detention-de-migrants

Gibney, Matthew J. 2013. "Deportation, Crime, and the Changing Character of Membership in the United Kingdom." In *The Borders of Punishment: Migration, Citizenship, and Social Exclusion*, edited by Katja Franko Aas and Mary Bosworth, 218–236. Oxford: Oxford University Press.

Glenn, Evelyn. Nakano. 2015. "Settler Colonialism as Structure: A Framework for Comparative Studies of U.S. Race and Gender Formation." *Sociology of Race and Ethnicity* 1 (01): 52–72.

Maria. 2015. *Deported: Immigrant Policing, Disposable Labor, and Global Capitalism*. New York: New York University Press.

Golash-Boza, Tanya Maria. 2016. "The Parallels between Mass Incarceration and Mass Deportation: An Intersectional Analysis of State Repression." *Journal of World-Systems Research* 22 (02): 484–509.

Goldring, Luin, Carolina Berinstein, and Judith K. Bernhard. 2009. "Institutionalizing Precarious Migratory Status in Canada." *Citizenship Studies* 13 (3): 239–265.

Gros, Hanna, and Paloma van Groll. 2015. ""We Have No Rights": Arbitrary Imprisonment and Cruel Treatment of Migrants with Mental Health Issues in Canada." University of Toronto Faculty of Law, Last Modified Summer, accessed 11 October. http://ihrp.law.utoronto.ca/We_Have_No_Rights.

Gros, Hanna, and Samer Muscati. 2020. "Canada's immigration detainees at higher risk in pandemic." Last Modified 23 March, accessed 03 April. https://ottawacitizen.com/opinion/columnists/gros-and-muscati-canadas-immigration-detainees-at-risk-in-pandemic/.

Guttin, Andrea. 2010. The Criminal Alien Program: Immigration Enforcement in Travis County, Texas. In *Immigration Policy Center's Special Reports*. Washington, DC: American Immigration Council.

Hall, Alexandra. 2012. *Border Watch: Cultures of Immigration, Detention, and Control, Anthropology, Culture and Society*. London: Pluto Press.

Hansen, Randall, and Demetrios G. Papademetriou. 2014. *Securing Borders: The Intended, Unintended, and Perverse Consequences*. New York City: Transatlantic Council on Migration.

Hasham, Nicole. 2016. "Detention centre workers suffering their own trauma in dealing with asylum seekers." Last Modified 26 February, accessed 02 March. http://www.standard.net.au/story/3754982/detention-centre-workers-suffering-their-own-trauma-in-dealing-with-asylum-seekers/?cs=7.

Jung, Maria. 2020. "Immigration and Crime in Canadian Cities: A 35-Year Study." *Canadian Journal of Criminology and Criminal Justice* 62 (1): 71–97.

Kaytaz, Esra S. 2021. "Held at the Gates of Europe: Barriers to Abolishing Immigration Detention in Turkey." *Citizenship Studies* 25 (2): 203–223.

Kennedy, Brendan. 2017. "Caged by Canada." *The Toronto Star*. Last Modified 17 March, accessed 20 March. http://projects.thestar.com/caged-by-canada-immigration-detention/part-1/.

Keung, Nicholas. 2017. "Asylum-seeker sues federal government over 'humiliating' 5-year imprisonment." *The Toronto Star*. Last Modified 01 October, accessed 11 October. https://www.thestar.com/news/immigration/2017/09/28/asylum-seeker-sues-federal-government-over-humiliating-5-year-imprisonment.html.

Kronick, Rachel, Cécile Rousseau, and Janet Cleveland. 2011. "Mandatory Detention of Refugee Children: A Public Health Issue?" *Paediatrics & Child Health* 16 (8): e65–e67.

Kronick, Rachel, Cecile Rousseau, and Janet Cleveland. 2016. "They Cut Your Wings Over Here… You Can't Do Nothing': Voices of Children and Parents Held in Immigration Detention in Canada." In *Detaining the Immigrant Other: Global and Transnational Issues*, edited by Rich Furman, Douglas Epps and Greg Lamphear, 195–208. Oxford: Oxford University Press.

Kukathas, Chandran. 2016. "Are Refugees Special?" In *Migration and Political Theory: The Ethics of Movement and Membership*, edited by Sarah Fine and Lea Ypi, 249–268. Oxford: Oxford University Press.

Last, Tamara, Giorgia Mirto, Orçun Ulusoy, Ignacio Urquijo, Joke Harte, Nefeli Bami, Marta Pérez, Flor Macias Delgado, Amélie Tapella, and Alexandra Michalaki. 2017. "Deaths at the Borders Database: Evidence of Deceased migrants' Bodies Found Along the Southern External Borders of the European Union." *Journal of Ethnic and Migration Studies* 43 (5): 693–712.

Leung, Jessica, Diana Elson, Kelsey Sanders, Mona Marin, Greg Leos, Brandy Cloud, Rebecca J. McNall, Carole J. Hickman, and Mariel Marlow. 2019. "Notes from the Field: Mumps in Detention Facilities That House Detained Migrants - United States, September 2018-August 2019." *MMWR. Morbidity and Mortality Weekly Report* 68 (34):749–750. doi: 10.15585/mmwr.mm6834a4.

Lister, Matthew. 2012. "Who Are Refugees?" *Law and Philosophy* 32 (05): 645–71.

Lister, Matthew. 2014. "Climate Change Refugees." *Critical Review of International Social and Political Philosophy* 17 (05): 618–34.

Lister, Matthew, and Adrian Little Children, Families, and Immigration Enforcement" In this volume. 2023. ". 2015. "The Complex Temporality of Borders: Contingency and Normativity." *European Journal of Political Theory* 14 (04): 429–47.

Little, Adrian. 2025. "The Complex Temporality of Borders: Contingency and Normativity." *European Journal of Political Theory* 14(04): 429–47.

Lydon, J. M. 2016. "Once There Was No Prison Rape: Ending Sexual Violence as Strategy for Prison Abolition." *philoSOPHIA* 6: 61–71.

Mainwaring, Ċetta, and Maria Lorena Cook. 2018. "Immigration Detention: An Anglo Model." *Migration Studies* 7 (04):455–476. doi: 10.1093/migration/mny015.

Mainwaring, Ċetta, and Stephanie J. Silverman. 2017. "Detention-as-Spectacle." *International Political Sociology* 11 (01): 21–38.

Massey, Douglas S., and Karen A. Pren. 2012. "Unintended Consequences of US Immigration Policy: Explaining the Post-1965 Surge from Latin America." *Population and Development Review* 38 (1): 1–29.

McNevin, Anne. 2011. *Contesting Citizenship: Irregular Migrants and New Frontiers of the Political*. New York: Columbia University Press.

Macedo, Stephen. 2007. "The Moral Dilemma of U.S. Immigration Policy: Open Borders Versus Social Justice?" In *Debating Immigration*, edited by C. Swain, 63–8. New York: Cambridge University Press.

Meng, Yunliang, Sulaimon Giwa, and Uzo Anucha. 2015. "Is There Racial Discrimination in Police Stop-and-Searches of Black Youth? A Toronto Case Study." *Canadian Journal of Family and Youth/Le Journal Canadien De Famille Et De La Jeunesse* 7 (01): 115–148.

Menjívar, Cecilia, and Leisy Abrego. 2012. ""Legal Violence: Immigration Law and the Lives of Central American Immigrants." *American Journal of Sociology* 117 (5): 000–000.

Menjívar, Cecilia, Andrea Gómez Cervantes, and Daniel Alvord. 2018.""The Expansion of "crimmigration," Mass Detention, and Deportation"" *Sociology Compass* 12 (4):1–15. doi: 10.1111/soc4.12573.

Miller, David. 2005. "Immigration: The Case for Limits." In *Contemporary Debates in Applied Ethics*, edited by A. Cohen and C. Wellman, 193–206. Malden, MA: John Wiley & Sons.

Miller, David. 2007. *National Responsibility and Global Justice*. Oxford: Oxford University Press.

Miller, David. 2016. *Strangers in Our Midst: The Political Philosophy of Immigration*. Boston: Harvard University Press.

Missbach, Antje. 2021. ""Substituting Immigration Detention Centres With 'open prisons' in Indonesia: Alternatives to Detention as the continuum of Unfreedom." *Citizenship Studies* 25 (2): 224–237.

Mountz, Alison. 2020. *The Death of Asylum: Hidden Geographies of the Enforcement Archipelago*. Minneapolis: University of Minnesota.

Ngai, M. M. 2004. *Impossible Subjects: Illegal Aliens and the Making of Modern America*. Oxford: Princeton University Press.

Oberman, Kieran. 2017. "Immigration, Citizenship, and Consent: What Is Wrong With Permanent Alienage?" *The Journal of Political Philosophy* 25 (1): 91–107.

Orrenius, Pia, and Madeline Zavodny. 2019. "Do Immigrants Threaten US Public Safety." *Journal on Migration and Human Security* 7 (3): 52–61.

PressProgress. 2018.""Jason Kenney Defended Locking Up Child Refugees in Heavy Security Detention Facilities"" Last Modified 20 June, accessed 04 February. https://pressprogress.ca/jason-kenney-defended-locking-up-child-refugees-in-heavy-security-detention-facilities/.

Rajendra, Tisha M. 2015. "The Rational Agent or the Relational Agent: Moving from Freedom to Justice in Migration Systems Ethics." *Ethical Theory and Moral Practice* 18 (02): 355–369.

Razack, Sherene H. 2021. "Human Waste and the Border: A Vignette." *Law, Culture and the Humanities* 17 (02): 322–334.

Reitano, Tuesday, Laura Adal, and Mark Shaw. 2014. Smuggled Futures: The Dangerous Path of the Migrant from Africa to Europe. In *The Global Initiative Against Transnational Organized Crime Series on Human Trafficking*. Geneva: The Global Initiative against Transnational Organized Crime.

Rodríguez, Dylan. 2010. "The Terms of Engagement: Warfare, White Locality, and Abolition." *Critical Sociology* 36 (1):151–173. doi: 10.1177/0896920509347145.

Sager, Alex. 2016. "Immigration Enforcement and Domination: An Indirect Argument for Much More Open Borders." *Political Research Quarterly* 70 (01): 42–55.

Sager, Alex. 2018. *Toward a Cosmopolitan Ethics of Mobility: The Migrant's-Eye View of the World, Mobility & Politics*. London: Palgrave Pivot.

Sampson, Robyn. 2015. "Does Detention Deter?" In *IDC Working Papers*. Sydney: International Detention Coalition.

Scott, David G. 2015. "Eating Your Insides Out: Cultural, Physical and Institutionally-Structured Violence in the Prison Place."." *Prison Service Journal* 221: 58–62.

Shantz, Jeff. 2023. Deaths in Shadows: Lethal and Unaccountable Migrant Detention in Canada. Border Criminologies. Accessed online on 08 May 2023 from https://blogs.law.ox.ac.uk/blog-post/2023/04/deaths-shadows-lethal-and-unaccountable-migrant-detention-canada

Silverman, Stephanie J. 2013. "In the Wake of Irregular Arrivals: Changes to the Canadian Immigration Detention System." *Refuge*: 27.

Silverman, Stephanie J. 2014. "Detaining Immigrants and Asylum Seekers: A Normative Introduction." *Critical Review of International Social and Political Philosophy* 17 (05: New Challenges in Immigration Theory):600–617.
Silverman, Stephanie J. 2021. "Springing *Amir*." *Migration and Society: Advances in Research* 4: 172–184.
Silverman, Stephanie J., and Esra S. Kaytaz. 2022. "Examining the 'National Risk Assessment for Detention' Process: an Intersectional Analysis of Detaining 'dangerousness' in Canada." *Journal of Ethnic and Migration Studies* 48 (03): 693–709.
Silverman, Stephanie J., and Petra Molnar. 2016. "Everyday Injustices: Barriers to Access to Justice for Immigration Detainees in Canada." *Refugee Survey Quarterly* 35 (01): 109–127.
Silverman, Stephanie J., and Petra Molnar. 2019. "Caged at the Border: Immigration Detention and the Denial of Human Rights to Asylum Seekers and Other Migrants." In *The Routledge History of Human Rights*, edited by Jean H. Quataert and Lora Wildenthal, 579–600. London: Routledge.
Stilz, Anna. 2011. "Nations, States, and Territory." *Ethics* 121 (03): 572–601.
Stumpf, Juliet. 2006. "The Crimmigration Crisis: Immigrants, Crime, and Sovereign Power." *American University Law Review* 56: 367.
Taylor, Luke. 2015. "Designated Inhospitality: the Treatment of Asylum Seekers Who Arrive by Boat in Canada and Australia." *McGill Law Journal/Revue De Droit De McGill* 60 (02): 333–379.
Trovall, Elizabeth. 2019. "More Than 400 Mumps Cases Confirmed in Texas Immigrant Facilities." Last Modified 29 July, accessed 04 April. https://www.houstonpublicmedia.org/articles/news/politics/immigration/2019/07/29/340973/more-than-400-mumps-cases-confirmed-in-texas-immigrant-facilities/.
Ugelvik, Thomas. 2016. "Techniques of Legitimation: The Narrative Construction of Legitimacy Among Immigration Detention Officers." *Crime Media Culture* 12 (02): 215–232.
Walia, Harsha, and Omar Chu. 2015. *Never Home: Legislating Discrimination in Canadian Immigration*. Vancouver: No One is Illegal - Vancouver.
Walzer, Michael. 1983. *Spheres of Justice: a Defense of Pluralism and Equality*. New York City: Basic Books.
Ware, S. J. R., and G. Dias. 2014. "It Can't Be Fixed Because It's Not Broken: Racism and Disability in the Prison Industrial Complex." In *Disability Incarcerated: Imprisonment and Disability in the United States and Canada*, edited by L. Ben-Moshe, C. Chapman and A. C. Carey, 163–184. New York: Palgrave Macmillan US.
Wellman, Christopher H. 2008. "Immigration and Freedom of Association." *Ethics* 119 (1): 109–141.
Wellman, Christopher Heath. 2011. "Refugees." In *Debating the Ethics of Immigration: Is There a Right to Exclude?* edited by Christopher Heath Wellman and Phillip Cole, 117–124. Oxford: Oxford University Press.
Wellman, Christopher Heath, and Phillip Cole. 2011. *Debating the Ethics of Immigration: Is There a Right to Exclude?* Oxford: Oxford University Press.
Whelan, Frederick G. 1988. "Citizenship and Freedom of Movement: An Open Admissions Policy?" In *Open Borders? Closed Societies? The Ethical and Political Issues*, edited by M. Gibney, 3–39. London: Greenwood Press.
White House Briefing Statements. 2020. "Remarks by President Trump in Roundtable on Border Security | Yuma, AZ." The White House, Last Modified 23 June, accessed 02 July. https://trumpwhitehouse.archives.gov/briefings-statements/remarks-president-trump-roundtable-border-security-yuma-az/.
Williams, Kira, and Alison Mountz. 2016. "Rising Tide: Analyzing the Relationship between Externalization and Migrant Deaths and Boat Losses." In *Externalizing Migration Management*, edited by Ruben Zaiotti, 31–49. London: Routledge.
Wilsher, Daniel. 2012. *Immigration Detention: Law, History, Politics*. Cambridge: Cambridge University Press.
Wolfe, P. 1999. *Settler Colonialism and the Transformation of Anthropology: The Politics and Poetics of an Ethnographic Event*. London: Cassell.

23
IMMIGRATION ENFORCEMENT

Alex Sager

23.1 Introduction

On June 24, 2022, Moroccan security forces and Spanish Guardia Civil officers clashed with migrants attempting to breach the Melilla border fence that separates Morocco from Spain. 189 guards were injured, and an estimated 37 migrants died in what civil society organizations have dubbed the #MasacreMelilla (Kassam 2022). Spanish president Pedro Sánchez blamed (without evidence) "the international mafias who organize these violent attacks" (Burgen 2022). Disturbingly, it is not nefarious criminal actors that deserve the blame here, but rather the banally violent business of border enforcement (Jones 2016).

The first observation of Joseph Carens' pioneering article, "Aliens and Citizens: The Case for Open Borders" is that "borders have guards and guards have guns" (Carens 1987: 251). While Carens' missive is frequently quoted, the guards and guns have faded into the background of the political theory of migration. Instead, theorists have primarily focused on rights and equality-based arguments for or against state restrictions on migration, with limited sustained attention to the details of enforcement. This neglect leaves a significant gap in our understanding of the normative issues.

This chapter provides an overview of the immigration enforcement and the issues that it raises for the political theory of migration. Immigration enforcement comprises the set of actors, institutions, laws, and policies for policing human migration. It includes agencies charged with controlling increasingly militarized borders and the technology necessary to surveil people. It also includes private actors across society tasked with denying access to goods and services based on immigration status and, in cases of some local police forces, carrying out enforcement directly. Moreover, it also relies on international cooperation, in which enforcement is delegated to foreign states, often states with troubling human rights records.

In what follows, I describe the domestic and international legal background that enables immigration enforcement and some of the central practices, such as immigrant detention, that states employ. I then turn to the normative issues that immigration enforcement raises within states, followed by a section on how it is carried out internationally. The final section looks at the permissibility of and possible obligations to resist immigration enforcement.

23.2 Understanding Immigration Enforcement

The legal environment of immigration enforcement grants sovereign states broad discretion over immigration policy. State discretion is not absolute, as most states are bound by the 1951 Convention relating to the Status of Refugees, the 1967 Protocol relating to the Status of Refugees, and customary international law, which prohibit the forcible return of refugees (Hathaway and Foster 2014). States are also constrained by regional and bilateral agreements and by widely accepted norms shaped by human rights law, trade law, labor law, and maritime law. Nonetheless, states are largely free to admit or exclude visitors and immigrants as they wish.

In the United States, the "plenary power doctrine" gives Congress and the Executive Branch broad discretion over foreign policy, including immigration, sharply limiting the scope of judicial review. Immigration authorities possess broad powers to prohibit foreigners from entering the country and to detain and deport them if they are present. In *Chae Chan Ping v. United States*, the "Chinese Exclusion Case", Chae Chan Ping, a resident of the United States from 1875 to 1887, challenged the *Chinese Exclusion Act*, which prohibited the immigration of Chinese laborers.[1] When he tried to return in 1888, he was denied entry and detained, despite having obtained a legal certificate permitting re-entry. The U.S. Supreme Court held:

> The power of exclusion of foreigners being an incident of sovereignty belonging to the government of the United States as a part of those sovereign powers delegated by the constitution, the right to its exercise at any time when, in the judgment of the government, the interests of the country require it, cannot be granted away or restrained on behalf of any one.

Plenary power was notoriously reaffirmed in *Korematsu v. United States, 323 U.S. 214*, which upheld the U.S. government's right to confine Japanese Americans in internment camps during World War II without judicial interference.

Plenary power, combined with the fact that immigration law is civil law, not criminal law, allows states to detain and deport people without many of the safeguards we take to be necessary for the legitimate and just exercise of power. In the United States, immigrants have limited Fourth, Fifth, Sixth, and Fourteenth Amendment rights. Immigration agents are permitted to consider national origin or ethnicity in stopping potential immigration law violators. Moreover, the "exclusionary rule", which prohibits the use of evidence obtained in unreasonable searches and seizures prohibited by the Fourth Amendment, does not apply to immigration cases. While subsequent case law has weakened the plenary power doctrine, so there are some protections against indefinite detention and deportation (Kagan 2015), this still falls far short of the justifications normally expected to deprive a person of their freedom or separate them from their family and community.

Despite (or perhaps because of) these limited protections, immigration law and criminal law have merged since the mid-1980s, something noted by "crimmigration" scholars (Menjívar, Gómez Cervantes, and Alvord 2018; Stumpf 2006). In the early stages of U.S. immigration law, the main intersection with criminal law was the denial of entry to people with a criminal history. Today, immigration crimes make up more than half of federal criminal prosecutions, with government spending on immigration enforcement agencies exceeding spending on all other agencies that enforce criminal federal law (Meissner et al. 2013).

Immigration is increasingly framed as a security issue, rather than as an economic or humanitarian issue. This framing is accompanied by expanded grounds for exclusion and deportation of non-U.S. citizens (including legal permanent residents who grew up in the U.S.) and by the transformation of immigration law so that civil violations are now criminal. Unlawful re-entry became a felony in 1929, as did voting as a non-citizen (which was widely permitted in the United States until the 20th century [Raskin 1993]). Immigration law is also used to detain and deport foreigners suspected of engaging in terrorism, since people do not have protections under immigration law that they would have if they were charged under criminal law, such as the right to legal representation or the right not to be detained without being charged with a crime (Stumpf 2006).

Immigrant detention is perhaps the most vivid illustration of how human mobility has been criminalized (García Hernández 2019). Immigrant detention is a global practice, with many countries shifting in recent decades from detention as an exceptional measure to a normal practice (Nethery and Silverman 2015). Detained immigrants, including children, are not limited to people who have illegally crossed a border or failed to leave the country at the expiration of their visas. It also includes people escaping oppressive regimes and extreme violence who have legally exercised their right to claim asylum only to find their trauma compounded by incarceration as they wait for their claims to be adjudicated. Since immigrant detention is classified as a civil remedy, not a criminal sanction, being locked up in a detention facility is *not* considered a punishment and therefore requires fewer safeguards. In practice, immigrant detention is in many cases indistinguishable from prison. In one respect, it can be worse: if you are convicted of a crime, you receive a sentence and can usually anticipate your release date. Immigrant detention can be indefinite (which is legally permitted in some countries, such as Canada) (Stauffer 2021).

Immigration enforcement raises many central questions for the political theory of migration. To begin, what, if anything, justifies the use of force to prevent people from crossing an international border? This question is particularly poignant when the people attempting to cross are fleeing persecution, violence, or famine or if they are poor and seeking work to better provide for themselves and their families. But even people who are not desperate or in danger are at least allowed an explanation for why they cannot pursue work, education, family life, or even tourism outside of their country of birth.

Almost all political theorists of migration agree that coercive border controls must be justified, if not directly to the people who are excluded directly, at least with compelling reasons. Theorists justifying coercive immigration controls have invoked national self-determination (Song 2019), freedom of association (Wellman 2008), national or cultural identity (Miller 2016), obligations toward the well-being of compatriots (Macedo 2018), and property rights (Pevnick 2011). Open borders theorists counter that none of these considerations outweigh immigrants' rights and interests in freedom of movement, opportunity, or welfare (Carens 2013; Cole 2000; Sager 2020).

These debates largely abstract from the legal and administrative institutions and structures that enable enforcement, leaving out what would be needed to implement a fair system of exclusion in practice. Currently, people who are denied a visa or turned away at the border do not typically have a process to contest the decision, even if it is based on incorrect information or discriminatory judgment. They may not even know why they have been excluded. If we are serious about the need to justify policies to immigrants, we need to think carefully about what systems need to be in place to give them the voice so that justifications have normative force.

23.3 Immigration Enforcement Within State Borders

Attention to the details of immigration enforcement also forces us to confront the fact that it does not just affect immigrants. It is misleading to treat immigration enforcement as confined to appointed officials at state borders checking foreigners' visas, assessing claims of credible fear of persecution, and turning away people who do not qualify for admission. As Chandran Kukathas points out, it is a mistake to only assume that

> guards sit at the border and they and their guns face outwards. The truth of the matter is very different: the guns face *inwards* more often than they face out, and the guards are to be found not merely well within the boundaries of the state but in every part of society.
>
> (Kukathas 2021: 4)

It is impossible to impose controls on immigrants without imposing controls on others. If we limit the freedom of immigrants, then we also limit the freedom of the local population, who find themselves subjected to stops at checkpoints (disproportionately targeting racialized groups) and to surveillance. The U.S. Border Patrol has the power to surveil, stop, and arrest people within 100 miles of the U.S. border (this includes most of the people in the United States). Immigration controls restrict citizens' ability to employ whom they choose (they can only employ those who can qualify under a work visa). They affect who people can live with or marry (with governments making invasive judgments about "legitimate" marriage in family-based immigration applications).

Furthermore, many families have mixed status, so they live in fear that their parent or partner may be deported. Many people denounced former U.S. Attorney General Jeff Sessions's Zero Tolerance Policy and his horrific decision to separate children from their parents at the border to deter people from arriving (Olivares 2019). Less attention was given to how immigration enforcement regularly leads to separation of parents and children, causing trauma and economic hardship (Chaudry et al. 2010; Lister x, this volume). Inevitably, some citizens and legal residents are wrongfully detained and deported (U.S. Government Accountability Office 2021).

One consideration in evaluating immigration enforcement is how it can change the character of organizations that are meant to serve the population. Medical care, housing, and education are human rights. Doctors, teachers, and landlords are not trained to enforce immigration law, so they may inadvertently deny essential goods and services to people legally and morally entitled to them. A particularly egregious example of this is former British Home Secretary and Prime Minister Theresa May's "hostile environment", in which landlords, educators, healthcare workers, and bank officials became part of immigration enforcement by preventing people who could not prove their right to reside in the country from accessing basic rights and services (Goodfellow 2020). The hostile environment came to a head with the Windrush Scandal, in which the British government refused services and, in some cases, deported longstanding, legal residents, largely from former Caribbean colonies (Hewitt 2020). Under these types of policies, immigrants (with and without legal status) will be reluctant to seek essential medical care, send their children to school, and find themselves confined to informal housing in low-income, *de facto* segregated neighborhoods.

Indeed, immigration enforcement cannot be evaluated without a frank discussion of racism and racialization. The history of immigration control is a history of racism, driven by explicit racist animus (FitzGerald and Cook-Martín 2014; Jones 2021). Immigrants are frequently portrayed not as people with a particular legal status but as threatening black or brown racial groups (Chávez 2013). Many theorists have examined the ways in which the criminalization of immigrants is a racial project (Mendoza 2016b; Provine and Doty 2011; Silva 2015), with dog whistles such as "illegal" replacing explicitly racist animus and policy (Menjívar 2021). Racial profiling risks targeting legal residents and citizens of the same ethnic group as immigrants. Amy Reed-Sandoval has argued that many people are "socially undocumented", suffering discrimination because their appearance associates them with groups stereotyped as having high numbers of illegalized residents (Reed-Sandoval 2020).

Notably, immigration enforcement need not be motivated by explicit racial bias. Institutional racism can cause racialized communities (immigrant and non-immigrant) to be disproportionately surveilled, policed, and punished in the name of facially colorblind laws (Hing 2009). This is amplified by practices such as creating a "hostile environment" so that people will "self-deport" or by programs such as the United States' Secure Communities, which co-opt local police forces into immigration enforcement. Institutional racism in the immigration system intersects with racism in other social institutions, such as policing, education, and housing.

There is also reason to be concerned that immigration enforcement has eluded democratic control, taking on an institutional logic at odds with its legitimate purposes. Agencies charged with immigration enforcement tend to perpetuate themselves. It is difficult to estimate how much money is spent on immigration enforcement, since it is carried out by many agencies not specifically tasked with immigration (e.g., local police forces) and by many organizations that provide services to immigrants and refugees (e.g., not to for profit groups providing legal aid or health care or running detention centers). Other facets of spending are difficult to track, for example, when foreign aid is contingent on sending and transit states preventing people from emigrating.

Nonetheless, Immigration and Customs Enforcement is the largest federal law enforcement body, and the Border Patrol has undergone exponential growth since 1986. Some figures are helpful to get a sense of the scope of spending. The FY 2022 President's Budget for the Department of Homeland Security dispersed nearly $30 billion of its $70 billion dollar budget between organizations such as the U.S. Customs and Border Protection (CBP) (18% of total budget), U.S. Immigration and Customs Enforcement (ICE) (9% of total budget), Transportation Security Administration (TSA) (10% of total budget), and the U.S. Citizenship and Immigration Services (USCIS) (5% of total budget).[2] The 2022 European Border and Coast Guard Agency (Frontex) budget totaled €754,375,142 (Frontex 2022).

The privatization of immigration enforcement also creates perverse incentives. Immigration enforcement is big business. In 2022, CBP and ICE awarded $7.5 billion in contracts to companies including Lockheed Martin, General Atomics, Palantir, CoreCivic, and the GEO Group (Miller 2023). Significant sums go to private companies, which is reflected in their lobbying; in the United States, the private prison company the GEO Group spent $920,000 lobbying the federal government in 2022.[3] Politicians beholden to rural economies dependent on border enforcement and the prison industry advocate for enforcement measures only vaguely connected to public interest or the realities of human mobility.

How should we respond to the effects of immigration enforcement within states? The ways in which immigration enforcement is enmeshed with racism is particularly troubling. Insofar as immigration enforcement embodies, contributes to, or sustains racism, we need to question its justice. This may have methodological consequences for how we approach migration, causing us to closely scrutinize race and racism in migration control (Bosworth, Parmar, and Vázquez 2018; Mendoza 2018) and to examine how colonial legacies continue to affect migration control and asylum (Mayblin 2017). It may also involve explicitly adopting an approach based on critical race theory so that normative analysis recognizes and engages with the institutional and structural nature of racism and white supremacy in immigration enforcement (Sanchez and Romero 2010).

More modestly, we should explore what measures are necessary so that immigration enforcement does not corrupt the character of institutions and prevent them from realizing their function. Joseph Carens has argued persuasively for a firewall that sharply separates immigration enforcement and law enforcement (Carens 2013). Communities that fear the police will be reluctant to report and testify about serious crime. When immigration status is based on family sponsorship, victims may choose not to report domestic violence (Nanasi 2018; Vladislava 2018).

Also, identifying and detaining immigrants diverts resources away from preventing and investigating violent crime and promoting public safety. This has led to "sanctuary cities" where local police are prohibited from enforcing immigration law, often because they see this as undermining public safety by creating fear and distrust among immigrant communities (Bauder 2017).

Finally, if we grant that coercive immigration controls are justified, we still need to assess their effects against competing rights and interests. What sort of harm is crossing a border without authorization or overstaying a visa? Immigration status is determined by policy choices, so many theorists have adopted the terminology *illegalized immigrant* to draw attention to how state laws and policies produced illegality (Bauder 2014). This encourages us to scrutinize the rationale for laws and sanctions, not only in immigration law, but also in related spheres such as labor, electoral, and education law.

There are also issues of proportionality. Turning away an affluent traveler who can return to a safe home or imposing a modest fine for failing to renew a visa may not raise major ethical concerns. In contrast, detention and deportation are serious punishments (even if they are not legally considered punishments). Theorists disagree on the reasons for regularization, but most agree that the harm of deporting long-term residents is disproportional to any wrong they committed by illegally crossing a border or overstaying a visa (Bosniak 2013; Carens 2013; Hosein 2016). Two-thirds of illegalized immigrants have lived in the United States for more than a decade (Manuel, Krogstad, and Cohn 2019). Over time, immigrants, regardless of their legal status, become community members. They have families with (often citizen) children in local schools. They contribute to the economy through their employment and to their community through public service. Deportation for a long-term resident is exile, a severe punishment that may be as or more harmful to the families left behind. Arguably, a just society will have clear procedures to allow people to regularize their status.

23.4 Extraterritorial Immigration Enforcement

So far, I have mainly considered how immigration enforcement affects people and institutions within the borders of the state. Another major issue is how immigration is enforced against people outside of the state. Immigration enforcement occurs at official state borders, in which people are screened for the right to enter, and within state borders, in which immigration authorities and their proxies surveil the population to determine legal rights to reside. It also takes place far from the official borders of states, with immigration restrictions being imposed by third-party states or by private actors. The United States, the EU, and Australia have outsourced immigration control to sending and transit states, effectively extending their borders thousands of miles. The visa regime is one of the most powerful tools for immigration control. Much of the world's population is unable to meet the criteria for a visa to travel to wealthy countries. Airlines subject to carrier sanctions prohibit people without the necessary visas or legal documents from boarding (Bloom and Risse 2014).

The ways that foreign states or private actors carry out immigration enforcement far from official state borders is often termed "border externalization". Even if we agree that the European Union, the United States, or Australia has a right to prevent people from entering their territory, this does not mean that they have the right to delegate enforcement to other countries. Despite all the challenges of effective public oversight of domestic immigration enforcement, citizens can criticize the federal government for the actions of private prison or security firms, protest injustice, and support legislation to remove immigration enforcement from local police forces. When foreign powers enforce immigration on behalf of receiving states, it becomes much more difficult to know what they are doing, let alone change their behavior.

Countries externalize migration controls to escape their own legal responsibilities. As Ayelet Shachar puts it:

> When it comes to controlling migration, states are willfully *abandoning* traditional notions of fixed and bounded territoriality, stretching their jurisdictional arm inward and outward with tremendous flexibility; but when it comes to granting rights and protections, the very same states snap back to a narrow and strict interpretation of spatiality which limits their responsibility and liability, by attaching it to the (illusionary) static notion of border control.
>
> *(Shachar 2020: 8)*

Again, we see ways in which immigration enforcement in practice undermines the character and function of a just immigration system. Migrants resort to risky and too often lethal routes, often with the assistance of smugglers. In the United States, "prevention-by-deterrence policies" funnel people away from safe crossings into lethal routes through the desert (Boyce and Chambers 2021). Even if the deaths of migrants are not intended, they are predictable. Indeed, Maurizio Albahari holds that "Thousands of deaths in the Mediterranean, over two decades, are not misfortunate accidents, inevitable fatalities, acts of God or of nature. They are crimes of peace…" (Albahari 2015: 21)

Moreover, many of these migrants are also refugees. Though there is considerable debate about the obligations that states owe to refugees and how they can discharge their responsibilities, a just international system depends on mechanisms that allow people persecuted or abandoned by their state to join a functional political community (Gibney 2004; Owen 2020). Rather than ensuring this is the case, affluent states have largely closed off legal routes to allow people to safely arrive and claim asylum. In too many cases, they have partnered with countries such as Libya and Guatemala that do not protect migrants' human rights, including their right to claim asylum.

Moving away from the practical effects of externalized border enforcement, the ways in which border control takes place far beyond the border and the complex political relationships that enable it have far-reaching consequences for sovereignty and democracy.

Matthew Longo suggests that the need for states to co-manage their borders challenges our understanding of sovereignty, conceived in terms of authority exercised within a system of territorial states: "borders are no longer simply marks of *division* between states but rather spaces of *joint maintenance* (such that borders are still *defining*, but not necessarily *unitary*)". (Longo 2018: 77) People in border zones increasingly find themselves subject to two sovereigns, suggesting a need for new forms of political representation and voice. Moreover, co-management of borders is frequently hierarchical, with powerful states such as the United States shaping the immigration policy of other states under the political logic of empire (Longo 2018: 95). Attention to immigration enforcement may thus force us to reevaluate how political theorists approach questions such as political authority, nationalism and cosmopolitanism, and global justice.

23.5 Resistance/Disobedience

Laws restricting human mobility are met with resistance, raising a further issue for political theory: how should people respond to immigration enforcement? How we answer depends in large part on our view of the justice of migration controls and immigration enforcement. Open borders theorists consider restrictive state border controls unjust, so they will need to weigh the injustice of border controls with obligations to obey even unjust laws, the availability of avenues to contest these laws through establishing legal and democratic procedures, and the probability that resistance will lead to meaningful change.

But one does not need to endorse open borders to have grave concerns about current immigration policies. As we have seen above, state enforcement may be illegitimate because of the means it employs (such as contracting with states that habitually violate human rights to prevent people from arriving). Its penalties, such as deporting people who have been part of the community for years or decades, may be grossly disproportionate to the wrongness of violating an immigration law. Furthermore, states may violate refugees' human rights by shutting off avenues that would give them a reasonable and fair opportunity to claim asylum.

There are three main groups of people resisting migration controls. First, migrants evade surveillance and cross borders without authorization. Second, non-migrants help migrants cross borders or assist them on their journey. Third, many people resist migration controls through civil disobedience and direct action because they consider them cruel or unjust.

What are the obligations of individual migrants who evade immigration authorities and break the law by crossing borders without legal authorization? A disingenuous refrain is that people who cross borders illegally are "queue jumpers". Since wealthy states have largely closed off legal avenues for much of the world's populations, there is no queue most people can stand in and wait their turn. Even when there is a "queue", applications for family migration can take years or even decades to be reviewed, undermining access to the right to family life.

Many migrants who choose irregular or unauthorized routes are escaping violence (which is not legal grounds in many jurisdictions to qualify for asylum) or poverty. In many cases, refugees need to choose between breaking an immigration law and exposing themselves to imprisonment, torture, rape, or death. It is hard to see how they could have a moral obligation to follow the law. A more complex case is when refugees receive a degree of protection in camps or transit countries, but are unable to resume their lives or reunite with family in other countries. Do they have an obligation to indefinitely wait for possible resettlement or for conditions in their country of origin to change? More broadly, do people have an obligation to live in poverty when the act of crossing a border would raise their income five-fold or more?

Javier Hidalgo has examined resistance to unjust border controls, drawing on a general principle: people subjected to an unjustified threat of harm are permitted to take measures to evade the harm, deceive the agent threatening the harm, and even employ proportional defensive force. He observes that there are some cases in which border agents threaten serious and plausibly unjustified harms to migrants, so it is sometimes permissible for migrants to evade, deceive, and use proportional defensive force to avoid these harms (Hidalgo 2015).

More radically, some theorists have argued that illegally crossing borders should be seen as a form of civil disobedience (Benli 2018) or radical politics (De Genova 2017). While many violations of immigration law are clandestine, migrants also participate in and lead protest movements, often exposing themselves to detention and deportation by publicly denouncing unjust laws (Caraus and Paris 2019). For some people, migration is a practice for prefiguring a world in which no human is illegal (King 2016). Rather than conceiving migrant journeys as individual narratives, we can see migrants participating in networks of solidarity enacting new and better relationships between people with and across borders.

Many people who are not migrants also violate immigration law. States' decision to largely eliminate opportunities to cross borders legally has raised the cost of clandestine travel, creating markets for smugglers and leading migrants to take out loans, which places them in a position of vulnerability. Governments that frame migration portray smugglers as members of organized crime, flattening the complexities of smuggling and the motivations of smugglers (many who act independently) (Zhang, Sanchez, and Achilli 2018). They often equate smugglers with human traffickers, who move people against their will, rather than entrepreneurs providing a service to people who want to travel without authorization (McCarthy 2014). While some smugglers abuse and exploit people under their power, the core issue is arguably not smuggling itself, but rather the criminal actions of some smugglers.

If it is sometimes permissible to evade border controls, it may also be the case that helping people do so is also permissible (Hidalgo 2016). In some cases, there may even be a moral obligation to resist migration controls, for example, when states shut off legal avenues for people fleeing persecution or life-threatening violence (Landry 2016). The complexities of the ethics of smuggling are compounded by the choice of some states to prosecute humanitarian actors who have intervened to protect human life by rescuing migrants at sea or providing food, water, and medical care to people crossing the desert (Devereaux 2019; Gionco and Kanics 2022).

The criminalization of humanitarian action raises questions for the obligations of civil society. Democratic societies justify the use of coercion by pointing to ways in which the people subject to coercion also authorize it. Another way of putting this is that coercion is exercised in the name of the people. A society's immigration laws and policies tell us a great deal about whether it values openness, diversity, and inclusivity or exclusion, homogeneity, and xenophobia, so we should ask what the society is prepared to defend with force.

Immigration enforcement includes examples such as prohibiting ship captains from rescuing migrants at sea and bringing them to shore where they can receive medical care. It is intertwined with the prison-industrial complex, with tens of thousands of people, including asylum seekers and families, confined in immigrant detention. Finally, it is not possible to enforce immigration law without interfering with the rights and freedom of non-immigrants.

Immigration enforcement affects us all, subjecting us all to levels of surveillance that we may find troubling and reinforcing institutional and systemic racism. When immigration policy is unjust, people need to ask what obligations they have to eliminate it. This includes contesting immigration laws through established legal and political channels, but also contemplating direct action (Delmas 2018).

A complete theory of justice in migration will need to take enforcement seriously. It is not enough to focus on principles that should govern immigration restriction without confronting the concrete practices of immigration enforcement. Rather than ending our inquiry with the question of if we can prevent people from migrating, we need to focus on who is doing the actual enforcing, how it affects the character of social institutions, and how it intersects with racism and colonial legacies. Doing so raises important questions for the nature of sovereignty and political authority and for broader questions of what it means to be a just society.

Notes

1 See Mendoza 2016a and Song 2019 for discussion.
2 https://www.dhs.gov/sites/default/files/publications/dhs_bib_-_web_version_-_final_8.pdf
3 https://www.opensecrets.org/federal-lobbying/clients/summary?cycle=2022&id=D000022003

Bibliography

Abizadeh, A. 2010. "Democratic Legitimacy and State Coercion: A Reply to David Miller." *Political Theory* 38 (1): 121–30. https://doi.org/10.1177/0090591709348192.
Albahari, Maurizio. 2015. *Crimes of Peace: Mediterranean Migrations at the World's Deadliest Border*. Philadelphia, Pennsylvania: University of Pennsylvania Press.
Bauder, H. 2014. "Why We Should Use the Term 'Illegalized' Refugee or Immigrant: A Commentary." *International Journal of Refugee Law* 26 (3): 327–32. https://doi.org/10.1093/ijrl/eeu032.
Bauder, Harald. 2017. "Sanctuary Cities: Policies and Practices in International Perspective." *International Migration* 55 (2): 174–87. https://doi.org/10.1111/imig.12308.
Benli, Ali Emre. 2018. "March of Refugees: An Act of Civil Disobedience." *Journal of Global Ethics* 14 (3): 315–31. https://doi.org/10.1080/17449626.2018.1502204.
Bloom, Tendayi, and Verena Risse. 2014. "Examining Hidden Coercion at State Borders: Why Carrier Sanctions Cannot Be Justified." *Ethics & Global Politics* 7 (2). https://doi.org/10.3402/egp.v7.24736.
Bosniak, Linda. 2013. "Amnesty in Immigration: Forgetting, Forgiving, Freedom." *Critical Review of International Social and Political Philosophy* 16 (3): 344–65. https://doi.org/10.1080/13698230.2013.795705.
Bosworth, Mary, Alpa Parmar, and Yolanda Vázquez, eds. 2018. *Race, Criminal Justice, and Migration Control: Enforcing the Boundaries of Belonging*. First edition. Oxford: Oxford University Press.
Boyce, Geoffrey Alan, and Samuel Norton Chambers. "The Corral Apparatus: Counterinsurgency and the Architecture of Death and Deterrence Along the Mexico/United States Border." *Geoforum* 120 (March 2021): 1–13. https://doi.org/10.1016/j.geoforum.2021.01.007.
Burgen, Stephen. 2022. "Moroccan Authorities Accused of Trying to Cover up Melilla Deaths Stephen Burgen." *Guardian*, June 27, 2022. https://www.theguardian.com/world/2022/jun/27/moroccan-authorities-accused-of-trying-to-cover-up-melilla-deaths
Carauș, Tamara, and Elena Paris, eds. 2019. *Migration, Protest Movements and the Politics of Resistance: A Radical Political Philosophy of Cosmopolitanism*. New York, NY: Routledge.
Carens, Joseph. 1987. "Aliens and Citizens: The Case for Open Borders." *Review of Politics* 49 (2): 251–73.
Carens, Joseph. 2013. *The Ethics of Immigration*. New York: Oxford University Press.

Chaudry, Ajay, Randy Capps, Juan Manuel Pedroza, Rosa Maria Castañeda, Robert Santos, and Molly M Scott. 2010. *Facing Our Future: Children in the Aftermath of Immigration Enforcement*. The Urban Institute.

Chávez, Leo R. 2013. *The Latino Threat: Constructing Immigrants, Citizens, and the Nation*. Second edition. Stanford, California: Stanford University Press.

Cole, Phillip. 2000. *Philosophies of Exclusion: Liberal Political Theory and Immigration*. Edinburgh: Edinburgh University Press.

De Genova, Nicholas, ed. 2017. *The Borders of "Europe": Autonomy of Migration, Tactics of Bordering*. Durham: Duke University Press.

Delmas, Candice. 2018. *A Duty to Resist*. New York, N.Y.: Oxford University Press. https://doi.org/10.1093/oso/9780190872199.001.0001.

Devereaux, Ryan. 2019. "Humanitarian Volunteer Scott Warren Reflects on the Borderlands and Two Years of Government Persecution." *The Intercept*, November 23, 2019. https://theintercept.com/2019/11/23/scott-warren-verdict-immigration-border/.

FitzGerald, David, and David Cook-Martín. 2014. *Culling the Masses: The Democratic Origins of Racist Immigration Policy in the Americas*. Cambridge, Massachusetts: Harvard University Press.

Frontex. 2022. "Budget 2022." Reg. No N 2022, Ref: FDS/FIN/NAAL/2022. Warsaw.

García Hernández, César Cuauhtémoc. 2019. *Migrating to Prison: America's Obsession With Locking up Immigrants*. New York: The New Press.

Gibney, Mark, ed. 1988. *Open Borders? Closed Societies? The Ethical and Political Issues*. New York: Greenwood Press.

Gibney, Matthew, J., 2004. *The ethics and politics of asylum: liberal democracy and the response to refugees*. Cambridge: Cambridge University Press.

Gionco, Marta, and Jyothi Kanics. 2022. "Resilience and Resistance in Defiance of the Criminalisation of Solidarity across Europe." Greens/EFA. https://picum.org/wp-content/uploads/2022/06/CriminalizationStudy_EN_web.pdf.

Goodfellow, Maya. 2020. *Hostile Environment: How Immigrants Became Scapegoats*. Second edition. London ; Brooklyn, NY: Verso.

Hathaway, James C., and Michelle Foster. 2014. *The Law of Refugee Status*. Second ed. Cambridge University Press. https://doi.org/10.1017/CBO9780511998300.

Hewitt, Guy. 2020. "The Windrush Scandal: An Insider's Reflection." *Caribbean Quarterly* 66 (1): 108–28. https://doi.org/10.1080/00086495.2020.1722378.

Hidalgo, Javier. 2015. "Resistance to Unjust Immigration Restrictions." *Journal of Political Philosophy* 23 (4): 450–70. https://doi.org/10.1111/jopp.12051.

Hidalgo, Javier. 2016. "The Ethics of People Smuggling." *Journal of Global Ethics* 12 (3): 311–26. https://doi.org/10.1080/17449626.2016.1245676.

Hing, Bill Ong. 2009. "Institutional Racism, ICE Raids, and Immigration Reform." *University of San Francisco Law Review* 44 (1): 1–49.

Hosein, Adam. 2016. "Arguments for Regularization." In *The Ethics and Politics of Immigration: Core Issues and Emerging Trends*, edited by Alex Sager, 159–79. Lanham: Rowman & Littlefield International.

Jones, Reece. 2016. *Violent Borders: Refugees and the Right to Move*. London New York: Verso.

Jones, Reece. 2021. *White Borders: The History of Race and Immigration in the United States, from Chinese Exclusion to the Border Wall*. Beacon: S.l.

Kagan, Michael. 2015. "Plenary Power Is Dead! Long Live Plenary Power!." *Michigan Law Review First Impressions* 114 (September): 21–29.

Kassam, Ashifa. 2022. "Calls for Investigation over Deaths in Moroccan-Spanish Border Crossing." *Guardian*, June 26, 2022. https://www.theguardian.com/world/2022/jun/26/calls-investigation-deaths-moroccan-spanish-border-melilla-enclave-crossing.

King, Natasha. 2016. *No Borders: The Politics of Immigration Control and Resistance*. London: Zed Books.

Kukathas, Chandran. 2021. *Immigration and Freedom*. Princeton: Princeton University Press.

Landry, Rachel. 2016. "The 'Humanitarian Smuggling' of Refugees: Criminal Offence or Moral Obligation?" *Refugee Studies Centre*, October. https://www.rsc.ox.ac.uk/publications/the-humanitarian-smuggling-of-refugees-criminal-offence-or-moral-obligation.

Lister, Matthew. Date TBD. "Children, Families, and Immigration Enforcement." *Routledge Handbook of the Ethics of Immigration*, edited by Sahar Akhtar, page #s TBD. New York: Routledge.

Longo, Matthew. 2018. *The Politics of Borders: Sovereignty, Security, and the Citizen after 9/11*. Problems of International Politics. Cambridge, United Kingdom: Cambridge University Press.

Macedo, Stephen. 2018. "The Moral Dilemma of U.S. Immigration Policy: Open Borders Versus Social Justice?" In *Debating Immigration, Second Edition*, edited by Carol M. Swain, 286–310. Cambridge ; New York: Cambridge University Press.

Manuel, Jens, Jeffrey S. Krogstad, and D'Vera Cohn. 2019. "5 Facts about Illegal Immigration in the U.S." Pew Research Center. https://www.pewresearch.org/fact-tank/2019/06/12/5-facts-about-illegal-immigration-in-the-u-s/.

Mayblin, Lucy. 2017. *Asylum after Empire: Colonial Legacies in the Politics of Asylum Seeking*. Kilombo : International Relations and Colonial Questions. London ; New York: Roman & Littlefield International.

McCarthy, Lauren A. 2014. "Human Trafficking and the New Slavery." *Annual Review of Law and Social Science* 10 (1): 221–42. https://doi.org/10.1146/annurev-lawsocsci-110413-030952.

Meissner, Doris, Donald M. Kerwin, Muzaffar Chishti, and Claire Bergerson. 2013. "Immigration Enforcement in the United States: The Rise of a Formidable Machinery." Migration Policy Institute. https://www.migrationpolicy.org/research/immigration-enforcement-united-states-rise-formidable-machinery.

Mendoza, José Jorge. 2016a. *The Moral and Political Philosophy of Immigration: Liberty, Security, and Equality*. Lanham: Lexington Books.

Mendoza, José Jorge. 2016b. "Illegal: White Supremacy and Immigration." In *The Ethics and Politics of Immigration: Core Issues and Emerging Trends*, edited by Alex Sager, 201–20. Lanham: Rowman & Littlefield International.

Mendoza, José Jorge. 2018. "Philosophy of Race and the Ethics of Immigration." In *The Routledge Companion to Philosophy of Race*, edited by Paul C. Taylor, Linda Martín Alcoff and Luvell Anderson, 507–19. New York, NY: Routledge.

Menjívar, Cecilia, Andrea Gómez Cervantes, and Daniel Alvord. 2018. "The Expansion of 'Crimmigration,' Mass Detention, and Deportation." *Sociology Compass* 12 (4): e12573. https://doi.org/10.1111/soc4.12573.

Menjívar, Cecilia. 2021. "The Racialization of 'Illegality.'" *Daedalus* 150 (2): 91–105.

Miller, David. 2010. "Why Immigration Controls Are Not Coercive: A Reply to Arash Abizadeh." *Political Theory* 38 (1): 111–20. https://doi.org/10.1177/0090591709348194.

Miller, David. 2016. *Strangers in Our Midst: The Political Philosophy of Immigration*. Cambridge, Massachusetts: Harvard University Press.

Miller, Todd. 2023. "The Border Industrial Complex Goes Big Time." *The Border Chronicle* (blog). January 19, 2023. https://www.theborderchronicle.com/p/the-border-industrial-complex-goes

Nanasi, Natalie. 2018. "The U Visa's Failed Promise for Survivors of Domestic Violence." *Yale Journal of Law & Feminism* 29: 273–320.

Nethery, Amy, and Stephanie Jessica Silverman, eds. 2015. *Immigration Detention: The Migration of a Policy and Its Human Impact*. London; New York: Routledge.

Olivares, Mariela. 2019. "The Rise of Zero Tolerance and the Demise of Family." *Georgia State University Law Review* 36 (2): 287–349.

Owen, David. 2020. *What Do We Owe to Refugees?* Political Theory Today. Cambridge, UK ; Medford, MA: Polity Press.

Pevnick, Ryan. 2011. *Immigration and the Constraints of Justice: Between Open Borders and Absolute Sovereignty*. Cambridge; New York: Cambridge University Press.

Provine, Doris Marie, and Roxanne Lynn Doty. 2011. "The Criminalization of Immigrants as a Racial Project." *Journal of Contemporary Criminal Justice* 27 (3): 261–77. https://doi.org/10.1177/1043986211412559.

Raskin, Jamin B. 1993. "Legal Aliens, Local Citizens: The Historical, Constitutional and Theoretical Meanings of Alien Suffrage." *University of Pennsylvania Law Review* 141: 1391–1446.

Reed-Sandoval, Amy. 2020. *Socially Undocumented: Identity and Immigration Justice*. Philosophy of Race. New York, NY, United States of America: Oxford University Press.

Sager, Alex. 2020. *Against Borders: Why the World Needs Free Movement of People*. Off the Fence: Morality, Politics, and Society. Lanham: Rowman & Littlefield International.

Sanchez, Gabriella, and Mary Romero. 2010. "Critical Race Theory in the US Sociology of Immigration." *Sociology Compass* 4 (9): 779–88.

Shachar, Ayelet. 2020. *The Shifting Border: Legal Cartographies of Migration and Mobility ; Ayelet Shachar in Dialogue*. Manchester University Press.

Silva, Grant J. 2015. "Embodying a 'New' Color Line: Racism, Anti-Immigrant Sentiment and Racial Identities in the 'Postracial' Era." *Knowledge Cultures* 3 (1): 65–90.

Song, Sarah. 2019. *Immigration and Democracy*. New York, NY: Oxford University Press.

Stauffer, Brian. 2021. "'I Didn't Feel Like a Human in There' : Immigration Detention in Canada and Its Impact on Mental Health." Human Rights Watch. https://www.hrw.org/report/2021/06/17/i-didnt-feel-human-there/immigration-detention-canada-and-its-impact-mental.

Stumpf, Julliet. 2006. "The Crimmigration Crisis: Immigrants, Crime, and Sovereign Power." *American University Law Review* 56 (2): 367–419.

U.S. Government Accountability Office. 2021. "Immigration Enforcement: Actions Needed to Better Track Cases Involving U.S. Citizenship Investigations." GAO-21-487. https://www.gao.gov/products/gao-21-487.

Vladislava, Stoyanova. 2018. "A Stark Choice: Domestic Violence or Deportation? The Immigration Status of Victims of Domestic Violence Under the Istanbul Convention." *European Journal of Migration and Law* 20 (1): 53–82.

Wellman, Christopher Heath, 2008. "Immigration and Freedom of Association." *Ethics* 119: 109–141. https://doi.org/10.1086/592311

Zhang, Sheldon X., Gabriella E. Sanchez, and Luigi Achilli. 2018. "Crimes of Solidarity in Mobility: Alternative Views on Migrant Smuggling." *The ANNALS of the American Academy of Political and Social Science* 676 (1): 6–15. https://doi.org/10.1177/0002716217746908.

24
THE ECONOMICS AND ETHICS OF U.S. INTERNAL IMMIGRATION ENFORCEMENT

Madeline Zavodny and George W. Rainbolt

24.1 Introduction

After remaining almost unchanged between 2007 and 2021, the number of unauthorized immigrants living in the U.S. surged in 2022 and 2023.[1] The increase reflected worsening conditions in many Latin American countries and changes in U.S. pandemic-related border policies. The strong U.S. economic recovery from the pandemic likely played an important role as well, with jobs acting as a magnet for many unauthorized migrant workers. Some of these unauthorized immigrants entered the U.S. without inspection, while others were admitted temporarily and overstayed the date they were required to leave.[2] (This chapter follows the U.S. Department of Homeland Security (DHS) in referring to foreign-born non-citizens who are not legal residents as unauthorized immigrants.) The growth in the unauthorized immigrant population was reminiscent of the period from the 1980s until the onset of the Great Recession in 2007. During that period, the unauthorized immigrant population swelled despite a large-scale legalization program enacted in 1986. Then, as now, tight labor markets motivated many migrants to enter or remain in the U.S. despite not having legal immigration status.

The latest wave of unauthorized immigrants faces a different U.S. immigration enforcement policy environment than earlier waves encountered. Most notably, internal enforcement policies adopted during the first two decades of the 21st century make living and working in the U.S. more challenging for many unauthorized immigrants. Some of these policies were enacted by the federal government, and others by states that believed that the federal government was not doing enough to reduce unauthorized immigration.

These internal enforcement policies are the focus of this chapter. It bears noting, however, that there are at least two other dimensions of immigration enforcement, namely, border enforcement and external enforcement. Border enforcement occurs as individuals attempt to enter the U.S. It includes physical barriers and border patrol personnel activity. Increased enforcement along the U.S.-Mexico border has made it more difficult for unauthorized immigrants to cross the border. External enforcement policies are initiatives by the U.S. to incentivize other countries to stem migration flows. For example, the U.S. has pressured Mexico to increase enforcement along that country's southern border and helped

DOI: 10.4324/9781003037309-32

fund Mexico's immigration control efforts (Ribando Seelke and Miro 2023). The goal of external enforcement policies is to make it more difficult for migrants to reach the U.S. border. As the name suggests, external enforcement policies take place in countries other than the U.S. Internal enforcement occurs after individuals have entered the U.S. The lines between external, border, and internal enforcement are necessarily somewhat vague. However, the concept of internal enforcement is important because many enforcement actions occur long after an individual has entered the U.S.

A growing literature examines the economic and social consequences of internal immigration enforcement policies in the U.S. Studies show that internal immigration enforcement policies deter some unauthorized immigrants from living and working in areas that enact tough policies. More broadly, the increase in internal enforcement likely contributed to the non-resumption of growth in the unauthorized immigrant population after the Great Recession ended until the recent surge began. Nonetheless, there is scant evidence that internal enforcement has economic benefits, while there is compelling evidence of undesirable economic and social consequences for both immigrants and U.S. natives. There are also good reasons to think that many current U.S. internal enforcement policies are unethical.

24.2 Description of Internal Immigration Enforcement Policies in the U.S.

Internal immigration enforcement policies can be categorized as privation or apprehension. Privation includes a wide variety of policies that deprive immigrants, primarily unauthorized ones, of rights that citizens and qualified immigrants possess. For example, before *Plyler v. Doe*, 457 U.S. 202 (1982), unauthorized immigrant children did not have the right to attend K-12 public schools in the U.S. The federal government bars unauthorized immigrants from participating in the Affordable Care Act (aka Obamacare), Medicare, Social Security, and many other federally funded programs. Many states bar unauthorized immigrants from obtaining a driver's license. Privation policies seek to reduce unauthorized immigration by making an area less attractive to unauthorized immigrants. Privation policies may require a variety of actors to screen individuals for immigration status. These actors may include employers, hospitals, landlords, banks, and schools, in addition to law enforcement and other government agencies. In effect, governments may require non-governmental actors to screen people for immigration status and to take or not take certain actions based on that status. These screens may be paired with a reporting requirement, a legal obligation to report unauthorized immigrants to a government agency.

Apprehension differs from privation in that it involves monitoring and/or confining individuals (e.g., with electronic monitoring devices or in prisons) and deporting them. Apprehension is carried out by law enforcement officials and is therefore sometimes called "police-based enforcement." The size and scope of police-based immigration enforcement in the U.S. is jaw-dropping. The federal agency in charge of removals from the U.S. interior, Immigration and Customs Enforcement (ICE), manages a sprawling immigration detention system, most of it contracted out to the private sector. Significantly more people are held each year in the immigration detention system than are serving sentences in federal prisons for all non-immigration-related federal crimes combined (Meissner et al. 2013). ICE also manages sizable alternatives-to-detention programs for non-citizens who are in the removal process.

Since the mid-1980s, most of the policy changes in the U.S. regarding internal enforcement directed toward unauthorized immigrants have focused on two areas: employment-based privation and apprehension.[3] Employment-based privation, or employer-based enforcement, makes it harder for unauthorized immigrants to work. Apprehension, or policed-based enforcement, has increasingly enlisted state and local law enforcement agencies to help enforce federal immigration laws and thus increases unauthorized immigrants' risk of being detained and ultimately deported. Although this chapter will discuss to some degree other forms of privation and apprehension, it will focus on employment-based enforcement and police-based enforcement.

24.2.1 Employment-Based Enforcement

Employment-based enforcement has its roots in the 1986 Immigration Reform and Control Act (IRCA), which prohibited employers from knowingly hiring people who are not authorized to work in the U.S. This prohibition has been carried out primarily by requiring employers to review employment eligibility documents for all new hires. Failure to do so can result in civil and criminal penalties for employers. DHS carries out criminal investigations, audits, and worksite raids to enforce the prohibition against knowingly hiring unauthorized workers. Such actions are uncommon, however, and raids usually result in arrests of workers, not employers (Bruno 2015; Sumption 2021).

After IRCA was enacted, employers and immigrants quickly realized that fraudulent documents could be used to evade the IRCA requirements. To address concerns about fraud, the 1996 Illegal Immigration Reform and Immigrant Responsibility Act (IIRIRA) mandated the creation of a system to authenticate worker-provided documents. That system, now known as E-Verify, confirms work eligibility by comparing information from the documents that new hires provide to employers, who enter the information onto a DHS website, with federal government records. Employers that use E-Verify are required to fire employees who cannot resolve discrepancies raised by the system.

Requiring some employers to use E-Verify has been the main way that states and the federal government have strengthened employment-based enforcement.[4] The majority of employment occurs without the use of E-Verify. As of early 2024, about two-fifths of states require at least some employers to use E-Verify to check hires' employment eligibility. Only eight states require all or virtually all employers to use E-Verify. The other E-Verify states require only public employers or government contractors to use the system. The federal government uses E-Verify to check the work eligibility of its employees and requires certain contractors to do so. Punishments for not complying with an E-Verify requirement typically include losing a business license, paying a fine, or being barred from receiving government contracts. However, these punishments are rare (Newkirk 2018).

24.2.2 Police-Based Enforcement

ICE, the DHS agency in charge of deportations from the interior, partners with state and local law enforcement agencies via two main programs to identify, detain, and remove people with immigration violations: 287(g) agreements and Secure Communities.[5] The 287(g) and Secure Communities programs overlap and can operate simultaneously within an area. Only the 287(g) program is voluntary.

In areas that have signed a 287(g) agreement with DHS, ICE-trained law enforcement officers can check DHS databases to determine people's immigration status and detain people with immigration violations until they can be taken into custody by ICE.[6] The first 287(g) agreement was signed in 2002. Some early 287(g) agreements allowed officers to use their delegated authority to check the immigration status of anyone whom officers encountered. Current agreements are limited to checking people who are already in custody. As of early 2024, almost 140 law enforcement agencies, including five state departments of corrections, participate in the 287(g) program.[7]

Like the 287(g) program, the Secure Communities program identifies people with immigration violations. When a state or local law enforcement official makes an arrest or books a person into custody, the person's fingerprints are sent to the Federal Bureau of Investigation (FBI). Under the Secure Communities program, the FBI forwards the fingerprints to DHS, which screens them for immigration violations. If DHS identifies a person who is deportable, it can issue a detainer for the person to be held for up to 48 hours so that ICE can take them into custody. Secure Communities is much larger than 287(g) in terms of geographic coverage. The first Secure Communities programs were implemented in 2008, and the program was in place nationwide by early 2013. In late 2014, Secure Communities was replaced by the Priority Enforcement Program (PEP), which focused on removable immigrants with records of violent crime. Secure Communities was reinstated nationwide in 2017, and PEP was disbanded. The Biden administration announced plans to end Secure Communities and return to PEP, but those plans have not been fully carried out because of litigation.

Police-based enforcement results in considerable numbers of arrests, detentions, and removals in a typical year. In the late 2000s and early 2010s, ICE removed about 200,000 people each fiscal year from the interior, and a similar number along the border.[8] In fiscal year 2023, ICE removed almost 45,000 people from the interior and almost 100,000 along the border.[9] The substantial overlap between criminal law and immigration law, as reflected in the large number of non-citizens affected by police-based internal immigration enforcement, has been dubbed "crimmigration" law.

In response to the rise in police-based enforcement, some areas have adopted sanctuary policies that restrict the ability of state or local law enforcement agencies to make arrests for immigration violations or detain people with immigration violations until they are taken into custody by ICE.

24.3 Evidence on Economic and Social Consequences

Internal immigration enforcement is intended to reduce the number of unauthorized immigrants in the U.S. by decreasing entries and increasing exits, either voluntarily or via deportation. The rise in internal immigration enforcement in the U.S. in the mid-2000s roughly coincided with the plateauing of the size of the unauthorized immigrant population. The Great Recession was the main reason the unauthorized immigrant population stopped growing in the mid-2000s, but tougher internal enforcement likely contributed to the non-resumption of growth in the unauthorized immigrant population once the recession ended and economic growth resumed.

Economists typically estimate the impact of internal immigration enforcement on the number of unauthorized immigrants by studying changes in internal enforcement policies that occurred in specific states or localities.[10] They compare the change in the estimated number of unauthorized immigrants in those areas with the change in the other, similar areas.[11] Empirical evidence indicates that employment- and police-based internal enforcement policies reduce the number of unauthorized immigrants living in areas that implement these policies (e.g., Bohn, Lofstrom, and Raphael 2014; Dee and Murphy 2020; Kostandini, Mykerezi, and Escalante 2014; Orrenius and Zavodny 2016; Watson 2014). Fewer unauthorized immigrants move into those areas, some move out to areas with laxer enforcement policies, and some leave the country altogether. However, employment- and police-based internal enforcement policies do not reduce the unauthorized immigrant population to anywhere near zero in areas that implement them, at least at the intensity at which they have thus far been implemented in the U.S.

24.3.1 Labor Market Impacts

Both employment- and police-based enforcement policies are intended to reduce the number of unauthorized immigrants working in an area. Effects on earnings, however, depend on the relative magnitude of effects on labor supply and labor demand. Labor supply falls if employment- or police-based enforcement reduces the number of unauthorized immigrants in an area. Employment-based enforcement causes labor demand to fall as employers become more reluctant to hire unauthorized workers because of concerns about potential punishment. Police-based enforcement does not directly affect labor demand since it only targets unauthorized immigrants, not employers. If labor demand falls more than labor supply, as might be the case with employment-based enforcement that focuses on employers, conventional labor market models predict that wages among remaining unauthorized immigrants will fall. But if labor supply falls more than labor demand, as is likely to be the case with police-based enforcement and relatively lax employment-based enforcement, then wages among remaining unauthorized immigrants will rise. Paradoxically, that increase in wages increases the incentive for unauthorized immigrants to live in those areas, assuming they are willing to risk tougher enforcement.

Studies conclude that employment- and police-based enforcement policies reduce the number and share of unauthorized immigrants working in an area (e.g., Amuedo-Dorantes and Bansak 2012; East et al. 2023; East and Velásquez 2022). Average hourly wages tend to fall among unauthorized immigrant men who remain employed in states that require all employers to use E-Verify (Amuedo-Dorantes and Bansak 2012; Orrenius and Zavodny 2015). Wage impacts among unauthorized immigrant women are more muted, perhaps because they are more likely to work in private households doing childcare and housecleaning and therefore not exposed to E-Verify (Amuedo-Dorantes and Bansak 2012; Orrenius and Zavodny 2015).

Empirical evidence on the impact of E-Verify requirements on legal immigrants' and U.S. natives' employment and wages is mixed but generally points to small, if any, effects among less-educated workers (e.g., Amuedo-Dorantes and Bansak 2014; Bohn, Lofstrom, and Raphael 2015; Orrenius and Zavodny 2015). Secure Communities appears to have reduced employment and wages among less-educated U.S. natives, suggesting that labor demand falls substantially as areas experience a drop in the number of unauthorized immigrants living there (East et al. 2023). Highly educated U.S.-born women with children reduce their labor supply in response to the Secure Communities-induced decrease in household services provided by unauthorized immigrants (East and Velásquez 2022). U.S.-born teenagers with unauthorized immigrant parents, in contrast, increase their labor supply in areas experiencing more deportations, suggesting they step up as family income providers when their parents reduce their labor supply to evade police-based enforcement (Rubalcaba, Bucheli, and Morales 2024).

Few studies have examined the economic impacts of internal enforcement policies on employers, such as whether profits fall in industries that typically hire larger shares of unauthorized immigrants.

24.3.2 Social Impacts

A large literature overwhelmingly concludes that immigrants are less likely to commit violent and property crimes than similar U.S. natives.[12] There is less evidence specific to unauthorized immigrants, but a study using arrest data from Texas found that unauthorized immigrants are less likely than U.S. natives to be arrested for violent or property crimes (Light, He, and Robey 2020). There is therefore little reason to expect that police-based enforcement programs would reduce crime rates. Empirical studies are consistent with this. For example, the rollout of Secure Communities had no observable effect on crime rates (Miles and Cox 2014). Further, implementing a sanctuary policy does not appear to affect crime rates in an area (Hausman 2020).

Police-based internal immigration enforcement can make immigrants, particularly unauthorized ones, reluctant to interact with police for fear of being detained or deported.[13] For example, during the period when the less-restrictive PEP program replaced the more-restrictive Secure Communities program, the number of crimes reported to local police by Hispanics in Dallas, Texas, rose, which is consistent with tougher police-based internal enforcement having a chilling effect on crime reporting (Jácome 2022). Sanctuary policies may increase immigrants' willingness to cooperate with police and thereby reduce some types of crimes. For example, domestic homicide rates among Hispanic women fell in areas that implemented sanctuary policies, suggesting immigrant women are more likely to report domestic violence and seek protection in sanctuary jurisdictions (Amuedo-Dorantes and Deza 2022). Hispanics are more likely to report to the police being the victim of a violent crime after an area adopts a sanctuary policy (Martínez-Schuldt and Martínez 2021).

Police-based enforcement appears to adversely affect health outcomes and reduce participation in means-tested programs among Hispanic immigrants who are likely to lack legal status. Hispanic immigrants report more mental stress in areas that have implemented police-based enforcement (e.g., Wang and Kaushal 2019), and a variety of health outcomes appear to worsen among children and adults after areas enter into partnerships with ICE (Perreira and Pedroza 2019). Unauthorized immigrants are ineligible for most means-tested programs, but their U.S. citizen children are eligible if they meet other program requirements. Participation of eligible Hispanic citizens in safety net programs, including Medicaid and the Supplemental Nutrition Assistance Program, falls as police-based enforcement intensifies in their area (e.g., Alsan and Yang 2022; Amuedo-Dorantes, Arenas-Arroyo, and Sevilla 2018; Watson 2014).

24.4 The Ethics of Internal Immigration Enforcement Policies in the U.S.

In philosophy, much of the literature on immigration focuses on the question of whether governments have the right to prohibit entry, aka the right to exclude. Some hold that governments have the right to exclude (e.g., Walzer 1983; Wellman 2008). Some hold that governments do not have the right to exclude. "Citizenship in Western liberal democracies is the modern equivalent of feudal privilege – an inherited status that greatly enhances one's life chances" (Carens 1987, 251). On one view, a commitment to the equality of all people implies that, with only a few exceptions, governments may not prohibit entry. If governments may not prohibit entry, then they may not enforce a prohibition on entry. A discussion of the ethics of internal immigration enforcement presupposes that governments may prohibit entry. Thus, this chapter assumes that governments may prohibit entry.[14]

The assumption that governments may prohibit entry does not imply that they may do anything and everything to enforce this prohibition. If a government has a right to prohibit some conduct, then there are some ways in which the government may enforce this prohibition and many ways it may not. This raises the general question: how may governments enforce the prohibition to enter? In particular, what are the ethical constraints on a government's internal enforcement? Here we set out four principles as guides to discussions of this question. The four principles are (a) protection of human rights, (b) respect for the rule of law, (c) proportional punishments and procedures, and (d) efficient, effective, and appropriate allocation of resources.

24.4.1 Human Rights

Those in philosophy and political theory who work on immigration disagree in many ways. However, one point is widely accepted: a government may not violate human rights. Although they disagree on many matters, Blake (2020), Brock (2020), Carens (2013), Ferracioli (2021), Hidalgo (2019), Miller (2016), Sager (2020), and Song (2019) all agree that human rights constrain a government's policies. Therefore, they all agree that a government's internal enforcement policies must not violate human rights.

Although there is wide agreement that internal immigration enforcement must be done within the bounds of human rights, the concept of human rights is contested. Two scholars can agree that a government's internal enforcement must not violate human rights while holding different views about matters such as what human rights we have, the importance of various human rights, and what specific actions violate a specific human right. The depth of the disagreement can be seen by comparing the human rights set out in the 30 articles of the Universal Declaration of Human Rights (United Nations, n.d.) (which includes, e.g., "the right to rest and leisure, including reasonable limitation of working hours and periodic holidays with pay") with the much more restrained list defended by Shue (1996).

The case of family connections illustrates that answering questions about internal immigration enforcement often seems to require a specific account of human rights. Suppose that Gregory, his wife, and his child overstay their visas. After his wife dies in an auto accident, Gregory remarries a U.S. citizen, and has another child who, being born in the U.S., is also a U.S. citizen. Do these family connections provide a reason to think that it would be a violation of Gregory's human rights to deport him? Ferracioli (2016; 2021), Lister (2018a), Song (2019), and Yong (2016) defend the view that, under certain conditions, family connections make it a violation of human rights to deport people. Suppose that Gregory was injured in the car accident. Do his human rights include a right to emergency health care? Because of *Plyler v. Doe*, under current U.S. law, Gregory's first child has a right to education. Is this a human right?

Although the concept of human rights is contested, there are cases in which there is wide agreement that certain policies would violate human rights. For example, a government may not use torture to find out the name of a person who is providing forged immigration documents. As Lister (2020) notes, it seems clear that certain detention conditions would violate human rights. For example, the government must provide adequate food and water to those in detention. There is a large literature on whether governments violate human rights if they consider race, ethnicity, gender, sex, or religion when making decisions about exclusion (e.g., Aitchison 2023; Akhtar 2022; Blake 2003, 2013, 2016; Brock 2020; Fine 2016; Hosein 2018; Mendoza 2014; Miller 2015; Reed-Sandoval 2020; Wellman 2022). There does not appear to be a literature on whether governments may consider these factors in the internal enforcement of exclusion. There appears to be a widespread but unargued assumption that if a government were to use these factors in internal immigration enforcement, that would be a violation of human rights.

Some have argued that police-based enforcement under 287(g) agreements and Secure Communities violates the human rights of unauthorized immigrants. For example, Mendoza has argued that unauthorized immigrants, "because of their susceptibility to deportation, are one of the most vulnerable sub-groups within any society. Their precarious situation leaves them virtually unprotected against various forms of exploitation and discrimination by both public…and private…institutions. This kind of oppression and discrimination is a violation of moral equality because, even if undocumented immigrants do not have the political right to be present…, as persons they are entitled to have their basic human rights respected" (2015, 86). One might hold that the phrase "virtually unprotected" is too strong. When it comes to the protection of human rights, the status of unauthorized immigrants in the U.S. today is far better than that of U.S. citizens of Japanese descent during World War II. However, in general, unauthorized immigrants are less protected from human rights abuses than citizens and authorized immigrants. Their unauthorized status is likely to make them significantly less willing to report violations of their human rights and thus make them more vulnerable to exploitation.

On these grounds, Carens (2013), Crépeau and Hastie (2015), Miller (2016), and Song (2019) have argued that there should be a "firewall" between internal immigration enforcement and the provision of public services (e.g., police protection, fire protection, health services, educational services, and welfare services). In other words, in order to secure the human rights of unauthorized immigrants, those who provide public services should not be allowed to provide information to those who carry out internal immigration enforcement policies. On this view, police-based enforcement under a 287(g) agreement or Secure Communities may be a breach of such a firewall and thus lead to violations of human rights.

In general, although the scope of the constraints that human rights place on internal immigration enforcement is a matter of debate, these constraints are significant. It is far from clear that policies such as 287(g) agreements and Secure Communities fall within these constraints. Reforms such as revising these programs so that only criminal convictions lead to a check of DHS records would significantly reduce these human rights concerns.

24.4.2 *The Rule of Law*

In general, the rule of law requires that "people in positions of authority…exercise their power within a constraining framework of well-established public norms rather than in an arbitrary, *ad hoc*, or purely discretionary manner" (Waldron 2023, 2).[15] Just as there does not appear to be literature that argues that, when internally enforcing immigration law, governments may violate human rights, there does not appear to be a literature that argues that internal enforcement activities are not subject to the constraints of the rule of law. For example, a government may not willfully turn a blind eye to the bribery of the officials charged with internal immigration enforcement. However, as is the case with human rights, a central reason for the wide agreement that internal immigration enforcement must be within the rule of law is that this concept is contested.

It is common to distinguish three aspects of the rule of law: formal, procedural, and substantive. Fuller (1964) is the *locus classicus* on the formal aspects of the rule of law. He lists eight formal conditions: generality, publicity, prospectivity, intelligibility, consistency, practicability, stability, and congruence. However, as the large literature on Fuller's work illustrates, each of these conditions is contested. These formal conditions are consistent with laws that a great many would consider to be unethical. For example, a prohibition on unauthorized immigrants having any counsel at immigration hearings could easily be written to be consistent with Fuller's conditions.

Waldron (2023) provides one list of procedural aspects of the rule of law. It includes a hearing by an impartial tribunal, a right to counsel, a right to present and confront witnesses, and a right to hear reasons from the tribunal.

While Raz (1977) argues that these formal and procedural aspects exhaust the rule of law, others (e.g., Bingham 2010; Gowder 2016) argue that the rule of law includes substantive aspects. For example, Gowder argues the rule of law requires that power "must be used under rules that give those over whom that power is exercised the opportunity to call the users of the power to account..." (2016, 4). This incorporates a substantive democratic requirement into the rule of law.

There is a large literature that argues that one or more aspects of the U.S.'s internal enforcement policies are not compatible with the rule of law (e.g., Aliverti 2017; Brock 2020, 2021; Ellermann 2014; Gibney 2008; Lister 2018b, 2020; Markowitz 2021; Mendoza 2015; Miller 2015; Silverman 2018; Song 2023; Song and Bloemraad 2022; Wirts and Mendoza 2022). These works do not set out a comprehensive view of the rule of law and then apply it to the enforcement of immigration law. Instead, they argue that some feature or features of immigrant enforcement are incompatible with some proposed part or parts of the rule of law.

Of particular relevance to internal immigration enforcement is the question of the degree to which discretion is compatible with the rule of law. Sager (2017; 2020) and Lenard (2015) have argued that it is not possible to control immigration without the removal of discretion and that the removal of discretion is required by the rule of law. Since there is discretion in the enforcement of the law against citizens, this argument would need to show that the levels of discretion in the internal enforcement of immigration law are higher than the levels found in the enforcement of the law against citizens. Nevertheless, Sager's and Lenard's arguments do seem to show that, all else being equal, we should favor internal immigration enforcement policies that minimize discretion. For example, rule of law considerations indicate that, when it comes to employment-based enforcement, a policy that requires all employers to verify the legal right to work of all hires is, all else being equal, preferable to a policy that gives officials discretion as to which employers must do this verification.

24.4.3 *Proportionality*

Two principles that govern punishments and procedures generally apply to the internal enforcement of immigration restrictions: (1) punishment should be proportional to the gravity of the offense, and (2) procedural protections should be proportional to the gravity of the punishment.

It is often said that the punishment should fit the crime. More precisely, the seriousness of a legal outcome should be proportional to the moral gravity of the offense. As Mendoza (2015) notes, it would be wrong if unauthorized immigrants received the death penalty. This is the principle of proportional punishment (Rainbolt and Reif 1997). There is an enormous literature on punishment, much of it focused on the justification of punishment. This literature is relevant to determining the gravity of an offense. For example, retributivists and consequentialists will offer different accounts of the gravity of offenses. The literature on immigration enforcement has been surprisingly silent on the gravity of the offense of unauthorized immigration as compared to other offenses.

The principle of proportional procedural protections is less well known than the principle of proportional punishment. Procedural protections are rules designed to reduce the chance that a legal penalty will be erroneously imposed. For example, the right to counsel reduces the chance that a tribunal will erroneously decide that a person has committed an offense. According to the principle of proportional procedural protections, the level of procedural protections should be proportional to the gravity of the possible punishment. The principle of proportional procedural protections stems from a conception of how serious an erroneous imposition of a penalty would be. If I were forced to pay a thirty-dollar fine for parking illegally when I did not park illegally, this would be an annoyance and a minor injustice. There is no need for a high level of procedural protection. On the other hand, if I were executed when I was not in any way involved with killing anyone, this would be a horrific injustice. If one risks death, procedural protections ought to be extremely high. There seem to be clear cases in which internal immigration enforcement would violate the principle of proportional procedural protections. We can imagine a policy according to which anyone found to not have their passport on their person would be deported without any hearing whatsoever. However, as was the case with the principle of proportional punishment, the philosophical literature on immigration enforcement is surprisingly silent on what level of procedural protections are appropriate for the internal enforcement of immigration violations as compared to other offenses.

One might argue that employer-based enforcement policies as currently implemented in the U.S. seem to violate the principle of proportional punishment. Currently, unauthorized immigrant workers face a punishment that may include deportation, whereas employers typically face fines that are small relative to their profits. Some might see the difference in the gravity of punishments between unauthorized immigrant workers and employers as a violation of the principle of proportional punishment. On the other hand, one might argue that unauthorized immigrant workers are doing their best to deceive employers, and therefore a stiffer punishment is warranted for the workers than for the employers. In response, some might claim that many employers are aware that some of their hires are unauthorized immigrants who presented falsified documents, and therefore employers should receive a punishment comparable to that received by workers.[16]

In applying the proportionality principles, governments often attach labels to sets of punishments and/or procedures. In the U.S., these labels include "infraction," "misdemeanor," "felony," "administrative," "civil," and "criminal." For example, generally speaking, a felony is a crime that is punishable by a prison sentence of more than one year, a misdemeanor is a crime punishable by a prison sentence of one year or less, and an infraction is not a crime and is not punishable by a prison sentence. Civil procedures offer a lower level of procedural protections than criminal procedures. These labels are one way governments try to implement the two proportionality requirements. They are not intrinsically relevant.

For example, that a particular offense is labeled "civil" does not matter when it comes to determining whether the proportionality requirements have been met. What matters is the seriousness of the possible consequences and the level of procedural protection. To avoid violations of proportionality, the labels must match the seriousness of the possible punishments and the rigor of the procedures.

In *Fong Yue Ting v. United States* 149 U.S. 698, 730 (1893), the U.S. Supreme Court held that deportation is not punishment for a crime. Although this precedent has been somewhat modified by cases such as *Padilla v. Kentucky*, 559 U.S. 356 (2010), the vast majority of U.S. deportation proceedings take place under the rules of civil procedure. That the U.S. Supreme Court attached the label "civil" to deportation does not imply that civil procedures are appropriate. Deportation is such a serious consequence that the principle of proportional procedural protections implies that criminal procedures (or some level of procedure that approaches criminal procedures) ought to be used. As it stands, because of *Ting*, U.S. law on internal immigration enforcement includes a clear violation of the principle of proportional procedural protections. (For a similar argument, see Markowitz 2011.)

24.4.4 Effective, Efficient, and Appropriately Resourced

Even if a set of policies for the internal enforcement of immigration restrictions respects human rights, the rule of law, and both proportionality principles, it could still be deeply flawed. It could be ineffective, inefficient, and/or inappropriately resourced. A perfectly effective set of immigration policies and procedures would result in no unauthorized immigrants and no deportations of those authorized to reside in the U.S. A perfectly efficient set of immigration policies and procedures would do these two things using the fewest possible resources.[17] In a perfectly resourced set of policies and procedures, the amount of resources expended on the enforcement of immigration laws would be proportional to the severity of the problems caused by unauthorized immigration. Of course, no part of any legal system is perfectly effective, perfectly efficient, or perfectly resourced. Nevertheless, a number of authors have argued that the U.S. internal immigration enforcement system is seriously flawed on one or more of these three criteria.

The fact that the number of unauthorized immigrants continues to rise supports the claim that internal immigration enforcement is not effective. Massey, Durand, & Pren argue that effective border enforcement combined with a lack of internal enforcement has "backfired by increasing the rate of undocumented population growth and turning what had been a circular flow of male workers going to three states into a settled population of families living in 50 states" (2016, 1558). In other words, they argue that, because crossing the border is harder than it was and internal immigration enforcement is ineffective, individuals who previously moved back and forth across the border without authorization as economic conditions ebbed and flowed now stay indefinitely in the U.S. instead of taking the risk of being detained while crossing the border. Others might argue that the current set of internal immigration enforcement policies does not result in many departures of unauthorized immigrants but instead creates an underclass of minority individuals who are vulnerable to exploitation.

It is hard to find anyone who defends the view that internal enforcement is efficient. On the contrary, both those who favor more immigration and those who favor less immigration believe that the U.S. internal enforcement system is extremely inefficient. To take only one example, it seems plausible that the U.S. internal immigration enforcement system would be more effective and efficient if it significantly increased sanctions on employers that knowingly employ unauthorized immigrants (e.g., Turley 2019). Doing so would reduce labor demand and weaken the job magnet that attracts many unauthorized immigrants.

When it comes to resources, studies indicate that unauthorized immigration has a positive economic impact in the U.S. (see, e.g., Chassamboulli and Peri 2015; Edwards and Ortega 2016; Hanson 2007). If that is the case, then the U.S. immigration enforcement system may be overresourced and the U.S. should spend less on immigration enforcement.

Sager (2020) and Mendoza (2014, 2017) have argued that it is impossible to implement a system of internal immigration enforcement that does not violate human rights, respects the rule of law, provides proportional punishments and procedures, and is efficiently effective. They then conclude that this means that the U.S. should have open borders. However, their argument is not clear on two key points. First, it is not clear whether Sager and Mendoza think that the U.S. (or any other country) has a general system of law enforcement (e.g., prohibitions on theft, embezzlement, and assault) that meets their standards in these four areas. If the U.S. has successfully implemented a general system of law enforcement that meets the requirements in these four areas, then it is not clear why it is impossible for the U.S. to do the same for internal immigration enforcement. Second, it is not clear how Sager and Mendoza are using the term "impossible." The barriers to reform of the internal immigration system that they point out mostly seem to be political, not conceptual. However, the political barriers to a policy of open borders are much larger than the political barriers to the adoption of the reforms necessary for the U.S. to have an effective and efficient system of internal immigration enforcement that adequately protects human rights, implements the rule of law, and respects the proportionality principles.

24.5 Conclusion

In a world of massive inequality of resources where technological change has caused a significant reduction in the cost of traveling from one country to another and a significant increase in the ability of people to get information about other countries, the increase in attempts to immigrate is not a surprise. Moreover, there is no reason to think that these fundamental factors driving increased attempts to immigrate will diminish anytime soon. Assuming governments may prohibit entry, a three-legged stool of external enforcement, border enforcement, and internal enforcement is necessary to effectively and efficiently control immigration. However, such a system of enforcement must not violate human rights, must respect the rule of law, and must honor the proportionality principles outlined above. While we do not have the space to make the argument here, there are good reasons to believe that current U.S. internal immigration enforcement policies, in addition to being lacking when it comes to efficiency and effectiveness, also violate human rights, fail to respect the rule of law, and do not follow the proportionality principles. On the other hand, unlike some authors, we think that changes to current U.S. internal immigration enforcement policies could lead to massive improvements in all four of these areas.

That said, we believe that any increase in U.S. internal immigration enforcement should be accompanied by a broad-based legalization program and expanded pathways for future immigrants to enter and remain in the U.S. legally. Otherwise, the economic costs of increased internal immigration enforcement would be considerable. A broad-based legalization program and expanded legal pathways for future immigrants would also begin to address some of the troubling ethical issues that surround immigration enforcement.

Notes

1 See, for example, estimates in Congressional Budget Office (2024) and Warren (2024).
2 It is unclear whether some groups of immigrants who have a temporary right to reside and work in the U.S. even though they entered without inspection or overstayed should be classified as unauthorized immigrants. These groups include recipients of Deferred Action for Childhood Arrivals (DACA) or Temporary Protected Status (TPS). Asylum seekers are another unclear group. In the post-pandemic period, a large number of migrants requested asylum and were released into the U.S. to await adjudication of their asylum claims. As of early 2024, those migrants can file for employment authorization 150 days after they file their asylum application. If they work before receiving their employment authorization document (EAD), they violate immigration law and are considered unlawfully present. The EAD process is severely backlogged, so many asylum seekers work without authorization.
3 The U.S. has enacted other major changes that affected unauthorized immigrants since the mid-1980s, most notably the 1996 Illegal Immigration Reform and Immigrant Responsibility Act (IIRIRA). The IIRIRA imposed three- or ten-year entry bars on immigrants who had entered the U.S. without inspection and returned to their home country to apply for U.S. lawful permanent resident (LPR) status. The re-entry bars have resulted in large numbers of unauthorized immigrants who could qualify for LPR status remaining in the U.S. without legal status since applying for LPR status would trigger the re-entry bar. See Bolter, Chisti, and Meissner (2021).
4 Another important form of employer-based enforcement in the U.S. was "no-match letters." In some years, the Social Security Administration (SSA) has notified employers when there is a discrepancy between SSA records and information that employers report to the federal government as part of tax withholding. Employers were required to fire employees who could not resolve discrepancies. The no-match letter program was most recently discontinued in 2021. DHS's IMAGE program also enlists employers in checking workers' employment eligibility but is small in scale and voluntary.
5 DHS has other programs that also apprehend, detain, and remove noncitizens, most notably the Criminal Apprehension Program (CAP). CAP focuses on noncitizens who are subject to removal because they have a felony conviction. The Biden administration changed the name of CAP from the Criminal Alien Program to the Criminal Apprehension Program.
6 The 287(g) program was created by the 1996 IIRIRA, which contained a provision that allowed state and local law enforcement agencies to sign agreements with DHS to carry out certain functions related to enforcing federal immigration law.
7 See https://www.ice.gov/identify-and-arrest/287g (accessed March 2, 2024).
8 See https://www.ice.gov/remove/removal-statistics/2015 and https://www.ice.gov/doclib/eoy/iceAnnualReportFY2023.pdf (accessed March 2, 2024).
9 See https://www.ice.gov/spotlight/statistics and https://www.ice.gov/doclib/eoy/iceAnnualReportFY2023.pdf (accessed March 2, 2024). The decrease from recent decades is presumably largely due to the increase in requests for asylum, which can take considerable time to be determined.
10 Empirical studies of the effects of specific programs tend to focus on E-Verify or 287(g) since there is more variation over time and across areas in those programs than in Secure Communities or CAP. Unlike E-Verify or 287(g), Secure Communities rolled out quickly nationwide, making it difficult for unauthorized immigrants to evade it by moving to another area. Studies that measure the intensity of police-based enforcement using data on removals measure the combined effects of 287(g), Secure Communities, and CAP.
11 Since few surveys ask about legal status, empirical studies typically use groups with a relatively high share of unauthorized immigrants, such as less-educated noncitizen Hispanics, as a proxy for unauthorized immigrants.
12 Orrenius and Zavodny (2019) provide a review of the literature.
13 Perreira and Pedroza (2019) provide a review of the literature.
14 Rainbolt is not sure that this assumption is plausible.
15 As philosophers use "the rule of law," only people in positions of authority can violate the rule of law. Neither an unauthorized immigrant nor a murderer violates the rule of law. They violate the law without violating the rule of law.

16 See, for example, claims by unauthorized immigrants who worked at the Trump National Golf Club that their supervisors knew they were unauthorized, as reported by Jordan (2018). Some employers may be more than aware of false documents: Fieldwork in California by Horton (2016) revealed agricultural supervisors providing unauthorized immigrant workers with false documents.

17 Economists are likely to determine whether policies are efficient based on whether their marginal benefit is equal to their marginal cost, not based on whether they minimize costs. The marginal cost of policies that would result in no unauthorized immigrants in the U.S. would almost certainly exceed the marginal benefit.

References

Aitchison, Guy. 2023. "Border-Crossing: Immigration Law, Racism and Justified Resistance." *Political Studies* 71 (3): 597–615. https://doi.org/10.1177/00323217211030184.

Akhtar, Sahar. 2022. "Race Beyond Our Borders: Is Racial and Ethnic Immigration Selection Always Morally Wrong?" *Ethics* 132 (2): 322–51. https://doi.org/10.1086/716870.

Aliverti, Ana. 2017. "The Wrongs of Unlawful Immigration." *Criminal Law and Philosophy* 11 (2): 375–391. https://doi.org/10.1007/s11572-015-9377-y.

Alsan, Marcella, and Crystal S. Yang. 2022. "Fear and the Safety Net: Evidence from Secure Communities." *The Review of Economics and Statistics*, forthcoming. https://doi.org/10.1162/rest_a_01250.

Amuedo-Dorantes, Catalina, and Cynthia Bansak. 2012. "The Labor Market Impact of Mandated Employment Verification Systems." *American Economic Review* 102 (3): 543–48. https://doi.org/10.1257/aer.102.3.543.

Amuedo-Dorantes, Catalina, and Cynthia Bansak. 2014. "Employment Verification Mandates and the Labor Market Outcomes of Likely Unauthorized and Native Workers." *Contemporary Economic Policy* 32 (3): 671–80. https://doi.org/10.1111/coep.12043.

Amuedo-Dorantes, Catalina, Esther Arenas-Arroyo, and Almudena Sevilla. 2018. "Immigration Enforcement and Economic Resources of Children with Likely Unauthorized Parents." *Journal of Public Economics* 158 (February): 63–78. https://doi.org/10.1016/j.jpubeco.2017.12.004.

Amuedo-Dorantes, Catalina, and Monica Deza. 2022. "Can Sanctuary Policies Reduce Domestic Violence?." *American Law and Economics Review* 24 (1): 116–70. https://doi.org/10.1093/aler/ahab014.

Bingham, Tom. 2010. *The Rule of Law*. London: Allen Lane.

Blake, Michael. 2003. "Immigration." In *A Companion to Applied Ethics*, edited by R.G. Frey and Christopher Heath Wellman, 224–37. Oxford: Blackwell Publishing.

Blake, Michael. 2013. "Immigration, Jurisdiction, and Exclusion." *Philosophy and Public Affairs* 41 (2): 103–30. https://doi.org/10.1111/papa.12012.

Blake, Michael. 2016. "Exclusion, Discretion, and Justice." In *The Ethics and Politics of Immigration*, edited by Alex Sager, 29–43. Lanham: Rowman & Littlefield.

Blake, Michael. 2020. *Justice, Migration, and Mercy*. New York: Oxford University Press.

Bohn, Sarah, Magnus Lofstrom, and Steven Raphael. 2014. "Did the 2007 Legal Arizona Workers Act Reduce the State's Unauthorized Immigrant Population?" *The Review of Economics and Statistics* 96 (2): 258–69. https://doi.org/10.1162/REST_a_00429.

Bohn, Sarah, Magnus Lofstrom, and Steven Raphael. 2015. "Do E-Verify Mandates Improve Labor Market Outcomes of Low-Skilled Native and Legal Immigrant Workers?" *Southern Economic Journal* 81 (4): 960–79. https://doi.org/10.1002/soej.12019.

Bolter, Jessica, Muzaffar Chisti, and Doris Meissner. 2021. *"Back on the Table: U.S. Legalization and the Unauthorized Immigrant Groups That Could Factor in the Debate."* Washington, DC: Migration Policy Institute. https://www.migrationpolicy.org/research/us-legalization-unauthorized-immigrant-groups.

Brock, Gillian. 2020. *Justice for People on the Move: Migration in Challenging Times*. Cambridge: Cambridge University Press.

Brock, Gillian. 2021. *Migration and Political Theory*. Cambridge: Polity.

Bruno, Andorra. 2015. *Immigration-Related Worksite Enforcement: Performance Measures*. Washington, DC: Congressional Research Service. https://crsreports.congress.gov/product/details?prodcode=R40002.

Carens, Joseph. 1987. "Aliens and Citizens: The Case for Open Borders." *Review of Politics* 49 (2): 251–73.

Carens, Joseph. 2013. *The Ethics of Immigration*. New York: Oxford University Press.

Chassamboulli, Andri, and Giovanni Peri. 2015. "The Labor Market Effects of Reducing the Number of Illegal Immigrants." *Review of Economic Dynamics* 18 (4): 792–821. https://doi.org/10.1016/j.red.2015.07.005.

Congressional Budget Office. 2024. *The Demographic Outlook: 2024 to 2054*. Washington, DC: Congressional Budget Office. https://www.cbo.gov/publication/59697.

Crépeau, François, and Bethany Hastie. 2015. "The Case for 'Firewall' Protection for Irregular Migrants: Safeguarding Fundamental Rights." *European Journal of Migration & Law* 17 (2): 157–83.

Dee, Thomas S., and Mark Murphy. 2020. "Vanished Classmates: The Effects of Local Immigration Enforcement on School Enrollment." *American Educational Research Journal* 57 (2): 694–727. https://doi.org/10.3102/0002831219860816.

East, Chloe N., Annie L. Hines, Philip Luck, Hani Mansour, and Andrea Velásquez. 2023. "The Labor Market Effects of Immigration Enforcement." *Journal of Labor Economics* 41 (4): 957–96. https://doi.org/10.1086/721152.

East, Chloe N., and Andrea Velásquez. 2022. "Unintended Consequences of Immigration Enforcement: Household Services and High-Educated Mothers' Work." *Journal of Human Resources* forthcoming. https://doi.org/10.3368/jhr.0920-11197R1.

Edwards, Ryan, and Francesc Ortega. 2016. "The Economic Contribution of Unauthorized Workers: An Industry Analysis." National Bureau of Economic Research Working Paper No. 22834. https://www.nber.org/papers/w22834.

Ellermann, Antje. 2014. "The Rule of Law and the Right to Stay: The Moral Claims of Undocumented Migrants." *Politics & Society* 42 (3): 293–308. https://doi.org/10.1177/0032329214543255.

Ferracioli, Luara. 2016. "Family Migration Schemes and Liberal Neutrality: A Dilemma." *Journal of Moral Philosophy* 13 (5): 553–75. https://doi.org/10.1163/17455243-4681056.

Ferracioli, Luara. 2021. *Liberal Self-Determination in a World of Immigration*. Oxford: Oxford University Press.

Fine, Sarah. 2016. "Immigration and Discrimination." In *Migration in Political Theory: The Ethics of Movement and Membership*, edited by Sarah Fine and Lea Ypi, 125–50. Oxford: Oxford University Press.

Fuller, Lon. 1964. *The Morality of Law*. New Haven: Yale University Press.

Gibney, Matthew. 2008. "Asylum and the Expansion of Deportation in the United Kingdom." *Government and Opposition* 43 (2): 146–67. https://doi.org/10.1111/j.1477-7053.2007.00249.x.

Gowder, Paul. 2016. *The Rule of Law in the Real World*. Cambridge: Cambridge University Press.

Hanson, Gordon H. 2007. *The Economic Logic of Illegal Immigration*. New York: Council on Foreign Relations.

Hausman, David K. 2020. "Sanctuary Policies Reduce Deportations Without Increasing Crime." *Proceedings of the National Academy of Sciences* 117 (44): 27262–67. https://doi.org/10.1073/pnas.2014673117.

Hidalgo, Javier S. 2019. *Unjust Borders: Individuals and the Ethics of Immigration*. New York: Routledge.

Horton, Sarah B. 2016. "Ghost Workers: The Implications of Governing Immigration Through Crime for Migrant Workplaces." *Anthropology of Work Review* 37: 11–23. https://doi.org/10.1111/awr.12081.

Hosein, Adam. 2018. "Racial Profiling and a Reasonable Sense of Inferior Political Status." *Journal of Political Philosophy* 26 (3): 1–20. https://doi.org/10.1111/jopp.12162.

Jácome, Elisa. 2022. "The Effect of Immigration Enforcement on Crime Reporting: Evidence from Dallas." *Journal of Urban Economics* 128 (March): 103395. https://doi.org/10.1016/j.jue.2021.103395.

Jordan, Miriam. 2018. "In America Illegally, and Employed by Trump." *The New York Times*, December 7, A1.

Kostandini, Genti, Elton Mykerezi, and Cesar Escalante. 2014. "The Impact of Immigration Enforcement on the U.S. Farming Sector." *American Journal of Agricultural Economics* 96 (1): 172–92.

Lenard, Patti Tamara. 2015. "The Ethics of Deportation in Liberal Democratic States." *European Journal of Political Theory* 14 (4): 464–80. https://doi.org/10.1177/1474885115584834.

Light, Michael T., Jingying He, and Jason P. Robey. 2020. "Comparing Crime Rates between Undocumented Immigrants, Legal Immigrants, and Native-Born US Citizens in Texas." *Proceedings of the National Academy of Sciences* 117 (51): 32340–47. https://doi.org/10.1073/pnas.2014704117.

Lister, Matthew. 2018a. "The Rights of Families and Children at the Border." In *Philosophical Foundations of Children's and Family Law*, edited by Elizabeth Brake and Lucinda Ferguson, 153–70. New York: Oxford University Press.

Lister, Matthew. 2018b. "'Dreamers' and Others: Immigration Protests, Enforcement, and Civil Disobedience." *American Philosophical Association Newsletters: Hispanic/Latino Issues in Philosophy* 17 (2): 15–17.

Lister, Matthew. 2020. "Enforcing Immigration Law." *Philosophy Compass* 15 (3): 1–11. https://doi.org/10.1111/phc3.12653.

Markowitz, Peter L. 2011. "Deportation Is Different." *Journal of Constitutional Law* 13 (5): 1299–1361.

Markowitz, Peter L. 2021. "Rethinking Immigration Enforcement." *Florida Law Review* 73: 1033–79.

Martínez-Schuldt, Ricardo D., and Daniel E. Martínez. 2021. "Immigrant Sanctuary Policies and Crime-Reporting Behavior: A Multilevel Analysis of Reports of Crime Victimization to Law Enforcement, 1980 to 2004." *American Sociological Review* 86 (1): 154–85. https://doi.org/10.1177/0003122420978406.

Massey, Douglas S., Jorge Durand, and Karen A. Pren. 2016. "Why Border Enforcement Backfired." *American Journal of Sociology* 121 (5): 1557–1600. https://doi.org/10.1086/684200.

Meissner, Doris, Donald M. Kerwin, Muzaffar Chisti, and Claire Bergeron. 2013. "Immigration Enforcement in the United States: The Rise of a Formidable Machinery." Washington, DC: Migration Policy Institute. https://www.migrationpolicy.org/research/immigration-enforcement-united-states-rise-formidable-machinery.

Mendoza, José Jorge. 2014. "Discrimination and the Presumptive Rights of Immigrants." *Critical Philosophy of Race* 2 (1): 68–83. https://doi.org/10.5325/critphilrace.2.1.0068.

Mendoza, José Jorge. 2015. "Enforcement Matters: Reframing the Philosophical Debate on Immigration." *Journal of Speculative Philosophy* 29 (1): 73–90. https://doi.org/10.5325/jspecphil.29.1.0073.

Mendoza, José Jorge. 2017. *The Moral and Political Philosophy of Immigration: Liberty, Security, and Equality*. Lanham: Lexington Books.

Miles, Thomas J., and Adam B. Cox. 2014. "Does Immigration Enforcement Reduce Crime? Evidence from Secure Communities." *The Journal of Law & Economics* 57 (4): 937–73. https://doi.org/10.1086/680935.

Miller, David. 2015. "Justice in Immigration." *European Journal of Political Theory* 14 (4): 391–408. https://doi.org/10.1177/1474885115584833.

Miller, David. 2016. *Strangers in Our Midst: The Political Philosophy of Immigration*. Cambridge, MA: Harvard University Press.

Newkirk, Margaret. 2018. "E-Verify Laws across Southern Red States Are Barely Enforced." *Bloomberg.com*, August 27. https://www.bloomberg.com/news/articles/2018-08-23/e-verify-laws-across-southern-red-states-are-barely-enforced.

Orrenius, Pia M., and Madeline Zavodny. 2015. "The Impact of E-Verify Mandates on Labor Market Outcomes." *Southern Economic Journal* 81 (4): 947–59. https://doi.org/10.1002/soej.12023.

Orrenius, Pia M., and Madeline Zavodny. 2016. "Do State Work Eligibility Verification Laws Reduce Unauthorized Immigration?" *IZA Journal of Migration* 5 (1): 5. https://doi.org/10.1186/s40176-016-0053-3.

Orrenius, Pia M., and Madeline Zavodny. 2019. "Do Immigrants Threaten US Public Safety?" *Journal on Migration and Human Security* 7 (3): 52–61. https://doi.org/10.1177/2331502419857083.

Perreira, Krista M., and Juan M. Pedroza. 2019. "Policies of Exclusion: Implications for the Health of Immigrants and Their Children." *Annual Review of Public Health* 40 (April): 147. https://doi.org/10.1146/annurev-publhealth-040218-044115.

Rainbolt, George, and Alison Reif. 1997. "Crime, Property, and Justice: The Ethics of Civil Forfeiture." *Public Affairs Quarterly* 11 (1): 39–55.

Raz, Joseph. 1977. *The Authority of Law*. Oxford: Oxford University Press.

Reed-Sandoval, Amy. 2020. *Socially Undocumented: Identity and Immigration Justice*. New York: Oxford University Press.

Ribando Seelke, Clare, and Ramon Miro. 2023. "Mexico's Immigration Control Efforts." Congressional Research Service. https://crsreports.congress.gov/product/pdf/IF/IF10215/28.

Rubalcaba, Joaquin Afredo-Angel, Jose R. Bucheli, and Camila Morales. 2024. "Immigration Enforcement and Labor Supply: Hispanic Youth in Mixed-Status Families." *Journal of Population Economics* 37: 43. https://doi.org/10.1007/s00148-024-01022-x.

Sager, Alex. 2017. "Immigration Enforcement and Domination: An Indirect Argument for Much More Open Borders." *Political Research Quarterly* 70 (1): 42–54. https://doi.org/10.1177/1065912916680036.

Sager, Alex. 2020. *Against Borders: Why the World Needs Free Movement of People*. London: Rowman & Littlefield International.

Shue, Henry. 1996. *Basic Rights: Subsistence, Affluence, and American Foreign Policy*. 2nd ed. Princeton, NJ: Princeton University Press.

Silverman, Stephanie. 2018. "Under the Umbrella of Administrative Law: Immigration Detention and the Challenges of Producing Just Immigration Law." *American Philosophical Association Newsletters: Hispanic/Latino Issues in Philosophy* 17 (2): 9–12.

Song, Sarah. 2019. *Immigration and Democracy*. New York: Oxford University Press.

Song, Sarah. 2023. "Justice, Collective Self-Determination, and the Ethics of Immigration Control." *Journal of Applied Philosophy* 40 (1): 26–34. https://doi.org/10.1111/japp.12557.

Song, Sarah, and Irene Bloemraad. 2022. "Immigrant Legalization: A Dilemma between Justice and The Rule of Law." *Migration Studies* 10 (3): 484–509. https://doi.org/10.1093/migration/mnac014.

Sumption, Rachel. 2021. "Shifting the Blame? Re-Evaluating Criminal Prosecution for Employers of Undocumented Workers." *American Criminal Law Review* 58: 227–56.

Turley, Jonathan. 2019. "Employers Must Be Prosecuted to End the Flow of Illegal Immigrants." *The Hill*, June 8.

United Nations. n.d. "Universal Declaration of Human Rights." United Nations. United Nations. Accessed April 12, 2024. https://www.un.org/en/about-us/universal-declaration-of-human-rights.

Waldron, Jeremy. 2023. "The Rule of Law." In *The Stanford Encyclopedia of Philosophy*, edited by Edward N. Zalta and Uri Nodelman. https://plato.stanford.edu/archives/fall2023/entries/rule-of-law/.

Walzer, Michael. 1983. *Spheres of Justice*. New York: Basic Books.

Wang, Julia Shu-Huah, and Neeraj Kaushal. 2019. "Health and Mental Health Effects of Local Immigration Enforcement." *International Migration Review* 53 (4): 970–1001. https://doi.org/10.1177/0197918318791978.

Warren, Robert. 2024. "After a Decade of Decline, the US Undocumented Population Increased by 650,000 in 2022." *Journal on Migration and Human Security*, January, 23315024241226624. https://doi.org/10.1177/23315024241226624.

Watson, Tara. 2014. "Inside the Refrigerator: Immigration Enforcement and Chilling Effects in Medicaid Participation." *American Economic Journal: Economic Policy* 6 (3): 313–38. https://doi.org/10.1257/pol.6.3.313.

Wellman, Christopher Heath. 2008. "Immigration and Freedom of Association." *Ethics* 119 (1): 109–41. https://doi.org/10.1086/592311.

Wellman, Christopher Heath. 2022. "Immigration." In *Stanford Encyclopedia of Philosophy*, edited by Edward N. Zalta and Uri Nodelman. https://plato.stanford.edu/archives/fall2022/entries/immigration/.

Wirts, Ameila M., and José Jorge Mendoza. 2022. "The Underming Mechanisms of "Rule of Law' Objections: A Response to Song and Bloemraad." In *The Ethics of Migration Policy Dilemmas Project*, 1–5. Migration Policy Center, European University Institute.

Yong, Caleb. 2016. "Caring Relationships and Family Migration Schemes." In *The Ethics and Politics of Immigration: Core Issues and Emerging Trends*, edited by A. Sager, 61–84. Lanham: Rowman & Littlefield.

25
CHILDREN, FAMILIES, AND IMMIGRATION ENFORCEMENT

Matthew Lister

25.1 Introduction

Although there is now a large and sophisticated literature on ethical or moral matters relating to family immigration (Lister 2007; Ferracioli 2016; Yong 2016; Lister 2018; Song 2019, 132–150; Honohan 2009) and immigration enforcement (Silverman 2014; Silva 2015; Mendoza 2017, 195–117; Sager 2018; Hosein 2019, 58–78; Lister 2020), the intersection of these topics has not been greatly explored. This is unfortunate, as particular and difficult normative issues arise in relation to immigration enforcement when applied to children and to families where some members are unauthorized migrants and others are citizens or authorized migrants ("mixed-status" families). This chapter addresses this deficit, explaining some of these special difficulties and providing suggestions as to how they may be addressed.

For the sake of this chapter, it will be assumed that states should have a significant degree of discretion in setting their own immigration policies. That is to say, I will assume that there is no general or basic right of free movement or a requirement of justice to establish open borders. This discretion is limited by obligations to protect refugees (Lister 2013; Cherem 2016; Owen 2020) and to provide for at least some degree of family migration. Family migration rights rest on the fundamental right to family life, and this right in turn provides strong reason to involuntarily separate families only in limited circumstances. I will also assume that, within limits, states may take steps to make immigration rules effective via enforcement. As will be shown, our topic poses special problems and complications for specific enforcement methods and policies but does not directly challenge the idea that enforcement is possible or acceptable.

Even if we accept the assumptions set out above, there are several special issues and concerns that arise when we look at children and families in relation to immigration enforcement. This chapter looks at these issues and addresses how the above assumptions need to be modified or adjusted in these cases. In doing so, I will look at four typical scenarios that arise repeatedly in many countries and explore the special moral considerations that come up in each of them. Three of these scenarios involve unauthorized migrants as an essential element:

1. Unauthorized and unaccompanied minor child
2. Families of unauthorized migrants including unauthorized children

3   Mixed-status families, where these have two main variants:
    a   Citizen child, unauthorized parents
    b   Unauthorized spouse/partner with citizen[1] partner/spouse

A final scenario also involves a non-citizen, but not one who was unauthorized:

4   Non-citizen who has/had legal status is removable for crime/character-based grounds, but has immediate relatives who are citizens – a partner/spouse or children.

25.2   Unauthorized Unaccompanied Minors

In this scenario, we consider an unauthorized[2] minor who is not accompanied by adult family members. Several issues arise in this situation immediately. Consider first the matter of detention.[3] Most states detain unauthorized migrants when they are encountered, at least for a short time, and we might accept that at least short-term detention to determine status and to facilitate removal for those without a right to remain can be acceptable for adults. The case of minors, however, poses particular problems. On the one hand, it will rarely be reasonable or acceptable to release an unaccompanied minor on his or her own recognizance, as we might with some adults. On the other hand, it will usually be unacceptable to detain unaccompanied minors in the same facilities as adults, especially in cases where these are jail-like.[4] So, what should be done in such situations?

In the short term, it will be necessary to provide safe short-term lodging to unaccompanied minors. How, exactly, this can and should be done will depend on the circumstances – whether authorities are dealing with individual cases, a small number of migrants, or a situation of mass flight, for example. Where the minor is first encountered – in a rural area, city, or unoccupied territory – may also matter for what sort of provisions can and should be provided, at least in the short term. A second necessary step will be to try to contact family – in the "home" country or the country of migration, both to potentially provide care and lodging, and to help determine the best path forward – that is, whether the child should remain in the country of migration or return home. This will be a necessary goal, if we are to seek the safety and the best interest of the minor, but will often in practice be complicated by the fact that the "in country" relatives may themselves be unauthorized, and so be uneager to interact with immigration officials.

Even if we assume that it is often acceptable to return many unauthorized migrants to their home country (perhaps especially if they have been in the country of migration for a short time), difficulties and complications arise in the case of unaccompanied minors. For example, if family members in the home country cannot be contacted, it may be unsafe to return the minor to the home country, even if it would be acceptable to return an adult. This might be so if the country does not have a well-functioning child welfare system, for example, meaning that return would likely mean living alone or on the streets. When this is the case, or when it would otherwise be unsafe to return an unaccompanied minor to her or his home country, a form of protection should be granted. While this need not necessarily be full permanent residence immediately, access to full residence will soon become the most acceptable result, given that the child in question will soon have spent a significant percentage of his or her formative years in the country of migration, and there is good reason to think that when this is the case, access to permanent residence is the best solution. (Lister 2010; Ferracioli 2022, 28–46) It is also important to note that some unaccompanied minors will be convention refugees, meaning that they should be granted refugee protection, but will usually have an even more difficult time than an adult showing this. Special care should be given to unaccompanied minors to ensure that rights owed to them under international and domestic law dealing with refugees are met. (UNHCR 1992, 50–51).

What sorts of concrete steps should be taken to comply with the conditions above? First, special advocates should be provided to unaccompanied minors, to help them find family members in either the country of migration or the home country, and to access what would be the safest and best course for the child. Sometimes this will involve removing the child and returning her or him to family members or government officials in the home country, but often it will involve a grant of legal status, which will have to also allow for basic needs to be met – by the government of the country of migration or by extended family members – including education, nutrition, and so on. This protection need not necessarily be permanent. If, say, a close family member is found in the home country and return would be safe after a few months or even one or two years, return may be the best course. But, if the child spends significant "formative" years in the country of migration, then arguments like those that support giving permanent resident status to so-called "Dreamers"[5] in the US will apply. (Note that one difference between "Dreamers" and unaccompanied minors that we might have first thought to be morally relevant – that "Dreamers" were typically brought to the US by their parents, and not of their own mature volition – is not actually relevant here, given that the people at question in this section would typically be too young to be held accountable for any moral fault in their entering without authorization, assuming we would find fault for that in an adult. We return briefly to this question below.)

Here we must address for the first time a worry that will come up for each of our scenarios, the question of moral hazard. That is, would taking this approach encourage more of the action that it seeks to remedy? If a state puts these plans in place, would it encourage more unaccompanied minors to cross state borders? While it is hard to be certain, I do not think this can be ruled out. Taking the path suggested above would make sending a child on his or her own, or sending for such a child, a better option than if the proposal was not in place, and we should always assume that migrants, like most people, are rational. However, even if this is so to a degree, this ought not cause us to reject the proposed path. First, if there is no presumptive default of permanent residence for unaccompanied minors, and no assumption of being able to sponsor family members for a visa, the increase in flows may not increase by too great of a level. Secondly, and more importantly, if an action is required by considerations of justice and accepted legal obligations, as will be the case in many instances of unaccompanied minors, then there can be an obligation to take the action, even if it imposes a cost on the one taking it.

25.3 Unauthorized Family with Minor Child

Our second major scenario involves an unauthorized family (or parent) with a minor child. Here we do not face the special issues that come up with an unaccompanied minor, since the child in question is "accompanied", but we still face important considerations that do not arise in the case of adults on their own, including the need to keep families together. To start with, if, as already argued, it will not normally be acceptable to keep minors in detention facilities where we might think it is acceptable to keep adults, then we will either have to provide special facilities for families, provide for their (perhaps monitored) released, or separate the family members.

The policy of separating families needs special consideration given that it was the recent policy of the Trump administration in the US. It is now beyond doubt that this was done with the specific intent of being a deterrent to migrants crossing the southern border of the US (Dickerson 2022). We must here ask why, if it is sometimes acceptable to separate parents from children (a point I will return to) it would be unacceptable to do this to deter unauthorized border crossings. There are several reasons. A first and important reason is that, in some cases, one or all of the family members in question will meet the requirements to be refugees under the Refugee Convention (and so under the domestic law of most signatory states.) When this is so, they have, under the Refugee Convention, a right to enter and apply for asylum without being subject to maltreatment (UNHCR 1992, 69; Goodwin-Gill 1996, 152–153). Only rarely, if ever, could family separation be justified in such cases, and then only for very short-term safety reasons, at most. This is especially the case given the generally recognized right to family unification for refugees (UNHCR 1992; Beaton 2023, 43–44). Here, though, the goal of deterrence is applied before an application for asylum can be made, let alone evaluated, indicating a naked attempt to avoid treaty and other legal obligations.

Even if the people in question are not convention refugees, they will often need and deserve humanitarian protection of some sort. States have different (usually insufficient) systems of complementary protection to respond to such situations, but these are again cases where deterrence of any sort is illegitimate, given that it is trying to prevent people from exercising rights or taking necessary steps for their own preservation where no risk of similar harm is imposed on others, and where there is no clear violation of a moral or legal obligation. (I return to this last point below.) We must also note that the form of deterrence used here involves an infringement (at least) of important rights – the rights to family life and family unity – and an obligation to protect the best interests of children (Ferguson 2018; Macleod 2018). Doing something we may not legitimately do in an especially bad way is, obviously enough, not acceptable.

A more interesting case involves unauthorized families who do not have good claims for asylum or other humanitarian protection. Could family separation as a deterrent be justified in these cases? One major issue is that it will normally be very difficult, if not impossible, to screen this group out from the one above before any harm is done. This should, perhaps, be sufficient to rule out deterrence through separation, but for now, assume that we could make this distinction. Would it then be acceptable to use family separation as a deterrent for unauthorized migrants? No, for a few reasons.

The first reason is that such a policy would impose disproportionate harm onto minors, who cannot be seen as morally blameworthy in any case. Most plausible accounts of deterrence require it to be restricted by a proportionality principle, and if the harm is inflicted on someone who is morally blameless, the proportionality principle will easily be violated (Bentham 1948, [1789] 178–88; Hart 1968, 24–5). Secondly, the deterrence is also unacceptable when directed towards parents. As will be discussed further below, separation of family members is sometimes widely accepted, such as when a parent has committed a significant crime and is therefore imprisoned, or when it is necessary to achieve an important and acceptable goal, such as in the case of a draft for the purpose of self-defence. But, there are two important differences between these cases and the use of family separation for deterrence of unauthorized migration.

First, in both cases just mentioned, the separation of families is an incidental, if necessary, side-effect of an otherwise legitimate goal, with it at least being very difficult to see how the goals – legitimate punishment and incapacitation of the dangerous and national self-defence – could be achieved otherwise. Now, even in these cases we have reason to limit the separation as much as is reasonably possible. We see this with policies in some states delaying the imprisonment of parents of young children, or providing them with different penalties, and in the common policy of giving lower draft priority to parents when possible. The Trump policy, however, specifically used family separation as a deterrent, imposing the separation to achieve its goal of reducing migration, and not as an unintentional side-effect to be minimized as far as possible. This makes it significantly harder to justify, even if it does deter people from behaviour that they have no right to do.

Here we may note another significant difference from the case of family separation that results from punishment for a serious crime. Even if we accept that states have a right to control migration, and even if we accept that they may take steps to control it via enforcement, it is not at all clear that unauthorized border crossing is itself a case of serious wrongdoing. This is especially so if we consider cases of unauthorized border crossing one by one, which seems to be required if we are to make a comparison with justified punishment for criminal wrongdoing. This is even more the case if we consider that it is not obvious, at least in the world we live in now, that non-citizens have an obligation to obey the immigration laws of other countries. This is to say, in our current world, the right to enforce migration laws by states may not imply an obligation by all non-members to respect these laws. While there are plausible arguments to be made that in a much more fully just world there could be such an obligation,[6] the necessary conditions for such an obligation do not generally obtain in our world, at least for many unauthorized migrants. So, if an unauthorized migrant does not commit a serious wrong in violating immigration law, and does not have a moral obligation to follow or respect the law, then using measures that involve significant infringements of rights and the imposition of significant harm to deter the behaviour will be unacceptable. Family separation policies fit this description, and so will almost always be unacceptable when used as a deterrent.[7]

25.4 Mixed-Status Families

The next scenario to consider involved mixed-status families. Here we may distinguish two main cases, first, one where there is one or more citizen-child with unauthorized parents, and second, one where a citizen has an unauthorized spouse or partner. (Other, more complex cases, some involving the mixture of the two above, are possible, but I will here focus on these two scenarios because, first, both involve relationships [minor child–parent and spouse–spouse] universally recognized to be especially important and which ground immigration rights in nearly all countries, as opposed to relationships such as those with adult siblings, grandparents, and other more distant relationships. Secondly, in many of the more complex cases, what we have can be seen as an iteration of the more basic cases, such as when an unauthorized person has both a citizen child and a citizen spouse.)

Importantly, at this point we are only considering cases where the unauthorized person has violated immigration laws (and perhaps laws on working without authorization or other essentially regulatory laws) but has not violated any criminal law[8] or otherwise shown themselves to be a danger to the community. In these cases we have, on the one side, a violation of immigration laws, and possibly other regulatory laws, and on the other a very important right – the right to live with one's immediate family members – spouses and minor children. That there is an obligation to allow at least close family migration is accepted by most people working on migration, and is reflected in the practice of most states. However, many states do not extend this right to all of the cases we are considering under this heading. In the US, for example, this right is in practice not available to most people who entered without inspection, and not available to unauthorized parents of minor children.[9]

Are the limits placed on mixed-status families acceptable? That is, is it reasonable to allow the removal of unauthorized aliens who have citizen spouses or minor children? There are two main arguments for allowing such removals. The first is that not doing so will "reward lawbreaking". This claim is not completely empty. In many normal cases like the ones we are considering, if the person had not violated the relevant immigration law, he or she would likely not have had the relationship in question, and so would not have this claim for changing status. Second, we should ask if making exceptions to normal immigration enforcement in these cases is likely to significantly increase unauthorized migration overall, and in particular if allowing these exceptions will increase the number of mixed-status families. Even if the answer to this question is yes, that may not settle the issue, but it will raise concerns about moral hazard[10] – a situation where attempting to address a problem gives rise to more of the same situation that needs to be addressed.

Let's start with the first concern, that of "rewarding lawbreaking". We can accept that the violation of an immigration rule will often be a "but for" cause of the relationship here without this implying that granting a right to stay in the country of migration and gaining legal status is "rewarding" the "lawbreaking" in question. To see this, consider how in some other cases where violation of an immigration rule is a "but for" cause of some benefit, it is generally accepted that the benefit must still be provided. To use a clear case, violating migration regulations and rules on employment by people without authorization is a "but for" cause of engaging in employment by unauthorized aliens, but it seems clear morally, and is generally accepted legally, that if an unauthorized alien performs work, he or she must still be paid for the work they do.[11] This comparison suggests that not every benefit that depends, in some way, on having violated a rule can properly be seen as a "reward for" violating the rule. If this is right, then this objection loses much of its force. (See also here (Motomura 2012)).

While our first concern seemed to apply both in the case of citizen children and citizen partners, our second concern may give different answers in these two cases. It does not seem especially likely that allowing spouses of citizens to avoid normal immigration enforcement will increase unauthorized migration. This is because it would be highly presumptuous to expect to be able to move to a country and find a citizen spouse. And, even if we (more plausibly) worried that allowing these benefits would increase the temptation to engage in marriage fraud so as to be able to remain in the country, the proper way to deal with this issue would be to impose increased evidentiary standards for marriages when one partner was unauthorized, and to have in place penalties for citizens who engage in marriage fraud.[12]

What seems more plausible, however, is that if having a child in the state of migration is enough to prevent unauthorized parents from being removed, this will encourage unauthorized migration by pregnant women and couples who might have children. This inference does not depend on the idea that unauthorized migrants would treat having children merely instrumentally, but only that the availability of relief from enforcement would influence these decisions. Given the already widespread practice of birth tourism to countries like the US with strong jus soli rules[13] it is not implausible to imagine that such rule changes would influence the behaviour of unauthorized migrants.

If we think that this is a significant concern, it might be addressed in a few ways. The most drastic, from the perspective of states that have strong *jus soli*[14] citizenship laws, would be to modify these laws to somewhat more closely resemble the law in Australia, which has only a weak *jus soli* rule. Without a strong *jus soli* rule, the problem of mixed-status families with citizen children and unauthorized parents will rarely arise, in that way "solving" the problem. While many countries have *jus soli* rules that are much weaker than those found in the US and many other countries in the Americas, these rules create their own problems insofar as they can create a class of children raised in a country who are de facto but not de jure members. (Lister 2010; Ferracioli 2022, 9–27; Cohen and Ghosh 2019, 99–120). If we wish to avoid these problems, while still reducing incentives to create more of the mixed-status families we hope to avoid, we should look to less drastic steps than changing citizenship law. For example, a restrictive rule might only refrain from normal immigration enforcement either when the child has lived in the country of birth for some significant amount of time, or where it could be shown that it would be unsafe and unreasonable to expect the citizen child to accompany his or her parents to their country of citizenship. (This is, of course, presupposing that the child would have easy access to the citizenship of his or her parents. This will usually be so, but not always, and the legal issue may be complicated in various ways. For the sake of this chapter, we must abstract from some of these complications, but people seeking to implement policy would obviously need to think them through carefully.) In the case that it would be unsafe or implausible for the child to move with her or his parents, a status less than full permanent resident status might be granted to the parents for some time. This status would not allow for the sponsorship of other relatives or access to citizenship until the time that the citizen child would be able to sponsor the parent under normal sponsorship rules, but would still maintain the ability of families to promote integration into the society of immigration.[15] Taking these steps would not fully eliminate the moral hazard in this case, but would reduce it and balance it against the hardship faced by mixed-status families and the best interests of the children. (On these hardships, see Zayas 2015.)

25.5 Mixed-Status Families and Criminal/Character Removal

Our final category involves non-citizens who are (or were[16]) lawful residents, but who face removal on criminal or character grounds, (where the latter need not require a criminal conviction) and who also have close citizen family members, focusing here again on minor children and spouses or partners. Unlike our prior scenarios, this case involves someone who has violated a criminal law or otherwise shown themselves to be "of bad character".[17] Removal is a collateral consequence of the criminal violation. (On "collateral consequences", see Hoskins (2019).) This is important in that removal is not, officially, part of the punishment for violating the underlying law. If it were, there would be grave worries about inequitable treatment – about non-citizens being subject to significantly harsher penalties than citizens. But if this outcome is not supposed to be punishment, what is it? What (supposedly) justifies it? The best answer has two parts. First, we might think that the non-citizen has violated a (perhaps implied) promise to be of good character in exchange for the privilege of being allowed to migrate. Second, we may think that removal in this case is done to promote the safety and well-being of the community – a dangerous element is removed, making the community overall better off.

Several problems arise almost immediately from this account. One is that the crimes that are used to justify removal are extremely diverse, and may not provide any significant indication of ongoing dangerousness. (That citizens who are punished for these crimes are typically not detained based on ongoing dangerousness after they have served their sentences is indicative but not dispositive, given that there may be other good reasons to not allow post-enforcement confinement for dangerousness.) This worry is furthered by the fact that these laws typically operate in a strict liability way – if the standard is met, the person is removable. There does not need to be any post-punishment showing of dangerousness before removal. Additionally, even if we could find that admission to a state involved an implied promise to be of good character (or if states modified their immigration policies to make such a promise explicit) it is unclear that such a promise could function to justify current policies in many states. Note that risk from removal for bad character or criminal grounds typically stops when an immigrant becomes a citizen. But, if having good character was a condition of migration, why would this be so? Why would the "promise" not still operate? On the other hand, we might reasonably doubt that a person could legitimately promise to comply with an arbitrarily long list of requirements in perpetuity, as is required by current policy. It seems implausible that we can promise to not do an indefinitely large list of things for an indefinitely long period of time. For these reasons, the "promise" account seems less than compelling.

The above worries about removal on criminal or character grounds are general, applying to anyone who faces removal on such grounds. But there are also specific reasons why we might question the appropriateness of removal when the person removed is part of a mixed-status family. The first reason is like those considered above, and to questions of family migration in general. That is, the situation involves not only a non-citizen, but a citizen as well, and an infringement of his or her rights to family life. Given that these are important rights, they should be infringed only for very weighty reasons. Even if we give credit to the arguments made for removing non-citizens of "bad character" above, these would need to be balanced against the rights of citizens to live with their family members. We might also come at this question from a slightly different direction. In Australia, for example, immigration officials who are considering whether a non-citizen who is purportedly of bad character should be removed are charged with considering the "good of the community".[18] The normal way to do this is to look at the broader "community". This is not wrong insofar as it goes, but we should also consider that families are themselves part of the "community", and often the part with the most at stake. We might see this as especially important for children, given the obligation of states to take the best interest of children into account (Ferguson 2018). Sometimes this might tell in favour of removing the non-citizen, but in many cases where the non-citizen has one or more citizen child, the "community interests" may tellin favour of allowing the non-citizen to remain, especially when there is no strong inference of ongoing dangerousness.

At this point, a proponent of removing non-citizens who have committed crimes might note that, with "domestic" criminals, we also regularly separate them from their families for significant periods of time, when they are in jail. This is true, but it is not obvious that it supports the removal of non-citizens in mixed-status families. Some of these issues have been discussed already above. Most relevantly here, we must note that, in the large majority of cases, the non-citizen who has been convicted of a crime has already been separated from his or her family to the same degree as would be a citizen. The question is whether this deprivation should be extended indefinitely. We must here remember that, in most cases, the non-citizen will have already served whatever penalty is generally thought appropriate for the crimes he or she has committed. Because of this, we should normally hold that whatever harm is "deserved" by the non-citizen has already been given to them. Keeping this in mind, and keeping in mind the rights of children and spouses/partners, what should we do in these cases?

One approach would be to hold that, if a non-citizen who is removable for criminal grounds has citizen immediate family members, the non-citizen may be removed only if it can be shown that there is a compelling need to do this that is significant enough to balance the harm that will come to family members if the non-citizen is removed. This approach would, to start, reverse the burden of proof required in many current legal systems, where the non-citizen must show that his or her removal would bring about bad results.[19] Under the proposal here, the state would be obliged to show that not removing the non-citizen would be likely to bring about specific harms. This might be done by showing that the non-citizen has continuing ties to organized crime, for example. However, the showing would need to be more specific and more significant than the normal risk of reoffending that exists for any particular person if the important rights of family members are to be appropriately respected.

25.6 Conclusion and Thoughts on Future Directions

In this chapter, I have tried to show that special and difficult issues arise for immigration enforcement when we consider the case of children and families, especially mixed-status families. If my arguments are correct, states wishing to have just immigration policies will need to make several changes to current practice. However, several important questions remain open for further study. For example, we may ask how far the arguments I have made in relation to citizens can and should be applied to permanent residents, and if they should be applied to all permanent residents or only long-term ones or ones who have difficulty naturalizing for some reason. We might also investigate whether the type of arguments I have made in relation to immediate relatives can or should be extended in some ways – perhaps to a lesser degree – to other family members and perhaps to other relationships. (On this idea see Ferracioli 2016). These and other questions remain to be solved, but I hope that the importance of the issues discussed above is clear.[20]

Notes

1 In many of the scenarios, I will consider we might get similar conclusion with a permanent resident immediate family member rather than a citizen family member. This seems more likely to me to be the case for spouses/partners than for children, but space considerations prevent me from exploring that issue in detail. Similarly, for space considerations, and to isolate a clear case at first, I will mostly focus on scenarios where at least one family member is a citizen. I will very briefly address how and why we might extend this analysis to permanent resident family members at the end of the chapter.
2 Note that it is not always completely straight-forward to determine unauthorized status even for adults, and that difficulty will likely be even higher for children, adding additional complexity to the scenario, but we will leave this issue aside here.
3 For a more detailed discussion of normative issues relating to immigration detention, see the chapter by Felix Bender and Stephanie Silverman in this volume, and (Silverman 2014).
4 Immigration detention facilities are sometimes literally situated in jails, though typically (but not always) in distinct wings. In other cases, the facilities are not located in a jail, but are physically very similar to jails. Some detention facilities are much less jail-like, though few would find them desirable places to spend significant time.

5 "Dreamers" are unauthorized residents in the US who were brought to the US by their parents when they were young and who have since grown up or otherwise spent significant time in the US.
6 Colin Grey (2015) has provided the most sustained discussion of when and how an immigration regime could have authority over would-be migrants. However, for this authority to be established, the states in question would have to implement many significant changes from their current immigration policy and practice of international relations. Given this, on Grey's account, nearly all, perhaps all, states currently lack at least full authority to enforce their immigration law on non-citizens. David Miller (2021) has developed an account of authority in immigration law resting on the idea of a natural duty of justice. Such an account has plausibility, but will, in our current world, be greatly restricted by the stringent requirements of a duty of natural justice to apply. In my own work (Lister 2020) I have tried to show what can be done in this area if we do not assume that migrants have a general obligation to comply with the immigration laws of other states.
7 For additional helpful discussion of closely related matters, see (Motomura 2012).
8 Of course, states may categorize immigration violations as "criminal" if they wish. The US does this for entry without inspection and for re-entry without permission after removal (see 8 USC § 1325 and § 1326 respectively.) However, these are, at worst, *malum prohibitum* offenses, with more in common with civil regulatory offenses than with core criminal laws.
9 While some unauthorized immigrants can "adjust status" if they marry a US citizen, this option is in practice largely foreclosed for people who entered without inspection, as they are required to leave the US before applying for adjustment of status, but then are barred from returning to the US for up to 10 years. See INA § 212(a)(9)(B)(ii). For a child to be able to sponsor his or her parent for immigration benefits, the child must be 21 years of age or older, excluding the scenario considered here. See INA § 201(b)(2)(A)(i). Somewhat similar laws apply in Australia.
10 For a helpful brief introduction to the idea of moral hazard, see (Heath 2010, pp. 117–33.)
11 For discussion, see US Department of Labor Fact Sheet #48, available at https://www.dol.gov/agencies/whd/fact-sheets/48-hoffman-plastics. Similar rules apply in Australia.
12 The US already has higher evidentiary standards for people applying for adjustment of status on the basis of marriage when one party is in removal proceedings. See INA § 245(e)(3). As noted above, this typically could not apply to people who entered without inspection. The proposal here might simply consist in applying this standard to people who entered without inspection as well. Penalties for marriage fraud exist in several countries. See 8 USC § 1325(c) (establishing penalties of up to five years in prison and a fine of up to $250,000) and Migration Act of 1958 s 240 (establishing a penalty of up to 10 years in prison) for Australia, for representative examples.
13 For one example, see, Department of Justice, "Chinese National Pleads Guilty to Running Birth Tourism Scheme", https://www.justice.gov/usao-cdca/pr/chinese-national-pleads-guilty-running-birth-tourism-scheme-helped-aliens-give-birth-us. For a wide-ranging discussion of some of the issues here, see Reed-Sandoval (2020).
14 "*Jus soli*" citizenship rules base citizenship on the location of birth. The strongest versions – such as those found in the US and many other countries in the Americas – grants citizenship upon birth in a territory without any other requirements. Weaker versions – more common in Europe and Australia – impose requirements other than mere birth in a territory before granting citizenship. In Australia, for example, a child born in Australia gains citizenship at birth only if at least one parent is a citizen or a permanent resident. See Australian Citizen Ship Act (2007) s 12(1)(a).
15 On this last point, see (Motomura 2006).
16 In Australia, for example, someone who "fails the character test" becomes an "unlawful non-citizen" as a matter of law. While this may be challenged, as a legal matter, the person automatically loses legal permanent resident status once he or she violates the character test. See Migration Act of 1958 s 501. In other states, loss of permanent resident status only comes after a ruling on removability. Because of this, in this scenario we have to consider both people who are, and ones who were, but no longer are, lawful permanent residents.
17 In Australia, a person may be found to be "of bad character" without a criminal conviction if certain other factors are present. This is troubling on its own, but as most cancellations of visas are due to criminal convictions, and the other grounds usually involve criminal activity, even if not convictions, we will here focus on cases where there has been a conviction. See Migration Act of 1958 s 501(6).
18 Immigration Direction 41.

19 In Australia, see Immigration Direction 17, 2.17(c). In the US, see INA § 240A(b)(1)(D).
20 A version of this chapter was presented at the Julius Stone Institute at the University of Sydney Law School. My thanks to the audience there, and especially to Kevin Walton, Luara Ferracioli, Sam Sphall, and Wojciech Sadurski for their comments, and to Caleb Yong for helpful conversation.

References

Beaton, Eilidh. 2023. "The Right to Family Unification for Refugees." *Social Theory and Practice* 49, no. 1: 1–28.
Bender, Felix, and Stephanie Silverman. 2024. "The Urgency of Addressing Immigration Detention in Normative Political Theory." In *The Routledge Handbook of the Ethics of Immigration*, edited by Sahar Akhtar. Abington, Routledge.
Bentham, Jeremy. 1948 [1789]. *The Principles of Morals and Legislation*. New York, NY, Hafner.
Cherem, Max G. 2016. "Refugee Rights: Against Expanding the Definition of 'Refugee' and Unilateral Protection Elsewhere." *The Journal of Political Philosophy* 24, no. 2: 183–205.
Cohen, Elizabeth F., and Cyril Ghosh. 2019. *Citizenship*. Cambridge, Polity.
Dickerson, Caitlin. 20220. "The Secret History of Family separation." *The Atlantic*. Aug. 2022.
Ferguson, Lucinda. 2018. "An Argument for Treating Children as a 'Special Case'." In *Philosophical Foundations of Children's and Family Law*, edited by Elizabeth Brake and Lucinda Ferguson, 227–256. Oxford, Oxford University Press.
Ferracioli, Luara. 2016. "Family Migration Schemes and Liberal Neutrality: A Dilemma." *Journal of Moral Philosophy* 13, no 5: 553–575.
Ferracioli, Luara. 2022. *Liberal Self-Determination in a World of Migration*. Oxford, Oxford University Press.
Goodwin-Gill, Guy S. 1996. *The Refugee in International Law*, 2nd Ed. Oxford, Oxford University Press.
Grey, Colin. 2015. *Justice and Authority in Immigration Law*. Portland, OR, Hart.
Hart, HLA. 1968. *Punishment and Responsibility: Essays in the Philosophy of Law*. Oxford, Oxford University Press
Heath, Joseph. 2010. *Economics Without Illusions: Debunking the Myths of Modern Capitalism*. New York, NY, Broadway Books.
Honohan, Iseult. 2009. "Reconsidering the Claims to Family Reunification in Migration." *Political Studies* 57, no. 4 (December): 768–787.
Hosein, Adam. 2019. *The Ethics of Migration: An Introduction*. Abingdon, Routledge.
Hoskins, Zachary. 2019. *Beyond Punishment: A Normative Account of the Collateral Legal Consequences of Conviction*. Oxford, Oxford University Press.
Lister, Matthew 2007. "A Rawlsian Argument for Extending Family-Based Immigration Benefits to Same-Sex Couples." *University of Memphis Law Review* 37: 745–780.
Lister, Matthew. 2010. "Citizenship, in the Immigration Context." *Maryland Law Review* 70: 170–233.
Lister, Matthew. 2013. "Who Are Refugees?" *Law and Philosophy*. 32, no. 5: 645–671.
Lister, Matthew. 2018. "The Rights of Families and Children at the Border." In *Philosophical Foundations of Children's and Family Law*, edited by Elizabeth Brake and Lucinda Ferguson, 153–173. Oxford, Oxford University Press.
Lister, Matthew. 2020. "Enforcing Immigration Law." *Philosophy Compass* 15, no. 3.
Macleod, Colin M. 2018. "Are Children's Rights Important?" In *Philosophical Foundations of Children's and Family Law*, edited by Elizabeth Brake and Lucinda Ferguson, 191–208. Oxford, Oxford University Press.
Mendoza, Jose Jorge. 2017. *The Moral and Political Philosophy of Immigration: Liberty, Security, and Equality*. Lanham, Lexington Books.
Miller, David. 2021. "Authority and Immigration." *Political Studies* 0(0) (on-line first) https://doi.org/10.1177/00323217211046423
Motomura, Hiroshi. 2006. "We Asked for Workers, But Families Came: Time, Law, and the Family in Immigration and Citizenship." *Virginia Journal of Social Policy and the Law* 17, no. 2: 239–254

Motomura, Hiroshi. 2012. "Making Legal: The Dream Act, Birthright Citizenship, and Broad-Scale Legalization." *Lewis & Clark Law Review* 16, no. 4: 1127–1148.
Owen, David. 2020. *What We Owe to Refugees*. Cambridge, Polity.
Reed-Sandovol, Amy. 2020. "Maternity and Migration." *Philosophy Compass* 15, no. 3.
Sager, Alex. 2018. "Private Contractors, Foreign Troops, and Offshore Detention Centers: The Ethics of Externalizing Immigration Controls." *American Philosophical Association Newsletter on Hispanic/Latino Issues in Philosophy*, 17, no. 2: 12–15.
Silva, Grant. 2015. "On the Militarization of the Border and the Juridical Right to Exclude." *Public Affairs Quarterly* 29, no. 2 (April): 217–234.
Silverman, Stephanie J. 2014. "Detaining Immigrants and Asylum Seekers: A Normative Introduction." *Critical Review of International Social and Political Philosophy* 17, no. 5: 600–617.
Song, Sarah. 2019. *Immigration and Democracy*. New York, NY, Oxford University Press.
UNHCR. 1992. *Handbook on Procedures and Criteria for Determining Refugee Status*. Geneva, Office of the United Nations High Commissioner for Refugees.
Yong, Caleb. 2016. "Caring Relationships and Family Migration Schemes." In *The Ethics and Politics of Immigration: Core Issues and Emerging Trends*, edited by Alex Sager, 61–84. London: Rowman and Littlefield.
Zayas, Louis. 2015. *Forgotten Citizens: Deportation, Children, and the Making of American Exiles and Orphans*. Oxford, Oxford University Press.

INDEX

Note: Page references in **bold** refer to tables and with "n" endnotes.

Abbot, Tony 270
ableism 281
Acemoglu, Daron 99, 108
Adams, Richard 29
admission 35–36, 50–52, 118, 121, 125–126, 171, 172, 174n3, 248n26, 277, 295, 329; agreements 48; automatic 157, 161; controls 49; differential 158; discretionary admissions 41; liberalized admissions 84–86; obligatory admissions 41; points-based 189; policies 157; regulating 146, 284
Affordable Care Act (Obamacare) 306
African-Americans 113; Jim Crow South 108; migration of 108
Akhtar, Sahar 51, 169, 196n2
Albahari, Maurizio 298
Alcoff, Linda Martín 181–182
Alesina, Alberto 91–92, 101–103
Algan, Yann 105, 113
"Aliens and Citizens: The Case for Open Borders" (Carens) 292
American Immigration Council 189
Amighetti, Sara 145
ancestry 100, 102–103, 111–112, 114, 162
Anderson, Benedict 140
Anderson, Elizabeth 182
Ang, James T. 109, 113
Antecol, Heather 102
anti-democratic power 138
Anzaldúa, Gloria 178, 184
arbitrary power 138

assimilation 4, 90–91, 100, 104–105, 108, 113–114, 118, 259
asylum 39, 58, 118–119, 241–243, 254; and free movement 50; necessitous migrants 43; and refugees 43; seekers 50, 58, 119, 268–269, 272–274, 278, 300, 317n2
asymmetrical bilingualism 123
asymmetrical multiculturalism 149
Attas, Daniel 219
attitude migration 101–108; and experimental correlates 105–108; intra-European 104–105; migration of familism 102–103; neoclassical examples 102; proxies for ancestry 103; *see also* migration
Auerbach, Nina 183
Australia 6, 99, 105, 203–204; 1901 Immigration Restriction Act 157; citizenship test 203–204; Department of Home Affairs website 189; "good of the community" 329; indefinite detention 286n2; *jus soli* rule 328; as Neo-Europes 99; points-based admissions systems 189; points-based migration systems 114; White Australia Policy 157–158, 161, 167, 169, 192–193; white immigration 119
Australian Citizenship Amendment (Citizenship Testing) Act 2007 203
Australian Citizenship Council 203
Australian Citizenship for a New Citizenship report 203
authoritarianism 138
automatic citizenship 145

Index

backlash: in liberal theory 130–137; and migration 128–138; in political practice 137–138
Ball-Blakely, Michael 194–195
Barry, Brian 24
Basu, Chandi 184
Bauböck, Rainer 143
Beaton, Eilidh 240, 248n25
Bender, Felix 330n3
Berg, Joyce 106
Berggren, Nicolas 91
Bertram, Christopher 215
Biden, Joe 202, 308, 317n5
Bigot's Veto 129–131, 135, 137–138
BioNTech 70
birthright citizenship 55
Blake, Michael 41–42, 52, 94n2, 147, 168–169, 170, 174n3, 311
Bologna Pavlik, Jamie 91
Bonilla-Silva, Eduardo 178, 182
Boochani, Behrouz 273
Boom, C. D. 240
border externalization 298
Borjas, George J. 80, 100, 114
Borrell-Porta, Mireia 104
Bracero Program 180, 185n13
Bradman, Sir Donald 203–204
brain drain 2, 6, 119, 224–230; arguments 226–227; debt-argument 228–229; and emigration 224–230; harm-argument 227–228
British Nationality Act 1981 205
Brock, Gillian 170, 175n7, 228–230, 311
Buchanan, James 90–91
Byravan, Sujatha 241, 247n14

Cahuc, Pierre 105, 113
Calderon, Alvaro 108
Canada: indefinite detention 286n2; Jewish population in 164n30; as Neo-Europes 99; points-based admissions systems 189; points-based migration systems 114; white immigration 119
Canada Border Services Agency (CBSA) 278–280
cantilever argument 52, 92
Caplan, Bryan 112
Capra, C. Mónica 107
Carens, Joseph H. 44, 52, 55, 67, 88, 92, 129–130, 134, 208, 215–218, 222n7, 239, 292, 297, 311, 312
Cargill 190
Chae Chan Ping 293
Chae Chan Ping v. United States 293
Chang, Howard F. 77, 80, 82–84

children 20–21, 121–124, 184; and immigration enforcement 322–330; minor 326–328; unauthorized immigrant 306
China 94, 101; Deep Roots outliers 112; Deep Roots scores for 111; millionaires in 165–166n44; research and development (R&D) in 99
Chinese ancestry 111–112
Chinese Exclusion Act 37, 157, 167, 293
Churchill, Sir Winston 206
circular migration 283
Citizens' Handbook (French Ministry 2015) 204
citizenship 2–3, 6, 15, 20; automatic 145; birthright 55; dual 56–57; non-citizenship 285; Olympic 188; right 47–59; social 54
citizenship premium 57, 212
citizenship right 3; demos boundary problem 55; free movement as 54–57
citizenship tests 201–208; Australia 203–204; European model 204–205; United Kingdom 205–208; United States 201–203
civil disobedience 299–300
Clemens, Michael A. 77, 100, 112–113, 190
climate change 1–2, 78, 93, 235–237, 239–244; beyond "climate refugees" 254–257; common but differentiated responsibilities 259–260; and immigration 253–261; and migration 2, 6–7; and protection 6–7; refugees 43
climate exiles 241, 244–246, 247n14, 249n30
climate migrants 7, 235, 247–248n15, 249n28, 255, 261n3, 265n53; are not refugees 235–246
climate refugees 2, 6–7, 119, 235–245, 247–248n15, 247n1, 247n2, 248n22, 253–260, 261n6
Climate Refugees 261n5
closed borders 29, 35–36, 39, 42, 282–283
coercive control 90
coercive philanthropist 229
coercive power 80, 90
collective political self-determination 244–246, 249n30
collective self-determination 3, 35–36, 39, 42, 45, 47
Collier, Paul 114
colonial powers 264n43
Comin, Diego 109
Commission on the Future of Multi-Ethnic Britain 205
"common but differentiated responsibilities" 259–260, 265n53
communal cohesion 80
"community of communities" 205
"community of equals" 182

Index

controlled borders and open doors: case for 39–42; overview 35; state sovereignty 36–39, 42–45
Convention Relating to the Status of Refugees (1951) 254, 293
CoreCivic 296
Cornell, Nicolas 246
correlation coefficients 115n3
Costa, Daniel 190
COVID-19 pandemic 67, 71, 187, 190, 226, 278, 279; vaccines 70–71
Crenshaw, Kimberle Williams 281
Crépeau, François 312
Crick, Sir Bernard 205
crime 171, 207, 255, 314–315, 325–326, 328–330; and immigrants 281, 293–294, 297, 308, 310; immigration restrictions 13; organized 300, 330; property 310; rate 13, 310
Criminal Apprehension Program (CAP) 317n5, 317n10
"Criminals in Our Land! Border Movement and Apprehension of Children from Bangladesh Within the Juvenile Justice System in India" (Basu) 184
criteria 2, 4–6, 118–122, 158, 160, 162, 167, 169–174, 236, 238–239, 242, 269, 298, 315
cross-border mobility 58
cross-boundary mobility 253
cultural communities 4, 85, 132; global social welfare 79–80; segregation of 79–80
cultural identity 1, 40, 144, 148, 282, 298
cultural integration 2, 4, 91
cultural nationalists 37
cultural transplant theory 4, 101, 104, 112–114
culture 36–37, 90–92, 144–145; and immigration 4–5; immigration restrictions 13; majority 144, 148, 150; and nationalism 4–5; societal 141; transplant, migration as 99–115
The Culture Transplant 101
Curtin, John 192

debt-argument 227, 228–229
Deep Roots literature 100–101, 108–109, 111, 114
Deferred Action for Childhood Arrivals (DACA) 317n2
degradation 158–159, 235
Del Savio, Lorenzo 131, 133, 134
democracy 54–59, 128, 298; deliberative institutions of 37; illegal immigration 19; liberal 5, 16, 87, 133, 138, 146; normative theories of 54; social 24–33
democratic equality 182
democratic self-determination 47

Denham, John 205
detention: immigrant 292, 294, 300; immigration (*see* immigration detention); indefinite 282, 286n2, 293; and normative theory 283–285
difference principle 25, 70
Dimant, Eugen 91
discretionary admissions 41
discretionary immigration policy 118–120
discretionary power 269
discrimination 158–159, 165n35; Christians 165n36; and immigration 2, 5–6; moral arbitrariness view of 191–192
"displaced persons" 50, 236, 245, 253–254, 256, 268
"Dreamers" 324, 331n5
dual citizenship 49, 56–57
Dummett, Michael 239–240
Dunn, John 140
duty 17–19, 36, 41, 43, 50–52, 145, 203, 215, 248n26, 283, 331n6
Dworkin, Ronald 24

Easterly, William 109
economic development 43, 93, 108–110, 240
economic freedom 2, 4; and immigration 65–73; overview 65–66
economic growth 4, 27, 72, 111, 145, 160, 260, 308
economic migrants 129, 238, 272
egalitarianism: and open borders 30–31; and social democracy 30–31
El-Hinnawi, Essam 237
Ellerman, Antje 171, 175n10
emigration 6, 224, 257–259; and brain drain 224–230; economic 49; free 49, 52, 56, 228–229; freedom of 51; Mexican 77; negative liberty of 52
employment authorization document (EAD) 317n2
employment-based enforcement 307, 309, 313
enforcement: employment-based 307, 309, 313; extraterritorial immigration 297–299; immigration (*see* immigration enforcement); police-based 307–308; and racism 295–296
Entry Denied: Controlling Sexuality at the Border (Luibheid) 183
entry of people 6
environmental disruptions 244
environmental protection 4, 77–79, 85
epidemiological approach, and cultural transmission 100
Equality Act 2000 173
ethics: analyses of skill-selective immigration policies 191–195; of skill-selective

Index

immigration policies 187–196; of U.S. internal immigration enforcement 305–316
ethics of immigration 224, 277, 285; Carens' argument 222n7; enforcement policies in the U.S. 310–316; illegal immigration 17–21; immigration restrictions 11–17; nationalism 140–151; overview 11
ethnicity: and immigration 157–158; and nationality 167–169; and race 167–169; and selective exclusion 159–162
"European model" 204–205
European Union (EU) 26–27, 48–50, 56, 140, 172, 265n55, 298
European Values Study (EVS) 104
E-Verify 307, 309, 317n10
exclusion 37, 158–162, 167, 293; *see also* right to exclude
exit of people 6
expatriate communities 258, 259
exploitation: humanitarian reason 271–274; worker 211–222
extraterritorial immigration enforcement 297–299

fair play 44, 272; illegal immigration 18–19
fair wage for temporary workers 218–221
false deterrent 282–283
families: and immigration enforcement 322–330; mixed-status 326–330
familism 102–103
Fassin, D. 267, 274
Federal Bureau of Investigation (FBI) 308
Fehr, Ernst 107
Fernández, Raquel 102
Ferracioli, Luara 168–169, 311
Fifth Amendment 293
Fine, Sarah 168, 174n4
Fiss, Owen 44
Fleischacker, Sam 143
Fong Yue Ting v. United States 315
forced migration 48, 58, 283
Foster, Michelle 247n4, 248n21
Fourteenth Amendment 293
Fourth Amendment 293
France 94, 102, 115n1, 123; citizenship test 204–205; Jewish population in 164n30; research and development (R&D) in 99
freedom of association 19–21, 36, 38–39, 193–194, 294; defined 19; illegal immigration 19–21
free emigration 49, 52, 56, 228–229
free internal movement 49, 52, 58
free international movement 48–49
Freeman, R.B. 213
Freeman, Samuel 28

free movement/freedom of movement 47–59; as citizenship right 54–57; conceptualizing 48–50; defined 48, 52; as human right 50–54; and international border controls 89; overview 47–48
Free to Move: Foot Voting, Migration, and Political Freedom (Somin) 72
Freiman, Christopher 31, 93
French Declaration of the Rights of Man and the Citizen 278
Fuchs-Schündeln, Nicola 102
Fuller, Lon 313
Functionalist Account 141, 145–148, **150–151**

Gans, Chaim 142
Gardner, John 174
Gemenne, Francois 247–248n15
General Atomics 296
General Social Survey (GSS) 100, 104
GEO Group 296
Germany 94, 102, 173; citizenship test 204–205; research and development (R&D) in 99
Giuliano, Paola 91–92, 103
GivingWhatWeCan 27
Glaeser, Edward L. 107
Glenn, Evelyn 281
Glick, Peter 136
Global Migration Matrix 108
Global North 6, 50, 57, 193, 269, 283
GlobalRichList 33n6
global social welfare: environmental protection 77–79; liberalized immigration policies 76–80; segregation of cultural communities 79–80
Global South 57, 172–173, 269, 283
Goenaga, Agustín 171, 175n10
Gong, Erick 109
Goodwin-Gill, Guy S. 248n21
Gowder, Paul 313
gratitude 229; illegal immigration 18
Great Depression 180
Great Recession 305, 308
Grey, Colin 331n6
Griggs v. Duke Power Co. 173
growth: economic 4, 27, 72, 111, 145, 160, 260, 308; population 77–78, 315; unauthorized immigrant population 305–306, 308
Gulf Cooperation Council 211
Gulf Cooperation Countries 29

H1-B visas 189
Habeas Corpus Acts of England 278
Hamilton, Bob 77
Hanson, Pauline 142
harm-argument 227–228
Harper, Stephen 282

337

Index

Hastie, Bethany 312
Hathaway, James C. 247n4, 248n21
Hayden, Sally 273
heteronormativity 281
Hidalgo, Javier 93, 299, 311
highly skilled migrants 6, 187–189, 195
Hindus 160
Hirschl, Ran 188–189, 191
Ho, Ben 105
Hobbes, Thomas 48
Holocaust 160
Holtug, Nils 146
Hosein, Adam 44, 170–171
Huemer, Michael 88
humanitarian reason 267–268; exploiting 271–274
human mobility 294, 296, 299
human rights 47–59, 92, 170, 239–241, 247n4, 269, 284–285, 311–312; and detention 283; frame of analysis for migration 236; free movement as 50–54; state interests 51–52; violations 224
hypothetical consent, and illegal immigration 18

identity: -based oppression 6, 179; cultural 1, 40, 144, 148, 282, 298; national 2, 27, 36–37, 40, 55, 134, 144–147, 151, 177; social 177–184; socially undocumented 178, 180–182, 184
I-Kiribati people 157, 162
illegal immigration 17–21, 38; democracy 19; fair play 18–19; freedom of association 19–21; gratitude 18; hypothetical consent 18; social contract 17–18; see also immigration
Illegal Immigration Reform and Immigrant Responsibility Act (IIRIRA) 307, 317n3, 317n6
illegalized immigrants 297
immigrant detention 292, 294, 300
immigration 1–3, 87–94, 224; and climate change 253–261; control powers 49–50, 52, 54, 56–57; and culture 4–5; and discrimination 2, 5–6; and economic freedom 65–73; enforcement 7–8; ethics of 140–151; and ethnicity 157–158; future directions 184; growth and distributional effects of 28–29; illegal 17–21, 38; more oppressive social identity formation 183–184; and nationalism 4–5, 140–151; and negative economic freedom 65, 66–69; policies 187–196; and political polarization 146; and positive economic freedom 69–72; and race 157–158; and religion 157–158; and social democracy 24–33; and social identity formation 177–184; socially undocumented oppression 179–183; see also illegal immigration

Immigration and Refugee Board (IRB) tribunal 278–279
immigration detention: analysis of "detainable" 280–282; detention and normative theory 283–285; facilities 280, 330n4; false deterrent 282–283; governing 278–280; legislating 278–280; in normative political theory 277–285
immigration enforcement 292–301; and children 322–330; extraterritorial 297–299; and families 322–330; mixed-status families 326–330; resistance/disobedience 299–301; within state borders 295–297; unauthorized family with minor child 324–326; unauthorized unaccompanied minors 323–324; understanding 293–294; see also enforcement
immigration holding centers (IHCs) 279–280
Immigration Reform and Control Act (IRCA), 1986 307
Immigration Restriction Act (Australia) 157–158, 169
immigration restrictions 3–6, 11, 17, 19, 21, 28, 65–70; crime 13; culture 13; as immoral 11–17; indirect selection 172–173; jobs 12; and nationality 167–174; nationality and 167–174; political self-defense 14–17; property rights 13–14; statistical generalisations 171–172
incorrect voting 15
indefinite detention 282, 286n2, 293
India 1; Citizenship Registration Act 140; Deep Roots outliers 112; greenhouse gas emissions 259–260; as one of the fastest-growing economies in 164n31
indirect selection 172–174
individual mobility 3
"Inherited Trust in 1935" 105–106
inhumanitarianism 266–274; justificatory 271–273; purposive 273
institutional racism 296–297, 301
institutions 4–5, 25–26, 28, 33, 37–40, 67, 72, 89, 91–94, 99–115, 124, 128–130, 135–136, 141–146, 205–206, 296
internal immigration enforcement policies: description of 306–308; economic and social consequences 308–310; effective/efficient/appropriately resourced 315–316; employment-based enforcement 307; ethics in the U.S. 310–316; human rights 311–312; labor market impacts 309–310; police-based enforcement 307–308; proportionality 313–315; rule of law 312–313; social impacts 310; in the U.S. 306–308
internally displaced persons (IDPs) 254, 268

International Covenant on Civil and Political Rights 39, 286n1
international mobility 257–259
International Refugee Organization 236
international refugee protection 50
intersectionality 281
intra-European migration 104–105
involuntary climate emigrants 253
Islamophobia 170
Islamophobic immigration practices 119
Italian Mare Nostrum policy of 2013–2014 271

Japan 87, 92, 94; health care system in 165–166n44; immigration policies in 169; millionaires in 165–166n44; per capita wealth 165–166n44; points-based migration systems 114; population decline in 169; research and development (R&D) in 99
Japanese Americans 165–166n44, 293
JBS 190
Jim Crow South 108
jobs 122, 180–182, 190–191, 213, 225, 227, 305; competition for 71–72; immigration restrictions 12; stealing and illegal immigrants 13, 195
Johansson-Stenman, Olof 107
Johnson, Noel D. 106
Johnson, Simon 99
Jones, Garett 91, 93–94
jus soli citizenship laws 328, 331n14
justificatory inhumanitarianism 271–273

Kafala system 211
Kahan, Dan 31
Kampala Declaration 247n7
Karlan, Dean S. 107
Kincaid, Jordan 241, 248n22
Knobloch, Thorben 132
Koopmans, Ruud 149
Korematsu v. United States 293
Kukathas, Chandran 88, 238, 295
Kymlicka, Will 134, 144

labor: mobility 28; rights of temporary workers 212–218
labor market 2, 4, 12, 77; access to 79, 84–85, 211–214, 218; behaviors 113; competition 222n8, 259; gains from trade in 79–80, 82–85; global 77; internal immigration enforcement policies 309–310; protecting native workers in 81; regulation 103–104; restrictions 219
language 4–5; as admissible criterion 120–122; as criterion of immigrant selection 118–126; discretionary immigration policy 118–120; vulnerable 122–125

League of Nations 236
legally undocumented migrants 5, 6, 179–182
Lenard, Patti Tamara 313
Lewis, E. G. 190
liberal democracy 5, 16, 87, 133, 138, 146
liberalized immigration policies: global social welfare 76–80; national interest 80–85; overview 76
liberal nationalism 141
liberal nationalists 37
liberal theory: backlash in 130–137; migration in 130–137
"Life in the UK" Advisory Group 205
"life options" 50, 181
Lim, Désirée 174, 175n6
Lincoln, Abraham 202
linguistic competence 118
Lippert-Rasmussen, Kasper 172–173, 175n9
Lister, Matthew 241–242, 246, 249n30, 311
living wage (LW) 217–219, 221
Lockean property theory 37
Lockheed Martin 296
Longo, Matthew 299
low-skilled migrants 187–188, 195–196
Luibhéid, Eithne 183

Macedo, Stephen 132–133
Mae Ngai 168
The Magna Carta 278
majority cultural rights 150
majority culture 144, 148, 150
majority nationalism 148
Majority Rights Account 141, 148–150, **150–151**
malum prohibitum offenses 331n8
market-clearing wage (MCW) 219, 221
market-dominant minority 108
market power 219
#MasacreMelilla 292
May, Theresa 295
Mayer, Robert 219
McAdam, Jane 248n21
Medicaid 83, 310
Medicare 306
Mendoza, José Jorge 312, 314, 316
mestiza consciousness 178, 185n10
methodological nationalism 141
Mexico City 134–135
Mieth, Corinna 132
migrants 6, 52, 66, 104, 111, 136–138, 149; climate 235, 261n3; economic 129, 238, 272; legally undocumented 5, 6, 179–182; low-skilled workers 211; necessitous 43, 45; "permanent alienage" of 44; socially undocumented 6, 178–182, 296; temporary workers 190–191, 211–222; unauthorized 43–44; in United States 190

Index

migration: attitude 101–108; and backlash 128–138; and climate change 2, 6–7; as culture transplant 99–115; of familism 102–103; forced 48; intra-European 104–105; in liberal theory 130–137; negative side effects on economic liberty 72–73; in political practice 137–138; -related oppression 178; state sovereignty over 36–39; temporary 211–222; trust 106; voluntary 48
migration restrictions: arguing for 224–226; group restrictions 225–226
Milanovic, Branko 212
Mill, John Stuart 145
Miller, David 37, 50–51, 132, 142, 168–169, 174n4, 191, 226–227, 228–230, 231n12, 240, 311, 312, 331n6
Mislin, Alexandra A. 106
mixed-status families 322–323, 326–328; and criminal/character removal 328–330; and *jus soli* rule 328; removal of non-citizens in 329
mobility: cross-border mobility 58; cross-boundary mobility 253; human 294, 296, 299; individual 3; international 257–259; labor 28; social 145
Moderna 70
Mohamad, Mahathirbin 143
Molnar, Petra 286n1
moral arbitrariness view of discrimination 191–192
moral hazard 191, 324, 327–328, 331n10
moral solidarity 267, 269
more oppressive social identity formation 183–184
Müller, Daniel 105
Muslim Americans 170
Muslims 161, 170; admission of 160; ban 140, 167, 170, 172; Hindu–Muslim relations 160; women 173
Myers, Norman 253
My Fourth Time, We Drowned (Hayden) 273

Nash, Michael 261n5
National Academies 83
National Beef 190
national interest: fiscal concerns 82–85; income distribution among natives 81–82; liberalized immigration policies 80–85
nationalism: and culture 4–5; ethics of immigration 140–151; Functionalist Account 141, 145–148, **150–151**; and immigration 4–5, 140–151; liberal 141; majority 148; Majority Rights Account 141, 148–150, **150–151**; methodological 141; perspectives on 140–141; Propertarian Account 141, 142–145, **150–151**

nationality: and ethnicity 167–169; and immigration restrictions 167–174; indirect selection 172–174; and race 167–169; and religion 169–171; statistical generalisations 171–172
Nationality, Immigration and Asylum Act 2002 205
National Origins Act 167–169, 172
National Origins Quota Act 37
National Research Council (NRC) 83
National Security Entry-Exit Registration System 167, 170
national self-determination 151n1
nation-state 5, 26, 141–143, 183, 285
Native Americans: descendants 41; land 41; tribes 202
natural disasters 237–239, 245, 247n1, 255, 268–269; man-made 237; victims 7, 236, 239, 245
necessitous migrants 43, 45
negative economic freedom 65, 66–69
Neo-Europes 99, 109
New Zealand 49; as Neo-Europes 99; points-based admissions systems 189; points-based migration systems 114; Recognised Seasonal Employer scheme 264n45
Ngai, Mae 168
No Friend But the Mountain (Boochani) 273
no-match letters 317n4
non-citizenship 285
nonrefoulement 43
nonworseness claim 222n3
normative political theory 277–285
Northern Triangle 286n4
Nowrasteh, Alex 112, 113
Nozick, Robert 25, 66
Nuti, Alasia 145

OAU convention 247n7
Oberman, Kieran 50, 88, 181, 231n13
obligatory admissions 41
Office of the United Nations High Commissioner for Refugees 235
Olson, Mancur 108
Olympic citizenship 188
Oostendorp, R.H. 213
open borders: defined 26; and egalitarianism 30–31; practical approaches 3–4; presumptive case for 87–89; and social democracy 26–27, 29–30; theoretical arguments 3; thesis 118–119
oppression 12, 158–159, 184, 195, 230, 312; identity-based 6, 179; migration-related 178; socially undocumented 179–183
Orgad, Liav 148, 149

Index

Organization for Economic Cooperation and Development Countries (OECD) 29, 91, 172
Ostrom, Elinor 91
Our Common Bond 204
Outstanding Americans by Choice Initiative 201

Padilla v. Kentucky 315
Page, John 29
Page Act of 1875 183
Palantir 296
Parekh, Lord (Bhikhu) 205
Pareto principle 222n5
Pellegrino, Gianfranco 241–243, 246, 248n23, 249n30
Peri, Giovanni 81
permanent alienage of migrants 44
persuasive power 248n21
Pevnick, Ryan 37–38, 87, 134
Pfizer 70
plenary power 293
Plyler v. Doe 306
Pogge, Thomas 228, 238
police-based enforcement 307–308
political membership 36
political power 48, 128, 146, 162
political self-defense 14–17
politicized economy 31–32
politics of inhumanitarianism 266–274
positive economic freedom 65–66; and immigration 69–72
Powell, Enoch 148
power: anti-democratic 138; arbitrary 138; coercive 80, 90; colonial powers 264n43; discretionary 269; immigration control powers 49–50, 52, 54, 56–57; inequalities of 51–52; linguistic 135; market 219; persuasive power 248n21; plenary 293; political 48, 128, 146, 162; predictive 109, 114; purchasing 122; salutary 267; state power 35–36, 285; statistical explanatory 109
PPP-adjusted world product 27
predictive power 109, 114
principle of fair play 44
Priority Enforcement Program (PEP) 308, 310
prison violence 286n3
Pritchett, Lant 112–113
progressive dilemma 146
Propertarian Account 141, 142–145, **150–151**
property rights 13–14, 21, 37–38, 89, 93, 143, 294
proportionality 297, 313–315
proportional procedural protections 314–315
Public Charge Rule 177, 183
purchasing power 122

purposive inhumanitarianism 273
Putterman, Louis 108, 109, 114

"queue jumpers" 299

race: and ethnicity 167–169; and immigration 157–158; and nationality 167–169; and selective exclusion 159–162
racialized social system 178
racial profiling 171–172, 296
racism 119, 140, 148, 160, 169, 171, 178, 194, 281; and immigration enforcement 295–296; institutional 296–297, 301; lived realities of 282; systemic 178, 301
radical politics 300
Rajan, Sudhir 241, 247n14
Rawls, John 24–27, 54, 70, 130–131, 133–134, 137, 219–220; difference principle 25, 70; on open borders 26–27
Raz, Joseph 313
Reagan, Ronald 136
reciprocity-based free movement 56
Reed-Sandoval, Amy 296
refugees: and asylum 43; climate 2, 119, 235, 237, 239–240, 242, 245, 248n22, 253–257, 259–260, 261n6; and climate migrants 235–246; defined 42, 236–241, 254; and politics of inhumanitarianism 266–274; resettlement of 43, 246, 258–259, 270, 272, 300; theoretical issues 242–246; Ukrainian war 50
regional free movement 56
religion 5, 31, 42, 119–120, 181, 203, 236, 254, 312; and immigration 157–158; and nationality 169–171; and selective exclusion 159–162
reservation price (RP) 219, 221
resettlement of refugees 43, 246, 258–259, 270, 272, 300
resistance/disobedience 299–301
resources: inequalities of 51–52; treating people as 224–230
reward lawbreaking 327
right-libertarianism 24, 33
rights-based argument 89–93
Rights-Numbers Tradeoff 211, 222n4
right to control borders: defined 26; and egalitarianism 30–31; practical approaches 3–4; presumptive case for 87–89; and social democracy 26–27, 29–30; theoretical arguments 3; thesis 118–119
right to discriminate 193
right to exclude 13–14, 38, 69–70, 94n2, 136, 142–143, 145–146, 168–169, 187, 193–194, 196n1, 283–284, 310
right to liberty 278, 286n1

Index

Rimmer, Sue Harris 203
Robinson, James A. 99
Roving and Stationary Bandits model 108
Royal Canadian Mounted Police 278
Rudd, Kevin 203
"the rule of law" 312–313, 317n15

Sager, Alex 141, 311, 313, 316
Sánchez, Pedro 292
sanctuary cities 297
Schmid, Lukas 58
Schmidtz, David 31
Scott, David G. 286n3
Scott, Matthew 247n1
Secure Communities 307–308, 317n10
selective exclusion: defined 158; and ethnicity 159–162; and race 159–162; and religion 159–162
self-determination 89, 193, 283; collective 3, 35–36, 39, 42, 45, 47; collective political self-determination 244–246, 249n30; democratic 47; national 151n1; state 3, 151n1
September 11, 2001 terrorist attacks 161, 170
Serena Parekh 270
Session, Jeff 295
sexism 281
Shachar, Ayelet 188–189, 191, 298
Shacknove, Andrew 239, 248n17
Shayo, Moses 138
Silverman, Stephanie J. 286n1, 330n3
Simmons, John 37
Simpson, Audra 177
Sixth Amendment 293
skill-selective immigration policies: ethical analyses of 191–195; ethics of 187–196; moral arbitrariness view of discrimination 191–192; and present-day examples 188–191; self-determination and the right to discriminate 193; status-harming view of wrongful discrimination 193–195
Smith, Rogers 145
Smithfield Foods 190
social citizenship 54
social contract 239; defined 17; illegal immigration 17–18
social democracy: and egalitarianism 30–31; growth and distributional effects of immigration 28–29; and immigration 24–33; and open borders 26–27, 29–30; politicized economy and openness 31–32; social justice nationalism 24–26; world poverty 27–28; *see also* democracy
social identity 178, 181–184

social identity formation: immigration and 177–184; more oppressive 183–184
social justice 24–26, 48, 54, 182–183
social justice nationalism 24–26
socially undocumented identity 178, 180–182, 184
Socially Undocumented: Identity and Immigration Justice (Reed-Sandoval) 178
socially undocumented migrants 6, 178–182, 296
socially undocumented oppression 179–183; social identity 181–182; social justice 182–183; socially *vs.* legally undocumented 179–181
social membership principle 44
social mobility 145
Social Security 306
Social Security Administration (SSA) 317n4
societal culture 141
Song, Sarah 92, 134, 311–312
Southeast Asia 111–112
South Korea 94, 99
"The Spaghetti Theory of Cultural Change" 108
Sparber, Chad 81
Spolaore, Enrico 93
'spontaneous arrivals' 272
Sreenivasan, Gopal 248n26
state: power 35–36, 285; right to exclude 196n1; self-determination 3, 151n1
state sovereignty: controlled borders and open doors 36–39, 42–45; over migration 36–39; qualifications 42–45; and unauthorized migrants 43–44
statistical explanatory power 109
status-harming view of wrongful discrimination 193–195
Steinberg, Oded 142
Stephen, Sir Ninian 203
Stevens, Jacqueline 69
Stilz, Anna 134
Stone, Bryan Arthur 279
Supplemental Nutrition Assistance Program 310
systematic inequality 44
systemic racism 178, 301
Szamko, Jan 278–279

Tamir, Yael 134
temporary migration and worker exploitation 211–222
Temporary Protected Status (TPS) 317n2
temporary workers: case against limiting the labor rights of 215–218; case for limiting the labor rights of 212–215; fair wage for 218–221

Index

Thöni, Christian 107
"Throwing Like A Girl" (Young) 182
Tiebout, Charles M. 79
Tiebout model 79
Tomalty, Jesse 175n7
Trump, Donald J. 37, 67, 135, 137, 167, 202, 286n4; Muslim ban 140, 167, 170, 172; "Zero Tolerance" policy 278
Trump National Golf Club 318n16
trust migration 106
Tyson Foods 190

Ukrainian war refugees 50
unauthorized family with minor child 324–326
unauthorized migrants: principle of fair play 44; and social membership principle 44; and state sovereignty 43–44; vulnerability of 44; *see also* migrants
unauthorized unaccompanied minors 323–324
UN Commission for the Unification and Rehabilitation of Korea (UNCURK) 247n5
UN Conciliation Commission for Palestine (UNCCP) 247n5
undemocratic values 16–17
undocumented migration 128
UN Human Rights Committee 54
United Kingdom (UK) 160, 205–208; citizenship test 205–208; Equality Act 2000 173; Jewish population in 164n30; "points-based" admissions systems 189; "Skilled Worker" visas 189
United Nations Environment Program 237
United Nations Framework Convention on Climate Change (UNFCCC) 247n14, 259
United Nations High Commissioner for Refugees (UNHCR) 236, 254, 273
United Nations Korean Reconstruction Agency 247n5
United Nations Relief and Works Agency for Palestine Refugees in the Near East 247n5
United States (US) 201–203; Border Patrol 295; Citizenship and Immigration Services 202; Citizenship and Integration Grant Program 201; citizenship test 201–203; Civil War 202; Deep Roots outliers 112; Department of Homeland Security 305, 307–308, 312, 317n5, 317n6; H2-A visa program 190; H2-B program 190; Immigration and Customs Enforcement 296, 306, 307–308, 310; internal immigration enforcement policies in 306–308, 310–316; Jewish population in 164n30; millionaires in 165–166n44; Nationality Act of 1790 187; National Security Entry-Exit Registration System 167; as "Neo-Europes" 99; "plenary power doctrine" 293; research and development in 99; Secure Communities 296; visa waiver programme 171
Universal Declaration of Human Rights 224, 286n1, 311
UN Refugee Convention 42–43, 236–237, 247n14, 269, 272, 286n1, 325
UNRWA 236, 247n8

Van Parijs, Philippe 26, 121
visible identities 181
voluntary deportations 283
voluntary migration 48
voluntary repatriation 245–246
voter psychology 31
vulnerable languages 122–125

Wacziarg, Romain 93
Waldron, Jeremy 313
Walzer, Michael 36–37, 44, 79, 84, 132, 144, 158, 193, 196n2, 213
Washington, George 202
Weil, David N. 108–109, 114
Welfare Reform Act of 1996 73
Wellman, Christopher Heath 38–39, 174n2, 193–195, 248n26
Weyl, Glen 29
Whalley, John 77
White, Stuart 38
White Australia Policy 167, 169; *see also* Immigration Restriction Act (Australia)
white nationalists 37
"Why Not a Political Coase Theorem?" 108
Why Trust Matters (Ho) 105
Windrush Scandal 295
Wolfe, Patrick 281
workers: exploitation 211–222; temporary 212–221
world poverty 27–28
World Values Survey (WVS) 100, 102, 104–106
World War I 238, 267
World War II 236, 293, 312
would-be immigrants 32, 41–42, 47, 56, 91, 167–174, 174n2, 174n3, 174n4

Young, Iris Marion 182

9780367479282